10th International Conference on Computational Semantics 2013

(IWCS 2013)

Includes Long Papers and Short Papers

Potsdam, Germany
19-22 March 2013

ISBN: 978-1-62748-395-7

Printed from e-media with permission by:

Curran Associates, Inc.
57 Morehouse Lane
Red Hook, NY 12571

Some format issues inherent in the e-media version may also appear in this print version.

Printed by Curran Associates, Inc. (2013)

For permission requests, please contact the Association for Computational Linguistics at the address below.

Association for Computational Linguistics
209 N. Eighth Street
Stroudsburg, Pennsylvania 18360

Phone: 1-570-476-8006
Fax: 1-570-476-0860

acl@aclweb.org

Additional copies of this publication are available from:

Curran Associates, Inc.
57 Morehouse Lane
Red Hook, NY 12571 USA
Phone: 845-758-0400
Fax: 845-758-2634
Email: curran@proceedings.com
Web: www.proceedings.com

TABLE OF CONTENTS

LONG PAPERS

SHORT PAPERS

UCCA: A Semantics-based Grammatical Annotation Scheme

Omri Abend* and Ari Rappoport
Institute of Computer Science
Hebrew University of Jerusalem
{omria01|arir}@cs.huji.ac.il

Abstract

Syntactic annotation is an indispensable input for many semantic NLP applications. For instance, Semantic Role Labelling algorithms almost invariably apply some form of syntactic parsing as pre-processing. The categories used for syntactic annotation in NLP generally reflect the formal patterns used to form the text. This results in complex annotation schemes, often tuned to one language or domain, and unintuitive to non-expert annotators. In this paper we propose a different approach and advocate substituting existing syntax-based approaches with semantics-based grammatical annotation. The rationale of this approach is to use manual labor where there is no substitute for it (i.e., annotating semantics), leaving the detection of formal regularities to automated statistical algorithms. To this end, we propose a simple semantic annotation scheme, UCCA for Universal Conceptual Cognitive Annotation. The scheme covers many of the most important elements and relations present in linguistic utterances, including verb-argument structure, optional adjuncts such as adverbials, clause embeddings, and the linkage between them. The scheme is supported by extensive typological cross-linguistic evidence and accords with the leading Cognitive Linguistics theories.

1 Introduction

Syntactic annotation is used as scaffolding in a wide variety of NLP applications. Examples include Machine Translation (Yamada and Knight, 2001), Semantic Role Labeling (SRL) (Punyakanok et al., 2008) and Textual Entailment (Yuret et al., 2010). Syntactic structure is represented using a combinatorial apparatus and a set of categories assigned to the linguistic units it defines. The categories are often based on distributional considerations and reflect the formal patterns in which that unit may occur.

The use of distributional categories leads to intricate annotation schemes. As languages greatly differ in their inventory of constructions, such schemes tend to be tuned to one language or domain. In addition, the complexity of the schemes requires highly proficient workforce for its annotation. For example, the Penn Treebank project (PTB) (Marcus et al., 1993) used linguistics graduates as annotators.

In this paper we propose a radically different approach to grammatical annotation. Under this approach, only semantic distinctions are manually annotated, while distributional regularities are induced using statistical algorithms and without any direct supervision. This approach has four main advantages. First, it facilitates manual annotation that would no longer require close acquaintance with syntactic theory. Second, a data-driven approach for detecting distributional regularities is less prone to errors and to the incorporation of implicit biases. Third, as distributional regularities need not be manually annotated, they can be arbitrarily intricate and fine-grained, beyond the capability of a human annotator to grasp and apply. Fourth, it is likely that semantic tasks that rely on syntactic information would be better served by using a semantics-based scheme.

We present UCCA (Universal Conceptual Cognitive Annotation), an annotation scheme for encoding semantic information. The scheme is designed as a multi-layer structure that allows extending it open-endedly. In this paper we describe the foundational layer of UCCA that focuses on grammatically-relevant information. Already in this layer the scheme covers (in a coarse-grained level) major semantic

*Omri Abend is grateful to the Azrieli Foundation for the award of an Azrieli Fellowship.

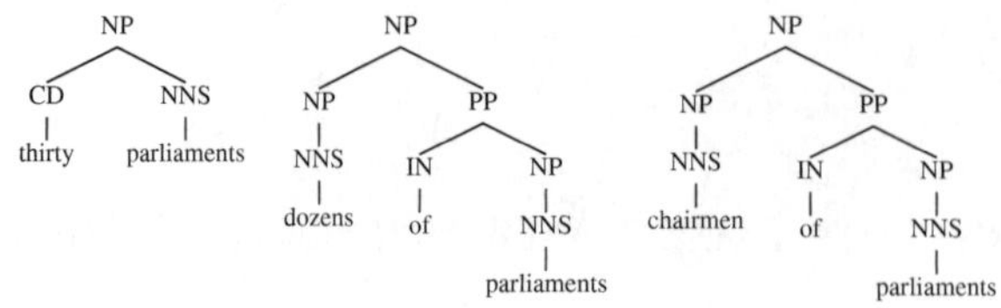

Figure 1: Demonstrating the difference between distributional and semantic representations. The central example is formally more similar to the example on the right, but semantically more similar to the example on the left.

phenomena including verbal and nominal predicates and their arguments, the distinction between core arguments and adjuncts, adjectives, copula clauses, and relations between clauses.

This paper provides a detailed description of the foundational layer of UCCA. To demonstrate UCCA's value over existing approaches, we examine two major linguistic phenomena: relations between clauses (linkage) and the distinction between core arguments and adjuncts. We show that UCCA provides an intuitive coarse-grained analysis in these cases.

UCCA's category set is strongly influenced by "Basic Linguistic Theory" (BLT) (Dixon, 2005, 2010), a theoretical framework used for the description of a great variety of languages. The semantic approach of BLT allows it to draw similarities between constructions, both within and across languages, that share a similar meaning. UCCA takes a similar approach.

The UCCA project includes the compilation of a large annotated corpus. The first distribution of the corpus, to be released in 2013, will consist of about 100K tokens, of which 10K tokens have already been annotated. The annotation of the corpus is carried out mostly using annotators with little to no linguistic background. Details about the corpus and its compilation are largely besides the scope of this paper.

The rest of the paper is constructed as follows. Section 2 explains the basic terms of the UCCA framework. Section 3 presents UCCA's foundational layer. Specifically, Section 3.1 describes the annotation of simple argument structures, Section 3.2 delves into more complex cases, Section 3.3 discusses the distinction between core arguments and adjuncts, Section 3.4 discusses linkages between different structures and Section 3.5 presents a worked-out example. Section 4 describes relevant previous work.

2 UCCA: Basic Terms

Distributional Regularities and Semantic Distinctions. One of the defining characteristics of UCCA is its emphasis on representing semantic distinctions rather than distributional regularities. In order to exemplify the differences between the two types of representations, consider the phrases "dozens of parliaments", "thirty parliaments" and "chairmen of parliaments". Their PTB annotations are presented in Figure 1. The annotation of "dozens of parliaments" closely resembles that of "chairmen of parliaments", and is considerably different from that of "thirty parliaments". A more semantically-motivated representation would have probably emphasized the similarity between "thirty" and "dozens of" and the semantic dissimilarity between "dozens" and "chairmen".

Formalism. UCCA's semantic representation consists of an inventory of relations and their arguments. We use the term *terminals* to refer to the atomic meaning-bearing units. UCCA's foundational layer treats words and fixed multi-word expressions as its terminals, but this definition can easily be extended to include morphemes. The basic formal elements of UCCA are called *units*. A unit may be either (i) a terminal or (ii) several elements that are jointly viewed as a single entity based on conceptual/cognitive considerations. In most cases, a non-terminal unit will simply be comprised of a single relation and its arguments, although in some cases it may contain secondary relations as well (see below). Units can be used as arguments in other relations, giving rise to a hierarchical structure.

UCCA is a multi-layered formalism, where each layer specifies the relations it encodes. For example, consider "big dogs love bones" and assume we wish to encode the relations given by "big" and "love". "big" has a single argument ("dogs"), while "love" has two ("big dogs" and "bones"). Therefore, the units of the sentence are the terminals (always units), "big dogs" and "big dogs love bones". The latter

Abb.	Category	Short Definition
		Scene Elements
P	Process	The main relation of a Scene that evolves in time (usually, action or movement).
S	State	The main relation of a Scene that does not evolve in time.
A	Participant	A participant in a Scene in a broad sense (including locations, abstract entities and Scenes serving as arguments).
D	Adverbial	A secondary relation in a Scene (including temporal relations).
		Elements of Non-Scene Relations
E	Elaborator	A relation (which is not a State or a Process) which applies to a single argument.
N	Connector	A relation (which is not a State or a Process) which applies to two or more arguments.
R	Relator	A secondary relation that pertains to a specific entity and relates it to some super-ordinate relation.
C	Center	An argument of an Elaborator or a Connector.
		Inter-Scene Relations
L	Linker	A relation between Scenes (e.g., temporal, logical, purposive).
H	Parallel Scene	A Scene linked to other Scenes by a Linker.
G	Ground	A relation between the speech event and the described Scene.
		Other
F	Function	Does not introduce a relation or participant. Required by some structural pattern.

Table 1: The complete set of categories in UCCA's foundational layer.

two are units by virtue of corresponding to a relation along with its arguments.

We can compactly annotate the unit structure using a directed graph. Each unit is represented as a node, and descendants of non-terminal units are the sub-units comprising it. Non-terminal nodes in the graph only represent the fact that their descendant units form a unit, and hence do not bear any features. Edges bear labels (or more generally feature sets) that express the descendant unit's role in the relation represented by the parent unit. Therefore, the internal structure of the unit is represented by its outbound edges and their features, while the roles a unit plays in relations it participates in are represented by its inbound edges. Figure 2(a) presents the graph representation for the above example "big dogs love bones". The labels on the figure's edges are explained in Section 3.

Extendability. Extendability is a necessary feature for an annotation scheme given the huge number of features required to formally represent semantics, and the ever-expanding range of distinctions used by the NLP community. UCCA's formalism can be easily extended with new annotation layers introducing new types of semantic distinctions and refining existing types. For example, a layer that represents semantic roles can refine a coarse-grained layer that only distinguishes between arguments and adjuncts. A layer that represents coreference relations between textual entities can be built on top of a more basic layer that simply delineates those entities.

3 The Foundational Layer of UCCA

This section presents an in-depth description of the foundational set of semantic distinctions encoded by UCCA. The three desiderata for this layer are: (i) covering the entire text, so each terminal is a part of at least one unit, (ii) representing argument structure phenomena of both verbal and nominal predicates, (iii) representing relations between argument structures (linkage). Selecting argument structures and their inter-relations as the basic objects of annotation is justified both by their centrality in many approaches for grammatical representation (see Section 4), and their high applicative value, demonstrated by the extensive use of SRL in NLP applications.

Each unit in the foundational layer is annotated with a single feature, which will be simply referred to as its *category*[1]. In the following description, the category names appear *italicized* and accompanied by an abbreviation. The categories are described in detail below and are also summarized in Table 1.

[1]Future extensions of UCCA will introduce more elaborate feature structures.

3.1 Simple Scene Structure

The most basic notion in this layer is the *Scene*. A Scene can either describe some movement or action, or otherwise a temporally persistent state. A Scene usually has a temporal and a spatial dimension. It may be specific to a particular time and place, but may also describe a schematized event which jointly refers to many occurrences of that event in different times and locations. For example, the Scene "elephants eat plants" is a schematized event, which presumably occurs each time an elephant eats a plant. This definition is similar to the definition of a clause in BLT. We avoid the term "clause" due to its syntactic connotation, and its association specifically with verbal rather than nominal predicates.

Every Scene contains one main relation, which is marked as a *Process (P)* if the Scene evolves in time, or otherwise as a *State (S)*. The main relation in an utterance is its "anchor", its most conceptually important aspect of meaning. We choose to incorporate the Process-State distinction in the foundational layer because of its centrality, but it is worth noting this distinction is not necessary for the completeness of the scheme.

A Scene contains one or more *Participants (A)*, which can be either concrete or abstract. Embedded Scenes are also considered Participants (see Section 3.4). Scenes may also include secondary relations, which are generally marked as *Adverbials (D)* using the standard linguistic term. Note that for brevity, we do not designate Scene units as such, as this information can be derived from the categories of its sub-units (i.e., a unit is a Scene if it has a P or an S as a sub-unit).

As an example, consider "Woody generally rides his bike home". The sentence contains a single Scene with three A's: "Woody", "his bike" and "home". It also contains a D: "generally" (see Figure 2(b)).

Non-Scene Relations. Not all relation words evoke a Scene. We distinguish between several types of non-Scene relations. *Elaborators (E)* apply to a single argument, while *Connectors (N)* are relations that apply to two or more entities in a way that highlights the fact that they have a similar feature or type. The arguments of non-Scene relations are marked as *Centers (C)*.

For example, in the expression "hairy dog", "hairy" is an E, and "dog" is a C. In "John and Mary", "John" and "Mary" are C's, while "and" is an N. Determiners are considered E's in the foundational layer, as they relate to a single argument.

Finally, any other type of relation between two or more units that does not evoke a Scene is a *Relator (R)*. R's have two main varieties. In one, R's relate a single entity to other relations or entities in the same context. For instance, in "I saw cookies in the jar", "in" relates "the jar" to the rest of the Scene. In the other, R's relate two units pertaining to different aspects of the same entity. For instance, in "bottom of the sea", "of" relates "bottom" and "the sea", two units that ultimately refer to the same entity.

As for notational conventions, in the first case we place the R inside the boundaries of the unit it relates (so "in the jar" would be an A in "I saw cookies in the jar"). In the second case, we place the R as a sibling of the related units (so "bottom", "of" and "sea" would all be siblings in "bottom of the sea").

Function Units. Some terminals do not refer to a participant or relation. They function only as a part of the construction they are situated in. We mark such terminals as *Function (F)*. Function units usually cannot be substituted by any other word. For example, in the sentence "it is likely that John will come tomorrow", the "it" does not refer to any specific entity or relation and is therefore an F.

Words whose meaning is not encoded in the foundational layer of annotation are also considered F's. For instance, auxilliary verbs in English (have, be and do) are marked as F's in the foundational layer of UCCA, as features such as voice or tense are not encoded in this layer.

Consider the sentence "John broke the jar lid". It describes a single Scene, where "broke" is the main (non-static) relation. The Participants are "John" and "the jar lid". "the jar lid" contains a part-whole relation, where "jar" describes the whole, and "lid" specifies the part. In such cases, UCCA annotates the "part" as an E and the "whole" as a C. The determiner "the" is also annotated as an E. In more refined layers of annotation, special categories will be devoted to annotating part-whole relations and the semantic relations described by determiners. Figure 2(c) presents the annotation of this example.

3.2 Beyond Simple Scenes

Nominal Predicates. The foundational layer of UCCA annotates the argument structure of nominal predicates much in the same fashion as that of verbal predicates. This accords with the standard practice in several NLP resources, which tend to use the same formal devices for annotating nominal and verbal argument structure (see, e.g., NomBank (Meyers et al., 2004) and FrameNet (Baker et al., 1998)). For example, consider "his speech against the motion". "speech" evokes a Scene that evolves in time and is therefore a P. The Scene has two Participants, namely "his" and "against the motion".

Multiple Parents. In general, a unit may participate in more than one relation. To this end, UCCA allows a unit to have multiple parents. Recall that in UCCA, a non-terminal node represents a relation, and its descendants are the sub-units comprising it. A unit's category is a label over the edge connecting

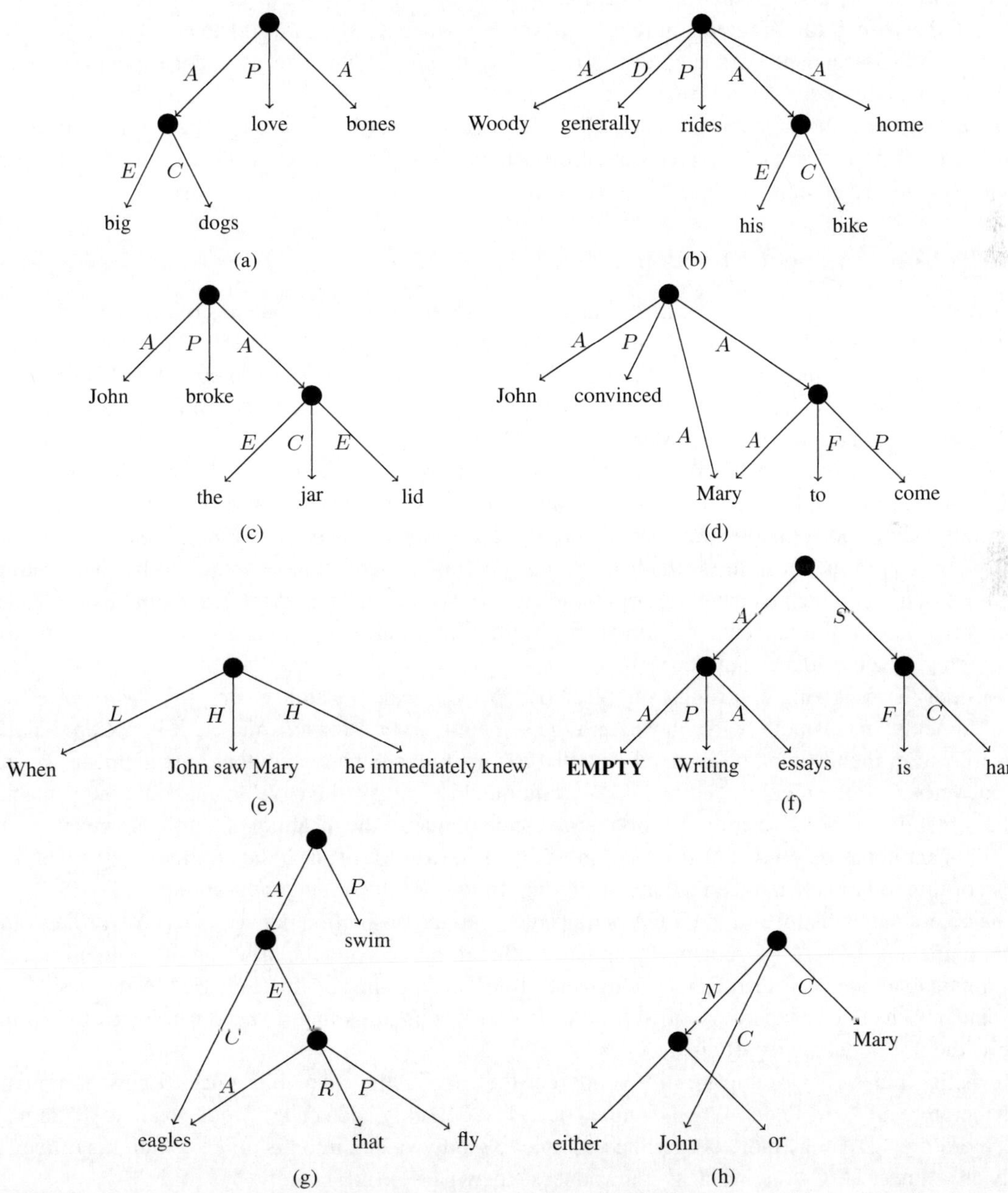

Figure 2: Examples of UCCA annotations.

it to its parent, that reflects the unit's role in the parent relation. A unit that participates in several relations (i.e., has several parents) may thus receive different categories in each of these relations.

For example, consider the sentence "John convinced Mary to come". The relation "convinced" has "John", "Mary" and "Mary to come" as Participants (Scenes may also be Participants, see below). The relation "come" has one Participant, namely "Mary". The resulting graph is presented in Figure 2(d).

The use of multiple parents leads to overlaps between the terminals of different units. It is sometimes convenient to define one of the terminal's parents as its base parent and the others as remote parents. In this paper we do not make this distinction.

Implicit Units. In some cases a relation or argument are clearly described in the text, but do not appear in it overtly. Formally, this results in a unit X that lacks one or more of its descendants. We distinguish between two cases. If that argument or relation corresponds to a unit Y that is placed in some other point in the text, we simply assign that Y as a descendant of X (using UCCA's capacity to represent multiple parents). Otherwise, if this argument or relation never appears in the text, we add an empty leaf node and assign it as X's descendant. We call such units *"Implicit Units"*. Other than not corresponding to any stretch of text, an implicit unit is similar to any other unit.

As an example, consider the sentence "Writing essays is hard". The participant who writes the essays is clearly present in the interpretation of the sentence, but never appears explicitly in the text. It is therefore considered an implicit A in this Scene (see Figure 2(f)).

3.3 The Core-Adjunct Distinction

The distinction between core arguments and adjuncts is central in most formalisms of grammar. Despite its centrality, the distinction lacks clear theoretical criteria for defining it, resulting in many borderline cases. This has been a major source of difficulty for establishing clear annotation guidelines. Indeed, the PTB describes the core-adjunct distinction as "very difficult" for the annotators, resulting in a significant slowdown of the annotation Process (Marcus et al., 1993).

Dowty (2003) claims that the pre-theoretic notions underlying the core-adjunct distinction are a conjunction of syntactic and semantic considerations. The syntactic distinction separates "optional elements" (adjuncts), and "obligatory elements" (cores). The semantic criterion distinguishes elements that "modify" or restrict the meaning of the head (adjuncts) and elements that are required by the meaning of the head, without which its meaning is incomplete (cores). A related semantic criterion distinguishes elements that have a similar semantic content with different predicates (adjuncts), and elements whose role is highly predicate-dependent (cores).

Consider the following opposing examples: (i) "Woody walked **quickly**" and (ii) "Woody cut **the cake**". "quickly" meets both the syntactic and the semantic criteria for an adjunct: it is optional and it serves to restrict the meaning of "walked". It also has a similar semantic content when appearing with different verbs ("walk quickly", "eat quickly", "talk quickly" etc.). "the cake" meets both the syntactic and the semantic criteria for a core: it is obligatory, and completes the meaning of "cut". However, many other cases are not as obvious. For instance, in "he walked **into his office**", the boldfaced argument is a core according to Framenet, but an adjunct according to PropBank (Abend and Rappoport, 2010).

The core-adjunct distinction in UCCA is translated into the distinction between D's (Adverbials) and A's (Participants). UCCA is a semantic scheme and therefore the syntactic criterion of "obligatoriness" is not applicable, and is instead left to be detected by statistical means. Instead, UCCA defines A's as units that introduce a new participant to the Scene and D's as units that add more information to the Scene without introducing a participant.

Revisiting our earlier examples, in "Woody cut the cake", "the cake" introduces a new participant and is therefore an A, while in "Woody walked quickly", "quickly" does not introduce a new participant and is therefore a D. In the more borderline example "Woody walked into his office", "into his office" is clearly an A under UCCA's criteria, as it introduces a new participant, namely "his office".

Note that locations in UCCA are almost invariably A's, as they introduce a new participant, namely the location. Consider "Woody walked in the park". "in the park" introduces the participant "the park" and is therefore an A. Unlike many existing approaches (including the PTB), UCCA does not distinguish between obligatory locations (e.g., "based in Europe") and optional locations (e.g., "walked in the park"), as this distinction is mostly distributional in nature and can be detected by automatic means.

Two cases which do not easily fall into either side of this distinction are subordinated clauses and temporal relations. Subordinated clauses are discussed as part of a general discussion of linkage in Section 3.4. The treatment of temporal relations requires a more fine-grained layer of representation. For the purposes of the foundational layer, we follow common practice and mark them as D's.

3.4 Linkage

Linkage in UCCA refers to the relation between Scenes. Scenes are invariably units, as they include a relation along with all its arguments. The category of the Scene units is determined by the relation they are situated in, as is the case with any other unit. The foundational layer takes a coarse-grained approach to inter-Scene relations and recognizes three types of linkage. This three-way distinction is adopted from Basic Linguistic Theory and is valid cross-linguistically.

First, a Scene can be a Participant in another Scene, in which case the Scene is marked as an A. For example, consider "writing essays is hard". It contains a main temporally static relation (S) "is hard" and an A "writing essays". The sentence also contains another Scene "writing essays", which has an implicit A (the one writing) and an explicit A ("essays"). See Figure 2(f) for the annotation of this Scene (note the empty node corresponding to the implicit unit).

Second, a Scene may serve as an Elaborator of some unit in another Scene, in which case the Scene is marked as an E. For instance, "eagles that fly swim". There are two Scenes in this sentence: (1) one whose main relation is "swim" and its A is "eagles that fly", (2) and another Scene whose main relation is "fly", and whose A is "eagles". See Figure 2(g) for the annotation graph of this sentence.

The third type of linkage covers inter-Scene relations that are not covered above. In this case, we mark the unit specifying the relation between the Scenes as a *Linker (L)* and its arguments as *Parallel Scenes (H)*. The Linker and the Parallel Scenes are positioned in a flat structure, which represents the linkage relation. For example, consider "When John saw Mary, he immediately knew" (Figure 2(e)). The sentence is composed of two Scenes "John saw Mary" and "he immediately knew" marked by H's and linked by the L "when". More fine-grained layers of annotation can represent the coreference relation between "John" and "he", as well as a more refined typology of linkages, distinguishing, e.g., temporal, logical and purposive linkage types.

UCCA does not allow annotating a Scene as an Adverbial within another Scene. Instead it represents temporal, manner and other relations between Scenes often represented as Adverbials (or sub-ordinate clauses), as linked Scenes. For instance, the sentence "I'm here because I wanted to visit you" is annotated as two Parallel Scenes ("I'm here" and "I wanted to visit you"), linked by the Linker "because".

Linkage is handled differently in other NLP resources. SRL formalisms, such as FrameNet and PropBank, consider a predicate's argument structure as the basic annotation unit and do not represent linkage in any way. Syntactic annotation schemes (such as the PTB) consider the sentence to be the basic unit for annotation and refrain from annotating inter-sentential relations, which are addressed only as part of the discourse level. However, units may establish similar relations between sentences as those expressed within a sentence. Another major difference between UCCA and other grammatical schemes is that UCCA does not recognize any type of subordination between clauses except for the cases where one clause serves as an Elaborator or as a Participant in another clause (see above discussion). In all other cases, linkage is represented by the identity of the Linker and, in future layers, by more fine-grained features assigned to the linkage structure.

Ground. Some units express the speaker's opinion of a Scene, or otherwise relate the Scene to the speaker, the hearer or the speech event. Examples include "in my opinion", "surprisingly" and "rumor has it". In principle, such units constitute a Scene in their own right, whose participants (minimally including the speaker) are implicit. However, due to their special characteristics, we choose to designate a special category for such cases, namely *Ground (G)*. For example, "Surprisingly" in "Surprisingly, Mary didn't come to work today" is a G linked to the Scene "Mary didn't come to work today".

Note that the distinction between G's and fully-fledged Scenes is a gradient one. Consider the above example and compare it to "I think Mary didn't come today" and "John thinks Mary didn't come today". While "John thinks" in the last example is clearly not a G, "I think" is a more borderline case. Gradience is a central phenomenon in all forms of grammatical representation, including UCCA. However, due to space limitations, we defer the discussion of UCCA's treatment of gradience to future work.

3.5 Worked-out Example

Consider the following sentence[2]:

After her parents' separation in 1976, Jolie and her brother lived with their mother, who gave up acting to focus on raising her children.

There are four Scenes in this sentence, with main relations "separation", "lived", "gave up acting" and "focus on raising". Note that "gave up acting" and "focus on raising" are composed of two relations, one central and the other dependent. UCCA annotates such cases as a single P. A deeper discussion of these issues can be found in (Dixon, 2005; Van Valin, 2005).

The Linkers are "after" (linking "separation" and "lived"), and "to" (linking "gave up acting" and "focus on raising"). The unit "who gave up acting to focus on raising her children" is an E, and therefore "who" is an R. We start with the top-level structure and continue by analyzing each Scene separately (non-Scene relations are not analyzed in this example):

- "After$_L$ [her parents' separation in 1976]$_H$, [Jolie and her brother lived with their mother, [who$_R$ [gave up acting]$_H$ to$_L$ [focus on raising her children]$_H$]$_E$]$_H$"
- "[her parents']$_A$ separation$_P$ [in 1976]$_D$"
- "[Jolie and her brother]$_A$ lived$_P$ [with their mother who abandoned ... children]$_A$"
- "mother$_A$ ... [gave up acting]$_P$"
- "mother$_A$ ... [focus on raising]$_P$ [her children]$_A$"

4 Previous Work

Many grammatical annotation schemes have been proposed over the years in an attempt to capture the richness of grammatical phenomena. In this section, we focus on approaches that provide a sizable corpus of annotated text. We put specific emphasis on English corpora, which is the most studied language and the focus language of this paper.

Semantic Role Labeling Schemes. The most prominent schemes to SRL are FrameNet (Baker et al., 1998), PropBank (Palmer et al., 2005) and VerbNet (Schuler, 2005) for verbal predicates and NomBank for nominal predicates (Meyers et al., 2004). They share with UCCA their focus on semantically-motivated rather than distributionally-motivated distinctions. However, unlike UCCA, they annotate each predicate separately, yielding shallow representations which are hard to learn directly without using syntactic parsing as preprocessing (Punyakanok et al., 2008). In addition, UCCA has a wider coverage than these projects, as it addresses both verbal, nominal and adjectival predicates.

Recently, the *Framenet Constructicon* project (Fillmore et al., 2010) extended FrameNet to more complex constructions, including a representation of relations between argument structures. However, the project is admittedly devoted to constructing a lexical resource focused on specific cases of interest, and does not attempt to provide a fully annotated corpus of naturally occurring text. The foundational layer of UCCA can be seen as being complementary to Framenet and Framenet Constructicon, as the UCCA foundational layer focuses on a high coverage, coarse-grained annotation, while Framenet focuses on more fine-grained distinctions at the expense of coverage. In addition, the projects differ in terms of their approach to linkage.

[2]Taken from "Angelina Jolie" article in Wikipedia (http://http://en.wikipedia.org/wiki/Angelina_Jolie).

Penn Treebank. The most influential syntactic annotation in NLP is probably the PTB. The PTB has spawned much subsequent research both in treebank compilation and in parsing technology. However, despite its tremendous contribution to NLP, the corpus today does not meet the community's needs in two major respects. First, it is hard to extend, both with new distinctions and with new sentences (due to its complex annotation that requires expert annotators). Second, its interface with semantic applications is far from trivial. Even in the syntactically-oriented semantic task of argument identification for SRL, results are of about 85% F-score for the in-domain scenario (Màrquez et al., 2008; Abend et al., 2009).

Dependency Grammar. An alternative approach to syntactic representation is Dependency Grammar. This approach is widely used in NLP today due to its formal and conceptual simplicity, and its ability to effectively represent fundamental semantic relations, notably predicate-argument and head-modifier relations. UCCA is similar to dependency grammar both in terms of their emphasis on representing predicate-argument relations and in terms of their formal definition[3]. The formal similarity is reflected in that they both place features over the graph's edges rather than over its nodes, and in that they both form a directed graph. In addition, neither formalism imposes contiguity (or projectivity in dependency terms) on its units, which facilitates their application to languages with relatively free word order.

However, despite their apparent similarity, the formalisms differ in several major respects. Dependency grammar uses graphs where each node is a word. Despite the simplicity and elegance of this approach, it leads to difficulties in the annotation of certain structures. We discuss three such cases: structures containing multiple heads, units with multiple parents and empty units. Cases where there is no clear dependency annotation are a major source of difficulty in standardizing, evaluating and creating clear annotation guidelines for dependency annotation (Schwartz et al., 2011). UCCA provides a natural solution in all of these cases, as is hereby detailed.

First, UCCA rejects the assumption that every structure has a unique head. Formally, instead of selecting a single head whose descendants are (the heads of) the argument units, UCCA introduces a new node for each relation, whose descendants are all the sub-units comprising that relation, including the predicate and its arguments. The symmetry between the descendants is broken through the features placed on the edges.

Consider coordination structures as an example. The difficulty of dependency grammar to capture such structures is exemplified by the 8 possible annotations in current use in NLP (Ivanova et al., 2012). In UCCA, all elements of the coordination (i.e., the conjunction along with its conjuncts) are descendants of a mutual parent, where only their categories distinguish between their roles. For instance, in "John and Mary", "John", "Mary" and "and" are all listed under a joint parent. Discontiguous conjunctions (such as "**either** John **or** Mary") are also handled straightforwardly by placing "either" and "or" under a single parent, which in turn serves as a Connector (Figure 2(h)). Note that the edges between "either" and "or" and their mutual parent have no category labels, since the unit "either ... or" is considered an unanalyzable terminal. A related example is inter-clause linkage, where it is not clear which clause should be considered the head of the other. See the discussion of UCCA's approach with respect to clause subordination in Section 3.4.

Second, a unit in UCCA can have multiple parents if it participates in multiple relations. Multiple parents are already found in the foundational layer (see, e.g., Figure 2(d)), and will naturally multiply with the introduction of new annotation layers introducing new relations. This is prohibited in standard dependency structures.

Third, UCCA allows implicit units, i.e., units that do not have any corresponding stretch of text. The importance of such "empty" nodes has been previously recognized in many formalisms for grammatical representation, including the PTB.

At a more fundamental level, the difference between UCCA and most dependency structures used in NLP is the latter's focus on distributional regularities. One example for this is the fact the most widely used scheme for English dependency grammar is automatically derived from the PTB. Another

[3]Dependency structures appear in different contexts in various guises. Those used in NLP are generally trees in which each word has at most one head and whose nodes are the words of the sentence along with a designated root node (Ivanova et al., 2012). We therefore restrict our discussion to dependency structures that follow these restrictions.

example is the treatment of fixed expressions, such as phrasal verbs and idioms. In these cases, several words constitute one unanalyzable semantic unit, and are treated by UCCA as such. However, they are analyzed up to the word level by most dependency structures. Finally, a major divergence of UCCA from standard dependency representation is UCCA's multi-layer structure that allows for the extension of the scheme with new distinctions.

Linguistically Expressive Grammars. Numerous approaches to grammatical representation in NLP have set to provide a richer grammatical representation than the one provided by the common phrase structure and dependency structures. Examples include Combinatory Categorial Grammar (CCG) (Steedman, 2001), Tree Adjoining Grammar (TAG) (Joshi and Schabes, 1997), Lexical Functional Grammar (LFG) (Kaplan and Bresnan, 1981) and Head-driven Phrase Structure Grammar (HPSG) (Pollard and Sag, 1994). One of the major motivations for these approaches is to provide a formalism for encoding both semantic and distributional distinctions and the interface between them. UCCA diverges from these approaches in its focus on annotating semantic information, leaving distributional regularities to be detected automatically.

A great body of work in formal semantics focuses on compositionality, i.e., how the meaning of a unit is derived from its syntactic structure along with the meaning of its sub-parts. Compositionality forms a part of the mapping between semantics and distribution, and is therefore modeled statistically by UCCA. A more detailed comparison between the different approaches is not directly relevant to this paper.

5 Conclusion

In this paper we proposed a novel approach to grammatical representation. Under this approach, only semantic distinctions are manually annotated, while distributional regularities are detected by automatic means. This approach greatly facilitates manual annotation of grammatical phenomena, by focusing the manual labor on information that can only be annotated manually.

We presented UCCA, a multi-layered semantic annotation scheme for representing a wide variety of semantic information in varying granularities. In its foundational layer, the scheme encodes verbal and nominal argument structure, copula clauses, the distinction between core arguments and adjuncts, and the relations between different predicate-argument structures. The scheme is based on basic, coarse-grained semantic notions, supported by cross-linguistic evidence.

Preliminary results show that the scheme can be learned quickly by non-expert annotators. Concretely, our annotators, including some with no linguistic background in linguistics, have reached a reasonable level of proficiency after a training period of 30 to 40 hours. Following the training period, our annotators have been found to make only occasional errors. These few errors are manually corrected in a later review phase. Preliminary experiments also show that the scheme can be applied to several languages (English, French, German) using the same basic set of distinctions.

Two important theoretical issues were not covered this paper due to space considerations. One is UCCA's treatment of cases where there are several analyses that do not exclude each other, each highlighting a different aspect of meaning of the analyzed utterance (termed *Conforming Analyses*). The other is UCCAs treatment of cases where a unit of one type is used in a relation that normally receives a sub-unit of a different type. For example, in "John's kick saved the game", "John's kick" describes an action but is used as a subject of "saved", a slot usually reserved for animate entities. Both of these issues will be discussed in future works.

Current efforts are devoted to creating a corpus of annotated text in English. The first distribution of the corpus consisting of about 100K tokens, of which 10K tokens have already been annotated, will be released during 2013. A parallel effort is devoted to constructing a statistical analyzer, trained on the annotated corpus. Once available, the analyzer will be used to produce UCCA annotations that will serve as input to NLP applications traditionally requiring syntactic preprocessing. The value of UCCA for applications and the learning algorithms will be described in future papers.

References

Abend, O. and A. Rappoport (2010). Fully unsupervised core-adjunct argument classification. In ACL '10.

Abend, O., R. Reichart, and A. Rappoport (2009). Unsupervised Argument identification for semantic role labeling. In ACL-IJCNLP '09.

Baker, C., C. Fillmore, and J. Lowe (1998). The berkeley framenet project. In ACL-COLING '98.

Dixon, R. (2005). A Semantic Approach To English Grammar. Oxford University Press.

Dixon, R. (2010). Basic Linguistic Theory: Grammatical Topics, Volume 2. Oxford University Press.

Dowty, D. (2003). The dual analysis of adjuncts/complements in categorial grammar. Modifying Adjuncts.

Fillmore, C., R. Lee-Goldman, and R. Rhodes (2010). The framenet constructicon. Sign-based Construction Grammar. CSLI Publications, Stanford.

Ivanova, A., S. Oepen, L. Øvrelid, and D. Flickinger (2012). Who did what to whom?: A contrastive study of syntacto-semantic dependencies. In LAW '12.

Joshi, A. and Y. Schabes (1997). Tree-adjoining grammars. Handbook Of Formal Languages 3.

Kaplan, R. and J. Bresnan (1981). Lexical-Functional Grammar: A Formal System For Grammatical Representation. Massachusetts Institute Of Technology, Center For Cognitive Science.

Marcus, M., M. Marcinkiewicz, and B. Santorini (1993). Building a large annotated corpus of english: The penn treebank. Computational Linguistics 19(2).

Màrquez, L., X. Carreras, K. Litkowski, and S. Stevenson (2008). Semantic role labeling: An introduction to the special issue. Computational Linguistics 34(2).

Meyers, A., R. Reeves, C. Macleod, R. Szekely, V. Zielinska, B. Young, and R. Grishman (2004). Annotating noun argument structure for nombank. In LREC '04.

Palmer, M., D. Gildea, and P. Kingsbury (2005). The proposition bank: An annotated corpus of semantic roles. Computational Linguistics 31(1).

Pollard, C. and I. Sag (1994). Head-driven Phrase Structure Grammar. University Of Chicago Press.

Punyakanok, V., D. Roth, and W. Yih (2008). The importance of syntactic parsing and inference in semantic role labeling. Computational Linguistics 34(2).

Schuler, K. (2005). VerbNet: A broad-coverage, comprehensive verb lexicon. Ph. D. thesis, University of Pennsylvania.

Schwartz, R., O. Abend, R. Reichart, and A. Rappoport (2011). Neutralizing linguistically problematic annotations in unsupervised dependency parsing evaluation. In ACL-NAACL '11.

Steedman, M. (2001). The Syntactic Process. MIT Press.

Van Valin, R. (2005). Exploring The Syntax-semantics Interface. Cambridge University Press.

Yamada, K. and K. Knight (2001). A syntax-based statistical translation model. In ACL '01.

Yuret, D., A. Han, and Z. Turgut (2010). Semeval-2010 task 12: Parser evaluation using textual entailments. The SemEval-2010 Evaluation Exercises On Semantic Evaluation '10.

Evaluating Topic Coherence Using Distributional Semantics

Nikolaos Aletras   Mark Stevenson
Department of Computer Science
University of Sheffield
Regent Court, 211 Portobello
Sheffield, S1 4DP, UK
{n.aletras, m.stevenson}@dcs.shef.ac.uk

Abstract

This paper introduces distributional semantic similarity methods for automatically measuring the coherence of a set of words generated by a topic model. We construct a semantic space to represent each topic word by making use of Wikipedia as a reference corpus to identify context features and collect frequencies. Relatedness between topic words and context features is measured using variants of Pointwise Mutual Information (PMI). Topic coherence is determined by measuring the distance between these vectors computed using a variety of metrics. Evaluation on three data sets shows that the distributional-based measures outperform the state-of-the-art approach for this task.

1 Introduction

Topic modelling is a popular statistical method for (soft) clustering documents (Blei et al., 2003; Deerwester et al., 1990; Hofmann, 1999). Latent Dirichlet Allocation (LDA) (Blei et al., 2003), one type of topic model, has been widely used in NLP and applied to a range of tasks including word sense disambiguation (Boyd-Graber et al., 2007), multi-document summarisation (Haghighi and Vanderwende, 2009) and generation of comparable corpora (Preiss, 2012).

A variety of approaches has been proposed to evaluate the topics generated by these models. The first to be explored were extrinsic methods, measuring the performance achieved by a model in a specific task or using statistical methods. For example, topic models have been evaluated by measuring their accuracy for information retrieval (Wei and Croft, 2006). Statistical methods have also been applied to measure the predictive likelihood of a topic model in held-out documents by computing their perplexity. Wallach et al. (2009) gives a detailed description of such statistical metrics.

However, these approaches do not provide any information about how interpretable the topics are to humans. Figure 1 shows some example topics generated by a topic model. The first three topics appear quite coherent, all the terms in each topic are associated with a common theme. On the other hand, it is difficult to identify a coherent theme connecting all of the words in topics 4 and 5. These topics are difficult to interpret and could be considered as "junk" topics. Interpretable topics are important in applications such as visualisation of document collections (Chaney and Blei, 2012; Newman et al., 2010a), where automatically generated topics are used to provide an overview of the collection and the top-n words in each topic used to represent it.

Chang et al. (2009) showed that humans find topics generated by models with high predictive likelihood to be less coherent than topics generated from others with lower predictive likelihood. Following Chang's findings, recent work on evaluation of topic models has been focused on automatically measuring the coherence of generated topics by comparing them against human judgements (Mimno et al., 2011; Newman et al., 2010b). Newman et al. (2010b) define topic coherence as the average semantic relatedness between topic words and report the best correlation with humans using the Pointwise Mutual Information (PMI) between topic words in Wikipedia.

1: oil, louisiana, coast, gulf, orleans, spill, state, fisherman, fishing, seafood
2: north, kim, korea, korean, jong, south, il, official, party, son
3: model, wheel, engine, system, drive, front, vehicle, rear, speed, power
4: drink, alcohol, indonesia, drinking, indonesian, four, nokia, beverage, mc-donald, caffeine
5: privacy, andrews, elli, alexander, burke, zoo, information, chung, user, regan

Figure 1: A sample of topics generated by a topic model over a corpus of news articles. Topics are represented by top-n most probable words.

Following this direction, we explore methods for automatically determining the coherence of topics. We propose a novel approach for measuring topic coherence based on the distributional hypothesis which states that words with similar meanings tend to occur in similar context (Harris, 1954). Wikipedia is used as a reference corpus to create a distributional semantic model (Padó and Lapata, 2003; Turney and Pantel, 2010). Each topic word is represented as a bag of highly co-occurring context words that are weighted using either PMI or a normalised version of PMI (NPMI). We also explore creating the vector space using differing numbers of context terms. All methods are evaluated by measuring correlation with humans on three different sets of topics. Results indicating that measures on the fuller vector space are comparable to the state-of-the-art proposed by Newman et al. (2010b), while performance consistently improves using a reduced vector space.

The remainder of this article is organised as follows. Section 2 presents background work related to topic coherence evaluation. Section 3 describes the distributional methods for measuring topic coherence. Section 4 explains the experimental set-up used for evaluation. Our results are described in Section 5 and the conclusions in Section 6.

2 Related work

Andrzejewski et al. (2009) proposed a method for generating coherent topics which used a mixture of Dirichlet distributions to incorporate domain knowledge. Their approach prefers words that have similar probability (high or low) within all topics and rejects words that have different probabilities across topics.

AlSumait et al. (2009) describe the first attempt to automatically evaluate topics inferred from topic models. Three criteria are applied to identify junk or insignificant topics. Those criteria are in the form of probability distributions over the highest probability words. For example, topics in which the probability mass is distributed approximately equally across all words are considered likely to be difficult to interpret.

Newman et al. (2010b) also focused on methods for measuring the semantic coherence of topics. The main contribution of this work is to propose a measure for the automatic evaluation of topic semantic coherence which has been shown to be highly correlated with human evaluation. It is assumed that a topic is coherent if all or the most of its words are related. Results showed that word relatedness is better predicted using the distribution-based Pointwise Mutual Information (PMI) of words rather than knowledge-based measures.

The method using PMI proposed by Newman et al. (2010b) relies on co-occurrences of words in an external reference source such as Wikipedia for automatic evaluation of topic quality. Mimno et al. (2011) showed that available co-document frequency of words in the training corpus can be used to measure semantic coherence. Topic coherence is defined as the sum of the log ratio between co-document frequency and the document frequency for the N most probable words in a topic. The intuition behind this metric is that the co-occurrence of words within documents in the corpus can indicate semantic relatedness.

Musat et al. (2011) associated words in a topic with WordNet concepts thereby creating topical subtrees. They rely on WordNet's hierarchical structure to find a common concept that best describes as many words as possible. It is assumed that the higher the coverage and specificity of a topical subtree, the more semantically coherent the topic. Experimental results showed high agreement with humans in the word intrusion task, in contrast to Newman et al. (2010b) who concluded that WordNet is not useful for topic evaluation.

Recent work by Ramirez et al. (2012) analyses and evaluates the semantic coherence of the results obtained by topic models rather than the semantic coherence of the inferred topics. Each topic model is treated as a partition of document-topic associations. Results are evaluated using metrics for cluster comparison.

3 Measuring Topic Coherence

Let $T = \{w_1, w_2, ..., w_n\}$ be a topic generated from a topic model which is represented by its top-n most probable words. Newman et al. (2010b) assume that the higher the average pairwise similarity between words in T, the more coherent the topic. Given a symmetric word similarity measure, $Sim(w_i, w_j)$, they define coherence as follows:

$$Coherence_{Sim}(T) = \frac{\sum_{\substack{1 \leq i \leq n-1 \\ i+1 \leq j \leq n}} Sim(w_i, w_j)}{\binom{n}{2}} \tag{1}$$

where $w_i, w_j \in T$.

3.1 Distributional Methods

We propose a novel method for determining topic coherence based on using distributional similarity between the top-n words in the topic. Each topic word is represented as a vector in a semantic space. Let $\vec{w_1}, \vec{w_2}, ..., \vec{w_n}$ be the vectors which represent the top n most probable words in the topic. Also, assume that each vector consists of N elements and $\vec{w_{ij}}$ is the jth element of vector $\vec{w_i}$. Then the similarity between the words, and therefore cohesion of the topic, can be computed using the following measures (Curran, 2003; Grefenstette, 1994):

- The **cosine** of the angles between the vectors:

$$Sim_{cos}(\vec{w_i}, \vec{w_j}) = \frac{\vec{w_i} \cdot \vec{w_j}}{\|\vec{w_i}\|\|\vec{w_j}\|} \tag{2}$$

- The **Dice** coefficient:

$$Sim_{Dice}(w_i, w_j) = \frac{2 \times \sum_{k=1}^{N} min(\vec{w_{ik}}, \vec{w_{jk}})}{\sum_{k=1}^{N} (\vec{w_{ik}} + \vec{w_{jk}})} \tag{3}$$

- The **Jaccard** coefficient:

$$Sim_{Jaccard}(w_i, w_j) = \frac{\sum_{k=1}^{N} min(\vec{w_{ik}}, \vec{w_{jk}})}{\sum_{k=1}^{N} max(\vec{w_{ik}}, \vec{w_{jk}})} \tag{4}$$

Each of these measures estimates the distance between a pair of topic words and can be substituted into equation 1 to produce a topic cohesion measure based on distributional semantics.

Alternatively, the cohesion of a set of topic words can be estimated with a single measure by computing the average distance between each topic word and the centroid:

$$Sim_{centroid} = \frac{\sum_{t \in T} sim_{cos}(T_c, t)}{n} \tag{5}$$

where T_c is the centroid of the vectors for topic T. For the experiments reported in this paper the distance of each vector to the centroid is computed using the cosine measure.

3.2 Constructing the Semantic Space

Vectors representing the topic words are constructed from a semantic space consisting of information about word co-occurrence. The semantic space was created using Wikipedia[1] as a reference corpus and a window of $\pm$ 5 words[2].

3.2.1 Weighting Vectors

Using the co-occurrence information to generate vectors directly does not produce good results so the vectors are weighted using two approaches.

For the first, **PMI**, the pointwise mutual information for each term in the context is used rather than the raw co-occurrence count. PMI is computed as follows:

$$\text{PMI}(w_i, w_j) = log_2 \frac{p(w_i, w_j)}{p(w_i)p(w_j)} \tag{6}$$

Note that this application of PMI for topic cohesion is different from one previously reported by Newman et al. (2010b) since we use PMI to weight vectors rather than to compute a similarity score between pairs of words.

In addition, vectors are also weighted using **NPMI** (Normalised PMI). This is an extension of PMI that has been used for collocation extraction (Bouma, 2009) and is computed as follows:

$$\text{NPMI}(w_i, w_j) = \frac{PMI(w_i, w_j)}{-log(p(w_i, w_j))} \tag{7}$$

Finally, we introduce γ which is a parameter to assign more emphasis on context features with high PMI (or NPMI) values with a topic word. Vectors are weighted using $PMI(w_i, f_j)^\gamma$ or $NPMI(w_i, f_j)^\gamma$ where w_i is a topic word and f_j is a context feature. For all of our experiments we set $\gamma = 2$ which was found to produce the best results.

3.2.2 Reducing the Basis

Including all co-occurring terms in the vectors leads to a high dimensional space. We also experimented with two approaches to reducing the number of terms to form a semantic space with smaller basis. Firstly, following Islam and Inkpen (2006), a **Reduced Semantic Space** is created by choosing the β_{w_i} most related context features for each topic word w_i:

$$\beta_{w_i} = \left(log(c(w_i))\right)^2 \frac{(log_2(m))}{\delta} \tag{8}$$

where δ is a parameter for adjusting the number of features for each word and m is the size of the corpus. Varying the value of δ did not effect performance for values above 1. This parameter was set of 3 for the results reported here. In addition a frequency cut-off of 20 was also applied. In addition, a smaller semantic space was created by considering only topic words as context features, leading to n features for each topic word. This is referred to as the **Topic Word Space**.

4 Experimental Set-up

4.1 Data

To the best of our knowledge, there are no standard data sets for evaluating topic coherence. Therefore we have developed one for this study which we have made publicly available[3]. A total of 300 topics are

[1] `http://dumps.wikimedia.org/enwiki/20120104/`

[2] We also experimented with different lengths of context windows

[3] The data set can be downloaded from `http://staffwww.dcs.shef.ac.uk/people/N.Aletras/resources/TopicCoherence300.tar.gz`

generated by running LDA over three different document collections:

- **NYT:** 47,229 New York Times news articles published between May and December 2010 from the GigaWord corpus. We generated 200 topics and randomly selected 100.
- **20NG:** The 20 News Group Data Collection[4] (20NG), a set of 20,000 newsgroup emails organised into 20 different subjects (e.g. sports, computers, politics). Each topic has 1,000 documents associated with it. 100 topics were generated for this data set.
- **Genomics:** 30,000 scientific articles published in 49 journals from MEDLINE, originally used in the TREC-Genomics Track[5]. We generated 200 topics and randomly selected 100.

All document were pre-processed by removing stop words and lemmatising. Topics are generated using *gensim*[6] with hyperparameters (α, β) set to $\frac{1}{num\_of\_topics}$. Each topic is represented by its 10 most probable words.

4.2 Human Evaluation of Topic Coherence

Human judgements of topic coherence were collected through a crowdsourcing platform, CrowdFlower[7]. Participants were presented with 10 word sets, each of which represents a topic. They asked to judge topic coherence on a 3-point Likert scale from 1-3, where 1 denotes a "Useless" topic (i.e. words appear random and unrelated to each other), 2 denotes "Average" quality (i.e. some of the topic words are coherent and interpretable but others are not), and 3 denotes a "Useful" topic (i.e. one that is semantically coherent, meaningful and interpretable). Each participant was asked to judge up to 100 topics from a single collection. The average response for each topic was calculated as the coherency score for the gold-standard.

To ensure reliability and avoid random answers in the survey, we used a number of questions with predefined answer (either totally random words as topics or obvious topics such as week days). Annotations from participants that failed to answer these questions correctly were removed.

We run three surveys, one for each topic collection of 100 topics. The total number of filtered responses obtained for the NYT dataset was $1,778$ from 26 participants, while for the 20NG dataset we collected $1,707$ answers from 24 participants. The participants were recruited by a broadcast email sent to all academic staff and graduate students in our institution. For the Genomics dataset the emails were sent only to members of the medical school and biomedical engineering departments. We collected $1,050$ judgements from 12 participants for this data set.

Inter-annotator agreement (IAA) is measured as the average of the Spearman correlation between the set of scores of each survey respondent and the average of the other respondents' scores. The IAA in the three surveys is 0.70, 0.64 and 0.54 for NYT, 20NG and Genomics respectively.

5 Results

Table 1 shows the results obtained for all of the methods on the three datasets. Performance of each method is measured as the average Spearman correlation with human judgements. The top row of each table shows the result using the average PMI approach (Newman et al., 2010b) while the next two rows show the results obtained by substituting PMI with NPMI and the method proposed by Mimno et al. (2011). The main part of each table shows performance using the approaches described in Section 3 using various combinations of methods for constructing the semantic space and determining the similarity between vectors.

[4]http://people.csail.mit.edu/jrennie/20Newsgroups
[5]http://ir.ohsu.edu/genomics
[6]http://radimrehurek.com/gensim
[7]http://crowdflower.com

NYT		
Newman et al. (2010b)		0.71
Average NPMI		0.74
Mimno et al. (2011)		-0.39
Reduced Semantic Space		
	PMI	NPMI
Cosine	0.69	0.68
Dice	0.63	0.62
Jaccard	0.63	0.61
Centroid	0.67	0.67
Topic Words Space		
	PMI	NPMI
Cosine	**0.76**	0.75
Dice	0.68	0.71
Jaccard	0.69	0.72
Centroid	**0.76**	0.75

20NG		
Newman et al. (2010b)		0.73
Average NPMI		0.76
Mimno et al. (2011)		0.34
Reduced Semantic Space		
	PMI	NPMI
Cosine	0.78	0.79
Dice	0.77	0.78
Jaccard	0.77	0.78
Centroid	0.77	0.78
Topic Words Space		
	PMI	NPMI
Cosine	0.79	**0.8**
Dice	0.79	**0.8**
Jaccard	**0.8**	**0.8**
Centroid	0.78	0.79

Genomics		
Newman et al. (2010b)		0.73
Average NPMI		0.76
Mimno et al. (2011)		-0.4
Reduced Semantic Space		
	PMI	NPMI
Cosine	0.74	0.73
Dice	0.69	0.68
Jaccard	0.69	0.76
Centroid	0.73	0.71
Topic Words Space		
	PMI	NPMI
Cosine	**0.8**	**0.8**
Dice	0.79	**0.8**
Jaccard	**0.8**	**0.8**
Centroid	**0.8**	**0.8**

Table 1: Performance of methods for measuring topic coherence (Spearman Rank correlation with human judgements).

Using the average PMI between topic words correlates well with human judgements, 0.71 for NYT, 0.73 for 20NG and 0.75 for Genomics confirming results reported by Newman et al. (2010b). However, NPMI performs better than PMI, with an improvement in correlation of 0.03 for all datasets. The improvement is down to the fact that NPMI reduces the impact of low frequency counts in word co-occurrences and therefore uses more reliable estimates (Bouma, 2009).

On the other hand, the method proposed by Mimno et al. (2011) does not correlate well with human judgements, (-0.39 for NYT, 0.34 for 20NG and -0.4 for Genomics) which is the lowest performance of all of the methods tested. This demonstrates that while co-document frequency helps to generate more coherent topics (Mimno et al., 2011), it is sensitive to the size of the collection.

Results obtained using the reduced semantic space and PMI are lower than the average PMI and NPMI approaches for the NYT and Genomics data sets. For the 20NG dataset the results are higher then the average PMI and NPMI using these approaches. The difference in relative performance is down to the nature of these corpora. The words found in topics in the NYT and Genomics datasets are often

Topic Terms	Human Rating
Top-3	
family wife died son father daughter life became mother born	2.63
election vote voter ballot state candidate voting percent party result	3
show television tv news network medium fox cable channel series	2.82
Bottom-3	
lennon circus rum whiskey lombardi spirits ranch idol make vineyard	1.93
privacy andrews elli alexander burke zoo information chung user regan	1.25
twitter board tweet followers conroy halloween kay hands emi post	1.53

Figure 2: Top-3 and bottom-3 ranked topics using Topic Word Space in NYT together with human ratings.

polysemous or collocate with terms which become context features. For example, one of the top context features of the word "coast" is "ivory" (from the country). However, that feature does not exist for terms that are related to "coast", such as "beach" or "sea". The majority of topics generated from 20NG contain meaningless terms due to the noisy nature of the dataset (emails) but these do not suffer from the same problems with ambiguity and prove to be useful for comparing meaning when formed into the semantic space.

Similar results are obtained for the reduced semantic space using NPMI as the association measure. Results in NYT and Genomics are normally 0.01 lower while for 20NG are 0.01 higher for the majority of the methods. This demonstrates that weighting co-occurrence vectors using NPMI produces little improvement over using PMI, despite the fact NPMI has better performance when the average similarity between each pair of topic terms is computed.

When the topic word space is used there is a consistent improvement in performance compared to the average PMI (Newman et al., 2010b) and NPMI approaches. More specifically, cosine similarity using PMI is consistently higher (0.05-0.06) than average PMI for all datasets and 0.02 to 0.04 higher than average NPMI (0.76, 0.79, 0.8 for NYT, 20NG and Genomics respectively). One reason for this improvement in performance is that the noise caused by polysemy and high dimensionality of the context features of the topic words is reduced. Moreover, cosine similarity scores in the reduced semantic space are higher than average PMI and NPMI in all of the datasets, demonstrating that vector-based representation of the topic words is better than computing their average relatedness. Table 2 shows the top-3 and bottom-3 ranked topics in NYT together with human ratings.

Another interesting finding is that the cosine metric produces better estimates of topic coherency compared to Dice and Jaccard in the majority of cases, with the exception of 20NG in reduced semantic space using PMI. Furthermore, similarity to the topic centroid achieves performance comparable to cosine.

6 Conclusions

This paper explored distributional semantic similarity methods for automatically measuring the coherence of sets of words generated by topic models. Representing topic words as vectors of context features and then applying similarity metrics on vectors was found to produce reliable estimates of topic coherence. In particular, using a semantic space that consisted of only the topic words as context features produced the best results and consistently outperforms previously proposed methods for the task.

Semantic space representations have appealing characteristics for future work on tasks related to topic models. The vectors used to represent topic words contain co-occurring terms that could be used for topic labelling (Lau et al., 2011). In addition, tasks such as determining topic similarity (e.g. to identify similar topics) could naturally be explored using these representations for topics.

Acknowledgments

The research leading to these results was carried out as part of the PATHS project (`http://paths-project.eu`) funded by the European Community's Seventh Framework Programme (FP7/2007-2013) under grant agreement no. 270082.

References

Loulwah AlSumait, Daniel Barbará, James Gentle, and Carlotta Domeniconi. Topic Significance Ranking of LDA Generative Models. *Machine Learning and Knowledge Discovery in Databases*, pages 67–82, 2009.

David Andrzejewski, Xiaojin Zhu, and Mark Craven. Incorporating Domain Knowledge into Topic Modeling via Dirichlet Forest Priors. In *Proceedings of the International Conference on Machine Learning*, pages 25–32, 2009.

David M. Blei, Andrew Y. Ng, and Michael I. Jordan. Latent Dirichlet Allocation. *Journal of Machine Learning Research*, 3:993–1022, 2003.

G. Bouma. Normalized (pointwise) mutual information in collocation extraction. In *Proceedings of the International Conference of the German Society for Computational Linguistics and Language Technology (GSCL '09)*, Potsdam, Germany, 2009.

Jordan Boyd-Graber, David Blei, and Xiaojin Zhu. A topic model for word sense disambiguation. In *Proceedings of the 2007 Joint Conference on Empirical Methods in Natural Language Processing and Computational Natural Language Learning (EMNLP-CoNLL '07)*, pages 1024–1033, 2007.

Allison June-Barlow Chaney and David M. Blei. Visualizing topic models. In *Proceedings of the 6th International AAAI Conference on Weblogs and Social Media (IWSCM)*, 2012.

Jonathan Chang, Jordan Boyd-Graber, and Sean Gerrish. Reading Tea Leaves: How Humans Interpret Topic Models. *Neural Information*, pages 1–9, 2009.

James R. Curran. From distributional to semantic similarity. *Ph.D. Thesis, University of Edinburgh*, 2003.

Scott Deerwester, Susan T. Dumais, George W. Furnas, Thomas K. Landauer, and Richard Harshman. Indexing by latent semantic analysis. *Journal of the American Society for Information Science*, 41(6): 391–407, 1990.

Gregory Grefenstette. *Explorations in Automatic Thesaurus Discovery*. Springer, 1994.

Aria Haghighi and Lucy Vanderwende. Exploring content models for multi-document summarization. In *Proceedings of Human Language Technologies: The 2009 Annual Conference of the North American Chapter of the Association for Computational Linguistics*, pages 362–370, Boulder, Colorado, 2009.

Zellig Sabbettai Harris. Distributional structure. *Word*, 10:146–162, 1954.

Thomas Hofmann. Probabilistic latent semantic indexing. In *Proceedings of the 22nd Annual International ACM SIGIR Conference on Research and Development in Information Retrieval (SIGIR '99)*, pages 50–57, Berkeley, California, United States, 1999.

Aminul Md. Islam and Diana Inkpen. Second Order Co-occurrence PMI for Determining the Semantic Similarity of Words. In *Proceedings of the 5th International Conference on Language Resources and Evaluation (LREC '06)*, pages 1033–1038, 2006.

Jey Han Lau, Karl Grieser, David Newman, and Timothy Baldwin. Automatic labelling of topic models. In *Proceedings of the 49th Annual Meeting of the Association for Computational Linguistics: Human Language Technologies*, pages 1536–1545, Portland, Oregon, USA, June 2011.

David Mimno, Hanna Wallach, Edmund Talley, Miriam Leenders, and Andrew McCallum. Optimizing semantic coherence in topic models. In *Proceedings of the 2011 Conference on Empirical Methods in Natural Language Processing*, pages 262–272, Edinburgh, Scotland, UK, 2011.

Claudiu C. Musat, Julien Velcin, Stefan Trausan-Matu, and Marian A. Rizoiu. Improving topic evaluation using conceptual knowledge. In *Proceedings of the Twenty-Second International Joint Conference on Artificial Intelligence (IJCAI '11)*, pages 1866–1871, Barcelona, Spain, 2011.

David Newman, Timothy Baldwin, Lawrence Cavedon, Eric Huang, Sarvnaz Karimi, David Martinez, Falk Scholer, and Justin Zobel. Visualizing search results and document collections using topic maps. *Web Semantics: Science, Services and Agents on the World Wide Web*, 8(23):169–175, 2010a.

David Newman, Jey Han Lau, Karl Grieser, and Timothy Baldwin. Automatic evaluation of topic coherence. In *Human Language Technologies: The 2010 Annual Conference of the North American Chapter of the Association for Computational Linguistics (NAACL-HLT '10)*, pages 100–108, Los Angeles, California, 2010b.

Sebastian Padó and Mirella Lapata. Constructing semantic space models from parsed corpora. In *Proceedings of the 41st Annual Meeting of the Association for Computational Linguistics*, pages 128–135, Sapporo, Japan, 2003.

Judita Preiss. Identifying comparable corpora using LDA. In *Proceedings of the 2012 Conference of the North American Chapter of the Association for Computational Linguistics: Human Language Technologies*, pages 558–562, Montréal, Canada, 2012.

Eduardo H. Ramirez, Ramon Brena, Davide Magatti, and Fabio Stella. Topic Model Validation. *Neurocomputing*, 76(1):125–133, 2012.

Peter D. Turney and Patrick Pantel. From frequency to meaning: Vector space models of semantics. *Journal of Artificial Intelligence Research*, 37:141–188, 2010.

Hanna M. Wallach, Iain Murray, Ruslan Salakhutdinov, and David Mimno. Evaluation Methods for Topic Models. In *Proceedings of the 26th Annual International Conference on Machine Learning (ICML '09)*, pages 1105–1112, Montreal, Quebec, Canada, 2009.

Xing Wei and W. Bruce Croft. LDA-based Document Models for Ad-hoc Retrieval. In *Proceedings of the 29th annual international ACM SIGIR conference on Research and Development in Information Retrieval (SIGIR '06)*, pages 178–185, 2006.

Automatically Deriving Event Ontologies for a CommonSense Knowledge Base

James Allen[1,2], Will de Beaumont[1], Lucian Galescu[1], Jansen Orfan[2], Mary Swift[2] and Choh Man Teng[1]

[1] Institute for Human and Machine Cognition, Pensacola, FL
[2] Dept. Of Computer Science, University of Rochester
{jallen, wbeaumont, lgalescu, cmteng}@ihmc.us
{jorfan, swift}@cs.rochester.edu

Abstract

We describe work aimed at building commonsense knowledge by reading word definitions using deep understanding techniques. The end result is a knowledge base allowing complex concepts to be reasoned about using OWL-DL reasoners. We show that we can use this system to automatically create a mid-level ontology for WordNet verbs that has good agreement with human intuition with respect to both the hypernym and causality relations. We present a detailed error analysis that reveals areas of future work needed to enable high-performance learning of conceptual knowledge by reading.

1. Introduction

Most researchers agree that attaining deep language understanding will require systems that have large amounts of commonsense knowledge. Such knowledge will need to be expressed in terms that support semantic lexicons as used by parsing systems, with concept hierarchies and semantic roles, and provide knowledge required for disambiguation as well as deriving key entailments. While there have been many attempts to hand-build such knowledge, most notably within the Cyc project (Lenat, 1995), as well as ontology-building efforts such as SUMO (Niles & Pease, 2001), GUM (Bateman et al., 1995), DOLCE (Gangemi et al., 2002) and EuroWordNet (Vossen, 1998), these fall short of encoding the range and depth of needed knowledge. This motivates work in building a commonsense knowledge base automatically from reading online sources. Learning by reading offers the opportunity not only to amass a significant knowledge base for processing online sources, but also allows for learning on demand - i.e., looking up something in a dictionary or Wikipedia when needed.

Recently, there has been significant interest in acquiring knowledge using information extraction techniques (e.g., Etzioni et al, 2011; Carlson et al, 2010). Such work, however, remains close to the surface level of language - involving mostly uninterpreted words and phrases and surface relations between them (e.g., is-a-subject-of, is-an-object-of), or a limited number of pre-specified relations. In addition, information extraction tends to focus more on learning facts (e.g., *Rome is the capital of Italy*) than conceptual knowledge (e.g., *kill* means *cause to die*).

We have been exploring the feasibility of building extensive knowledge bases by reading definitional sources such as online dictionaries and encyclopedias such as Wikipedia. So far, we have focussed on what knowledge can be derived by reading the glosses in WordNet (Fellbaum, 1998). This is a good start for the project for several reasons. First, WordNet is the most used lexical resource in computational linguistics, and so a knowledge base indexed to WordNet would be most readily accessible for use in other projects. Second, a significant portion (i.e., about 50%) of the content words in WordNet glosses have been sense tagged by hand, thus giving us considerable help on tackling the word sense disambiguation problem. And third, WordNet has hand-built semantic structures, such as the hypernym and troponym hierarchies, as well as tagged relations such as *cause*, and *part-of*, which give us a hand-coded standard to compare against. While most previous work on extracting knowledge from WordNet has focused on exploiting these hand-built relations, we focus solely on what can be extracted by understanding the glosses, which consist of short definitions (e.g., kill: *cause to die*) and a few examples (e.g., *This man killed several people when he tried to rob a bank*), and use the hand-built relations for evaluation. The goal is a system that is not WordNet specific, but could be used on any source of definitional knowledge. This projects shares some of the same goals with the work of Nichols et al. (2005), who convert definitions from a machine readable dictionary of Japanese into underspecified semantic representations using Robust Minimal Recursion Semantics (Frank, 2004) and construct an ontology based on extracted hypernyms and synonyms.

While many complain about WordNet, it is an unparalleled lexical resource. Attempts to use WordNet as an ontology to support reasoning have mainly focussed on nouns, because the noun hypernym hierarchy provides a relatively good subclass hierarchy (e.g., Gangemi et al. 2003). The situation is not the same for verbs however. Verbs in WordNet have no organization into an ontology of event types in terms of major conceptual categories such as states, processes, accomplishments and achievements (cf. Vendler 1957). Instead, WordNet has a set of 15 semantic domains that serve as unique beginners for verbs, such as verbs of motion and verbs of communication. The verbs are then organized around a troponym hierarchy - capturing manner modifications (e.g., destroy is a killing done in a particular way). Fellbaum (1998) argues against a top-level verb distinction between events and states, or *be* and *do* as suggested in Pulman (1983), for several reasons. A goal of WordNet was to reflect human lexical organization, and there is a lack of psycholinguistic evidence that humans have strong associations between abstract concepts such as *do* and more specific verbs. This lack of a hierarchical mid-level[1] ontology for events creates a significant obstacle to unifying WordNet with ontologies that are built to encode commonsense knowledge and support reasoning.

In this paper, we report on work that attempts to address this problem and bring formal ontologies and lexical resources together in a way that captures the detailed knowledge implicit in the lexical resources. Specifically, we focus on building an ontology by reading word definitions -- and use WordNet glosses as our test case for evaluating the feasibility of doing so. It is important to remember here that our goal is to develop new techniques for building knowledge bases by reading definitions in general, and our work is not specific to WordNet, though we use WordNet for evaluation.

It is always difficult to evaluate the usefulness and correctness of ontologies. We resort to using several focussed evaluations of particular types of knowledge using human judgement. In some of these cases, we find that WordNet itself provides some information related to these aspects, so we can compare the coverage and accuracy of our automatically constructed ontology with the explicitly coded information in WordNet. For example, we can evaluate the coverage of our event hierarchy by comparing to the WordNet troponym hierachy, and we can compare the causal relationships we derive between events with the explicitly annotated *cause* relations in WordNet.

2. Encoding Knowledge in WordNet Glosses

There have been several prior attempts to process glosses in WordNet to produce axioms that capture entailments. For the most part, these representations are fairly shallow, and look more like an encoding of the syntactic information in a logical notation, with each word represented as a predicate. Furthermore, some of the encodings resist a formal interpretation. For instance, the representations in eXtended WordNet (Harabagiu et al. 2003) contain variables that are free, predicates that have variable arity, and lack a principled representation of logical operators, particularly disjunction. As such, it cannot support sound inference procedures. Furthermore the predicates are just words, not disambiguated senses. Clark et al. (2008) produce a representation where the predicates are senses, but share many of the other weaknesses of eXtended WordNet. Agerri & Peñas (2010) resolve a number of these issues and generate intermediate logical forms that have no free variables nor unconnected predicates in the definitions, but the formalism still resembles an encoding of syntax as opposed to a semantic representation. As an example, Figure 1 shows the representation generated for the definition of the adjective *bigheaded* as *overly conceited or arrogant*. It is not clear what the semantics of the encoding of disjunction (i.e., *conj_or(x3,x5)*) plays in the definition, as it appears that both modifiers *conceited* and *arrogant* appear in parallel *amod* relations to the variable *x1*. It is hard to imagine an inference mechanism that would handle the disjunction correctly given this representation.

---

[1] we distinguish between the upper ontology (identifying the fundamental conceptual distinctions underlying knowledge), the mid-level ontology (capturing general knowledge of events), and the domain ontology, capturing specific knowledge about particular domains.

something(x1) ^ amod(x1,x3) ^ amod(x1,x5) ^ overly(x2) ^ conceited(x3)

^ advmod(x3,x2) ^ conj_or(x3,x5) ^ arrogant(x5)

Figure 1: Agerri & Peñas (2010) representation of the gloss "overly conceited or arrogant"

Building a good ontology requires more than natural language processing--it requires sophisticated reasoning to identify subsumption relations implicit in the definitions. We pick our target formalism for the ontology to be description logic, specifically OWL, and use its associated reasoners to compute the subsumption relations. As an example, we encode the definition of *bigheaded* as

$$\text{bigheaded} \sqsubseteq \forall\_\text{of.(person)} \sqcap ((\text{conceited} \sqcap \forall\_\text{of}^{-1}.(\text{degree-modifier and overly})) \sqcup \text{arrogant})$$

i.e., *bigheaded* is a predicate that applies to people, and which is a subclass of the union of things that are conceited (with degree modifier overly) with things that are arrogant. Note that OWL allows types defined by relations and their inverses: $\forall\_\text{of.(person)}$ is the class of all objects that are in the domain of an of relation with only people (i.e., person) in the range, whereas $\forall\_\text{of}^{-1}.\text{(person)}$ would be the class of all objects that are in the range of a relation with only person in the domain. While description logic is less expressive than first order logic, our experience has shown that it provides a good formalism for capturing much of the content in definitions and produces a representation that supports provably tractable inference about hierarchical relationships over complex types, making it suitable for encoding ontologies.

3. Parsing Glosses

We parse WordNet glosses with a slightly modified TRIPS parser (Allen et al., 2008). The TRIPS semantic lexicon provides information on semantic roles and selectional restrictions for about 5000 verbs, and the parser constructs a semantic representation of the language that is rich enough for reasoning. TRIPS has already shown promise in parsing WordNet glosses in order to build commonsense knowledge bases (Allen et al., 2011). The logical form is a graphical formalism that captures an unscoped modal logic (Manshadi et al. 2008). Figure 2 shows the logical form graph for the definition of *kill* as to *cause to die*. The graph consists of nodes that specify the word senses for each word (both its sense in the TRIPS ontology and the WordNet Sense) and quantification information, and relations between the nodes are labelled with semantic roles. The IMPRO nodes are derived from the gaps in the definition and become the arguments for the new concept, namely kill%2:35:00[2].

WordFinder

To attain broad lexical coverage beyond its hand-defined lexicon, the TRIPS parser uses input from a variety of external resources. WordFinder is a subsystem that accesses WordNet when an unknown word is encountered. The WordNet senses have hand-built mappings to semantic types in the TRIPS ontology, although sometimes at a fairly abstract level. WordFinder uses the combined information from WordNet and the TRIPS lexicon and ontology to dynamically build lexical entries with approximate semantic and syntactic structures for words not in the core lexicon.

WordFinder offers a powerful tool for increased lexical coverage. However, the information in entries constructed by WordFinder is frequently underspecified, so the parser must deal with significantly increased levels of ambiguity when dealing with dynamically constructed words. There are several

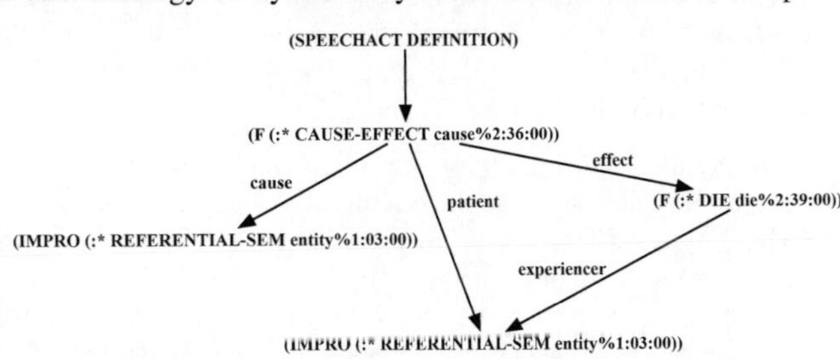

Figure 2: TRIPS parser output for definition "to cause to die"

[2] We use the WordNet sense key notation throughout, which uses three values to identify a sense: kill%2:35:00 is a verb (2), is a verb of contact (35), and has a unique identifier (00) within this group.

settings that can be used to control how WordFinder is used during parsing. First, users can specify the number of senses returned from WordNet. WordNet may have multiple fine-grained senses for a given word, but depending on the application, selecting the most frequent senses listed in WordNet will suffice (cf. McCarthy et al. 2004).

Word Sense Disambiguation

As we mentioned earlier, one thing that makes WordNet glosses a good experimental dataset for our initial experiments is that many of the words in the glosses have been hand-tagged with their word senses (though see section 6 for an analysis of errors in the tagging). The remainder of the words, however, need to be tagged. We use a set of heuristic strategies to identify the WordNet senses for these words. First, for words that appear in the hand-built TRIPS lexicon, we simply use these TRIPS-WordNet mappings to identify the possible WordNet senses for each TRIPS sense, and then have the parser select the best interpretation in its usual manner, based on syntactic templates possible for each word, the selectional preferences, and finally frequency-based preferences among the senses. For words not in the TRIPS lexicon, we generate lexical entries for a small number of WordNet senses using WordFinder, drawing first from the Core WordNet senses (Boyd-Graber et al, 2006), and/or the most frequent senses (i.e., the first senses listed in WordNet).

4. Building Event Classes from Definitions

Because many glosses are complex, often highly elliptical and hard to parse, we depend on the ability of the TRIPS parser to produce semantically meaningful fragments when a full spanning parse cannot be found. In addition, we apply several strategies to create simplified definitions that are used as backup in case the full definition doesn't parse: These simplifications are

- if the definition starts with "verb or verb ....", truncate the first two words
- If the definition contains "or", "and", or comma, truncate the definition starting at that token

We parse the full definition and any simplifications produced, and then find the fragment or full interpretation that covers the greatest amount of the gloss while producing a definition that is semantically compatible with the target word (e.g., verbs must map to events, adjectives must map to predicates). Note that natural definitions, including those in WordNet, sometimes indicate necessary conditions while at other times indicate necessary and sufficient conditions, and do not reliably signal such cases. For the present, we treat all definitions as specifying only necessary conditions. Because of this, when we define a sense based on only part of its definition, it typically still produces useful knowledge.

We identify the likely arguments (i.e., semantic roles) of the concept using signals in the logical form such as the presence of gaps and the use of a few indefinite pro-forms such as *someone, somewhere, etc.* Note that most roles are **not** explicit in the definition. For example, the definition of *kill*, *cause to die,* does not explicitly express the subject or the object of the cause and the LF recovers this missing information, producing something like *<something> causes <something> to die*. We identify the semantic roles for these arguments by checking the TRIPS lexicon for the roles involved in the verb *cause*, or if there is no explicit entry in the lexicon, we use WordFinder to derive the likely roles by employing the WordNet to TRIPS ontology mapping. In this case, the roles for *kill%2:35:00* would be identified as *AGENT* and *PATIENT.*

To refine the roleset and compute selectional restrictions, we then try to parse the examples provided in WordNet, plus additional examples involving the current word sense being defined from the SEMCOR corpus[3]. These examples provide some evidence as to the range of syntactic templates and semantic roles that can occur with the verb, as well as providing examples of possible fillers. We compute a selectional preference for each role by attempting to find the most common subsumer of all the examples in either the WordNet hypernym

New Concept Name: kill%2:35:00
Roles: AGENT person%1:03:00
PATIENT organism%1:03:00
Definition: LF graph in Figure 2

Figure 3: The information derived for the concept corresponding to kill%2:35:00

[3] http://www.cse.unt.edu/~rada/downloads.html#semcor

hierarchy, or in the TRIPS ontology (and then mapping from this value back to the equivalent WordNet senses). At the end of this first phase of processing the definition, we have derived the information shown in Figure 3 for *kill%2:35:00*.

The next phase is to convert this information into OWL DL. In most cases we are performing a one-to-one mapping from the LF to OWL where concepts in the LF become OWL classes and roles are mapped to corresponding OWL object role restrictions. For example, we begin converting kill%2:35:00 with the selectional preferences by asserting that it is a subclass of the expression: ∀_agent.person%1:03:00 ⊓ ∀_patient.organism%1:03:00 (i.e., all things that have agents that are person%1:03:00 and have patients that are organism%1:03:00). Note that the we can use the more informative universal restriction instead of an existential because we assume that verbs have at most one of each core role.

Next, we handle the conversion of the LF graph of the gloss shown in Figure 2. We begin at the head of the definition, the CAUSE-EFFECT node, by creating a new OWL class that uniquely represents that node, we will call C1, and assert, kill%2:35:00 ⊑ C1. Next we define C1 simply as the subclass of the conjunction of its WordNet class, cause%2:36:00, and its semantic restrictions. To translate the :EFFECT role we first create a new class, D1, and then create the object role restriction ∀_effect.D1. Doing this for each of C1's roles produces the axiom

C1 ⊑ cause%2:36:00 ⊓ ∀_effect.D1 ⊓ ∀_patient.R1 ⊓ ∀_cause.R2.

We then recursively define any new classes; in this example, D1 ⊑ die%2:39:00 ⊓ ∀_experiencer.R1 , R1 ⊑ entity%1:03:00, R2 ⊑ entity%1:03:00.

We next must handle the multiple references to R1. The LF treats each object as a unique instance so when it is referred to more than once in an LF we know that each reference indicates the same instance. When we convert the LF to OWL the objects are no longer instances but are instead classes. In the above example, we no longer have the meaning that the patient and experiencer are the same individual - only that they belong to the same class, R1. In order to capture the intended meaning we introduce an OWL data property called varID which uniquely names the reference. varID acts as an indicator that when the classes are grounded those with the same varID are the same OWL instance. Using this methodology, we have the final set of assertions for the definition:

kill%2:35:00 ⊑ ∀_agent.person%1:03:00 ⊓ ∀_patient.organism%1:03:00 ⊓ C1
C1 ⊑ cause%2:36:00 ⊓ ∀_effect.D1 ⊓ ∀patient.(R1 ⊓ varID="r1") ⊓ ∀_cause.R2
D1 ⊑ die% 2.39.00 ⊓ ∀_experiencer.(R1 ⊓ varID="r1")
R1 ⊑ entity%1:03:00
R2 ⊑ entity%1:03:00

Note that we are using a hierarchical roleset similar to the combining of VerbNet and LIRICS roles as described in Bonial et al (2011), with slight variations in the role names. Specifically, the Agent role is a specialization of the Cause role (i.e., the axiom agent ⊑ cause is in the OWL KB), thus we know that the the agent of kill%2:35:00 is the same as the cause role in the definition of C1.

Modifiers are indicated with a relation :MOD (see Figure 4) that indicates the presence of a backlink with semantic meaning but do not add any semantics itself. We remove these cycles and replace them with inverse object roles meant to represent the backlink. For the example, the concept defined in Figure 4 would be a subclass of die%2:39:00 ⊓ ∃_OF^{-1}.quickly%4:02:00. Notice that modifiers use the less restrictive existential rather than the universal since we do not restrict objects to have only one modifier. This is a very simple example. The same technique works for more complex cases like dealing with relative clauses.

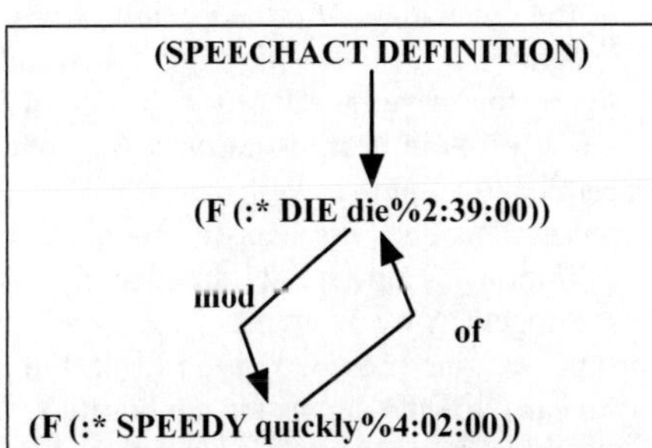

Figure 4: An LF graph with a modifier

	0	*1*	*2*	*3*	*4*	*5*	*6*	*7*	*8*	*9*	*10*	*11*	*12*
# new verb senses	559	255	169	150	99	75	66	41	34	29	15	15	10
# new senses	559	853	988	970	748	543	437	318	230	163	106	64	46

Table 1: The number of new senses introduced with each iteration

Logical operators such as conjunction, disjunction and negation are converted directly into the corresponding OWL operators, allowing the conversion of arbitrarily complex logical forms.

The translation process described above captures enough of the meaning in the LF to support the system described in the rest of the paper but it does not capture all the possible entailments one might be able to derive. In the future, we would like to encode core semantic roles in the gloss (not the ones found in selectional preferences) as the more appropriate exactly-one cardinality constraint coupled with an existential constraint. For instance, ∀_effect.D1 (if there is an effect then it is of type D1) becomes =1_effect.⊤ ⊓ ∃_effect.D1 (there is only one effect and it is of type D1). We are also exploring how to better handle negation in glosses. Consider the gloss for acquitted, "declared not guilty of a specific offense or crime; legally blameless". What "not guilty" actually indicates is the opposite of guilty, i.e., innocent. While it would be correct to say that the _effect of the declare action is of the class ¬guilty, it isn't very useful. A lot of unrelated things could be ¬guilty: dog, blue, running, etc.

5. Building a Mid-Level Ontology for WordNet Verbs

As mentioned earlier, defining a mid-level ontology was not one of the goals of the WordNet designers. The hierarchical organization of verbs is the troponym hierarchy, which captures *manner* specialization (e.g., *beating* is a type of *striking* which is a type of *touching*). The sense *touch%2:35:00* is a top-level sense and has no more abstract characterization. There are 559 such synsets in WordNet that have no hypernyms, and these concepts range from concepts that would serve as useful primitives (like *touch, breathe)* to more specific senses such as three senses of the verb *keep up* (prevent from going to bed, keep informed, and maintain a required pace or level). The sense of *kill* we have used as an example is also one of the top-level verbs. In addition, over 200 of these verbs have no troponyms either, leaving these sense essentially unrelated hierarchically to any other verbs in WordNet.

The idea underlying this experiment is that we can build a mid-level ontology by reading the glosses of these words. The consequence of this is that each of the previous top-level verb synsets will now have a superclass concept, e.g., kill%2:35:00 will now have a superclass of cause%2:36:00 ⊓ ∃_effect.die%2:30:00 (i.e., "cause to die") which of course is a specialization of the general class cause%2:36:00. Note that while many linguistic ontologies capture only subclass links between atomic types, we are generating much richer information that captures the definition in terms of a complex type. In this example, we not only have derived a hierarchical relation between kill%2:35:00 and cause%2:36:00, but also the causal relationship between kill%2:35:00 and die%2:30:00.

After this first iteration, we will have introduced a new set of word senses, both verbs and non verbs, that have not yet been defined. So we then iterate using the same procedure on this new set of words to define them. In principle, we continue this iteration as long as new undefined senses are introduced. In the evaluation described below, we stopped after twelve iterations and completed the remaining undefined terms by adding the hypernym chain for the concept. Table 1 shows the number of new senses that were introduced with each iteration. It takes another dozen iterations, each one adding just a few verbs in order to exhaust the generation of new undefined senses. One might think that this continual defining of verb senses would produce a full event hierarchy rooted at some "mother" verb-sense! This does not happen however, because of the presence of cycles in the definitions. Circular definitions "short-circuit" the identification of more abstract classes and tend to collapse sets of synsets together. We examined these circular classes by hand and found that most result from errors in the sense tagging provided in the Princeton WordNet Gloss Corpus. By correcting these tagging errors, we can avoid the unwanted circularities. Other cycles appear to cluster around core definitional primitives that simply are hard to define in any formal decompositional way, and we leave them as they are.

Class	*Definition*
Air%2:32:03	be broadcast%2:32:01
broadcast%2:32:01	**broadcast%2:32:00** over the airwave%1:10:00, as in radio or television%1:06:01
broadcast%2:32:00	cause to become widely known%3:00:00

Table 2: The definitions used to infer that 'airing something' causes it 'to become known'

We discuss our analysis of the cycles generated from processing the top-level WordNet verb classes in a later section. The evaluation examines systems with and without these word sense corrections.

Empirical Evaluation

While we have built a knowledge base containing significant amounts of conceptual information by reading the glosses, here we focus on evaluating just two aspects of this knowledge base. First is the hierarchical relations between the bare WordNet classes, which is a mid-level ontology for WordNet verbs. The second involves causal relationships that can be derived from the knowledge. Some of these are trivial (e.g., *kill%2:35:00* causes *die%2:39:00*), while others are revealed from inference. For instance, the subsumption algorithm will compute that the verb class *air%2:32:03* causes the event of something becoming *known%3:00:00*. There is much more information in this knowledge base than we are going to evaluate here. For instance, it contains knowledge about the changes of state and transitions that serve to define many verbs, and in Allen et al (2011) we demonstrate an ability to perform temporal inference using the knowledge base. But in this paper we focus solely on evaluating just the hierarchical and causal relations between bare WordNet classes in order to enable a direct comparison with WordNet.

We randomly selected 6N (N=8) pairs of verb concepts (A, B) from those that our system successfully processed (columns 0-11 in Table 1), such that at least N of them fell into each of the four categories "{WordNet, our OWL-DL knowledge base} says that A {is a kind of, causes} B", and such that 2N pairs were unrelated in either source. We then presented the pairs in different randomized orders to a set of human judges and asked them to identify whether there was a causal or hierarchical relation between the events, or whether they were unrelated. As judges, we used six researchers who had been involved with the project as well as five people who have no relation to the work. We computed the inter-rater agreement (IRA) using Cohen's kappa score (Cohen, 1960). Kappa was computed for each pair of judges, then averaged to provide a single index of IRA (Light, 1971). The resulting kappa indicated substantial agreement, $\varkappa = 0.63$ (Landis & Koch, 1977). In order to eliminate the cases where their was no consensus among the judges, we only consider the cases in which eight or more judges agreed, which was 83% of the samples, and used the majority decision as the gold standard. We can then evaluate the accuracy of the hand-coded relations in WordNet against two versions of our system: one processing the raw glosses in WordNet and the other with 79 corrected word sense tags out of over 5000 glosses processed.

The precision and recall results are shown in Table 3. The most important property we desire is that the knowledge produced is accurate, i.e., the precision score. This reflects the ability of the systems to produce accurate knowledge from processing glosses. If precision is high, we could always improve recall by processing more definitional sources. We see that the precision scores for the system generated relations are quite good, over 80% for the hypernym relations and a perfect 100% for the causal relations.

Regarding WordNet, we see that the hand-coded relations had a 100% precision, indicating that the structural information in WordNet is highly accurate. The recall numbers, however, show that a significant number of possible relations are missed, especially for causal relations. This suggests that it is worth exploring whether the information implicit in the glosses is redundant given the hand-coding, or whether they serve as an important additional source of knowledge. We can explore this by comparing the sets of relations produced by the system with the relations in WordNet. If they overlap significantly, then the hand-built WordNet relations are fairly complete. If they are disjoint, then the glosses contain an important additional source of these structural relations. The analysis is summarized in Table 4. We look at each relation proposed by WordNet or the system, and look at the overlap

Source	*Hypernym*			*Causal*		
	P	R	F1	P	R	F1
Processing Raw Glosses	80%	33%	47%	100%	36%	53%
Processing Corrected Glosses	83%	42%	56%	100%	55%	71%
Explicit WordNet relations	100%	83%	91%	100%	55%	71%

Table 3: Precision and Recall Scores Against Human Judgement

Relation	*WordNet*	*System*	*count*	*Human Judgement*	
				yes	*no*
Causation	Yes	Yes	1	1	0
	Yes	No	5	5	0
	No	Yes	5	5	0
	No	No	29	0	29
Hypernym	Yes	Yes	3	3	0
	Yes	No	7	7	0
	No	Yes	3	2	1
	No	No	27	0	27

Table 4: Comparing the Redundancy between WordNet & System-generated relations

and disjoint cases. The data show a surprising disjointness between what is explicitly coded in WordNet and the information derived from the glosses. Out of 11 cases of causal relations, there is only one overlap between WordNet and the system, and the remaining relations are equally divided, with five causal relations in WordNet that were not derivable by the system, and five causal relations the system derived that are not coded in WordNet. Thus there is significant causal knowledge derivable from the glosses that is not currently encoded in WordNet. With hypernyms, results are similarly disjoint, with only three out of thirteen cases both encoded in WordNet and derived by the system.

6. Error Analysis

Consider the cases where a hand-coded hypernym relation was not derived from the definitions. In general, the most common reasons for this include problems in parsing and an inability to reason from the provided definitions to the desired entailments. Interestingly, virtually all the errors in the evaluation set are problems the reasoning side. Some of these are because the definitions simply don't provide enough information, and in other cases the system lacked of an ability to resolve vagueness in the definitions. For instance, by failing to make a connection between "deprive of life" and "cause to die", the system misses that *annihilate%2:30:00* is a subclass of *kill%2:35:00*. In another case, it fails to note the relationship between *compose* and *create* due to the definition creating a disjunction that cannot be reasoned through. Specifically, *compose%2:36:01* is found to be a subclass of the class (OR create%2:36:00 construct%2:36:01). In other cases, the conclusion is not found because of sense tagging errors. For instance, the system cannot conclude that *corrupt%2:41:00* is a subclass of *alter%2:30:01* in either version of the system. The system running on uncorrected tags ended in a circular definition of *corrupt%2:41:00*. The system running with corrected tags infers that corrupting is making a mess of someone morally, and cannot relate this to causing a change in someone. As a final example, definitions sometimes involve phrasal verbs that are not defined in WordNet. For instance, *posit%2:32:02* is defined as "put%2:35:00 before" where the system knows nothing about a sense of *put before* as a verb of communication, and this phrasal verb is not defined in WordNet.

The one false positive in the evaluation was when the system derived that *excogitate%2:36:00*, defined by "come up with (an idea, plan, explanation, theory, or principle) after a mental effort", is a subclass of *execute%2:36:00*, defined as "put into effect". This conclusion results from a long chain of reasoning through definitions of *come up with*, to *bring forth*, to *bring*, to *take* and finally to *accomplish%2:36:00*, which is in the same synset as *execute%2:36:00*. It is hard to identify a specific flaw in this chain, but the human judges resoundingly judged this pair as being unrelated.

In general, exploring the results beyond this specific evaluation, the most common problem found was word sense tagging errors, mostly by the system on words that were not tagged in the glosses (and one hand-tagged in the WordNet files). Most of these were light verbs, specifically *have, give* and *put*, and generally the system tagged a more common concrete sense (e.g., *have* as possession) rather than the abstract causal sense (e.g., *have* as causing something). We believe such errors can be reduced by specializing the WSD algorithm to more specifically bias the senses useful in definitions. Other cases arose because the system identified the incorrect semantic roles in the definition, thereby losing the required entailments, and the system has significant problems in getting the right scoping for definitions containing disjunctions. We explore the sense tagging issues in more detail below.

Word Sense Corrections

As mentioned before, the initial, automatically generated ontology contained a number of senses with circular definitions that prevented deriving desired entailments. For example, we have in WordNet the following definition (showing only the relevant sense keys) for the synset *stick%2:35:00*: (stick%2:35:00 to firmly).

In general, cycles indicate equivalence of the senses involved and logically collapse the synsets into one single class. We manually examined these cycles and determined that many of their definitions had been mis-tagged, and used the follow strategies to break many of the cycles.

- *Selecting an Alternative Sense:* We re-tagged the offending lemma with a different sense of the lemma. In the example of stick%2:35:00:: above, its definition should refer to a more basic sense stick%2:35:01:: (come or be in close contact with; stick or hold together and resist separation)
- *Replacing with a Hypernym:* There may not always be an alternative sense that seems appropriate. We replaced some of these circular senses with their hypernyms. For the circular definition *cast_away%2:40:00: (throw_away%2:40:00 or cast_away%2:40:00),* we replaced both words in the definition with their (common) hypernym: *cast_away%2:40:00: (get_rid_of%2:40:01::)*
- *Unpacking Phrases:* In WordNet phrasal verbs are often defined in entries separate from those of their head verbs. For example, *go_into%2:42:00* has its own definition *(be used or required for).* However, WordNet also includes an entry for the non-phrasal-verb sense of "go into" *go_into%2:38:00: (to come or go_into%2:38:00).* In this second example, "go into" literally means "go" + "into". We broke the phrase into these two components in the definition: *go_into%2:38:00: (to come or go%2:38:00 into)*
- *Simplifying Definitions:* Some definitions contain elaborate, detailed and slightly redundant information. For example: *pronounce%2:32:01: (speak, pronounce%2:32:01, or utter in a certain way)* Logically, with one of the disjuncts being identical to the sense being defined, the definition is vacuous. However, here "speak", "pronounce" and "utter" are closely related. We could break the cycle by deleting "pronounce" in the definition. Arguably this strategy could lose some information, but we only apply this simplification when the disjunct is nearly synonymous with some of the other elements in the definition.

There remain, however, some cycles that represent core concepts not easily reducible to other even more basic concepts. For example, the four-synset cycle containing

change%2:30:00 < undergo%2:39:04 < pass%2:38:00 < go%2:38:00 < change%2:30:00

are all related to the concept of change. We elected not to contrive a re-definition but rather leave these cycles in place. Such cycles are prime candidates for core concepts that would benefit from being hand axiomatized in an upper ontology.

7. Discussion

We have described initial steps in constructing common-sense knowledge bases by reading word definitions. The focus of this work is to derive conceptual knowledge, i.e., definitions of concepts associated with word senses, to facilitate deeper language understanding. This stands in contrast to much current work on learning by reading, which is focused on building surface level word/phrase relationships. For instance, Etzioni et al (2011) have an impressive system that scans the web and extracts surface patterns such as (Starbucks, has, a new logo). NELL (Carlson et al, 2010) derives similar knowledge by learning extraction patterns for a predefined set of relations. Neither of these systems attempt to disambiguate word senses or construct definitional knowledge. The evaluation is performed

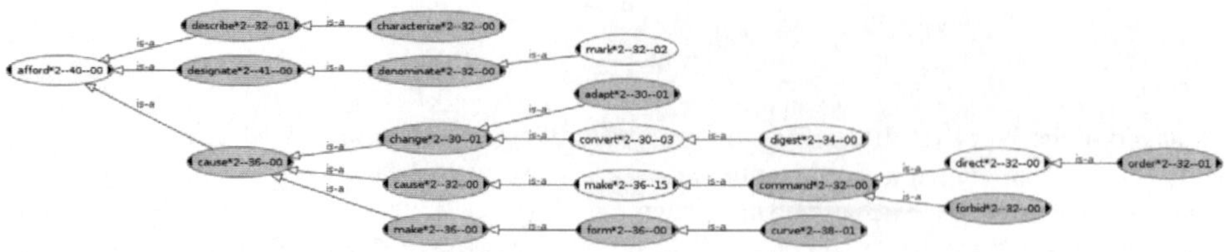

Figure 5: A fragment of the event hierarchy derived from the glosses

by human judges who, of course, used their ability to understand natural language in order to validate the data (e.g.., picking word senses that make sense).

As a demonstration of the promise of our techniques, we have shown that we can construct a mid-level ontology for WordNet verbs from the WordNet glosses, starting from the 559 verb senses in WordNet that have no hypernym. We evaluate the results using human judges comparing relations between word senses in WordNet, where each sense is carefully defined in the evaluation. We have shown that the knowledge we derive is not only quite accurate, but is substantially different from the information already in the explicitly defined WordNet relations (e.g., hypernym and cause relations). As such, our techniques have the potential to produce an expanded set of WordNet style relations that could be very useful for improving current techniques that use WordNet as a source of entailments.

Most prior work linking WordNet to ontologies has involved producing mappings from the synsets into an upper ontology, without developing the intermediate detail. For instance, SUMO has a comprehensive mapping from WordNet to its upper ontology, but 670 WordNet verb synsets are mapped to the single SUMO class *IntentionalProcess* (3 equivalences and 667 subsumptions), including senses as diverse as *postdate* (establish something as being later relative to something else), *average* (achieve or reach on average), *plug* (persist in working hard), *diet* (follow a regimen or a diet, as for health reasons), *curtain off* (separate by means of a curtain) and *capture* (succeed in representing or expressing something intangible). While these links connect WordNet into SUMO, they don't provide significant extra knowledge to enable entailments. Our work can provide links to an upper ontology with significant additional structure providing an opportunity for entailment. As an example, Figure 5 shows a small part of the derived ontology. This encodes such information like *forbidding* is a form of *commanding*, which involves *making someone do something*, which itself is a form of *causation*. With each of the concepts along this chain having a detailed definition in the style described in Section 4, we can use reasoning systems developed for OWL-DL to draw a rich set of entailments about the consequences of performing a *forbidding* act.

Much remains to be done to realize our dream of building rich knowledge bases by reading. There are short term issues and longer term issues. On the short term, the biggest improvement would result from improving word sense disambiguation, especially for the light verbs such as *have* and *go*. It is not a coincidence that these verbs generally are not tagged in the Princeton Gloss corpus. They are difficult to tag, and it is not clear that the senses offered in WordNet always provide the right set of choices. We are considering special processing of these abstract senses, possibly encoding them directly in a hand-built upper ontology. In the longer term, we need to expand our evaluation methods to verify that the knowledge derived beyond hypernym and causal relations is accurate and useful. This will presumably involve more complex entailment tests. Finally, in the long run, we do not believe that effective knowledge bases can be derived entirely from processing individual definitions without some inferentially-based "knowledge cleaning" where raw knowledge is combined from several sources, abstracted and revised in order to create more consistent and coherent knowledge.

8. Acknowledgements

This work was supported in part by the National Science Foundation under grant 1012205, by DARPA grant 1012205 FA8750-09-C-0179 in the Machine Reading program, and ONR grant N000141110417.

9. References

Agerri, R., Anselmo Peñas (2010) On the Automatic Generation of Intermediate Logic Forms for WordNet Glosses. CICLing 2010: 26-37.

Allen, J., W. de Beaumont, N. Blaylock, G. Ferguson, J. Orfan, M. Swift (2011) Acquiring Commonsense Knowledge for a Cognitive Agent. AAAI Advances in Cognitive Systems (ACS 2011), Arlington, VA.

Allen, J., M. Swift and W. de Beaumont. Deep Semantic Analysis for Text Processing. Symposium on Semantics in Systems for Text Processing (STEP 2008) Shared Task: Comparing Semantic Representations. Venice, Italy, September 22-24, 2008.

Bateman, J.A., B. Magnini, and G. Fabris (1995) The generalized upper model knowledge base: Organization and use. In N.J.I. Mars (Ed.). Towards very large knowledge bases: Knowledge building and knowledge sharing. Amsterdam: IOS Press.

Bonial, C., Brown, S.W., Corvey, W., Palmer, M., Petukhova, V., and Bunt, H. (2011). An Exploratory Comparison of Thematic Roles in VerbNet and LIRICS, Proceedings of the Sixth Joint ISO - ACL SIGSEM Workshop on Interoperable Semantic Annotation (ISA-6).

Boyd-Graber, J., Fellbaum, C., Osherson, D., and Schapire, R. (2006). "Adding dense, weighted connections to WordNet." In: Proceedings of the Third Global WordNet Meeting, Jeju Island, Korea, January 2006

Carlson, A. Justin Betteridge, Bryan Kisiel, Burr Settles, Estevam R. Hruschka Jr., and Tom M. Mitchell. Toward an architecture for never-ending language learning. In AAAI'10, 2010.

Clark, P., Fellbaum, C., Hobbs, J.R., Harrison, P., Murray, W.R., Thompson, J. (2008) Augmenting WordNet for Deep Understanding of Text. In: Bos, J., Delmonte, R. (eds.) Semantics in Text Processing. STEP 2008 Conference Proceedings. Research in Computational Semantics, vol. 1. College Publications.

Cohen, J. (1960). A coefficient of agreement for nominal scales. *Educational and Psychological Measurement*, 20(1), 37-46.

Etzioni, O., A. Fader, J. Christiansen, S. Soderland, and Mausam. Open Information Extraction: The next generation, IJCAI, 2011.

Fellbaum, S. (1998, ed.) WordNet: An Electronic Lexical Database. Cambridge, MA: MIT Press.

Frank, A. (2004) Constraint-based RMRS construction from shallow grammars. COLING-2004, Geneva.

Gangemi, A., N. Guarino, C. Masolo, A. Oltramari, and L. Schneider (2002). Sweetening ontologies with DOLCE. In A. Gómez-Pérez and V. Benjamins (Eds.), Knowledge Engineering and Knowledge Management: Ontologies and the Semantic Web, Berlin, Heidelberg: Springer Berlin.

Gangemi, A., Navigli, R., Velardi, P. Axiomatizing WordNet Glosses in the OntoWordNet Project (2003) Workshop on Human Language Technology for the Semantic Web and Web Services, 2nd International Semantic Web Conference (ISWC2003). Sanibel Island, Florida.

Harabagiu, S.M., Miller, G.A., Moldovan, D.I. (2003): eXtended WordNet - A Morphologically and Semantically Enhanced Resource, http://xwn.hlt.utdallas.edu.

Landis, J. R., & Koch, G. G. (1977). The measurement of observer agreement for categorical data. *Biometrics*, 33(1), 159-174.

Lenat, D. B. (1995): Cyc: A Large-Scale Investment in Knowledge Infrastructure. The Communications of the ACM 38(11):33-38.

McCarthy, D., R. Koeling, J. Weeds, and J. Carroll, (2004) Finding predominant senses in untagged text. In Proc. of the 42nd Annual Meeting of the Association for Computational Linguistics. Barcelona, Spain..

Mehdi H. Manshadi, James Allen, Mary Swift, "Towards a Universal Underspecified Semantic Representation", Proc. 13th Conference on Formal Grammar (FG 2008), Hamburg, Germany, August 9-10, 2008

Nichols, E., F. Bond, and D. Flickinger, Robust ontology acquisition from machine-readable dictionaries, IJCAI-2005.

Niles, I. and Pease, A. Towards a Standard Upper Ontology (2001) In Proc. 2nd International Conf. on Formal Ontology in Information Systems (FOIS-2001), Chris Welty and Barry Smith, eds, Ogunquit, Maine.

Pulman, S. G. (1983) Word meaning and belief. London: Croom Helm.

Vendler, Z. Verbs and Times. The Philosophical Review, Vol. 66, No. 2. (Apr., 1957), pp. 143-160.

Vossen, P. (Ed.). (1998). EuroWordNet: A Multilingual Database with Lexical Semantic Networks. Dordrecht: Kluwer Academic Publishers.

Intensionality was only alleged:
On adjective-noun composition in distributional semantics

Gemma Boleda
The University of Texas at Austin
gboleda@cs.utexas.edu

Marco Baroni
University of Trento
marco.baroni@unitn.it

Nghia The Pham
University of Trento
thenghia.pham@unitn.it

Louise McNally
Universitat Pompeu Fabra
louise.mcnally@upf.edu

Abstract

Distributional semantics has very successfully modeled semantic phenomena at the word level, and recently interest has grown in extending it to capture the meaning of phrases via semantic composition. We present experiments in adjective-noun composition which (1) show that adjectival modification can be successfully modeled with distributional semantics, (2) show that composition models inspired by the semantics of higher-order predication fare better than those that perform simple feature union or intersection, (3) contrary to what the theoretical literature might lead one to expect, do not yield a distinction between intensional and non-intensional modification, and (4) suggest that head noun polysemy and whether the adjective corresponds to a typical attribute of the noun are relevant factors in the distributional representation of adjective phrases.

1 Introduction

Distributional semantics (see Turney and Pantel, 2010, for an overview) has been very successful in modeling lexical semantic phenomena, from psycholinguistic facts such as semantic priming (McDonald and Brew, 2004) to tasks such as picking the right synonym on a TOEFL exercise (Landauer and Dumais, 1997). More recently, interest has increased in using distributional models to account not only for word meaning but also for phrase meaning, i.e. semantic composition (Mitchell and Lapata, 2010; Baroni and Zamparelli, 2010; Socher et al., 2012; Garrette et al., 2012).

Adjectival modification of nouns is a particularly useful and at the same time challenging testbed for different distributional models of composition, because syntactically it is very simple, while the semantic effect of the composition is very variable and potentially complex due to the frequent context dependence of the relation between the adjective and the noun (Asher, 2011, provides recent discussion). As a comparatively underexplored area of semantic theory, it is also an empirical domain where distributional models can give feedback to theoreticians about how adjectival modification works. In the formal semantic tradition, the analysis of adjectives has been largely motivated by the general entailment patterns in which they participate (Parsons, 1970; Kamp, 1975, and subsequent work). For example, if something is a *white towel*, then it is both white and a towel. This use of *white* is *intersective*: it yields an adjective-noun phrase (hereafter, AN phrase) whose denotation is the intersection of the denotations of the adjective and the noun. If someone is a *skillful surgeon*, then she is a surgeon but not necessarily skillful in general. Such adjectives are *subsective*: The denotation of the phrase is a subset of that of the noun. Finally, if someone is an *alleged murderer*, we cannot be sure that she is a murderer, and it is not even grammatical to say that she is "alleged". Intensional adjectives thus do not appear to describe attributes or relations; rather, they are almost universally modeled as higher-order properties, whereas intersective and subsective (hereafter, non-intensional) adjectives have been given both first-order and higher-order analyses.

Given these facts, we can expect that intensional adjectives will be more difficult to model computationally than non-intensional adjectives. Moreover, they raise specific issues for the increasingly popular distributional approaches to semantics. First, as intensional adjectives cannot be modeled as first-order properties, it is hard to predict what their representations might look like or what their semantic effect would be in standard distributional models of composition based on vector addition or multiplication. This is so because addition and multiplication correspond to feature combination (see Section 2 for discussion), and it is not obvious what set of distinctive distributional features an intensional adjective would contribute on a consistent basis.

In Boleda et al. (2012), we presented a first distributional semantic study of intensional adjectives. However, our study was limited in two ways. First, it compared intensional adjectives with a very narrow class of non-intensional adjectives, namely color terms; this raises doubts about the generality of our results. Second, the study had methodological weaknesses, as we did not separate training and test data, nor did we do any systematic parameter tuning prior to carrying out our experiments. This paper adresses these limitations by covering a wider variety of adjectives and using a better implementation of the composition functions, and performs several qualitative analyses on the results.

Our results confirm that high quality adjective composition is possible in distributional models: Meaningful vectors can be composed, if we take phrase vectors directly extracted from the corpus as a benchmark. In addition, we find (perhaps unsurprisingly) that models that replicate higher-order predication within a distributional approach, such as Baroni and Zamparelli (2010) and Guevara (2010), fare better than models based on vector addition or multiplication (Mitchell and Lapata, 2010). However, unlike our previous study, we find no difference in the relative success of the different composition models on intensional vs. non-intensional modification, nor in relevant aspects of the distributional representations of corpus-harvested phrases. Rather, two relevant effects involve the polysemy of the noun and the extent to which the adjective denotes a typical attribute of the entity described by the noun.

These results indicate that, in general, adjectival modification is more complex than simple feature intersection, even for adjectives like *white* or *ripe*. We therefore find tentative support for modeling adjectives as higher-order functors as a rule, despite the fact that entailment phenomena do not force such a conclusion and certain facts have even been used to argue against it (Larson, 1998, and others). The results also raise deeper and more general questions concerning the extent to which the entailment-based classification is cognitively salient, and point to the need for clarifying how polysemy and typicality intervene in the composition process and how they are to be reflected in semantic representations.

2 Composition functions in distributional semantics

Distributional semantic models represent words with vectors that record their patterns of co-occurrence with other words (or other linguistic contexts) in corpora. The raw counts are then typically transformed by reweighting and dimensionality selection or reduction operations (see Clark, 2012; Erk, 2012; Turney and Pantel, 2010, for recent surveys). Although there has always been interest in how these models could encode the meaning of phrases and larger constituents, the last few years have seen a huge increase in the number of studies devoted to *compositional* distributional semantics. We will now briefly review some of the composition methods that have been proposed and that we re-implemented here, focusing in particular on how they model AN phrases.

Mitchell and Lapata, in a set of very influential recent studies summarized in Mitchell and Lapata (2010), propose three simple and effective approaches to composition, showing that they outperform more complex models from the earlier literature. Their **weighted additive** model derives a phrase vector $\mathbf{p}$ by a weighted sum of its parts $\mathbf{u}$ and $\mathbf{v}$ (in our study, the $\mathbf{u}$ and $\mathbf{v}$ vectors to be composed will stand for adjectives and nouns, respectively):

$$\mathbf{p} = \alpha\mathbf{u} + \beta\mathbf{v}$$

The **multiplicative** model proceeds by component-wise multiplication:

$$p_i = u_i v_i$$

Assuming that one of the words in the phrase acts as its "head", the **dilation** model performs composition by analyzing the head vector $\mathbf{v}$ in terms of components parallel and orthogonal to the modifier vector $\mathbf{u}$, and stretching only the parallel component by a factor λ:

$$\mathbf{p} = (\lambda - 1)(\mathbf{u} \cdot \mathbf{v})\mathbf{u} + (\mathbf{u} \cdot \mathbf{u})\mathbf{v}$$

The natural assumption, in our case, is that the noun acts as head (**v**) and the adjective as modifier (**u**). We experimented with the other direction as well, obtaining, unsurprisingly, worse results than those we report below for dilation with noun as head. Note that dilation can be seen as a special way to estimate the parameters of weighted addition on a phrase-by-phrase basis ($\alpha = (\lambda - 1)(\mathbf{u} \cdot \mathbf{v})$; $\beta = \mathbf{u} \cdot \mathbf{u}$).

If we interpret the components of distributional vectors as *features* characterizing the meaning of a target word, the Mitchell and Lapata models amount to essentially feature union or intersection, where the components of a phrase are those features that are active in either (union; additive model) or both (intersection; multiplicative model) the noun and/or adjective vectors. Thus, the result is "adjective-like" and/or "noun-like". Indeed, in our experiments below the nearest neighbors of phrase vectors built with these models are very often the adjective and noun components.[1] This makes intuitive sense: for example, as discussed in Boleda et al. (2012), for *white dress* feature combination makes the phrase more similar to *wedding* than to *funeral*, through the association between *white* and *wedding*. However, as formal semanticists have long observed, adjective-noun composition is often *not* a feature combination operation. Most obviously in the case of intensional adjectives, it is not correct to think of an *alleged murderer* as somebody who possesses an intersection (or union, for that matter) of features of *murderers* and features of *alleged* things.

Guevara (2010) explores the **full additive** model, an extension of the additive model where, before summing, the two n-dimensional input vectors are multiplied by two $n \times n$ weight matrices:

$$\mathbf{p} = \mathbf{A}\mathbf{u} + \mathbf{B}\mathbf{v}$$

Unlike weighted addition and dilation, the full additive method derives the value in each component of the output vector by a weighted combination of *all* components of both input vectors, providing more flexibility. Still, a single weight matrix is used for all adjectives, which fails to capture the intuition that adjectives can modify nouns in very different ways (again, compare *white* to *alleged*).

Baroni and Zamparelli (2010) go one step further, taking the classic Fregean view of composition as function application, where certain words act as functions that take other words as input to return the semantic representation of the phrase they compose. Given that matrices encode linear functions, their **lexical function** model treats composition as the product of a matrix $\mathbf{U}$ representing the word acting as the functor and a vector $\mathbf{v}$ representing the argument word (essentially the same idea is put forth also by Coecke et al., 2010):

$$\mathbf{p} = \mathbf{U}\mathbf{v}$$

In our case, adjectives are functors and nouns arguments. Each adjective is represented by a separate matrix, thus allowing maximum flexibility in the way in which adjectives produce phrases, with the goal of capturing relevant adjectival modification phenomena beyond union and intersection.

As mentioned in the Introduction, "matrix-based" models such as the full additive and lexical function models are more similar to higher-order modification in formal semantics than feature combination models are. Thus, we expected them to perform better in modeling intensional modification, while it could be the case that for non-intensional modification feature combination models work just as well. As will be shown in Section 4, what we find is that the matrix-based model perform best across the board, and that no model finds intensional modification more difficult.

[1]Nearest neighbors are the semantic space elements having the highest cosines with the phrase of interest. These can be any of the 42K elements presented in Section 3.3: adjectives, nouns, or AN phrases.

3 Experimental setup

3.1 Semantic space

A distributional semantic space is a matrix whose rows represent target elements in terms of (functions of) their patterns of co-occurrence with contexts (columns or dimensions). Several parameters must be manually fixed or tuned to instantiate the space.

Our source corpus is given by the concatenation of the ukWaC corpus, a mid-2009 dump of the English Wikipedia and the British National Corpus,[2] for a total of about 2.8 billion tokens. The corpora have been dependency-parsed with the MALT parser (Hall, 2006), so it is straightforward to extract all cases of adjective-noun modification. We use part-of-speech-aware lemmas as our representations both for target elements and dimensions. (e.g., we distinguish between noun and verb forms of *can*).

The target elements in our semantic space are the 4K most frequent adjectives, the 8K most frequent nouns, and approximately 30K AN phrases. The phrases were composed only of adjectives and nouns in the semantic space, and were chosen as follows: a) all the phrases for the dataset that we evaluate on (see Section 3.3 below), and b) the top 10K most frequent phrases, excluding the 1,000 most frequent ones to avoid highly collocational / non-compositional phrases. The phrases were used for training purposes, and also entered in the computation of the nearest neighbors.

The dimensions of our semantic space are the top 10K most frequent content words in the corpus (nouns, adjectives, verbs and adverbs). We use a bag-of-words representation: Each target word or phrase is represented in terms of its co-occurrences with content words within the same sentence. Note that this also applies to the AN phrases: We build vectors for phrases in the same way we do for adjectives and nouns, by collecting co-occurrence counts with the dimensions of the space (Baroni and Zamparelli, 2010; Guevara, 2010). This way, we have the same type of representation for, say, *hard*, *rock*, and *hard rock*. We will call the vectors directly extracted from the corpus (as opposed to derived compositionally) **observed vectors**.

We optimized the remaining parameters of our semantic space construction on the independent task of maximizing correlation with human semantic relatedness ratings on the MEN benchmark[3] (see the references on distributional semantics at the beginning of Section 2 above for an explanation of the parameters). We found that the best model on this task was one where all dimensions where used (as opposed to removing the 50 or 300 most frequent dimensions), the co-occurrence matrix was weighted by Pointwise Mutual Information (as opposed to: no weighting, logarithm transform, Local Mutual Information), dimensionality reduction was performed by Nonnegative Matrix Factorization[4] (as opposed to: no reduction, Singular Value Decomposition), and the dimensionality of the reduced space was 350 (among values from 50 to 350 in steps of 50). The best performing model achieved very high 0.78 (Pearson) and 0.76 (Spearman) correlation scores with the MEN dataset, suggesting that we are using a high-quality semantic space.

3.2 Parameters of composition models

Except for the multiplication method, all composition models have parameters to be tuned. Following Guevara (2010) and Baroni and Zamparelli (2010), we optimize the parameters of the models by minimizing (with standard least squares regression methods) the average distance of compositionally derived vectors representing a phrase to the corresponding observed vectors extracted from the corpus (e.g., minimize the distance between the *hard rock* vector constructed by a model and the corresponding *hard rock* vector directly extracted from the corpus). There is independent evidence that such observed phrase vectors are semantically meaningful and provide a good optimization criterion. Baroni et al. (2013) report an experiment in which subjects consistently prefer the nearest neighbors of observed phrase vectors

[2]`http://wacky.sslmit.unibo.it/; http://en.wikipedia.org; http://www.natcorp.ox.ac.uk/`

[3]`http://clic.cimec.unitn.it/~elia.bruni/MEN`

[4]Unlike the more commonly used Singular Value Decomposition method, Nonnegative Matrix Factorization produces reduced dimensions that have no negative values, and are not fully dense.

I	alleged	former	future	hypothetical	impossible	likely	mere	mock
N	loose	wide	white	naive	severe	hard	intelligent	ripe
I	necessary	past	possible	potential	presumed	probable	putative	theoretical
N	modern	black	free	safe	vile	nasty	meagre	stable

Table 1: Evaluated adjectives. Intensional (I) and non-intensional (N) adjectives are paired by frequency.

over challenging foils. Turney (2012) shows how the observed vectors outperform any compositionally-derived model in a paraphrasing task. Grefenstette et al. (2013) reach state-of-the-art performance on widely used sentence similarity test sets with composition functions optimized on the observed vectors (see also Baroni et al., 2012; Baroni and Zamparelli, 2010; Boleda et al., 2012).

Since we use the same criterion to evaluate the quality of the models, we are careful to separate training phrases from those used for evaluation (we introduce the test set in the next section). The weighted additive, dilation and full-additive models require one single set of parameters for all adjectives, and we thus use the top 10K most frequent phrases in our semantic space (excluding test items) for training. For the lexical function model, we need to train a separate weight matrix for each adjective. We do this by using as training data, for each adjective, all phrase vectors in our semantic space that contain the adjective and are not in the test set. These range between 52 (*ripe*) and 1,789 (*free*). For weighted additive, we find that the best weights are $\alpha = 0.48$, $\beta = 0.61$, giving only marginally more weight to the noun. For dilation, $\lambda = 1.69$.

3.3 Evaluation set

We evaluate the models on a set of 16 intensional adjectives and a set of 16 non-intensional adjectives, paired according to frequency (see Table 1). The intensional adjectives were chosen starting from the candidate list elaborated for Boleda et al. (2012), with two modifications. First, the frequency criteria were altered, allowing the addition of seven more adjectives (e.g., *alleged* and *putative*). Second, we removed adjectives that can be used predicatively with the same intensional interpretation despite having been claimed to meet the entailment test for intensionality; this excludes, e.g., *false* (cp. *This sentence is false*). Adjectives that have a non-intensional predicative use alongside a non-predicative intensional one, e.g., *possible* (cp. *The possible winner* vs. ??*The winner was possible*, but *Peace was possible*) were left in, despite the potential for introducing some noise. The non-intensional adjectives were chosen by generating, for each intensional adjective, a list of the 20 adjectives closest in frequency and taking from that list the closest match in frequency that was morphologically simple (excluding, e.g., *unexpected* or *photographic*) and unambiguously an adjective (excluding, e.g., *super* and *many*).

We used all the AN phrases in the corpus with a frequency of at least 20 for all adjectives except the underrepresented ones (*nasty*, *mock*, *probable*, *hypothetical*, *impossible*, *naive*, *presumed*, *putative*, *vile*, *meagre*, *ripe*), for which we selected at most 200 phrases, taking phrases down to a frequency of 5 if needed. For each adjective, we randomly sampled 50 phrases for testing (total: 1,600).[5] The rest were used for training, as described above. The results and analyses in sections 4 and 5 concern the test data only.

4 Results

4.1 Overall results

Table 2 (first column) shows the results of the main evaluation: Average cosine of phrase vectors produced by composition models (henceforth, **predicted vectors**) with the corresponding observed vectors. As a baseline (last row in the table), we take doing no composition at all, that is, taking as the predicted vector simply the noun vector. This is a hard baseline: Since AN phrases in general denote a set closely related to the noun, noun-phrase similarities are relatively high.

[5]The dataset is available from the first author's webpage.

Model	Global	Intensional	Non-intensional	NN=A	NN=N
observed	-	-	-	*8.2*	*3.3*
lexical function	**0.60**±0.11	**0.60**±0.10	**0.60**±0.10	0.9	0.6
full additive	0.52±0.13	0.52±0.13	0.51±0.12	10.0	4.8
weighted additive	0.48±0.14	0.48±0.14	0.48±0.14	23.2	13.3
dilation	0.42±0.18	0.42±0.17	0.42±0.17	31.0	11.6
multiplicative	0.32±0.21	0.32±0.20	0.32±0.20	29.9	16.6
noun only	*0.40±0.18*	*0.40±0.17*	*0.40±0.17*	-	-

Table 2: Predicted-to-observed vector cosines for each model (mean ± standard deviation), globally and by adjective type. The last two columns show the average % of the 50 nearest neighbors that are adjectives (NN=A) and nouns (NN=N), as opposed to AN phrases.

The global results show that the matrix-based models (lexical function and full additive) clearly outperform the models based on a simple combination of the component vectors, and the lexical function model ranks best, with a high cosine score of 0.6.[6] It is also robust, as it exhibits the lowest standard deviation (0.11). The models that are based on some form of weighted addition[7] score in the middle, above the baseline but clearly below matrix-based models. Contrary to Mitchell and Lapata's results, where often multiplicative is the best performing model, multiplication in our experiments performs worst, and actually below the noun-only baseline. Moreover, the multiplicative model has the highest standard deviation (0.21), so it is the least robust model. This matches informal qualitative analysis of the nearest neighbors: The multiplicative model does very well on some phrases, and very poorly on others. Given the aggressive feature intersection that multiplication performs (zeroing out dimensions with no shared counts, inflating the values of shared dimensions), our results suggest that it is in general better to perform a "smoothed" union as in weighted addition. We leave it to further work to compare our results and task with Mitchell and Lapata's.

The table (columns *Intensional*, *Non-intensional*) also shows that, contrary to expectation, no model finds intensional modification more difficult, or indeed any difference between the two types of modification: The mean predicted-to-observed cosines for the two types of phrases are the same. This holds for both matrix-based and feature-combination-based models. For further discussion, see Section 5.

The last two columns of Table 2 show the average percentage of adjectives and nouns, respectively, among the 50 nearest neighbors of the phrase vectors. Observed phrases have few such single word neighbors (8.2% and 1.6% on average). We observe the same pattern as with the global evaluation: Matrix-based models also have low proportions of single word neighbors, thus corresponding more closely to the observed data,[8] while the other models exhibit a relatively high proportion of such neighbors. Single word neighbors are not always bad (e.g., the weighted additive model proposes *dolphin* for *white whale*), but their high proportion suggests that feature combination models often produce more general and therefore less related nearest neighbors. This was confirmed in a small qualitative analysis of nearest neighbors for the weighted additive model.

To sum up, the superior results of matrix-based models across the board suggest that adjectival modification is not about switching features on and off, but rather about a more complex type of transformation. Indeed, our results suggest that this is so not only for intensional adjectives, which have traditionally already been treated as higher-order predicates, but also for adjectives like *white*, *hard*, or *ripe*, whose analysis has been more controversial. If this is so, then it is not so surprising that in general the models do not find intensional adjectives any more difficult to model.

[6]Despite the large standard deviations, even the smallest difference between the models is highly significant, as is the smallest difference in the table: dilation vs. baseline (noun only), paired t-test, $t = 38.2$, df = 1599, $p < 2.2\text{e-}16$, mean of differences = 0.02.

[7]That dilation is essentially another way to estimate weighted addition, as discussed in section 2, is empirically confirmed by the fact that the correlation between the predicted-to-observed cosines for weighted additive and dilation is 0.9.

[8]In fact, the lexical function model is a bit extreme, producing almost no adjective and noun nearest neighbors.

Indeed, once an adjective is composed with a noun, the result is something that is not merely the sum of its parts. We associate with *black voter* something much more specific than merely *a voter that is black*, for instance, in the US, strong connotations of likely political inclinations. In this respect, an adjective does not just help to pick out a subset of the noun's denotation; it enriches the description contributed by the noun. This is in line with observations in the cognitive science literature on concept combination, essentially a counterpart of semantic composition. Murphy (2002, 453-453) discusses the case of *dog magazine* (with a noun modifier, but the same point holds for adjectives), arguing that its meaning is not just *magazine about dogs*: People "can infer other properties of this concept. A dog magazine probably is directed toward dog owners and breeders;... unlike many other magazines, it probably does not contain holiday recipes, weight-loss plans... Importantly, these kinds of properties... are not themselves properties of the concepts of dog or magazine but arise through the interaction of the two."

4.2 Comparing the quality of predicted and observed vectors

We have used observed data for phrases both to train and tune our models and to evaluate the results. If we can work with the observed data, what do we need composition for? Due to Zipf's Law, there is only a limited amount of phrases for which we can have enough data to build a meaningful representation. Perfectly plausible modifiers of nouns may never be observed in actual corpora. Thus, we need a way to combine semantic representations for words, and this is partly what drives the research on composition in distributional semantics. It is natural to hypothesize that, for rare phrases, predicted vectors will actually be more useful than observed vectors. We carried out a pilot study that supports this hypothesis.

A native speaker of English and linguist evaluated the quality of the nearest neighbors of frequent versus (relatively) rare phrases, comparing the lexical function model and the observed data. As frequent phrases, we took the top 100 most frequent phrases in the semantic space. As rare phrases, the 95 phrases with corpus frequency 20-21. The task of the judge was to choose, for a given target phrase, which of two randomly ordered nearest neighbors was more semantically related to it (we found, in earlier studies, that this type of choice is easier than assigning absolute scores to separate items). For instance, the judge had to choose whether *modern study* or *general introduction* was a semantically closer neighbor to *modern textbook*. The items were two nearest neighbors with the same rank, where the rank was randomly picked from 2-10 (the top nearest neighbor was excluded because it is trivially always the target phrase for observed vectors). The judge obviously did not know which model generated which nearest neighbor.

The results indicate that observed vectors yield better nearest neighbors for frequent phrases, as they were chosen 60% of the times (but note that the lexical function also fared well, since its nearest neighbors were preferred in 40% of the cases). However, for rare phrases we find the inverse pattern: The lexical function neighbor is preferred in 59% of the cases. For instance, the lexical function produces *nasty cold* for *nasty cough*, which was preferred to the observed nearest neighbor *medical attention*. This suggests that the composed vectors offer a better representation of rare phrases, and in tasks that depend on such phrases, they should yield better results than the observed ones.

5 Analysis

As mentioned in the Introduction, in Boleda et al. (2012) we found differences between intensional adjectives and color adjectives. We attributed these differences to the type of modification, intensional or not. We failed to to replicate these results here, with a wider range of adjectives.

Figure 5 shows the cosine distribution of the measures used in our previous work (compare to Figure 1 in Boleda et al., 2012), namely the cosines between the observed vectors for adjectives, nouns, and the corresponding phrase vectors for each AN phrase.[9] The figure shows that, contrary to expectation

[9]Each boxplot represents the distribution of cosine values across the relevant vector pair comparisons. The horizontal lines in the rectangles mark the first quartile, median, and third quartile, respectively. Larger rectangles correspond to a more widely spread distribution, and their (a)symmetry mirrors the (a)symmetry of the distribution. The lines above and below each rectangle stretch to the minimum and maximum values, at most 1.5 times the length of the rectangle. Values outside this range (outliers) are represented as points.

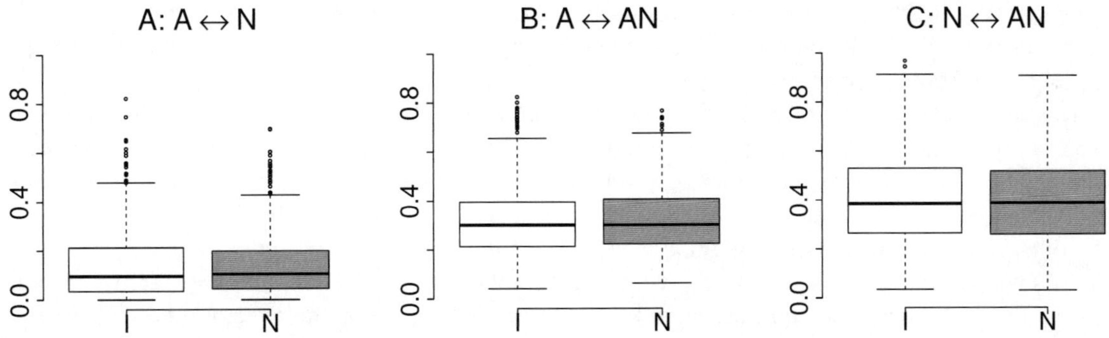

Figure 1: Distribution of cosines for observed vectors, by adjective type (intensional, I, or non-intensional, N). From left to right, adjective vs. noun, adjective vs. phrase, and noun vs. phrase cosines.

	Monosemous	**Polysemous**
I	*alleged accomplice, former surname, necessary competence*	*mock charge, putative point, past range*
N	*modern aircraft, severe hypertension, wide disparity*	*nasty review, ripe shock, meagre part*
	Typical	**Nontypical**
I	*former mayor, likely threat, alleged killer*	*former retreat, likely base, alleged fact*
N	*severe pain, free download, wide perspective*	*severe budget, free attention, wide detail*

Table 3: Examples of adjective-noun phrases for the two factors analyzed (polysemy of the head noun, typicality of the attribute) by adjective type: I(ntensional), N(on-intensional). See text for details.

and the previous results, in the observed data there is absolutely no difference in these measures between intensional and non-intensional modification: The distributions overlap completely. In a preliminary study, we paired phrases on the basis of the noun (e.g. *former bassist-male bassist*) instead of on the basis of the adjective as in the present experiments. With that design, too, we obtained no difference between the two types of phrases. We therefore take this to be a robust negative result, which suggests that the differences observed in our previous work were due to our having chosen a very narrow set of adjectives (color terms) for comparison to the intensional adjectives.

This result is surprising insofar as intensional and non-intensional adjectives have often been assumed to denote very different types of properties. One possibility is that the tools we are using are not the right ones: Perhaps using bags-of-words as the dimensions cannot capture the differences, or perhaps these differences are not apparent in the cosines between phrase and adjective/noun vectors. However, these results may also mean that all kinds of adjectival modification share properties that have gone unappreciated.

If the type of modification does not explain the differences in the observed data, what does? An analysis reveals two relevant factors. The first one is the polysemy of the head noun. We find that, the more polysemous a noun is, the less similar its vector is to the corresponding phrase vector. It is plausible that modifying a noun has a larger impact when the noun is polysemous, as the adjective narrows down the meaning of the noun; indeed, adjectives have been independently shown to be powerful word sense disambiguators of nouns (Justeson and Katz, 1995). In distributional terms, the adjective notably "shifts" the vector of polysemous nouns, but for monosemous nouns there is just not much shifting room.

This is reasonable but unsurprising; what is more worthy of attention is that this effect is invariant to adjective type. Both non-intensional and intensional adjectives have meaning modulating power, as shown in Table 3. For example, *ripe* selects for the sense of *shock* that has to do with a pile of sheaves of grain or corn. Similarly, *past* is incompatible with physical senses of *range* such as that referring to mountains or a cooking appliance.

The second effect that we find is that, the more typical the attribute described by an adjective is for the sort of thing the noun denotes, the closer the phrase vector is to both its adjective and its noun vector components. This can be explained along similar lines as the first factor: A ripe raspberry is probably more like other raspberries than, say, a humongous raspberry is. Similarly, a ripe raspberry is more like most other ripe things than a ripe condition is. Therefore, the effect of the adjective on the noun is larger if it does not describe a typical attribute of whatever the noun describes. The difference is mirrored in the contexts in which the phrases appear, which leads to larger differences in their vector representations.[10]

Interestingly, we find that typicality is also invariant across adjective type, as the examples in Table 3 show. Intensional adjectives do seem to describe typical attributes of some nouns. For example, nouns like *mayor* arguably have a temporal component to their semantics (see, e.g., Musan, 1995), the meaning of *threat* involves future intention and it is thus inherently modal, and it is culturally highly relevant whether a description like *killer* holds of a particular individual or not. Note also that typicality is not a matter of the specific adjective, but of the combination of the adjective and the noun, as illustrated by the fact that the same adjectives appear in both columns of the table: *Wide* arguably corresponds to a typical attribute of perspectives, but not of details.

The interpretation just presented is supported by a statistical analysis of the data. We estimated polysemy using the number of synsets in which a given noun appears in WordNet,[11] and typicality using an association measure, Local Mutual Information (Evert, 2005).[12] When fitting a mixed-effects model to the observed data with adjective as random effect, we find that intensionality plays no significant role in predicting the cosines between observed vectors (neither adjective vs. phrase nor noun vs. phrase cosines). Polysemy has a strong negative effect on noun vs. phrase cosines (and no effect on adjective vs. phrase cosines). Typicality has a strong positive effect on both adjective-phrase and noun-phrase cosines. We also find that these factors (but not intensionality) play a role in the difficulty of modeling a given AN phrase, since they are also highly significant (in the same directions) in predicting observed-to-predicted cosines for the lexical function model.

To sum up, in this section we have shown that there are semantic effects that are potentially relevant to adjectival modification and cut across the intensionality range, and that distributional representations of words and phrases capture such semantic effects. Thus, the analysis also provides support for the use of distributional representations for phrases.

6 Conclusion

In this paper we have tackled the computational modeling of adjective-noun composition. We have shown that adjective modification can be successfully modeled with distributional semantics, both in terms of approximating the actual distribution of phrases in corpora and in terms of the quality of the nearest neighbors they produce. We have also shown that composition models inspired in higher-order predication fare better than those that essentially intersect or combine features. Finally, contrary to what the theoretical linguistics literature might lead one to expect, we did not find a difference between intensional and non-intensional modifers in the distributional representation of phrases, nor did we find that composition functions have a harder time with intensional modification. Together, these results suggest that adjective-noun composition rarely corresponds to a simple combination of attributes of the noun and

[10] A similar explanation is provided in Boleda et al. (2012) to explain the difference between intersective and subsective uses of color terms. Here we generalize it.

[11] `http://wordnet.princeton.edu/`

[12] An association measure is not all there is to typicality; for instance, multi-word expressions like *black hole* will score high on LMI despite *black* not describing a typical attribute of holes. However, we find it a reasonable approximation because typical attributes can be expected to score higher than nontypical ones, an expectation that receives support from qualitative exploration of the data. We leave it to future work to identify alternative sources of information about typicality, such as the WordNet-based adjectival attributes in Hartung and Frank (2011).

the modifier (in line with research in cognitive science), but rather that adjectives denote functions that operate on nouns to yield something that is more than the sum of its parts. Thus, at least when used as modifiers, they denote properties of properties, rather than properties of entities.

The results of our study also indicate that intensional adjectives share a significant number of properties with non-intensional adjectives. We are of course not claiming that there are no differences between the two: For instance, there are clearly relevant semantic differences that are mirrored in the syntax. Rather, we claim that the almost exclusive focus on entailment relations in the formal semantic tradition has obscured factors that are potentially relevant, and that cut across the intensionality parameter. These are related to graded phenomena such as the polysemy of the head noun or the typicality of the attribute contributed by the adjective. We hope that our results promote closer scrutiny of these factors by theoretical semanticists, and ultimately a more complete understanding of the semantics of modification.

Acknowledgements

We thank Miquel Cornudella for help in constructing the dataset. We acknowledge the support of Spanish MICINN grant FFI2010-09464-E (McNally, Boleda), the ICREA Foundation (McNally), Catalan AGAUR grant 2010BP-A00070, MICINN grant TIN2009-14715-C04-04, EU grant PASCAL2, FP7-ICT-216886, the DARPA DEFT program under AFRL grant FA8750-13-2-0026 (Boleda) and the ERC under the 2011 Starting Independent Research Grant 283554 to the COMPOSES project (Baroni, Pham). Any opinions, findings, and conclusions or recommendations expressed in this material are those of the authors and do not necessarily reflect the view of DARPA, AFRL or the US government.

References

Asher, N. (2011). *Lexical Meaning in Context: A Web of Words*. Cambridge University Press.

Baroni, M., R. Bernardi, N.-Q. Do, and C.-C. Shan (2012). Entailment above the word level in distributional semantics. In *Proceedings of EACL*, Avignon, France, pp. 23–32.

Baroni, M., R. Bernardi, and R. Zamparelli (2013). Frege in space: A program for compositional distributional semantics. Submitted, draft at http://clic.cimec.unitn.it/composes.

Baroni, M. and R. Zamparelli (2010). Nouns are vectors, adjectives are matrices: Representing adjective-noun constructions in semantic space. In *Proceedings of EMNLP*, Boston, MA, pp. 1183–1193.

Boleda, G., E. M. Vecchi, M. Cornudella, and L. McNally (2012). First order vs. higher order modification in distributional semantics. In *Proceedings of EMNLP*, Jeju Island, Korea, pp. 1223–1233.

Clark, S. (2012). Vector space models of lexical meaning. In S. Lappin and C. Fox (Eds.), *Handbook of Contemporary Semantics, 2nd edition*. Malden, MA: Blackwell. In press.

Coecke, B., M. Sadrzadeh, and S. Clark (2010). Mathematical foundations for a compositional distributional model of meaning. *Linguistic Analysis 36*, 345–384.

Erk, K. (2012). Vector space models of word meaning and phrase meaning: A survey. *Language and Linguistics Compass*. In press.

Evert, S. (2005). *The Statistics of Word Cooccurrences*. Dissertation, Stuttgart University.

Garrette, D., K. Erk, and R. Mooney (2012). A formal approach to linking logical form and vector-space lexical semantics. In H. Bunt, J. Bos, and S. Pulman (Eds.), *Computing Meaning, Vol. 4*. In press.

Grefenstette, E., G. Dinu, Y.-Z. Zhang, M. Sadrzadeh, and M. Baroni (2013). Multi-step regression learning for compositional distributional semantics. In *Proceedings of IWCS*, Potsdam, Germany. In press.

Guevara, E. (2010). A regression model of adjective-noun compositionality in distributional semantics. In *Proceedings of the ACL GEMS Workshop*, Uppsala, Sweden, pp. 33–37.

Hall, J. (2006). *MaltParser: An Architecture for Labeled Inductive Dependency Parsing*. Licentiate thesis, Växjö University, Växjö, Sweden.

Hartung, M. and A. Frank (2011). Exploring supervised lda models for assigning attributes to adjective-noun phrases. In *Proceedings of EMNLP 2011*, Stroudsburg, PA, USA, pp. 540–551.

Justeson, J. S. and S. M. Katz (1995). Principled disambiguation: Discriminating adjective senses with modified nouns. *Computational Linguistics 21*(1), 1–27.

Kamp, J. A. W. (1975). Two theories about adjectives. In E. L. Keenan (Ed.), *Formal Semantics of Natural Language*, pp. 123–155. Cambridge: Cambridge University Press.

Landauer, T. and S. Dumais (1997). A solution to Plato's problem: The latent semantic analysis theory of acquisition, induction, and representation of knowledge. *Psychological Review 104*(2), 211–240.

Larson, R. K. (1998). Events and modification in nominals. In *Proceedings of SALT*, Ithaca, NY.

McDonald, S. and C. Brew (2004). A distributional model of semantic context effects in lexical processing. In *Proceedings of ACL*, pp. 17–24.

Mitchell, J. and M. Lapata (2010). Composition in distributional models of semantics. *Cognitive Science 34*(8), 1388–1429.

Murphy, G. L. (2002). *The Big Book of Concepts*. Cambridge, MA (etc.): The MIT Press.

Musan, R. (1995). *On the temporal interpretation of noun phrases*. Ph. D. thesis, MIT.

Parsons, T. (1970). Some problems concerning the logic of grammatical modifiers. *Synthese 21*(3-4), 320–324.

Socher, R., B. Huval, C. Manning, and A. Ng (2012). Semantic compositionality through recursive matrix-vector spaces. In *Proceedings of EMNLP*, Jeju Island, Korea, pp. 1201–1211.

Turney, P. (2012). Domain and function: A dual-space model of semantic relations and compositions. *Journal of Artificial Intelligence Research 44*, 533–585.

Turney, P. and P. Pantel (2010). From frequency to meaning: Vector space models of semantics. *Journal of Artificial Intelligence Research 37*, 141–188.

Sentiment Composition Using a Parabolic Model

Baptiste Chardon[12] Farah Benamara[1] Yannick Mathieu[3]
Vladimir Popescu[1] Nicholas Asher[1]

[1] IRIT-CNRS, Toulouse University,
[2] Synapse Développement, Toulouse,
[3] LLF-CNRS, Paris 7 University
{chardon, benamara, popescu, asher}@irit.fr
yannick.mathieu@linguist.jussieu.fr

Abstract

In this paper, we propose a computational model that accounts for the effects of negation and modality on opinion expressions. Based on linguistic experiments informed by native speakers, we distil these effects according to the type of modality and negation. The model relies on a parabolic representation where an opinion expression is represented as a point on a parabola. Negation is modelled as functions over this parabola whereas modality through a family of parabolas of different slopes; each slope corresponds to a different certainty degree. The model is evaluated using two experiments, one involving direct strength judgements on a 7-point scale and the other relying on a sentiment annotated corpus. The empirical evaluation of our model shows that it matches the way humans handle negation and modality in opinionated sentences.

1 Introduction

Sentiment composition is the process of computing the sentiment orientation of an expression or a sentence (in terms of polarity and / or strength) on the basis of the sentiment orientation of its constituents. This process, similar to the *principle of compositionality* (Dowty et al., 1989), aims to capture how opinion expressions interact with each other and with specific linguistic operators such as intensifiers, negations or modalities. For instance, the sentiment expressed in the sentence *This restaurant is good but expensive* is a combination of the prior sentiment orientation of the words *restaurant*, *good*, *but* and *expensive*. Similarly, in *My wife confirms that this restaurant is not good enough*, sentiment composition has to deal with the verb *confirm*, the adjective *good* and the adverbs *not* and *enough*.

Several computational models were proposed to account for sentiment composition. (Moilanen and Pulman, 2007) use a syntactic tree representation where nodes are associated to a set of specific hand-made composition rules that treat both negation and intensifier via three models: sentiment propagation, polarity conflict resolution and polarity reversal. (Shaikh et al., 2007) use verb frames representation for sentence-level classification and show that their compositional model outperfoms a non-compositional rule-based system. (Yessenalina and Cardie, 2011) represent each word as a matrix and combine words using iterated matrix multiplication, which allows for modelling both additive (for negations) and multiplicative (for intensifiers) semantic effects. This matrix-space model is learned in order to assign ordinal sentiment scores to sentiment-bearing phrases. (Socher et al., 2011) model sentences in a vectorial representation and propose an approach based on semi-supervised recursive autoencoders in order to predict sentence-level sentiment distributions. (Wu et al., 2011) propose a graph-based method for computing a sentence-level sentiment representation. The vertices of the graph are the opinion targets, opinion expressions and modifiers of opinion and the edges represent relations among them (mainly, opinion restriction and opinion expansion). Finally (Socher et al., 2012) propose a matrix-vector representations with a recursive neural network. The model is build on a parse tree where the nodes are associated to a vector. The matrix captures how each constituent modifies its neighbour. The model was applied to predict fine-grained sentiment distributions of adverb-adjective pairs.

Based on linguistic experiments informed by native speakers (Benamara et al., 2012), we propose a sentiment composition model based on a parabolic representation where an opinion expression is represented as a point on a parabola. Our model is designed to handle the interactions between opinion expressions and specific linguistic operators at the sub-sentential level. This paper focus particularly on modality and negation but our model can be used to treat intensifier as well. Within the model, negation are modelled as functions over this parabola whereas modality through a family of parabolas of different slopes; each slope corresponds to a different certainty degree. The model is applied for French but it can be easily instantiated for other languages like English. Its empirical evaluation shows that it has good agreement with the way humans handle negation and modality in opinionated sentences. Our approach is novel:

- it takes into account both negation and modality in a uniform framework. In our knowledge, our approach is the first study dealing with the semantic of modality for sentiment analysis,
- it distills the effect of these linguistic phenomena on opinion expressions depending on different types of negation and modality. We distinguish between three types of negation (Godard, 2013): *negative operators*, such as "not", "without", *negative quantifiers*, such as "ever", "nobody" and *lexical negations*, such as "absence" and between three types of modality (Larreya, 2004) (Portner, 2009): *bouletic*, such as "hope", "wish", *epistemic* such as "definitely", "probably" and *deontic*, such as "must". (Benamara et al., 2012) empirically show that each type of negation and modality has a specific effect on the opinion expression in its scope: both on the polarity and the strength for negation and on the strength and/or the certainty degree for modality. These empirical results provide a basis for our computational model.
- it provides a lexicon independent representation of extra-propositional aspects of meaning.

The paper is organized as follow. We first give an overview of how existing sentiment analysis systems deal with negation and modality. We then give in section 3 the linguistic motivations behind our approach. The parabolic model and its evaluation are respectively described in section 4 and section 5.

2 Related Works

The computational treatment of negation and modality has recently become an emerging research area. These complex linguistic phenomena have been shown to be relevant in several NLP applications such as sentiment analysis (Wiegand et al., 2010), information retrieval (Jia and Meng, 2009), recognizing contrasts and contradictions (de Marneffe and Manning, 2008) and biomedical text processing (Szarvas, 2008). Due to the emergence of this field, several workshops and conferences have been organized such as the Negation and Speculation in Natural Language Processing (NeSp-NLP 2010) workshop, the Extra-Propositional Aspects of Meaning in Computational Linguistics (ExPRom 2012) workshop, and the publication of a special issue of the journal Computational Linguistics. A number of resources annotated with factuality information are also available. Among them, we can cite the BioScope corpus (Vincze et al., 2008) and FactBank (Saurí and Pustejovsky, 2009).

In sentiment analysis, the presence of modalities is generally used as a feature in a supervised learning setting for sentence-level opinion classification (Kobayakawa et al., 2009). However, to our knowledge, no work has investigated how modality impacts on opinions. There are two ways of treating negation when computing the contextual polarity an opinion expression at the sentense-level: (a) *polarity reversal* (Polanyi and Zaenen, 2006; Moilanen and Pulman, 2007; Choi and Cardie, 2008) that flips the prior polarity of the expression to its opposite value. For instance, if the score of the adjective "excellent" is +3, then the opinion in "this student is not excellent" is -3 ; (b) *polarity shift* (Taboada et al., 2011) that assumes that negation affects both the polarity and the strength. For instance, the opinion in "this student is not excellent" cannot be -3 ; it rather means that the student is not good enough. Two main types of negation were taken into account in these models: negators such as "not" and / or *content word negators* (Choi and Cardie, 2008) that can be positive polarity shifters (like *abate*) or negative polarity shifters (like *lack*). Few studies take into account other types of negation. (Taboada et al., 2011) treat negative polarity items (NPIs) (as well as modalities) as "irrealis blockers" by ignoring the semantic orientation of the word under their scope. For example, the opinion word "good" will just be ignored in "any good movie in this theater". We think that ignoring NPIs is not suitable and a more accurate analysis is needed. In addition, no work has investigated the effect of multiple negatives on opinions.

All the previous studies have focused on English. In French, as far as we know, main existing research in sentiment analysis treat negation as polarity reversal and do not take into account modality (Vernier et al., 2007). Thus, there is little existing work for us to compare ourselves to.

3 Linguistic motivations

Our analysis of negation is based on the lexical-syntactic classification of (Godard, 2013) as part of the "Grande Grammaire du Français" project (Abeillé and Godard, 2010). We distinguish between four types of negation in French[1].

- *Negative operators*, denoted by `NEG`: they are the adverbs "pas" ("not"), "plus" ("no more"), "non" ("no one"), the preposition "sans" ("without") and the conjunction "ni" ("neither"). These operators always appear alone in the sentence and they cannot be combined with each other. The semantic of negative operators are similar to the negation used in logic since they can be paraphrased by "it is not true".

- *Negative quantifiers*, denoted by `NEG_quant`, express both a negation and a quantification. They are, for example, the nouns and pronouns "aucun" ("none"), "nul" ("no"), "personne" ("nobody"), "rien" ("nothing"), or the adverbs "jamais" ("never") and "aucunement"/"nullement" ("in no way")[2]. `Neg_quant` have three main properties: (i) they can occur in positive sentences (that is not negated), particularly in interrogatives, when they are employed as indefinite (as in *Jean travaille toute la semaine mais jamais le dimanche (Jean works all the week but never on Sunday)* or when they appear after the relative pronoun "que" ("that") (as in *Il a réussi sans qu'il ait jamais fait d'efforts (He was successful without doing any efforts)*, (ii) in negative contexts, they are always associated to the adverb "ne" ("not") and (iii) they can be combined with each other as well as with negative operators. Here are some examples of this type of negation extracted form our corpus of French movie reviews: "on ne s'ennuie jamais" ("you will never be bored"), "je ne recommande cette série à personne" ("I do recommend this movie to nobody")

- *Lexical negations* denoted by `NEG_lex` which are implicit negative words, such as "manque de" ("lack of"), "absence de"("absence of"), "carence" ("deficiency"), "manquer de" ("to lack"), " dénué de" ("deprived of"). `NEG_lex` can be combined with each other as well as with the two previous types of negation.

- *Multiple negatives.* In some languages, double negatives cancel the effect of negation, while in negative-concord languages like French, double negations usually intensify the effect of negation[3]. In French, multiple negatives that preserve negation concern two cases: the combinations composed of negative quantifiers and the combination of a negative quantifier and a negative operator. Note that the combination of a lexical negation with a lexical quantifier or a lexical negation with a negative operator cancel the effect of `NEG_lex`. Here is an example of a positive opinion

[1] This classification does not cover words such as *few* or *only*, since we consider them as weak intensifiers (strength diminishers) rather than negations.

[2] In this paper, all examples are in French along with their direct translation in English. Note however that there are substantial semantic differences between the two languages.

[3] In French, there are at most three negative words in a multiple negative. However, this case is relatively rare in opinion text and we only deal with two negatives

extracted from our corpus of French movie reviews: *Cette série télé n'a jamais manqué de me surprendre (This TV series never fails to amaze me)* where we have two negatives: the negative quantifier *jamais (never)* and the lexical negation *manqué (fail)*.

Drawing partly on (Portner, 2009) and on (Larreya, 2004) for French, we have chosen to split modality in three categories:

- *Bouletic*, denoted by `Mod_B`. It indicates the speaker's desires/wishes. This type of modality is expressed via a closed set of verbs denoting hope e.g. "I *wish* he were kind".
- *Epistemic*, denoted by `Mod_E`. It indicates the speaker's belief in the propositional content he asserts. They are expressed via adverbs expressing doubt, possibility or necessity such as "perhaps", "definitely", "certainly", etc., and via the French verbs "devoir" ("have to"), "falloir" ("need to/must") and "pouvoir" ("may/can"), e.g. "The movie *might* be good",
- *Deontic*, denoted by `Mod_D`. It indicates a possibility or an obligation (with their contrapositives, impossibility and permission, respectively). They are only expressed via the same modal verbs as for epistemic modality, but with a deontic reading, e.g., "You *must* go see the movie".

(Benamara et al., 2012) consider that effect of each modal category on opinion expression is on their *strength* – for instance, the strength of the recommendation "You must go see the movie, it's a blast" is greater than for "Go see the movie, it's a blast", and *certainty degree* – for instance, "This movie is *definitely* good" has a greater certainty than "This movie is good". The certainty degree has three possible values, in line with standard literature (Saurí and Pustejovsky, 2009): *possible*, *probable* and *certain*. However, as in (Benamara et al., 2012), we consider that, in an opinion analysis context, the frontier between the first two values is rather vague, hence we conflate them into a value that we denote by *uncertain*. We thus obtain two certainty degrees, from which we build a three-level scale, by inserting between these values a "default" certainty degree for all expressions which are not modalities or in the scope of a modality.

(Benamara et al., 2012) structure the effects of each negation type as a set of hypotheses *PolNeg, StrNeg, QuantNeg, LexNeg* and *MultiNeg* that have been empirically validated by volunteer native French speakers through two protocols: one for *PolNeg* and *StrNeg*, with 81 subjects and one for the three other hypotheses with 96 subjects. Similarly, the effects of modality are structured as a set of six hypotheses that have been empirically validated via a set of three evaluation protocols. Respectively 78, 111 and 78 subjects participated in these studies. The table 1 gives an overview of our set of hypotheses, as well as the results (as the average agreement and disagreement between the subjects' answers and the hypotheses). Regarding these results, only valid hypotheses (i.e that obtain more that 50% agreement) are plugged in our parabolic model. We leave lexical negations for future work since their effect is closely related to the semantic of the word used to express negation.

4 Parabolic Model

Let T be an explicitly subjective phrase that contains one opinion expression exp about one topic. exp can be an adjective, a noun or a verb, and can be modified by a set of linguistic operators (e.g., intensifier, negation, modality) that we denote by OP_i for $i = 1 \dots n$. Their cumulative effect on exp is represented by the nesting $OP_1(OP_2...(OP_n((exp)))$, where the order of operators reflects their scope over exp. Here are some examples of T, along with their corresponding semantic representations, operators are in bold font:

(1) *Cet étudiant est brillant (this student is brilliant)*, $T = brilliant$

(2) *Cet étudiant* **n'est pas** *brillant (this student is* **not** *brilliant)*, $T = NEG(brilliant)$

(3) **Personne n**'*est brillant* (**nobody** *is brilliant)*, $T = NEG\_quant(brilliant)$

Hypothesis	Description	Results
PolNeg	The negation always reverses the polarity of an opinion expression. Exp. *exceptionnel (exceptional)* and *pas exceptionnel (not exceptional).*	90.7 %
StrNeg	The strength of an opinion expression in the scope of a negation is not stronger than of the opinion expression alone.	100 %
QuantNeg	The strength of an expression when in the scope of a `NEG_quant` is greater than when in the scope of a `NEG`. Exp. *jamais exceptionnel (never exceptional)* is stronger than *pas exceptionnel (not exceptional).*	67 %
LexNeg	`NEG_lex` has the same effect as `NEG`. Exp. *lack of taste* and *no taste*	43 %
MultiNeg	The strength of an expression when in the scope of multiple negatives is greater than when in the scope of each negation alone. Exp. *plus jamais bon (no longer ever good)* is stronger than *plus bon (no longer good)*	64 %
BoulMod	`Mod_B` alters the certainty degree of opinion expressions in their scope and is weaker than the certainty degree of the opinion expression itself. Exp. *I hope this movie is funny* there is less certainty than in *This movie is funny*	86.5 %
EpisMod1	`Mod_E` alters the certainty degree of opinion expressions in their scope. For adverbial `Mod_E`, this degree is altered according to the certainty of the respective adverb: if the latter is uncertain, then the certainty of the opinion in the scope of the adverb is reduced; otherwise, the certainty is augmented	72 %
EpisMod2	The certainty of opinion expressions in the scope of a verbal `Mod_E` is always lower than when not in the scope of such a modality and varies according to the certainty of the respective verb, from *pouvoir* – lowest certainty, as in "the film *might* be good", to *devoir* and *falloir* – greater certainty, as in "the film *must* be good".	79 %
EpisMod3	The certainty degrees of opinion expressions in the scope of epistemic *devoir* and *falloir* are the same.	57 %
DeonMod1	`Mod_D` alters the strength of opinion expressions in their scope. Hence, strength varies according to the verb: *pouvoir* reduces the strength of the opinion, whereas *devoir* and *falloir* boost it.	54 %
DeonMod2	The strengths of opinion expressions in the scope of deontic *devoir* and *falloir* are the same.	60 %

Table 1: An overview of our set of hypotheses and their associated results

(4) *Cet étudiant n'apportera* **jamais rien** *de bon (This student will* **never** *bring* **anything** *good)*, $T = NEG\_quant(NEG\_quant(bon))$

(5) *Cet étudiant* **n'est definitivement pas** *brillant (this student is* **definitely not** *brilliant)*, $T = Mod\_E(NEG(brilliant))$

We assume that exp is characterized by a prior score $s = pol \cdot str$ encoded in a lexicon, where $pol \in \{-1, +1\}$ is the polarity of exp and $str \in (0, MAX]$ is its strength. For example, if we have a three-value scale to encode opinion strength, we can put $s(brilliant) = +3$. The key question is: how can we compute the contextual score of exp ? i.e what is the value of $s(T)$? Knowing contextual score of opinion expressions at the sub-sentential level is a necessary step in a sentiment analysis system since the $s(T)$ scores have to be aggregated in order to determine the overall polarity orientation and/or the overall rating at the document level.

To compute the contextual polarity of exp, we propose a parabolic model where an opinion expression exp is represented by a point E of the parabola of focus F and summit O, such that $E \neq O$[4]. This parabola belongs to a family of three parabolas of the same focus and different slopes. The slopes correspond to certainty degrees. By convention, we set a reference value p_0 for "default" certainty degrees, $p_1 > p_0$ for "certain" and $p_2 < p_0$ for "uncertain". The certainty degree of exp being "default", we place it on the parabola of slope p_0. The polarity and strength of exp on this parabola are then characterized by the angle θ between the lines EF and OF (see Figure 1).

Our model is parametrises by pol, str and MAX. Hence, θ is obtained as a mapping $\phi : \{pol\} \times \{str\} \rightarrow (0; \pi)$, such that: $\phi = \varphi_2 \circ \varphi_1$ where $\varphi_1 : \{str\} \rightarrow (0; 1)$ and $\varphi_2 : \{pol\} \times (0; 1) \rightarrow (0; \pi)$. To compute φ_1, we rely on a "pivot" word exp_0, such that when in the scope of a negative operator (see Section 3), its polarity is reversed, while its strength, denoted by str_0, is preserved. This generally corresponds to words with relatively weak strengths like "good" or "bad" in English. We set $\varphi_1(str_0)$ to $\frac{1}{2}$. This parameter is set to this value in order to be consistent with our elementary operation for negation operators Σ_{neg} (cf. description below). Then, for any expression exp, its new strength is computed as follows:

[4] E cannot be on the summit of the parabola, since this would correspond to a non-opinionated expression, and our model does not apply to such expressions.

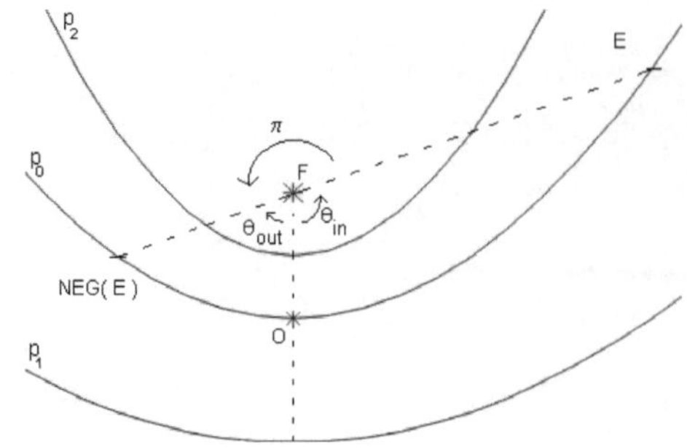

Figure 1: Parabolic model, with negation and modality.

$$\varphi_1(str) = \begin{cases} \frac{str}{str_0} \cdot \frac{1}{2} & \text{, if } str \leq str_0 \\ \frac{1}{2} + (\frac{str - str_0}{MAX + 1 - str_0} \cdot \frac{1}{2}) & \text{, else} \end{cases}$$

Then, we determine the angle corresponding to exp from its polarity and new strength as follows:

$$\theta \equiv \varphi_2(pol; \varphi_1(str)) = pol \cdot \varphi_1(str) \cdot \pi$$

The table 2 below shows normalized values in case of a three-points discrete strength such that the "pivot" word *good* is associated to the score $+1$:

Opinion score s	**Normalized angular score** θ	**Example**
$+1$	$\pi/2$	good
$+2$	$2\pi/3$	brilliant
$+3$	$5\pi/6$	excellent
-1	$-\pi/2$	bad
-2	$-2\pi/3$	disgusting
-3	$-5\pi/6$	outrageous

Table 2: Normalization on a 3-points scale

The next step is to compute the score of T, given that T contains one single phrase of the type $OP_1(OP_2...(OP_n((exp)))$. Negations and modalities are modeled as functions Σ over the angle θ and the slope p of the parabola where the expressions are placed: $\Sigma : (\theta_{in}; p_{in}) \mapsto (\theta_{out}; p_{out})$. Σ is customized with respect to the operator type: we have both "primitive" and "composition" functions. We have four "primitive" functions:

- Σ_{neg} for negative operators NEG. It consists in adding/subtracting π to/from θ, which ensures that negating of a high-strength opinion expression yields a low-strength one, which is in line with observed behaviour in Hypotheses *PolNeg* and *StrNeg* (cf. table 1):

$$\theta_{out} = \begin{cases} \theta_{out} = \theta_{in} + \pi & \text{, if } \theta_{in} < 0 \\ \theta_{out} = \theta_{in} - \pi & \text{, if } \theta_{in} > 0 \end{cases} ; p_{out} = p_{in}$$

  Table 3 shows how this formula can be applied in case of a three-points strength scale for positive values. As expected, "not good" has a stronger score than "not excellent".

- Σ_{int} for intensity modifiers, i.e. deontic modalities (MOD_D) or intensity adverbs. This operation consists in an angle adjustment: it can either increase or decrease the value of θ. We denote these effects by the two sub-functions Σ_{int+} and Σ_{int-}, respectively:

$$\Sigma_{int+}(\theta) = \begin{cases} 2 \cdot \frac{|\theta|}{\theta} \cdot |\theta| & \text{, if } |\theta| \leq \frac{\pi}{3} \\ \frac{|\theta|}{\theta} \cdot \left(\frac{\pi}{2} + \frac{|\theta|}{2}\right) & \text{, else;} \end{cases}$$

θ_{in}	$\Sigma_{neg}(\theta_{in})$	**Example**
$\pi/2$	$-\pi/2$	good / not good
$2\pi/3$	$-\pi/3$	brilliant / not brilliant
$5\pi/6$	$-\pi/6$	excellent / not excellent

Table 3: Negation primitive function on a 3-points scale

$\Sigma_{int-}(\theta) = \pi - \Sigma_{neg}(\pi - \theta)$

Table 4 shows an example of these functions in case of a three-points strength scale for positive values.

θ_{in}	$\Sigma_{int+}(\theta_{in})$	**Example**	$\Sigma_{int-}(\theta_{in})$	**Example**
$\pi/2$	$3\pi/4$	definitely good	$\pi/4$	possibly good
$2\pi/3$	$5\pi/6$	definitely brilliant	$\pi/3$	possibly brilliant

Table 4: Modality primitive functions on a 3-points scale

- Σ_{cert} for modalities that alter the certainty degree of the expressions in their scope (epistemic MOD_E), according to Hypotheses *BoulMod, EpisMod1* to *EpisMod3*. It consists in altering the slope of the parabola, according to the certainty degree c of the modality:

$$\theta_{out} = \theta_{in};\ p_{out} = \begin{cases} 2 & \text{, if } c = \text{"certain"} \\ 0.5 & \text{, if } c = \text{"uncertain"}, \end{cases}$$

- Σ_{cert0} for buletic modalities. This operation consists in cancelling the opinion by setting the parameter p to 0.

We have two "composition" functions, Σ_{neg_quant} and Σ_{neg_m}, that account for negative quantifiers and multiple negations, respectively. These functions adjust the output angle yielded by Σ_{neg} and ϕ according to Hypotheses *QuantNeg, DeonMod1, DeonMod2* and *MultiNeg*. These "composition" functions are defined as follows.

$\Sigma_{neg\_quant} : \theta_{out} = \Sigma_{int+}(\Sigma_{neg}(\theta_{in}; p_{in})),\ p_{out} = p_{in}.$

$\Sigma_{neg\_m} : \theta_{out} = \Sigma_{int+}(\Sigma_{int+}(\Sigma_{neg}(\theta_{in}; p_{in})));\ p_{out} = p_{in}.$

Table 5 illustrates these functions.

θ_{in}	$\Sigma_{neg\_quant}(\theta_{in})$	**Example**	$\Sigma_{neg\_m}(\theta_{in})$	**Example**
$\pi/2$	$-3\pi/4$	good / never good	$-7\pi/8$	good / no longer ever good
$2\pi/3$	$-2\pi/3$	brilliant / never brilliant	$-5\pi/6$	brilliant / no longer ever brilliant

Table 5: Composition functions on a 3-points scale

5 Empirical validation

In order to validate empirically our model, we conducted two complementary evaluations. The first one relies on a set of linguistic protocols that aims at evaluating at what extent our model matches the way humans handle negation and modality in opinionated sentences. The second one relies on manually annotated review product corpus and aims at comparing the score that annotators give to elementary discourse segments to the score computed by our model. In both evaluation settings, we compare our model with some baselines and with the (Taboada et al., 2011)'s system which is the state-of-the art model that is the most closer to our. Indeed, (Taboada et al., 2011)'s model shifts the score of an expression to the opposite polarity by a fixed amount. Thus a $+2$ adjective is negated to a -2, but the negation of a -3 adjective (for instance, *sleazy*) is only slightly positive.

5.1 Assessing the parabolic model via linguistic protocols

We designed three protocols: *P_NegOp1* and *P_NegOp2* to assess our model with respect to negative operators and one protocol, namely *P_NegQuantMulti*, to evaluate our model with respect to negative quantifiers and to multiple negatives. Since the function Σ_{cert} simply alters the slop of the parabola following the already validated hypothesis *BoulMod* and *EpisMod1* to *EpisMod3* (cf. Table 1), we do not give its evaluation here (see (Benamara et al., 2012) for more details).

In our framework, the strength of the opinion is discretized on a three-level scale, going from 1 (minimal strength) to 3 (maximal strength). Several types of scales have been used in sentiment analysis research, going from continuous scales to discrete ones. Since our negation hypotheses have to be evaluated against human subjects, the chosen length of the scale has to ensure a trade-off between a fine-grained categorisation of subjective words and the reliability of this categorisation with respect to human jugments. We thus use in our framework a discrete 7-point scale, going from -3 (which corresponds to "extremely negative" opinions) to $+3$ (for "extremely positive" ones) to quantify the strenght of an opinion expression. Note that 0 corresponds to cases where in the absence of any context, the opinion expression can be neither positive nor negative.

5.1.1 The experimental setup

The first protocol *P_NegOp1* was already used for evaluating Hypothesis *PolNeg*. It is needed to check whether the scores yielded by the parabolic model match those elicited from human subjects. A set of six questions are shown to subjects. In each question, an opinionated sentence is presented, along with its negation using negative operators, as in "This student is brilliant" and "This student is *not* brilliant". The strengths of the opinions vary from one question to another on a discrete scale. A set of 81 native French speakers were asked to indicate the strength of each sentence in a question on the same 7-point scale. In the second protocol *P_NegOp2*, the same subjects are given 6 couples of sentences with negative operators, where we vary the strength of the opinion expression in the scope of the negation, while keeping their polarity, e.g. "This student is not brilliant" and "This student is not exceptional". We ask them to compare, within each couple, the strengths of its members. A set of 96 native French speakers participated in this study. *P_NegOp2* is needed in order to discriminate between our model and different, baseline or state-of-the-art ones (see below), in case of equal performance according to the first protocol. In the third and last protocol, named *P_NegQuantMulti*, we give subjects a set of sentences where each contains an opinion expression of a distinct strength. Each sentence is presented with three forms: one with a negative operator, one with a negative quantifier and one with multiple negation. We then ask subjects to rank each sentence on our 7-point scale. 96 volunteers participate in this protocol.

Given that negation alters only the polarity and strength of an expression (and hence its angle in the model), we first perform a mapping between the angle obtained by applying Σ_{neg}, Σ_{neg_quant} and Σ_{neg_m}, and the 7-point scale, used by human subjects. This mapping is based on the fact that, φ_1 and φ_2 being bijections, their composition $\phi = \varphi_2 \circ \varphi_1$ is a bijection as well. Hence, the inverse mapping $\phi^{-1} = \varphi_1^{-1} \circ \varphi_2^{-1}$ is also a bijective function. Thus, for any angle θ, we get a real-numbered score σ_θ in $[-3, 3]$, which is further discretized via the nearest integer function, yielding the integer $\lfloor \sigma_\theta \rceil$ on the 7-point scale. The evaluation is performed in two steps: (i) verifying, via *P_NegOp1*, and *P_NegQuantMulti* that, for a given expression, its $\lfloor \sigma_\theta \rceil$ corresponds to the score given by the subjects; (ii) verifying, via *P_NegOp2*, that, for a set of expressions, the ordering of their $\lfloor \sigma_\theta \rceil$s is identical to the ordering of the scores given by subjects. The assessments are quantified as subjects-model agreements.

P_NegOp1 and *P_NegOp2* aim, in addition, to assess our model, along with three other negation models: (i) a "switch" model, which only changes the polarity of the prior score of an expression, while keeping the strength unchanged; (ii) a "flat" model, where the strengths of expressions in the scope of negations are either $+1$ for negative expressions or -1 for positive ones; (iii) "Tab et al." model, standing for (Taboada et al., 2011)'s model. In this model negation boils down to a ± 4 shift of the scores of the opinion expressions on a scale of $\{-5, -4, \dots, 4, 5\}$; hence, polarity is not preserved (Hypothesis *PolNeg* not validated). The assessment according to *P_NegOp1* allows us to indirectly compare these three models to our model. To this end, we first need to perform a scale adjustment for prior scores in (Taboada et al., 2011)'s model: first, our prior scores are linearly mapped to Taboada et al.'s scale, then their model is applied and finally the results are re-mapped to our scale.

5.1.2 Results

In Table 6 we evaluate the subjects-model agreement measure of the four models. We thus assess their ability to provide scores that reflect subjects' intuition (protocol *P_NegOp1*). In case of equal performance according to this measure, the models are further assessed with respect to their ability to provide the same score orderings as the subjects (protocol *P_NegOp2*). Concerning the correspondence between subject and model scores (*P_NegOp1*), we observe that the "flat" and parabolic models perform best. The "switch" and "Tab et al." models reflect to a lesser extent subjects' assessments. The "Tab et al." model exhibits lower performance figures because, unlike the "flat" and parabolic models, it does not systematically reverse polarity, whereas subjects do so. The parabolic and flat models show the same performance because in both models negation boils down to assigning ± 1 strengths to negated expressions and, in fact, discretizing the output of the parabolic model on the $\{-3, \dots 3\}$ scale boils down to applying the same formula as for the "flat" model. Hence, in order to further distinguish between the "flat" and parabolic models, we performed the second evaluation, with respect to score orderings (*P_NegOp2*). In this setting, we remark that (Taboada et al., 2011)'s and our parabolic model perform best, which shows that the "switch" and "flat" models fail to provide a score ranking in agreement with subjects' intuitions. Our model has the same performance as (Taboada et al., 2011)'s model because both are order-preserving shifting models and hence yield the same score ordering for the negated expressions, starting from the same prior score ordering for the expressions.

Model	*P_NegOp1*	*P_NegOp2*
Switch	27.03 %	5.80 %
Flat	61.43 %	21.16 %
Tab et al.	47.77 %	73.04 %
Parabolic	61.43 %	73.04 %

Table 6: Empirical validation of the parabolic model

Finally, using *P_NegQuantMulti*, the agreement between the parabolic model and subjects that are in concordance with Hypothesis *PolNeg* is 85.96% for negative quantifiers and 78 % for multiple negatives. Our results show that the adjustment function Σ_{int+} perfoms well.

5.2 Assessing the parabolic model on manually annoted data

In order to validate our model as a whole, we conducted an experiment on manually annotated data. The data consists in a set of 133 reviews on various subjects: films, TV series, books, and video games. The annotation includes opinion information both at the expression level, with polarity and strength on a three-point scale for opinion words, and with the operators associated to them, and at the discourse segment level, with polarity and strength after application of the operators. While annotating, annotators are not asked to determine the semantic category of negation and modality. For our evaluation, we first automatically determine the type of each operator (i.e negative operator, negative quantifier, multiple negative, epistemic modality, boulic modality as well as intensifiers where we distinguish between adverbs that increase (vs. decrease) the opinion strength) using a dedicated lexicon. Then, we compare the score of discourse segments with those given by annotators. The corpus used for the evaluation contains 393 segments. Table 7 shows the results obtained in terms of accuracy.

We observe that the three models obtain good results, especially in case of intensifiers. Indeed, this kind of operation is usually well supported by each model. Concerning negation, switch model loses an

Model	Accuracy
Switch	59.5 %
Tab et al.	64.7 %
Parabolic	68.8 %

Table 7: Empirical validation of the parabolic model

important part of discourse segments when dealing with high strength opinions; Tab et al. model performs better on most negation, but loses some segments especially when high intensity opinion expression are concerned: Tab et al model doesn't forecast a polarity switch, and we showed with hypothesis *PolNeg* that this is not the best behaviour for French. On the contrary our model deals correctly with in these cases. In addition, our model performs well on multiple negative and negative quantifiers, which are not taken into account neither in the switch nor in the Tab et al. model. Finally, we also observe that our results for modality are very good, with a F-measure of 88%. However, these results need to be assessed on a larger corpus (we had few instances of epistemic and deontic modalities in our corpus).

6 Conclusion

In this paper, we propose a way to compute the opinion orientation at the sub-sentencial level using a parabolic model. Our approach takes into account both negation and modality in a uniform framework and distils the effect of these linguistic phenomena on opinion expressions depending on different types of negation and modality. The empirical evaluation of our model shows that it has good agreement with the way humans handle negation and modality in opinionated sentences. In further work, we plan to study the effect of cumulative modalities, as in "you definitely must see this movie" and of co-occurring negation and modality, as in *you should not go see this movie*, on opinion expressions. At the moment, our model is based on the assumption that a subjective text span contains a single opinion expression. This assumption is far from being verified. Hence, we plan to extend our parabolic model so that it can compute the overall opinion of a text containing several opinion expressions. The focus of the family of three parabolas can correspond to a couple (topic, holder), hence we have as many families of parabolas as opinions expressed towards different topics and/or by different holders. Sentiment composition can then be parametrized by the topic or the holder of the opinion. Finally, we plan to instantiate our model in other languages in order to compare its prediction on standard datasets available in the literature.

Acknowledgement

This work was supported by a DGA-RAPID project under grant number 0102906143.

References

Abeillé, A. and D. Godard (2010). The grande grammaire du français project. In *Proceedings of the 7th LREC*.

Benamara, F., B. Chardon, Y. Mathieu, V. Popescu, and N. Asher (2012). How do negation and modality impact on opinions? In *Proceedings of the Workshop on Extra-Propositional Aspects of Meaning in Computational Linguistics*, pp. 10–18. Association for Computational Linguistics.

Choi, Y. and C. Cardie (2008). Learning with compositional semantics as structural inference for subsentential sentiment analysis. In *Proceedings of EMNLP*, pp. 793–801.

de Marneffe, Marie-Catherine, A. N. R. and C. D. Manning (2008). Finding contradictions in text. In *In Proceedings of ACL 2008*, pp. 10391047.

Dowty, D. R., R. E. Wall, and S. Peters (1989). *Introduction to Montague Semantics*, Volume 11. D. Reidel.

Godard, D. (2013). Les négateurs. In *La Grande Grammaire du français*. Godard Danièle, Anne Abeillé and Annie Delaveau. Actes Sud.

Jia, L. Yu, C. T. and W. Meng (2009). The effect of negation on sentiment analysis and retrieval effectiveness. In *CIKM*, pp. 1827–1830.

Kobayakawa, T., T. Kumano, H. Tanaka, N. Okazaki, J. Kim, and J. Tsujii (2009). Opinion classification with tree kernel svm using linguistic modality analysis. In *Proceedings of the 18th ACM conference on Information and knowledge management*, pp. 1791–1794.

Larreya, P. (2004). L'expression de la modalité en français et en anglais (domaine verbal). *Revue belge de philologie et d'histoire 82*(3), 733–762.

Moilanen, K. and S. Pulman (2007, September 27-29). Sentiment composition. In *Proceedings of RANLP*, pp. 378–382.

Polanyi, L. and A. Zaenen (2006). Contextual valence shifters. In *Computing Attitude and Affect in Text: Theory and Applications*, Volume 20 of *The Information Retrieval Series*, pp. 1–10.

Portner, P. (2009). *Modality*, Volume 1. Oxford University Press, USA.

Saurí, R. and J. Pustejovsky (2009). FactBank: a corpus annotated with event factuality. *Language Resources and Evaluation 43*(3), 227–268.

Shaikh, M. A. M., H. Prendinger, and M. Ishizuka (2007). Assessing sentiment of text by semantic dependency and contextual valence analysis. In *Affective Computing and Intelligent Interaction, Second International Conference, ACII 2007, Lisbon, Portugal, September 12-14, 2007, Proceedings*, Lecture Notes in Computer Science, pp. 191–202. Springer.

Socher, R., B. Huval, C. D. Manning, and A. Y. Ng (2012). Semantic Compositionality Through Recursive Matrix-Vector Spaces. In *Proceedings of EMNLP*.

Socher, R., J. Pennington, E. H. Huang, A. Y. Ng, and C. D. Manning (2011, July). Semi-supervised recursive autoencoders for predicting sentiment distributions. In *Proceedings of EMNLP*, pp. 151–161.

Szarvas, G. (2008). Hedge classification in biomedical texts with a weakly supervised selection of keywords. In *In Proceedings of ACL 2008*, pp. 281289.

Taboada, M., J. Brooke, M. Tofiloski, K. Voll, and M. Stede (2011). Lexicon-based methods for sentiment analysis. *Computational Linguistics 37*, 267–307.

Vernier, M., Y. Mathet, F. Rioult, T. Charnois, S. Ferrari, and D. Legallois (2007). Classification de textes d'opinions: une approche mixte n-grammes et sémantique. *DEFT'07*.

Vincze, V., G. Szarvas, R. Farkas, G. Móra, and J. Csirik (2008). The bioscope corpus: biomedical texts annotated for uncertainty, negation and their scopes. *BMC bioinformatics 9*(Suppl 11), S9.

Wiegand, M., A. Balahur, B. Roth, D. Klakow, and A. Montoyo (2010). A survey on the role of negation in sentiment analysis. In *Proceedings of the Workshop on Negation and Speculation in Natural Language Processing*, NeSp-NLP '10, pp. 60–68.

Wu, Y., Q. Zhang, X. Huang, and L. Wu (2011). Structural opinion mining for graph-based sentiment representation. In *Proceedings of EMNLP*, pp. 1332–1341.

Yessenalina, A. and C. Cardie (2011). Compositional matrix-space models for sentiment analysis. In *Proceedings of EMNLP*, pp. 172–182.

Temporal Relation Classification Based on Temporal Reasoning

Francisco Costa
University of Lisbon
fcosta@di.fc.ul.pt

António Branco
University of Lisbon
Antonio.Branco@di.fc.ul.pt

Abstract

The area of temporal information extraction has recently focused on temporal relation classification. This task is about classifying the temporal relation (precedence, overlap, etc.) holding between two given entities (events, dates or times) mentioned in a text. This interest has largely been driven by the two recent TempEval competitions.

Even though logical constraints on the structure of possible sets of temporal relations are obvious, this sort of information deserves more exploration in the context of temporal relation classification. In this paper, we show that logical inference can be used to improve—sometimes dramatically—existing machine learned classifiers for the problem of temporal relation classification.

1 Introduction

Recent years have seen renewed interest in extracting temporal information from text. Evaluation campaigns like the two TempEval challenges (Verhagen et al., 2010) have brought an increased interest to this topic. The two TempEval challenges focused on ordering the events and the dates and times mentioned in text. Since then, temporal processing has expanded beyond the problems presented in TempEval, like for instance the work of Pan et al. (2011), which is about learning event durations.

Temporal information processing is important and related to a number of applications, including event co-reference resolution (Bejan and Harabagiu, 2010), question answering (Ahn et al., 2006; Saquete et al., 2004; Tao et al., 2010) and information extraction (Ling and Weld, 2010). Another application is learning narrative event chains or scripts (Chambers and Jurafsky, 2008b; Regneri et al., 2010), which are "sequences of events that describe some stereotypical human activity" (i.e. eating at a restaurant involves looking at the menu, then ordering food, etc.).

This paper focuses on assessing the impact of temporal reasoning on the problem of temporal information extraction. We will show that simple classifiers trained for the TempEval tasks can be improved by extending their feature set with features that can be computed with automated reasoning.

2 Temporal Information Processing

The two TempEval challenges made available annotated data sets for the training and evaluation of temporal information systems. Figure 1 shows a sample of these annotations, taken from the English data used in the first TempEval. The annotation scheme is called TimeML (Pustejovsky et al., 2003).

Temporal expressions are enclosed in `TIMEX3` tags. A normalized representation of the time point or interval denoted by time expressions is encoded in the `value` attribute of `TIMEX3` elements.

Event terms are annotated with `EVENT` tags. The annotations in Figure 1 are simplified and do not show all attributes of TimeML elements. For instance, the complete annotation for the term *created* in that figure is: `<EVENT eid="e1" class="OCCURRENCE" stem="create" aspect= "NONE" tense="PAST" polarity="POS" pos="VERB">`*created*`</EVENT>`.

Several attributes describe lexical and morpho-syntactic features of these terms, such as `stem` (its dictionary form), `pos` (its part-of-speech), `tense` (its grammatical tense, if it is a verb), `aspect` (its grammatical aspect), `polarity` (whether it occurs in a positive or negative context). The `class`

```
<TIMEX3 tid="t190" type="TIME" value="1998-02-06T22:19:00"
functionInDocument="CREATION_TIME">02/06/1998 22:19:00</TIMEX3>
<s>WASHINGTON _ The economy <EVENT eid="e1">created</EVENT> jobs at a surprisingly robust pace in
<TIMEX3 tid="t191" type="DATE" value="1998-01">January</TIMEX3>, the government <EVENT
eid="e4">reported</EVENT> on <TIMEX3 tid="t193" type="DATE"
value="1998-02-06">Friday</TIMEX3>, evidence that America's economic stamina has <EVENT
eid="e6">withstood</EVENT> any <EVENT eid="e7">disruptions</EVENT> <EVENT
eid="e224">caused</EVENT> so far by the financial <EVENT eid="e228">tumult</EVENT> in Asia.</s>
<TLINK lid="l1" relType="OVERLAP" eventID="e4" relatedToTime="t193" task="A"/>
<TLINK lid="l2" relType="AFTER" eventID="e4" relatedToTime="t191" task="A"/>
<TLINK lid="l26" relType="BEFORE" eventID="e4" relatedToTime="t190" task="B"/>
```

Figure 1: Example of the TempEval annotations (simplified) for the fragment: *WASHINGTON _ The economy created jobs at a surprisingly robust pace in January, the government reported on Friday, evidence that America's economic stamina has withstood any disruptions caused so far by the financial tumult in Asia.*

attribute includes some information about aspectual type, in the spirit of Vendler (1967)—it distinguishes states from non-stative situations—, and whether the term introduces an intensional context, among other distinctions. One time expression is especially important. This is the one denoting the document's creation time (DCT) and it is annotated with the value `CREATION_TIME` for the attribute `functionInDocument`.

Temporal relations are represented with `TLINK` elements. In the TempEval data, the first argument of the relation is always an event and is given by the attribute `eventID`. The second argument can be another event or the denotation of a time expression, and it is annotated in a `relatedToEvent` or `relatedToTime` attribute in `TLINK` elements. The attribute `relType` describes the type of temporal relation holding between these two ordered entities: `BEFORE`, `AFTER` or `OVERLAP`.[1]

The TempEval challenges consider three kinds of temporal relations.[2] These correspond to the three tasks of TempEval, whose goal was to correctly assign the relation type to already identified temporal relations. Task A considers temporal relations holding between an event and a time mentioned in the same sentence, regardless of whether they are syntactically related or not. Task B considers temporal relations holding between the main event of sentences and the DCT. Finally, task C focuses on temporal relations between the main events of two consecutive sentences.

The systems participating in TempEval had to guess the relation type of temporal relations (the value of the feature `relType` of `TLINK`s), but all other annotations were given and could be used as features for classifiers. The second TempEval included additional tasks whose goal was to obtain also these remaining annotations from raw text.

The best results for the two TempEval competitions are indicative of the state-of-the-art of temporal information processing. For task A, the best participating system correctly classified 62% of the held-out test relations. For task B this was 80% and, for task C, 55%. The best results of the second TempEval show some improvement (65%, 81% and 58% respectively), but the first task was slightly different and arguably easier (only pairs of event terms of temporal expressions that are syntactically related were considered).

In this paper, we will also be working with these three types of temporal relations and dealing with similar data. Our purpose is to check whether existing solutions to the TempEval problems can be improved with the help of a temporal reasoning component.

[1]There are also the disjunctive types `BEFORE-OR-OVERLAP`, `OVERLAP-OR-AFTER` and `VAGUE`. Because they were used only for those cases where the human annotators could not agree, they are quite rare, to the point where machine learned classifiers are seldom or never able to learn to assign these values.

[2]The second TempEval considers a fourth type, which we ignore here.

2.1 Temporal Relation Classification and Reasoning

The problem of temporally ordering events and times is constrained by the logical properties of temporal relations, e.g. temporal precedence is a strict partial order. Therefore, it is natural to incorporate logical information in the solutions to the problem of ordering events and time intervals. Perhaps surprisingly, little work has explored this idea.

Our working hypothesis is that classifier features that explore the logical properties of temporal relations can be used effectively to improve machine learned classifiers for the temporal information tasks of TempEval.

The motivation for using logical information as a means to help solving this problem can be illustrated with an example from Figure 1.

There, we can see that the date `1998-02-06`, denoted by the expression *Friday*, includes the document's creation time, which is `1998-02-06T22:19:00`. We know this from comparing the normalized value of these two expressions, annotated with the `value` attribute of `TIMEX3` elements. From the annotated temporal relation with the id `l26` (the last one in the figure) we also know that the event identified with `e4`, denoted by the form *reported*, precedes the document's creation time.

From these two facts one can conclude that this event either precedes the time denoted by *Friday* or they overlap; this time cannot however precede this event. That is, the possible relation type for the relation represented with the `TLINK` named `l1` is constrained—it cannot be `AFTER`.

What this means is that, in this example, solving task B can, at least partially, solve task A. The information obtained by solving task B can be utilized in order to improve the solutions for task A.

3 Related Work

The literature on automated temporal reasoning includes important pieces of work such as Allen (1984); Vilain et al. (1990); Freksa (1992). A lot of the work in this area has focused on finding efficient methods to compute temporal inferences.

Katz and Arosio (2001) used a temporal reasoning system to compare the temporal annotations of two annotators. In a similar spirit, Setzer and Gaizauskas (2001) first compute the deductive closure of annotated temporal relations so that they can then assess annotator agreement with standard precision and recall measures.

Verhagen (2005) uses temporal closure as a means to aid TimeML annotation, that is as part of a *mixed-initiative* approach to annotation. He reports that closing a set of manually annotated temporal relations more than quadruples the number of temporal relations in TimeBank (Pustejovsky et al., 2003), a corpus that is the source of the data used for the TempEval challenges.

Mani et al. (2006) use temporal reasoning as an oversampling method to increase the amount of training data. Even though this is an interesting idea, the authors recognized in subsequent work that there were methodological problems in this work which invalidate the results (Mani et al., 2007).

Since the advent of TimeBank and the TempEval challenges, machine learning methods have become dominant to solve the problem of temporally ordering entities mentioned in text. One major limitation of machine learning methods is that they are typically used to classify temporal relations in isolation, and therefore it is not guaranteed that the resulting ordering is globally consistent. Yoshikawa et al. (2009) and Ling and Weld (2010) overcome this limitation using Markov logic networks (Richardson and Domingos, 2006), or MLNs, which learn probabilities attached to first-order formulas. One participant of the second TempEval used a similar approach (Ha et al., 2010). Denis and Muller (2011) cast the problem of learning temporal orderings from texts as a constraint optimization problem. They search for a solution using Integer Linear Programming (ILP), similarly to Bramsen et al. (2006), and Chambers and Jurafsky (2008a). Because ILP is costly (it is NP-hard), the latter two only consider *before* and *after* relations.

Most of these approaches are similar to ours in that they can use knowledge about one TempEval task to solve the other tasks. However, these studies do not report on the full set of logical constraints

```
<TIMEX3 tid="t190" type="TIME" value="1998-02-06T22:19:00"
functionInDocument="CREATION_TIME">06/02/1998 22:19:00</TIMEX3>
<s>WASHINGTON - A economia <EVENT eid="e1">criou</EVENT> empregos a um ritmo surpreendentemente
robusto em <TIMEX3 tid="t191" type="DATE" value="1998-01">janeiro</TIMEX3>, <EVENT
eid="e4">informou</EVENT> o governo na <TIMEX3 tid="t193" type="DATE"
value="1998-02-06">sexta-feira</TIMEX3>, provas de que o vigor económico da América <EVENT
eid="e6">resistiu</EVENT> a todas as <EVENT eid="e7">perturbações</EVENT> <EVENT
eid="e224">causadas</EVENT> até agora pelo <EVENT eid="e228">tumulto</EVENT> financeiro na
Ásia.</s>
<TLINK lid="l1" relType="OVERLAP" eventID="e4" relatedToTime="t193" task="A"/>
<TLINK lid="l2" relType="AFTER" eventID="e4" relatedToTime="t191" task="A"/>
<TLINK lid="l26" relType="BEFORE" eventID="e4" relatedToTime="t190" task="B"/>
```

Figure 2: Example of the Portuguese data used (simplified). The fragment is: *WASHINGTON - A economia criou empregos a um ritmo surpreendentemente robusto em janeiro, informou o governo na sexta-feira, provas de que o vigor económico da América resistiu a todas as perturbações causadas até agora pelo tumulto financeiro na Ásia.*

used or explore little information (e.g. the transitivity of temporal precedence only). Our work does not have these shortcomings: we employ a comprehensive set of reasoning rules (see Section 5.1).

Our approach of encoding in features information that is obtained from automated reasoning does not guarantee that, at the end, the automatically classified temporal relations are consistent. This is a limitation of our approach that is not present in some of the above mentioned work. However, our approach is not sensitive to the size of the training data, since the reasoning rules are hand-coded. With MLNs, even though the rules are also designed by humans, the weight of each rule still has to be learned in training.

One participant of the first TempEval used "world-knowledge axioms" as part of a symbolic solution to this challenge (Puşcaşu, 2007). This world-knowledge component includes rules for reasoning about time. Closest to our work is that of Tatu and Srikanth (2008). The authors employ information about task B and temporal reasoning as a source of classifier features for task C only. This is more limited than our approach: we also explore the other tasks as sources of knowledge, besides task B, and we also experiment with solutions for the other tasks, not just task C.

4 Annotation Scheme and Data

For the experiments reported in this paper we used TimeBankPT (Costa and Branco, 2012), which is an adaptation to Portuguese of the English data used in the first TempEval. These data were produced by translating the English data used in the first TempEval and then adapting the annotations so that they conform to the new language.

Figure 2 shows a sample of that corpus. As before, that figure is simplified. For instance, the full annotation for the first event event term in that example is: `<EVENT eid="e1" class="OCCURRENCE" stem="criar" aspect="NONE" tense="PPI" polarity="POS" pos="VERB">`*criou*`</EVENT>`.

TimeBankPT is similar in size to the English TempEval data. It contains 60K word tokens for training and close to 9K words for evaluation (the word counts are somewhat higher than those for its English counterpart because of language differences). Overall (i.e. for all tasks combined), the number of temporal relations (i.e. instances for classification) is 5,781 for training and 758 for evaluation. The two corpora are quite similar to each other, as one is the translation of the other.

5 Feature Design

The main rationale behind our approach is that, when a system annotates raw text, it may split the annotation process in several steps, corresponding to the different TempEval tasks. In this scenario, the information annotated in previous steps can be used. That is, e.g. if one has already classified the temporal relations between the events in a text and its creation time (task B, which is also the easiest), this information can then be used to help classify the remaining temporal relations.

Our goal is then to evaluate new features for machine learned classifiers for these three tasks. These new features are meant to help predict the class feature by computing the temporal closure of a set of initial temporal relations. This initial set of temporal relations is composed of relations coming from two sources:

- Temporal relations between pairs of dates or times corresponding to annotated temporal expressions. Because the annotations for time expressions contain a normalized representation of them, it is possible to order them symbolically. That is, they are ordered according to the `value` attribute of the corresponding `TIMEX3` element.[3]

- The temporal relations annotated for the other tasks.

The values for these features reflect the possible values of the class feature (i.e. the temporal relation being classified), after applying temporal reasoning to these two sets of relations.

The possible values for these classifier features are the six class values (`BEFORE`, `AFTER`, `OVERLAP`, `BEFORE-OR-OVERLAP`, `OVERLAP-OR-AFTER` and `VAGUE`).[4]

For the sake of experimentation, we try all combinations of tasks:

- Predict task A after temporally closing the relations annotated for tasks B and C (and the temporal relations between the times mentioned in the document). These are the features **Ab** (based on the temporal relations annotated for task B only), **Ac** (based on the relations for task C only) and **Abc** (based on the relations for both tasks).

- Similarly, predict task B, based on tasks A and C: the features **Ba** (based on the relations for task A only), **Bc** (based on the relations for task C only) and **Bac** (based on the relations for both tasks).

- Predict task C after temporally closing the relations annotated for tasks A and B: the features **Ca** (based on the relations for task A only), **Cb** (based on the relations for task B only) and **Cab** (based on the relations for both of them).

The usefulness of these classifier features is limited in that they have very good precision but low recall, as temporal reasoning is unable to restrict the possible type of temporal relation for many instances. In fact, we did not test some of these features, because they produced the `VAGUE` value for all training instances. This was the case of the features **Ac** and **Bc** (and also **Avc** and **Bvc**, which are presented below).

For this reason, we additionally experimented with another set of features that, instead of trying to predict the class value directly, may provide useful heuristics to the classifiers. These are:

- For task B, from all annotated temporal expressions in the same sentence as the event being related to the DCT, the majority temporal relation between those temporal expressions and the DCT, based on their annotated `value` attributes. This is the feature **Bm**.

[3]Chambers and Jurafsky (2008a) also perform this step, but they consider far fewer possible formats of dates and times than we do. The full set of rules used to order times and dates can be found in Costa (2013).

[4]It must be noted that the values `BEFORE-OR-OVERLAP` or `OVERLAP-OR-AFTER` are output when none of the three more specific values (`BEFORE`, `OVERLAP` and `AFTER`) can be identified by the temporal reasoner but one of them can be excluded (i.e. `OVERLAP-OR-AFTER` is used when `BEFORE` can be excluded). Similarly, `VAGUE` is output when no constraint can be identified from the initial set of temporal relations. These underspecified values do not necessarily correspond to the cases when the annotated data contain these values (those are the cases when the human annotators could not agree on a more specific value). It often is the case that the human annotation is more specific, as humans have access to further information.

- For task B, the temporal relation between the time expression closest to the event being ordered with the DCT and the DCT. This is the feature **Bt**.
- A vague temporal relation for task A based on the relations annotated for tasks B and C. These are the classifier features **Avb**, **Avc** and **Avbc**.
- A vague temporal relation for task B based on the relations annotated for tasks A and C: classifier features **Bva**, **Bvc** and **Bvac**.
- A vague temporal relation for task C based on the relations annotated for tasks A and B: features **Cva**, **Cvb** and **Cvab**.

These temporal relations that we call vague are useful when the reasoning component does not identify a precise temporal relation between the two relevant entities in the temporal relation (due to insufficient information). In these cases, it may be useful to known that e.g. both of them temporally overlap a third one, as this may provide some evidence to the classifiers that they are likely to overlap. This is what these vague features encode. Their possible values are: (i) a third entity precedes the two entities, (ii) a third entity overlaps both entities, (iii) a third entity follows the two entities (iv) any combination of any of the above, (v) the first entity in the relation to be guessed overlaps a third entity that temporally follows the second entity in the relation to be guessed, (vi) the first entity in the relation to be guessed overlaps a third entity that temporally precedes the second entity in the relation to be guessed, (vii) the two entities are not even connected in the temporal graph for the document, whose edges correspond to overlap and precedence relations, (viii) none of the above.

5.1 Temporal Reasoning Rules

The rules implemented in our reasoning component are: (i) temporal precedence is transitive, irreflexive and antisymmetric; (ii) temporal overlap is reflexive and symmetric; (iii) if A overlaps B and B precedes C, then C does not precede A.

Because we also consider temporal relations between times and dates, we also deal with temporal inclusion, a type of temporal relation that is not part of the annotations used in the TempEval data, but that is still useful for reasoning. We make use of the following additional rules, dealing with temporal inclusion: (i) temporal inclusion is transitive, reflexive and antisymmetric; (ii) if A includes B, then A and B overlap; (iii) if A includes B and C overlaps B, then C overlaps A; (iv) if A includes B and C precedes A, then C precedes B; (v) if A includes B and A precedes C, then B precedes C; (vi) if A includes B and C precedes B, then either C precedes A or A and C overlap (A cannot precede C); (vii) if A includes B and B precedes C, then either A precedes C or A and C overlap (C cannot precede A).

As mentioned, temporal expressions are ordered according to their normalized value. For instance, the date `2000-01-03` is ordered as preceding the date `2010-03-04`. Since all temporal expressions are normalized in the annotated data, we order temporal expressions before applying any temporal reasoning. This increases the number of temporal relations we start with, and the potential number of relations we end up with after applying temporal reasoning.

To this end, we used Joda-Time 2.0 (`http://joda-time.sourceforge.net`). Each normalized date or time is converted to an interval.

In many cases it is possible to specify the start and end points of this interval, e.g. the date of January 3, 2000 is represented internally by an interval with its start point at `2000-01-03T00:00:00.000` and ending at `2000-01-03T23:59:59.999`. Many different kinds of normalized expressions require many rules. For instance, an expression like *last Winter* could be annotated in the data as `2010-WI`, and dedicated rules are used to get its start and end points.

Some time expressions are normalized as `PRESENT_REF` (e.g. *now*), `PAST_REF` (*the past*) or `FUTURE_REF` (*the future*). These cases are not represented by any Joda-Time object. Instead we need to account for them in a special way. They can be temporally ordered among themselves (e.g. `PRESENT_REF` precedes `FUTURE_REF`), but not with other temporal expressions. We further stipulate

Feature	Task A	Task B	Task C
event-aspect	d--kn	----n	d--kn
event-polarity	d--kn	--r-n	----n
event-POS	--r-n	---k-	----n
event-stem	-jrk-	--r-n	-----
event-string	--r-n	-j---	-----
event-class	djr-n	-jrk-	djrkn
event-tense	--r--	djrkn	djrkn

Feature	Task A	Task B	Task C
o-event-first	djrkn	N/A	N/A
o-event-between	djrkn	N/A	N/A
o-timex3-between	-jrk-	N/A	N/A
o-adjacent	-j--n	N/A	N/A
timex3-mod	----n	---k-	N/A
timex3-type	d-rk-	--rk-	N/A

Table 1: Features used in the baseline classifiers. Key: `d` means the feature is used with `DecisionTable`; `j`, with `J48`; `r`, with `JRip`; `k`, with `KStar`; `n`, with `NaiveBayes`.

that `PRESENT_REF` includes each document's creation time (which therefore precedes `FUTURE_REF`, etc.). So, in additional to the representation of times and dates as time intervals, we employ a layer of *ad-hoc* rules.

The variety of temporal expressions makes it impossible to provide a full account of the implemented rules in this paper, but they are listed in full in Costa (2013).

6 Experiment and Results

Our goal is to test the features introduced in Section 5. Our methodology is to extend existing classifiers for the problem of temporal relation classification with these features, and check whether their performance improves.

For the first TempEval, Hepple et al. (2007) used simple classifiers that use the annotations present in the annotated data as features. They trained Weka (Witten and Frank, 1999) classifiers with these features and obtained competitive results. 10-fold cross-validation on the training data was employed to evaluate different combinations of features.

For our baselines, we use the same approach as Hepple et al. (2007), with the Portuguese data mentioned above in Section 4.

6.1 Experimental Setup

The classifier features used in the baselines are also similar to the ones used by Hepple et al. (2007).

The *event* features correspond to attributes of `EVENT` elements according to the data annotations, with the exception of the `event-string` feature, which takes as value the character data inside the corresponding TimeML `EVENT` element. In a similar fashion, the *timex3* features are taken from the attributes of `TIMEX3` elements with the same name.

The *o(rder)* features are the attributes computed from the document's textual content. The feature `order-event-first` encodes whether the event terms precedes in the text the time expression it is related to by the temporal relation to classify. The classifier feature `order-event-between` describes whether any other event is mentioned in the text between the two expressions for the entities that are in the temporal relation, and similarly `order-timex3-between` is about whether there is an intervening temporal expression. Finally, `order-adjacent` is true if and only if both `order-timex3-between` and `order-event-between` are false (even if other linguistic material occurs between the expressions denoting the two entities in the temporal relation).

Just like Hepple et al. (2007), we experimented with several machine learning algorithms. Table 1 shows the classifier features that we selected for each algorithm. For each algorithm and task, we tried all possible combinations of features and selected the one that performed best, according to 10-fold cross-validation on the training data.

	Task A		Task B		Task C	
Classifier	bl.	best	bl.	best	bl.	best
DecTable	52.1	**58.6** (Ab,Abc)	77.0	77.0	49.6	49.6 (Cva)
J48	55.6	**58.0** (Ab,Avb)	77.3	**77.9** (Ba,Bva)	52.7	52.7
JRip	59.2	**68.0** (Ab,Avbc)	72.8	**76.7** (Bt,Ba,Bva)	54.3	54.3 (Ca,Cva,Cb,Cab)
KStar	54.4	**59.8** (Ab,Avb,Abc)	73.4	72.8 (Ba,Bva)	53.1	**53.9** (Cva,Cb)
NBayes	53.3	**56.2** (Ab,Avb)	75.2	**75.3** (Ba)	53.9	53.5 (Ca,Cva)
Average	54.9	**60.1**	75.1	**75.9**	52.7	**52.8**

Table 2: Classifier accuracy on test data (bl.: baseline; best: baseline extended with best combination of the new features, shown in parentheses, determined with cross-validation on train data). Boldface highlights improvements on test data.

We essentially used the same algorithms as Hepple et al. (2007).[5] We also experimented with J48 (Weka's implementation of the C4.5 algorithm). The classifiers obtained this way are used as baselines. To compare them with solutions incorporating temporal reasoning, we retrained them with the entire training data and evaluated them on the held-out test data. The results are shown in the columns of Table 2 labeled with *bl.* (baselines). We chose these baselines because they are very easy to reproduce: the algorithms are open-source and the classifier features are straightforwardly extractable from the annotated data and only require simple string manipulation.

For each task (A, B and C) and algorithm, we extended the best classifier previously found with the features that were presented above in Section 5. We kept the basic features, listed in Table 1 (i.e. the ones selected in the manner just reported), constant and tried all combinations of the new features, based on temporal reasoning. We then selected the feature combination that produced the best results for each algorithm and task, using 10-fold cross-validation on the train data, and, once again, evaluated the combination thus chosen on the held-out test data.

6.2 Results and Discussion

The results can be seen in Table 2. They vary by task. The tested classifier features are quite effective for task A. The new features are, however, much less effective for the other tasks. This is perhaps more surprising in the case of task C. It is mostly a problem with recall (the new reasoning-based features are able to restrict the possible type of temporal relation only for a few instances, because the data are not very densely annotated for temporal relations). That is, reasoning is very precise but leaves many instances unaccounted for. For instance, out of 1735 train instances for task C, 1589 have the value VAGUE for the feature **Cb**. In the test data, this is 241 instances out of 258.

For task A, we inspected the final decision tree (obtained with J48), the decision table (DecisionTable) and the rules (JRip) induced by the learning algorithms from the entire training set. The tree for task A checks the feature **Ab** and outputs the same type of temporal relation as the one encoded in that feature. When the value of this feature is one of the disjunctive values (VAGUE, BEFORE-OR-OVERLAP and OVERLAP-OR-AFTER), it consults the remaining features. Because of the way that trees are built by this algorithm (J48, an implementation of the C4.5 algorithm), this means that the feature **Ab** is the classifier feature with the highest information gain, among those used by this classifier. The same feature **Ab** appears frequently in the antecedent of the rules induced by JRip for task A (it occurs in the antecedent of 5 of the 8 induced rules), another indication that it is quite useful. When learning a table that associates combinations of feature values with class values, the DecisionTable algorithm

[5]These are: Weka's implementation of decision tables, Dec(ision)Table; the RIPPER algorithm, JRip; N(aive)Bayes, a Bayesian classifier; and KStar, a k-NN algorithm with an entropy-based distance function. We left out support vector machines, which are too slow for exhaustive search to be practical, even with this limited set of features. Hepple et al. (2007) tried this algorithm, but selected classifier features using a greedy search method.

Classifier	Task A bl.	Task A best	Task B bl.	Task B best	Task C bl.	Task C best
`DecTable`	52.1	**54.4** (Ab,Abc,Avbc)	77.0	77.0	49.6	49.6 (Cvb,Cvab)
`J48`	55.6	54.4 (Ab,Avb)	77.3	**79.5** (Ba)	52.7	51.9 (Cvb)
`JRip`	59.2	**64.5** (Avb,Abc)	72.8	**74.0** (Bt,Ba,Bac,Bvac)	54.3	54.3
`KStar`	54.4	**58.6** (Ab,Avb)	73.4	71.9 (Bva)	53.1	52.7 (Cva)
`NBayes`	53.3	**55.6** (Ab,Avbc)	75.2	**75.5** (Bm,Bac)	53.9	**54.3** (Cb)
Average	54.9	**57.5**	75.1	**75.6**	52.7	52.6

Table 3: Classifier accuracy on test data, with the reasoning-based features computed from the temporal relations classified by the baseline classifiers.

prunes some of the classifier features: the feature **Abc** is pruned, but the feature **Ab** is kept, another indication that task B relations are useful when classifying task A relations.

Inspection of the learned models thus suggests that information about task C is not as useful to solve task A as the information coming from task B. This is easy to understand: task A relates entities in the same sentence, whereas task C relates entities in different sentences; they also relate different kinds of entities (task C temporal relations are between two events whereas task A relations are between an event and a time). As such, temporal relations with arguments in common are not found between these two tasks, and only long chains of relations can support inferences,[6] but they are infrequent in the data.

The results in Table 2 are obtained with reasoning based on the gold standard annotations. That is, a feature such as **Ab** tries to predict the class of task A relations on the basis of task B temporal relations, and these task B relations are taken from the gold standard. In a real system, we do not have access to this information. Instead, we have temporal relations classified with some amount of error. We would have to look at the output of a classifier for task B in order to compute this feature **Ab**. An interesting question is thus how our approach performs when the initial temporal relations given to the reasoning component are automatically obtained. Table 3 presents these results. In this table, the reasoning component acts on the output of the baseline classifiers. For instance, the feature **Ab** tries to predict task A temporal relations using the reasoning rules on the output of the corresponding baseline classifier for task B (i.e. task B temporal relations that have been automatically classified by the baseline classifier employing the same learning algorithm).[7]

As can be seen from Table 2, the results are slightly worse, but there is still a noticeable and systematic improvement in task A. Under both conditions (Table 2 and Table 3), the differences between the baseline classifiers and the classifiers with the new features are statistically significant for task A ($p < 0.05$, according to Weka's `PairedCorrectedTTester`), but not for the other tasks. For this task at least, reasoning is a useful means to improve the temporal relation classification. Comparing the two tables, we can conclude that as temporal relation classification improves (and the error present in the initial temporal relations on which reasoning is based goes down), so does the positive impact of reasoning increase: the results in Table 2 are better than the ones in Table 3 because the initial temporal relations on which temporal reasoning is based are better quality. Therefore, as the performance of existing temporal relation classification technology improves, so should the potential impact of these features based on reasoning. Another conclusion is that, even with the current technology, these features are already useful, as Table 3 presents statistically significant improvements on task A.

In a real system for temporal processing, these new features cannot be used for all tasks. When temporally annotating text automatically, assuming one classifier for each task, one must choose an order

[6]For instance, according to task C, an event e_1 precedes another event e_2, which precedes the document creation time according to task B, which precedes a time t_3 according to their annotated `value`, therefore event e_1 must precede t_3.

[7]In this case, the input relations may be inconsistent. We can detect sets of inconsistent temporal relations, but we cannot know which temporal relations in such a set are misclassified. For this reason, we simply add temporal relations to the reasoning component according to textual order, and a relation is skipped if it is inconsistent with the previously added ones.

of processing the three tasks, and this determines which features are available for each classifier. Since task A benefits considerably from these features, a practical system incorporating our proposal would classify the temporal relations for tasks B and C first (taking advantage of none of the new features, as they do not improve these two tasks), and then a classifier for task A, trained using these new features, can be run, based on the output for the other tasks.

7 Concluding Remarks

In this paper we showed that features based on logical information improve existing classifiers for the problem of temporal information processing in general and temporal relation classification in particular. Even though temporal reasoning has been used in the context of temporal information processing to oversample the data (Mani et al., 2006), to check inter-annotator agreement (Setzer and Gaizauskas, 2001), as part of an annotation platform (Verhagen, 2005), or as part of symbolic approaches to the TempEval problems (Puşcaşu, 2007), to the best of our knowledge the present paper is the first to report on the use temporal reasoning as a systematic source of features for machine learned classifiers.

References

Ahn, D., S. Schockaert, M. D. Cock, and E. Kerre (2006). Supporting temporal question answering: Strategies for offline data collection. In *5th International Workshop on Inference in Computational Semantics*, Buxton.

Allen, J. (1984). Towards a general theory of action and time. *Artificiall Intelligence 23*, 123–154.

Bejan, C. A. and S. Harabagiu (2010). Unsupervised event coreference resolution with rich linguistic features. In *Proceedings of the 48th Annual Meeting of the ACL*, Uppsala, pp. 1412–1422. ACL.

Bramsen, P., P. Deshpande, Y. K. Lee, and R. Barzilay (2006). Inducing temporal graphs. In *Proceedings of EMNLP 2006*, Sydney, pp. 189–198.

Chambers, N. and D. Jurafsky (2008a). Jointly combining implicit constraints improves temporal ordering. In *Proceedings of EMNLP 2008*, Honolulu, pp. 698–706. ACL.

Chambers, N. and D. Jurafsky (2008b). Unsupervised learning of narrative event chains. In *Procedings of the 46th Annual Meeting of the ACL*, Columbus, pp. 789–797. ACL.

Costa, F. (2013). *Processing Temporal Information in Unstructured Documents*. Ph. D. thesis, Universidade de Lisboa, Lisbon. To appear.

Costa, F. and A. Branco (2012). TimeBankPT: A TimeML annotated corpus of Portuguese. In *Proceedings of LREC 2012*, Istanbul, pp. 3727–3734. ELRA.

Denis, P. and P. Muller (2011). Predicting globally-coherent temporal structures from texts via endpoint inference and graph decomposition. In *Proceedings of IJCAI 2011*.

Freksa, C. (1992). Temporal reasoning based on semi-intervals. *Artificial Intelligence 54*(1), 199–227.

Ha, E. Y., A. Baikadi, C. Licata, and J. C. Lester (2010). NCSU: Modeling temporal relations with Markov logic and lexical ontology. In *Proceedings of SemEval 2010*, Uppsala, pp. 341–344. ACL.

Hepple, M., A. Setzer, and R. Gaizauskas (2007). USFD: Preliminary exploration of features and classifiers for the TempEval-2007 tasks. In *Proceedings of SemEval-2007*, Prague, pp. 484–487. ACL.

Katz, G. and F. Arosio (2001). The annotation of temporal information in natural language sentences. In *Proceedings of the 2001 ACL Workshop on Temporal and Spatial Information Processing*, Toulouse.

Ling, X. and D. S. Weld (2010). Temporal information extraction. In *Proceedings of the Twenty-Fourth AAAI Conference on Artificial Intelligence (AAAI-10).*

Mani, I., M. Verhagen, B. Wellner, C. M. Lee, and J. Pustejovsky (2006). Machine learning of temporal relations. In *Proceedings of the 44th Annual Meeting of the ACL*, Sydney. ACL.

Mani, I., B. Wellner, M. Verhagen, and J. Pustejovsky (2007). Three approaches to learning TLINKs in TimeML. Technical Report CS-07-268, Brandeis University.

Pan, F., R. Mulkar-Mehta, and J. R. Hobbs (2011). Annotating and learning event durations in text. *Computational Linguistics 37*(4), 727–752.

Puşcaşu, G. (2007). WVALI: Temporal relation identification by syntactico-semantic analysis. In *Proceedings of SemEval-2007*, Prague, pp. 484–487. ACL.

Pustejovsky, J., J. Castaño, R. Ingria, R. Saurí, R. Gaizauskas, A. Setzer, and G. Katz (2003). TimeML: Robust specification of event and temporal expressions in text. In *IWCS-5, Fifth International Workshop on Computational Semantics.*

Pustejovsky, J., P. Hanks, R. Saurí, A. See, R. Gaizauskas, A. Setzer, D. Radev, B. Sundheim, D. Day, L. Ferro, and M. Lazo (2003). The TIMEBANK corpus. In *Proceedings of Corpus Linguistics 2003.*

Regneri, M., A. Koller, and M. Pinkal (2010). Learning script knowledge with web experiments. In *Proceedings of the 48th Annual Meeting of the ACL*, Uppsala, pp. 979–988. ACL.

Richardson, M. and P. Domingos (2006). Markov logic networks. *Machine Learning 62*(1), 107–136.

Saquete, E., P. Martínez-Barco, R. Muñoz, and J. L. Vicedo (2004). Splitting complex temporal questions for question answering systems. In *Proceedings of the 42nd Meeting of the ACL*, Barcelona. ACL.

Setzer, A. and R. Gaizauskas (2001). A pilot study on annotating temporal relations in text. In *ACL 2001 Workshop on Temporal and Spatial Information Processing.*

Tao, C., H. R. Solbrig, D. K. Sharma, W.-Q. Wei, G. K. Savova, and C. G. Chute (2010). Time-oriented question answering from clinical narratives using semantic-web techniques. In *Proceedings of the 9th International Conference on the Semantic Web*, Volume 2, Berlin, pp. 241–256.

Tatu, M. and M. Srikanth (2008). Experiments with reasoning for temporal relations between events. In *Proceedings of COLING 2008*, Volume 1.

Vendler, Z. (1967). Verbs and times. In *Linguistics in Philosophy*, pp. 97–121. Ithaca, New York: Cornell University Press.

Verhagen, M. (2005). Temporal closure in an annotation environment. In *Language Resources and Evaluation*, Number 39, pp. 211–241.

Verhagen, M., R. Saurí, T. Caselli, and J. Pustejovsky (2010). SemEval-2010 task 13: TempEval-2. In *Proceedings of SemEval-2010.*

Vilain, M., H. Kautz, and P. van Beek (1990). Constraint propagation algorithms for temporal reasoning: A revised report. In *Readings in Qualitative Reasoning about Physical Systems*, pp. 373–381. San Francisco: Morgan Kaufmann.

Witten, I. H. and E. Frank (1999). *Data Mining: Practical Machine Learning Tools and Techniques with Java Implementations.* San Francisco: Morgan Kaufmann.

Yoshikawa, K., S. Riedel, M. Asahara, and Y. Matsumoto (2009). Jointly identifying temporal relations with Markov logic. In *Proceedings of the 47th Annual Meeting of the ACL.*

Empirical Validation of Reichenbach's Tense Framework

Leon Derczynski
Department of Computer Science
University of Sheffield, UK
leon@dcs.shef.ac.uk

Robert Gaizauskas
Department of Computer Science
University of Sheffield, UK
robertg@dcs.shef.ac.uk

Abstract

There exist formal accounts of tense and aspect, such as that detailed by Reichenbach (1947). Temporal semantics for corpus annotation are also available, such as TimeML. This paper describes a technique for linking the two, in order to perform a corpus-based empirical validation of Reichenbach's tense framework. It is found, via use of Freksa's semi-interval temporal algebra, that tense appropriately constrains the types of temporal relations that can hold between pairs of events described by verbs. Further, Reichenbach's framework of tense and aspect is supported by corpus evidence, leading to the first validation of the framework. Results suggest that the linking technique proposed here can be used to make advances in the difficult area of automatic temporal relation typing and other current problems regarding reasoning about time in language.

1 Introduction

In his 1947 account, Reichenbach offers a three-point framework for describing the tenses of verbs. The framework uses the concepts of *speech*, *event* and *reference* points and the relations between them in order to give descriptions of tenses. This framework has since been widely adopted and scrutinised by those working in the fields of linguistics and type-theoretic semantics.

Within computational linguistics, increased interest in temporal semantics, automatic annotation of temporal information, and temporal information extraction has led to temporally annotated resources being created and the discovery of many interesting problems. One of the most difficult problems in temporal information extraction is that of automatically determining the nature of the temporal order of times and events in a given discourse.

Temporal ordering is an important part of language – it allows us to describe history, to communicate plans and to discuss change. When automatic temporal annotation is broken into a tripartite task of detecting events, detecting times, and automatically determining the ordering of events and times, the third part – determining temporal ordering – is the most difficult. This is illustrated by, for example, the low performance scores at the most recent TempEval exercise (Verhagen et al., 2010), which focuses on automatic annotation of temporal relations. Event-event ordering is the hardest temporal relation typing task, and the focus of this paper.

Reichenbach's framework not only offers a means of formally describing the tenses of verbs, but also rules for temporally arranging the events related by these verbs, using the its three abstract points. This can, for a subset of cases, form a basis for describing the temporal ordering of these events.

The framework is currently used in approaches to many computational linguistics problems. These include language generation, summarisation, and the interpretation of temporal expressions. When automatically creating text, it is necessary to make decisions on when to shift tense to properly describe events. Elson and McKeown (2010) relate events based on a "perspective" which is calculated from the reference and event times of two verbs that each describe events. They construct a natural language generation system that uses reference times in order to correctly write stories. Further, reference point management is critical to medical summary generation. In order to helpfully unravel the meanings of tense shifts in minute-by-minute patient reports, Portet et al. (2009) required understanding of the reference point. The framework also helps interpret linguistic expressions of time (timexes). Reference time is required to interpret anaphoric expressions such as *"last April"*. Creation of recent timex corpora prompted the comment that there is a "need to develop sophisticated methods for temporal focus tracking if we are to extend current time-stamping technologies" (Mazur and Dale, 2010) – focus as a rôle filled by Reichenbach's reference point. In fact, demand for accurate reference time management is so persistent that state of the art systems for converting times expressed in natural language to machine-readable format now contain extra layers solely for handling reference time (Llorens et al., 2012).

Given the difficulty of automatically determining the orderings, or temporal relations, between events, and the suggested ability of Reichenbach's framework to provide information for this, it is natural to apply this framework to the temporal ordering task. Although tense has played a moderately useful part in machine learning approaches to the task (Hepple et al., 2007), its exact role in automatic temporal annotation is not fully understood. Further, though it was not the case when the framework was originally proposed, there now exist resources annotated with some temporal semantics, using TimeML (Pustejovsky et al., 2005). Comparing the explicit temporal annotations within these resources with the modes of interaction proposed by Reichenbach's framework permits an evaluation of the validity of this established account of tense and aspect.

This paper addresses the following questions:

1. How can Reichenbach's framework be related to a modern temporal annotation schema?
2. Between which event-relating verbs should the framework be applied?
3. Given Reichenbachian descriptions of pairs of verbs in English, how can one automatically determine the temporal relation between the events described by the verbs?
4. Do the behaviours that Reichenbach proposes agree with human-annotated, ground-truth data?

The main contributions made by this paper are twofold. Firstly, it provides an account of how tensed verb events, described according to Reichenbach, can be linked with each other to extract information about their temporal ordering. Secondly, it provides the first corpus-based validation of Reichenbach's framework against human-annotated ground truth data.

The rest of this paper is constructed as follows. Firstly Reichenbach's framework is introduced with accompanying examples (Section 2). Relevant parts of the TimeML annotation scheme are covered in Section 4. Discussion of how event-signifying verbs may be associated and then ordered is in Section 3. Section 5 introduces a way of connecting TimeML with Reichenbach's three time points. A corpus-based evaluation of Reichenbach's framework is in Section 6, and conclusion in Section 7.

2 Reichenbach's Framework

The core of the framework comprises three time points – speech time, event time and reference time. These are ordered relative each other using equality (e.g. simultaneity), precedence or succession operators. The tense and aspect of each verb is described using these points and the relations between them.[1] Interactions between verbs can be described in terms of relations between the time points of each verb.

2.1 Time Points

Reichenbach introduces three abstract time points to describe tenses. Firstly, there is speech time, S.[2] This represents the point at which the tensed verb described is uttered or written. Secondly, event time E is the time that the event introduced by the verb occurs. The position of this point relative to other verbs' Es reveals the temporal order of events related by a discourse. Thirdly, there is reference time R; this is an abstract point, from which events are viewed. Klein (1994) describes R as "the time to which a claim is constrained." In Example 1, speech time S is the point when the author created the discourse.

(1) *By then, she had left the building.*

[1]Although Reichenbach's suggests the framework is for describing tense, it also provides an account of perfective aspect. For example, Reichenbach's anterior tenses correspond to perfective aspect in English.

[2]For this paper, it is assumed that speech time is equivalent to DCT, unless otherwise explicitly positioned by discourse. Following the description of discourse deixis by Fillmore (1971), this is the same as always setting speech time S equal to his encoding time *ET* and not decoding time *DT*.

Relation	*Reichenbach's Tense Name*	*English Tense Name*	*Example*
E<R<S	Anterior past	Past perfect	*I had slept*
E=R<S	Simple past	Simple past	*I slept*
R<E<S			
R<S=E	Posterior past		*I expected that I would sleep*
R<S<E			
E<S=R	Anterior present	Present perfect	*I have slept*
S=R=E	Simple present	Simple present	*I sleep*
S=R<E	Posterior present	Simple future	*I will sleep (Je vais dormir)*
S<E<R			
S=E<R	Anterior future	Future perfect	*I will have slept*
E<S<R			
S<R=E	Simple future	Simple future	*I will sleep (Je dormirai)*
S<R<E	Posterior future		*I shall be going to sleep*

Table 1: Reichenbach's tenses; from Mani et al. (2005)

In this sentence, one perceives the events from a point S after they occurred. Reference time R is *"then"* – abstract, before speech time, and after event time E, the leaving of the building.

2.2 Tense Structure

Using these points, Reichenbach details the structure of nine tenses (see Table 1). The tenses detailed by Reichenbach are past, present or future, and may take a simple, anterior or posterior form. In English, the tenses apply to single non-infinitive verbs and to verbal groups consisting of a head verb and auxiliaries. Reichenbach's tense system describes the arrangement of the time points for each tensed verb.

In Reichenbach's view, different tenses specify different relations between S, E and R. Table 1 shows the six tenses conventionally distinguished in English. As there are more than six possible ordering arrangements of S, E and R, some English tenses might suggest more than one arrangement. Reichenbach's named tenses names also suffer from this ambiguity when converted to $S/E/R$ structures, albeit to a lesser degree. Past, present and future tenses imply $R < S$, $R = S$ and $S < R$ respectively. Anterior, simple and posterior tenses imply $E < R$, $E = R$ and $R < E$ respectively.

3 Associating Event Verbs

This validation relies on assessing temporal orderings suggested by Reichenbach's framework. These temporal orderings are between event-describing verbs. Therefore, we must determine which verbs may be directly temporally associated with one another. The simplest case is to examine relations between the smallest set of events which contains at least one relation: an event pair. So, in order to proceed, the following must be defined:

1. How does connecting a pair of verbs affect the relative positions of one verb's $S/E/R$ to anothers;
2. Which pairs of events can be linked;
3. How the results of linking events can be propagated from Reichenbach's framework to TimeML.

3.1 Reichenbachian Event-Event Relations

When sentences are combined to form a compound sentence, verbs interact, and implicit grammatical rules may require tenses be adjusted. These rules operate in such a way that the reference point is the same in all cases in the sequence. Reichenbach names this principle **permanence of the reference point**:

> We can interpret these rules as the principle that, although the events referred to in the clauses may occupy different time points, the reference point should be the same for all clauses.

Example 2 show a sentence in which this principle applies.

(2) *John told me the news, but I had already sent the letter.*

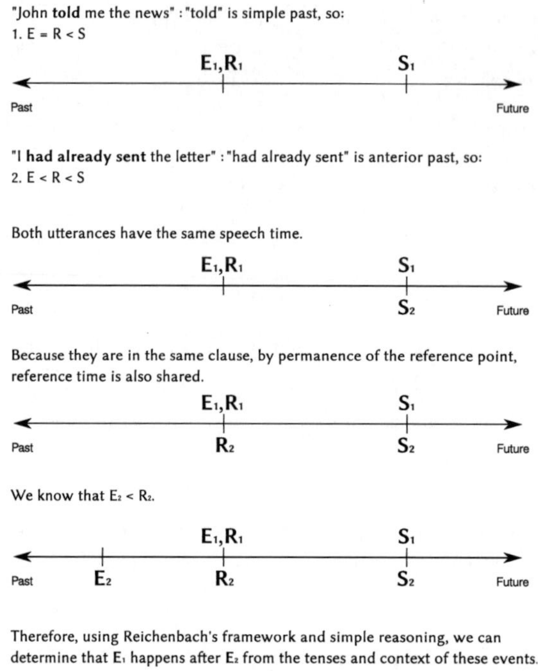

Figure 1: An example of permanence of the reference point.

Example 2 shows a sentence with two verb events – *told* and *had sent*. Using Reichenbach's framework, these share their speech time S (the time of the sentence's creation) and reference time R, but have different event times (see Figure 1). In the first verb, reference and event time have the same position. In the second, viewed from when John told the news, the letter sending had already happened – that is, event time is before reference time. As reference time R is the same throughout the sentence, we know that the letter was sent before John mentioned the news. Arranging S, E and R for each verb in a discourse and linking these points with each other ensures correct temporal ordering of events that the verbs describe.

3.2 Temporal Context

In the linear order that events and times are introduced in discourse, speech and reference points persist until changed by a new event or time. Observations during the course of this work suggest that the reference time from one sentence will roll over to the next sentence, until it is repositioned explicitly by a tensed verb or time. To make discussion of sets of verbs with common reference times easy, following Derczynski and Gaizauskas (2011a), we call each of these pragmatic groups a **temporal context**.

Temporal contexts may be observed frequently in natural language discourse. For example, the main body of a typical news article shares the same reference point, reporting other events and speech as excursions from this context. Each conditional world of events invoked by an "if" statement will share the same context. Events or times linked with a temporal signal will share a reference point, and thus be explicitly placed into the same temporal context. Reichenbach constrains the verbs which may be linked under his framework by using a grammatical device – the sequence of tenses. This is the only description in his paper of which in contexts the framework applies.

Several previous studies have indicated temporal context-like bounds in discourse. Dowty (1986) describes something similar to temporal context with the idea of the **temporal discourse interpretation principle** (TDIP). This states:

> Given a sequence of sentences S_1, S_2, ..., S_n to be interpreted as a narrative discourse, the reference time of each sentence S_i (for i such that $1 < i - n$) is interpreted to be:
>
> (a) a time consistent with the definite time adverbials in S_i, if there are any;
>
> (b) otherwise, a time which immediately follows the reference time of the previous sentence S_{i-1}.

The TDIP accounts for a set of sentences which share a reference and speech point. However, as with other definitions of temporal context, this principle involves components that are difficult to automatically determine (e.g. "consistent with definite time adverbials"). Webber (1987) introduces a listener model, incorporating R as a means of determining temporal focus. Her focus resumption and embedded discourse heuristics capture the nesting behaviour of temporal contexts. Further, Eijck and Kamp (2010) describe context-bounding, tense-based rules for applicability of Reichenbach's framework. These comprise a qualitative model of temporal context.

As described in Chapter 4 of Hornstein (1990), permanence of the reference point does not apply between main verb events and those in embedded phrases, relative clauses or quoted speech. These latter events occur within a separate temporal context, and it is likely that they will have their own reference time (and possibly even speech time, for example, in the case of quoted speech).

To handle such subordinate clauses, one must add a caveat – S and R persist as a discourse is read in textual order, for each temporal context. A context is an environment in which events occur, and may be the main body of the document, a tract of reported speech, or the conditional world of an *if* clause (Hornstein, 1990). For example:

(3) *Emmanuel had said "This will explode!," but changed his mind.*

Here, *said* and *changed* share speech and reference points. Emmanuel's statement occurs in a separate context, which the opening quote instantiates and is ended by the closing quote, and begins with an S that occurs at the same time as *said* – or, to be precise, *said*'s event time E_{said}.

However, temporal context information is not overt in TimeML annotations (Section 4) and not readily available from discourse. We therefore have the problem of needing to model temporal context, in order to decide to which event verb-event verb pairs the framework should be applied.

In order to temporally relate verb events using Reichenbach's framework, we must filter verb event pairs so that only those in which both events are in the same temporal context are considered. This requires a model of temporal context. If events in a pair are not both in the same context, Reichenbach's framework may not directly apply, and the pair should not be further analysed.

Simple techniques for achieving temporal context modelling could work based on sentence proximity. Proximity alone may not be sufficient, given this paper's earlier observations about quoted speech, re-positioning of the reference point and so on. Further techniques for temporal context modelling are detailed in experiments below in Section 6.

3.3 Progressive Aspect

While Reichenbach's basic framework provides an explicit, point-based account of the perfective, it does not do the same for the progressive. This section proposes a point-based solution for the progressive, within Reichenbach's framework.

Consider that event time E is a temporal interval, and therefore may be split into start and finish points E_s and E_f between which the event obtains. Given this, it becomes possible to place reference or speech time *within* the event interval – later than E_s but before E_f. This enable construction of scenarios where one is reporting on an ongoing process that starts before and ends after the reporting point – the same concept related by use of progressive aspect – and corresponds to Reichenbach's illustration of "extended tenses."

Examples of the Reichenbachian structure of progressive-aspect events are included in Table 3. For the simple tenses (where $R = E$) which TimeML describes aspect of NONE, it is assumed not that the event is a point, but that the event is an interval (just as in the progressive) and the reference time is *also* an interval, starting and finishing at the same times as the event (e.g. $R_s = E_s$ and $R_f = E_f$).

4 TimeML Schema and Dataset

TimeML (Pustejovsky et al., 2005)[3] is an annotation markup language for temporal semantics. It defines annotations for events and temporal expressions (both also called "intervals," because they are modelled

[3] or, in its current incarnation, ISO-TimeML

Relation	Explanation of A-relation-B
BEFORE	A finishes before B starts
AFTER	A starts after B ends
INCLUDES	A start before and finishes after B
IS_INCLUDED	A happens between B's start and finish
DURING	A occurs within duration B
DURING_INV	A is a duration in which B occurs
SIMULTANEOUS	A and B happen at the same time
IAFTER	A happens immediately after B
IBEFORE	A happens immediately before B
IDENTITY	A and B are the same event/time
BEGINS	A starts at the same time as B, but finishes first
ENDS	A starts after B, but they finish at the same time
BEGUN_BY	A starts at the same time as B, but goes on for longer
ENDED_BY	A starts before B, but they finish at the same time

Table 2: TimeML temporal interval relations

as periods of time between a start and end point). TimeML also defines annotations for the temporal relations that exist between intervals, in the form of binary interval relations.

4.1 Tense System

Under TimeML, event annotations have a part-of-speech feature. This permits easy identification of verbs, which are the relevant events for this study. Each verb has both tense and aspect features, which take values from three "tenses[4]" (PAST, PRESENT and FUTURE) and four "aspects" (NONE, PERFECTIVE, PROGRESSIVE and PERFECTIVE_PROGRESSIVE) respectively.

In many ways, TimeML's tense system is less expressive than that of Reichenbach's. It provides a maximum of 12 tense/aspect combinations, whereas the framework provides 19. The TimeML system cannot express anterior tenses according to Reichenbach's scheme. Further, TimeML does not account for the reference point, making shifts of reference time difficult to express other than by describing their end results. In its favour, TimeML does explicitly cater for progressive aspect – something that Reichenbach does not, a solution for which is proposed later in Section 3.3.

4.2 TimeML Temporal Relations

In TimeML, temporal relations may be annotated using one of thirteen interval relations. This set of relations is based on Allen's temporal interval algebra (Allen, 1983).

Temporal relations obtain between two intervals. They describe the natural of temporal ordering between those intervals. Those intervals may be either times or events, and need not be of the same type. Accordingly, a temporal relation annotation must specify two intervals and a relation that obtains from the first to the second; see Example 4. Additional information may be included, such as references to phrases that help characterise the relation (Derczynski and Gaizauskas, 2011b). Descriptions of the TimeML interval relations, based on Allen (1983)'s interval relation set, are given in Table 2.

(4)
```
John <EVENT eiid="e1" tense="PAST" aspect="NONE">told</EVENT>
me the news, but I had already
<EVENT eiid="e2" tense="PAST" aspect="PERFECTVE">told</EVENT>
the letter.
<TLINK eventInstanceID="e1" relType="BEFORE" relatedToInstance="e2" />
```

4.3 TimeBank

TimeBank v1.2 is a TimeML annotated corpus. It contains 6 418 temporal link annotations, 1 414 time annotations and 7 935 event annotations. TimeBank's creation involved a large human annotator effort and multiple versions (Pustejovsky et al., 2003); it is currently the largest temporally-annotated corpus containing explicit temporal relations.

[4] In TimeML v1.2, the tense attribute of events has values that are conflated with verb form. This conflation is deprecated in the most versions of TimeML, though no significant volume of ground-truth data is annotated under these later schemas.

TimeML Tense	TimeML Aspect	Reichenbach structure
PAST	NONE	$E = R < S$
PAST	PROGRESSIVE	$E_s < R < S, R < E_f$
PAST	PERFECTIVE	$E_f < R < S$
PRESENT	NONE	$E = R = S$
PRESENT	PROGRESSIVE	$E_s < R = S < E_f$
PRESENT	PERFECTIVE	$E_f < R = S$
FUTURE	NONE	$S < R = E$
FUTURE	PROGRESSIVE	$S < R < E_f, E_s < R$
FUTURE	PERFECTIVE	$S < E_s < E_f < R$

Table 3: TimeML tense/aspect combinations, in terms of the Reichenbach framework.

Inter-annotator agreement (IAA) describes the quality of annotation in TimeBank. Events were annotated with agreement 0.78; given events, their tenses were annotated with agreement 0.96 and aspect with agreement of 1.00 (complete agreement). For temporal relations between intervals, the type of relation reached agreement of 0.77. TimeBank is the ground truth used to validate Reichenbach's framework.

5 Mapping from TimeML to Reichenbach

Given the above accounts of the two schemas for describing events, tense and aspect, we shall now consider how they may be joined. TimeML and Reichenbach's framework do not use the same temporal semantics, so some work is required to map descriptions from one format to the other.

5.1 Interval Disjunctions

Based on our above accounts of Reichenbach's framework, TimeML, progressive aspect, temporal context, and temporal ordering, it is now possible to derive a mapping from TimeML to Reichenbach based on three-point algebra. Accordingly, the TimeML tenses and aspects may be mapped to $S/E/R$ structures using the translations shown in Table 3.

Working on the hypothesis that Reichenbach's framework may constrain a TimeML relation type to more than just four possible groupings, the table of tense-tense interactions is rebuilt, giving for each event pair a disjunction of TimeML relations instead of one of four labels. In TimeML, aspect values are composed of two "flags", PERFECTIVE and PROGRESSIVE, which may both be independently asserted on any verb event annotation. For simplicity, PERFECTIVE_PROGRESSIVE aspect was converted to PERFECTIVE; this feature value accounts for 20 of 5974 verb events, or 0.34% – a minority that does not greatly impact overall results. Another simplification is that participle "tenses" in TimeML (PASTPART and PRESPART) are interpreted the same way as their non-participle equivalents.

When determining corresponding TimeML TLINK `relType` values given two Reichenbachian tense structures, there is often more than one possible `relType`. In fact, multiple potential TimeML interval relation types apply in many cases. Given the events and tenses in Example 4, the relation could be not only BEFORE but also IBEFORE. Instead of specifying the exact relation, this *constrains* the type of temporal ordering.

The disjunctions of interval relations indicated by various tense/aspect pair combinations frequently recur, and are not unique to each tense/aspect pair combination. In fact, this approach to event-event ordering causes the framework to generate a limited set of such disjunctions, which matches the interval relation disjunctions corresponding to semi-intervals.

5.2 Emergence of Semi-intervals

Where an interval is defined by its start and end bounds, and both of these are required in order to perform interval reasoning, a semi-interval is defined using only one of its bounds. The sets of interval relation disjunctions indicated by the above tense/aspect combinations overlaps with the relation types present in a semi-interval temporal algebra. This algebra, identified by Freksa (1992), differs from the conventional interval reasoning described above by only make one bound of each interval finite. A full list of Freksa's semi-interval relations is provided in Table 4.

Freksa semi-interval relations can be described in terms of groups of Allen relations. The disjunctions

Relation	Illustration	TimeML relType disjunction
X is *older* than Y Y is *younger* than X	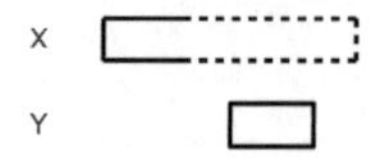	X [BEFORE, IBEFORE, ENDED_BY, INCLUDES, DURING] Y
X is *head to head* with Y	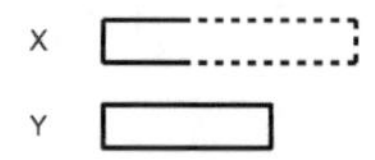	X [BEGINS, SIMULTANEOUS, IDENTITY, BEGUN_BY] Y
X *survives* Y Y is *survived by* X	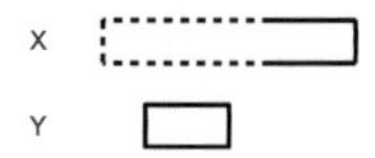	X [INCLUDES, BEGUN_BY, IAFTER, AFTER] Y
X is *tail to tail* with Y	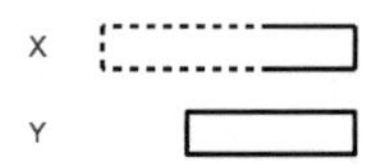	X [ENDED_BY, SIMULTANEOUS, IDENTITY, ENDS] Y
X *precedes* Y Y *succeeds* X	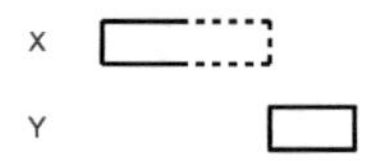	X [BEFORE, IBEFORE, ENDED_BY, INCLUDES, DURING_INV] Y
X is a *contemporary* of Y	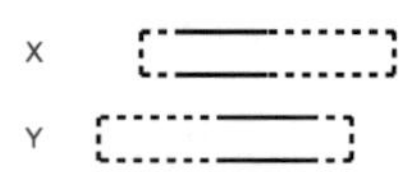	X [INCLUDES, IS_INCLUDED, BEGUN_BY, BEGINS, DURING, DURING_INV, SIMULTANEOUS, IDENTITY, ENDS, ENDED_BY] Y
X is *born before death* of Y Y *dies after birth* of X	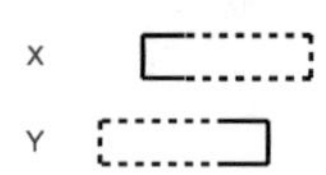	X [IS_INCLUDED, ENDS, DURING_INV, BEFORE, IBEFORE, INCLUDES, DURING, ENDED_BY] Y

Table 4: Freksa semi-interval relations; adapted from Freksa (1992). The superset of relations is omitted here but related there.

of TimeML full-interval relations suggested by our interpretation of Reichenbach's framework always match one of the groups of Allen relations used to represent a Freksa semi-interval relation.

For example, for two events E_1 and E_2, if the tense arrangement suggests that E_1 starts before E_2 (for example, E_1 is simple past and E_2 simple future), the available relation types for E_1 / E_2 are BEFORE, IBEFORE, DURING, ENDED_BY and INCLUDES.

The ambiguity of one interval bound in a semi-interval relation gives rise to a disjunction of possible interval relation types. For example, given that $E_{1s} < E_{2s}$, and $E_s < E_f$ for any proper interval event (e.g. its start is before its finish), the arrangement of E_1 and E_2's finish points is left unspecified. The disjunction of possible interval relation types is as follows:

- $E_{1f} < E_{2s}$: before;
- $E_{1f} = E_{2s}$: ibefore;
- $E_{1f} > E_{2s}$, $E_{1f} < E_{2f}$: during;
- $E_{1f} = E_{2f}$: ended_by;
- $E_{1f} > E_{2f}$: includes.

In each case, these disjunctions correspond to the Freksa semi-interval relation E_1 YOUNGER E_2.

5.3 Linking TimeML Events Using Reichenbach's Framework

Reichenbach's framework suggests temporal relation constraints based on the tenses and aspects of a pair of verbs. Given permanence of the reference point between the verbs, these constraints can be described using semi-interval relations. Accordingly, the full TimeML tense/aspect event-event interaction matrix according to this paper's interpretation of the framework is given in Table 5.

e1 ↓ e2 →	PAST-NONE	PAST-PROG.	PAST-PERF.	PRESENT-NONE	PRESENT-PROG.
PAST-NONE	*all*	contemporary	succeeds	survived by	survived by
PAST-PROGRESSIVE	contemporary	*contemporary*	survives	older	all
PAST-PERFECTIVE	precedes	survived by	*all*	precedes	survived by
PRESENT-NONE	survives	younger	succeeds	*contemporary*	contemporary
PRESENT-PROGRESSIVE	survives	all	survives	contemporary	*contemporary*
PRESENT-PERFECTIVE	all	all	succeeds	survived by	survived by
FUTURE-NONE	succeeds	younger	after	succeeds	younger
FUTURE-PROGRESSIVE	survives	dies after birth	survives	younger	dies after birth
FUTURE-PERFECTIVE	after	younger	after	younger	younger

e1 ↓ e2 →	PRESENT-PERF.	FUTURE-NONE	FUTURE-PROG.	FUTURE-PERF.
PAST-NONE	all	precedes	survived by	before
PAST-PROGRESSIVE	all	older	born before death	older
PAST-PERFECTIVE	precedes	before	survived by	before
PRESENT-NONE	survives	precedes	older	older
PRESENT-PROGRESSIVE	survives	older	born before death	older
PRESENT-PERFECTIVE	*all*	before	survived by	before
FUTURE-NONE	after	*all*	contemporary	survived by
FUTURE-PROGRESSIVE	survives	contemporary	*contemporary*	survives
FUTURE-PERFECTIVE	after	survived by	survived by	*all*

Table 5: TimeML tense/aspect pairs with the Freksa semi-intervals relations they suggest, according to this paper's interpretation of Reichenbach's framework. These semi-intervals correspond to disjunctions of TimeML interval relations.

6 Validating the Framework

So far, this paper has discussed the temporal relation typing problem, the differing tense representations provided by Reichenbach and TimeML, and an interpretation of Reichenbach's framework that permits temporal relation type constraint in TimeML. This section details the method for and presents results of validating Reichenbach's framework.

6.1 Context Modelling

Temporal context (detailed in Section 3.2) is defined as a set of events that have a common reference time, where the grammatical rule of sequence of tenses is followed. Lacking tools for annotating temporal context, it may instead be modelled in a variety of ways, based on arrangements of speech time and reference time, and the sentence-distance between a given pair of verb events.

Based on the hypothesis that events in a single temporal context will generally be distributed closely to one another in a text, proximity-based modelling of temporal context is evaluated. This assumes that all verbs within a certain proximity bound are considered to be in the same context. This is tested for single-sentence (e.g. all verbs in the same sentence are in the same temporal context, and no others), and for adjacent-sentence (verbs in adjacent sentences are in the same temporal context).

Because permanence of the reference point requires a shared reference time, for tenses to be meaningful in their context, the speech time must remain static. The "same SR" context refers to modelling of temporal context as a situation where the ordering of reference and speech times remains constant (in terms of one preceding, occurring with or following the other). This simple same-ordering constraint on S and R does not preclude situations where speech or reference time move, but still remain in roughly the same order (e.g. if reference time moves from 9pm to 9.30pm when speech time is 3pm), which are in fact changes of temporal context (either because R is no longer shared or because S has moved).

6.2 Results

Results are given in Table 6. In this table, a "consistent TLINK" is one where the relation type given in the ground truth is a member of the disjunction of relation types suggested by Reichenbach's framework. Separate figures are provided for performance including and excluding cases where the disjunction of all link types is given. This is because consistency given "no constraint" is not useful.

Context model	TLINKs	Consistent	Non-"all"	Non-"all" consistent
None (all pairs)	1 167	81.5%	481	55.1%
Same sentence, same SR	300	88.0%	95	62.1%
Same sentence	600	71.2%	346	50.0%
Same / adjacent sentence, same SR	566	**91.9%**	143	**67.8%**
Same / adjacent sentence	913	78.3%	422	53.1%

Table 6: Consistency of temporal orderings suggested by Reichenbach's framework with ground-truth data. The non-all columns refer to cases in which there was relation constraint, e.g., the framework did not suggest "all relation types possible".

6.3 Analysis

Interpreted in this way, Reichenbach's framework is generally consistent with TimeBank, supporting the framework's suggestions of event-event ordering among pairs of tensed verb events.

Although the proportion of inconsistent links (ignoring unconstrained cases) is noticeable – 32.2% in the best scenario – it is sufficiently strong to support the framework. The magnitude of inconsistency is comparable with inter-annotator *dis*agreement on TimeBank's temporal relation labels (0.23) when the crudeness of the proposed temporal context models is taken into account. IAA for tense and aspect labels in TimeBank – critical to correct application of Reichenbach's framework – are much higher (see Section 4.3). The fact that temporal context is derived from models and not explicit gold-standard annotation is also likely a significant source of noise in agreement.

The "same SR" context yields good results, though has limited applicability (e.g., it halves the set of considered same-sentence pairings). As both arguments having the same S and R occurs when they have the same TimeML tense, the only effective variant in these cases – in terms of data that contributes to Reichenbachian interpretation – is the TimeML aspect value. When given the constraint that both arguments have the same TimeML tense, the measured consistency of the framework increases. This hints that the ordering and positions of S and R are critical factors in relating tensed events, and considering them may lead to improvements in temporal relation labelling techniques that rely on aspect, such as that of Costa and Branco (2012).

Enlarging the context "window" to include adjacent sentences improves consistency. It may be that linked events within sentences are often between main events and embedded clauses or reported speech. It is also possible that single sentences may contain repositionings of the reference point that persist in following sentences, so that a single sentence does not exhibit internal permanence but permanence exists between it and following sentences. Close investigation into the typical scoping and switching of temporal context could help explain this phenomenon and lead to better models of temporal context.

The results suggest Reichenbach's framework is accurate and capable of temporally ordering events.

7 Conclusion

This paper set out to validate Reichenbach's framework of tense and aspect in the context of event ordering. The framework was found to be supported by human-annotated ground-truth data. This result provides empirical support for this established account of tense and aspect. In its finding, this paper also details a technique for reasoning about the temporal order of verb events in discourse.

Reichenbach's framework is a powerful tool for ordering events (and times) within a given context. It transparently informs approaches to many complex tasks, including automatic temporal ordering, timex normalisation, machine translation, clinical summarisation, and natural language generation. The approach detailed here requires *temporal context* to exploit the framework. However, it is not yet clear *how* to automatically determine the bounds of temporal contexts. To this end, future work can consider the annotation of temporal context, in order to aid high-precision temporal information extraction from discourse. Further, the argument that semi-interval reasoning is suitable for temporal information from text is supported by this empirical work, prompting more investigation into its use in the linguistic context.

Acknowledgments Thanks is due James Pustejovsky for early discussions on Reichenbach's framework and TimeML, and to the anonymous reviewers for their helpful feedback.

References

Allen, J. (1983). Maintaining knowledge about temporal intervals. *Communications of the ACM 26*(11), 832–843.

Costa, F. and A. Branco (2012). Aspectual type and temporal relation classification. In *Proc. EACL*, pp. 266–275.

Derczynski, L. and R. Gaizauskas (2011a). An Annotation Scheme for Reichenbach's Verbal Tense Structure. In *Proc. Joint ACL-ISO Workshop on Interoperable Semantic Annotation.*

Derczynski, L. and R. Gaizauskas (2011b). A corpus-based study of temporal signals. In *Proc. Conference on Corpus Linguistics.*

Dowty, D. (1986). The effects of aspectual class on the temporal structure of discourse: semantics or pragmatics? *Linguistics and philosophy 9*(1), 37–61.

Eijck, J. v. and H. Kamp (2010). Discourse representation in context. In J. v. Benthem and A. ter Meulen (Eds.), *Handbook of Logic and Language*, pp. 181 – 252. Elsevier.

Elson, D. and K. McKeown (2010). Tense and Aspect Assignment in Narrative Discourse. In *Proc. International Conference in Natural Language Generation.*

Fillmore, C. (1971). *Lectures on deixis.* CSLI Publications Stanford, California.

Freksa, C. (1992). Temporal reasoning based on semi-intervals. *Artificial intelligence 54*(1), 199–227.

Hepple, M., A. Setzer, and R. Gaizauskas (2007). USFD: preliminary exploration of features and classifiers for the TempEval-2007 tasks. In *Proc. International Workshop on Semantic Evaluation*, pp. 438–441.

Hornstein, N. (1990). *As time goes by: Tense and universal grammar.* MIT Press.

Klein, W. (1994). *Time in language.* Germanic linguistics. London [u.a.]: Routledge.

Llorens, H., L. Derczynski, R. Gaizauskas, and E. Saquete (2012). TIMEN: An Open Temporal Expression Normalisation Resource. In *Proc. International Conference on Language Resources and Evaluation*, pp. 3044–3051.

Mani, I., J. Pustejovsky, and R. Gaizauskas (2005). *The Language of Time: A Reader.* Oxford University Press.

Mazur, P. and R. Dale (2010). WikiWars: A new corpus for research on temporal expressions. In *Proc. EMNLP*, pp. 913–922.

Portet, F., E. Reiter, A. Gatt, J. Hunter, S. Sripada, Y. Freer, and C. Sykes (2009). Automatic generation of textual summaries from neonatal intensive care data. *Artificial Intelligence 173*(7-8), 789–816.

Pustejovsky, J., P. Hanks, R. Sauri, A. See, R. Gaizauskas, A. Setzer, D. Radev, B. Sundheim, D. Day, L. Ferro, and M. Lazo (2003). The TimeBank corpus. In *Proc. Conference on Corpus Linguistics*, pp. 647–656.

Pustejovsky, J., B. Ingria, R. Sauri, J. Castano, J. Littman, R. Gaizauskas, A. Setzer, G. Katz, and I. Mani (2005). The specification language TimeML. In *The Language of Time: A Reader*, pp. 545–557. Oxford University Press.

Reichenbach, H. (1947). The tenses of verbs. In *Elements of Symbolic Logic.* Macmillan.

Verhagen, M., R. Sauri, T. Caselli, and J. Pustejovsky (2010). SemEval-2010 task 13: TempEval-2. In *Proc. International Workshop on Semantic Evaluation*, pp. 57–62.

Webber, B. (1987). The interpretation of tense in discourse. In *Proc. ACL*, pp. 147–154.

Generating Natural Language from Linked Data: Unsupervised template extraction

Daniel Duma Ewan Klein
School of Informatics, University of Edinburgh
danielduma@gmail.com, ewan@inf.ed.ac.uk

Abstract

We propose an architecture for generating natural language from Linked Data that automatically learns sentence templates and statistical document planning from parallel RDF datasets and text. We have built a proof-of-concept system (LOD-DEF) trained on un-annotated text from the Simple English Wikipedia and RDF triples from DBpedia, focusing exclusively on factual, non-temporal information. The goal of the system is to generate short descriptions, equivalent to Wikipedia stubs, of entities found in Linked Datasets. We have evaluated the LOD-DEF system against a simple generate-from-triples baseline and human-generated output. In evaluation by humans, LOD-DEF significantly outperforms the baseline on two of three measures: non-redundancy and structure and coherence.

1 Introduction

In recent years, work on the Semantic Web has undergone something of a split. At one end of the continuum, considerable energy has been invested into the construction of detailed domain ontologies expressed in some variant of OWL,[1] with considerable attention paid to maintaining logical consistency. At the other end, the so-called Linked Data framework has given rise to the publication of quite large scale datasets, with relatively little concern for ensuring consistency. Although the language, namely RDF,[2] in which Linked Data is encoded can be regarded as a restricted form of first-order predicate logic, existing Linked Datasets are closer in many ways to large, distributed databases than the kind of carefully constructed knowledge base that is familiar from AI research. The work that we report here takes as its starting point the following question: can Linked Data be used as the input to a Natural Language Generation (NLG) system? There are at least a couple of reasons why a positive answer would be interest. First, it is still relatively hard for non-experts to browse unfamiliar Linked Data sets, and a natural language representation could potentially ameliorate this problem. Second, cultural heritage institutions (e.g., museums, art galleries, and libraries) are increasingly interested in publishing their data in the form of Linked Data.[3] Such institutions are typically committed to presenting information about their holdings in multiple forms, and consequently generation of natural language that utilises a single Linked Data source would be highly attractive. Moreover, the very nature of Linked Data should make it easier for an NLG system to supplement institution-specific data with encyclopaedic information drawn from sources such as DBpedia.[4]

In the light of these motivations, we propose an architecture for a trainable NLG system for Linked Data that can automatically learn sentence templates and document planning from parallel RDF data and text, with the communicative goal of describing Wikipedia-style factual descriptions of entities.

[1] http://www.w3.org/TR/owl2-overview/
[2] We describe RDF in more detail in the next section
[3] See http://museum-api.pbworks.com for many examples.
[4] http://dbpedia.org

2 Background

2.1 Natural Language Generation

Natural Language Generation is the task of producing natural language text from an input of domain-dependent semantic information. Reiter and Dale (2000) describe a modular architecture for a deep NLG system as a pipeline composed of three main modules: (1) document planning, where the information to include in the final text is selected (*content determination*) and ordered (*text structuring*), (2) *microplanning*, where lexicalisation, referring expression generation and aggregation (coordination and subordination of sentences) are performed, and (3) *surface realisation*, where possible verbalisations are typically over-generated, ranked and selected. This has been called "deep" NLG, in contrast to "shallow" methods based on templates.

We will adopt some of this terminology, but nevertheless propose a shallow approach, in which text realisation uses RDF data to fill slots in sentence templates. Templates are learned on the basis of parallel text-data — cf. the Text-Knowledge Resources (TKRs) proposed by Duboue and Mckeown (2003). They describe these as "a set of human written text and knowledge base pairs", where the knowledge base includes data that a concept-to-text system could use to generate output achieving the same communicative goals as the human-authored text. Wide-scale unsupervised learning of templates and document plans opens the prospect of designing NLG systems that are inexpensive to develop and deploy, easier to transfer to other domains, and potentially multilingual.

The system is trained from a TKR by performing four main actions. First it aligns the text and the data by matching data values from RDF statements with strings in the text. Second, it extracts and modifies sentences that express these values, so as to build a set of sentence templates. Third, it collects statistics about how the matched values are ordered in text. Finally, it determines the class of entity that a TKR pair describes and assembles a set of templates and associated information to form a 'model' for that class.

We describe LOD-DEF, a proof-of-concept system trained on text from the Simple English Wikipedia[5] and data from DBpedia (Mendes et al., 2012). Our goal is to demonstrate that such an architecture is feasible, and that a system trained in this way can generate texts which are perceived as intelligible and informative by human judges.

2.2 Linked Data and RDF

The term *Linked Data* refers to a set of best practices for publishing and interlinking structured data on the Web (Heath and Bizer, 2011). These so-called "Linked Data Principles" mandate the use of a number of web based open formats for publishing data, such as HTTP as a transport layer and the Resource Description Framework (RDF)[6] for representing and linking datasets. The central claim of Linked Data is that the general architecture of the World Wide Web can be generalised to the task of sharing structured data on global scale. The rate of publication of Linked Open Data (i.e., data freely accessible without restrictions on use) has been steadily increasing over last years, forming a big data cloud (Heath and Bizer, 2011) which includes information about an extensive variety of topics. DBpedia is the *de facto* central hub of this Web of Data. It is a broad-purpose knowledge base containing over a billion RDF statements, which have been extracted by mining Wikipedia "infoboxes", the tables of attribute-value pairs appearing alongside an article. These contain much factual information, such as birth and death dates for people, names of capitals and political leaders for countries, and so on.

RDF uses a graph-based data model for representing knowledge. Statements in RDF are expressed as so-called triples of the form `(subject predicate object)`, where `predicate` is a binary relation taking `subject` and `object` as arguments. RDF subjects and predicates are Uniform Resource Identifiers (URIs) and objects are either URIs or literals. For example, the following (using Turtle[7] syntax for serialising triples) is intended to say that the J. S. Bach's date of birth is 1685-03-21 and his place of birth is Eisenach:

(1)
```
:Johann_Sebastian_Bach dbont:birthDate "1685-03-21" .
:Johann_Sebastian_Bach dbont:birthPlace :Eisenach .
```

[5] http://dumps.wikimedia.org/simplewiki/latest/simplewiki-latest-pages-articles.xml.bz2

[6] http://www.w3.org/RDF/

[7] http://www.w3.org/TeamSubmission/turtle/

The notation dbont:birthDate makes use of an abbreviatory syntax for URIs involving the prefix dbont followed by a colon and a "local name". A prefix can be thought of as determining a namespace within which a given identifier, such as :Johann_Sebastian_Bach, is unique. To be complete, we also need to declare what the prefix dbont stands for. If, say, it is defined to be http://dbpedia.org/ontology/, then the unabbreviated version of dbont:birthDate would be http://dbpedia.org/ontology/birthDate. In the remainder of the paper, we use prefixed names and often use the empty prefix (e.g., as in :Eisenach) to stand for the default namespace. Example (1) illustrates another important feature of RDF, namely that the objects of predicates can be literals (like "1685-03-21") or URIs (like :Eisenach). Although literals are often just strings, they can also be assigned to other XML Schema datatypes, such as xsd:float.

We will also adopt an abbreviatory convention from Turtle which allows a sequence of triples that share the same subject to be condensed with a semi-colon, as shown in (2).

```
(2)  :Johann_Sebastian_Bach dbont:birthDate "1685-03-21" ;
                            dbont:birthPlace :Eisenach .
```

This is equivalent to (1).

Sets of RDF triples can also be thought of as graphs, where the subject and object provide labels for nodes in the graph, and the predicate labels the edge between the nodes. This is illustrated in Fig. 1.

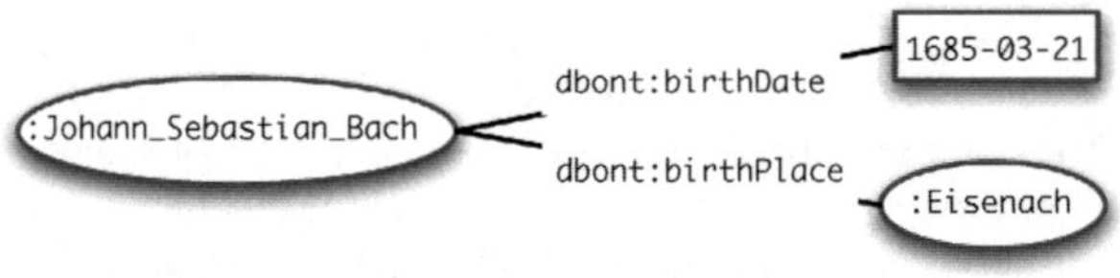

Figure 1: RDF Graph

RDF statements of the kind shown in (1) are equivalent to unquantified atomic sentences of first order logic.[8] For example, the graph in Fig. 1 translates to

(3) *birthDate(Johann_Sebastian_Bach, 1685-03-21)* ∧
birthPlace(Johann_Sebastian_Bach, Eisenach)

3 Related Work

NLG for the Semantic Web Most previous approaches to Natural Language Generation from Semantic Web formalisms have been concerned with verbalising OWL ontologies (e.g. Stevens et al., 2011; Hewlett et al., 2005; Liang et al., 2012)). By contrast, the textual realisation of factual data in RDF has received relatively little attention. One interesting exception is Sun and Mellish (2007), whose Triple-Text system generates strings directly from RDF with a minimum of hand-coded rules. Sun and Mellish note that RDF predicates typically encode useful linguistic information. That is, while URIs are officially expected to be semantically opaque, in practice they often provide good clues as to their intended interpretation; examples are the predicates ex:hasProperty and ex:industryOfArea. Triple-Text exploits this information to lexicalise URIs and the triples they occur in without using domain knowledge. That is, since "camel-case" is often used to indicate implicit word boundaries in RDF predicates, it is straightforward to split up a predicate such as hasProperty into a sequence of tokens [has, property], as a prelude to further processing. In Triple-Text, the tokens are POS-tagged and classified into categories via pattern-matching, and the categories then trigger the application of an appropriate realization rule to derive an output sentence. For example, given the triple (4), the system generates the sentence (5).

(4) ex:North ex:industryOfArea ex:manufacturing_sector.

(5) The industry of the North is manufacturing sector.

Although Triple-Text is fast and inexpensive to deploy, its expressiveness is limited by the fact that triples are processed in isolation from each other. As a result, only binary relations can be +expressed (since that is all that can be stated by a single RDF statement). A related consequence is that the

[8]Note that there is no way of expressing negation in RDF. Although existential quantification is allowed, we shall not have need of it in this paper.

information contained in a set of RDF statements cannot be aggregated or placed within the context of a larger discourse structure. Finally, the output is not always grammatically correct and cannot easily be tailored to a specific domain, since lexical choice is determined by the form of URIs in the triples.

Trainable NLG As mentioned above, we learn templates from parallel text-knowledge base pairs (TKRs) as originally proposed by Duboue and Mckeown (2003). Data in a TKR is aligned with the text (the "matching" stage) in a two-step process. First, the system identifies spans of text that are string-identical to values in the data. Second, it builds a statistical language model and uses the entropy of these to determine if other spans of text are indicative of similar values being expressed. The output of Duboue and Mckeown's system is dependent on hand-written rules and is specifically targeted at content determination for the constrained domain of biography generation. The approach we are adopting is less sophisticated, and is similar to the first matching step in their algorithm, where values in the data are matched to identical or near-identical strings in the text.

Automatic summarisation Our approach is related to multi-document summarisation and text-to-text generation insofar as they deal with the extraction and arrangement of sentences to create a new document. Text-to-text NLG only deals with processing documents that are about the same entity or topic and extracts the most relevant sentences from those documents to create a new document. In contrast, we want to generate natural language describing an instance in an ontology for which there may be no prior text available. To achieve this goal, we need to identify sentences about an entity that will be "transferable", that is, will be true of other entities of the same type (see § 4.2). Where such sentences are not directly derivable from the text, we can try to modify them to make them transferable. This is similar to the task of sentence compression in automatic summarisation (e.g. Cohn and Lapata, 2009; Filippova and Strube, 2008). Compression is often effected by tree operations over a parse tree, with the most frequent operation being the deletion of constituents. For summarisation, constituents are removed because they are deemed of lesser importance, while in our approach they are deleted when there is no evidence for them in the data. We adopt a syntactic pruning approach inspired by Gagnon and Da Sylva (2006), where sentences are first parsed and then the resulting structures are simplified by applying hand-built rules and filters.

4 The Task

4.1 Overview

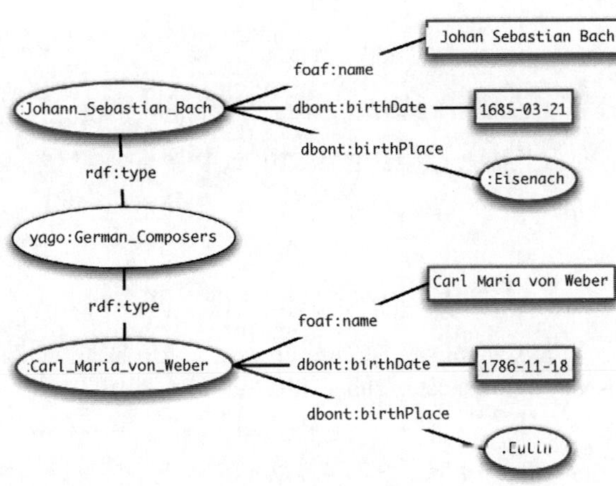

Figure 2: RDF Graph of Two Composers

We begin this section with a simplified example of how templates are extracted and then filled to produce a new sentence. Let's assume that our TKR is a pairing of the text

(6) Johan Sebastian Bach (b. Eisenach, 21 March 1685) was a German composer of the Baroque period.

with the RDF graph in Fig. 2. Note that a triple using the predicate `rdf:type` is the standard way of expressing class membership in RDF. By comparing the text with the part of the graph rooted in the node `:Johann_Sebastian_Bach`, we can figure out that certain substrings of (6) correspond to values of predicates in the RDF. For example, the string *Johan Sebastian Bach* matches the value of the predicate `foaf:name`. If we delete any string in (6) that can be mapped to the value of an RDF predicate in Fig. 2, then the result is a sentence template like that shown in (7), where we've use an underscore (___) to indicate 'slots' in the template.

(7) ___ (b. ___, ___) was a ___ of the Baroque period.

Although (7) is a template, it is not MINIMAL, since it contains information (*of the Baroque period*) that fails to correspond to any values in the graph. However, once we have pruned away non-minimal text, we are left with a transferable template which can be used to generate new sentences. In particular, we can use the subgraph of Fig. 2 rooted in the node `Carl_Maria_von_Weber` to fill the slots in the template, giving us the result in (8).

(8) Carl Maria von Weber (b. Eutin, 18 November 1786) was a German composer.

4.2 Extracting Templates

Automatically aligning the RDF data with the text can be viewed a special case of Named Entity Recognition (NER), or as a similar task to that of Wikification, which aims to annotate keywords in the document with their most relevant Wikipedia page (Mihalcea and Csomai, 2007). In our more restricted scenario, we only need to match spans of text with literal values that occur as objects of triples in the RDF. For instance, we want to be able to match the text string *Eisenach* with the literal that occurs as object of the predicate `dbont:birthPlace`. Rather than labelling named entity mentions with classes, we label them with the predicate of the triple in which the corresponding data value occurs. Let's write $\alpha \sim \mathrm{o}$ to mean that a string α is matched to an RDF object o. Then we say that α *has object-type* p if $\alpha \sim$ o and for some subject s, a triple of the form (s p o) occurs in the relevant RDF graph.

To illustrate, let's consider the slightly more complex example in Fig. 3.

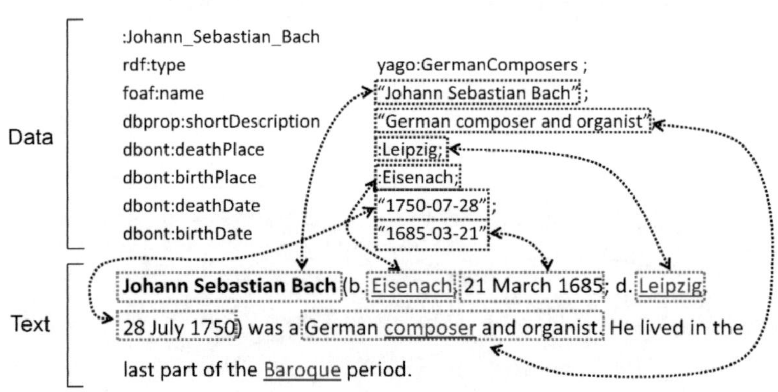

Figure 3: Aligning Data and Text

The template extracted from this alignment is represented as a text string with interpolated slots of the form `[p]`, where `p` is an RDF predicate. This is illustrated in (9).

(9) `[foaf:name]` (b. `[dbont:birthPlace]`, `[dbont:birthDate]`, d. `[dbont:deathPlace]`, `[dbont:deathDate]`) was a `[dbprop:shortDescription]`.

Selecting the RDF predicates whose values are to be matched in the text is dependent on the domain of the text and on the way data is encoded in RDF. We can think of the domain in terms of a subgraph of a given depth within the overall RDF graph in our dataset. In the present approach, we only retrieve the triples whose subject corresponds to the main topic of the Wikipedia article being processed. This restriction to subgraphs of depth 1 turned out to be sufficient for our task, and retrieving longer paths through the graph was found to significantly increase the complexity of the extraction without corresponding benefit.

Following Grice's Maxim of Quality, the output of the system should be constrained to be "truthful", in the sense that the textual output should be supported by evidence in the input data. As mentioned earlier, the sentence templates extracted for a given subject `s` should be minimal with respect to `s`, in that they do not contain substantive information unless it is licensed by a triple `(s p o)`. If a template $\mathcal{T}$ is minimal for `s`, and there is some `s'` which has the same class and (at least) the same attributes as `s`, then the result of filling $\mathcal{T}$'s slots with property values of `s'` should be a true sentence. As we pointed out earlier, we adopt a similar approach to (Gagnon and Da Sylva, 2006) by first parsing[9] the source sentences and then pruning away any constituents which fail to be licensed by the RDF data.

We will call the following grammatical categories PRUNABLE: noun, adjective, adverb and numeral. Pruning proceeds in three stages. First, if a word w belongs to a prunable category, then we delete w if it fails to match a data value in the relevant graph. Second, we delete any subtree T whose head has been deleted; for example, if w of category N has been deleted, then we also delete the NP (and any remaining daughters) which w headed. Finally, templates are discarded unless they contain slots corresponding to both the subject of the triple set and at least one property value, and remaining templates undergo post-processing to ensure correct punctuation by deleting empty brackets, duplicate commas, and so on.

The template extraction algorithm was informally evaluated by running it on 268 articles. 199 candidate templates were extracted, of which 124 were discarded after pruning and other filtering, leading to 74 templates. We judged 60 of these to be minimal, and 43 (58%) to be grammatically acceptable.

4.3 Document Planning

For content determination, we implement the baseline of (Duboue and Mckeown, 2003). We collect unigrams of matched RDF predicates in the text, and if the frequency of a predicate is below a threshold in the articles for a given class of entity, even if an instance of this class has this property in the data, the system should not output it. According to Reiter and Dale (2000), document structuring carries out more complex selection and ordering of information than just sequencing; it treats the text as a tree structure and clusters related items of information. Given that the sentences templates extracted from the text contain several properties expressed, we can think of them as partial trees, part of the bigger tree required for document structuring, so we expect that extracting these templates and ordering them in the right way will yield good results. We never attempt to assess the relative importance of a sentence to a text; we aim to extract as many templates as possible and treat them as equally important.

We need to deal with the fact that, for a given subject, an RDF predicate can have more than one value and that more than one property can have the same value. Indeed this is often the case and LOD tends to show very high redundancy. To deal with this, we cluster predicates into equivalence classes, or PREDICATE POOLS, when they appear to take the same value for the subject with frequency over a given threshold. For example, `foaf:name`, `rdfs:label` and `dbprop:name` are clustered together in a single pool for all classes used in the experiments.

Sentence templates that have been selected for inclusion in the final text are ordered using trigram probabilities of the predicate pools they verbalise. For each step, the probability score of each template is computed using the trigram probability of the last two verbalised pools and the first one in the template and the one with the highest probability is chosen.

4.4 Class Models

The NLG system has a single communicative goal: to describe an instance of a class (for example, J. S. Bach as an instance of `GermanComposer`). However, attributes that are relevant to, say, a rock band, are unlikely to be relevant to an antelope or other animal species. Similarly, given predicates need not be expressed in the same order for all classes. Finally, sentence templates can also be expected to depend on the class of the entity, because of the RDF predicates they realise and also because of their lexical and syntactic composition. In order to capture this dependence, we associate with classes a bundle of information including the relevant RDF predicate pools, a preferred ordering

[9] We used the Stanford Parser version 1.6.5, from 30/11/2010 with the pre-trained PCFG English model (Klein and Manning, 2003).

for realising the corresponding object-types, and the appropriate sentence templates. This bundle is termed a CLASS MODEL.

This means that when we want to generate text about a given entity, we need to choose, from those available, the class that it would be most prototypical of (cf. Rosch, 1973). This class must have the right granularity and level of detail, both for training and generating. It must not be so general that its attributes are too generic, or so specific that the extracted templates do not generalise to other entities of the same class. This task is surprisingly nontrivial, since not only can instances be members of multiple classes (via triples of the form `s rdf:type C`), but classes also allow multiple inheritance (via triples of the form `C rdfs:subClassOf SC`). An initial exploratory analysis of the Wikipedia data shows that a single entity typically belongs to a large number of classes. This is illustrated by Figure 4, which shows the classes to which J. S. Bach belongs according to DBPedia.[10]

```
AnglicanSaints              ComposersForViolin
Person                      ComposersForCello
GermanComposers             GermanClassicalOrganists
ComposersForPipeOrgan       PeopleCelebratedInTheLutheranLiturgicalCalendar
ComposersForLute            OrganistsAndComposersInTheNorthGermanTradition
18th-centuryGermanPeople    PeopleFromSaxe-Eisenach
BaroquEComposers            ClassicalComposersOfChurchMusic
PeopleFromEisenach
```

Figure 4: Class membership of `Johann_Sebastian_Bach`

Choosing the "right" class for an entity is a challenging problem. For the present approach we have adopted baseline algorithm which rests on the heuristic that if a substring occurs frequently in the terms used as class names for some entity, then it is likely to correspond to a core class for that entity. For example, inspection of Figure 4 shows that *Composers* occurs as a substring in 8 of the 15 class names (and will also occur in the literal value of the `rdfs:label` predicate for those classes). The algorithm has the following steps:

1. Collect the `rdfs:label` values for each of the classes as a bag-of-words, and combine this with the words from the first sentence of the Wikipedia article. Create a word vector *tf* (term frequency) whose values are each word's raw frequency in the bag.
2. Compute a score for every class label, which is the normalized sum of *tf* scores of every work in it, using the formula:

$$score(w) = \frac{1}{M} \sum_{i=0}^{N} tf(w_i)$$

   where w is the list of tokens derived from the class label string (e.g. *["People", "from", "Eisenach"]*), w_i is the ith element in this list and N is the total number of elements in w. M is set to be N if $N > 1$, otherwise it is set to an arbitrary higher value to reflect a dispreference against one-word class names.
3. Select the classes with the n-highest scores. We train for several models at the same time, given that we cannot be confident the class we chose is the only one that the entity is prototypical of. During the experiments, we set the value of n to 5.

As an example, the 5-best class list (with their scores) for `:Johann_Sebastian_Bach` is shown in (10). For each of these classes, a class model is created (or updated if already present).

(10) `yago:GermanComposers (6.0), yago:BaroquEComposers (3.3)`
`yago:ComposersForViolin (3.0), yago:ComposersForCello (3.0),`
`yago:ComposersForLute (3.0)`

4.5 Generation

The LOD-DEF generation algorithm takes as input a collection of class models, and the URI of the entity to be described. The five best classes are chosen (using the approach described above, but without the addition of article text to the bag of words) and the corresponding model classes are

[10]To ease presentation, we have omitted the namespace qualifiers of these classes.

scored according to the number of predicate pools that would be instantiated via the model's sentence templates.

In order to check instantiation, we need to access the RDF properties of the subject entity, and this is carried out by running a sequence of SPARQL queries against the DBPedia endpoint. That is, we execute a query for each predicate pool in the class model. As mentioned earlier, a predicate pool may contain a number of different RDF predicates, but since these are considered to be semantically equivalent, as soon as the value of one of them has been successfully returned by the query, this value is taken as the representative for the whole pool and querying is terminated. Where a single pool has multiple values, it is treated as a list for the purpose of aggregation, e.g. if ":X dbont:birthPlace :A" and ":X dbont:birthPlace :B" then "X was born in A and B".

To illustrate the scoring procedure, let's suppose that we have selected the classes shown in (10) for the topic `:Johann_Sebastian_Bach`. The scores for two class models are shown in Table 1.

	Models	
	`GermanComposers`	`ComposersForCello`
Number of templates	2	3
Predicates with values in the data	7	6
Predicates instantiated in templates	5	6

Table 1: Scoring class models

The chosen model would be `ComposersForCello`, even though it received a lower score in the first step, because a higher number of values would be (potentially) expressed through templates. The motivation behind this choice is that an extracted sentence template is expected to generate higher quality text, so a model instantiating more predicates through extracted templates is preferred.

We use chart generation: all sentence templates in the model for which there are enough triples in the data are put on a chart and combinations of them are generated. The following steps are taken: (1) We discard templates whose object-types involve predicate pools for which no data values have been found and put the remaining ones on the chart. (2) For each pool in the model, a default sentence template of the form `[possessive] [property] is [value]` is generated and added to the chart. This deals with the situation where a retrieved data value would failed to be expressed for a lack of an appropriate template.

We select and order sentence templates from the chart to produce a text. Ideally, we would want to find the combination of sentences that expresses all the values of the predicate pools in the model, while employing as many extracted templates and as few default templates as possible. We also want to order the templates in the most plausible order according to the RDF predicate trigrams collected during training. In order to deal with the combinatorial explosion we compute scores for all the options at every step, select the combination with the highest score and discard all the others, thus only ever keeping one possible combination. One important constraint is that a given predicate pool should only be instantiated once per generated article. When a template is chosen that requires the value of a predicate pool, any other template on the chart also requiring that information will not be considered for the combination. This is not guaranteed to be the optimal solution to the requirements outlined above, but it is a satisfactory trade-off between quality and speed and keeps the algorithm to $O(n^2 log(n))$.

5 Evaluation

5.1 Method and Materials

Given the exploratory nature of this project, the evaluation relies on human evaluation of the system's output compared to output from two other systems: the baseline and expert human output. We adopt a two-panel (i.e., two separate groups of subjects) approach to compare the three outputs, similarly to Sun and Mellish (2007). Subjects in Panel I generate descriptions of the same 12 entities [11] while subjects in Panel II rate the different outputs of System A (baseline), System B (LOD-DEF) and System C (human generation) across a number of dimensions. The hypothesis is that subjects will rate LOD-DEF higher on average than a baseline system generating exclusively from English words in RDF predicate labels. The system is also ranked against human-generated text for the same data.

[11] For a full list of the entities used and more in-depth details of our implementation, see Duma (2012).

Human-generated text need not always be an upper bound in subjective evaluation, but given the simplicity of the two NLG systems, this is a reasonable expectation.

Subjects were asked to complete an online survey. For this survey, the same 12 entities were described by the three systems, which produced 36 short texts, rated by 25 subjects. The participants were self-identified as having an upper-intermediate or above level of English. The texts were presented to the subjects in pseudo-random order, to avoid texts about the same entity occurring within a page of each other (four texts were presented on every page). Subject were asked to rate each text on a measure of 1 (lowest) to 5 (highest) on the following three criteria, adapted from the DUC 2007 criteria: grammaticality; non-redundancy; and structure and coherence.[12] No direct evaluation of content determination is carried out, but this is assumed to evaluated implicitly through the dimension of *non-redundancy*, given that its main effect in the implementation is filtering out redundant and unnecessary information. LOD-DEF does not select more relevant triples, but it omits irrelevant ones. It was not disclosed to the subjects that humans generated the texts of one of the systems being tested.

Data One of the aims was to evaluate the effectiveness of extracted sentence templates used by the LOD-DEF system. Consequently, classes for evaluation were not chosen at random, but were selected with a bias towards maximising the number of RDF predicates matched in text and the number of templates; this correlated with classes for which more factual information (strings and quantities) was available on DBpedia. Subject to this constraint, an attempt was made to vary the selected classes as much as possible.

Baseline	Jennifer Saunders is an English television actor. Her birth date is 6 July 1958. Her description is British comedienne. Her place of birth is Sleaford, Lincolnshire, England.
Humans	Jennifer Saunders (Born 06/07/1958) is an English comedienne, originally from Sleaford, Lincolnshire.
LOD-DEF	Jennifer Saunders (6 July 1958, Sleaford and Lincolnshire) is a British comedienne.

Figure 5: Sample outputs of baseline, human and LOD-DEF

Baseline Our baseline NLG system employs direct generation from RDF triples in the style of Sun and Mellish (2007). Each triple is realised as a single sentences and a shallow linguistic analysis of the words in the RDF predicate determines the structure of these sentences. The label values (from `rdfs:label`) of predicates are used for this when available, otherwise a tokenisation of the predicate URI was used. The initial sentence created by the baseline is realises the class of the entity, formed by the name of the entity (its `rdfs:label`) followed by *is a* and the `rdfs:label` of the class of the entity, e.g., *Johann Sebastian Bach is a German composer*. The relevant class is chosen using the class selection algorithm detailed earlier.

The collection of triples we are dealing with encodes information about a single entity, and we wish to present this information as a coherent text made up of several sentences. To aid coherence, the baseline implements a very simple Referring Expression Generation algorithm, where subsequent references to the topic entity use a personal pronouns rather than the full name. The system selects the correct personal and possessive pronoun on the basis of the value of the `foaf:gender` predicate. This baseline makes no attempt at document planning, but simple heuristics filter out properties with inappropriate values (e.g., values containing more than ten words).

Human Upper Bound Panel I, formed by two native speakers of English (linguistics postgraduate students), were given triples related to the chosen entities and instructions to write summary descriptions of the entities the data is about, expressing in text as much of this data as possible. The information was raw but presented in a human-friendly format as illustrated in (11).

(11)
```
birth date = 1958-07-06
place of birth = Sleaford, Lincolnshire, England
```

The triples were based on the same data as that used by by the LOD-DEF system except that they were manually filtered to remove redundancy and to randomize their order. We avoided giving the subjects examples of what kind of output we expected, thus taking care not to prime them. Fig. 5 shows short examples of each kind of output.

[12] `http://www-nlpir.nist.gov/projects/duc/duc2007/quality-questions.txt`

5.2 Results

An exploratory analysis of the data collected showed clear differences in means between for the rating of the three systems (Table 2). We ran a One-Way ANOVA for each of the three criteria the texts were rated on. All three ANOVAs were statistically significant: for grammaticality $F(2, 72) = 119.001, p < 0.001$, for non-redundancy $F(2, 72) = 129.053, p < 0.001$ and for structure and coherence $F(2, 72) = 129.053, p < 0.001$. Tukey's Post-Hoc test established which comparisons were significant for each; Tables 3 and 4 show the differences in mean and their significance.

As expected, human generation was judged to be consistently superior to the other two systems. LOD-DEF does not improve on the perception of grammaticality of the baseline, but it does significantly outperform the baseline on non-redundancy and structure and coherence. The most significant improvement of LOD-DEF over the baseline is on the non-redundancy metric, with a difference of 1.14.

System	Grammaticality	Non-redundancy	Structure & coherence
A (baseline)	2.29	1.89	1.95
B (LOD-DEF)	2.58	3.03	2.70
C (humans)	4.48	4.66	4.49

Table 2: Means

Baseline vs. LOD-DEF	Grammaticality	Non-redundancy	Structure & coherence
Difference	0.29	1.14	0.75
Significance	p = 0.151	p < 0.001	p < 0.001
Significant	No	Yes	Yes

Table 3: Differences and significance

LOD-DEF vs. Humans	Grammaticality	Non-redundancy	Structure & coherence
Difference	1.14	1.63	1.79
Significance	p < 0.001	p < 0.001	p < 0.001
Significant	Yes	Yes	Yes

Table 4: Differences and significance

6 Conclusion

We have implemented and tested a trainable shallow Natural Language Generation system for verbalising factual RDF data based on the extraction of sentence templates and document planning via content n-grams. We trained this system on text from the Simple English Wikipedia and RDF triples from DBpedia, and also implemented a baseline system, based on direct generation from triples.

We conducted human evaluation of the two systems, together with text generated by humans from the same information, where LOD-DEF significantly outperformed the baseline on *non-redundancy* and *structure and coherence*. These are encouraging results that suggest shallow systems like this one can be easily built and trained from Text-Knowledge Resources. While any structured representation of meaning could be used as the "knowledge" resource, we have dealt specifically with Linked Open Data, which required specific solutions to some of its inherent challenges.

It is conceivable that most, if not all, components of an NLG system could be trained from these TKR. More sophisticated approaches applying a deeper understanding of natural language and deeper NLG would be required for this, together with much reasoning and inference to connect the data and text. Our results, preliminary as they are, suggest that this vision is worth pursuing.

7 Acknowledgements

This research was partially supported by European Commission FP7 project ROBOT-ERA (grant agreement ICT-288899).

References

Cohn, T. and M. Lapata (2009). Sentence compression as tree transduction. *Journal of Artificial Intelligence Research 34*, 637–674.

Duboue, P. A. and K. R. Mckeown (2003). Statistical acquisition of content selection rules for natural language generation. In *Proceedings of the 2003 conference on Empirical Methods in Natural Language Processing (EMNLP)*, pp. 121–128.

Duma, D. (2012). Natural language generation for the semantic web: Unsupervised template extraction. MSc Dissertation. http://www.scribd.com/doc/111024287/Natural-Language-Generation-for-the-Semantic-Web-Unsupervised-Template-Extraction.

Filippova, K. and M. Strube (2008). Dependency tree based sentence compression. In *Proceedings of the Fifth International Natural Language Generation Conference*, pp. 25–32. Association for Computational Linguistics.

Gagnon, M. and L. Da Sylva (2006). Text compression by syntactic pruning. *Advances in Artificial Intelligence 1*, 312–323.

Heath, T. and C. Bizer (2011). *Linked Data: Evolving the Web into a Global Data Space*. Synthesis Lectures on the Semantic Web: Theory and Technology. Morgan & Claypool.

Hewlett, D., A. Kalyanpur, V. Kolovski, and C. Halaschek-Wiener (2005). Effective NL paraphrasing of ontologies on the Semantic Web. In *Workshop on End-User Semantic Web Interaction, 4th Int. Semantic Web conference, Galway, Ireland.*

Klein, D. and C. Manning (2003). Accurate unlexicalized parsing. In *Proceedings of the 41st Annual Meeting on Association for Computational Linguistics-Volume 1*, pp. 423–430. Association for Computational Linguistics.

Liang, S., R. Stevens, D. Scott, and A. Rector (2012). OntoVerbal: a Protegé plugin for verbalising ontology classes. In *Proceedings of the Third International Conference on Biomedical Ontology*.

Mendes, P., M. Jakob, and C. Bizer (2012). DBpedia: A multilingual cross-domain knowledge base. In *Proceedings of the International Conference on Language Resources and Evaluation (LREC 2012)*.

Mihalcea, R. and A. Csomai (2007). Wikify!: linking documents to encyclopedic knowledge. In *Proceedings of the sixteenth ACM conference on Conference on information and knowledge management*, pp. 233–242. ACM.

Reiter, E. and R. Dale (2000). *Building natural language generation systems*. Cambridge Univ Press.

Rosch, E. (1973). Natural categories. *Cognitive psychology 4*(3), 328–350.

Stevens, R., J. Malone, S. Williams, R. Power, and A. Third (2011). Automating generation of textual class definitions from OWL to English. *Journal of Biomedical Semantics 2*(Suppl 2), S5.

Sun, X. and C. Mellish (2007). An experiment on free generation from single RDF triples. In *Proceedings of the Eleventh European Workshop on Natural Language Generation*, pp. 105–108. Association for Computational Linguistics.

Towards a semantics for distributional representations

Katrin Erk
University of Texas at Austin
katrin.erk@mail.utexas.edu

Abstract

Distributional representations have recently been proposed as a general-purpose representation of natural language meaning, to replace logical form. There is, however, one important difference between logical and distributional representations: Logical languages have a clear semantics, while distributional representations do not. In this paper, we propose a semantics for distributional representations that links points in vector space to mental concepts. We extend this framework to a joint semantics of logic and distributions by linking intensions of logical expressions to mental concepts.

1 Introduction

Distributional similarity can model a surprising range of phenomena (e.g., Lund et al. (1995); Landauer and Dumais (1997)) and is useful in many NLP tasks (Turney and Pantel, 2010). Recently, it has been suggested that a general-purpose framework for representing natural language semantics should be distributional, such that it could represent word similarity and phrase similarity (Coecke et al., 2010; Baroni and Zamparelli, 2010; Grefenstette and Sadrzadeh, 2011; Clarke, 2012). Another suggestion has been to combine distributional representations and logical form, with the argument that the strengths of the two frameworks are in complementary areas (Garrette et al., 2011).

One important difference between logic and distributional representations is that logics have a semantics. For example, a model[1] in model-theoretic semantics provides a truth assignment to each sentence of a logical language. More generally, it associates expressions of a logic with set-theoretic structures, for example the constant cat' could be interpreted as the set of all cats in a given world. But what is the interpretation of a distributional representation? What does a point in vector space, where the dimensions are typically uninterpretable symbols, stand for? [2] In this paper, we propose a semantics in which distributional representations stand for mental concepts, and are linked to intensions of logical expressions. This gives us a joint semantics for distributional and logical representations.

Distributional representations stand for mental concepts. One central function of models is that they evaluate sentences of a logic as being either true or false. Distributional representations have been evaluated on a variety of phenomena connected to human concept representation (e.g., Lund et al. (1995); Landauer and Dumais (1997); Burgess and Lund (1997)). Here, evaluation means that predictions based on distributional similarity are compared to experimental results from human subjects. So we will interpret distributional representations over a conceptual structure.

Distributional representations stand for intensions. Gärdenfors (2004) suggests that the intensions of logical expressions should be mental concepts. By adopting this view, we can link distributional representations and logic through a common semantics: Both the intensions of logical expressions and the interpretations of distributional representations are mental concepts. However, there is a technical

[1] In the context of logical languages, "models" are structures that provide interpretations. In the context of distributional approaches, "distributional models" are particular choices of parameters. To avoid confusion, this paper will reserve the term "model" for the model-of-a-logic sense.

[2] Clark et al. (2008) encode a model in a vector space in which natural language sentences are mapped to a single-dimensional space that encodes truth and falsehood. This is a vector space representation, but it is not distributional as it is not derived from observed contexts. In particular, it does not constitute a semantics for a distributional representation.

$$\frac{\exists x\big(woodchuck(x) \wedge see(John, x)\big) \quad sim(woodchuck, groundhog) > \theta}{\exists x\big(groundhog(x) \wedge see(John, x)\big)}$$

Figure 1: Sketch of an example interaction of distributional and logical representations

problem: If intensions are mental concepts, they cannot be mappings from possible worlds to extensions, which is the prevalent way of defining intensions. We address this problem through *hyper-intensional semantics*. Hyper-intensional approaches in formal semantics (Fox and Lappin, 2001, 2005; Muskens, 2007) were originally introduced to address problems in the granularity of intensions. Crucially, some hyper-intensional approaches have intensions that are abstract objects, with minimal requirements on the nature of these objects. So we can build on them to link some intensions to conceptual structure.

Why design a semantics for distributional representations? Our aim is not to explicitly construct conceptual models; that would be at least as hard as constructing an ontology. Rather, our aim is to support inferences. Distributional representations induce synonyms and paraphrases automatically based on distributional similarity (Lin, 1998; Lin and Pantel, 2001). As Garrette et al. (2011) point out, and as illustrated in Figure 1, these can be used as inference rules within logical form. But when is such inference projection valid? Our main aim for constructing a joint semantics is to provide a principled basis for answering this question.

In the current paper, we construct a first semantics along the lines sketched above. In order to be able to take this first step, we simplify distributional predictions greatly by discretizing them. We want to stress, however, that this is a temporary restriction; our eventual aim is to make use of the ability of distributional models to handle graded and uncertain information as well as ambiguity.

2 Related work

Predicting sentence similarity with distributional representations. The distributional representation for a word is typically based on the textual contexts in which it has been observed (Turney and Pantel, 2010). The distributional representation of a document is typically based on the words that it contains, or on latent classes derived from co-occurrences of those words (Landauer and Dumais, 1997; Blei et al., 2003). Phrases and sentences occupy an unhappy middle ground between words and documents. They re-appear too rarely for a representation in terms of the textual contexts in which they have been observed, and they are too short for a document-like representation. There are multiple approaches to predicting similarity between sentences based on distributional information. The first computes a single vector space representation for a phrase or sentence in a compositional manner from the representations of the individual words (Coecke et al., 2010; Baroni and Zamparelli, 2010; Grefenstette and Sadrzadeh, 2011). This approach currently still faces big hurdles, including the problem of encoding the meaning of function words and the problem of predicting similarity for sentences of different structure. The second approach compares two phrases or sentences by computing multiple pairwise similarity values between components (words or smaller phrases) of the two sentences and then combining those similarity values (Socher et al., 2011; Turney, 2012). The third approach seeks to transform the representation of one sentence into another through term rewriting, where the rewriting rules are based on distributional similarity between words and smaller phrases (Bar-Haim et al., 2007). The approach of Garrette et al. (2011) can be viewed as falling into the third group. It represents sentences not as syntactic graphs as Bar-Haim et al. (2007) but through logic, and injects weighted inference rules derived from distributional similarity. Our approach belongs into this third group. The aim of the semantics that we present in Section 3 is to show that the use of distributional rewriting rules does not change the semantics of a logical expression. A fourth approach is the taken by Clarke (2007, 2012), who formalizes the idea of "meaning as context" in an algebraic framework that replaces concrete corpora with a generative corpus model that can assign probabilities to arbitrary word sequences. This eliminates the sparseness problem of finite corpora, such that both words and arbitrary phrases can be given distributional representations. Clarke also combines vector spaces and logic-based semantics by proposing a space in which the dimensions

(IHTT1) $p \vdash \top$ (IHTT2) $\bot \vdash p$ (IHTT3) $\vdash \neg p \leftrightarrow p \to \bot$ (IHTT4) $r \vdash p \wedge q$ iff $r \vdash p$ and $r \vdash q$ (IHTT5) $p \vee q \vdash r$ iff $p \vdash r$ or $q \vdash r$ (IHTT6) $p \vdash q \to r$ iff $p \wedge q \vdash r$ (IHTT7) $p \vdash \forall x_B \phi_{\langle B,\Pi\rangle}$ iff $p \vdash \phi$ (IHTT8) $\phi(a) \vdash \exists x_B \phi(x)$ (where $\phi \in \langle B, \Pi\rangle$, and a is a constant in B)	(IHTT9) $\vdash \lambda u \phi(v) \cong \phi[u/v]$ (where u is a variable in A, $v \in A$, $\phi \in \langle A, B\rangle$, and v is not bound when substituted for u in ϕ) (IHTT10) $\vdash \forall s, t_\Pi (s \cong t \leftrightarrow (s \leftrightarrow t))$ (IHTT11) $\vdash \forall \phi, \psi_{\langle A,B\rangle} (\forall u_A (\phi(u) \cong \psi(u)) \to \phi \cong \psi)$ (IHTT12) $\vdash \forall u, v_A \forall \phi_{\langle A,B\rangle} (u = v \to \phi(u) \cong \phi(v))$ (IHTT13) $\vdash \forall t_\Pi (t \vee \neg t)$

Table 1: Axioms of the intensional higher-order type theory IHTT of Fox and Lappin (2001)

• If α_A is a non-logical constant, then $\|\|\alpha\|\|^{M,g} = F(I(\alpha))$ • If α_A is a variable, then $\|\|\alpha\|\|^{M,g} = g(\alpha)$ • $\|\|\alpha_{\langle A,B\rangle}(\beta_A)\|\|^{M,g} = \|\|\alpha\|\|^{M,g}(\|\|\beta\|\|^{M,g})$ • If α is in A and u is a variable in B, then $\|\|\lambda u \alpha\|\|^{M,g}$ is a function $h : D_A \to D_B$ such that for any $a \in D_A$, $h(a) = \|\|\alpha\|\|^{M,g[u/a]}$ • $\|\|\neg\phi_\Pi\|\|^{M,g} = t$ iff $\|\|\phi\|\|^{M,g} = f$ • $\|\|\phi_\Pi \wedge \psi_\Pi\|\|^{M,g} = t$ iff $\|\|\phi\|\|^{M,g} = \|\|\psi\|\|^{M,g} = t$	• $\|\|\phi_\Pi \vee \psi_\Pi\|\|^{M,g} = t$ iff $\|\|\phi\|\|^{M,g} = t$ or $\|\|\psi\|\|^{M,g} = t$ • $\|\|\phi_\Pi \to \psi_\Pi\|\|^{M,g} = t$ iff $\|\|\phi\|\|^{M,g} = f$ or $\|\|\psi\|\|^{M,g} = t$ • $\|\|\phi_\Pi \leftrightarrow \psi_\Pi\|\|^{M,g} = t$ iff $\|\|\phi\|\|^{M,g} = \|\|\psi\|\|^{M,g}$ • $\|\|\alpha_A \cong \beta_A\|\|^{M,g} = t$ iff $\|\|\alpha\|\|^{M,g} = \|\|\beta\|\|^{M,g}$ • $\|\|\alpha_A = \beta_A\|\|^{M,g} = t$ iff $I(\alpha) = I(\beta)$ • $\|\|\forall u_A \phi_\Pi\|\|^{M,g} = t$ iff for all $a \in D_A(\|\|\phi\|\|^{M,g[u/a]} = t)$ • $\|\|\exists u_A \phi_\Pi\|\|^{M,g} = t$ iff for some $a \in D_A(\|\|\phi\|\|^{M,g[u/a]} = t)$ • ϕ_Π is true in M (false in M) iff $\|\|\phi\|\|^{M,g} = t\ (f)$ for all g. • ϕ_Π is logically true (false) iff ϕ is true (false) in every M • $\phi_\Pi \models \psi_\Pi$ iff for every M such that ϕ is true in M, ψ is true in M

Table 2: Interpretation of IHTT expressions

correspond to logic formulas. A word or phrase x is linked to formulas for sequences uxv in which it occurs, and each formula F is generalized to other formulas G that entail F. But it is not clear yet how this representation could be used for inferences.

Distributions, extensions, and intensions Like the current paper, Copestake and Herbelot (2012) consider the connection between distributional representations and the semantics of logical languages. However, they reach a very different conclusion. They propose using distributional representations as intensions of logical expressions. In addition, they link distributions to extensions by noting that each sentence that contributes to the distributional representation for the word "woodchuck" is about some member of the extension of $woodchuck$. They define the *ideal distribution* for a concept, for example "woodchuck", as the collection of all true statements about all members of the category, in this case all woodchucks in the world.

In our view, distributions describe general, intensional knowledge, and do not provide reference to extensions, so we will link distributional representations to intensions and not extensions. Concerning the Copestake and Herbelot proposal of distributions as intensions, we consider distributions as representations in need of an interpretation or intension, rather than representations that constitute the intension. [3] Also it is a somewhat unclear how the intension would be defined in practice in the Copestake and Herbelot framework, as it is based on the hypothetical ideal distribution with its potentially infinite number of sentences.

Hyper-intensional semantics The axiom of Extensionality states that if two expressions have the same extension, then they share all their properties. Together with the standard formulation of intensions as functions from possible worlds to extensions, this generates the problem that logically equivalent statements like "John sleeps" and "John sleeps, and Mary runs or does not run" become intersubstitutable in

[3]Though it should be noted that there is a debate within psychology on whether mental conceptual knowledge is actually distributional in nature (Landauer and Dumais, 1997; Barsalou, 2008; Andrews et al., 2009).

all contexts, even in contexts like "Sue believes that..." where they should not be exchangeable. Hyperintensional semantics addresses this problem. In particular, some approaches (Fox and Lappin, 2001, 2005; Muskens, 2007) address the problem by (1) dropping the axiom of Extensionality, (2) mapping expressions of the logic first to intensions and then mapping the intensions to extensions, and (3) adopting a notion of intensions as abstract objects with minimal restrictions. This makes these approaches relevant for our purposes, as we can add the axioms that we need for a joint semantics of logical and distributional representations. Muskens (2007) has one constraint on intensions that makes the approach unusable for our purposes in its current form: It has intensions and extensions be objects from the same collections of domains – but we would not want to force extensions to be mental objects. Instead we build on the intensional higher-order type theory IHTT from Fox and Lappin (2001). The set of types of IHTT contains the basic types e (for entity) and Π (proposition), and if A, B are types, then so is $\langle A, B\rangle$. The logic contains all the usual connectives, plus "$\cong$" for extensional equality and "=" for intensional equality. Fox and Lappin adopt the axioms shown in Table 1, which do not include the axiom of Extensionality. [4] A model for IHTT is a tuple $M = \langle D, S, L, I, F\rangle$, where D is a family of non-empty sets such that D_A is the set of possible extensions for expressions of type A. S is the set of possible intensions, and $L \subseteq S$ is the set of possible intensions for non-logical constants of the logic. I is a function that maps arbitrary expressions of IHTT to the set S of intensions. If α is a non-logical constant, then $I(\alpha)$ is in L, otherwise $I(\alpha)$ is in $S - L$. The function F is a mapping from L (intensions of non-logical constants) to members of D (extensions). A valuation g is a function from the variables of IHTT to members of D such that for all v_A it holds that $g(v) \in D_A$. A model of IHTT has to satisfy the following constraints: [5]

(M1) If v is a variable, then $I(v) = v$.

(M2) For a model M, if $I(\alpha) = I(\beta)$, then for all g, $||\alpha||^{M,g} = ||\beta||^{M,g}$.

Table 2 shows the definition of extensions $||.||^{M,g}$ of expressions of IHTT.

3 A joint semantics for distributional and logical representations

In this section we construct a first implementation of the semantics for distributional representations sketched in the introduction. In this semantics, distributional interpretations are interpreted over mental concepts and are linked to the intensions of some logical expressions. We use as a basis the hyperintensional logic IHTT of Fox and Lappin (2001) (Section 2), which does not require intensions to be mappings from possible worlds to extensions, such that we are free to link intensions to mental concepts. The central result of this section will be that the interpretation of sentences of the logic is invariant to rewriting steps such as the one in Figure 1, which replace a non-logical constant by another based on distributional similarity. The semantics that we present in this paper constitutes a first step. It leaves some important questions open, such as paraphrasing beyond the word level, or graded concept membership.

3.1 Distributional representations

Typically, the distributional representation for a target word t is computed from the occurrences, or *usages*, of t in a given corpus. Minimally, a usage is a sequence of words in which the target appears at least once. We will allow for two additional pieces of information in a usage, namely larger discourse context, and non-linguistic context. (Recently, there have been distributional approaches that make use of non-linguistic context, in particular image data (Feng and Lapata, 2010; Bruni et al., 2012).)

Let W be a set of words (the lexicon), and let $Seq(W)$ be the set of finite sequences over W. Then a *usage* over W is a tuple $\langle s, t, \delta, \omega\rangle$, where $s \in Seq(W)$ is a sequence of words such that a word form of $t \in W$ occurs in s at least once, $\delta \in \Delta \cup \{NA\}$ is a (possibly empty) discourse context, and

[4] We write α_A to indicate that expression α is of type A.

[5] Fox and Lappin mention that one could add the constraint that if α, α' differ only in the names of bound variables, then $I(\alpha) = I(\alpha')$. We do not do that here, since we are only concerned with replacing non-logical constants in the current paper.

$\omega \in \Omega \cup \{NA\}$ is a (possibly empty) non-linguistic context. We write $\mathcal{U}(W, \Delta, \Omega)$ for the set of all usages over W (and Δ and Ω). For any usage $u = \langle s, t, \delta, \omega \rangle$, we write $target(u) = t$. Given a set $U \subseteq \mathcal{U}(W, \Delta, \Omega)$ of usages, we write $U_t = \{u \in U \mid target(u) = t\}$ for the usages of a target word t. Furthermore, we write $W_U = \{t \in W \mid U_t \neq \emptyset\}$ for the set of words that have usages in U.

In distributional approaches, the vector space representation for a target word t is computed from such a set U of usages, typically by mapping U to a single point in vector space (Lund et al., 1995; Landauer and Dumais, 1997) or a set of points (Schütze, 1998; Reisinger and Mooney, 2010). This makes it possible to use linear algebra in modeling semantics. However, for our current purposes, we do not need to specify any particular mapping to a vector space, and can simply work with the underlying set U of usages: A finite set U of usages over W constitutes a *distributional representation* for W_U. The distributional representation for a word $t \in W$ is U_t.

3.2 A semantics for distributional representations

We want to interpret distributional representations over conceptual structure. But what is conceptual structure? We know that concepts are linked by different semantic relations, including is-a, and part-of (Fellbaum, 1998), they can overlap, and they are associated with definitional features (Murphy, 2002). Eventually, all of these properties may be useful to include in the semantics of distributional representations. But for this first step we work with a much simpler definition. We define a conceptual structure simply as a set of (atomic, unconnected) concepts.

An individual usage of a word t can refer to a single mental concept. For example, the usage of "bank" in (1) clearly refers to a "financial institution" concept, not the land at the side of a river. But an individual usage can also refer to multiple mental concepts when there is ambiguity as in (2), or when there is too little information to determine the intended meaning as in (3). [6][7]

(1) $\langle$The bank engaged in risky stock trades, bank, δ, $\omega\rangle$

(2) $\langle$Why fix dinner when it isn't broken, fix, δ, $\omega\rangle$[8]

(3) $\langle$bank, bank, NA, NA$\rangle$

From this link between individual usages and concepts, we can derive a link between distributional representations and concepts: The representation U_t of a word t is connected to all concepts to which the usages in U_t link. Formally, a *conceptual model* for $\mathcal{U}(W, \Delta, \Omega)$ is a tuple $\mathcal{C} = \langle I_u, C \rangle$, where C is a set of concepts, and the function $I_u : \mathcal{U}(W, \Delta, \Omega) \rightarrow 2^C$ is an interpretation function for usages that maps each usage to a set of concepts. [9] A conceptual model $\mathcal{C}$ together with a finite set $U \subseteq \mathcal{U}(W, \Delta, \Omega)$ of usages define a conceptual mapping for words. We write $I_{\mathcal{C},U}(w) = \bigcup_{u \in U_w} I_u(u)$ for the set of concepts associated with w.

Distributional approaches centrally use some similarity measure, for example cosine similarity, on pairs of distributional representations, usually pairs of points in vector space. Since we represent a word t directly by its set U_t of usages rather than a point in vector space derived from U_t, we instead have a similarity measure $sim(U_1, U_2)$ on sets of usages. We assume a range of $[0, 1]$ for this similarity measure. A conceptual model can be used to evaluate the appropriateness of similarity predictions: A prediction is appropriate if it is high for two usage sets that refer to the same concepts, or low for two usage sets that refer to different concepts. Formally, a similarity prediction $sim(U_1, U_2)$ is *appropriate* for a conceptual model $\mathcal{C} = \langle I_u, C \rangle$ and threshold θ iff

- either $sim(U_1, U_2) \geq \theta$ and $\bigcup_{u \in U_1} I_u(u) = \bigcup_{u \in U_2} I_u(u)$,

[6] For the purpose of this paper we make the simplifying assumption that concepts have "strict boundaries": A usage either does or does not refer to a concept. We do not model cases where a usage is related to a concept, but is not a clear match.

[7] Another possible reason for one usage mapping to multiple mental concepts is concept overlap (Murphy, 2002).

[8] Advertisement for a supermarket in Austin, Texas..

[9] We write 2^S for the power set of a set S.

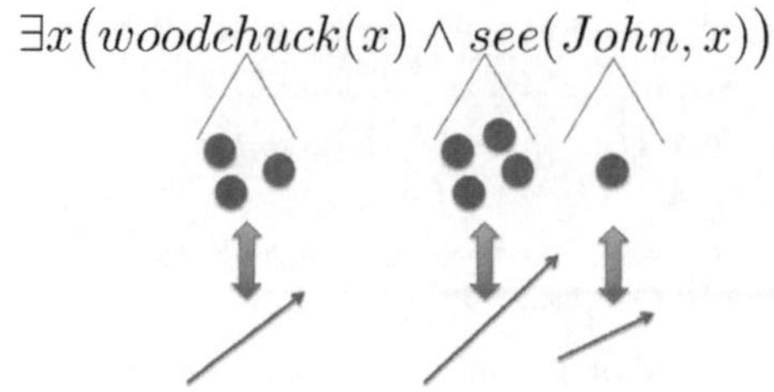

Figure 2: Enriching the information about non-logical constants: Constants are associated with sets of concepts (circles) and, through them, with distributional representations

- or $sim(U_1, U_2) < \theta$ and $\bigcup_{u \in U_1} I_u(u) \neq \bigcup_{u \in U_2} I_u(u)$.

This formulation of appropriateness is simplistic in that it discretizes similarity predictions into two classes: above or below threshold θ. This is due to our current impoverished view of concepts as disjoint atoms. When we introduce a conceptual similarity measure within conceptual models, a more fine-grained evaluation of distributional similarity ratings becomes available. Such a conceptual similarity measure would be justified, as humans can judge similarity between concepts (Rubenstein and Goodenough, 1965), but we do not do it here in order to keep our models maximally simple.

3.3 A joint semantics for logical form and distributional representations

We now link the intensions of some logical expressions to mental concepts, using the logic IHTT as a basis. We will need to constrain the behavior of intensions more than Fox and Lappin do. In particular, we add the following two requirements to models $M = \langle D, S, L, I, F \rangle$ of IHTT.

(M3) If the expression $\alpha \in A$ is the result of beta-reducing the expression $\beta \in A$, then $I(\alpha) = I(\beta)$.

(M4) If $I(u_A) = I(v_A)$, then for all $\phi \in \langle A, B \rangle$, $I(\phi(u)) = I(\phi(v))$.

(M4) allows for the exchange of an intensionally equal expression without changing the intension of the overall expression.

We now define models that join an intensional model of IHTT with a conceptual model for a distributional representation. In particular, we link constants of the logic to sets of concepts, and through them, to distributional representations, as sketched in Figure 2. If the word "woodchuck" is associated with the concept set $C_{\text{woodchuck}} = I_{\mathcal{C},U}(\text{woodchuck})$, then the intension of the constant $woodchuck$ will also be $C_{\text{woodchuck}}$. We proceed in two steps: In the definition of joint models, we require the existence of a mapping from words to non-logical constants that share the same interpretation. In a second step, we require semantic constructions to respect this mapping, such that the logical expression associated with "woodchuck" will be $\lambda x(woodchuck(x))$ rather than $\lambda x(guppy(x))$. Note that only words in W_U have distributional representations associated with them; for words in $W - W_U$, neither their translation to logical expressions nor the intensions of those expressions are constrained in any way.

Let $M = \langle D, S, L, I, F \rangle$ be a model for IHTT, let $\mathcal{C} = \langle I_u, C \rangle$ be a conceptual model for $\mathcal{U}(W, \Delta, \Omega)$, and let U be a finite subset of $\mathcal{U}(W, \Delta, \Omega)$. Then $M_{\mathcal{C}} = \langle D, S, L, I, F, I_u, C \rangle$ is an *intensional conceptual model* for IHTT and $\mathcal{U}(W, \Delta, \Omega)$ *based on* U if

(M5) There exists a function h from W_U to the non-logical constants of IHTT such that for all $w \in W_U$, $I_{\mathcal{C},U}(w) = I(h(w))$

(M6) For all $w_1, w_2 \in W_U$, if $I_{\mathcal{C},U}(w_1) = I_{\mathcal{C},U}(w_2)$ then $h(w_1)$ and $h(w_2)$ have the same type.

We say that the model $M_{\mathcal{C}}$ *contains* M and $\mathcal{C}$.

Constraint (M5) links each word to a non-logical constant such that the distributional interpretation of the word and the intension of the constant are the same. (M6) states that if two words have the same distributional interpretation, their associated constants have the same type. We next define semantic constructions sem in general, and semantic constructions that connect the translation $sem(w)$ of a word w to its associated constant $h(w)$. A *semantic construction function* for a set W of words and a logical language $\mathcal{L}$ is a partial function $sem : Seq(W) \to \mathcal{L}$ such that $sem(w)$ is defined for all $w \in W$. $sem(.)$ maps sequences of words over W to expressions from $\mathcal{L}$. A sequence $s \in Seq(W)$ is called *grammatical* if $sem(s)$ is defined. A semantic construction sem is an *intended semantic construction* for an intensional conceptual model $M = \langle D, S, L, I, F, I_u, C\rangle$ based on U if the following constraint holds for the function h from (M5):

(M7) For each type A there exists some expression ϕ^A such that for all $w \in W_U$, $sem(w)$ is equivalent (modulo beta-reduction) to $\phi^A(h(w))$.

(M7) states that the construction of translations $sem(w)$ from non-logical constants $h(w)$ must be uniform for all words of the same semantic type. For example, if for the word "woodchuck" we have $h(\text{woodchuck}) = woodchuck$, an expression of type $\langle e, \Pi\rangle$, then the expression $\phi_{\langle e,\Pi\rangle} = \lambda P \lambda x(P(x))$ will map $woodchuck$ to $\lambda x(woodchuck(x)) = sem(\text{woodchuck})$.

3.4 Synonym replacement

In Section 2 we have sketched a framework for the interaction of logic and distributional representations based on Bar-Haim et al. (2007). Distributional representations can be used to predict semantic similarity between pairs of words and in particular to predict synonymy between words (Lin, 1998). Distributionally induced synonym pairs can be used as rewriting rules that transform sentence representations. In our case, the representations to be transformed are expressions of the logic. Two sentences count as synonymous if it is possible to transform the representation of one sentence into the representation of the other, using both distributional rewriting rules and the axioms of the logic.

We start out by showing that the application of a rewriting rule that exchanges one non-logical constant of IHTT for another constant with the same intension leaves both the intension and the extension of the overall logical expression unchanged. Given a logical expression ϕ, we write $\phi[\text{some } b/a]$ for the set of expressions obtained from ϕ by replacing zero or more occurrences of a by b.

Proposition 1: Soundness of non-logical constant rewriting. Let $M = \langle D, S, L, I, F\rangle$ be an intensional model for IHTT, and let a, b be non-logical constants of IHTT of type A such that $I(a) = I(b)$. Then for any expression ϕ of IHTT and any $\phi' \in \phi[\text{some } b/a]$, $I(\phi) = I(\phi')$, and for any valuation g, $||\phi||^{M,g} = ||\phi'||^{M,g}$.

Proof. Let x_A be a variable that does not occur in ϕ. Then for each $\phi' \in \phi[\text{some } b/a]$ there exists an expression $\psi \in \phi[\text{some } x/a]$ such that $(\lambda x \psi)(a)$ beta-reduces to ϕ and $(\lambda x \psi)(b)$ beta-reduces to ϕ'. As $I(a) = I(b)$, we have $I((\lambda x \psi)(a)) = I((\lambda x \psi)(b))$ by (M4). So by (M3), $I(\phi) = I(\phi')$. From this it follows that for any valuation g, $||\phi||^{M,g} = ||\phi'||^{M,g}$ by (M2). □

We call two words synonyms if they refer to the same set of concepts. Formally, let U be a finite subset of $\mathcal{U}(W, \Delta, \Omega)$ that is a distributional representation for W_U, and $\mathcal{C} = \langle I_u, C\rangle$ a conceptual model for $\mathcal{U}(W, \Delta, \Omega)$. A word $p \in W_U$ is a *synonym* for $t \in W_U$ by $\mathcal{C}$ and U if $I_{\mathcal{C},U}(t) = I_{\mathcal{C},U}(p)$.

We would like to show that if t and p are synonyms, then exchanging t for p changes neither the intension nor the extension of the logical translation for the sentence. To do so, we first show that exchanging t for p corresponds to applying constant rewriting on the sentence representation.

Note, however, that the logical translation of a sentence depends not only on the words, but also on the syntactic structure of the sentence. If a given syntactic analysis framework only allows for the bracketing "(small (tree house))" and at the same time only allows for the bracketing "((little tree) house)", then the two phrases will not receive the same semantics even if the model considers "small" and "little" to be synonyms. So we will show that if replacement by a synonym *within a given syntactic structure* again yields a valid syntactic structure, then the semantics of the sentence remains unchanged. For any sequence $s \in Seq(W)$ of words over W, we write $T(s)$ for the set of constituent structure analyses for s. For $\tau \in T(s)$, we write $\tau[p/t]$ for the syntactic graph that is exactly like τ except that all leaves labeled t are replaced by leaves labeled p. We write $sem(\tau)$ for the logical translation of s that is based on the syntactic structure of τ. We assume that there exists exactly one translation $sem(\tau)$ for each syntactic structure τ.

Lemma 2. Let $M_{\mathcal{C}}$ be be an intensional conceptual model for IHTT and $\mathcal{U}(W, \Delta, \Omega)$ based on $U \subseteq \mathcal{U}(W, \Delta, \Omega)$ that contains $M = \langle D, S, L, I, F\rangle$ and $\mathcal{C} = \langle I_u, C\rangle$. Let $t, p \in W_U$ be synonyms by $\mathcal{C}$ and U, and let $s \in Seq(W)$ be a sequence with syntactic analysis $\tau \in T(s)$ such that $\tau[p/t] \in T(s[p/t])$. Then for any intended semantic construction sem for $M_{\mathcal{C}}$ and U, $sem(\tau[p/t])$ is equivalent modulo beta-reduction to some member of $sem(\tau)[\text{some } h(p)/h(t)]$.

Proof. We proceed by induction over the structure of τ. If s consists of a single word, then $\tau = s$, and either $s = t$ or $s = w$ for a word $w \neq t$. If $s = w$ for some $w \neq t$, then $sem(\tau[p/t]) = sem(\tau) \in sem(\tau)[\text{some } h(p)/h(t)]$.

If $s = t$, then $sem(\tau) = sem(t)$ and $sem(\tau[p/t]) = sem(p)$. By (M5) and because t and p are synonyms, we have $I(h(t)) = I_{\mathcal{C},U}(t) = I_{\mathcal{C},U}(p) = I(h(p))$. From this it follows by (M6) that the non-logical constants $h(t)$ and $h(p)$ have the same semantic type A. Then by (M7) there exists a logical expression ϕ^A such that $sem(\tau) = sem(t)$ is equivalent modulo beta-reduction to $\phi^A(h(t))$. At the same time, $sem(\tau[p/t]) = sem(p)$ is equivalent modulo beta-reduction to $\phi^A(h(p))$, which is equivalent modulo beta-reduction to a member of $\big(\phi^A(h(t))\big)[\text{some } h(p)/h(t)]$, which in turn is equivalent modulo beta-reduction so a member of $sem(\tau)[\text{some } h(p)/h(t)]$.

Now assume that s comprises more than one word. Let the root of τ have n children that are the roots of subtrees $\tau_1 \ldots \tau_n$. There is some semantic construction rule associated with the root of τ that can be written as an expression ϕ of IHTT such that $\phi(sem(\tau_1))\ldots(sem(\tau_n))$ beta-reduces to $sem(\tau)$. By the inductive hypothesis, $sem(\tau_i[p/t])$ is equivalent modulo beta-reduction to some $\psi_i \in sem(\tau_i)[\text{some } h(p)/h(t)]$ for $1 \leq i \leq n$. The expression ϕ remains unchanged between $sem(\tau)$ and $sem(\tau[p/t])$ because only leaves of the tree were changed and the overall constituent structure remained the same. So the expression $sem(\tau[p/t])$ is equivalent modulo beta-reduction to $\phi(\psi_1)\ldots(\psi_n) \in \big(\phi(sem(\tau_1))\ldots(sem(\tau_n))\big)[\text{some } h(p)/h(t)]$, which in turn is equivalent modulo beta-reduction to $sem(\tau)[\text{some } h(p)/h(t)]$. □

The reason why we have used $\phi[\text{some } b/a]$ rather than replacement of all occurrences is that there is no guarantee that the corresponding non-logical constant $h(t)$ for a word t is used only in the lexical entry of t. For example, the expression $\phi^{\langle e,\Pi\rangle}$ of (M7) could be $\lambda P \lambda x\big(woodchuck(x) \wedge P(x)\big)$, making the lexical entry for "guppy" $\lambda x\big(woodchuck(x) \wedge guppy(x)\big)$. Or the semantic construction expression ϕ for NPs could contain the constant $woodchuck$. However, now we are in a position to show that this does not matter, and that a constant rewriting rule can be applied to all occurrences of $h(t)$, whether in the lexical entry for t or elsewhere. At the same time, we show that replacement of a word by a synonym does not change the interpretation of the sentence.

Proposition 3: Synonym replacement as constant replacement. Let $M_{\mathcal{C}}$ be be an intensional conceptual model for IHTT and $\mathcal{U}(W, \Delta, \Omega)$ based on $U \subseteq \mathcal{U}(W, \Delta, \Omega)$ that contains $M = \langle D, S, L, I, F\rangle$ and $\mathcal{C} = \langle I_u, C\rangle$. Let $t, p \in W_U$ be synonyms by $\mathcal{C}$ and U, and let $s \in Seq(W)$ be a sequence with syntactic analysis $\tau \in T(s)$ such that $\tau[p/t] \in T(s[p/t])$. Then for any valuation g, and any intended semantic construction sem for $M_{\mathcal{C}}$ and U, $I(sem(\tau)) = I(sem(\tau[p/t])) = I(sem(\tau)[h(p)/h(t)])$, and $||sem(\tau)||^{M,g} = ||sem(\tau[p/t])||^{M,g} = ||sem(\tau)[h(p)/h(t)]||^{M,g}$.

Proof. By Lemma 2, the semantic representation of the changed syntactic tree, $sem(\tau[p/t])$, is equivalent modulo beta-reduction to some $\psi \in sem(\tau)[\text{some } h(p)/h(t)]$. So by Proposition 1, $I(\psi) =$

$I(sem(\tau))$, and by (M3), $I(sem(\tau)[p/t]) = I(\psi)$. Thus, $I(sem(\tau)) = I(sem(\tau[p/t]))$. By Proposition 1, the intension is the same for all members of $sem(\tau)$[some $h(p)/h(t)$], so we have $I(sem(\tau)) = I(sem(\tau)[h(p)/h(t)]$. And by (M2), if $sem(\tau)$, $sem(\tau[p/t])$ and $sem(\tau)[h(p)/h(t)]$ have the same intension, they also have the same extension. □

3.5 Inference

We extend the list of axioms for IHTT from Table 1 by two additional axioms that correspond to the constraints (M3) and (M4).

(IHTT14) $\vdash \lambda u \phi(v) = \phi[u/v]$ (where u is a variable in A, $v \in A$, $\phi \in \langle A, B\rangle$, and v is not bound when substituted for u in ϕ)

(IHTT15) $\vdash \forall u, v_A \forall \phi_{\langle A,B\rangle} (u = v \rightarrow \phi(u) = \phi(v))$

These axioms parallel (IHTT9) and (IHTT12) but state intensional rather than extensional equality.

Synonymy predictions from the distributional representation can be transformed into rewriting rules: If the words t and p are synonyms by the distributional representation U, then we generate the rewriting rule $h(t) \mapsto h(p)$. As Proposition 3 shows, this rewriting rule can be applied indiscriminately to a logical expression, and is not restricted to the lexical entry for t. But since the logic is equipped with inference capability and is not a passive representation like the syntactic graphs that Bar-Haim et al. (2007) used, we can alternatively just inject an expression $h(t) = h(p)$, which states intensional equality, into the logical representation for the parsed sentence τ. The logical representation for $\tau[p/t]$ can then be inferred using (IHTT14) and (IHTT15).

4 Conclusion and outlook

In this paper we have proposed a semantics for distributional representations, namely that each point in vector space stands for a set of mental concepts. We have provided a coarse-grained evaluation for distributional representations in which their similarity predictions are evaluated against conceptual equality or inequality. We have extended this approach to a joint semantics of distributional and logical representations by linking the intensions of some logical expressions to mental concepts as well: If the distributional representation for a word w is interpreted as a set C of concepts, then the non-logical constant linked to the lexical entry for w will have as its intension the same set C. We have used hyperintensional semantics as a basis for this joint semantics. We have been able to show that distributional rewriting rules that exchange non-logical constants with the same intension do not change the intension or extension of the overall logical expression. These rewriting rules can be used to compute the logical representation of a sentence after exchanging a word for its synonym.

The current joint semantics is, however, only a first step, and leaves many important questions open. We consider the following three to be especially important. *(1) Polysemy.* Many synonym pairs can only be substituted for one another in particular sentence contexts. For example "correct" is a synonym for "fix" that can be substituted in the context of "The programmer fixed the error", but not in "The cook fixed dinner." This means that the words "fix" and "correct" do not map to the same set of concepts, but they are exchangeable in particular contexts. So we would want to say that "fix" and "correct" are synonyms with respect to a usage $u = \langle s, \text{fix}, \delta, \omega\rangle$ if $I_u(u) = I_u(\langle s[\text{correct}/\text{fix}], \text{correct}, \delta, \omega\rangle)$. The main challenge for incorporating polysemy is to have intensions change based on the context of use.

(2) Distributional similarity of larger phrases. There is considerable work both on the distributional similarity of phrases and sentences (Coecke et al., 2010; Baroni and Zamparelli, 2010; Grefenstette and Sadrzadeh, 2011) and on the distributional similarity of phrases with open argument slots, such as "X solves Y" and "X finds a solution to Y" (Lin and Pantel, 2001; Szpektor and Dagan, 2008; Berant et al., 2011). We would like to use these results to do distributionally driven replacement of multi-word paraphrases in a joint distributional and logical framework. But this requires a semantics for distributional representations of larger phrases. If we assume some sort of conceptual structures as semantics, the next

question is whether all logical expressions should be associated with conceptual structures: Should the intension of a variable be something conceptual?

(3) Gradience. In this paper we have assumed that the link from usage to concept is binary – either present or not –, and also that there are no relations between concepts. Both assumptions are simplifications: Concepts have "fuzzy boundaries" (Hampton, 2007), and cognizers can distinguish degrees of similarity between concepts (Rubenstein and Goodenough, 1965). By modeling this gradience, we could then talk about degrees of similarity between words and phrases, not just a binary choice of either synonymy or non-synonymy. But this will require dealing with probabilities or weights in the model and also in the logic.

Acknowledgements. This research was supported in part by the NSF CAREER grant IIS 0845925 and by the DARPA DEFT program under AFRL grant FA8750-13-2-0026. Any opinions, findings, and conclusions or recommendations expressed in this material are those of the author and do not necessarily reflect the view of DARPA, AFRL or the US government. Warmest thanks to John Beavers and Gemma Boleda, as well as the members of the Austin Computational Linguistics Tea and the anonymous reviewers, for very helpful discussions.

References

Andrews, M., G. Vigliocco, and D. Vinson (2009). Integrating experiential and distributional data to learn semantic representations. *Psychological Review 116*(3), 463–498.

Bar-Haim, R., I. Dagan, I. Greental, and E. Shnarch (2007). Semantic inference at the lexical-syntactic level. In *Proceedings of AAAI*, Vancouver, Canada.

Baroni, M. and R. Zamparelli (2010). Nouns are vectors, adjectives are matrices: Representing adjective-noun constructions in semantic space. In *Proceedings of EMNLP*, Cambridge, MA.

Barsalou, L. W. (2008). Grounded Cognition. *Annual Review of Psychology 59*(1), 617–645.

Berant, J., I. Dagan, and J. Goldberger (2011). Global learning of typed entailment rules. In *Proceedings of ACL*, Portland, OR.

Blei, D. M., A. Ng, and M. I. Jordan (2003). Latent Dirichlet allocation. *Journal of Machine Learning Research 3*, 993–1022.

Bruni, E., G. Boleda, M. Baroni, and N. Tran (2012). Distributional semantics in technicolor. In *Proceedings of ACL*, Jeju Island, Korea.

Burgess, C. and K. Lund (1997). Modelling parsing constraints with high-dimensional context space. *Language and Cognitive Processes 12*, 177–210.

Clark, S., B. Coecke, and M. Sadrzadeh (2008). A compositional distributional model of meaning. In *Proceedings of QI*, Oxford, UK, pp. 133–140.

Clarke, D. (2007). *Context-theoretic Semantics for Natural Language: an Algebraic Framework*. Ph. D. thesis, University of Sussex.

Clarke, D. (2012). A context-theoretic framework for compositionality in distributional semantics. *Computational Linguistics 38*(1).

Coecke, B., M. Sadrzadeh, and S. Clark (2010). Mathematical foundations for a compositional distributed model of meaning. *Lambek Festschrift, Linguistic Analysis 36*.

Copestake, A. and A. Herbelot (2012, July). Lexicalised compositionality. Unpublished draft.

Fellbaum, C. (Ed.) (1998). *WordNet: An electronic lexical database*. Cambridge, MA: MIT Press.

Feng, Y. and M. Lapata (2010). Visual information in semantic representation. In *Proceedings of HLT-NAACL*, Los Angeles, California.

Fox, C. and S. Lappin (2001). A framework for the hyperintensional semantics of natural language with two implementations. In P. de Groote, G. Morrill, and C. Retore (Eds.), *Proceedings of LACL*, Le Croisic, France.

Fox, C. and S. Lappin (2005). *Foundations of Intensional Semantics*. Wiley-Blackwell.

Gärdenfors, P. (2004). *Conceptual spaces*. Cambridge, MA: MIT press.

Garrette, D., K. Erk, and R. Mooney (2011). Integrating logical representations with probabilistic information using markov logic. In *Proceedings of IWCS*, Oxford, UK.

Grefenstette, E. and M. Sadrzadeh (2011). Experimental support for a categorical compositional distributional model of meaning. In *Proceedings of EMNLP*, Edinburgh, Scotland, UK.

Hampton, J. A. (2007). Typicality, graded membership, and vagueness. *Cognitive Science 31*, 355–384.

Landauer, T. and S. Dumais (1997). A solution to Platos problem: the latent semantic analysis theory of acquisition, induction, and representation of knowledge. *Psychological Review 104*(2), 211–240.

Lin, D. (1998). Automatic retrieval and clustering of similar words. In *Proceedings of COLING-ACL*, Montreal, Canada.

Lin, D. and P. Pantel (2001). Discovery of inference rules for question answering. *Natural Language Engineering 7*(4), 343–360.

Lund, K., C. Burgess, and R. Atchley (1995). Semantic and associative priming in high-dimensional semantic space. In *Proceedings of the Cognitive Science Society*, pp. 660–665.

Murphy, G. L. (2002). *The Big Book of Concepts*. MIT Press.

Muskens, R. (2007). Intensional Models for the Theory of Types. *The Journal of Symbolic Logic 72*(1), 98–118.

Reisinger, J. and R. Mooney (2010). Multi-prototype vector-space models of word meaning. In *Proceeding of NAACL*.

Rubenstein, H. and J. Goodenough (1965). Contextual correlates of synonymy. *Computational Linguistics 8*, 627–633.

Schütze, H. (1998). Automatic word sense discrimination. *Computational Linguistics 24*(1).

Socher, R., E. Huang, J. Pennin, A. Ng, and C. Manning (2011). Dynamic pooling and unfolding recursive autoencoders for paraphrase detection. In J. Shawe-Taylor, R. Zemel, P. Bartlett, F. Pereira, and K. Weinberger (Eds.), *Proceedings of NIPS*.

Szpektor, I. and I. Dagan (2008). Learning entailment rules for unary templates. In *Proceedings of COLING*.

Turney, P. and P. Pantel (2010). From frequency to meaning: Vector space models of semantics. *Journal of Artificial Intelligence Research 37*, 141–188.

Turney, P. D. (2012). Domain and function: A dual-space model of semantic relations and compositions. *Journal of Artificial Intelligence Research 44*, 533–585.

Probabilistic induction for an incremental semantic grammar*

Arash Eshghi Matthew Purver
Julian Hough
Cognitive Science Research Group
School of Electronic Engineering and Computer Science
Queen Mary University of London
{arash,mpurver,jhough}@eecs.qmul.ac.uk

Abstract

We describe a method for learning an incremental semantic grammar from a corpus in which sentences are paired with logical forms as predicate-argument structure trees. Working in the framework of Dynamic Syntax, and assuming a set of generally available compositional mechanisms, we show how lexical entries can be learned as probabilistic procedures for the incremental projection of semantic structure, providing a grammar suitable for use in an incremental probabilistic parser. By inducing these from a corpus generated using an existing grammar, we demonstrate that this results in both good coverage and compatibility with the original entries, without requiring annotation at the word level. We show that this semantic approach to grammar induction has the novel ability to learn the syntactic and semantic constraints on pronouns.

1 Introduction

Dynamic Syntax (DS) is an inherently incremental semantic grammar formalism (Kempson et al., 2001; Cann et al., 2005) in which semantic representations are projected on a word-by-word basis. It recognises no intermediate layer of syntax (see below), but instead reflects grammatical constraints via constraints on the incremental construction of partial logical forms (LFs). Given this, and its definition of parsing and generation in terms of the same incremental processes, it is in principle capable of modelling and providing semantic interpretations for phenomena such as unfinished utterances, co-constructions and interruptions, beyond the remit of standard grammar formalisms but important for dialogue systems.

However, its definition in terms of semantics (rather than the more familiar syntactic phrase structure) makes it hard to define or extend broad-coverage grammars: expert linguists are required. Here, we present a method for automatically inducing DS grammars, by learning lexical entries from sentences paired with complete, compositionally structured, propositional LFs. By assuming only the availability of a small set of general compositional semantic operations, reflecting the properties of the lambda calculus and semantic conjunction, we ensure that the lexical entries learnt include the grammatical constraints and corresponding compositional semantic structure of the language; by additionally assuming a general semantic copying operation, we can also learn the syntactic and semantic properties of pronouns.

2 Previous work on grammar induction

Existing grammar induction methods can be divided into two major categories: supervised and unsupervised. Fully supervised methods use a parsed corpus as the training data, pairing sentences with syntactic trees and words with their syntactic categories, and generalise over the phrase structure rules to learn a grammar which can be applied to a new set of data. By estimating probabilities for production rules that

*We would like to thank Ruth Kempson and Yo Sato for helpful comments and discussion. This work was supported by the EPSRC, RISER project (Ref: EP/J010383/1), and in part by the EU, FP7 project, SpaceBook (Grant agreement no: 270019).

share the same LHS category, this produces a grammar suitable for probabilistic parsing and disambiguation (e.g. PCFGs, Charniak, 1996). Such methods have shown great success, but presuppose detailed prior linguistic information (and are thus not adequate as human grammar learning models). Unsupervised methods, on the other hand, proceed from unannotated raw data; they are thus closer to the human language acquisition setting, but have seen less success. In its pure form —positive data only, without bias— unsupervised learning has been demonstrated to be computationally too complex ('unlearnable') in the worst case (Gold, 1967). Successful approaches involve some prior learning or bias, e.g. a fixed set of known lexical categories, a probability distribution bias (Klein and Manning, 2005) or a hybrid, semi-supervised method with shallower (e.g. POS-tagging) annotation (Pereira and Schabes, 1992).

More recently, another interesting line of work has emerged: *lightly* supervised learning guided by *semantic* rather than syntactic annotation, using sentence-level propositional logical form rather than detailed word-level annotation (more justifiably arguable to be 'available' to a human learner in a real-world situation, with some idea of what a string in an unknown language could mean). This has been successfully applied in Combinatorial Categorial Grammar (Steedman, 2000), as it tightly couples compositional semantics with syntax (Zettlemoyer and Collins, 2007; Kwiatkowski et al., 2010, 2012); as CCG is a lexicalist framework, grammar learning involves inducing a lexicon assigning to each word its syntactic and semantic contribution. Moreover, the grammar is learnt ground-up in an 'incremental' fashion, in the sense that the learner collects data over time and does the learning sentence by sentence.

Here we follow this spirit, inducing grammar from a propositional meaning representation and building a lexicon which specifies what each word contributes to the target semantics. However, taking advantage of the DS formalism, we make two novel contributions: first, we bring an added dimension of incrementality: not only is learning sentence-by-sentence incremental, but the grammar learned is word-by-word incremental, commensurate with psycholinguistic results showing incrementality to be a fundamental feature of human parsing and production Lombardo and Sturt (1997); Ferreira and Swets (2002). While incremental parsing algorithms for standard grammar formalisms have seen much research (Hale, 2001; Collins and Roark, 2004; Clark and Curran, 2007), to the best of our knowledge, a learning system for an explicitly incremental grammar is yet to be presented. Second, by using a grammar in which syntax and parsing context are defined in terms of the growth of semantic structures, we can learn lexical entries for items such as pronouns the constraints on which depend on semantic context.

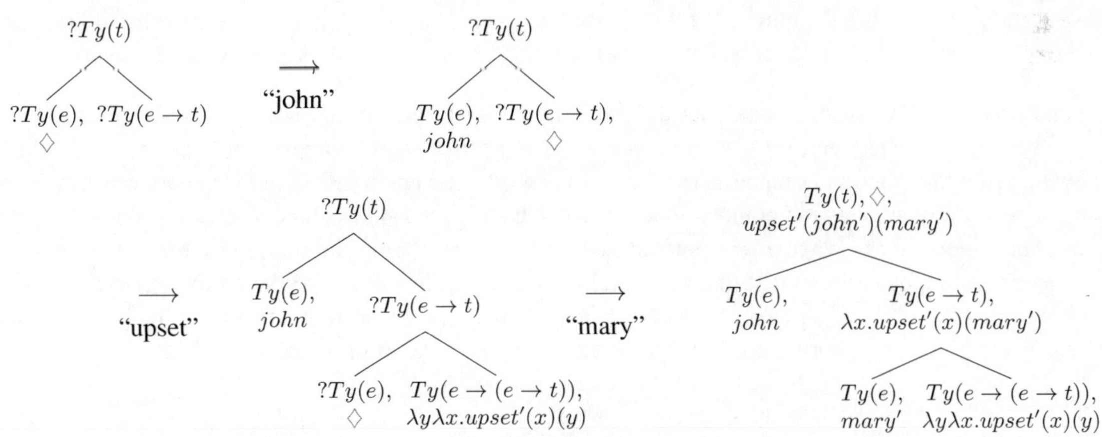

Figure 1: Incremental parsing in DS producing semantic trees: *"John upset Mary"*

3 Dynamic Syntax

Dynamic Syntax is a parsing-directed grammar formalism, which models the word-by-word incremental processing of linguistic input. Unlike many other formalisms, DS models the incremental building up of *interpretations* without presupposing or indeed recognising an independent level of syntactic processing. Thus, the output for any given string of words is a purely *semantic* tree representing its predicate-argument structure; tree nodes correspond to terms in the lambda calculus, decorated with labels expressing their semantic type (e.g. $Ty(e)$) and formula, with beta-reduction determining the type and formula at a mother node from those at its daughters (Figure 1).

These trees can be *partial*, containing unsatisfied requirements for node labels (e.g. $?Ty(e)$ is a requirement for future development to $Ty(e)$), and contain a *pointer* $\diamondsuit$ labelling the node currently under development. Grammaticality is defined as parsability: the successful incremental construction of a tree with no outstanding requirements (a *complete* tree) using all information given by the words in a sentence. The input to our induction task here is therefore sentences paired with such complete, *semantic* trees, and what we learn are constrained lexical procedures for the incremental construction of such trees. Note that in these trees, leaf nodes do not necessarily correspond to words, and may not be in linear sentence order (see Figure 1); and syntactic structure is not explicitly represented, only the structure of semantic predicate-argument combination.

3.1 Actions in DS

The parsing process is defined in terms of conditional *actions*: procedural specifications for monotonic tree growth. These take the form both of general structure-building principles (*computational actions*), putatively independent of any particular natural language, and of language-specific actions induced by parsing particular lexical items (*lexical actions*). The latter are what we here try to learn from data.

Computational actions These form a small, fixed set, and we assume them as given here. Some merely encode the properties of the lambda calculus and the logical tree formalism itself (LoFT Blackburn and Meyer-Viol, 1994) – these we term *inferential* actions. Examples include THINNING (removal of satisfied requirements) and ELIMINATION (beta-reduction of daughter nodes at the mother). These actions are entirely language-general, cause no ambiguity, and add no new information to the tree; as such, they apply non-optionally whenever their preconditions are met.

Other computational actions reflect the fundamental predictivity and dynamics of the DS framework. For example, *ADJUNCTION introduces a single unfixed node with underspecified tree position (replacing feature-passing concepts for e.g. long-distance dependency); and LINK-ADJUNCTION builds a paired ("linked") tree corresponding to semantic conjunction (licensing relative clauses, apposition and more). These actions represent possible parsing strategies and can apply optionally at any stage of a parse if their preconditions are met. While largely language-independent, some are specific to language type (e.g. INTRODUCTION-PREDICTION in the form used here applies only to SVO languages).

Lexical actions The lexicon associates words with lexical actions; like computational actions, these are sequences of tree-update actions in an IF..THEN..ELSE format, and composed of explicitly procedural *atomic* tree-building actions such as `make`, `go`, `put`. `make` creates a new daughter node, `go` moves the pointer, and `put` decorates the pointed node with a label. Figure 2 shows an example for a proper noun, *John*. The action checks whether the pointed node (marked as $\diamondsuit$) has a requirement for type e; if so, it decorates it with type e (thus satisfying the requirement), formula $John'$ and the bottom restriction $\langle\downarrow\rangle\bot$ (meaning that the node cannot have any daughters). Otherwise (if no requirement $?Ty(e)$), the action aborts, meaning that the word *'John'* cannot be parsed in the context of the current tree.

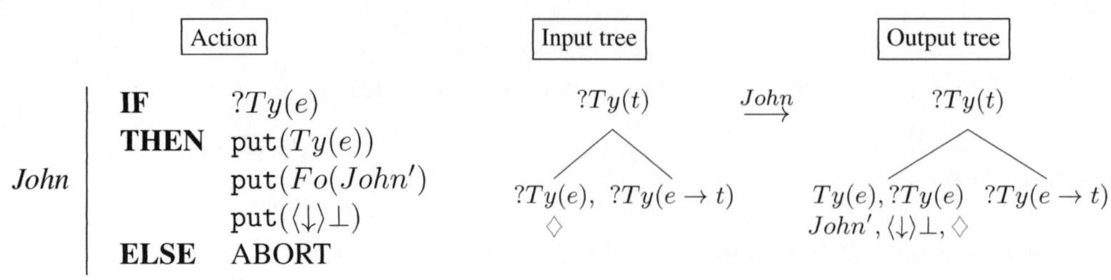

Figure 2: Lexical action for the word 'John'

3.2 Graph Representation of DS Parsing

These actions define the parsing process. Given a sequence of words $(w_1, w_2, ..., w_n)$, the parser starts from the *axiom* tree T_0 (a requirement $?Ty(t)$ to construct a complete tree of propositional type), and applies the corresponding lexical actions $(a_1, a_2, \ldots, a_n)$, optionally interspersing computational actions – see Figure 1. Sato (2011) shows how this parsing process can be modelled on a *Directed Acyclic Graph* (DAG), rooted at T_0, with partial trees as nodes, and computational and lexical actions as edges (i.e. transitions between trees):

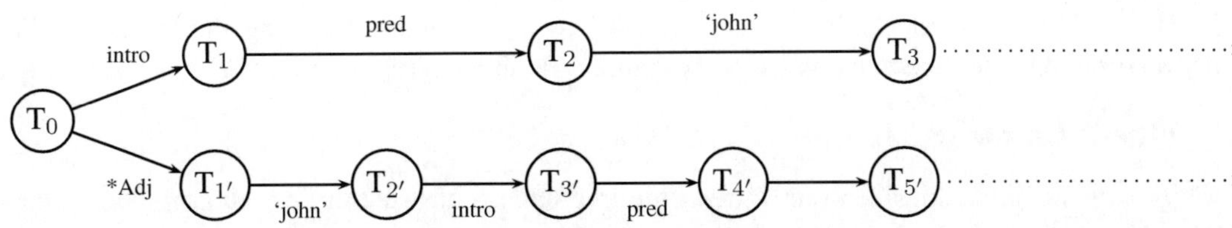

In this DAG, *intro*, *pred* and **Adj* correspond to the computational actions INTRODUCTION, PREDICTION and *-ADJUNCTION respectively; and 'john' is a lexical action. Different paths through the DAG represent different parsing strategies, which may succeed or fail depending on how the utterance is continued. Here, the path $T_0 - T_3$ will succeed if 'John' is the subject of an upcoming verb ("John upset Mary"); $T_0 - T_4$ will succeed if 'John' turns out to be a left-dislocated object ("John, Mary upset").

This DAG makes up the *parse state* at any point, and contains all information available to the parser. This includes semantic tree and tree-transition information taken to make up the *linguistic context* for ellipsis and pronominal construal (Purver et al., 2011). It also provides us with a basis for probabilistic parsing (see Sato, 2011): given a conditional probability distribution $P(a|w, T)$ over possible actions a given a word w and (some set of features of) the current partial tree T, the DAG can then be incrementally constructed and traversed in a best-first, breadth-first or beam parsing manner.

4 Learning lexical actions

4.1 Problem Statement

Our task here is data-driven, probabilistic learning of lexical actions for all the words occurring in the corpus. Throughout, we will assume that the (language-independent) *computational actions* are known. We also assume that the supervision information is structured: i.e. our dataset pairs sentences with complete DS trees encoding their predicate-argument structures, rather than just a flat logical form (LF) as in e.g. Zettlemoyer and Collins (2007). DS trees provide more information than LFs in that they disambiguate between different possible predicate-argument decompositions of the corresponding LF; note however that this provides *no* extra information on the mapping from words to meaning. The input to the induction procedure is now as follows:

- the set of computational actions in Dynamic Syntax, G.
- a set of training examples of the form $\langle S_i, T_i \rangle$, where $S_i = \langle w_1 \ldots w_n \rangle$ is a sentence of the language and T_i – henceforth referred to as the *target tree* – is the complete semantic tree representing the compositional structure of the meaning of S_i.

The output is a grammar specifying the possible lexical actions for each word in the corpus. Given our data-driven approach, we take a probabilistic view: we take this grammar as associating each word w with a probability distribution θ_w over lexical actions. In principle, for use in parsing, this distribution should specify the posterior probability $p(a|w, T)$ of using a particular action a to parse a word w in the context of a particular partial tree T. However, here we make the simplifying assumption that actions are conditioned solely on one feature of a tree, the semantic type Ty of the currently pointed node; and that actions apply exclusively to one such type (i.e. ambiguity of type leads to multiple actions). This effectively simplifies our problem to specifying the probability $p(a|w)$.

In traditional DS terms, this is equivalent to assuming that all lexical actions have a simple IF clause of the form IF $?Ty(X)$; this is true of most lexical actions in existing DS grammars (see examples above), but not all. This assumption will lead to some over-generation – inducing actions which can parse some ungrammatical strings – we must rely on the probabilities learned to make such parses unlikely, and evalute this in Section 5. Given this, the focus of what we learn here is effectively the THEN clause of lexical actions: a sequence of DS atomic actions such as *go*, *make*, and *put* (see Fig. 2), but now with an attendant posterior probability. We will henceforth refer to these sequences as *lexical hypotheses*. We first describe our method for constructing lexical hypotheses with a single training example (a sentence-tree pair). We then discuss how to generalise over these outputs, while updating the corresponding probability distributions incrementally as we process more training examples.

4.2 Hypothesis Construction

DS is *strictly monotonic*: actions can only *extend* the tree under construction, deleting nothing except satisfied requirements. Thus, hypothesising lexical actions consists in an incremental search through the space of all monotonic, and well-formed extensions of the current tree, T_{cur}, that subsume (i.e. can be extended to) the target tree T_t. This gives a bounded space which can be described by a DAG equivalent to the parsing DAG of section 3.2: nodes are trees, starting with T_{cur} and ending with T_t, and edges are possible extensions. These extensions may be either DS's basic computational actions (already known) or new *lexical hypotheses*.

This space is further constrained by the fact that not all possible trees and tree extensions are well-formed (meaningful) in DS, due to the properties of the lambda-calculus and those of the modal tree logic LoFT. Mother nodes must be compatible with the semantic type and formula of their daughters, as would be derived by beta-reduction; formula decorations cannot apply without type decorations; and so on. We also prevent arbitrary type-raising by restricting the types allowed, taking the standard DS assumption that noun phrases have semantic type e (rather than a higher type as in Generalized Quantifier theory) and common nouns their own type cn (see Cann et al., 2005, chapter 3 for details).

We implement these constraints by packaging together permitted sequences of tree updates as macros (sequences of DS atomic actions such as `make`, `go`, and `put`), and hypothesising possible DAG paths based on these macros. We can divide these into two classes of lexical hypothesis macros: (1) *tree-building* hypotheses, independent of the target tree, and in charge of building appropriately typed daughters for the current node; and (2) *content decoration* hypotheses in charge of the semantic decoration of the leaves of the current tree (T_{cur}), with formulae taken from the leaves of the target tree (T_t).

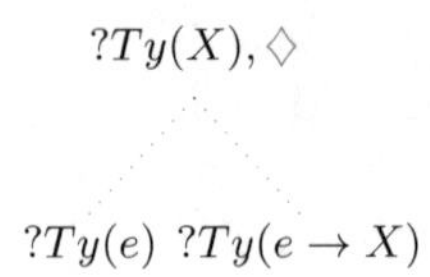

IF	$?Ty(X)$
	$X \neq e$
THEN	$make(\langle\downarrow_0\rangle); go(\langle\downarrow_0\rangle)$
	$put(?Ty(e)); go(\langle\uparrow\rangle)$
	$make(\langle\downarrow_1\rangle); go(\langle\downarrow_1\rangle)$
	$put(?Ty(e \rightarrow X)); go(\uparrow)$
ELSE	ABORT

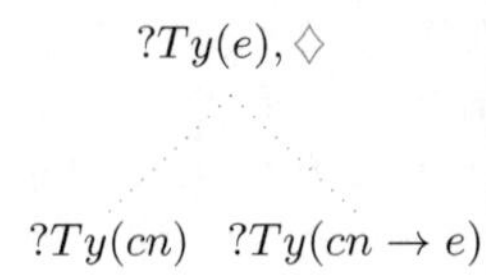

IF	$?Ty(e)$
THEN	$make(\langle\downarrow_0\rangle); go(\langle\downarrow_0\rangle)$
	$put(?Ty(cn)); go(\langle\uparrow\rangle)$
	$make(\langle\downarrow_1\rangle); go(\langle\downarrow_1\rangle)$
	$put(?Ty(cn \rightarrow e)); go(\uparrow)$
ELSE	ABORT

Figure 3: Target-independent tree-building hypotheses

Figure 3 shows example *tree-building* hypotheses which extend a mother node with a type requirement to have two daughter nodes which would (once themselves developed) combine to satisfy that requirement. On the left, an general rule in which a currently pointed node of some type X can be hypothesised to be formed of types e and $e \rightarrow X$ (e.g. if $X = e \rightarrow t$, the daughters will have types e and $e \rightarrow (e \rightarrow t)$). This reflects only the fact that DS trees correspond to lambda calculus terms, with e being a possible type. The other is more specific, suitable only for a type e node, allowing it to be composed of nodes of type cn and $cn \rightarrow e$ (where $cn \rightarrow e$ turns out to be the type of determiners), but again reflects only general semantic properties which would apply in any language.

Content decoration hypotheses on the other hand depend on the target tree: they posit possible addition of semantic content, via sequences of `put` operations (e.g. `content-dec: put(Ty(e)); put(Fo(john))` which develop the pointed node on T_{cur} towards the corresponding leaf node on T_t.

They are constrained to apply only to *leaf* nodes (i.e. nodes in T_{cur} whose counterparts on T_t are leaf nodes), other nodes being assumed to receive their content via beta-reduction of their daughters.

4.3 Hypothesis Splitting

Hypothesis construction therefore produces, for each training sentence $\langle w_1 \ldots w_n \rangle$, all possible sequences of actions that lead from the axiom tree T_0 to the target tree T_t (henceforth, the *complete* sequences); where these sequences contain both lexical hypotheses and general computational actions. To form discrete lexical entries, we must split each such sequence into n sub-sequences, $\langle cs_1 \ldots cs_n \rangle$, with each *candidate subsequence* cs_i, corresponding to a word w_i, by hypothesising a set of word boundaries.

This splitting process is subject to two constraints. Firstly, each candidate sequence cs_i must contain exactly one *content decoration* lexical hypothesis (see above); this ensures both that every word has some contribution to the sentence's semantic content, and that no word decorates the leaves of the tree with semantic content more than once. Secondly, candidate subsequences cs_i are *computationally maximal* on the left: cs_i may begin with (possibly multiple) computational actions, but must end with a lexical hypothesis. This reduces the splitting hypothesis space, and aids lexical generalisation (see below).

Each such possible set of boundaries corresponds to a *candidate sequence tuple* $\langle cs_1 \ldots cs_n \rangle$. Importantly, this means that these cs_i are not independent, e.g. when processing "John arrives", a hypothesis for 'John' is only compatible with certain hypotheses for 'arrives'. This is reflected below in how probabilities are assigned to the word hypotheses.

4.4 Hypothesis Generalisation

DS's general computational actions can apply at any point before the application of a lexical action, thus providing strategies for adjusting the syntactic context in which a word is parsed. Removing computational actions on the left of a candidate sequence will leave a more general albeit equivalent hypothesis: one which will apply successfully in more syntactic contexts. However, if a computational subsequence seems to occur *whenever* a word is observed, we would like to lexicalise it, including it within the lexical entry for a more efficient and constrained grammar. We therefore want to generalise over our candidate sequence tuples to partition them into portions which seem to be achieved lexically, and portions which are better achieved by computational actions alone.

First Training Example: 'john' in fixed object position;
Sequence intersected: $\langle LH : \textit{content-dec} : \textit{put}(Ty(e)); \textit{put}(Fo(John')) \rangle$:

Second Training Example: 'john' in subject position;
Sequence intersected: $\langle CA : \textit{intro}, CA : \textit{predict}, LH : \textit{content-dec} : \textit{put}(Ty(e)); \textit{put}(Fo(John')) \rangle$

Third Training Example: 'john' on unfixed node, i.e. left-dislocated object;
Sequence intersected: $\langle CA : \textit{star-adj}, LH : \textit{content-dec} : \textit{put}(Ty(e)); \textit{put}(Fo(John')) \rangle$

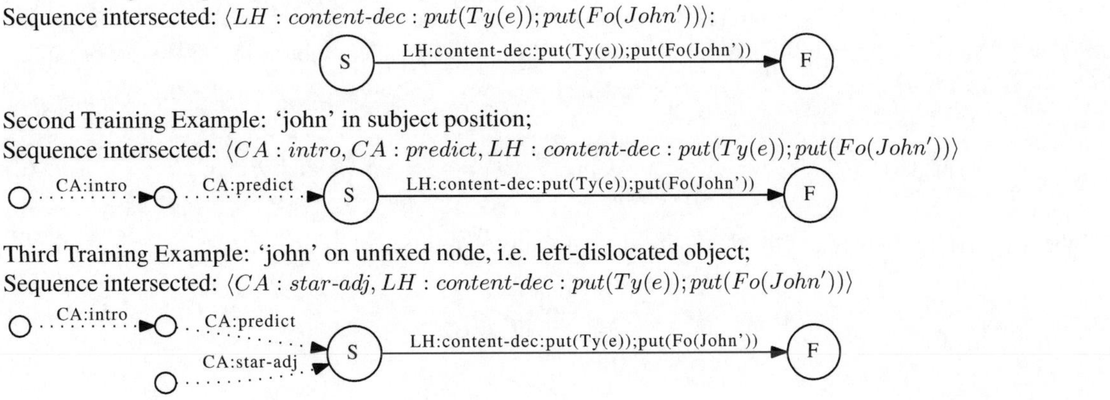

Figure 4: Incremental intersection of candidate sequences; CA=Computational Action, LH=Lexical Hypothesis

We therefore group the candidate sequence tuples produced by splitting, storing them as members of equivalence classes which form our final *word hypotheses*. Two tuples belong to the same equivalence class if they can be made identical by removing *only* computational actions from the beginning of either one. We implement this via a single packed data-structure which is again a DAG, as shown in Fig. 4; this represents the full set of candidate sequences by their intersection (the solid central common path) and differences (the dotted diverging paths at beginning). Nodes here therefore no longer represent single trees, but sets of trees. Figure 4 shows this process over three training examples containing the unknown word 'John' in different syntactic positions. The 'S' and 'F' nodes mark the start and finish of the intersection – initially the entire sequence. As new candidate sequences arrive, the intersection – the maximal common path – is reduced as appropriate. Word hypotheses thus remain as general as possible.

In our probabilistic framework, these DAGs themselves are our lexical entries, with associated probabilities (see below). If desired, we can form traditional DS lexical actions: the DAG intersection corresponds to the THEN clause, with the IF clauses being a type requirement obtained from the pointed node on all partial trees in the initial 'S' node. As lexical hypotheses within the intersection are identical, and were constrained when formed to add type information before formula information (see Section 4.2), any type information must be common across these partial trees. In Figure 4 for 'john', this is $?Ty(e)$, i.e. a requirement for type e, common to all three training examples.

4.5 Probability Estimation

The set of possible word hypotheses induced as above can of course span a very large space: we must therefore infer a probability distribution over this space to produce a useful grammar. This can be estimated from the observed distribution of hypotheses, as these are constrained to be compatible with the target tree for each sentence; and the estimates can be incrementally updated as we process each training example. For this process of probability estimation, the input is the output of the splitting and generalisation procedure above, i.e. for the current training sentence $S = \langle w_1 \ldots w_n \rangle$ a set HT of *Hypothesis Tuples* (sequences of word hypotheses), each of the form $HT_j = \langle h_1^j \ldots h_n^j \rangle$, where h_i^j is the word hypothesis for w_i in HT_j. The desired output is a probability distribution θ_w over hypotheses for each word w, where $\theta_w(h)$ is the posterior probability $p(h|w)$ of a given word hypothesis h being used to parse w.

Re-estimation Given some prior estimate of θ'_w, we can use a new training example to produce an updated estimate θ''_w directly. We assign each hypothesis tuple HT_j a probability based on θ'_w; the probability of a sequence $\langle h_1^j \ldots h_n^j \rangle$ is the product of the probabilities of the h_i's within it (by the Bayes chain rule):

$$p(HT_j|S) = \prod_{i=1}^{n} p(h_i^j|w_i) = \prod_{i=1}^{n} \theta'_{w_i}(h_i^j) \tag{1}$$

Now, for any word w and possible hypothesis h, we can re-estimate the probability $p(h|w)$ as the normalised sum of the probabilities of all observed tuples HT_j which contain h, that is the set of tuples, $HT^h = \{HT_j | h \in HT_j\}$:

$$\theta''_w(h) = p(h|w) = \frac{1}{Z} \sum_{HT_j \in HT^h} p(HT_j|S) = \frac{1}{Z} \sum_{HT_j \in HT^h} \prod_{i=1}^{n} \theta'_{w_i}(h_i^j) \tag{2}$$

where Z, the normalising constant, is the sum of the probabilities of all the HT_j's:

$$Z = \sum_{HT_j \in HT} \prod_{i=1}^{n} \theta'_{w_i}(h_i^j)$$

Incremental update Our procedure is now to update our overall esimate θ_w incrementally: after the Nth example, our new estimate θ_w^N is a weighted average of the previous estimate θ_w^{N-1} and the new value from the current example θ''_w from equation (2), with weights reflecting the amount of evidence on which these estimates are based:

$$\theta_w^N(h) = \frac{N-1}{N}\theta_w^{N-1}(h) + \frac{1}{N}\theta''_w(h) \tag{3}$$

Note that for training example 1, the first term's numerator is zero, so θ_w^{N-1} is not required and the new estimates are equal to θ''_w. However, to produce θ''_w we need some prior estimate θ'_w; in the absence of any information, we simply assume uniform distributions $\theta'_w = \theta^0_w$ over the lexical hypotheses observed in the first training example.

In subsequent training examples, there will arise new hypotheses h not seen in previous examples, and for which the prior estimate θ'_w gives no information. We incorporate these hypotheses into θ'_w by discounting the probabilities assigned to known hypotheses, reserving some probability mass which we then assume to be evenly distributed over the new unseen hypotheses. For this we use the same weight as in equation (3):

$$\theta'_w(h) = \begin{cases} \frac{N-1}{N}\theta^{N-1}_w(h) & \text{if } h \text{ in } \theta^{N-1}_w \\ \frac{1}{N_u}\sum_{h\in\theta^{N-1}_w}\frac{1}{N}\theta^{N-1}_w(h) & \text{otherwise} \end{cases} \tag{4}$$

where N_u here is number of new unseen hypotheses in example N. Given (4), we can now more accurately specify the update procedure in (3) to be:

$$\theta^N_w(h) = \theta'_w(h) + \frac{1}{N}\theta''_w(h) \tag{5}$$

Non-incremental estimation Using this incremental procedure, we use the estimates from previous sentences to assign prior probabilities to each hypothesis tuple (i.e. each possible path through the hypothesised parse DAG), and then derive updated posterior estimates given the observed distributions. Such a procedure could similarly be applied non-incrementally at each point, by repeatedly re-estimating and using the new estimates to re-calculate tuple probabilities in a version of the Expectation-Maximisation algorithm (Dempster et al., 1977). However, this would require us to keep all HT sets from every training example; this would be not only computationally demanding but seems psycholinguistically implausible (requiring memory for all lexical and syntactic dependencies for each sentence). Instead, we restrict ourselves here to assuming that this detailed information is only kept in memory for one sentence; intermediate versions would be possible.

4.6 Pronouns

Standard approaches to grammar induction treat pronouns simply as entries of a particular syntactic category. Here, as we learn from semantic annotations, we can learn not only their anaphoric nature, but syntactic and semantic constraints on their resolution. To achieve this, we assume one further general strategy for lexical hypothesis formation: a copying operation from context whereby the semantic content (formula and type decorations) can be copied from any existing type-compatible and complete node on T_{cur} (possibly more than one) accessible from the current pointed node via some finite tree modality. This assumption therefore provides the general concept of anaphoricity, but nothing more: it can be used in hypothesis formation for any word, and we rely on observed probabilities of its providing a successful parse to rule it out for words other than pronouns. By requiring access via some tree modality ($\uparrow_0, \downarrow_*$ etc), we restrict it to intrasentential anaphora here, but the method could be applied to intersentential cases where suitable LFs are available.

This modal relation describes the relative position of the antecedent; by storing this as part of the hypothesis DAG, and subjecting it to a generalisation procedure similar to that used for computational actions in Section 4.4, the system learns constraints on these modal relations. The lexical entries resulting can therefore express constraints on the possible antecedents, and grammatical constraints on their presence, akin to Principles A and B of Government and Binding theory (see Cann et al. (2005), chapter 2); in this paper, we evaluate the case of relative pronouns only (see below).

5 Evaluation

5.1 Parse coverage

This induction method has been implemented and tested over a 200-sentence artificial corpus. The corpus was generated using a manually defined DS grammar, with words randomly chosen to follow the

Word class	Type	Token	Type%	Token%
noun	119	362	76.3%	48.7%
verb	29	263	18.6%	35.4%
determiner	3	56	1.9%	7.5%
pronoun	5	62	3.2%	8.4%
Total	156	743	100.00%	100.00%
Total of 200 sentences				
Min, Max and Mean sentence lengths : 2, 6, 3.7 words				
Mean tokens per word = 4.01				

Table 1: Training and test corpus distributions and means

	Parsing Coverage	Same Formula
Top one	26%	77%
Top two	77%	79%
Top three	100%	80%

Table 2: Test parse results: showing percentage parsability, and percentage of parses deriving the correct semantic content for the whole sentence

distributions of the relevant POS types and tokens in the CHILDES maternal speech data (MacWhinney, 2000) - see Table 1. 90% of the sentences were used as training data to induce a grammar, and the remaining 10% used to test it. We evaluate the results in terms of both parse coverage and semantic accuracy, via comparison with the logical forms derived using the original, hand-crafted grammar.

The induced hypotheses for each word were ranked according to their probability; three separate grammars were formed using the top one, top two and top three hypotheses and were then used independently to parse the test set. Table 2 shows the results, discounting sentences containing words not encountered in training at all (for which no parse is possible). We give the percentage of test sentences for which a complete parse was obtained; and the percentage of those for which one of the top 3 parses resulted in a logical form identical to the correct one.

As Table 2 shows, when the top three hypotheses are retained for each word, we obtain 80% formula derivation accuracy. Manual inspection of the individual actions learned revealed that the words which have incorrect lexical entries at rank one were those which were sparse in the corpus - we did not control for the exact frequency of occurrence of each word. The required frequency of occurrence varied across different categories; while transitive verbs require about four occurrences, intransitive verbs require just one. Count nouns were particularly sparse (see type/token ratios in Table 1).

As we have not yet evaluated our method on a real corpus, the results obtained are difficult to compare directly with other baselines such as that of Kwiatkowski et al. (2012) who achieve state-of-the-art results; cross-validation of this method on the CHILDES corpus is work in progress, which will allow direct comparison with Kwiatkowski et al. (2012).

5.2 Lexical Ambiguity

We introduced lexically ambiguous words into the corpus to test the ability of the system to learn and distinguish between their different senses; 10% of word types were ambiguous between 2 or 3 different senses with different syntactic category. Inspection of the induced actions for these words shows that, given appropriately balanced frequencies of occurrence of each separate word sense in the corpus, the system is able to learn and distinguish between them. 57% of the ambiguous words had lexical entries with both senses among the top three hypotheses, although in only one case were the two senses ranked one and two. This was the verb 'tramped' with transitive and intransitive readings, with 4 and 21 occurrences in the corpus respectively.

5.3 Pronouns

For pronouns, we wish to learn both their anaphoric nature (resolution from context) and appropriate syntactic constraints. Here, we tested on relative pronouns such as 'who' in "John likes Mary, who runs": the most general lexical action hypothesis learned for these is identical to hand-crafted versions of the action (see Cann et al. (2005), chapter 3):

who	**IF**	$?Ty(e)$
		$\langle\uparrow_*\uparrow_L\rangle Fo(X)$
	THEN	$put(Ty(e))$
		$put(Fo(X))$
		$put(\langle\downarrow\rangle\bot)$
	ELSE	ABORT

This action instructs the parser to copy a semantic type and formula from a type $Ty(e)$ node at the modality $\langle\uparrow_*\uparrow_L\rangle$, relative to the pointed node. The system has therefore learnt that pronouns involve resolution from context (note that many other hypotheses are possible, as pronouns are paired with different LFs in different sentences). It also expresses a syntactic constraint on relative pronouns, that is, the relative position of their antecedents $\langle\uparrow_*\uparrow_L\rangle$ (the first node above a dominating LINK tree relation – i.e. the head of the containing NP).

Of course, relative pronouns are a special case: the modality from which their antecedents are copied is relatively fixed. Equivalent constraints could be learned for other pronouns, given generalisation over several modal relations; e.g. locality of antecedents for reflexives is specified in DS via a constraint $\langle\uparrow_0\uparrow_1^*\downarrow_0\rangle$ requiring the antecedent to be in *some* local argument position. In learning reflexives, this modal relation can come from generalisation over several different modalities obtained from different training examples; this will require larger corpora.

6 Conclusions and Future work

In this paper we have outlined a novel method for the probabilistic induction of new lexical entries in an inherently incremental and semantic grammar formalism, Dynamic Syntax, with no independent level of syntactic phrase structure. Our method learns from sentences paired with semantic trees representing the sentences' predicate-argument structures, assuming only very general compositional mechanisms. While the method still requires evaluation on real data, evaluation on an artificial but statistically representative corpus demonstrates that the method achieves good coverage. A further bonus of using a semantic grammar is that it has the potential to learn both semantic and syntactic constraints on pronouns: our evaluation demonstrates this for relative pronouns, but this can be extended to other pronoun types.

Our research now focusses on evaluating this method on real data (the CHILDES corpus), and on reducing the level of supervision by adapting the method to learn from sentences paired not with trees but with less structured LFs, using Type Theory with Records Cooper (2005) and/or the lambda calculus. Other work planned includes the integration of the actions learned into a probabilistic parser.

References

Blackburn, P. and W. Meyer-Viol (1994). Linguistics, logic and finite trees. *Logic Journal of the Interest Group of Pure and Applied Logics 2*(1), 3–29.

Cann, R., R. Kempson, and L. Marten (2005). *The Dynamics of Language*. Oxford: Elsevier.

Charniak, E. (1996). *Statistical Language Learning*. MIT Press.

Clark, S. and J. Curran (2007). Wide-coverage efficient statistical parsing with CCG and log-linear models. *Computational Linguistics 33*(4), 493–552.

Collins, M. and B. Roark (2004). Incremental parsing with the perceptron algorithm. In *Proceedings of the 42nd Meeting of the ACL*, Barcelona, pp. 111–118.

Cooper, R. (2005). Records and record types in semantic theory. *Journal of Logic and Computation 15*(2), 99–112.

Dempster, A., N. Laird, and D. B. Rubin (1977). Maximum likelihood from incomplete data via the EM algorithm. *Journal of the Royal Statistical Society. Series B (Methodological) 39*(1), 1–38.

Ferreira, F. and B. Swets (2002). How incremental is language production? evidence from the production of utterances requiring the computation of arithmetic sums. *Journal of Memory and Language 46*, 57–84.

Gold, E. M. (1967). Language identification in the limit. *Information and Control 10*(5), 447–474.

Hale, J. (2001). A probabilistic Earley parser as a psycholinguistic model. In *Proceedings of the 2nd Conference of the North American Chapter of the Association for Computational Linguistics*, Pittsburgh, PA.

Kempson, R., W. Meyer-Viol, and D. Gabbay (2001). *Dynamic Syntax: The Flow of Language Understanding*. Blackwell.

Klein, D. and C. D. Manning (2005). Natural language grammar induction with a generative constituent-context mode. *Pattern Recognition 38*(9), 1407–1419.

Kwiatkowski, T., S. Goldwater, L. Zettlemoyer, and M. Steedman (2012). A probabilistic model of syntactic and semantic acquisition from child-directed utterances and their meanings. In *Proceedings of the Conference of the European Chapter of the Association for Computational Linguistics (EACL)*.

Kwiatkowski, T., L. Zettlemoyer, S. Goldwater, and M. Steedman (2010, October). Inducing probabilistic CCG grammars from logical form with higher-order unification. In *Proceedings of the 2010 Conference on Empirical Methods in Natural Language Processing*, Cambridge, MA, pp. 1223–1233. Association for Computational Linguistics.

Lombardo, V. and P. Sturt (1997). Incremental processing and infinite local ambiguity. In *Proceedings of the 1997 Cognitive Science Conference*.

MacWhinney, B. (2000). *The CHILDES Project: Tools for Analyzing Talk* (Third ed.). Mahwah, New Jersey: Lawrence Erlbaum Associates.

Pereira, F. and Y. Schabes (1992, June). Inside-outside reestimation from partially bracketed corpora. In *Proceedings of the 30th Annual Meeting of the Association for Computational Linguistics*, Newark, Delaware, USA, pp. 128–135. Association for Computational Linguistics.

Purver, M., A. Eshghi, and J. Hough (2011, January). Incremental semantic construction in a dialogue system. In J. Bos and S. Pulman (Eds.), *Proceedings of the 9th International Conference on Computational Semantics*, Oxford, UK, pp. 365–369.

Sato, Y. (2011). Local ambiguity, search strategies and parsing in Dynamic Syntax. In E. Gregoromichelaki, R. Kempson, and C. Howes (Eds.), *The Dynamics of Lexical Interfaces*. CSLI Publications.

Steedman, M. (2000). *The Syntactic Process*. Cambridge, MA: MIT Press.

Zettlemoyer, L. and M. Collins (2007). Online learning of relaxed CCG grammars for parsing to logical form. In *Proceedings of the Joint Conference on Empirical Methods in Natural Language Processing and Computational Natural Language Learning (EMNLP-CoNLL)*.

Towards Weakly Supervised Resolution of Null Instantiations

Philip Gorinski
Saarland University
philipg@coli.uni-saarland.de

Josef Ruppenhofer
Hildesheim University
ruppenho@uni-hildesheim.de

Caroline Sporleder
Trier University
sporledc@uni-trier.de

Abstract

This paper addresses the task of finding antecedents for locally uninstantiated arguments. To resolve such null instantiations, we develop a weakly supervised approach that investigates and combines a number of linguistically motivated strategies that are inspired by work on semantic role labeling and corefence resolution. The performance of the system is competitive with the current state-of-the-art supervised system.

1 Introduction

There is a growing interest in developing algorithms for resolving locally unrealized semantic arguments, so-called *null instantiations (NIs)*. Null instantiations are frequent in natural discourse; only a relatively small proportion of the theoretically possible semantic arguments tend to be locally instantiated in the same clause or sentence as the target predicate. This even applies to core arguments of a predicate i.e., those that express participants which are necessarily present in the situation which the predicate evokes. However, null instantiated arguments can often be 'recovered' from the surrounding context.

Consider example (1) below (taken from Arthur Conan Doyle's "The Adventure of Wisteria Lodge"). In a frame-semantic analysis of (1), *interesting* evokes the `Mental_stimulus_stimulus_focus` (`Mssf`) frame. This frame has two core semantic arguments, EXPERIENCER and STIMULUS, as well as eight peripheral arguments, such as TIME, MANNER, DEGREE. Of the two core arguments, neither is realized in the same sentence. Only the peripheral argument DEGREE (DEG) is instantiated and realized by *most*. To fully comprehend the sentence, it is necessary to infer the fillers of the EXPERIENCER and STIMULUS roles, i.e., the reader needs to make an assumption about what is interesting and to whom. For humans this inference is easy to make since the EXPERIENCER (EXP) and STIMULUS (STIM) roles are actually filled by *he* and *a white cock* in the previous sentence. Similarly, in (2) *right* evokes the `Correctness` (`Corr`) frame, which has four core arguments, only one of which is filled locally, namely SOURCE (SRC), which is realized by *You* (and co-referent with *Mr. Holmes*). However, another argument, INFORMATION (INF), is filled by the preceding sentence (spoken by a different speaker, namely Holmes), which provides details of the fact about which Holmes was right.

(1) ["A white cock,"]$_{Stim}$ said [he]$_{Exp}$. "[Most]$_{Deg}$ **interesting**$_{Mssf}$!"

(2) A. ["Your powers seem superior to your opportunities."]$_{Inf}$

B. "[You]$_{Src}$'re **right**$_{Corr}$, Mr. Holmes."

Semantic role labeling (SRL) systems typically only label arguments that are locally realised (e.g., within the maximal projection of the target predicate); they tacitly ignore all roles that are not instantiated locally. Previous attempts to resolve null instantiated arguments have obtained mixed results. While Gerber and Chai (2010, 2012) obtain reasonable results for NI resolution within a restricted PropBank-based scenario, the accuracies obtained on the FrameNet-based data set provided for the SemEval 2010

Shared Task 10 (Ruppenhofer et al., 2010; Chen et al., 2010; Tonelli and Delmonte, 2010, 2011; Silberer and Frank, 2012) are much lower. This has two reasons: Semantic role labelling in the FrameNet framework is generally harder than in the PropBank framework, even for overt arguments, due to the fact that FrameNet roles are much more grounded in semantics as opposed to the shallower, more syntactically-driven PropBank roles. Second, the SemEval 2010 data set consists of running text in which null instantiations are marked and resolved, while the data set used by Gerber and Chai (2010, 2012) consists of annotated examples sentences for just a few predicates. This makes the latter data set easier as there are fewer predicates to deal with and more examples per predicate to learn from. However, this set-up is somewhat artificial and unrealistic (Ruppenhofer et al., to appear). Independently of whether the NI annotation is done on individual predicates or running texts, it is unlikely that we will ever have sufficient amounts of annotated data to address large-scale NI resolution in a purely supervised fashion.

In this paper, we present a system that uses only a minimal amount of supervision. It combines various basic NI resolvers that exploit different types of linguistic knowledge. Most of the basic resolvers employ heuristics; however, we make use of semantic representations of roles learnt from FrameNet. Note that the system does not require data annotated with NI information, only data annotated with overt semantic roles (i.e., FrameNet). Our paper is largely exploratory; we aim to shed light on what types of information are useful for this task. Similarly to Silberer and Frank (2012) , we focus mainly on NI *resolution*, i.e., we assume that it is known whether an argument is missing, which argument is missing, and whether the missing argument has a definite or indefinite interpretation (DNI vs. INI, see Section 2 for details).[1]

2 Arguments and Null Instantiations in FrameNet

A predicate argument structure in FrameNet consists of a *frame* evoked by a target predicate. Each frame defines a number of *frame elements* (FEs). For some FEs, FrameNet explicitly specifies a *semantic type*. For instance, the EXPERIENCER of the `Mental_stimulus_stimulus_focus` frame (see (1)) is defined to be of type 'sentient'. We make use of this information in the experiments. The FEs are categorized into core arguments, peripheral arguments, and extra-thematic arguments. *Core arguments* are taken to be essential components of a frame; they distinguish it from other frames and represent participants which are necessarily present in the situation evoked by the frame, though may not be overtly realized every time the frame is evoked. *Peripheral arguments* are optional and generalize across frames, in that they can be found in all semantically appropriate frames. Typical examples of peripheral arguments are TIME or MANNER. Finally, *extra-thematic arguments* are those that situate the event described by the target predicate against another state-of-affairs. For example, *twice* can express the extra-thematic argument ITERATION. Since only core arguments are essential to a frame, only they are analyzed as null instantiated if missing. Peripheral and extra-thematic arguments are optional by definition.

(3) [A drunk burglar]$_{Sspct}$ was **arrested**$_{Arrest}$ after accidentally handing his ID to his victim.

(4) [We]$_{Thm}$ **arrived**$_{Arrive}$ [at 8pm]$_{Tm}$.

NIs can be classified into definite NIs (DNIs) or indefinite NIs (INI). The difference is illustrated by examples (3) and (4). Whereas, in (3) the protagonist making the arrest is only existentially bound within the discourse (an instance of indefinite null instantiation, INI), the GOAL location in (4) is an entity that must be accessible to speaker and hearer from the discourse or its context (definite null instantiation, DNI). As INIs do not need to be accessible within a context, the task of resolving NIs is restricted to DNIs. The complete task can then be modeled as a pipeline consisting of three sub-tasks: (i) identifying potential NIs by taking into account information about core arguments, (ii) automatically distinguishing between DNIs and INIs, and (iii) resolving NIs classified as DNI to a suitable referent in the text. In this paper, we focus largely on the last subtask.

[1]The first two questions are the focus of recent work on motion predicates by Feizabadi and Padó (2012).

3 Related work

Null instantiations were the focus of the SemEval-10 Task-10 (Ruppenhofer et al., 2010). The two participating systems which addressed the NI resolution task took very different approaches. Tonelli and Delmonte (2010) developed a knowledge-based system called VENSES++ that builds on an existing text understanding system (Delmonte, 2008). Different resolution strategies are employed for verbal and nominal predicates. For the former, NIs are resolved by reasoning about the semantic similarity between an NI and a potential filler using WordNet. For nominal predicates, the system makes use of a common sense reasoning module that builds on ConceptNet (Liu and Singh, 2004). The system is conservative and has a relatively high precision but a low recall, identifying less than 20% of the NIs correctly. To address the low recall, Tonelli & Delmonte in later work (Tonelli and Delmonte, 2011) developed a simpler role linking strategy that is based on computing a relevancy score for the nominal head of each potential antecedent. The intuition is that heads which serve often as role fillers and occur close to the target NI are more likely to function as antecedents for the NI. Compared to the earlier model, the new method led to a noticeable increase in recall and f-score but a drop in precision.

The second SemEval system (Chen et al., 2010) is statistical and extends an existing semantic role labeler (Das et al., 2011). Resolving DNIs is modeled in the same way as labeling overt arguments, with the search space being extended to pronouns, NPs, and nouns outside the sentence.[2] When evaluating a potential filler, the syntactic features which are used in argument labeling of overt arguments are replaced by two semantic features: The system checks first whether a potential filler in the context fills the null-instantiated role overtly in one of the FrameNet sentences, i.e. whether there is a precedent for a given filler-role combination among the overt arguments of the frame in FrameNet. If not, the system calculates the distributional similarity between filler and role. The surface distance between a potential filler and an NI is also taken into account. While Chen et al.'s system has a higher recall than VENSES++, its performance is still relatively low. The authors argue that data sparseness is the biggest problem.

Silberer and Frank (2012) also used supervised machine learning to model NI resolution for the SemEval data. However, while Tonelli & Delmonte and Chen et al. view NI resolution as an extension of semantic role labelling, Silberer and Frank explicitly cast the problem as a coreference resolution (CR) task, employing an entity-mention model, i.e. the potential fillers are taken to be entity chains rather than individual mentions of discourse referents. They experiment with a variety of features, both from SRL and CR and automatically expand the training set with examples generated from a coreference corpus. They find that CR features, such as salience, perform somewhat better than SRL features.

Gerber and Chai (2010; 2012) present a study of implicit arguments for a group of frequent nominal predicates. They also use an entity mention approach and model the problem as a classical supervised task, implementing a number of syntactic, semantic, and discourse features such as the sentence distance between an NI and its potential filler, their mutual information, and the discourse relation holding between the spans containing the target predicate and the potential filler. Gerber and Chai report results that are noticeably higher than those obtained for the SemEval data. However, this is probably largely due to the fact that the two data sets are very different. Gerber and Chai's corpus consists of newswire texts (Wall Street Journal), which are annotated with NomBank/PropBank roles. The data cover 10 nominal predicates from the commerce domain, with—on average—120 annotated instances per predicate. The Task-10 corpus consists of narrative texts annotated under the FrameNet paradigm. Crucially, this corpus provides annotations for running texts not for individual occurrences of selected target predicates. It thus treats many different general-language predicates of all parts of speech. While the overall size of the corpus in terms of sentences is comparable to Gerber and Chai's corpus, the SemEval corpus contains many more target predicates and fewer instances for each.[3] NI resolution results obtained by the Task-10 participants are significantly below those reported by Gerber and Chai (2010).

[2]This disregards other role fillers such as whole sentences as in example (2) above.

[3]E.g., Ruppenhofer et al. (2010) report that there are 1,703 frame instances covering 425 distinct frame types, which gives an average of 3.8 instances per frame.

data set	sentences	tokens	frame instances	frame types	overt frame elements	DNIs (resolved)	INIs
Wisteria	438	7,941	1,370	317	2,526	303 (245)	277
Hound	525	9,131	1,703	452	3,141	349 (259)	361

Table 1: Statistics for the SemEval-10 Task-10 corpus

4 Data

In our experiments we used the corpus distributed for SemEval-10's Task-10 on "Linking Events and Their Participants in Discourse" (Ruppenhofer et al., 2010). The data set consists of two texts by Arthur Conan Doyle, "The Adventure of Wisteria Lodge"(1908) and "The Hound of the Baskervilles" (1901/02). The annotation consists of frame-semantic argument structure, co-reference chains, and information about null instantiation, i.e., the NI type (DNI vs. INI) and the filler, if available in the text. Table 1 provides basic statistics about this data set.

The Wisteria data were given out for training in the SemEval task. We use these data for parameter tuning and error analysis. We also use the overt FE annotations in Wisteria to compute semantic vectors of roles. For comparison with previous systems, the final results we report are for the unseen Hound data (the test set in SemEval).

5 Modeling NI Resolution

While the complete NI resolution task consists of three steps, detecting NIs, classifying NIs as DNIs or INIs, and resolving DNIs, in this paper, we focus exclusively on the third task as this is by far the most difficult one. We model the problem as a weakly supervised task, where the only type of supervision is the use of a corpus annotated with overtly realised semantic roles. We do not make use of the NI annotations in the training set. This distinguishes our work from the approaches by Gerber and Chai (2012; 2010) and Silberer and Frank (2012). However, like these two we employ an entity mention model, that is, we take into account the whole coreference chain for a discourse entity when assessing its likelihood of filling a null instantiated role. For this, we make use of the gold standard coreference chains in the SemEval data. So as not to have an unfair advantage, we also create singleton chains for all noun phrases without an overt co-referent, since such cases could, in theory, be antecedents for omitted arguments. Finally, since NIs can also refer to complete sentences, we augment the entity set by all sentences in the document.

We implemented four linguistically informed resolvers plus a baseline resolver. Each resolver returns the best antecedent entity chain according to its heuristics or null, if none can be found. If two or more chains score equally well for a given resolver, the one whose most recent mention is closest to the target predicate is chosen, i.e., we employ recency/salience as a tie breaker. To arrive at the final decision over the output of all (informed) resolvers, we experimented with various weighting schemes but found that majority weighting works best.

5.1 Semantic Type Based Resolver (Stres)

One approach we pursue for identifying a suitable mention/chain relies on the semantic types that FrameNet specifies for frame elements. Specifically, we look up in FrameNet the semantic type(s) of the FE that is unexpressed. With that information in hand, we consider all the coreference chains that are active in some window of context, where being active means that one of the member mentions of the chain occurs in one of the context sentences. We try to find chains that share at least one semantic type with the FE in question. This is possible because for each chain, we have percolated the semantic types associated with any of their member mentions to the chain.[4] If we find no chain at all within the window that has semantic types compatible with our FE, we guess that the FE has no antecedent.[5] Note also that in our current set-up we have defined the semantic type match to be a strict one. For instance, if our FE has the semantic type *Entity* and an active chain is of the type *Sentient*, we will not get a match even though the type *Sentient* is a descendant of *Entity* in the hierarchy in which semantic types are arranged.

5.2 String Based Resolver (String)

Another way of finding a correct filler is the frame-independent search for realizations of the null instantiated frame element in a given context window. This is based on the assumption that a constituent which has taken a given role before is likely to fill out that role again.

An example is (5), where *house* fills the role of GOAL in an instance of the `Cotheme` frame evoked by *led* and is the correct antecedent for the omitted GOAL FE in a later instance of the `Arriving` frame.

(5) s2: The curved and shadowed drive **led**$_{Cotheme}$ us [to a low , dark house , pitchblack against a slate-coloured sky]$_{Goal}$. ... s11: "I am glad you have **come**$_{Arriving}$, sir . ... "

Investigating the active chains in the context, we try to find any chain containing a mention that is annotated with a frame element of the same name as the null instantiated FE. We do so concentrating on the FE name only and disregard the actual annotated frame, making use of the observation that FrameNet tends to assign similar names to similar roles across frames. In our current set-up, the matching of FE names is strict. Note that this constraint could be weakened by also considering frame elements that have *similar* names to the FE under investigation. For example, many 'numbered' FE names such as PROTAGONIST_1 could be treated as equivalent to simple unnumbered names such as PROTAGONIST. Note that a similar feature is used by Chen et al. (2010). The difference is that they compute the feature on the FrameNet data while we use the SemEval data.

5.3 Participant Based Resolver (Part)

Instead of concentrating on the null instantiated FE itself, another approach is to investigate the other participants of the frame in question. Based on the assumption that roles occuring together with similar other roles can be instantiated with the same filler, we search the coreference chains for mentions with the highest overlap of roles with the frame under investigation. For this, the set of roles excluding the null instantiated FE is checked against the role sets of frames in the context window. In case of an overlap between those sets, we choose the mention as a possible filler that is annotated with an FE that is not in the set. In case of there being multiple mentions fulfilling this criterion, the mention closest to the NI is chosen. The mention that is finally chosen as the filler is that mention whose annotated frame shares the most participants with the null instantiation's frame.

5.4 Vector Based Resolver (Vec)

Another semantics-based approach next to the Semantic Type Based Resolver is to calculate the similiarity between the mentions in a coreference chain and the known fillers of a null instantiated frame element. For each annotated (overt) FE in FrameNet and Wisteria, we calculate a context vector for the filler's head word, consisting of the 1000 most frequent words in the English Gigaword corpus.[6] The vectors are calculated on the Gigaword corpus and the training data in addition, and the mean vector of all vectors for a particular FE fillers' head words is calculated as the target vector for said frame element. In the actual process of resolving a given null instantiation, we investigate all coreference chains in the

[4] In the official FrameNet database, not every frame element is assigned a semantic type. We modified our copy of FrameNet so that every FE does have a semantic type by simply looking up in WordNet the path from the name of a frame element to the synsets that FrameNet uses to define semantic types.

[5] Alternatively, we could have widened the window of context in the hope of hitting upon a suitable chain.

[6] http://www.ldc.upenn.edu/Catalog/CatalogEntry.jsp?catalogId=LDC2003T05

context window, and calculate the mean vectors of their mentions' head words. We use the cosine for measuring the similarity of each mean vector to the null instantiated frame element's vector, and choose as an antecedent the chain that bears the highest similarity. A similar feature is employed by Chen et al. (2010) who also make use of distributional similarity.

5.4.1 Baseline Resolver (Base)

The baseline resolver is based on the intuition that the (entity chain of the) mention closest to the NI might be a good filler in the absence of more sophisticated knowledge. There are essentially two filler types: NPs and sentences. The FrameNet definition of the null instantiated FE is used to determine whether its filler's semantic type should be a *living thing* or another kind of general *physical object*, in which case we link to the closest NP, or if the element is a *Topic or Message* FE, in which case we link to the preceding sentence.

6 Experiments

We first applied all individual resolvers as well as the combination of the four informed resolvers (by majority vote) to the Wisteria data set. As Table 2 shows, the string and the participant (part) resolvers behave similarly as well as the semantic type (stres) and vector (vec) resolvers: the former two have a relatively high precision but very low recall, while the latter two obtain a higher recall and f-score. This is not surprising since string and part on the one hand and stres and vec on the other hand model very similar types of information. Moreover, the string and part resolvers suffer more from sparse data since they are based on information about argument structures seen before. The more strongly semantic resolvers stres and vec are more robust.

The combination of all resolvers by majority voting outperforms each individual resolver. However, the difference is not huge, which suggests that there is a certain amount of overlap between the resolvers, i.e. they are not disjoint. We experimented with other voting schemes besides majority voting, however none led to significant improvements. As expected, the baseline resolver performs fairly poorly.

	Prec.	Rec.	F-Score	TPs
stres	0.23	0.2	0.21	51
string	0.53	0.06	0.11	16
part	0.66	0.01	0.02	2
vec	0.21	0.18	0.19	46
all	0.26	0.24	0.25	62
base	0.07	0.02	0.03	4

Table 2: Results for the individual resolvers on Wisteria

6.1 Qualitative Analysis

To shed further light on the behaviour of the resolvers as well as on the challenges of the task we performed a detailed qualitative analysis for a run on the training data in which we use a window of 3 sentences prior to the target sentence. (The results for slightly greater windows sizes up to 5 are essentially the same.)

Performance by frame For the semantic type-based resolver and the vector resolver we looked in detail at their performance on individual frames. We did not similarly look at the other two resolvers as they only identified antecedents for relatively few DNIs, thus rendering the analysis a bit unreliable. The vector and the semantic type-based resolvers behave similarly and, for reasons of space, we focus on the latter here. We traced the system's handling of all frame instances with a DNI-FE from start to finish, providing us with detailed information on why particular cases cannot be resolved. Table 3 shows information for those FEs that are most often omitted as DNI. The resolver setting employed is one where the resolver looks backward only for coreferent mentions of the missing referent. All mentions in a window of three sentences before the DNI are considered. For instance, the first line in Table 3 shows that the FE GOAL in the `Arriving` frame occurs 14 times overall. In 12 cases, a resolution within the text is possible. However, in only 4 cases is the correct coreference chain among the set of active candidates that the resolver considers within the 3-sentence window. None of these 4 cases were resolved successfully. By comparison, performance is much higher for the FE INITIAL_SET of the `Increment` frame, where 5 of 8 resolvable instances are correctly resolved. Note that for the same frame, performance seems much lower for the FE CLASS, which, however, is also less often resolvable than its sister FE INITIAL_SET. Likewise, the numbers for WHOLE in `Calendric_unit` suggest that for some FEs in particular frames resolution to an explicit mention within the text is rarely possible and typically results in false positives. Taken together, these facts suggest that ideally we would have resolution strategies more specifically attuned to particular frame-FE combinations.

Framename	FE	Instances	Resolvable	Active	Correct
Arriving	Goal	14	12	4	0
Increment	Initial_set	9	8	5	**1**
Increment	Class	6	2	0	0
Risky_situation	Asset	6	6	5	0
Attempt	Goal	6	5	2	0
Time_vector	Landmark_event	6	3	1	0
Observable_bodyparts	Possessor	6	6	6	2
Locative_relation	Ground	5	5	4	**1**
Social_interaction_evaluation	Judge	5	4	**2**	1
Calendric_unit	Whole	5	0	0	0
		...			
Personal_relationship	Partner_2	3	3	3	**0**

Table 3: STRES performance on training data for frequent DNI-FEs (forward- and backward-looking)

Performance by search direction When resolving a DNI we considered all entity chains with mentions in a window of 3 sentences before the target predicate. We experimented with larger window sizes but this did not lead to improved performance. We also experimented with looking at the following sentences, too. In some cases, such as example (6), looking forward is the only way to get at an antecedent within a given window size (*he-his-the black-eyed , scowling , yellow devil*).

(6) s292: They pushed her into the carriage s293: She fought her way out again . s294: I took her part , got her into a cab , and here we are . s295: I shan 't forget the **face**$_{Observable\_Bodypart}$ at the carriage window as I led her away . s296: I 'd have a short life if he had his way - the black-eyed , scowling , yellow devil . "

We may thus wonder what the effect of also looking forward might be. Table 4 shows the information for the same set of frequent DNI-FEs as Table 3 but now for the resolver setting where the resolver looks forward 3 sentences as well as backward.

Comparison of the tables suggests that looking forward does not usually give us access to chains that we wouldn't have available by only looking backward. We have only one such case–Social interaction evaluation.Judge–in our tables. Overall, among the 303 DNI cases in the data, the gold chain is within range in 143 cases when we only look back and in 156 cases when we look forward, too. (+9%) Looking forward more often results in the resolution of the right candidate (chain/mention) going wrong; e.g. Increment.Initial_set is a good example from the tables above. Overall, across all cases of DNI we have a 41.9 % drop in correct resolutions.

Framename	FE	Instances	Resolvable	Active	Correct
Arriving	Goal	14	12	4	0
Increment	Initial_set	9	8	5	**5**
Increment	Class	6	2	0	0
Risky_situation	Asset	6	6	5	0
Attempt	Goal	6	5	2	0
Time_vector	Landmark_event	6	3	1	0
Observable_bodyparts	Possessor	6	6	6	2
Locative_relation	Ground	5	5	4	**2**
Social_interaction_evaluation	Judge	5	4	**1**	1
Calendric_unit	Whole	5	0	0	0
	...				
Personal_relationship	Partner_2	3	3	3	**2**

Table 4: STRES performance on training data for frequent DNI-FEs (backward-looking only)

Number of candidate chains On average there are about 26.5 different candidate chains available for a case of DNI if the system only looks back 3 sentences. Even with various constraints in place that filter out chains, the number of viable chains is still high. Consider example 7, where an antecdent needs to be found for the missing OFFENDER. That sentence alone, not including earlier ones, mentions multiple distinct human individuals and groups. Given that the correct referent (*he*) is farthest away from the frame's target, it is not surprising that resolution did not succeed given that the system has no understanding that all other mentioned individuals and groups are among the revenge-seeking PROTAGONISTs and thus highly unlikely to also fill the role of OFFENDER.

(7) s371: Knowing that he would return there , Garcia , who is the son of the former highest dignitary in San Pedro , was waiting with two trusty companions of humble station , all three fired with the same reasons for **revenge**$_{Revenge}$.

Performance by target POS The distribution of DNI cases across targets of different parts of speech is not even, as can be seen from Table 5. Neither is the performance of our systems equal for all POS, as illustrated by Table 6. On the Wisteria data resolution performance is lowest for verbs. This is somewhat surprising because traditional SRL tends to be easier for verbal predicates than for other parts-of-speech. Similarly, in our experience, we have found performance on the two steps preceding antecedent resolution, that is, on NI detection and NI-type recognition, to usually be better on verbs (and adjectives) than on nouns. However, the difference is small and may be accidental, especially since on the test data verbs, along with adjectives, again perform better than nouns.

Adjective	Noun	Prep	Adverb	Verb	Other
48	160	2	10	79	4

Table 5: Distribution of DNI instances across targets of different POS in the training data

POS	Instances	Resolvable	Gold in CandidateSet	Correct
Adj	48	38	25	8 (16.7%)
Noun	160	133	81	26 (16.25%)
Verb	79	65	33	7 (8.9%)

Table 6: Performance of the semantic type-based resolver for major POS types in the training data

Performance on specific semantic domains While our training dataset is small, we also decided to group related frames for three important semantic domains (Motion, Communication, Cognition & Perception) that are relatively frequent in the training data. We compare the resolution performance for the frame instances covered by the different groups in Table 7. Our intuition is that there may be differences between the domains. For instance, as suggested by the example of the GOAL FE in the `Arriving` frame (discussed in 6.1 above) Source and Goal FEs in motion-related frames may be relatively difficult to resolve. However, the differences between the domains are not statistically significant on the amount of data we have: the p-value of a Fisher's exact test using the Freeman-Halton extension is 0.17537655.

Domain	Instances	Resolvable	Gold in CandidateSet	Correct
Motion	33	27	11	1 (3.0%)
Communication	19	19	13	3 (15.8%)
Cognition & Perception	15	15	10	1 (6.7%)

Table 7: Resolution performance of STRES for three well-represented domains

6.2 Quantitative Analysis

For comparison with previous work, we also report our results on the SemEval test set (Hound) for the best parameter setting (majority vote, window of 5 sentences preceding the target sentence) as obtained from the development set (Wisteria). Tables 8 and 9 give the results for the role linking task only, i.e. assuming that NIs have been identified and correctly classified as DNI or INI. Tables 10 and 11 give the results for the full NI resolution task. In the latter set-up we use heuristics to identify NIs and determine DNIs. Our system is most comparable to the model by Silberer and Frank (2012), however, the latter is supervised while our model only makes use of minimal supervision. Despite this, the best results by Silberer and Frank for the role linking task are only slightly higher than ours (0.27 F1-Score). While this is encouraging, the overall performance of all NI resolution systems proposed so far for FrameNet argument structures is, of course, still relatively low. Comparing our results for the role linking (gold) vs. the full NI resolution task (non gold) indicates that there is also still room for improvement regarding NI identification and DNI vs. INI classification. The scores drop noticably for the non-gold setting. The tables below also list the performance for different parts-of-speech of the FEE. Surprisingly adjective FEEs seem to be easiest, while nouns seem more difficult than verbs. The low result for the category 'Other' can probably be explained by the fact that this category is very infrequent.

	Verb	Noun	Adj	Other	All
Precision	0.27	0.23	0.33	0.0	0.25
Recall	0.26	0.22	0.33	0.0	0.23
F1-Score	0.27	0.22	0.33	0.0	0.24

Table 8: Results on Hound Chapter 13 (gold)

	Verb	Noun	Adj	Other	All
Precision	0.32	0.22	0.38	0.0	0.27
Recall	0.29	0.21	0.33	0.0	0.24
F1-Score	0.31	0.22	0.35	0.0	0.25

Table 9: Results on Hound Chapter 14 (gold)

	Verb	Noun	Adj	Other	All
Precision	0.23	0.14	0.23	0.0	0.17
Recall	0.13	0.12	0.25	0.0	0.13
F1-Score	0.17	0.13	0.24	0.0	0.15

Table 10: Results on Hound Chapter 13 (non gold)

	Verb	Noun	Adj	Other	All
Precision	0.18	0.08	0.1	0.0	0.12
Recall	0.16	0.08	0.22	0.0	0.12
F1-Score	0.17	0.08	0.13	0.0	0.12

Table 11: Results on Hound Chapter 14 (non gold)

7 Conclusion

In this paper, we presented a weakly supervised approach to finding the antecedents for definite null instantiations. We built four different resolvers for the task, each drawing on slightly different aspects of semantics. The semantic type-based and the vector resolver focused on the properties of potential role fillers; the participant-based filler focused on the set of co-occurring roles; and the string-based resolver represents a bet that a constituent which has filled a given role before is likely to fill the same role again. While the semantic type-based and vector resolvers proved to be more robust than the others, the best system consisted in a combination of all four resolvers. The combined system produced results competitive with the current best supervised system, despite being largely unsupervised.

A detailed performance analysis for the semantic type-based resolver on the training data confirmed some prior findings and yielded several new insights into the task. First, resolution attempts could benefit from knowledge about the particulars of frames or of semantic domains. For instance, there seem to be some omissible FEs such as WHOLE in the `Calendric_unit` frame that are almost never resolvable and which we therefore might best guess to have no antecedent. Similarly, while for some FEs in some frames (e.g. INITIAL_SET in `Increment`) a very narrow window of context is sufficient, for others such as SOURCE, PATH or GOAL FEs in motion-related frames it might make sense to widen the window of context that is searched for antecedents. Second, while it is clear that definite null instantiations normally have to have prior mentions at the point when they occur, it was not obvious that also considering active chains in a window *following* the occurrence of the FEE would in fact lower performance as it does for STRES. Third, while verbs unexpectedly performed worse than nouns and adjectives on the training data, the usual pattern was observed on the test data: role labeling and NI resolution perform better on verbs than on nouns. Finally, the detailed analysis illustrates that the antecedent-finding step is indeed a hard one given that on average the correct chain has to be found among more than 25 candidates.

Acknowledgements

This work was partly funded by the German Research Foundation, DFG (Cluster of Excellence *Multimodal Computing and Interaction*).

References

Chen, D., N. Schneider, D. Das, and N. A. Smith (2010, July). SEMAFOR: Frame argument resolution with log-linear models. In *Proceedings of the 5th International Workshop on Semantic Evaluation*, Uppsala, Sweden, pp. 264–267. Association for Computational Linguistics.

Das, D., N. Schneider, D. Chen, and N. Smith (2011). Probabilistic frame-semantic parsing. In *Proc. of NAACL-HLT-10*.

Delmonte, R. (2008). *Computational Linguistic Text Processing Lexicon, Grammar, Parsing and Anaphora Resolution*. New York: Nova Science.

Feizabadi, P. and S. Padó (2012). Automatic identification of motion verbs in wordnet and framenet. In *Proceedings of KONVENS 2012*, Vienna, Austria.

Gerber, M. and J. Y. Chai (2010). Beyond nombank: a study of implicit arguments for nominal predicates. In *Proceedings of the 48th Annual Meeting of the Association for Computational Linguistics*, ACL '10, Stroudsburg, PA, USA, pp. 1583–1592. Association for Computational Linguistics.

Gerber, M. and J. Y. Chai (2012). Semantic role labeling of implicit arguments for nominal predicates. *Computational Linguistics 38*(4), 755–798.

Liu, H. and P. Singh (2004). ConceptNet: A practical commonsense reasoning toolkit. *BT Technology Journal 22*(4), 211–226.

Ruppenhofer, J., R. Lee-Goldman, C. Sporleder, and R. Morante (to appear). Beyond sentence-level semantic role labeling: linking argument structures in discourse. *Language Resources and Evaluation*.

Ruppenhofer, J., C. Sporleder, R. Morante, C. Baker, and M. Palmer (2010). SemEval-2010 task 10: Linking events and their participants in discourse. In *The ACL Workshop SemEval-2010: 5th International Workshop on Semantic Evaluations*.

Silberer, C. and A. Frank (2012, 7-8 June). Casting implicit role linking as an anaphora resolution task. In **SEM 2012: The First Joint Conference on Lexical and Computational Semantics – Volume 1: Proceedings of the main conference and the shared task, and Volume 2: Proceedings of the Sixth International Workshop on Semantic Evaluation (SemEval 2012)*, Montréal, Canada, pp. 1–10. Association for Computational Linguistics.

Tonelli, S. and R. Delmonte (2010, July). Venses++: Adapting a deep semantic processing system to the identification of null instantiations. In *Proceedings of the 5th International Workshop on Semantic Evaluation*, Uppsala, Sweden, pp. 296–299. Association for Computational Linguistics.

Tonelli, S. and R. Delmonte (2011, June). Desperately seeking implicit arguments in text. In *Proceedings of the ACL 2011 Workshop on Relational Models of Semantics*, Portland, Oregon, USA, pp. 54–62. Association for Computational Linguistics.

Multi-Step Regression Learning for Compositional Distributional Semantics

E. Grefenstette[*], G. Dinu[†], Y. Zhang[‡], M. Sadrzadeh[*] and M. Baroni[†]

[*]University of Oxford Department of Computer Science
[†]University of Trento Center for Mind/Brain Sciences
[‡]University of Tokyo Department of Computer Science

Abstract

We present a model for compositional distributional semantics related to the framework of Coecke et al. (2010), and emulating formal semantics by representing functions as tensors and arguments as vectors. We introduce a new learning method for tensors, generalising the approach of Baroni and Zamparelli (2010). We evaluate it on two benchmark data sets, and find it to outperform existing leading methods. We argue in our analysis that the nature of this learning method also renders it suitable for solving more subtle problems compositional distributional models might face.

1 Introduction

The staggering amount of machine readable text available on today's Internet calls for increasingly powerful text and language processing methods. This need has fuelled the search for more subtle and sophisticated representations of language meaning, and methods for learning such models. Two well-researched but *prima-facie* orthogonal approaches to this problem are formal semantic models and distributional semantic models, each complementary to the other in its strengths and weaknesses.

Formal semantic models generally implement the view of Frege (1892)—that the semantic content of an expression is its logical form—by defining a systematic passage from syntactic rules to the composition of parts of logical expressions. This allows us to derive the logical form a of sentence from its syntactic structure (Montague, 1970). These models are fully compositional, whereby the meaning of a phrase is a function of the meaning of its parts; however, as they reduce meaning to logical form, they are not necessarily adapted to all language processing applications such as paraphrase detection, classification, or search, where topical and pragmatic relations may be more relevant to the task than equivalence of logical form or truth value. Furthermore, reducing meaning to logical form presupposes the provision of a logical model and domain in order for the semantic value of expressions to be determined, rendering such models essentially *a priori*.

In contrast, distributional semantic models, suggested by Firth (1957), implement the linguistic philosophy of Wittgenstein (1953) stating that meaning is associated with use, and therefore meaning can be learned through the observation of linguistic practises. In practical terms, such models learn the meaning of words by examining the contexts of their occurrences in a corpus, where 'context' is generally taken to mean the tokens with which words co-occur within a sentence or frame of n tokens. Such models have been successfully applied to various tasks such as thesaurus extraction (Grefenstette, 1994) and essay grading (Landauer and Dumais, 1997; Dumais, 2003). However, unlike their formal semantics counterparts, distributional models have no explicit canonical composition operation, and provide no way to integrate syntactic information into word meaning combination to produce sentence meanings.

In this paper, we present a new approach to the development of *compositional* distributional semantic models, based on earlier work by Baroni and Zamparelli (2010), Coecke et al. (2010) and Grefenstette et al. (2011), combining features from the compositional distributional framework of the latter two with the learning methods of the former. In Section 2 we outline a brief history of approaches to compositional distributional semantics. In Section 3 we overview a tensor-based compositional distributional model resembling traditional formal semantic models. In Section 4 we present a new multi-step regression algorithm for learning the tensors in this model. Sections 5–7 present the experimental setup and results of two experiments evaluating our model against other known approaches to compositionality in distributional semantics, followed by an analysis of these results in Section 8. We conclude in Section 9 by suggesting future work building on the success of the model presented in this paper.

2 Related work

Although researchers tried to derive sentence meanings by composing vectors since the very inception of distributional semantics, this challenge has attracted special attention in recent years. Mitchell and Lapata (2008, 2010) proposed two broad classes of composition models (additive and multiplicative) that encompass most earlier and related proposals as special cases. The simple additive method (summing the vectors of the words in the sentence or phrase) and simple multiplicative method (component-wise multiplication of the vectors) are straightforward and empirically effective instantiations of the general models. We re-implemented them here as our Add and Multiply methods (see Section 5.2 below).

In formal semantics, composition has always been modeled in terms of function application, treating certain words as functions that operate on other words to construct meaning incrementally according to a calculus of composition that reflects the syntactic structure of sentences (Frege, 1892; Montague, 1970; Partee, 2004). Coecke et al. (2010) have proposed a general formalism for composition in distributional semantics that captures the same notion of function application. Empirical implementations of Coecke's et al.'s formalism have been developed by Grefenstette et al. (2011) and tested by Grefenstette and Sadrzadeh (2011a,b). In the methods they derive, a verb with r arguments is a rank r tensor to be combined via component-wise multiplication with the Kronecker product of the vectors representing its arguments, to obtain another rank r tensor representing the sentence:

$$S = V \odot (\mathbf{a}_1 \otimes \mathbf{a}_2 \otimes ... \otimes \mathbf{a}_r)$$

Grefenstette and Sadrzadeh (2011b) propose various ways to estimate the components of verb tensors in the two-argument (transitive) case, with the simple method of constructing the rank 2 tensor (matrix) by the Kronecker product of a corpus-based verb vector with itself giving the best results. The Kronecker method outperformed the best method of Grefenstette and Sadrzadeh (2011a), referred to as the Categorical model. We re-implement the Kronecker method for our experiments below. It was not possible to efficiently implement the Categorial method across our large corpus, but we still provide a meaningful indirect comparison with this method.

Baroni and Zamparelli (2010) propose a different approach to function application in distributional space, that they apply to adjective-noun composition (see also Guevara (2010) for similar ideas). Adjectives are functions, encoded as linear maps, that take a noun vector as input and return another nominal vector representing the composite meaning as output. In linear algebraic terms, adjectives are matrices, and composition is matrix-by-vector multiplication:

$$\mathbf{c} = A \times \mathbf{n}$$

Baroni and Zamparelli (2010) estimate the adjective matrices by linear regressions on corpus-extracted examples of their input and output vectors. In this paper, we derive their approach as a special case of a more general framework and extend it, both theoretically and empirically, to two-argument functions (transitive verbs), as well as testing the original single argument variant in the verbal domain. Our generalisation of their approach is called Regression in the experiments below.

In the MV-RNN model of Socher et al. (2012), *all* words and phrases are represented by both a vector and a matrix, and composition also involves a non-linear transformation. When two expressions are combined, the resulting composed vector is a non-linear function of the concatenation of two linear transformations (multiplying the first element matrix by the second element vector, and *vice versa*). In parallel, the components of the matrices associated with the resulting phrase are linear combinations of the components of the input matrices. Socher and colleagues show that MV-RNN reaches state-of-the-art performance on a variety of empirical tasks.

While the proposal of Socher et al. is similar to our approach in many respects, including syntax-sensitivity and the use of matrices in the calculus of composition, there are three key differences. The first is that MV-RNN requires task-specific labeled examples to be trained for each target semantic task, which our framework does not, attempting to achieve greater generality while relying less on manual annotation. The second difference, more theoretical in nature, is that all composition in MV-RNN is pairwise, whereas we will present a model of composition permitting functions of larger arity, allowing the semantic representation of functions that take two or more arguments simultaneously. Finally, we follow formal semantics in treating certain words as functions and other as arguments (and can thus directly import intuitions about the calculus of composition from formal semantics into our framework), whereas Socher and colleagues treat each word equally (as both a vector and a matrix). However, we make no claim at this stage as to whether or not these differences can lead to richer semantic models, leaving a direct comparison to future work.

Several studies tackle word meaning in context, that is, how to adapt the distributional representation of a word to the specific context in which it appears (e.g., Dinu and Lapata, 2010; Erk and Padó, 2008; Thater et al., 2011). We see this as complementary rather than alternative to composition: Distributional representations of single words should first be adapted to context with these methods, and then composed to represent the meaning of phrases and sentences.

3 A general framework for distributional function application

A popular approach to compositionality in formal semantics is to derive a formal representation of a phrase from its grammatical structure by representing the semantics of words as functions and arguments, and using the grammatical structure to dictate the order and scope of function application. For example, formal semantic models in the style of Montague (1970) will associate a semantic rule to each syntactic rule in a context-free grammar. A sample formal semantic model is shown here:

Syntax	Semantics
S ⇒ NP VP	$[\![S]\!] \Rightarrow [\![VP]\!]([\![NP]\!])$
NP ⇒ N	$[\![NP]\!] \Rightarrow [\![N]\!]$
N ⇒ ADJ N	$[\![N]\!] \Rightarrow [\![ADJ]\!]([\![N]\!])$
VP ⇒ Vt NP	$[\![VP]\!] \Rightarrow [\![Vt]\!]([\![NP]\!])$
VP ⇒ Vi	$[\![VP]\!] \Rightarrow [\![Vi]\!]$

Syntax (cont'd)	Semantics (cont'd)
Vt ⇒ $\{verbs_t\}$	$[\![Vt]\!] \Rightarrow [\![verb_t]\!]$
Vi ⇒ $\{verbs_i\}$	$[\![Vi]\!] \Rightarrow [\![verb_i]\!]$
ADJ ⇒ $\{adjs\}$	$[\![ADJ]\!] \Rightarrow [\![adj]\!]$
N ⇒ $\{nouns\}$	$[\![N]\!] \Rightarrow [\![noun]\!]$

Following these rules, the parse of a simple sentence like 'angry dogs chase furry cats' yields the following interpretation: $[\![chase]\!]([\![furry]\!]([\![cats]\!]))([\![angry]\!]([\![dogs]\!]))$. This is a simple model, where typically lambda abstraction will be liberally used to support quantifiers and argument inversion, but the key point remains that the grammar dictates the translation from natural language to the functional form, e.g. predicates and logical relations. Whereas in formal semantics these functions have a set theoretic form, we present here a way of defining them as multilinear maps over geometric objects. This geometric framework is also applicable to other formal semantic models than that presented here. This is particularly important, as the version of the model presented here is overly simple compared to modern work in formal semantics (which, for example, apply NPs to VPs instead of VPs to NPs, to model quantification), and only serves as a model frame within which we illustrate how our approach functions.

The bijective correspondence between linear maps and matrices is a well known property in linear algebra: Every linear map $f : A \to B$ can be encoded as a $dim(B)$ by $dim(A)$ matrix M, and conversely every such matrix encodes a class of linear maps determined by the dimensionality of the domain and co-domain. The application of a linear map f to a vector $\mathbf{v} \in A$ producing a vector $\mathbf{w} \in B$ is equivalent to the matrix multiplication:

$$f(\mathbf{v}) = M \times \mathbf{v} = \mathbf{w}$$

In the case of multilinear maps, this correspondence generalises to a correlation between n-ary maps and rank $n+1$ tensors (Bourbaki, 1989; Lee, 1997). Tensors are generalisations of vectors and matrices; they have *larger degrees of freedom* referred to as tensor ranks, which is one for vectors and two for matrices. To illustrate this generalisation, consider how a row/column vector may be written as the weighted superposition (summation) of its basis elements: any vector $\mathbf{v}$ in a vector space V with a fixed basis $\{\mathbf{b}_i\}_i$, can be written

$$\mathbf{v} = \sum_i c_i^{\mathbf{v}} \mathbf{b}_i = \left[c_1^{\mathbf{v}}, \ldots, c_i^{\mathbf{v}}, \ldots, c_{dim(V)}^{\mathbf{v}}\right]^{\top}$$

Here, the weights $c_i^{\mathbf{v}}$ are elements of the underlying field (e.g. $\mathbb{R}$), and thus vectors can be fully described by such a one-index summation. Likewise, matrices, which are rank 2 tensors, can be seen as a collection of row vectors from some space V_r with basis $\{\mathbf{a}_i\}_i$, or of column vectors from some space V_c with basis $\{\mathbf{d}_j\}_j$. Such a matrix M is an element of the space $V_r \otimes V_c$, and can be fully described by the two index summation:

$$M = \sum_{ij} c_{ij}^{M} \mathbf{a}_i \otimes \mathbf{d}_j$$

where, once again, c_{ij}^{M} is an element of the underlying field which in this case is simply the element from the ith row and jth column of the matrix M, and the basis element $\mathbf{a}_i \otimes \mathbf{d_j}$ of $V_r \otimes V_c$ is formed by a pair of basis elements from V_r and V_c. The number of indices (or degrees of freedom) used to fully describe a tensor in this superposition notation is its rank, e.g., a rank 3 tensor $T \in A \otimes B \otimes C$ would be described by the superposition of weights c_{ijk}^{T} associated with basis elements $\mathbf{e}_i \otimes \mathbf{f}_j \otimes \mathbf{g}_k$.

The notion of matrix multiplication and inner product both generalise to tensors as the non-commutative tensor contraction operation ($\times$). For tensors $T \in A \otimes \ldots \otimes B \otimes C$ and $U \in C \otimes D \otimes \ldots \otimes E$, with bases $\{\mathbf{a}_i \otimes \ldots \otimes \mathbf{b}_j \otimes \mathbf{c}_k\}_{i...jk}$ and $\{\mathbf{c}_k \otimes \mathbf{d}_l \otimes \ldots \otimes \mathbf{e}_m\}_{kl...m}$, the tensor contraction of $T \times U$ is calculated:

$$\sum_{i...jkl...m} c_{i...jk}^{T} c_{kl...m}^{U} \mathbf{a}_i \otimes \ldots \otimes \mathbf{b}_j \otimes \mathbf{d}_l \otimes \ldots \otimes \mathbf{e}_m$$

where the resulting tensor is of rank equal to two less than the sum of the ranks of the input tensors; the subtraction reflects the elimination of matching basis elements through summation during contraction.

For every curried multilinear map $g : A \to \ldots \to Y \to Z$, there is a tensor $T^g \in Z \otimes Y \otimes \ldots \otimes A$ encoding it (Bourbaki, 1989; Lee, 1997). The application of a curried n-ary map $h : V_1 \to \ldots \to V_n \to W$ to input vectors $\mathbf{v_1} \in V_1, \ldots, \mathbf{v_n} \in V_n$ to produce output vector $\mathbf{w} \in W$ corresponds to the tensor contraction of the tensor $T^h \in W \otimes V_n \otimes \ldots \otimes V_1$ with the argument vectors:

$$h(\mathbf{v_1}) \ldots (\mathbf{v_n}) = T^h \times \mathbf{v_1} \times \ldots \times \mathbf{v_n}$$

Using this correspondence between n-ary maps and tensors of rank $n+1$ we can turn any formal semantic model into a compositional distributional model. This is done by first running a type inference algorithm on the generative rules and obtaining types, then assigning to each basic type a vector space and to each function type a tensor space, and representing arguments by vectors and functions by tensors, finally, model function application by tensor contraction.

To give an example, in the simple formal semantic model given above, a type inference algorithm would provide us with basic types $[\![N]\!]$ and $[\![S]\!]$; we assign vector spaces N and S to these respectively. Nouns and noun phrases are vectors in N, whereas sentences are vectors in S. Verb phrases map noun phrase interpretations to sentence interpretations, hence they are of type $[\![VP]\!] : \mathit{type}([\![NP]\!]) \to \mathit{type}([\![S]\!])$, in vector space terms we have $[\![VP]\!] : N \to S$. Intransitive verbs map noun phrases to verb phrases, therefore have the tensor form $T^{\text{vi}} \in S \otimes N$. Transitive verbs have type $[\![Vt]\!] : [\![NP]\!] \to [\![VP]\!]$, expanded to $[\![Vt]\!] : N \to N \to S$, giving us the tensor form $T^{\text{vt}} \in S \otimes N \otimes N$. Finally, adjectives are of type $[\![ADJ]\!] : [\![N]\!] \to [\![N]\!]$, and hence have the tensor form $T^{\text{adj}} \in N \otimes N$. Putting all this together with tensor contraction ($\times$) as function application, the vector meaning of our sample sentence "angry dogs chase furry cats" is obtained by calculating the following operations, for lexical semantic vectors T^{cats} and T^{dogs}, square matrices T^{furry} and T^{angry} , and a rank 3 tensor T^{chase}:

$$\left(T^{\text{chase}} \times \left(T^{\text{furry}} \times T^{\text{cats}}\right)\right) \times \left(T^{\text{angry}} \times T^{\text{dogs}}\right)$$

An important feature of the proposed approach is that elements with the same syntactic category will always be represented by tensors of the same rank and dimensionality. For examples, all phrases of type S (namely sentences) will be represented by vectors with the same number of dimensions, making a direct comparison of sentences with arbitrary syntactic structures possible.

4 Learning functions by multi-step regression

The framework described above grants us the ability to determine the rank of the tensors needed to encode functions, as well as their dimensions relative to those of the vectors used to represent arguments.

It leaves open the question of how to learn tensors of specific ranks. This, very much like in the case of the DisCoCat framework of Coecke et al. (2010) from which it originated, is intentional: There may be more than one suitable semantic representation for arguments, functions, and sentences, and it is a desirable feature that we may alternate between such representations or combine them while leaving the mechanics of function composition intact. Furthermore, there may be more than one way of learning the tensors and vectors of a particular representation. Previous work on learning tensors has been described independently by Grefenstette and Sadrzadeh (2011a,b) for transitive verbs, and by Baroni and Zamparelli (2010) for adjective-noun constructions. In this section, we describe a new way to learn such tensors, based on ideas from both aforementioned approaches, namely that of multi-step regression.

Multi-step regression learning is a generalisation of linear regression learning for tensors of rank 3 or higher, as procedures already exist for tensors of rank 1 (lexical semantic vectors) and rank 2 (Baroni and Zamparelli, 2010). For rank 1 tensors, we suggest learning vectors using any standard lexical semantic vector learning model, and present sample parameters in Section 5.1 below. Learning rank 2 tensors (matrices) can be treated as a multivariate multiple regression problem, where the matrix components are chosen to optimise (in a least square error sense) the mapping from training instances of input (argument) to output (composed expression) vectors. Consider for example the task of estimating the components of the matrix representing an intransitive verb, that maps subject vectors to (subject-verb) sentence vectors (Baroni and Zamparelli discuss the analogous adjective-noun composition case):

$$\mathbf{s} = V \times \mathbf{subj}$$

The weights of the matrix are estimated by least-squares regression from example pairs of input subject and output sentence vectors directly extracted from the corpus. For example, the matrix for *sing* is estimated from corpus-extracted vectors representing pairs such as <*mom, mom sings*>, <*child, child sings*>, etc. Note that if the input and output vectors are n dimensional, we must estimate an $n \times n$ matrix, each row corresponding to a separate regression problem (the i-th row vector of the estimated matrix will provide the weights to linearly combine the input vector components to predict the i-th output vector component). Regression is a supervised technique requiring training data. However, we can extract the training data automatically from the corpus and so this approach does not incur an extra knowledge cost with respect to unsupervised methods.

Learning tensors of higher rank by linear regression involves iterative application of the linear regression learning method described above. The idea is to progressively learn the functions of arity two or higher encoded by such tensors by recursively learning the partial application of these functions, thereby reducing the problem to the same matrix-learning problem as addressed by Baroni and Zamparelli. To start with an example: the matrix-by-vector operation of Baroni and Zamparelli (2010) is a special case of the general tensor-based function application model we are proposing, where a 'mono-argumental' function (intransitive verbs) corresponds to a rank 2 tensor (a matrix). The approach is naturally extended to bi-argumental functions, such as transitive verbs, where the verb will be a rank 3 tensor to be multiplied first by the object vector and then by the subject, to return a sentence-representing vector:

$$\mathbf{s} = V \times \mathbf{obj} \times \mathbf{subj}$$

The first multiplication of a $n \times n \times n$ tensor by a n-dimensional vector will return a n-by-n matrix (equivalent to an intransitive verb, as it should be: both *sings* and *eats meat* are VPs requiring a subject to be saturated). Note that given n-dimensional input vectors, the ij-th n-dimensional vector in the estimated tensor provides the weights to linearly combine the input object vector components to predict the ij-th output component of the unsaturated verb-object matrix. The matrix is then multiplied by the subject vector to obtain a n-dimensional vector representing the sentence. Again, we estimate the tensor components by linear regression on input-output examples. In the first stage, we apply linear regression to obtain examples of semi-saturated matrices representing *verb-object* constructions with a specific verb. These matrices are estimated, like in the intransitive case, from corpus-extracted examples of <subject, subject-verb-object> pairs. After estimating a suitable number of such matrices for a variety of objects of the same verb, we use pairs of corpus-derived object vectors and the corresponding estimated verb-object matrices as input-output pairs for another regression, where we estimate the verb tensor components. The estimation procedure is schematically illustrated for *eat* in Fig. 1.

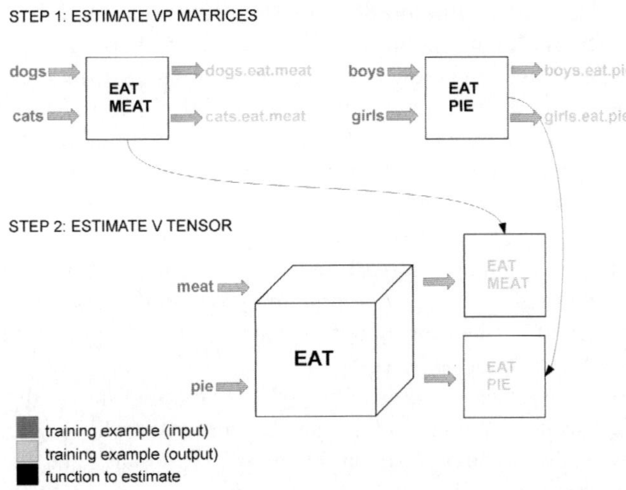

Figure 1: Estimating a tensor for *eat* in two steps. We first estimate matrices for the VPs *eat-meat*, *eat-pie* etc. by linear regression on input subject and output sentence vector pairs. We then estimate the tensor for *eat* by linear regression with the matrices estimated in the previous step as output examples, and the vectors for the corresponding objects as input examples.

We can generalise this learning procedure to functions of arbitrary arity. Consider an n-ary function $f : X_1 \to \ldots \to X_n \to Y$. Let L_i be the set of i-tuples $\{w_1^j, \ldots, w_i^j\}_{i\in[1,k]}$, where $k = |L_i|$, corresponding to the words which saturate the first i arguments of f in a corpus. For each tuple in some set L_i, let $f\ w_1^j \ldots w_i^j = f_i^j : X_{i+1} \to \ldots \to X_n \to Y$. Trivially, there is only one such f_0^j—namely f itself—since $L_0 = \emptyset$ (as there are no arguments of f to saturate for $i = 0$). The idea behind multi-step regression is to learn, at each step, the tensors for functions f_i^j by linear regression over the set of pairs $(w_{i+1}^{j'}, f_{i+1}^{j'})$, where the tensors $f_{i+1}^{j'}$ are the expected outcomes of applying f_i^j to $w_{i+1}^{j'}$ and are learned during the previous step. We bootstrap this algorithm by learning the vectors in Y of the set $\{f_n^j\}_j$ by treating the word which each f_n^j models combined with the words of its associated tuple in L_n as a single token. We then learn the vector for this token from the corpus using our preferred distributional semantics method. By recursively learning the sets of functions from $i = n$ down to 0, we obtain smaller and smaller sets of increasingly de-saturated versions of f, which finally allow us to learn $f_0 = f$.

To specify how the set of pairs used for recursion is determined, let there exist a function *super* which takes the index of a tuple from L_i and returns the set of indices from L_{i+1} which denote tuples identical to the first tuple, excluding the last element:

$$super : \mathbb{N} \times \mathbb{N} \to \mathcal{P}(\mathbb{N}) :: (i, j) \mapsto \{j' | \forall j' \in [1, k'].[w_1^j = w_1^{j'} \wedge \ldots \wedge w_i^j = w_i^{j'}]\} \text{ where } k' = |L_{i+1}|$$

Using this function, the regression set for some f_i^j can be defined as $\{(w_{i+1}^{j'}, f_{i+1}^{j'}) | j' = super(i, j)\}$.

While we just demonstrated how our model generalises to functions of arbitrary arity, it remains to be seen if in actual linguistic modeling there is an effective need for anything beyond tri-argumental functions (ditransitive verbs).

5 Experimental procedure

5.1 Construction of distributional semantic vectors

We extract co-occurrence data from the concatenation of the Web-derived ukWaC corpus (`http://wacky.sslmit.unibo.it/`), a mid-2009 dump of the English Wikipedia (`http://en.wikipedia.org`) and the British National Corpus (`http://www.natcorp.ox.ac.uk/`). The corpus has been tokenised, POS-tagged and lemmatised with TreeTagger (`http://www.ims.uni-stuttgart.de/projekte/corplex/TreeTagger/`) and dependency-parsed with MaltParser (`http://www.maltparser.org/`). It contains about 2.8 billion tokens.

We collect vector representations for the top 8K most frequent nouns and 4K verbs in the corpus, as well as for the subject-verb (320K) and subject-verb-object (1.36M) phrases containing one of the verbs to be used in one of the experiments below and subjects and objects from the list of top 8K nouns. For all target items, we collect within-sentence co-occurrences with the top 10K most frequent content words (nouns, verbs, adjectives and adverbs), save for a stop list of the 300 most frequent words. We extract co-occurrence statistics at the lemma level, ignoring inflectional information. Following standard practice, raw co-occurrence counts are transformed into statistically weighted scores. We tested various weighting schemes of the semantic space on a word similarity task, observing that non-negative pointwise mutual information (PMI) and local mutual information (raw frequency count multiplied by PMI score) generally outperform other weighting schemes by a large margin, and that PMI in particular works best when combined with dimensionality reduction by non-negative matrix factorization (described below). Consequently, we pick PMI weighting for our experiments.

Reducing co-occurrence vectors to lower dimensionality is a common step in the construction of distributional semantic models. Extensive evidence suggests that dimensionality reduction does not affect, and might even improve the quality of lexical semantic vectors (Bullinaria and Levy, 2012; Landauer and Dumais, 1997; Sahlgren, 2006; Schütze, 1997). In our setting, dimensionality reduction is virtually necessary, since working with 10K-dimensional vectors is problematic for the Regression approach (see Section 5.2 below), that requires learning matrices and tensors with dimensionalities which are quadratic and cubic in the dimensionality of the input vectors, respectively. We consider two dimensionality reduction methods, the Singular Value Decomposition (SVD) and Non-negative Matrix Factorization (NMF). SVD is the most common technique in distributional semantics, and it was used by Baroni and Zamparelli (2010). NMF is a less commonly adopted method, but it has also been shown to be an effective dimensionality reduction technique for distributional semantics (Dinu and Lapata, 2010). It has a fundamental advantage from our point of view: The Multiply and Kronecker composition approaches (see Section 5.2 below), because of their multiplicative nature, cannot be meaningfully applied to vectors containing negative values. NMF, unlike SVD, produces non-negative vectors, and thus allows a fair comparison of all composition methods in the same reduced space.[1]

We perform the Singular Value Decomposition of the input matrix X: $X = U\Sigma V^T$ and, like Baroni and Zamparelli and many others, pick the first $k = 300$ columns of $U\Sigma$ to obtain reduced representations. Non-negative Matrix Factorization factorizes a $(m \times n)$ non-negative matrix X into two $(m \times k)$ and $(k \times n)$ non-negative matrices: $X \approx WH$ (we normalize the input matrix to $\sum_{i,j} X_{ij} = 1$ before applying NMF). We use the Matlab implementation[2] of the projected gradient algorithm proposed in Lin (2007), which minimizes the squared error of Frobenius norm $F(W, H) = \|X - WH\|_F^2$. We set $k = 300$ and we use W as reduced representation of input matrix X.[3]

5.2 Composition methods

Verb is a baseline measuring the cosine between the verbs in two sentences as a proxy for sentence similarity (e.g., similarity of *mom sings* and *boy dances* is approximated by the cosine of *sing* and *dance*).

We adopt the widely used and generally successful multiplicative and additive models of Mitchell and Lapata (2010) and others. Composition with the **Multiply** and **Add** methods is achieved by, respectively, component-wise multiplying and adding the vectors of the constituents of the sentence we want to represent. Vectors are normalised before addition, as this has consistently shown to improve Add performance in our earlier experiments.

Grefenstette and Sadrzadeh (2011b) proposed a specific implementation of the general DisCoCat approach to compositional distributional semantics (Coecke et al., 2010) that we call **Kronecker** here.

[1] We ran the experiments reported below in full space for those models for which it was possible, finding that Multiply obtained better results there (approaching those of reduced-spaced Regression). This suggests that, although in our preliminary word similarity tests the original 10K-dimensional space and the two reduced spaces produced very similar results, it is still necessary to look for better low-dimensionality approximations of the full space.

[2] Available at `http://www.csie.ntu.edu.tw/~cjlin/nmf/`.

[3] For both SVD and NMF, the latent dimensions are computed using a "core" matrix containing nouns and verbs only, subsequently projecting phrase vectors onto the same space. In this way, the dimensions of the reduced space do not depend on the ad-hoc choice of phrases required by our experiments.

Under this approach, a transitive sentence is a matrix S derived from:

$$S = (\mathbf{v} \otimes \mathbf{v}) \odot (\mathbf{subj} \otimes \mathbf{obj})$$

That is, if nouns and verbs live in a n-dimensional space, a transitive sentence is a $n \times n$ matrix given by the component-wise multiplication of two Kronecker products: that of the verb vector with itself and that of the subject and object vectors. Grefenstette and Sadrzadeh show that this method outperforms other implementations of the same formalism and is the current state of the art on the transitive sentence task of Grefenstette and Sadrzadeh (2011a) we also tackle below. For intransitive sentences, the same approach reduces to component-wise multiplication of verb and subject vectors, that is, to the Multiply method.

Composition of nouns and verbs under the proposed (multi-step) **Regression** model is implemented using Ridge Regression (RR) (Hastie et al., 2009). RR, also known as L_2 regularized regression, is a different approach from the Partial Least Square Regression (PLSR) method that was used in previous related work (Baroni and Zamparelli, 2010; Guevara, 2010) to deal with the multicollinearity problem. When multicollinearity exists, the matrix $X^T X$ (X here is the input matrix after dimensionality reduction) becomes nearly singular and the diagonal elements of $(X^T X)^{-1}$ become quite large, which makes the variance of weights too large. In RR, a positive constant λ is added to the diagonal elements of $X^T X$ to strengthen its non-singularity. Compared with PLSR, RR has a simpler solution for the learned weight matrix $B = (X^T X + \lambda I)^{-1} X^T Y$ and produces competitive results at a faster speed. For each verb matrix or tensor to be learned, we tuned the parameter λ by generalized cross-validation (Golub et al., 1979). The objective function used for tuning minimizes least square error when predicting corpus-observed sentence vectors or intermediate VP matrices (the data sets we evaluate the models on are *not* touched during tuning!). Training examples are found by combining the 8K nouns we have vectors for (see Section 5.1 above) with any verb in the evaluation sets (see Sections 6 and 7 below) into subject-verb-(object) constructions, and extracting the corresponding vectors from the corpus, where attested (vectors are normalised before feeding them to the regression routine). We use only example vectors with at least 10 non-0 dimensions before dimensionality reduction, and we require at least 3 training examples per regression. For the first experiment (intransitives), these (untuned) constraints result in an average of 281 training examples per verb. In the second experiment, in the verb-object matrix estimation phase, we estimate on average 324 distinct matrices per verb, with an average of 15 training examples per matrix. In the verb tensor estimation phase we use all relevant verb-object matrices as training examples.[4]

6 Experiment 1: Predicting similarity judgments on intransitive sentences

We use the test set of Mitchell and Lapata (2008), consisting of 180 pairs of simple sentences made of a subject and an intransitive verb. The stimuli were constructed so as to ensure that there would be pairs where the sentences have high similarity (*the fire glowed* vs. *the fire burned*) and cases where the sentences are dissimilar while having a comparable degree of lexical overlap (*the face glowed* vs. *the face burned*). The sentence pairs were rated for similarity by 49 subjects on a 1-7 scale. Following Mitchell and Lapata, we evaluate each composition method by the Spearman correlation of the cosines of the sentence pair vectors, as predicted by the method, with the individual ratings produced by the subjects for the corresponding sentence pairs.

The results in table 1(a) show that the Regression-based model achieves the best correlation when applied to SVD space, confirming that the approach proposed by Baroni and Zamparelli for adjective-noun constructions can be successfully extended to subject-verb composition. The Regression model also achieves good performance in NMF space, where it is comparable to Multiply. Multiply was found to be the best model by Mitchell and Lapata, and we confirm their results here (recall that Multiply can also be seen as the natural extension of Kronecker to the intransitive setting). The correlations attained by Add and Verb are considerably lower than those of the other methods.

[4] All materials and code used in these experiments that are not already publicly available can be requested to the first author.

(a) Intransitive Sentences

method	ρ
Humans	0.40
Multiply.nmf	0.19
Regression.nmf	0.18
Add.nmf	0.13
Verb.nmf	0.08
Regression.svd	0.23
Add.svd	0.11
Verb.svd	0.06

(b) Transitive Sentences

method	ρ
Humans	0.62
Regression.nmf	0.29
Kronecker.nmf	0.25
Multiply.nmf	0.23
Add.nmf	0.07
Verb.nmf	0.04
Regression.svd	0.32
Add.svd	0.12
Verb.svd	0.08

Table 1: Spearman correlation of composition methods with human similarity intuitions on two sentence similarity data sets (all correlations significantly above chance). Humans is inter-annotator correlation. The multiplication-based Multiply and Kronecker methods are not well-suited for the SVD space (see Section 5.1) and their performance is reported in NMF space only. Kronecker is only defined for the transitive case, Multiply functioning also as its intransitive-case equivalent (see Section 5.2).

7 Experiment 2: Predicting similarity judgments on transitive sentences

We use the test set of Grefenstette and Sadrzadeh (2011a), which was constructed with the same criteria that Mitchell and Lapata applied, but here the sentences have a simple transitive structure. An example of a high-similarity pair is *table shows result* vs. *table expresses result*; whereas *map shows location* vs. *map expresses location* is a low-similarity pair. Grefenstette and Sadrzadeh had 25 subjects rating each sentence. Model evaluation proceeds like in the intransitive case.[5]

As the results in table 1(b) show, the Regression model performs very well again, better than any other methods in NMF space, and with a further improvement when SVD is used, similarly to the first experiment. The Kronecker model is also competitive, confirming the results of Grefenstette and Sadrzadeh's experiments. Neither Add nor Verb achieve very good results, although even for them the correlation with human ratings is significant.

8 General discussion of the results

The results presented here show that our iterative linear regression algorithm outperforms the leading multiplicative method on intransitive sentence similarity when using SVD (and it is on par with it when using NMF), and outperforms both the multiplicative method and the leading Kronecker model in predicting transitive sentence similarity. Additionally, the multiplicative model, while commendable for its extreme simplicity, is of limited general interest, since it cannot take word order into account. We can trivially make this model fail by testing it on transitive sentences with subject and object inverted: For Multiply, *pandas eat bamboo* and *bamboo eats pandas* are identical statements, whereas for humans they are obviously very different.

Confirming what Grefenstette and Sadrzadeh found, we saw that Kronecker performs very well also in our experimental setup (although not as well as Regression). The main advantage of Kronecker over Regression lies in its simplicity: there is no training involved, all it takes is two outer vector products and a component-wise multiplication. However, as pointed out by Grefenstette and Sadrzadeh (2011b), this method is ad hoc compared to the linguistically motivated Categorical method they initially presented in Grefenstette and Sadrzadeh (2011a). It is conceivable that the Kronecker model's good performance is primarily tied to the nature of the evaluation data-set, where only verbs change while subject and object stay the same in sentence pairs.

While our regression-based model's estimation procedure is considerably more involved than for Kronecker, the model has much to recommend it, both from a statistical and from a linguistic point of view. On the statistical side, there are many aspects of the estimation routine that could be tuned on automatically collected training data, thus bringing up the Regression model performance. We could for

[5]Kronecker produces matrix representations of transitive sentences, so technically the similarity measure used for this method is the Frobenius inner product of the normalised matrices, equivalent to unfolding the matrices into vectors and computing cosine similarity.

example harvest a larger number of training phrases (not limiting them to those that contain nouns from the 8K most frequent in the corpus, as we did), or *vice versa* limit training to more frequent phrases, whose vectors are presumably of better quality. Moreover, Ridge Regression is only one of of many estimation techniques that could be tried to come up with better matrix and tensor weights. On the linguistic side, the model is clearly motivated as an instantiation of the vector-space "dual" of classic composition by function application via the tensor contraction operation, as discussed in Section 3 above. Moreover, Regression produces vectors of the same dimensionality for sentences formed with intransitive and transitive verbs, whereas for Kronecker, if the former are n-dimensional vectors, the second are $n \times n$ matrices. Thus, under Kronecker composition, sentences with intransitive and transitive verbs are not directly comparable, which is counter-intuitive (being able to measure the similarity of, say, *kids sing* and *kids sing songs* is both natural and practically useful).

Finally, we remark that in both experiments SVD-reduced vectors lead to Regression models outperforming their NMF counterparts. Regression, unlike the multiplication-based models, is not limited to non-negative vectors, and it can thus harness the benefits of SVD reduction (although of course it is precisely because of the large regression problems we must solve that we need to perform dimensionality reduction at all!).

9 Conclusion

The main advances introduced in this paper are as follows. First, we discussed a tensor-based compositional distributional semantic framework in the vein of that of Coecke et al. (2010) which has the compositional mechanism of Baroni and Zamparelli (2010) as a specific case, thereby uniting both lines of research in a common framework. Second, we presented a generalisation of Baroni and Zamparelli's matrix learning method to higher rank tensors, allowing us to induce the semantic representation of functions modelled in this framework. Finally, we evaluated this new semantic tensor learning model against existing benchmark data-sets provided by Mitchell and Lapata (2008) and Grefenstette and Sadrzadeh (2011a), and showed it to outperform other models. We furthermore claim that the generality of our extended regression method allows it to capture more information than the multiplicative and Kronecker models, and will allow us to canonically model more complex and subtle relations where argument order and semantic roles matter more, such as quantification, logical operations, and ditransitive verbs.

Among the plans for future work, we intend to improve regression-based tensor estimation, focusing in particular on automated ways to choose informative training examples. On the evaluation side, we want to construct a larger test set to directly compare sentences with different argument counts (e.g., transitive vs. intransitive constructions) and word orders (e.g., sentences with subject and object inverted), as well as extending modeling and evaluation to other syntactic structures and types of function application (including the challenging cases we listed in the previous paragraph). We want moreover to test the Regression model against the Categorical model of Grefenstette and Sadrzadeh (2011a) and to design evaluation scenarios allowing a direct comparison with the MV-RNN model of Socher et al. (2012).

Acknowledgments

Edward Grefenstette is supported by EPSRC Project *A Unified Model of Compositional and Distributional Semantics: Theory and Applications* (EP/I03808X/1). Georgiana Dinu and Marco Baroni are partially supported by the ERC 2011 Starting Independent Research Grant to the COMPOSES project (n. 283554). Mehrnoosh Sadrzadeh is supported by an EPSRC Career Acceleration Fellowship (EP/J002607/1).

References

Baroni, M. and R. Zamparelli (2010). Nouns are vectors, adjectives are matrices: Representing adjective-noun constructions in semantic space. In *Proceedings of EMNLP*, Boston, MA, pp. 1183–1193.

Bourbaki, N. (1989). *Commutative Algebra: Chapters 1-7.* Springer-Verlag (Berlin and New York).

Bullinaria, J. and J. Levy (2012). Extracting semantic representations from word co-occurrence statistics: Stop-lists, stemming and SVD. *Behavior Research Methods 44*, 890–907.

Coecke, B., M. Sadrzadeh, and S. Clark (2010). Mathematical foundations for a compositional distributional model of meaning. *Linguistic Analysis 36*, 345–384.

Dinu, G. and M. Lapata (2010). Measuring distributional similarity in context. In *Proceedings of EMNLP*, Cambridge, MA, pp. 1162–1172.

Dumais, S. (2003). Data-driven approaches to information access. *Cognitive Science 27*, 491–524.

Erk, K. and S. Padó (2008). A structured vector space model for word meaning in context. In *Proceedings of EMNLP*, Honolulu, HI, USA, pp. 897–906.

Firth, J. (1957). *Papers in linguistics, 1934-1951.* Oxford University Press.

Frege, G. (1892). Über Sinn und Bedeutung. *Zeitschrift fuer Philosophie un philosophische Kritik 100*, 25–50.

Golub, G., M. Heath, and G. Wahba (1979). Generalized cross-validation as a method for choosing a good Ridge parameter. *Technometrics 21*, 215–223.

Grefenstette, E. and M. Sadrzadeh (2011a). Experimental support for a categorical compositional distributional model of meaning. In *Proceedings of EMNLP*, Edinburgh, UK, pp. 1394–1404.

Grefenstette, E. and M. Sadrzadeh (2011b). Experimenting with transitive verbs in a DisCoCat. In *Proceedings of GEMS*, Edinburgh, UK, pp. 62–66.

Grefenstette, E., M. Sadrzadeh, S. Clark, B. Coecke, and S. Pulman (2011). Concrete sentence spaces for compositional distributional models of meaning. In *Proceedings of IWCS*, pp. 125–134.

Grefenstette, G. (1994). *Explorations in Automatic Thesaurus Discovery.* Boston, MA: Kluwer.

Guevara, E. (2010). A regression model of adjective-noun compositionality in distributional semantics. In *Proceedings of the ACL GEMS Workshop*, Uppsala, Sweden, pp. 33–37.

Hastie, T., R. Tibshirani, and J. Friedman (2009). *The Elements of Statistical Learning, 2nd ed.* New York: Springer.

Landauer, T. and S. Dumais (1997). A solution to Plato's problem: The latent semantic analysis theory of acquisition, induction, and representation of knowledge. *Psychological Review 104*(2), 211–240.

Lee, J. (1997). *Riemannian manifolds: An introduction to curvature*, Volume 176. Springer Verlag.

Lin, C.-J. (2007). Projected gradient methods for nonnegative matrix factorization. *Neural Computation 19*(10), 2756–2779.

Mitchell, J. and M. Lapata (2008). Vector-based models of semantic composition. In *Proceedings of ACL*, Columbus, OH, pp. 236–244.

Mitchell, J. and M. Lapata (2010). Composition in distributional models of semantics. *Cognitive Science 34*(8), 1388–1429.

Montague, R. (1970). English as a formal language. *Linguaggi nella società e nella tecnica*, 189–224.

Partee, B. (2004). *Compositionality in Formal Semantics.* Malden, MA: Blackwell.

Sahlgren, M. (2006). *The Word-Space Model.* Dissertation, Stockholm University.

Schütze, H. (1997). *Ambiguity Resolution in Natural Language Learning.* Stanford, CA: CSLI.

Socher, R., B. Huval, C. Manning, and A. Ng (2012). Semantic compositionality through recursive matrix-vector spaces. In *Proceedings of EMNLP*, Jeju Island, Korea, pp. 1201–1211.

Thater, S., H. Fürstenau, and M. Pinkal (2011). Word meaning in context: A simple and effective vector model. In *Proceedings of IJCNLP*, Chiang Mai, Thailand, pp. 1134–1143.

Wittgenstein, L. (1953). *Philosophical Investigations.* Oxford: Blackwell. Translated by G.E.M. Anscombe.

Domain Adaptable Semantic Clustering in Statistical NLG

Blake Howald, Ravikumar Kondadadi and Frank Schilder
Thomson Reuters, Research & Development
610 Opperman Drive, Eagan, MN 55123
firstname.lastname@thomsonreuters.com

Abstract

We present a hybrid natural language generation system that utilizes Discourse Representation Structures (DRSs) for statistically learning syntactic templates from a given domain of discourse in sentence "micro" planning. In particular, given a training corpus of target texts, we extract semantic predicates and domain general tags from each sentence and then organize the sentences using supervised clustering to represent the "conceptual meaning" of the corpus. The sentences, additionally tagged with domain specific information (determined separately), are reduced to templates. We use a SVM ranking model trained on a subset of the corpus to determine the optimal template during generation. The combination of the conceptual unit, a set of ranked syntactic templates, and a given set of information, constrains output selection and yields acceptable texts. Our system is evaluated with automatic, non–expert crowdsourced and expert evaluation metrics and, for generated *weather, financial* and *biography* texts, falls within acceptable ranges. Consequently, we argue that our DRS driven statistical and template–based method is robust and domain adaptable as, while content will be dictated by a target domain of discourse, significant investments in sentence planning can be minimized without sacrificing performance.

1 Introduction

In this paper, we propose a sentence (or "micro") planning system that can quickly adapt to new domains provided a corpus of sentences from the target domain is supplied. First, all sentences from the corpus are parsed and a semantic representation is generated. We used predicate and domain general named entities from Discourse Representation Structures (DRSs) derived by *Boxer*, a robust analysis tool that creates DRSs from text (Bos (2008)). Second, the sentences are automatically clustered by their conceptual meaning with a *k*-means clustering algorithm and then manually reviewed for consistency and purity. Third, named entity and domain specific content tagging creates banks of templates (syntactic representations) associated with the respective cluster (a "conceptual unit"). Finally, a ranking algorithm is used to train a ranker that determines the optimal template at a given point in the generated discourse given various features based on the conceptual units and the text derived so far.

Our system generates sentences from templates given a semantic representation as part of a larger Natural Language Generation ("NLG") system for three domains: *financial, biography* and *weather* (from the SUMTIME-METEO corpus (Reiter et al. (2005))). NLG is traditionally seen as a multistage process whereby decisions are made on the type of text to be generated (communicative goal); entities, events and relationships that express the content of that text; and forging grammatical constructions with the content into a "natural" sounding text. These stages are articulated in a variety of architectures - for example, Bateman and Zock summarize NLG as follows: (1) Macro Planning creating a document plan; (2) Micro Planning sentence planning; (3) Surface Realization concatenating the information from (1-2) into coherent and grammatical text; and (4) Physical Presentation document layout considerations (formatting, titles, etc.) (Bateman and Zock (2003)). Each one of these stages can have several subtasks and vary considerably in terms of complexity (*see generally,* McKeown (1985); Hovy (1993); Reiter and Dale (2000)). However, in general, some abstract representation is developed in (1-2) and (3-4) deal with translating the abstraction to natural language largely through either rule–based or statistical approaches.

Significant human investments often need to be made to create systems from scratch. But while these systems may perform very well for a specific domain, extending to alternative domains may require starting over. Statistical approaches can streamline some human investment, but domain adaptability remains a concern. Finding the appropriate balance between investing in input and achieving an appropriate level of evaluated acceptance of the output, let alone whether or not the approach is adaptable, can be problematic. More abstracted representations may require more rules to process and generate acceptable texts while less abstract representations may require less rules but more investment in human resources. When evaluated, we find that our system produces texts that fall within acceptable ranges for automatic metrics (BLEU and METEOR), non-expert crowdsourced evaluations via CrowdFlower and expert evaluations of the *biography* domain (based on similar evaluation comparisons for other NLG systems).

Basile and Bos suggest that DRSs provide an appropriate form of abstraction for NLG tasks (Basile and Bos (2011)). The reason being that DRSs provide deep semantic content in the form of named entities, relationships between entities, identity relations and logical implications (e.g. negation, scope) all of which have a straight forward mapping to syntactic parses (e.g., within Combinatorial Categorial Grammar) and, in sum, provide a useable architecture to perform a myriad of NLG tasks. We adopt Discourse Representation Theory (Kamp and Reyle (1993)) as a starting point for our experiments for domain adaptable NLG. And while we only use a few features of the DRS in the current work, we anticipate that the logical representations in DRT can be useful for future work, as in improving the clustering of conceptual units in the training corpus, for example.

The main contributions of this paper are:

- A hybrid approach to sentence planning that combines a statistical system with a template-based system where templates are generated semi-automatically with minimal human review
- Domain adaptability is shown in three different domains (*financial, biography* and *weather*).
- Non-expert human evaluation is carried out by means of crowdsourcing. The evaluation provides scores for overall fluency of the generated text as well as sentence-level preferences between generated and original texts. These evaluations are supplemented by expert evaluations for the *biography* domain.

This article is structured as follows. Section 2 describes existing rule-based and statistical NLG approaches and domain adaptability. Section 3 explains our methodology; including DRSs and their use in clustering the three corpora and how the generated clusters are ranked and deployed in the generation of texts. Section 4 presents sample generated texts and the results of automatic and crowdsourced evaluations. Section 5 concludes with limitations and avenues of future research.

2 NLG: Templates, Rules and Statistics

This section discusses current approaches to NLG. We argue that a combination of a statistical approach and templates has an advantage over purely rule-based or statistical NLG systems.

Overall, NLG systems tend to be rule–based where some type of text is sought to be generated and different stores of data are manipulated to generate texts. The rules exist at all levels of the system from selecting content, to choosing a grammatical output to post-processing constraints (e.g. sentence aggregation and pronoun generation). For example, the SUMTIME-METEO project (Reiter et al. (2005)) generates weather forecasts from numerical data. First, the numerical data is analyzed, then decisions are made about what content to convey based on the analysis and how to grammatically represent the content at the document and sentence level. These decisions are implemented by hand crafted rules with input from multiple experts. Hence, rule–based systems come with a potentially high development cost due to the necessity of domain experts and system developers creating the rules.[1]

[1]Anja Belz references a personal communication with Ehud Reiter and Somayajulu Sripada where 12 person months where spent on the SUMTIME-METEO microplanner and realizer alone (Belz (2007)).

Statistical NLG systems, on the other hand, look to bypass or minimize extensive construction of rules by using corpus data to "learn" rules for one or more components of an NLG system (Langkilde and Knight (1998)). Alternative generations are then created from the rules and a decision model governs which alternative to choose at a given point in a generated discourse. For example, the *p*CRU system, which also generates weather texts from numerical data, starts with a small number of relations that are trained on a corpus (Belz (2007)). Other statistical systems such as the SPaRKy (Stent et al. (2004)) for generating restaurant recommendations uses a ranking algorithm for training rules for sentence generation. Statistical systems have less of a reliance on human input, but they require robust training data and it is harder to control the output – often leading to texts that are shorter, less natural and possible ungrammatical (but *see e.g.*, van Deemter et al. (2005)).

Our system relys on both statistical and template–based approaches. We first statistically learn the semantic structure of a given domain of discourse which is then used to produce templates for our system (combining the Micro Planning and Surface Realization stages). Next, to pick the best template, we train a ranker which ranks the different sentence templates (the SPaRKy system that also employs a ranking algorithm, but it ranks different *rules* rather than the *sentences*). This combination avoids pitfalls stemming from a statistical model generating the input for a realizer (also avoiding the need for an extensive grammar) and, in contrast to some systems which rely only in part on statistical learning (e.g., for template selection but not for generating underlying semantic structures (Galley et al. (2001))), we find that our approach is not only efficient in terms of processing and generating data, but also highly adaptable to different domains with minimized human involvement.

3 Methodology

In order to generate the different templates, it is necessary to rely on some formalism to capture the semantics of a given training corpus. Reducing the training corpus to semantic expressions works to ensure that use of human experts would be minimized and flexibility in domain adaptability could be preserved while not compromising the quality of the generated texts. To this end, we utilized *Boxer* which relies on a combination of CCG parsing, part–of–speech tagging and a store of lexical semantic representations from the CCGbank (Hockenmaier and Steedman (2005)) to create the structures. Each DRS is a combination of domain general named entities (DATE, PERSON, etc.) and predicates (typically content words, but also shallow semantic categories such as AGENT and EVENT) which are related by different relational elements (typically function words) (*in, by*). For our system, we extract only those words and categories marked as predicates and the domain general entity tags. To illustrate, consider (1):

(1) a. The consensus recommendation for the financial services peergroup is a buy.
b. T. Rowe Price led the group last quarter with a 3.6% average per share price increase.
c. The increase is projected to level off during the current quarter.

The predicate and domain general entity information created by *Boxer* for (1) is as follows:

(2) a. CONSENSUS | RECOMMENDATION | EVENT | SERVICE | PEERGROUP | BUY | ...
b. COMPANY | LEAD | DATE | SHARE | EVENT | AVERAGE | INCREASE | ...
c. INCREASE | EVENT | PROJECT | OFF | DATE | ...

The DRS-based predicates and domain general entities in (2) provide a lexical semantic representation of the sentence which captures the conceptual meaning of the sentence. Our assumption is that each grouping of DRS-based predicates represents the semantic "concept" of the sentence. The highly abstracted representation that does not utilize, for example, the relational information between the predicates, is a good starting point for grouping sentences and creating clusters (via *k*-means, discussed below in Section 3.1) by semantic concept. In viewing each sentence in a training corpus as such (indicated with an identifier ("*CuId*")), and a document as a sequence of "conceptual units" associated with templates and a store of predetermined information (domain specific tagging), we can categorize sentences by concept and create an organized bank of syntactic representations. For example, consider (3) (assuming, for the sake of presentation, that each utterance in (1) conveys a separate conceptual units):

(3) a. $\{CuId : 001\}$
Information: **industry**: financial services peergroup; **recommendation**: buy
b. $\{CuId : 002\}$
Information: **company**: T.Rowe Price; **time**: last quarter; **value**: 3.6%;
industry: the group; **financial**: average per share price; **movement**: increase
c. $\{CuId : 003\}$
Information: **movement**: increase, level off; **time**: the current quarter

The associated template representation (assigned to sentence in (1)) would be as follows:

(4) a. $\{CuId : 001\}$: The consensus recommendation for the **[industry]** is a **[recommendation]**.
b. $\{CuId : 002\}$: **[company]** led **[industry]** **[time]** with a **[value]** **[financial]** **[movement]**.
c. $\{CuId : 003\}$: The **[movement]** is projected to **[movement]** during **[time]**.

For domain adaptability in NLG, the key is to find a method that allows for the extraction of the appropriate level of semantics to be useable for generation across different corpora. The level of semantics can be relatively course or fine grained, weighed against a number of relevant factors (e.g., the communicative goal and the selection of content). The selection of content for our system is relatively fixed and is based on domain specific (not discussed here) and general tagging (e.g., COMPANY, DATE, PERSON from *Boxer* or other open source tools). Domain specific tags were not considered in the extraction of predicates from our training corpora. The following example from the *biography* domain illustrates the types of semantic content extracted for purposes of clustering the semantics of different training corpora.

(5) *Training Sentence*
a. Mr. Mitsutaka Kambe has been serving as Managing Director of the 77 Bank, Ltd. since June 27, 2008.
b. Earlier in his career, he was Director of Market Sales, Director of Fund Securities and Manager of Tokyo Branch in the Bank.
c. He holds a Bachelor's in finance from USC and a MBA from UCLA.

Conceptual Meaning
d. SERVING | MANAGING | DIRECTOR | PERSON | COMPANY | DATE | ...
e. EARLY | CAREER | DIRECTOR | MARKET | SALES | MANAGER | ...
f. HOLDS | BACHELOR | FINANCE | MBA | HOLD | EVENT | ...

Content Mapping
g. $\{CuId : 004\}$
Information: **person**: Mr. Mitsutaka Kambe; **title**: Managing Director;
company: 77 Bank, Ltd.; **date**: June 27, 2008
h. $\{CuId : 005\}$
Information: **person**: he; **title**: Director of Market Sales, Director of Fund Securities, Manager; **organization**: Tokyo Branch; **company**: the Bank
i. $\{CuId : 006\}$
Information: **person**: he; **degree**: Bachelor's, MBA; **subject**: finance; **institution**: USC; UCLA

Templates
j. $\{CuId : 004\}$: **[person]** has been serving as **[title]** of the **[company]** since **[date]**.
k. $\{CuId : 005\}$: Earlier in his career, **[person]** was **[title]**, **[title]** and **[title]** of **[organization]** in **[company]**.
l. $\{CuId : 006\}$: **[person]** holds a **[degree]** in **[subject]** from **[institution]** and a **[degree]** from **[institution]**.

As shown in (4-5), predicate and domain general information from *Boxer* captures significant variability in the different domains of discourse which becomes less problematic with our approach than compared with, for example, rule–based sentence planning. This is with the proviso that a sufficiently sized and variable training corpus is available. Example generations for each domain are included in (6).

(6) *Financial*

a. First quarter profit per share for Brown-Forman Corporation expected to be $0.91 per share by analysts.
b. Brown-Forman Corporation July first quarter profits will be below that previously estimated by Wall Street with a range between $0.89 and $0.93 per share and a projected mean per share of $0.91 per share.
c. The consensus recommendation is Hold.
d. The recommendations made by ten analysts evaluating the company include one Strong Buy, one Buy, six Hold and two Underperform.
e. The average consensus recommendation for the Distillers peer group is a Hold.

Biography

f. Mr. Satomi Mitsuzaki has been serving as Managing Director of Mizuho Bank since June 27, 2008.
g. He was previously Director of Regional Compliance of Kyoto Branch.
h. He is a former Managing Executive Officer and Chief Executive Officer of new Industrial Finance Business Group in Mitsubishi Corporation.

Weather

i. Complex low from southern Norway will drift slowly nne to the Lofoten Islands by early tomorrow.
j. A ridge will persist to the west of British Isles for Saturday with a series of weak fronts moving east across the North Sea.
k. A front will move ene across the northern North Sea Saturday.

Because of the nature of our statistical plus template–based approach, it was not necessary to utilize all that *Boxer* has to offer. We only used predicates, which, for all intense and purposes, could be captured with content words, and domain general entity tagging. However, there are several additional aspects of *Boxer* which may prove useful such as exploiting the relation information, rhetorical relations and drawing further inferences based on the logical structure of the DRS are left to future work.

In sum, for our system, given some training sentence clustered on relatively simple semantics, coupled with domain specific tagging, templates can easily be generated and organized in a logical manner. With a large enough training corpus, there would be multiple templates (cf. Table 1) within each *CuId* and the one selected for generation would be statistically learned. The next section provides more detail about the data and clustering of semantic information in the creation of conceptual units and template banks from which the selection model generates text.

3.1 Data and Clustering

As indicated in Table 1, the *financial* domain includes 1067 machine generated texts from a commercially available NLG system covering mutual fund performance reports (n=162) and broker recommendations (n=905) from a commercially available NLG system, ranging from 1 to 21 segments (period ended sentences). The *biography* domain includes 1150 human generated texts focused on corporate office biographies, ranging from 3-17 segments. The *weather* domain includes 1045 human generated weather reports for offshore oil rigs from the SumTime-Meteo corpus (Reiter et al. (2005)).

For each domain, the corpus was processed with *Boxer* and those items identified as predicates and named entity tags by the system were extracted. Each sentence then, represented as string of predicates and domain general tags, was clustered using *k*–means (in the WEKA toolkit (Witten and Frank (2005))) with *k* set to 50 for the *financial* domain and 100 for the *biography* and *weather* domains. The resulting clusters were manually checked to determine consistency - i.e., that all strings of predicates and

Table 1: Data and Semantic Cluster Distribution.

	Financial	*Biography*	*Weather*
Texts	1067	1150	1045
Conceptual Units	38	19	9
Templates	1379	2836	2749
Average Template/CU (Range)	36 (6–230)	236 (7–666)	305 (6–800)

tags assigned to a cluster conveyed the same or similar concept.[2] Clusters can be thought of as groups of most common words, for example the "recommend" cluster in the *financial* domain included RECOMMEND, CONSENSUS, COMPANY, the "current position" cluster in the *biography* domain included PERSON, POSITION, COMPANY, JOIN, DATE, and the "ridge" cluster in the *weather* domain included RIDGE, PRESSURE, DIRECTION.

The *biography* and *weather* domains, despite being human generated, are semantically less interesting (19 and 9 conceptual units respectively) but exhibit significantly more variability – 236 and 305 average number of templates per conceptual unit as compared to 36 for the *financial* domain (which is machine generated). The end result of the semantic preprocessing (along with domain specific entity tagging) is a training corpus reduced to templates (cf. 4,5j-l) organized by semantic concept. We use a ranking model to select a template corresponding to a semantic concept.

3.2 Ranking Model

For each conceptual unit, we rank all the matching templates and select the best ranked template. In order to train a ranking model, we do a 70/30 split of the data for training and testing. We represent each training document as a series of conceptual units along with the input information. For each conceptual unit, we first filter out all the non-matching templates by entity type and number - selecting only those templates that match the type of domain specific tagging present in the data and also have the same number of entities for each entity type. We rank the remaining templates based on the Levenshtein (Levenshtein (1966)) edit distance from the gold template (Template extracted from the original sentence in the training document). Additionally, several features are extracted for the top 20 ranked templates (to ease processing time) and are used in building the model: (1) N-grams: Word n-grams extracted from the template. We used 1-3 grams; and (2) Length: Normalized length of the input template. We used a ranking support vector machine (Joachims (2002)) with a linear kernel to train a model and each feature in the model will have an associated weight.

During testing, the system is presented with a sequence of conceptual units and the input data associated with each conceptual unit. All the templates associated with the conceptual units are extracted from the template bank and are filtered according to the filtering criteria used in the training phase. For each of the remaining templates, the model weights are applied to compute a score and the highest scored template is selected for generation. This embodiment constitutes the *system* generations. For the purpose of evaluation, we compared the *system* generations against the *original* texts and texts created without the ranking model - where any template associated with a conceptual unit is selected at random (rather than based on score) after applying the filter (*random* generations). The next section discusses the generated texts and a series of automatic and human (non-expert crowdsourced and expert) evaluations of the texts.

[2]To this end, we initialized k to an arbitrarily large value to facilitate collapsing of similar clusters during manual verification. We assume this to be an easier task than reassigning individual sentences from existing clusters. As indicated in Table 1, this proved useful as the most semantically varied domain turned out to be the *financial* domain with 38 clusters (each cluster corresponds to a different conceptual unit).

4 Experimental Results

Table 2 provides generation comparisons for the system (*_Sys*), random (*_Rand*) and the original (*_Orig*) text from each domain. The variability of the generated texts ranges from a close similarity to the original text to slightly shorter, which, as mentioned in Section 2, is not an uncommon (Belz and Reiter (2006)), but not necessarily detrimental, observation for NLG systems (van Deemter et al. (2005)). The generated sentences can be equally informative and semantically similar to the original texts (e.g., the *financial* sentences in Table 2). The generated sentences can also be less informative, but semantically similar to the original texts (e.g., leaving out "manager" in *Bio_Sys*). However, there can be a fair amount of gradient semantic variation (e.g., moving northeast *to* a location vs. moving northeast *across* a location in *Weather_Sys* and "Director of Sales Planning" vs. "Director of Sales" in *Bio_Rand*).

Table 2: Example Texts.

System	Text
Fin_Orig	Funds in Small-Cap Growth category increase for week.
Fin_Sys	Small-Cap Growth funds increase for week.
Fin_Rand	Small-Cap Growth category funds increase for week.
Weather_Orig	Another weak cold front will move ne to Cornwall by later Friday.
Weather_Sys	Another weak cold front will move ne to Cornwall during Friday.
Weather_Rand	Another weak cold front from ne through the Cornwall will remain slow moving.
Bio_Orig	He previously served as Director of Sales Planning and Manager of Loan Center.
Bio_Sys	He previously served as Director of Sales in Loan Center of the Company.
Bio_Rand	He previously served as Director of Sales of the Company.

Some semantic differences are introduced in our system despite generating grammatical sentences. For example, "remain slow moving" (*Weather_Rand*) is not indicated in the original text. These types of differences are more common for *random* rather than *system* generations. However, the ultimate impact of these and other changes is best understood through a comparative evaluation of the texts with automatic and human evaluations.

4.1 Evaluations and Discussion

We evaluate our NLG system with automatic and human metrics and the correlations between them. The human evaluations can (and, in some circumstances, must be) performed by both non-experts and experts. We provide non-expert crowdsourced evaluations to determine grammatical, informative and semantic appropriateness and the same evaluations by several experts in biography generation.

The automatic metrics used here are BLEU–4 (Papineni et al. (2002)) and METEOR (v.1.3) (Denkowski and Lavie (2011)) and originate from machine translation research. BLEU–4 measures the degree of 4-gram overlap between documents. METEOR uses a unigram weighted *f*–score less a penalty based on chunking dissimilarity. We also calculated an error rate as an exact match between strings of a document. Table 3 provides the automatic evaluations of *financial, biography* and *weather* domains for both *random* and *system* for all of the testing documents in each domain (*financial* (367); *weather* (209); *biography* (350)).[3]

For each domain, the general trend is that *random* exhibits a higher error rate and lower BLEU–4 and METEOR scores as compared to *system*. This suggests that the *system* is more informative than the *random* text. However, scores for the *financial* domain exhibit a smaller difference compared to *weather* and *biography*. Further, the BLEU–4 and METEOR scores are very similar. This is arguably related to the fact that the average number of templates is significantly lower for the *financial* disourses than the *weather* and *biography* domains. That is to say, there is a greater chance of the *random* system selecting

[3]If comparing originals, the Error Rate would equal 0 and BLEU–4 and METEOR would equal 1.

Table 3: Automatic Metric Evaluations of *Biography*, *Financial* and *Weather Domains*.

Metric	*Bio_Rand*	*Bio_Sys*	*Fin_Rand*	*Fin_Sys*	*Weather_Rand*	*Weather_Sys*
Error Rate	0.815	0.350	0.571	0.477	0.996	0.698
BLEU–4	0.174	0.750	0.524	0.577	0.057	0.469
METEOR	0.198	0.520	0.409	0.386	0.256	0.436

the same template as *system*. So, from an automatic metric standpoint, applying model weights increases "performance" of the generation (based on coarse content overlap). However, human evaluations of the texts are necessary to confirm and augment what the automatic metrics indicate.

Two sets of crowdsourced human evaluation tasks (run on CrowdFlower) were constructed to compare against automatic metrics: (1) an understandability evaluation of the entire text on a three-point scale: **Fluent** = no grammatical or informative barriers; **Understandable** = some grammatical or informative barriers; **Disfluent** = significant grammatical or informative barriers; and (2) a sentence–level preference between sentence pairs (e.g., "Do you prefer Sentence A (from *original*) or the corresponding Sentence B (from *random/system*)"). 100 different texts and sentence pairs for *system*, *random* and the *original* texts from each domain were selected at random. Figure 1 presents the text understanding task and Figure 2 presents the sentence preference task (The aggregate percentage agreement for the text–understandability is .682 and .841 for the sentence–preference tasks based on four judgments per text and sentence pair).[4]

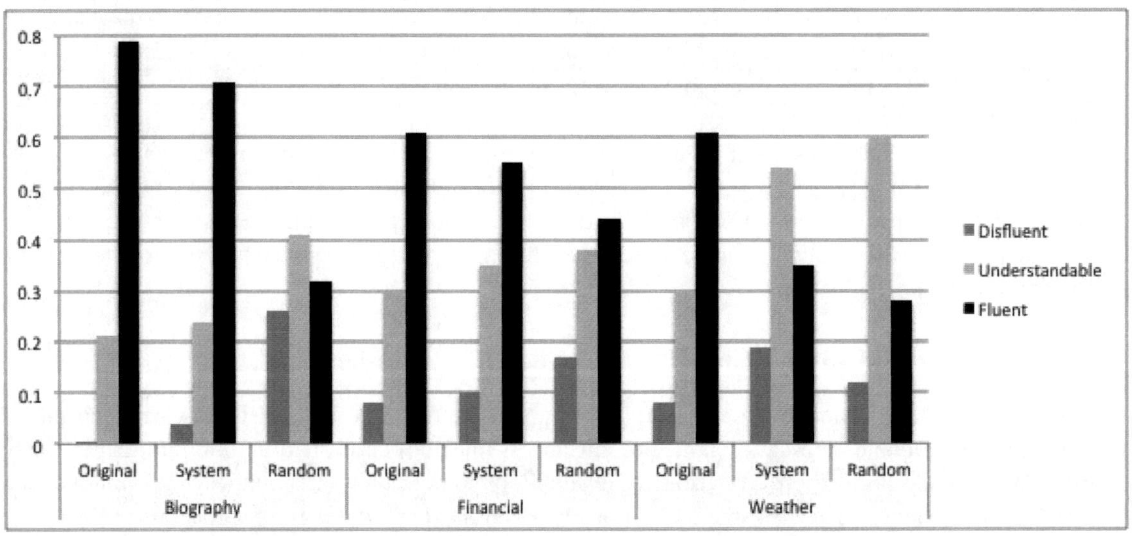

Figure 1: Human Text–Understandability Evaluations.

In all cases, the *original* texts in each domain demonstrate the highest comparative **fluency** and the lowest comparative **disfluency**. Further, the *system* texts demonstrate the highest **fluency** and the lowest **disfluency** compared to the *random* texts. However, the difference between the *system* and *random* for the *financial* and *weather* domains are fairly close whereas the differences for the *biography* domain is much greater. This makes sense as the *biography* domain is human generated and exhibits a high amount of variability. Given that the *weather* domain is also human generated and exhibits more variability compared to the *financial* domain, but they read more like the *financial* domain because of their narrow geographic and subject matter vernacular.

[4]Over 100 native English speakers contributed, each one restricted to providing no more than 50 responses and only after they sucessfully answered 4 "gold data" questions correctly. We also omitted those evaluators with a disproportionately high response rate. No other data was collected on the contributors (although geographic data (country, region, city) and ip addresses were available). Radio buttons were separated from the text to prevent click bias.

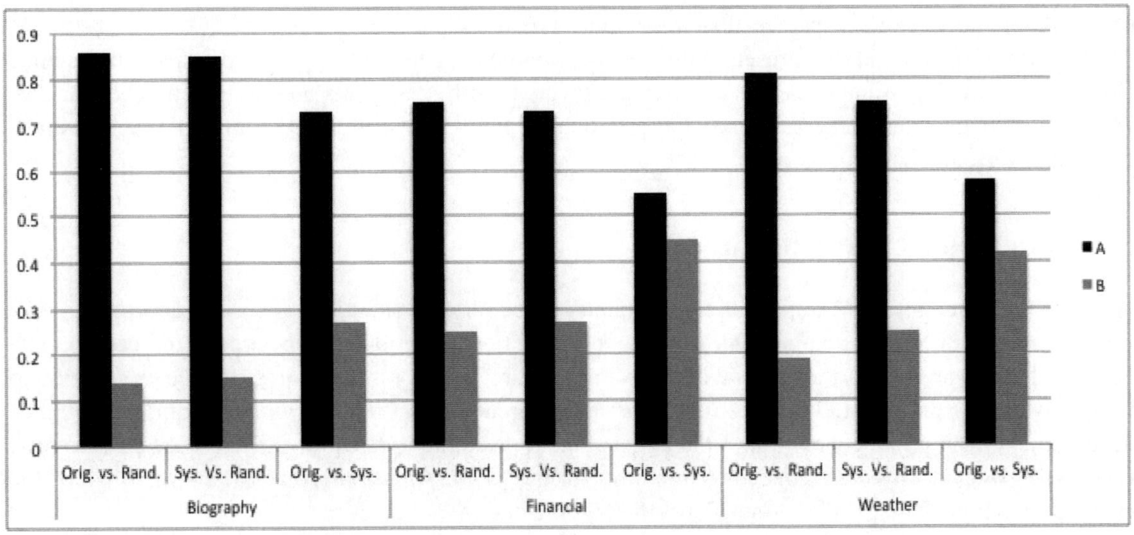

Figure 2: Human Sentence–Preference Evaluations.

Similar trends are demonstrated in the sentence preferences (Figure 2). In all cases, the *original* and *system* sentences are preferred to *random*. The *original* sentences are also preferred to *system* sentences, but the difference is very close for the *financial* and *weather* domains. This indicates that, at the sentence level, our *system* is performing similar to the *original* texts.

As indicated in Table 4, Pearson Correlation, based on 300 documents (100 from each domain), between the automatic metrics are high with the appropriate direction (e.g., error rate correlates negatively with BLEU–4 and METEOR scores, which correlate positively with each other). The human ratings - a consolidated score (**Fluent** = 1, **Understandable** = .66, **Disfluent** = .33) averaged over four raters per document - behave similar to the BLEU–4 and METEOR automatic metrics, but much less stong. There is more variability captured in the human judgments as compared to the automatic metrics which are both stricter and more consistent.

Table 4: Human–Automatic Pearson Correlation ($p \leq .0001$)).

	Error Rate	BLEU–4	METEOR	**Human**
Error Rate	1	-.719	-.715	-.406
BLEU–4		1	.827	.520
METEOR			1	.490
Human				1

Extreme cases aside, there is no exact formula for translating automatic and human evaluations to a true estimation for how the generated texts are performing. It is a relative determination at best and, in all actuality, deference is paid to the human evaluations. Human understandability of the texts is key.

We were able to perform expert evaluation of the *biography* domain. Three experts journalists, who write short biographies for news archives, performed the same two non–expert crowdsourced tasks. For the text evaluation, the experts rated both the *original* and *system* texts to be 100% **Fluent** (with the *random* texts following a similar distribution of non-expert ratings). For the sentence evaluations, the experts still preferred the *original* to the *system* sentences, but with an increase in preference for the *system* as compared to the non-experts - 27% preference by non-experts versus a 35% preference by experts. This trend is a reverse of what is reported for weather texts. For example, Belz and Reiter report a reduction in acceptability with experts as compared to non-experts (Belz and Reiter (2006)). This makes sense as the expert should be more discriminant based on experience. For the present texts, it could be the case that our system is capturing nuances of biography writing that experts are sensitive to. However, more critical expert feedback is required before saying more.

The performances that we present here are comparable to other rule–based and statistical systems. However, comparing systems can be problematic given the different goals and architectures. Nonetheless, the evaluations and generated texts indicate that we have been able to appropriately capture interesting and varied semantic structures.

5 Conclusions and Limitations

We have presented a hybrid statistical and template–based NLG system that generates acceptable texts for a number of different domains. Our experiments with both experts and non–experts indicate that the generated text is as good as the original text. From a resource standpoint, it is an attractive proposition to have a method to create NLG texts for a number of different subject matters with a minimal amount of development. The initial generation of the conceptual units and templates for the *financial* domain took two person weeks. This was reduced to two days for the *weather* and *biography* domains. Most of the development time was spent on domain specific tagging and model creation.

As compared to other NLG systems, there are several limitations to what we have presented here. First of all, our system assumes the document plan is given as an input; but this is not always necessarily true. In addition to the document plan, we also use domain specific tags from the original text. For example, we use phrases like *last quarter* as our input whereas a typical NLG system receives pure data like an exact date indicating the end of the quarter. It is the NLG system's responsibility to generate the corresponding referring expression appropriate for the current context. We are currently working on an extension of our framework that includes document planning and referring expression generation. This will also enable us to compare our system with existing state-of-the-art statistical NLG systems such as *p*CRU. We have not done expert evaluation for the *financial* and *weather* domains. While non-experts can provide useable judgments on the well–formedness of generated texts, evaluating the finer grained semantics of the text falls with the expert and will be included in future development. Finally, our system will only work with domains that have significant historical data. If only limited data is available, our system potentially cannot capture the variety of linguistic expressions used to express a semantic concept and will thus fail to avoid redundancy across texts.

Future work will focus on additional domains, and the integration of more discourse–level features into the model. Also, as we have only focused on a small part of what DRSs contain, deepening the semantics with the inclusion of relational elements may improve generation as well. We are in particular interested in utilizing the semantic representation for an improved clustering of conceptual units. As indicated in this article, attention to semantic structures is central to NLG and captures a large portion of the theoretical construction of such systems.

Acknowledgments

This research is made possible by Thomson Reuters Global Resources with particular thanks to Peter Pircher, David Rosenblatt and Jaclyn Sprtel for significant support. Thank you also to Khalid Al-Kofahi for encouragment and to Ben Hachey and three anonymous reviewers for critical feedback.

References

Basile, V. and J. Bos (2011). Towards generating text from discourse representation structures. In *Proceedings of the 13th European Workshop on Natural Language Generation (ENLG)*, pp. 145–150.

Bateman, J. and M. Zock (2003). Natural language generation. In R. Mitkov (Ed.), *Oxford Handbook of Computational Linguistics*, Research in Computational Semantics, pp. 284–304. Oxford University Press, Oxford.

Belz, A. (2007). Probabilistic generation of weather forecast texts. In *Proceedings of Human Language Technologies 2007: The Annual Conference of the North American Chapter of the Association for Computational Linguistics (NAACL-HLT'07)*, pp. 164–171.

Belz, A. and E. Reiter (2006). Comparing automatic and human evaluation of NLG systems. In *Proceedings of the European Association for Computational Linguistics (EACL'06)*, pp. 313–320.

Bos, J. (2008). Wide-coverage semantic analysis with *Boxer*. In J. Bos and R. Delmonte (Eds.), *Semantics in Text Processing. STEP 2008 Conference Proceedings*, Volume 1 of *Research in Computational Semantics*, pp. 277–286. College Publications.

Denkowski, M. and A. Lavie (2011). Meteor 1.3: Automatic metric for reliable optimization and evaluation of machine translation systems. In *Proceedings of the EMNLP 2011 Workshop on Statistical Machine Translation*, pp. 85–91.

Galley, M., E. Fosler-Lussier, and A. Potamianos (2001). Hybrid natural language generation for spoken dialogue systems. In *Proceedings of the 7th European Conference on Speech Communication and Technology*, pp. 1735–1738.

Hockenmaier, J. and M. Steedman (2005). CCGBANK: Users' manual. In *Department of Computer and Information Science Technical Report MS-CIS-05-09*. University of Pennsylvania, Philadelphia, PA.

Hovy, E. H. (1993). Automated discourse generation using discourse structure relations. *Artificial Intelligence 63*, 341–385.

Joachims, T. (2002). *Learning to Classify Text Using Support Vector Machines*. Kluwer.

Kamp, H. and U. Reyle (1993). *From Discourse to Logic; An Introduction to Modeltheoretic Semantics of Natural Language, Formal Logic and DRT.* Kluwer, Dordrecht.

Langkilde, I. and K. Knight (1998). Generation that exploits corpus-based statistical knowledge. In *Proceedings of the 36th Annual Meeting of the Association for Computational Linguistics (ACL'98)*, pp. 704–710.

Levenshtein, V. (1966). Binary codes capable of correcting deletions, insertions, and reversals. *Soviet Physics Doklady 10*, 707–710.

McKeown, K. R. (1985). *Text Generation: Using Discourse Strategies and Focus Constraints to Generate Natural Language Text.* Cambridge University Press.

Papineni, K., S. Roukos, T. Ward, and W.-J. Zhu (2002). BLEU: A method for automatic evaluation of machine translation. In *Proceedings of the 40th Annual Meeting of the Association for Computational Linguistics (ACL'02)*, pp. 311–318.

Reiter, E. and R. Dale (2000). *Building Natural Language Generation Systems.* Cambridge University Press.

Reiter, E., S. Sripada, J. Hunter, and J. Yu (2005). Choosing words in computer-generated weather forecasts. *Artificial Intelligence 167*, 137–169.

Stent, A., R. Prasad, and M. Walker (2004). Trainable sentence planning from complex information presentations in spoken dialog systems. In *Proceedings of the 42nd Annual Meeting of the Association for Computational Linguistics (ACL'04')*, pp. 79.

van Deemter, K., M. Theune, and E. Krahmer (2005). Real *vs.* template-based natural language generation: a false opposition? *Computational Linguistics 31*(1), 15–24.

Witten, I. and E. Frank (2005). *Data Mining: Practical Machine Learning Techniques with Java Implementation (2nd Ed.).* Morgan Kaufmann, San Francisco, CA.

Sources of Evidence for Implicit Argument Resolution

Egoitz Laparra
IXA Group
Basque Country University
San Sebastian, Spain
egoitz.laparra@ehu.es

German Rigau
IXA Group
Basque Country University
San Sebastian, Spain
german.rigau@ehu.es

Abstract

Traditionally, semantic role labelling systems have focused on searching the fillers of those explicit roles appearing within sentence boundaries. However, when the participants of a predicate are implicit and can not be found inside sentence boundaries, this approach obtains incomplete predicative structures with null arguments. Previous research facing this task have coincided in identifying the implicit argument filling as a special case of anaphora or coreference resolution. In this work, we review a number of theories that model the behaviour of discourse coreference and propose some adaptations to capture evidence for the implicit argument resolution task. We empirically demonstrate that exploiting such evidence our system outperforms previous approaches evaluated on the SemEval-2010 task 10 dataset. We complete our study identifying those cases that traditional coreference theories can not cover.

1 Introduction

One of the most relevant tasks in the semantic processing of texts is identifying the arguments of a predicate. Several systems have been developed to perform this task, called Semantic Role Labelling (SRL) (Gildea and Jurafsky, 2000). However they have traditionally focused on searching the fillers for the overtly realized arguments in the local context of the predicate. In other words, only exploring those participants that share a syntactical relation with the predicate. Since traditional SRL systems depend strongly on these syntactic relations, they cannot perform predictions when the candidate instantiation of the argument is not explicit. Nevertheless, *some* null instantiated arguments can be inferred from the context. Using the nominal predicates of NomBank (Meyers et al., 2004), Gerber and Chai (Gerber and Chai, 2010) pointed out that the implicit arguments can add up to 65% to the coverage of the instantiations. As a consequence, increasing the number of connections between the predicates and their participants could help dramatically text understanding.

In FrameNet (Baker et al., 1998), the predicates, called *lexical-units* (LU), evoke frames which roughly correspond to different events or scenarios. For each frame, a set of possible arguments are defined. These arguments are called *Frame Elements* (FE) and when they are not explicitly instantiated they are called Null Instantiations (NI). When they can be inferred implicitly they are called *Definite Null Instantiations* (DNI). In the next example, the LU **tenant**$_n$ evoking the frame **Residence** has an instantiated FE, *Resident*, whose filler is [the tenants]. The correct filler for the DNI corresponding to FE *Location*, [*the house*], appears two sentences before:

> "Now, Mr. Holmes, with your permission, I will show you round the house." The various bedrooms and sitting-rooms had yielded nothing to a careful search. Apparently [the **tenants**$_{Residence}$]$_{Resident}$ had brought little or nothing with them. DNI$_{Location}$

Early studies on implicit arguments described this problem as a special case of anaphora or coreference resolution (Palmer et al., 1986; Whittemore et al., 1991; Tetreault, 2002). Also recent works cast this problem as an anaphora resolution task (Silberer and Frank, 2012).

In this work we present a detailed study of a set of features that have been traditionally used to model anaphora and coreference resolution tasks. We describe how these features manifest in a FrameNet based corpus for modeling implicit argument resolution, including an analysis of their benefits and drawbacks.

The paper is structured as follows: section 2 discusses the related work. Section 3 describes the SemEval-2010 task 10 dataset. Section 4 reviews a number of sources of evidence applied to the anaphora or coreference resolution tasks. We also propose how to adapt these features to select the appropriate fillers for the implicit arguments. Section 5 presents some experiments we have carried out to test these features. Section 6 discusses the initial results. Finally, section 7 offers some concluding remarks and presents some future researching.

2 Related Work

Task 10 of SemEval-2010 focused on the evaluation of SRL systems based on the FrameNet paradigm[1] (Ruppenhofer et al., 2009). This task was divided in two different sub-tasks:

(i) Argument annotation in a traditional SRL manner.
(ii) Filling null instantiatios over the document.

The systems participating in the second subtask identified those missing *Frame Elements* that were really *Null Instantiations*, decided which of those NI were definite, and finally located the correct fillers of the DNIs. Two systems participated in the second sub-task: VENSES++ and SEMAFOR.

VENSES++ (Tonelli and Delmonte, 2010) builds logical rules from syntactic parsing and uses hand-crafted lexicons. They apply a rule based anaphora resolution procedure before employing semantic similarity between a NI and a potential filler using WordNet (Fellbaum, 1998). More recently, the same authors have tried to improve the performance of their system (Tonelli and Delmonte, 2011).

SEMAFOR (Chen et al., 2010) is a supervised system that extends an existing semantic role labeller replacing the features defined for regular arguments with two new semantic features. First, their system checks if a potential filler in the context fills the null-instantiated role in one of the FrameNet sentences, and second, it calculates the distributional semantic similarity between the fillers and the roles. Although this system obtained the best performance in the task, data sparseness strongly affected the results.

In a different approach, (Ruppenhofer et al., 2011) explore a number of linguistic strategies in order to enhance the DNI identification. They conclude that a more sophisticated approach for DNI identification can improve significantly the performance of the whole pipeline, even if the method for the DNI filling is simple. For filling DNIs they propose to use the semantic types specified for FEs in FrameNet. Following this line (Laparra and Rigau, 2012) presented a novel strategy for the DNI identification exploiting explicit Frame Elements annotations. Their approach gets the best results in the state of the art for DNI identification and showed its relevance in the DNI filling process.

(Silberer and Frank, 2012) propose to solve the task adapting an entity-based coreference resolution model. In this work, the authors also extend automatically the training corpus to avoid data sparseness.

Finally, (Gerber and Chai, 2010) define a closely related task characterizing the implicit arguments of some predicates appearing in NomBank (Meyers et al., 2004). They use a set of syntactic and semantic features to train a logistic regression classifier. The documents, obtained from the Wall Street Journal corpus, were already annotated with explicit arguments. Unlike SemEval-2010 task, the resulting dataset contains 1.253 predicate instances with an average of 1,8 roles annotated per instance. However just a set of ten different predicates is taken into account.

3 SEMEVAL-2010 dataset

In the experiments reported in this paper, we have used the dataset distributed in SemEval-2010 for Task 10 "Linking Events and their Participants in Discourse". The corpus contains some chapters extracted

[1] http://www.coli.uni-saarland.de/projects/semeval2010_FG/

from two Arthur Conan Doyle's stories. "The Tiger of San Pedro" chapter from "The Adventure of Wisteria Lodge" was selected for training, while chapters 13 and 14 from "The Hound of the Baskervilles" were selected for testing. The texts are annotated using the frame-semantic structure of FrameNet 1.3 including null instantiations, the type of the NI and the corresponding fillers for each DNI. Table 1 shows the number of DNI in the dataset.

data-set	DNIs (solved)	Explicit FE
train	303 (245)	2,726
test-13	158 (121)	1,545
test-14	191 (138)	1,688

Table 1: Number of DNI and Explicit FE annotations for the SemEval-10 Task-10 corpus.

The dataset also includes the annotation files for the lexical units and the full-text annotated corpus from FrameNet. The annotations are enriched with a constituent-based parsing and for the training document there are manual coreference annotations available.

4 Sources of evidence

Many sources of evidence have proved their utility in reference resolution (Burger and Connolly, 1992). In this section, we adapt them to the specific characteristics of the DNI linking task. We also present their behaviour over the training data. Two main differences must been taken into account with respect to anaphora and coreference tasks. First, in anaphora and coreference tasks, mentions occur explicitly and they can be exploited to check particular constrains. Without an explicit argument, in some cases, we decided to obtain the evidences from the predicate (that is, the lexical-unit) of the target DNI. Second, the referenced entities are not just nouns or pronouns but also verbs, adjectives, etc. Therefore, some features must be generalized. We introduce the sources of evidence grouped in four different types.

4.1 Syntactic

Some of the earliest theories studying pronoun resolution focused on the syntactic relations between the referenced entities. Here we present two syntactic features that also exploit this source of evidence. In both cases, we also include an artificial node covering all document sentence trees in order to generalize its behaviour beyond sentence boundaries.

Command: C-command (Reinhart, 1976) is a syntactic relationship between nodes in a constituency tree. One node N1 is said c-commanded by another N2 if three requirements are satisfied:

- N1 does not dominate N2
- N2 does not dominate N1
- The first upper node that dominates N1, also dominates N2

This syntactic relation has proved to be useful to locate anaphoric references. Now, we study if this relationship can also be of utility for DNI resolution. We implemented this relation as a distance measure between the candidate filler node and the nearest common ancestor with respect the lexical-unit of the target DNI (see a simple example in figure 1). Note that a value equal to zero means that either the filler dominates the target or the target dominates the filler. Besides, those fillers having a command value equal to one satisfy the c-command theory. Figure 2 presents the frequency distribution of our distance measure on the training data. It seems that most fillers have a command value equal or close to one.

Nearness: The constituency tree can also be exploited for anaphora resolution using breadth-first search techniques. A widely known algorithm based in this search is the Hobbs' algorithm (Hobbs, 1977). This algorithm follows a traversal search of the tree looking for a node that satisfies some constraints. Because of the nature of these constraints this algorithm cannot be directly applied to the implicit argument annotation task. Instead, we studied if the breadth distance can be an evidence through a measure we call **nearness**. We calculate **nearness** N as follows:

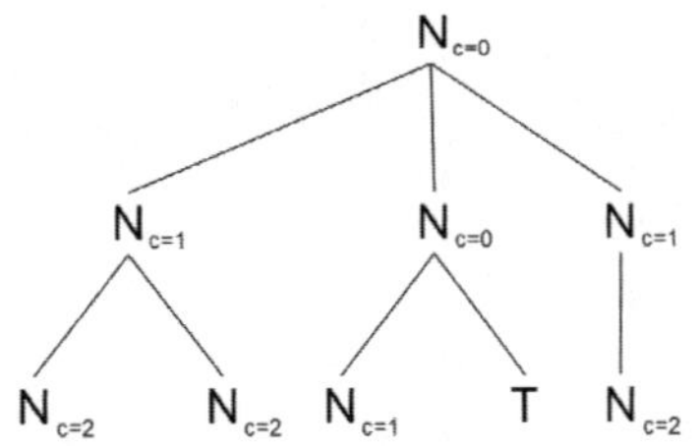

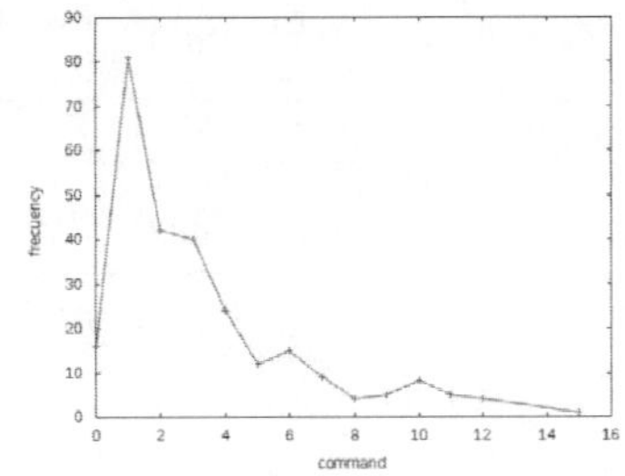

Figure 1: Sample values of **command** for different nodes in a constituency tree. T represents the lexical-unit of the target DNI

Figure 2: Frequency distribution of the different values of **command** in the training data

- P is the first upper node that dominates the lexical-unit T and the filler F
- B is the tree branch containing F whose parent is P
- If F precedes T, N is the number of following siblings of F in B
- If F follows T, N is the number of preceding siblings of F in B
- If T dominates F or F dominates T, N is equal to 0

Figure 3 presents some examples of values obtained using this measure. Figure 4 shows the frequency distribution of the different values of **nearness** in the training data. It also seems that most fillers prefer small **nearness** values.

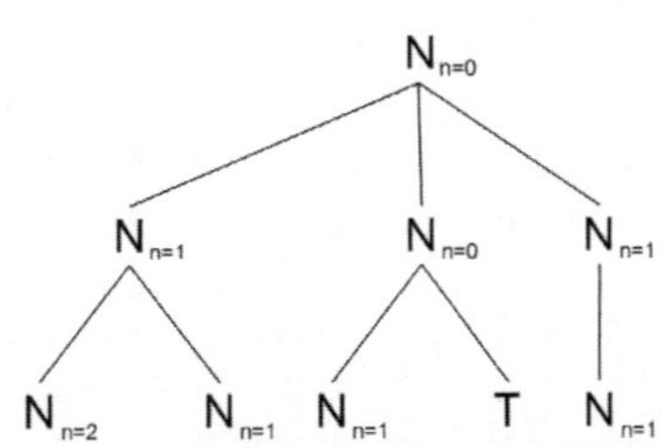

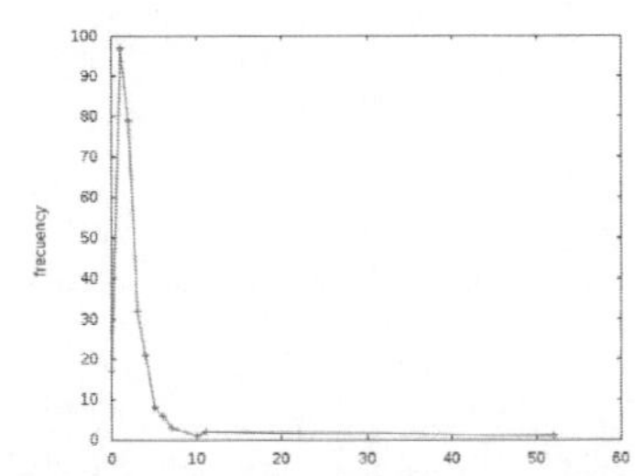

Figure 3: Sample values of **nearness** for different nodes in a constituency tree. T represents the lexical-unit of the target DNI

Figure 4: Frequency distribution of the different values of **nearness** in the training data

4.2 Morpho-syntactic and Semantic Agreement

Anaphora and coreference solvers usually apply morpho-syntactic and semantic agreement tests. These constraints check for the consistency between the properties of the target entities and the referents. Several agreement tests such as gender, number or semantic class can be applied. Since most of these tests can not be applied to this task, in this work we have studied part of speech and semantic type agreement.

Semantic Type: To extract the semantic type of the filler of a frame element, we first perform a very simple Word Sense Disambiguation (WSD) process assigning to each word, whenever possible, the most frequent sense of WordNet (Fellbaum, 1998). This heuristic has been used frequently as a baseline in the evaluation of WSD systems. As WordNet senses have been mapped to several ontologies, this disambiguation method allows us to label the documents with ontological features that can work as semantic types. In this work we have used the Top Ontology (TO) (Álvez et al., 2008). We assign to each filler the ontological features of its syntactic head. In this way, we can learn from the training data and for each frame element a probability distribution of its semantic types. Table 2 contains some examples.

Part of Speech: We also calculate the probability distribution of the part of speech (POS) of the head of the fillers similarly as for the semantic types.

Frame#FrameElement	SemanticType	Probability
Expectation#Cognizer	Human	0.93
	Group	0.07
Residence#Location	Building	0.77
	Place	0.33
Attempt#Goal	Purpose	0.41
	UnboundEvent	0.37
	Object	0.13
	Part	0.09

Table 2: Some examples of semantic types assigned to frame elements.

4.3 Discursive

Recency: Recent entities are more likely to be a coreferent than more distant ones. This fact can be easily represented as the sentence distance between the lexical-unit of the target DNI and its referent. This feature has been used frequently not only in coreference and anaphora resolution but also in implicit argument resolution. (Gerber and Chai, 2010) noticed that the vast majority of the fillers of an implicit argument can be found either in the same sentence of the predicate or in the two preceding sentences. In our training data, this fact accounts for 70% of cases. Moreover, only around 2% of the fillers are located in posterior sentences. Figure 5 presents a frequency distribution of the different **recency** values.

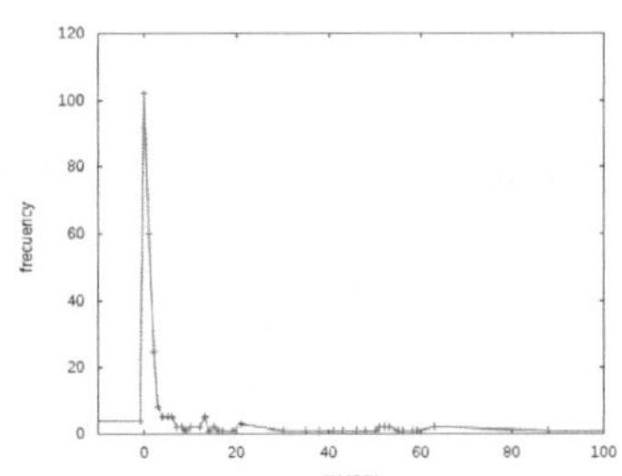

Figure 5: Frequency distribution of the different values of **recency** in the training data

filler LU	dialogue	monologue
dialogue	77.8%	5.4%
monologue	22.2%	94.6%

Table 3: Dialogue vs. monologue distributions

Dialogue: Since the corpus data consists of different chapters of a novel, it contains many dialogues inserting a narrative monologue. The resolution of pronoun and coreference in dialogues dealing with a multi-party discourse have been largely studied (e.g. (Byron and Stent, 1998; Poesio et al., 2006; Stent and Bangalore, 2010)). In this work, we just studied how referents are maintained with respect the two different levels of discourse. Table 3 shows that, in the vast majority of cases, both lexical-unit and filler belong to the same level of discourse[2]. Consequently, this fact can be used to promote those candidates that are at the same discourse level of the lexical-unit of the target DNI.

4.4 Coreference chains

An important source of evidence for anaphora resolution is the focus. The entity or topic which is salient in a particular part of the discourse is the most likely to be coreferred in the same part of the discourse. Thus, given a coreference annotation of a document it is possible to know how the focus varies along the discourse. As we explained in Section 3, the training data contains a full coreference annotation that we use to study three sources of evidence related to both focus and coreference chains.

Non singleton: Using the same training data, (Silberer and Frank, 2012) found that 72% of the DNIs are linked to referents that belong to non-singleton coreference chains. This means that candidate entities that are mentioned just once are less likely to be a referent filler of an implicit argument.

[2]Moreover, as expected, it is more frequent to refer from a monologue to a dialogue entity than the opposite.

Focus: The **focus** refers to the entities that are most likely to be coreferred in a given point in the discourse (Sidner, 1978; Grosz and Sidner, 1986). Now, we study if this is also satisfied for DNI referents by checking if the filler of a DNI corresponds to the **focus** of a near context. We define the **focus** in a near context as follows. Consider the following definitions:

- F is the mention of an entity that is annotated as a filler of a target DNI.
- T is the lexical-unit of the target DNI.
- E is any entity between F and T.
- F-1 is the previous mention of F in the coreference chain.
- Nf is the number of mentions of F from F-1 to T.
- Ne is the number of mentions of E from F-1 to T.

If F-1 is the previous mention of F in the coreference chain, then Nf is equal to two. If there are no previous mentions of F, then F-1 is equal to F, and Nf is equal to one. F is the focus of the near context of T if and only if there is no E complying with Ne>Nf.

From our training data, we also observe that the **focus** matches the filler of a DNI in 72% of the cases.

Centering: **Centering** (Grosz et al., 1995; Brennan et al., 1987) is a theory that tracks the continuity of the focus to explain the coherence of the referential entities in a discourse. The theory establishes three different types of focus transition depending on the relation within the previous focus, Cb(Un-1), the actual focus, Cb(Un), and the element that is most likely to be the focus, Cp(Un), according to its grammatical function. Figure 6 shows the three different kinds of **centering** transitions.

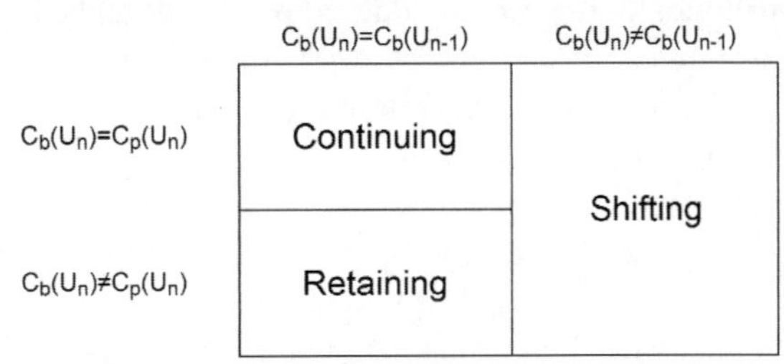

Figure 6: Types of **centering** transitions

The theory establishes that the most common transition is **continuing**. The second most common transition is **retaining** and the least common transition is **shifting**. Applying this schema to the training data, we found that the following probability distribution:

- Continuing: 41.0%
- Retaining: 25.2%
- Shifting: 18.8%
- Other: 15.0%

Since in the DNI filling task the referents can be of any kind of POS and the grammatical function only takes into account nouns or pronouns, the **centering** theory is not always applicable. When the filler is not a noun or a pronoun we have created a fake **centering** category called **other**. Thus, according to the training data, it seems that the preference order of the transitions matches the original theory being **continuing** the most common transition.

5 Experiments

In the previous section we have proposed an adaptation to the implicit argument filling task of some theories traditionally applied to capture evidence for anaphora and coreference resolution. Since the implicit role reference is a special case of coreference, we expect a similar behaviour also for this case. In fact, our analysis using the training data of SemEval seems to confirm our initial hypothesis. In order to evaluate the potential utility of these sources of evidence we have performed a set of experiments using the SemEval-2010 Task 10 testing-data. In this section, we describe our strategy for solving the implicit arguments and the scorer system used in the evaluation.

Processing Steps: Any system presented to the implicit argument resolution subtask had to follow the following three steps:

1. Select the *frame elements* that are Null Instantiations.
2. Decide if the *null instantiations* are Definite.
3. In case of definite *null instantiation*, locate the corresponding filler.

For the first two steps, we have followed the strategy proposed by (Laparra and Rigau, 2012). This method learns patterns of concurrent *Frame Elements* from explicit annotations. The most common patterns help to identify a missing FE when the rest of the FEs appears explicitly. Following this simple approach, 66% of DNIs in the testing data can be recognized correctly.

For the last step of the subtask, we have modelled the sources of evidence presented in the previous section as features to train a Naive-Bayes algorithm. We applied a maximum-likelihood method without any smoothing function. Thus, having a set of features *f*, for each DNI we select as filler the candidate *c* that satisfies:

$$\arg\max P(c) \prod_i P(f_i|c)$$

Non-singleton, focus and centering features require a coreference annotation of the document to be analysed. As we explain in Section 3, the training data of the SemEval task contains manually annotated coreference chains that can be used to exploit these features. However, as the testing data does not contain this type of annotations, we applied an automatic coreference resolution system. We used the software provided by Stanford [3]. In the following experiments, we present the results obtained using manual and predicted coreference.

Score measures: The scorer provided for the NI SemEval subtask works slightly different than previous scorers for traditional SRL tasks. Since the participants can appear repeatedly along the document, the scorer needs to take into account the coreference chains of the possible fillers. Thus, if a system selects any of the mentions of the correct filler, the scorer will count it as correct. For this purpose, the dataset provides a full manual coreference annotation. In this subtask, the NI linking precision is defined as the number of all true positive links divided by the number of links made by a system. NI linking recall is defined as the number of true positive links divided by the number of links between an NI and its equivalence set in the gold standard. NI linking F-Score is then calculated as the harmonic mean of precision and recall.

However, since any prediction including the head of the correct filler is scored positively, selecting very large spans of text would obtain very good results[4]. For example, [*madam*] and [*no good will, madam*] would be evaluated as positive results for a [*madam*] gold-standard annotation. Therefore, the scorer also computes the overlap (Dice coefficient) between the words in the predicted filler (P) of an NI and the words in the gold standard one (G):

$$\textbf{NI linking overlap} = \frac{2|P \cap G|}{|P| + |G|}$$

Results on the SemEval-2010 test: Table 4 shows available precision, recall, F-score and overlapping figures of the different systems using predicted and gold-standard coreference chains[5]. Our simple strategy clearly outperforms (Tonelli and Delmonte, 2010) in terms of both precision and recall. (Chen et al., 2010) seems to solve more accurately but a more limited number of cases. We also include the results from (Silberer and Frank, 2012) obtained when using for training a larger corpus extended heuristically (best) and the results obtained with no additional training data (no extra train). Our approach

[3] `http://nlp.stanford.edu/software/dcoref.shtml`

[4] In particular, returning the whole document would obtain perfect precision and recall.

[5] Surprisingly, previous research do not report results of overlapping. The authors of (Laparra and Rigau, 2012) kindly provided their overlapping results through personal communication.

obtains better results in all the cases except when they use extended training data with the gold-standard coreference chains. In this case, our approach seems to achieve a similar performance but without exploiting extra training data. Apparently, (Laparra and Rigau, 2012) presents better results but, as we explained previously, a low overlapping score means vague answers. Although our approach outperforms previous approaches, such a low figures clearly reflect the inherent difficulty of the task.

	Auto Coref				GS Coref			
System	**P**	**R**	**F1**	**Over.**	**P**	**R**	**F1**	**Over.**
(Tonelli and Delmonte, 2010)	-	-	0.01	-				
(Chen et al., 2010)	**0.25**	0.01	0.02	-				
(Tonelli and Delmonte, 2011)	0.13	0.06	0.08	-				
(Silberer and Frank, 2012) no extra train	0.06	0.09	0.07	-	-	-	0.13	-
(Silberer and Frank, 2012) best	0.09	0.11	0.10	-	-	-	**0.18**	-
(Laparra and Rigau, 2012)	0.15	**0.25**	**0.19**	0.54				
This work	0.14	0.18	0.16	**0.89**	0.16	0.20	**0.18**	0.90

Table 4: Results using SemEval-2010 dataset.

DNI linking experiment: In order to check the sources of evidence independently of the rest of processes, we have performed a second experiment where we assume perfect results for the first two steps. In other words, we apply our DNI filling strategy just to the correct DNIs in the document. Table 5 shows the relevance of a correct DNI identification (the first two steps of the process). Once again, without extra training data our strategy outperforms the model of (Silberer and Frank, 2012)[6]. Again, when using extended training data their model seems to perform similar to ours.

	Auto Coref				GS Coref			
System	**P**	**R**	**F1**	**Over.**	**P**	**R**	**F1**	**Over.**
(Silberer and Frank, 2012) no extra train					0.26	**0.25**	0.25	-
(Silberer and Frank, 2012) best					0.31	**0.25**	**0.28**	-
This work	0.30	0.22	0.26	0.89	**0.33**	0.24	**0.28**	0.89

Table 5: Results using SemEval-2010 dataset on the correct DNIs.

Ablation tests: Table 6 presents the results using the gold-standard coreference, when leaving out a type of feature one at a time. The table empirically demonstrates that all feature types contribute positively to solve this task. The morpho-syntactic and semantic agreement seem to be the most relevant evidence in terms of precision and recall. That is, identifying the head of the correct filler. On the other hand, syntactic features are the most relevant to detect the correct span of the fillers.

Source Set	**P**	**R**	**F1**	**Over.**
all	0.33	0.24	0.28	0.89
no-coref	0.30	0.22	0.25	0.86
no-semagree	0.22	0.22	0.22	0.90
no-discursive	0.29	0.22	0.25	0.82
no-syntactic	0.28	0.21	0.24	0.75

Table 6: Ablation tests using the gold-standard coreference.

6 Discussion

In order to analyse the limits of the different types of evidence, we used as reference the results obtained using the gold-standard DNIs and coreference chains (see table 5). As an overall remark, all previous

[6]The rest of the systems do not perform any experiments with gold-standard DNI identification.

works facing this task agree on the sparsity of the training data. We also observed that this problem affects all sources of evidence we have studied. This can be seen clearly when studying the agreement of semantic types.

Data sparsity for semantic types: The semantic types do not cover the full set of frame elements. The testing data contains a total of 209 different Frame#FrameElements. 73 of them (out of 35%) do not appear on the training data. Another problem appears when the FEs have too many different semantic types with very similar probabilities. Without enough information to discriminate correctly the filler, this source of evidence becomes damaging (see table 7).

Outside the same sentence: Recency strongly prioritises the window formed by the same sentence of the lexical-unit of the target DNI and the two previous sentences. However, in 19% of the cases the filler belongs to a sentence outside that window. Furthermore, syntactic based evidences rely on relations between entities in the same sentence. Obviously, adding an artificial node covering the whole document analysis is quite arbitrary. Table 8 shows how the performance of our approach decreases strongly when the filler and the lexical-unit are in different sentences.

P	R	F1	Over.
0.21	0.09	0.13	0.61

Table 7: Performance of FE having more than 5 semantic types

same sentence				another sentence			
P	R	F1	Over.	P	R	F1	Over.
0.50	0.34	0.40	0.87	0.20	0.16	0.18	0.96

Table 8: Performance when the filler and the lexical-unit are in the same sentence or in another one

Discursive structure: The particular structure of the documents can also affect seriously the performance of the sources of evidence. Table 9 presents the results on contexts with at least 10% of entities on monologue or dialogue. According to the recency feature, each context is formed by the sentence of the lexical-unit of the target DNI and the two previous sentences. We can observe that the results on mixed contexts are better than in general. Obviously, dialogue features are totally useless in contexts with only monologues or only dialogues.

Singleton fillers: Most of the fillers are entities that belong to a coreference chain. Therefore, these cases heavily depends on a correct coreference annotation. This is why worse results are obtained when using predicted coreferent chains. Table 10 shows the results when the filler belongs or not to a coreference chain. It is important to remind that in this work we have adapted a set of sources of evidence and theories traditionally used is anaphora and coreference resolution. Originally these theories focused just on noun and pronoun entities.

P	R	F1	Over.
0.38	0.29	0.33	0.93

Table 9: Performance in mixed contexts with at least 10% of entities of each level

coref-chain				no-coref-chain			
P	R	F1	Over.	P	R	F1	Over.
0.45	0.35	0.39	0.94	0.06	0.04	0.05	0.31

Table 10: Performance when the filler belongs to a coreference-chain or not

7 Conclusions and Future Work

We have presented a first attempt to study the behaviour of traditional coreference and anaphora models for the implicit argument resolution task, a special case of coreference. Our analysis shows that these theories and models can be successfully applied as sources of evidence in an existing dataset. In fact, their joint combination improves state of the art results.

However, the sources of evidence presented in this work are adaptations that focus on nominal entities and pronouns, and on relations within entities and referents belonging to the same sentence. It seems that for these cases it is possible to capture useful evidence. But for the rest (singletons, non nominal POS, beyond sentence boundaries, etc.), further investigation is needed.

We have also observed, that the training data of the SemEval-2010 task 10 is too small. Possibly, the results could be improved using an extended training data (Silberer and Frank, 2012).

Following the line of research presented by Roth and Frank (Roth and Frank, 2012b,a) we will study the influence between the implicit arguments resolution and the predicate alignment.

Finally, we plan to perform a similar study on the NomBank dataset (Gerber and Chai, 2010).

References

Álvez, J., J. Atserias, J. Carrera, S. Climent, E. Laparra, A. Oliver, and G. Rigau (2008). Complete and consistent annotation of wordnet using the top concept ontology. In *LREC*.

Baker, C. F., C. J. Fillmore, and J. B. Lowe (1998). The berkeley framenet project. In *COLING-ACL*, pp. 86–90.

Brennan, S. E., M. W. Friedman, and C. J. Pollard (1987). A centering approach to pronouns. In *Meeting of the Association for Computational Linguistics*.

Burger, J. D. and D. Connolly (1992). Probabilistic resolution of anaphoric reference. In *AAAI Fall Symposium on Probabilistic Approaches to Natural Language*, Cambridge, MA, USA, pp. 17–24.

Byron, D. K. and A. Stent (1998). A Preliminary Model of Centering in Dialog. In *Meeting of the Association for Computational Linguistics*, pp. 1475–1477.

Chen, D., N. Schneider, D. Das, and N. A. Smith (2010). Semafor: Frame argument resolution with log-linear models. In *Proceedings of the 5th International Workshop on Semantic Evaluation*, SemEval '10, Stroudsburg, PA, USA, pp. 264–267. Association for Computational Linguistics.

Fellbaum, C. (Ed.) (1998). *WordNet: an electronic lexical database.* MIT Press.

Gerber, M. and J. Y. Chai (2010). Beyond nombank: a study of implicit arguments for nominal predicates. In *Proceedings of the 48th Annual Meeting of the Association for Computational Linguistics*, ACL '10, Stroudsburg, PA, USA, pp. 1583–1592. Association for Computational Linguistics.

Gildea, D. and D. Jurafsky (2000). Automatic labeling of semantic roles. In *ACL*.

Grosz, B. J., A. K. Joshi, and S. Weinstein (1995). Centering: A Framework for Modeling the Local Coherence of Discourse. *Computational Linguistics 21*, 203–225.

Grosz, B. J. and C. L. Sidner (1986). Attention, Intentions, and the Structure of Discourse. *Computational Linguistics 12*, 175–204.

Hobbs, J. R. (1977). Pronoun resolution. *Intelligence/sigart Bulletin*, 28–28.

Laparra, E. and G. Rigau (2012). Exploiting explicit annotations and semantic types for implicit argument resolution. In *6th IEEE International Conference on Semantic Computing*, ICSC '12, Palermo, Italy.

Meyers, A., R. Reeves, C. Macleod, R. Szekely, V. Zielinska, B. Young, and R. Grishman (2004, May 2 - May 7). The nombank project: An interim report. In A. Meyers (Ed.), *HLT-NAACL 2004 Workshop: Frontiers in Corpus Annotation*, Boston, Massachusetts, USA, pp. 24–31. Association for Computational Linguistics.

Palmer, M., D. A. Dahl, R. J. Schiffman, L. Hirschman, M. C. Linebarger, and J. Dowding (1986). Recovering implicit information. In *ACL*, pp. 10–19.

Poesio, M., A. Patel, and B. D. Eugenio (2006). Discourse Structure and Anaphora in Tutorial Dialogues: An Empirical Analysis of Two Theories of the Global Focus. *Research on Language and Computation 4*, 229–257.

Reinhart, T. (1976). *The syntactic domain of anaphora.* MIT Linguistics Dissertations. Massachusetts Institute of Technology.

Roth, M. and A. Frank (2012a). Aligning predicate argument structures in monolingual comparable texts: A new corpus for a new task. In *Proceedings of *SEM 2012: The First Conference on Lexical and Computational Semantics*, Montreal, Canada.

Roth, M. and A. Frank (2012b). Aligning predicates across monolingual comparable texts using graph-based clustering. In *Proceedings of the 2012 Conference on Empirical Methods in Natural Language Processign (EMNLP)*, Jeju, Republic of Korea.

Ruppenhofer, J., P. Gorinski, and C. Sporleder (2011). In search of missing arguments: A linguistic approach. In G. Angelova, K. Bontcheva, R. Mitkov, and N. Nicolov (Eds.), *Recent Advances in Natural Language Processing, RANLP 2011, 12-14 September, 2011, Hissar, Bulgaria*, pp. 331–338. RANLP 2011 Organising Committee.

Ruppenhofer, J., C. Sporleder, R. Morante, C. Baker, and M. Palmer (2009). Semeval-2010 task 10: linking events and their participants in discourse. In *Proceedings of the Workshop on Semantic Evaluations: Recent Achievements and Future Directions*, DEW '09, Stroudsburg, PA, USA, pp. 106–111. Association for Computational Linguistics.

Sidner, C. L. (1978). The use of focus as a tool for disambiguation of definite noun phrases. In *Proceedings of the 1978 workshop on Theoretical issues in natural language processing*, TINLAP '78, Stroudsburg, PA, USA, pp. 86–95. Association for Computational Linguistics.

Silberer, C. and A. Frank (2012). Casting implicit role linking as an anaphora resolution task. In **SEM 2012: The First Joint Conference on Lexical and Computational Semantics*, Montréal, Canada, pp. 1–10. Association for Computational Linguistics.

Stent, A. J. and S. Bangalore (2010). Interaction between dialog structure and coreference resolution. In *IEEE Workshop on Spoken Language Technology.*

Tetreault, J. R. (2002). Implicit role reference. In *International Symposium on Reference Resolution for Natural Language Processing*, Alicante, Spain, pp. 109–115.

Tonelli, S. and R. Delmonte (2010). Venses++: Adapting a deep semantic processing system to the identification of null instantiations. In *Proceedings of the 5th International Workshop on Semantic Evaluation*, SemEval '10, Stroudsburg, PA, USA, pp. 296–299. Association for Computational Linguistics.

Tonelli, S. and R. Delmonte (2011, June). Desperately seeking implicit arguments in text. In *Proceedings of the ACL 2011 Workshop on Relational Models of Semantics*, Portland, Oregon, USA, pp. 54–62. Association for Computational Linguistics.

Whittemore, G., M. Macpherson, and G. Carlson (1991). Event-building through role-filling and anaphora resolution. In *Proceedings of the 29th annual meeting on Association for Computational Linguistics*, ACL '91, Stroudsburg, PA, USA, pp. 17–24. Association for Computational Linguistics.

Recognising Sets and Their Elements: Tree Kernels for Entity Instantiation Identification

Andrew McKinlay and Katja Markert
School of Computing
University of Leeds, UK
{scs4ajm,markert}@comp.leeds.ac.uk

Abstract

We apply tree kernels to *entity instantiations*. An entity instantiation is an entity relationship, in which a set of entities is mentioned, and then a member or subset of this set is introduced. We present the first reliably annotated intrasentential entity instantiation corpus, along with an extension to the intersentential annotations in McKinlay and Markert (2011). We then apply tree kernels to both inter- and intrasentential entity instantiations, showing comparable results to an extensive set of unstructured features. The combination of tree kernels and unstructured features leads to significant improvements over either method in isolation.

1 Introduction

In a previous paper, we define an entity instantiation as follows (McKinlay and Markert, 2011):

> An Entity Instantiation is a non-coreferent entity relationship, where a *set* of entities is mentioned, and then a *member* or *subset* is introduced.

Examples 1 and 2 show a set membership instantiation and a subset instantiation, respectively[1].

(1) a. **The two lawmakers** sparred in a highly personal fashion, violating usual Senate decorum.
b. Their tone was good-natured, with *Mr. Packwood* saying he intended to offer [...]

(2) a. To the extent that the primary duty of personal staff involves local benefit-seeking, this indicates that political philosophy leads **congressional Republicans** to pay less attention to narrow constituent concerns.
b. First, economists James Bennett and Thomas DiLorenzo find that *GOP senators* turn back roughly 10% more of their allocated personal staff budgets than Democrats do.

Entity Instantiations are highly context dependent and their interpretation requires careful consideration of prior mentions of both set and member/subset. In Example 3, one must refer back 2 sentences to establish that *'they'* is coreferent with *'the Montreal Protocol's legions of supporters'*, and the set from which *'Peter Teagan, a specialist in heat transfer'* is drawn. In Example 4, we need the knowledge that Mr. Mason is Jewish from the first sentence to establish the instantiation in the final sentence.

(3) But even though by some estimates it might cost the world as much as $100 billion between now and the year 2000 to convert to other coolants, foaming agents and solvents and to redesign equipment for these less efficient substitutes, <u>the Montreal Protocol's legions of supporters</u> say it is worth it. They insist that CFCs are damaging the earth's stratospheric ozone layer, which screens out some of the sun's ultraviolet rays. Hence, as **they** see it, if something isn't done earthlings will become ever more subject to sunburn and skin cancer.

[1] All examples in this paper are taken from the Penn Treebank Wall Street Journal corpus (Marcus et al., 1993) unless stated otherwise, and are occasionally abbreviated. Sets are highlighted in **bold** and members or subsets are shown in *italics*.

Peter Teagan, a specialist in heat transfer, is running a project at Arthur D. Little Inc., of Cambridge, Mass., to find alternative technologies that will allow industry to eliminate CFCs.

(4) [...] Or so it must seem to Jackie Mason, the veteran Jewish comedian appearing in a new ABC sitcom airing on Tuesday nights (9:30-10 p.m. EDT). Not only is Mr. Mason the star of "Chicken Soup," he's also the inheritor of a comedic tradition dating back to "Duck Soup," and he's currently a man in hot water. Here, in neutral language, is the gist of Mr. Mason's remarks, quoted first in the Village Voice while he was a paid spokesman for the Rudolph Giuliani mayoral campaign, and then in Newsweek after he and the campaign parted company. [...]

He said that **Jews** have contributed more to black causes over the years than vice versa.

Entity instantiations vary a great deal, in terms of internal structure, ordering and overlap with other phenomena. Example 1 shows a set member entity instantiation between an NP headed by a plural noun, and a named entity. In Example 5 the set member is coupled with an apposition — *'an analyst with Drexel Burnham Lambert'*. In Example 6, neither set nor set member are named entities, and the set is a complex plural noun phrase (NP) which is made up of several constituents. In Example 7, the member NP precedes the set NP, and recognition needs the interpretation of *'Capitol Hill'* as a metonymic reference to the U.S. Congress.

(5) a. But **other analysts** said that having Mr. Phillips succeed Mr. Roman would make for a smooth transition.

b. "Graham Phillips has been there a long time [...]", said *Andrew Wallach, an analyst with Drexel Burnham Lambert.*

(6) a. And Democrats, who are under increasing pressure from their leaders to reject the gains-tax cut, are finding **reasons to say no, at least for now.**

b. *A major reason* is that they believe the Packwood-Roth plan would lose buckets of revenue over the long run.

(7) a. However, the disclosure of the guidelines, first reported last night by NBC News, is already being interpreted on *Capitol Hill* as an unfair effort to pressure Congress.

b. It has reopened the bitter wrangling between **the White House and Congress** over who is responsible for the failure to oust Mr. Noriega and, more broadly, for difficulties in carrying out covert activities abroad.

In contrast to our previous work in McKinlay and Markert (2011), we also consider *intrasentential* entity instantiations. This introduces further variety, and the possibility of nested instantiations. In Example 8, the set member is nested within the conjunction that forms the set. In Example 9, the set member is also nested in the set, but this time as a subtree of the prepositional phrase that complements the set NP. Example 10 exhibits a different sort of nesting — the set is nested within the set member. There are also many intrasentential instantiations where the participant NPs do not overlap, such as Example 11.

(8) So if anything happened to me, I'd want to leave behind enough so that my 33-year-old husband would be able to pay off ***the mortgage*** **and some other debts**.

(9) [...] **several firms, including discount broker Charles Schwab & Co. and *Sears, Roebuck & Co. 's Dean Witter Reynolds Inc. unit***, have attacked program trading as a major market evil.

(10) When he is presented with a poster celebrating the organization's 20th anniversary, he recognizes a photograph of *one of* ***the founders*** and recalls time spent together in Camden.

(11) **Banking stocks** were the major gainers Monday amid hope that interest rates have peaked, as *Deutsche Bank and Dresdner Bank* added 4 marks each to 664 marks and 326 marks, respectively.

These complexities make entity instantiations difficult to identify. We address this complexity by using *tree kernels*, a method of learning from tree data.

In this paper we introduce the first corpus of intrasentential entity instantiations, and an expanded corpus of intersentential entity instantiations. We present the first algorithm for the classification of intrasentential instantiations, and the first application of tree kernels for both inter- and intrasentential instantiations.

2 Related Work

The only prior research which has tackled the problem of entity instantiations is our own in McKinlay and Markert (2011). We annotated a 25-text corpus of entity instantiations between adjacent sentences but not *within* sentences, and experimented with unstructured features, including lexical, contextual and world-knowledge features. We achieved good results on an artificially balanced set, but on the original, highly skewed data reported a highest F-Score of only 0.19 for set members and 0.14 for subsets.

Entity instantiations are also closely related to at least two important natural language processing problems: *relation extraction* and *bridging anaphora*.

Relation Extraction. Relation extraction (RE) is the detection and classification of binary semantic relationships between entities, such as Part-Of, Employed-By or Located-In. A considerable amount of research in this field is connected to the important MUC (MUC, 1998) and ACE programs (ACE, 2005), both of which provided RE corpora and shared evaluation metrics.

RE and detecting entity instantiations are similar problems; they both involve the discovery of binary semantic relations in context. There are two fundamental differences, however. Firstly the participants of entity instantiations are not restricted to mentions of entities representing concrete, real-world objects, but instead consider heterogeneous NPs. Secondly, whilst the evidence for an entity instantiation can be drawn from anywhere in the document or from existing world knowledge, RE schemes restrict the scope of their relations to within a sentence. Set membership and subset relations are not annotated as part of the RE corpora which formed part of the MUC and ACE programs.

SemEval-2 had a shared task, *Multi-Way Classification of Semantic Relations Between Pairs of Nominals* (Hendrickx et al., 2010), which does include a *Member-Collection* relation, and is somewhat different to the ACE/MUC RE paradigm. However, their task differs from ours in several ways. Firstly, they only consider relations which exist only between base NPs with common noun heads — named entities and pronouns are excluded. Additionally, and similarly to ACE/MUC, they do not mark relations which rely on discourse knowledge and restrict annotations to sentence internal relations. Also, rather than annotating full texts they focus on single sentences extracted from web searches.

Despite these important distinctions, the similarities mean that many of the methods used are relevant to entity instantiations, including the use of *kernel* methods. A range of work has applied tree kernels to the RE problem, applying kernels to shallow parses (Zelenko et al., 2003), dependency trees (Culotta and Sorensen, 2004; Bunescu and Mooney, 2005) and full constituency parses (Zhang et al., 2006; Zhou et al., 2007; Swampillai and Stevenson, 2011). Refinements include automatically deciding the portion of the tree required to learn the relation (Zhou et al., 2007) and combining unstructured features with tree kernels (Zhou et al., 2007; Swampillai and Stevenson, 2011).

Almost all RE research considers solely intrasentential relations. Swampillai and Stevenson (2011), however, apply tree kernels to the problem of *intersentential* RE. As a constituency parse tree pertains only to a single sentence, they join the two sentences containing the entities under a new ROOT node.

Other work has focused on unstructured features. Approaches include Bayesian networks (Roth and Yih, 2002), maximum entropy models (Kambhatla, 2004), Support Vector Machines (SVMs) (Zhou et al., 2005) and the inclusion of background knowledge (Chan and Roth, 2010; Sun et al., 2011).

Bridging Anaphora. Bridging anaphora are those anaphora which require inference from the reader to *bridge* the gap between anaphor and antecedent (Clark, 1975). The classical example is in the form of meronymy, as in Example 12[2] but bridging anaphora can also be connected to their antecedent by set membership, such as Example 13 (and Example 6). However, not all entity instantiations are bridged — Examples 1, 2, 5, 7, 8, 9, and 11 are amongst those that have non-anaphoric set members and subsets.

(12) I looked into *the room*. **The ceiling** was very high.

(13) I met *two people* yesterday. **The woman** told me a story.

[2]Examples 12 and 13 are from Clark (1975). The anaphor is in **bold**, the antecedent is in *italics*.

Theoretical linguistic literature has discussed set membership and subset bridging (Clark, 1975; Prince, 1981), and the phenomenon has been annotated in at least three corpora (Poesio, 2003; Nissim et al., 2004; Markert et al., 2012). Early computational approaches either used hand-crafted rules (Markert et al., 1996; Poesio et al., 1997; Vieira and Poesio, 2000) or focused solely on meronymy-based bridging (Markert et al., 2003; Poesio et al., 2004). More recent work has focused on learning the *information status* (IS) of an entity, rather than identifying its antecedent. The IS of an entity represents whether it is *new* to the reader, *old* because it is coreferent to a prior mention, or can be *mediated* from prior text, often by bridging. Most relevant to our work is the learning of fine-grained IS, which involves learning subtypes of the mediated category, including set membership. Rahman and Ng (2012) use the Switchboard corpus (Nissim et al., 2004), which includes a restricted version of set membership, and employ a feature set based on unigrams, markables and binary features based on hand-coded rules. Markert et al. (2012) learn fine-grained IS on a portion of OntoNotes corpus. They couple local features with a collective learning model, using links between instances based upon syntactic parent-child and precedence relations.

3 Annotation, Agreement and Corpus Study

We created a substantial corpus annotated for both inter- and intrasentential entity instantiations. Our initial corpus study in McKinlay and Markert (2011) covered 25 Penn Treebank (PTB) Wall Street Journal corpus (Marcus et al., 1993) texts, annotating solely between adjacent sentences. We first extended our intersentential annotation to cover an additional 50 PTB texts, and then added a second layer of intrasentential annotation to the same 75 texts.

3.1 Potential difficulties and Borderline Cases

We took inspiration from the Recognising Textual Entailment (RTE) task (Dagan et al., 2006). In RTE, the challenge is to automatically ascertain whether a text (T) *entails* a hypothesis (H). Rather than framing the problem as an issue of logical implicature, they regard RTE as an applied, empirical task:

> *We say that T entails H if, typically, a human reading T would infer that H is most likely true.* (Dagan et al. (2006))

We, as well, were interested in the phenomena from the perspective of a human reading the text, and so did not apply strict logical rules for identifying entity instantiation, and instead took an applied approach. While successful, this approach is not without drawbacks, and leads to a number of borderline cases.

The plural NPs[3] which act as sets in our corpus fall into 4 rough categories; extensionally defined, clearly intensionally defined, vaguely intensionally defined and generic. For those NPs which are either extensionally defined or are clearly intensional, set members are easy to identify. Examples 7 and 8 show extensionally defined sets, and the sets in Examples 2, 4 and 11 are clearly defined intensional examples.

The other two categories cause more difficulties. Not knowing the members in a vaguely intensionally defined set makes it difficult judging whether the relationship between NPs is a subset, coreference or set overlap. In Example 14, for instance, it is difficult to know for certain whether *'175'* and *'136'* are subsets of *'The 189 Democrats who supported the override yesterday'*, though it may be assumed to be the case.

(14) The 189 Democrats who supported the override yesterday compare with 175 who initially backed the rape-and-incest exemption two weeks ago and 136 last year.

In our annotation scheme, we make no distinction between those plural NPs which represent sets and those which represent generics, and allow instantiations to be drawn from both. This leads to annotation that is more akin to hyponymy than set membership or subset relationships, such as in Example 15.

[3]We restrict our set NPs to plural NPs, in order to reduce annotation effort. This does lead to the exclusion of some singular nouns which would be valid sets, such as *family, set* or *group*. In the future, we intend to include such nouns, either by means of a manually constructed list or using lexicosyntactic patterns.

Entity Instantiation	M&M (2011) corpus		Full corpus	
	# NP Pairs	%	# NP Pairs	%
Set Member	468	1.62	1477	1.89
Subset	180	0.62	641	0.82
No instantiation plural-singular NP pair	18 758	64.76	46 128	59.11
No instantiation plural-plural NP pair	9 560	33.00	29 793	38.18
Total	28 966	100.00	78 039	100.00

Table 1: Frequency of Intersentential Annotations, compared with 25 text corpus from McKinlay and Markert (2011).

(15) a. A customs official said the arrests followed a "Snake Day" at Utrecht University in the Netherlands, an event used by some collectors as an opportunity to obtain **rare snakes**.

b. British customs officers said they'd arrested eight men sneaking *111 rare snakes* into Britain [...]

Despite these problems, we still achieved substantial agreement. This is likely due to the genre of the texts involved; the financial-based newswire texts annotated tend to include many sets, subsets and members which are concrete, such as companies, countries and people. Applying this scheme to a genre of texts that contains more generics and less straightforwardly defined NPs, for example a philosophy text, could lead to a more problematic annotation. One possible way to improve agreement would be to introduce a layer of annotation that identified generic NPs, such as that employed by Reiter and Frank (2010), and prevent these generic NPs from participating in instantiations.

3.2 Intersentential Annotation

We follow our previous annotation method (McKinlay and Markert, 2011), automatically identifying plural and singular NPs, and separately displaying plural-plural NP pairs for subset annotation and plural-singular NP pairs for set member annotation. We also remove NPs that are appositions or predicates, and include the option to mark NPs as *"Not a mention"*, for excluding instances of non-referential *it*, idiomatic NPs and generic pronouns. The task of the annotator is then to indicate whether each NP pair is an instantiation. Each sentence pair is annotated both with sets in the first sentence and members/subsets in the second sentence, and sets in the second sentence and members/subsets in the first.

We annotated 50 PTB texts following this scheme, which combined with our original 25 texts gave us a corpus of 75 texts annotated for intersentential entity instantiations. Table 1 shows the frequency distribution of set members and subsets in both our original 25 texts and the full 75 text corpus.

3.3 Intrasentential Annotation

We added a layer of *intrasentential* entity instantiation annotation to the same 75 texts. We followed the same scheme of annotation as for the intersentential entity instantiations. However, we also included nested instantiations, such as those in Examples 8, 9 and 10.

3.3.1 Agreement Study and Gold Standard Corpus

Despite the differences between inter- and intrasentential annotation being minor, and the intersentential annotation scheme being previously shown to be reliable, we undertook a short agreement study. Five randomly selected texts were annotated by the two authors of this paper independently, and agreement was measured in the same three ways as in McKinlay and Markert (2011):

1. Does this pair of candidate NPs participate in a set membership/subset relationship or not?
2. Does this candidate set member/subset participate in a set membership/subset relationship with any potential set or not?
3. Is there an Entity Instantiation in this sentence?

Method	# Items Tested	Kappa	Agreement
1	3098 NP pairs	0.7493	97.81%
2	1414 NPs	0.7742	96.39%
3	237 sentences	0.7277	89.87%

Table 2: Intrasentential Agreement Statistics

Entity Instantiation	# NP pairs	%
Set Member	1 538	3.51
Subset	865	1.98
No instantiation plur-sing pair	24 363	55.63
No instantiation plur-plur pair	17 028	38.88
Total	43 794	100.00

Table 3: Frequency of Intrasentential Entity Instantiations in 75 texts

Relationship	Set Member		Other Sing-Plur pair	
Set NP Parent	1 065	(69.2%)	2 294	(9.4%)
Member NP Parent	55	(3.6%)	1 843	(7.6%)
Same Clause	84	(5.5%)	7 068	(29.0%)
Different Clause	334	(21.7%)	13 158	(54.0%)
Total	1 538	(100.0%)	24 363	(100.0%)

Table 4: Frequency of syntactic relationships between NPs in set member instantiations.

Relationship	Subset		Other Sing-Plur pair	
Set NP Parent	615	71.1%	1 489	8.7%
Subset NP Parent	85	9.8%	1 991	11.7%
Same Clause	90	10.4%	4 945	29.0%
Different Clause	75	8.7%	8 603	50.5%
Total	865	100.0%	17 028	100.0%

Table 5: Frequency of syntactic relationships between NPs in subset instantiations.

We achieve substantial agreement with all three metrics (see Table 2). Common disagreements consisted of matters of interpretation rather than any systematic problem with the scheme. One common disagreement, related to the issues mentioned in Section 3.1, was deciding whether two sets were in a subset relationship or overlapping, such as *'the key districts'* and *'the state's major cities'* in Example 16.

(16) With ballots from *most of the state's major cities* in by yesterday morning, the Republicans came away with 10% of the vote in several of **the key districts**.

The intrasentential annotation was then completed over the remaining 70 texts by the first author of this paper. The frequency distribution of these annotations is shown in Table 3. The final corpus of intersentential and intrasentential instantiations will be made publicly available, in a stand-off form, at `http://www.comp.leeds.ac.uk/markert/data.html`.

3.3.2 Intrasentential Syntactic Relationships

To gain an insight into the patterns tree kernels might learn, we computed the syntactic relationship between the two participant NPs in an entity instantiation, and compared this to the distribution of non-instantiations. We organised the relationships into four classes: the set NP was a parent of the member/subset NP (e.g Example 8), the member/subset NP was a parent of the set NP (e.g Example 10), the two NPs were not in a parent/child relationship but were in the same clause, and the two NPs were in different clauses (e.g. Example 11).

The results are shown in Tables 4 and 5. We found that in the majority of instantiations, the Set NP was a parent of the Member or Subset NP, and that the distribution of instantiations was significantly different from that of non-instantiations in both set members and subsets[4].

4 Experiments

We used a supervised machine learning approach to identify entity instantiations, treating set membership and subsets separately (see also McKinlay and Markert (2011)). We therefore divide our data set into two; plural-singular NP pairs that are labelled either *set member* or *no-instantiation* and plural-plural NP pairs that are labelled either *subset* or *no-instantiation*. We use the same feature set for both, employing two types of features; traditional unstructured features, and tree kernels.

[4] We used a χ^2 test for consistency in a 4×2 table with 3 degrees of freedom, giving $\chi^2 = 4605$ for set members and $\chi^2 = 3123$ for subsets, both corresponding to $p < 0.00000001$.

4.1 Unstructured features

Our unstructured features are identical to those presented in McKinlay and Markert (2011). They comprise five categories; *surface*, *salience*, *syntactic*, *contextual* and *knowledge*, and contain features that relate to a single NP, and those that represent cross-NP relationships. We list them briefly below, further details of the features can be found in McKinlay and Markert (2011).

Surface features. The unigrams, part-of-speech tags, lemmas and head words of each NP. Also included is Levenshtein's distance between the corresponding strings, the distance in characters and words between NP pairs, and a boolean feature which represents the order of the NPs.

Salience features. The grammatical role of each NP, whether it is the first mention of that entity in the sentence or document, the number of prior mentions and the overall number of mentions of the entity in the document.

Syntactic features. Syntactic parallelism and pre- and post-modification of each NP. The modification type includes values that represent apposition, conjunction, pre modification and bare nouns.

Contextual features. The Levin class (Levin, 1993) of each NP's head verb, as well as the verb itself, whether each NP is in a quotation, and an approximation of the discourse relations present in the two sentences by identifying likely discourse connectives and mapping them to their most frequent explicit relation in the Penn Discourse Treebank (PDTB) (Prasad et al., 2008).

Knowledge-based features. WordNet-based features which express synonymy/hyponymy between potentials members/subsets and sets. A feature which searches Freebase (Bollacker et al., 2008), for potential set member/subset NPs and compares the *topics* (loosely hyponyms) of matching entries to the potential set NP. A Point-wise Mutual Information feature derived from Google hit counts, based on the notion that the pattern "X and other Y", where X is a potential set member or subset and Y is a potential set, indicates hyponymy (Hearst, 1992; Markert and Nissim, 2005). A feature which establishes whether the animacy of the two NPs matches.

4.2 Tree Kernels

The unstructured features discussed in Section 4.1 are presented to the machine learner as a vector. Tree features are instead presented as structured data, and the learner works directly with this structured form.

We used two trees — Shortest Path Enclosed Tree (SPET) and Shortest Path Tree (SPT), which have been previously used for RE (Zhang et al., 2006; Swampillai and Stevenson, 2011). We also included two variations in the lexicalisation of these trees; full delexicalisation, in which all terminal nodes are removed, and partial delexicalisation, in which all terminals which represent nouns are removed.

The SPET is the shortest path between the two NPs, inclusive of all nodes in between. SPT is identical, but *exclusive* of all nodes in between. Example 17 shows a sentence with two NPs underlined. Figure 1(a) and 1(b) show the SPET and SPT that connects them, respectively. We replace the node label of the subtree that represents the set member/subset NP with the node MEMBER, and node label of the subtree that represents the set NP with SET.

(17) In a highly unusual meeting in Sen. DeConcini's office in April 1987, the five senators asked federal regulators to ease up on Lincoln.

For intersentential entity instantiations we followed Swampillai and Stevenson (2011), joining the trees of the two sentences under a single node called ROOT and then extracting the trees as above.

4.3 Experimental Set Up

We considered the problems of intersentential and intrasentential instantiations separately, reasoning that intrasentential instantiations are a sufficiently different phenomena, and occur in patterns not found in intersentential instantiations. Our intuition was that syntax played a stronger role in identifying intrasentential instantiations, and that the tree kernels would have a greater impact on the intrasentential data.

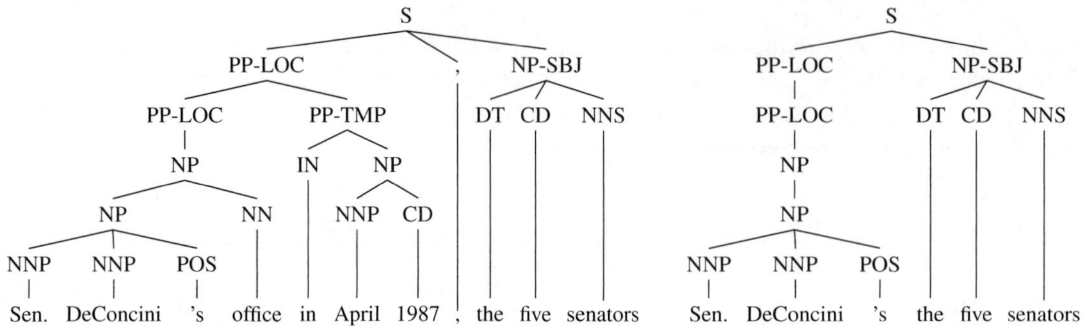

(a) Shortest Path Enclosed Tree (SPET)
(b) Shortest Path Tree (SPT)

Figure 1: Examples of trees used for tree kernel learning.

We applied 10-fold cross-validation for testing and training in all our experiments, keeping pairs of NPs from the same text in the same fold to avoid over-training based on specific topical unigrams that may occur in a single text. We used SVM-LIGHT-TK (Moschitti, 2006b), an extension to SVM^{light} (Joachims, 1999) as our learner. We found that a linear kernel gave best results for flat features, and so used it in all experiments. For all tree kernel experiments we used the Subset tree kernel. We used addition, rather than multiplication, to combine tree and flat feature kernels.

The data contains many more negative examples than positive ones (only 3.7% of the 121,833 candidate pairs are positive). Previously we experimented with *balanced* data sets (McKinlay and Markert, 2011) — data sets in which the numbers of Entity Instantiations and non-Instantiations are equal — to demonstrate the utility of their features. We, however, focus on the original skewed data sets.

For comparison we include two baselines: *majority*, which predicts the majority class in each fold, and *unigram* which has two features, representing the unigrams of the two NPs.

4.4 Intrasentential Results and Discussion

The results of our intrasentential experiments are shown in Table 6. Precision, Recall and F-Score are calculated for the positive instances and SPTP represents SPT, Partially Lexicalised where as SPETF represents SPET, Fully Lexicalised and so on. We also include results of a feature ablation study, in which we removed each group of features in turn. We performed a similar experiment with our tree kernels, based on removing each of the 4 tree kernels in turn. We then combined the full set of tree kernels with the full feature set, and the best performing feature set with the best performing tree kernel combination according to the results of our ablation.

All our algorithms beat the baselines significantly[5]. In the unstructured feature ablation, the best performing algorithm involves the omission of contextual features for both set members and subsets.

The tree kernels have a slightly worse accuracy than the unstructured features but provide a higher precision. There are no significant differences between the performance of each tree kernel combination; there seems to be no difference between partial and full lexicalisation or between including or omitting intervening context in terms of accuracy. This suggests that a few structural features that all 4 representations have in common are important.

The combination of the best unstructured features and best tree kernels leads to significant improvements over either method in isolation for both set members and subsets. Also, the combination of all trees and all features is significantly better than the best unstructured and tree methods for subsets.

[5]McNemar's χ^2 test (1 d.f.) was used for all significance tests on results. Minimum χ^2 values were 280 for set members and 101 for subsets, both corresponding to $p < 0.00000001$.

	Set Members				Subsets			
Feature set	**Accuracy**	**P**	**R**	**F**	**Accuracy**	**P**	**R**	**F**
Majority	94.1%	—	—	—	95.2%	—	—	—
Unigrams	94.1%	—	—	—	95.2%	—	—	—
Unstructured Features								
All features	96.9%	0.847	0.578	0.687	96.8%$^{\eta}$	0.842	0.425	0.565
All features - Surface	96.2%$^{\delta}$	0.805	0.475	0.597	96.1%$^{\gamma}$	0.774	0.282	0.414
All features - Salience	95.7%$^{\gamma}$	0.836	0.337	0.481	96.2%$^{\gamma}$	0.867	0.265	0.406
All features - Syntax	96.6%	0.835	0.538	0.654	96.1%$^{\gamma}$	0.791	0.271	0.404
All features - Contextual	97.0%$^{\alpha}$	0.849	0.597	0.701	97.0%$^{\alpha}$	0.834	0.471	0.602
All features - World Knowledge	96.7%$^{\delta}$	0.834	0.552	0.665	96.6%$^{\gamma}$	0.852	0.788	0.833
Tree kernels								
SPTP+SPTF+SPETP+SPETF	96.7%	0.894	0.495	0.637	96.7%	0.937	0.342	0.501
SPTF+SPETP+SPETF	96.6%	0.897	0.486	0.630	96.7%	0.940	0.345	0.504
SPTP+SPETF+SPETP	96.7%$^{\beta}$	0.914	0.491	0.638	96.7%	0.937	0.343	0.504
SPTP+SPTF+SPETF	96.6%	0.892	0.492	0.634	96.7%$^{\beta}$	0.940	0.345	0.504
SPTP+SPTF+SPETP	96.7%	0.908	0.494	0.640	96.7%	0.934	0.343	0.502
Combination kernels								
All Trees + All features	97.0%	0.884	0.579	0.699	97.2%$^{\epsilon}$	0.934	0.461	0.618
SPTF + SPTP + SPETF + All - Contextual	97.1%$^{\epsilon}$	0.889	0.591	0.710	97.3%$^{\epsilon}$	0.936	0.476	0.631
SPTP + SPETF + SPETP + All - Contextual	97.1%	0.886	0.586	0.705	97.3%$^{\epsilon}$	0.935	0.479	0.633

Table 6: Intrasentential results.

α SVM flat-feature algorithm with highest accuracy
β Tree Kernel Algorithm with highest accuracy
γ Significantly *worse* than α, $p < 0.001$.
δ Significantly *worse* than α, $p < 0.05$.
ϵ Significantly *better* than α ($p < 0.05$) and β ($p < 0.001$)

4.5 Intersentential Results and Discussion

Intersentential instantiation identification is a more difficult problem than its intrasentential counterpart. The best F-scores achieved by us on the original data, rather than the artificially created balanced set, were 0.1938 and 0.1414 for set members and subsets respectively, and involved oversampling the positive instances (McKinlay and Markert, 2011). Our classifier had very poor recall without oversampling — 0.0289 for set members, 0.0266 for subsets — leading to F-Scores of 0.0527 and 0.0465.

In our experiments on the expanded corpus, we found that SVM-LIGHT-TK with the same options as our intrasentential experiments led to a classifier which always predicted the majority class, giving us a Precision, Recall and F-Score of 0. We had more success by using the cost-factor parameter to penalise errors on positive examples more heavily in the training process[6]. The value of the cost-parameter was set to $f(\text{Negative Examples})/f(\text{Positive Examples})$.

The results of our intersentential experiments are shown in Table 7. We improve over our previous non-oversampled results for set members and subsets, and the oversampled results for set members. However, as the corpus is triple the size, direct comparison is difficult. We find that whilst our tree kernels are more accurate than their unstructured counterparts, recall is much poorer, meaning that the unstructured features in isolation have the best F-Scores. The only algorithms that perform significantly differently to the unigram baseline are the unstructured set member classifier, which has worse accuracy but an increased F-Score, and the two subset classifiers which use tree kernels, which have higher accuracy but lower F-Scores. Our intuition that tree kernels would have less impact on intersentential instantiations, as they are not as syntax-dependent, appears accurate.

[6]Applying this additional setting to our intrasentential data produced classifiers with similar accuracy as before, but with reduced precision and increased recall. For example, on the All Trees + All Features combination, the classifier using the cost factor parameter scored an Accuracy/P/R/F of 96.5/71.0/69.5/70.2 for set members and 97.1/78.8/54.1/64.2 for subsets.

	Set Members				Subsets			
Feature set	**Accuracy**	**P**	**R**	**F**	**Accuracy**	**P**	**R**	**F**
Majority	96.9%	—	—	—	97.9%	—	—	—
Unigrams	95.1%	0.166	0.143	0.153	97.1%	0.058	0.023	0.033
All Unstructured	94.8%†	0.216	0.257	0.235	97.0%	0.146	0.086	0.108
All Trees	95.2%	0.217	0.214	0.215	97.8%†	0.042	0.002	0.003
All Trees + All Unstructured	95.2%	0.217	0.214	0.215	97.7%†	0.250	0.041	0.070

Table 7: Intersentential results.

† Significantly different from unigram baseline, $p < 0.001$.

5 Conclusion and Future Work

In this paper we make two novel contributions; the introduction of intrasentential entity instantiations, and the application of tree kernels to the detection of both intra- and intersentential entity instantiations. Our corpus of intrasentential entity instantiations is annotated with good agreement, and our statistics show that the majority of intrasentential instantiations have strong syntactic links between participating NPs. We then use tree kernels to learn directly from constituency parse tree data. Our tree kernels perform comparably to much larger and more varied set of unstructured features, that needed access to outside world knowledge sources. In addition, the combination of those unstructured features and tree kernels leads to significant improvements over either method in isolation on intrasentential data. Our best algorithms are highly precise.

In the future, we wish to explore the annotation of entity instantiations beyond adjacent sentences, and apply our scheme to genres other than newswire. We wish to explore different tree representations, such as those based on dependency structures, and different tree kernels, such as the more general Partial Tree Kernel (Moschitti, 2006a). We intend to improve our classification results by employing a global model for the joint learning of inter- and intrasentential entity instantiations.

Entity instantiations also have the potential to be useful for a number of applications, including discourse relation classification, sentiment analysis and summarisation. We wish to investigate the impact of entity instantiations on these applications.

Acknowledgements

Andrew McKinlay is funded by an EPSRC Doctoral Training Grant.

References

ACE (2000-2005). Automatic Content Extraction. `http://www.ldc.upenn.edu/Projects/ACE/`.

Bollacker, K., C. Evans, P. Paritosh, T. Sturge, and J. Taylor (2008). Freebase: a collaboratively created graph database for structuring human knowledge. In *Proceedings of ACM SIGMOD 2008*, pp. 1247–1250.

Bunescu, R. and R. Mooney (2005). A shortest path dependency kernel for relation extraction. In *Proceedings of HLT/EMNLP 2005*, pp. 724–731.

Chan, Y. and D. Roth (2010). Exploiting background knowledge for relation extraction. In *Proceedings of COLING 2010*, pp. 152–160.

Clark, H. (1975). Bridging. In *Proceedings of the 1975 Workshop on Theoretical Issues in Natural Language Processing*, pp. 169–174.

Culotta, A. and J. Sorensen (2004). Dependency tree kernels for relation extraction. In *Proceedings of ACL 2004*, pp. 423.

Dagan, I., O. Glickman, and B. Magnini (2006). The PASCAL Recognising Textual Entailment Challenge. In J. Quiñonero Candela, I. Dagan, B. Magnini, and F. d'Alché Buc (Eds.), *Machine Learning Challenges*, Volume 3944, Chapter 9, pp. 177–190. Springer Berlin Heidelberg.

Hearst, M. (1992). Automatic acquisition of hyponyms from large text corpora. In *Proceedings of COLING 1992*, pp. 539–545.

Hendrickx, I., S. N. Kim, Z. Kozareva, P. Nakov, D. Ó Séaghdha, S. Padó, M. Pennacchiotti, L. Romano, and S. Szpakowicz (2010). Semeval-2010 task 8: Multi-way classification of semantic relations between pairs of nominals. In *Proceedings of the 5th International Workshop on Semantic Evaluation*, pp. 33–38.

Joachims, T. (1999). Making large-scale support vector machine learning practical. In *Advances in kernel methods*, pp. 169–184. MIT Press.

Kambhatla, N. (2004). Combining lexical, syntactic, and semantic features with maximum entropy models for extracting relations. In *Proceedings of ACL 2004*, pp. 22.

Levin, B. (1993). *English verb classes and alternations: A preliminary investigation*. University of Chicago press.

Marcus, M., M. Marcinkiewicz, and B. Santorini (1993). Building a large annotated corpus of English: The Penn Treebank. *Computational Linguistics 19*(2), 313–330.

Markert, K., Y. Hou, and M. Strube (2012). Collective classification for fine-grained information status. In *Proceedings of ACL 2012*, pp. 8–14.

Markert, K., N. Modjeska, and M. Nissim (2003). Using the web for nominal anaphora resolution. In *Proceedings of EACL 2003 Workshop on the Computational Treatment of Anaphora*, pp. 39–46.

Markert, K. and M. Nissim (2005). Comparing knowledge sources for nominal anaphora resolution. *Computational Linguistics 31*(3), 367–402.

Markert, K., M. Strube, and U. Hahn (1996). Inferential realization constraints on functional anaphora in the centering model. In *Proceedings of CogSci 1996*, pp. 609–614.

McKinlay, A. and K. Markert (2011, September). Modelling entity instantiations. In *Proceedings of RANLP 2011*, pp. 268–274.

Moschitti, A. (2006a). Efficient convolution kernels for dependency and constituent syntactic trees. In *Proceedings of ECML 2006*, pp. 318–329.

Moschitti, A. (2006b). Making tree kernels practical for natural language learning. In *Proceedings of EACL 2006*, Volume 6, pp. 113–120.

MUC (1987-1998). Message Understanding Conferences. The NIST MUC website: `http://www.itl.nist.gov/iaui/894.02/related_projects/muc/`.

Nissim, M., S. Dingare, J. Carletta, and M. Steedman (2004). An annotation scheme for information status in dialogue. In *Proceedings of LREC 2004*.

Poesio, M. (2003). Associative descriptions and salience: A preliminary investigation. In *Proceedings of the EACL 2003 Workshop on The Computational Treatment of Anaphora*.

Poesio, M., R. Mehta, A. Maroudas, and J. Hitzeman (2004). Learning to resolve bridging references. In *Proceedings of ACL 2004*, pp. 143.

Poesio, M., R. Vieira, and S. Teufel (1997). Resolving bridging references in unrestricted text. In *Proceedings of Workshop on Operational Factors in Practical, Robust Anaphora Resolution for Unrestricted Texts*, pp. 1–6.

Prasad, R., N. Dinesh, A. Lee, E. Miltsakaki, L. Robaldo, A. Joshi, and B. Webber (2008). The Penn Discourse TreeBank 2.0. In *Proceedings of LREC 2008*, pp. 2961–2968.

Prince, E. (1981). Toward a Taxonomy of Given-New Information. *Radical Pragmatics 3*, 223–255.

Rahman, A. and V. Ng (2012). Learning the fine-grained information status of discourse entities. In *Proceedings of EACL 2012*.

Reiter, N. and A. Frank (2010). Identifying generic noun phrases. In *Proceedings of ACL 2010*, pp. 40–49.

Roth, D. and W. Yih (2002). Probabilistic reasoning for entity & relation recognition. In *Proceedings of COLING 2002*, pp. 1–7. ACL.

Sun, A., R. Grishman, and S. Sekine (2011). Semi-supervised relation extraction with large-scale word clustering. In *Proceedings of ACL-HLT 2011*, pp. 521–529.

Swampillai, K. and M. Stevenson (2011, September). Extracting relations within and across sentences. In *Proceedings of RANLP 2011*, pp. 25–32. RANLP 2011 Organising Committee.

Vieira, R. and M. Poesio (2000). An empirically based system for processing definite descriptions. *Computational Linguistics 26*(4), 539–593.

Zelenko, D., C. Aone, and A. Richardella (2003). Kernel methods for relation extraction. *The Journal of Machine Learning Research 3*, 1083–1106.

Zhang, M., J. Zhang, J. Su, and G. Zhou (2006). A composite kernel to extract relations between entities with both flat and structured features. In *Proceedings of COLING/ACL 2006*, pp. 825–832.

Zhou, G., J. Su, J. Zhang, and M. Zhang (2005). Exploring various knowledge in relation extraction. In *Proceedings of ACL 2005*, pp. 427–434.

Zhou, G., M. Zhang, D. Ji, and Q. Zhu (2007). Tree Kernel-Based Relation Extraction with Context-Sensitive Structured Parse Tree Information. In *Proceedings of EMNLP-CoNLL 2007*, pp. 728–736.

A corpus study of clause combination

Olga Nikitina
Institut für Computerlinguistik
Universität Heidelberg
nikitina@cl.uni-heidelberg.de

Sebastian Padó
Institut für Computerlinguistik
Universität Heidelberg
pado@cl.uni-heidelberg.de

Abstract

We present a corpus-based investigation of cases of clause combination that can be expressed both through coordination or with subordination. We analyse the data with a two-step computational model which first distinguishes subordination from coordination and then determines the direction for cases of subordination. We find that a wide range of features help with the prediction, notably frequency of predicate participants, presence of adjuncts and sharing of participants between the clause predicates.

1 Introduction

Subordination and coordination are the two primary ways to combine syntactic phrases into sentences. Coordination is a paratactic way of combining constituents (typically) of the same category, where the whole construction has the same type as its daughters. Coordination stands in opposition to subordination, where one constituent is syntactically dependent on another, and where the whole construction has the same type as only one of its daughters, the head daughter. Figure 1 shows examples of both constructions.

In subordinate structures, the dependent constituent can occupy the position of either argument or adjunct. In this paper, we ignore cases of subordinated argument clauses, since their occurrence is mandated mainly by the subcategorization properties of the main clause predicate. Instead, we focus on subordinated clauses that are adjuncts of the main clauses, such as gerund constructions or clauses introduced by subordinating conjunctions (*when, because, ...*). Such adjunctive clauses typically describe independent events that stand in some relation to the main clause event.

For such cases, the question arises what determines the speaker's choice between subordination and coordination. It is discussed controversially in the literature. Matthiessen and Thompson (1988) argue that subordination and coordination constructions are grammaticalized discourse relations, with coordination representing the paratactic discourse relations such as *Sequence* and adjunctive subordination constructions representing subjective hypotactic discourse relations such as *Condition* or *Circumstance*. Goldsmith (1985) and Culicover and Jackendoff (1997) list instances of coordination constructions with semantics that is different from that of a sequence, and demonstrate that coordination constructions can express, for example, condition (cf. the example in Figure. 1, a simplified version of their original example *You drink one more can of beer and I'm leaving*). Similarly, there are coordination constructions with causal, concessive, and other meanings.

The goal of our study is to analyze a broader range of factors and their influence on the coordination/subordination choice. To this end, we perform a corpus-based analysis that investigates properties of predicates (and the events which they express) that correlate with the choice between subordination and coordination.

Our study considers three groups of features that are useful for the prediction of clause combination type between two clauses: the frequency and recency of predicates' participants, the presence of adjuncts and the sharing of semantic arguments between predicates. We show that the subordination-coordination choice is not based exclusively on discourse factors, but also correlates with the presence of common participants of predicates as well as with the number and type of predicate modifiers.

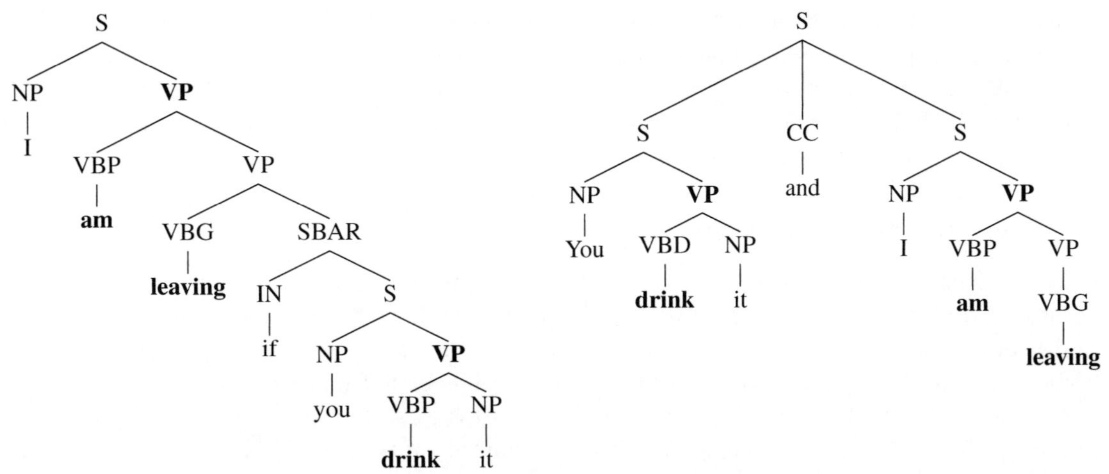

Figure 1: Examples of subordination (left) and coordination (right). The VP projections of the predicates are marked in boldface.

Plan of the paper. In Section 2 we formulate the task and present our method of feature evaluation. In Section 3, we present the features and analyze their usefulness for the prediction tasks. Section 4 contains the evaluation of our model against a majority-case baseline and a model that relies on morphological features. We relate our research to previous studies in Section 5 and summarize the results and give conclusions in Section 6.

2 Method

We adopt a corpus-based method to study the coordination vs. subordination choice. We use the OntoNotes corpus (Pradhan et al., 2007) to extract cases of coordination and subordination and analyze various classes of features that can be suspected in correlating with the coordination/subordination distinction. We evaluate the predictions of our classifiers against the relations between clauses in the original text, which we treat as the gold standard.

This section formulates our task more precisely. We begin by describing our operationalization of the terms "coordination" and "subordination". Then we propose a way to estimate the correlations between the type of clause combination and features of the clauses. Finally, we describe the corpus that we exploit in our experiments.

2.1 Operationalizing Subordination and Coordination

For the analysis, we need to define subordination and coordination constructions in terms of Penn Treebank parse trees and other layers of corpus annotation. For all predicates marked in the PropBank layer of the corpus annotation we define their VP projections (see examples in Figure 1). If the VPs (or their dominating S-nodes) are located at the same level in the tree and if their mother node is also a VP (or an S, respectively), and if they are linked by a coordination conjunction (a word with the part-of-speech CC), we consider these pairs of predicates as *coordination constructions*. *Subordination constructions* are pairs of predicates where one VP is embedded in another VP. More specifically, we define X to be subordinate to Y if there are exactly two VPs on the path between X and Y which correspond to the projections of X and Y, respectively.[1]. Additionally, we restrict our attention to subordinate clauses that are adjucts as motivated in Section 1. We use the PropBank annotation layer to filter out all pairs where one of the

[1]For a deeper analysis of syntactic and semantic differences between coordinate and subordinate structures see, for example, Haspelmath (2004).

predicates is marked as an argument of the second predicate, or where a predicate is the main verb of a sentence that occupies a position of an argument. The semantic information from PropBank allows us to distinguish between syntactically identical argument and adjunct clauses, e.g. "*I liked singing*" and "*I stood singing*". We also exclude all relative clauses and other clausal noun modifiers. For this, we make sure that the path between predicate projections does not contain NPs.

2.2 Statistical Model and Evaluation

Given a pair of predicates (p_1,p_2), we are faced with two binary decision tasks: (a) p_1 and p_2 can be coordinated or one of them can be subordinated to another, and (b) if the predicates form a subordination construction, either of them can be the main predicate. The first task is the task of prediction the clause combination type, the second is the task of predicting the direction of subodination.

For the purposes of computational modeling, we treat these two decisions as independent and sequential. For each task, we train a binary classifier on sets of features that can influence the clause combination type. More specifically, we make use of logistic regression models, a method that in the past furnished estimates of the importance of different factors in explaining linguistic variation, see e.g. Bresnan et al. (2007) or Hayes and Wilson (2008).

Formally, logistic regression models assume that datapoints consist of a set of predictors x and a binary response variable y. They have the form

$$p(y=1) = \frac{1}{1+e^{-z}} \text{ with } z = \sum_i \beta_i x_i \quad (1)$$

where p is the probability of a datapoint x, β_i is the weight assigned to the predictor x_i. Model estimation sets the parameters β so that the likelihood of the observed (training) data is maximized.

We construct one classifier for each task and for each response variable: $\mathrm{subord\text{-}type}(p_1, p_2)$ computes the probability for p_1 and p_2 being linked by a subordination relation, $\mathrm{coord\text{-}type}(p_1, p_2)$ computes the probablity for the two predicates to be coordinated, $\mathrm{subord\text{-}dir}(p_1, p_2)$ calculates the probablity the probability for p_2 being subordinated to p_1, and $\mathrm{subord\text{-}type}(p_2, p_1)$ computes the probability that p_2 dominates p_1. For the first task, we compute the outcome as $\arg\max\{\mathrm{coord\text{-}type}(p_1, p_2),$ $\mathrm{subord\text{-}type}(p_1, p_2)\}$, and for the second task as $\arg\max\{\mathrm{subord\text{-}dir}(p_1, p_2), \mathrm{subord\text{-}dir}(p_2, p_1)\}$, respectively. Note that we assume that coordination is a symmetrical relation and we do neither predict nor utilize the linear order of predicates in the original sentence.

Within this scenario, we perform an analysis of individual features and feature groups according to standard practice in the statistics community by considering the effect of features on the models' residual deviance. Residual deviance describes the ratio of the likelihood of the data under a "saturated" model to the likelihood of the data under the actual model (Baayen, 2011). Large decreases in residual deviance that result from the addition of a feature indicate that the feature has substantially increased the ability of the model to explain the data. The statistical significance of the decrease can be determined with the chi-square test.

Since this analysis considers only the training set, it is amenable to overfitting. We therefore add a second kind of analysis that evaluates the model trained on an unseen test set. As the figure of merit, we use simple accuracy (percentage of correctly predicted clause combination types) and compare it against two different baselines (Section 4).

2.3 Corpus

We run our training and testing on the release 4.0 of the OntoNotes corpus (Pradhan et al. (2007)). It contains several layers of annotation, including the PropBank annotation of predicate-argument structures (Palmer et al., 2005), Penn Treebank-style parses (Marcus et al., 1993), and a coreference annotation layer (BBN Technologies, 2007). The WSJ sections 00, 02-04, 09-12, 14, and 17 are used for training and section 20 is used for testing. There are in total 732 documents in the training part of the corpus and 76 in the testing subcorpus. Documents include an average of 46.4 sentences and 109.3 predicates, respectively.

Training corpus		Testing corpus	
Subordinate pairs	7691	Subordinate pairs	736
Coordinate pairs	2187	Coordinate pairs	182
Other pairs	625	Other pairs	61
Total number of pairs	10530	Total number of pairs	979

Table 1: Training and testing corpora

Our training and testing corpora contain three types of predicate pairs. Pairs of the first type are those that joined by the subordination relation, and pairs of the second type are coordination pairs. Third type pairs are those that resemble coordination, but are not linked by any conjunction. We do not consider these cases. Table 1 shows the most important statistics.

Note that while the labels for our first task (subordination vs. coordination, cf. Section 2.2) are "read off" the corpus instances, the relation between the predicates in each subordination pair is not correlated with the actual order of the predicates in the text. In our representation of the data, we broke down all subordination pairs randomly in two classes of comparable size (3833 and 3858 pairs in each class, respectively). In one case all features for p_1 correspond to the features of the main verb, and in another class all features of p_1 describe the dependent verb.

3 Features and Feature Analysis

Table 2 lists the features that we consider in our study. Most features describe *predicates* p_1 or p_2, i.e., the head verbs of adjacent clauses. Each predicate describes an event, typically with one or more participants. Formally, we model *participants* as collections of coreferent NPs (as manually annotated on the coreference level of the corpus). The relationship between participants and predicates is captured on the level of *semantic roles* as annotated on the predicate-argument (PropBank) level of the corpus (e.g., ARG0 is the agent, ARG1 is the patient). Participants can fill more than one role for one predicate, or roles of more than one predicate. In these cases, we talk about *sharing* of participants.

Our features fall into three groups:

Salience features exploit the idea that the discourse status of events is reflected in their syntactic position in the sentence (Matthiessen and Thompson, 1988): key events that are necessary for the understanding of the story cannot be expressed as subordinate clauses. If this holds, it could be expected that such events have more salient participants of the discourse as arguments, and that their discourse status is at least partially determined by the salience of their participants. We assess the salience of participants with a total of 20 features, using some of the features used in anaphora resolution tasks: participant frequency and distance to the previous mention (see Chiarcos (2011) and Mitkov (1998), among others). Participant frequency should show how salient the participant is for the overall document. The distance to the previous mention helps to trace down smaller topics and characterize the participant's role in the local discourse.

Adjunct features cover the expression of adjuncts of the predicates. This group is designed to test whether presence of non-clausal modifiers of predicates influence their syntactic combination. The idea behind including these features is two-fold: on the one hand, they might account for the size of the clauses that should be combined. On the other hand, they might give a clue to us, what properties of events are referred to in the context of the two clause combinations.

Shared participant features test the hypothesis that clauses are syntactically connected because they share content, namely they describe events with identical participants. It was shown before that mentions of same entities may be employed to detect global discourse structure (see Section 5), therefore, it might be possible that they also act on a more local level.

Feat. id	Feature description
Salience features	
f_{1-2}	Number of mentions of the most frequent participant of a predicate
f_{3-4}	Average frequency of all participants of a predicate
f_{5-6}	Average participant frequency, discounted by log of document length in clauses
f_{7-8}	Number of mentions of the most frequent participant, discounted by log of document length in clauses
f_{9-10}	Average participant frequency, discounted by log of number of participants in the document
f_{11-12}	Number of mentions of the most frequent participant, discounted by log of number of participants in the document
f_{13}	Are the most frequent participants of the two predicates equally frequent?
f_{14}	Is the most frequent participant of p_1 mentioned more often than that of p_2?
f_{15-16}	Have any of the participants of a predicate been mentioned previously in text
f_{17-18}	Distance to the previous mention of the participant, minimum over all participants
f_{19}	Has the most recently mentioned participant of p_2 appeared in the document is the same sentence as the most recent participant of p_1?
f_{20}	Has the most recently mentioned participant of p_2 appeared in the document in a sentence that comes before the sentence, where the most recent participant of p_1 was mentioned for the first time?
Adjunct features	
f_{21-22}	Number of adjuncts (of any type)
f_{23-24}	Number of temporal adjuncts
f_{25-26}	Number of locative adjuncts
f_{27-28}	Number of purpose adjuncts
f_{29-30}	Number of causal adjuncts
f_{31-32}	Number of manner adjuncts
Shared participant features	
f_{33}	Are there any shared participants between the predicates?
f_{34}	Number of shared participants between the predicates
f_{35-36}	Does the agent of a predicate coincide with other participants?
f_{37-38}	Does the patient of a predicate coincide with other participants?
f_{39}	Does the agent of p_1 coincide with the patient of p_2?
f_{40}	Does the patient of p_1 coincide with the agent of p_2?
f_{41}	Do the agents of predicates coincide?
f_{42}	Do the patients of predicates coincide?

Table 2: Features for clause combination type prediction. Features with double feature id (e.g. f_{3-4}) are computed separately for each predicate (one for the predicate p_1, one for the predicate p_2)

In the rest of this section, we model the feature groups individually to assess their contribution overall and in terms of single features (cf. Section 2.2).

3.1 Salience Features

The results for predicting subordination/coordination based on salience features are given in Table 3. We find that of all salience features, only features that estimate participant frequency and novelty are useful for the prediction of clause combination type. In fact, predicates with equally frequent participants are more likely to be coordinated than form a subordination construction. This feature has a far greater impact on the model performance than any other feature.

In subordination constructions, verbs with old participants are dispreferred in subordinated positions, while simultaneously verbs with overall more frequent participants are more likely to be dependent on other verbs. We interpret this result, surprising at first sight, to mean that "early" mentions of frequent participants are often found in subordinate clauses. Indeed, this situation is common for news articles, where main participants of the news story are introduced in the first sentence. In the following example, the NP *the American Bar Association* that will be subsequently mentioned in the text several times is first introduced in the subordinate clause: *The Bush administration's nomination of Clarence Thomas to a seat*

Feature id and description	Response variable					
	Clause comb. type is subord.			*p_2 subordinated to p_1*		
	Coefficient	$-\Delta$ RD	Sig.	Coefficient	$-\Delta$ RD	Sig.
Intercept	1.58196	–	–	0.214595	–	–
f_3: Average participant freq. of p_1	-0.04649	35.288	***	0.008190	0.977	
f_4: Average participant freq. of p_2	-0.03265	6.259	*	0.004631	0.044	
f_{15}: A participant of p_1 is not new	0.06243	20.348	***	0.501011	4.978	*
f_{16}: A participant of p_2 is not new	0.03532	4.398	*	-0.503871	16.493	***
f_{13}: Equally frequent participants	-0.59391	180.477	***	0.268878	0.002	
f_{14}: Participants of p_1 are more frequent	-0.02845	0.064		-0.547673	33.708	***
f_{20}: Participants of p_1 are more recent	0.31972	9.994	**	0.008335	0.028	
f_{19}: Equally recent participants	-0.02007	0.031		0.034358	0.105	.

Table 3: Frequency-related features ($-\Delta$ RD: drop in residual deviance; Sig.: Statistical significance, .: $p<0.1$; *: $p<0.05$; **: $p<0.01$; ***: $p<0.001$)

on the federal appeals court here received a blow this week when the American Bar Association gave Mr. Thomas only a "qualified" rating, rather than "well qualified".

In sum, the analysis of salience features shows that the discourse status of participants correlates with the syntactic structure of the sentences only mildly. They may be relevant mostly for the prediction of clause combination, but not for the prediction of direction of subordination.

3.2 Adjunct Features

The model that explores the influence of expressed adjuncts is given in Tables 4. The model includes features that describe the number of expressed non-clausal adjuncts. Verbs with temporal and, in particular, locative modifiers tend to be coordinated. Presence of causal adjuncts, on the other hand, increases the probablity of a subordination relation.

A possible explanation is that texts that involve descriptions of locations of different objects and events include more coordination constructions. When the text discusses cause and effects, it is more likely to contain subordination constructions which allow a more precise expression of the semantic relation through subordinating conjunctions. This idea extends the hypothesis that RST relations such as *Cause* are grammaticalized as subordination relations by suggesting that subordination is also likely to be used for other phrasal adjucts of clauses with causal adjuncts.

Within the category of subordination constructions, main clauses tend to contain less adjuncts than subordinated clauses. Clauses that are "heavy" with adjuncts generally reside lower in the syntactic tree; this may be due to considerations similar to those involved in the "heavy NP shift" within clauses (Ross, 1967). The presence of locative adjuncts is the only feature that has a significant effect on the prediction and that runs counter to this pattern.

3.3 Shared Participant Features

Table 5 shows an analysis of the participant features. The features f_{39-40} are most useful for the prediction of dependency direction in the subordination construction. Sharing of the patient of p_1 with the agent of p_2 (f_{39}) is a very strong indicator that p_1 assumes the position of main verb. On the other hand, coinciding agents (f_{41}) and patients (f_{42}) suggest that the verbs are most likely coordinated. The coefficient for the feature f_{34} suggests that the more participants two predicates have in common, the more likely it is that they form a subordination construction.

However, in our experiments we found out that the feature that indicates the presence of shared participants (f_{33}) has the opposite impact on the prediction of clause combination type. In fact, if we treat the f_{34} as a discrete variable, we obtain clearer results. Exactly one common participant increases the chances that the predicates are coordinated, but as the number of shared participants grows, the subordination becomes a more probable alternative (see Table 6).

Feature id and description	Response variable					
	Subordinative combination			p_2 *subordinated to* p_1		
	Coefficient	$-\Delta$ RD	Sig.	Coefficient	Drop $-\Delta$ RD	Sig.
Intercept	1.06692	–	–	0.007055	–	–
f_{23}: Number of temp. adjuncts of p_1	-0.07231	3.5674	.	-0.246345	20.2885	***
f_{24}: Number of temp. adjuncts of p_2	-0.13936	8.3621	**	0.230160	17.5562	***
f_{25}: Number of loc. adjuncts of p_1	-0.36687	19.9467	***	0.127297	1.5190	
f_{26}: Number of loc. adjuncts of p_2	-0.25236	7.6491	**	-0.201170	3.9508	*
f_{27}: Number of purp. adjuncts of p_1	0.39889	0.9586		0.364775	0.9158	
f_{28}: Number of purp. adjuncts of p_2	0.79290	2.0314		-0.437820	0.9268	
f_{29}: Number of cause adjuncts of p_1	0.84954	11.4742	***	-0.028193	0.0160	
f_{30}: Number of cause adjuncts of p_2	0.32878	2.8584	.	0.410857	5.2560	*
f_{21}: Number of manner adjuncts of p_1	0.03634	0.0960		-0.190564	5.8010	*
f_{32}: Number of manner adjuncts of p_2	-0.18875	5.8788	*	0.040456	0.2218	

Table 4: Features characterizing non-clausal adjuncts of the predicates ($-\Delta$ RD: drop in residual deviance; Sig.: Statistical significance, .: p<0.1; *: p<0.05; **: p<0.01; ***: p<0.001)

Feature id and description	Response variable					
	Subordinative combination			p_2 *subordinated to* p_1		
	Coefficient	$-\Delta$ RD	Sig.	Coefficient	$-\Delta$ RD	Sig.
Intercept	1.31168	–	–	-0.0003424	–	–
f_{34}: Number of shared participants	0.18660	205.41	***	0.0137141	0.326	
f_{39}: The agent of p_1 is the patient of p_2	-0.59652	8.02	**	-1.5567667	113.404	***
f_{40}: The agent of p_2 is the patient of p_1	-0.68431	2.23		1.6358964	100.761	***
f_{41}: The agents are the same entity	-1.72330	391.99	***	-0.1119343	1.651	
f_{42}: The patients are the same entity	-1.66920	153.62	***	0.1537697	0.652	

Table 5: Features describing the sharing of participants ($-\Delta$ RD: drop in residual deviance; Sig.: Statistical significance, .: p<0.1; *: p<0.05; **: p<0.01; ***: p<0.001)

Thus, there is a non-linear dependency between participant sharing features and clause combination type. Subordination and coordination constructions have distinct patterns of participant sharing. For coordination, it is often exactly one participant that occupies the same semantic role in the frames of both predicates. More shared participants mean that the verbs are more likely to be subordinated. These constructions are distinguished by the tendency to share participants between the patient of the main verb and the agent of the dependent verb.

We have also tested models with less specific features f_{35-38} and noticed that in subordination constructions, the dependent verb is generally likely to share its agent with one of other participants of the main predicate. In the task of the prediction of clause combination type, having shared participants in almost any role is more likely for coordination constructions, with higher coefficients for agent sharing (f_{35-36}).

4 Prediction of Clause Combination Type

In this Section, we build a model that incorporates all the features that we have discussed in the previous section and use it to predict the test portion of our dataset.

This model (the *Semantic/Discourse Model*), is created on the basis of the most successful features according to our previous analyses. Specifically, it includes 14 features which (a) estimate and compare the frequency of the participants of the verbs in the pair ($f_{3,13,14}$), which (b) register whether any of the participants were mentioned previously ($f_{15,16,20}$), (c) the number of expressed temporal, locative and causal adjuncts ($f_{23-26,29}$), and (d) that report on whether participants are shared between agent and patient roles of the two predicates ($f_{34,39-42}$). We build one classifier for each class and combine them as described in Section 2.2.

Feature id and description	Response variable					
	Subordinative combination			*p_2 subordinated to p_1*		
	Coefficient	$-\Delta$ RD	Sig.	Coefficient	$-\Delta$ RD	Sig.
Intercept	1.45711	–	–	0.004735	–	–
f_{34}=1: One shared participants	-0.99505			-0.013430		
f_{34}=2: Two shared participants	0.05641			-0.261963		
f_{34}=3: Three shared participants	0.92524	766.36	***	0.090377	9.938	.
f_{34}=4: Four shared participants	0.72261			0.004918		
f_{34}=5: Five shared participants	-0.50095			0.682436		
f_{39}: The agent of p_1 is the patient of p_2	-0.50048	4.90	*	-1.493254	112.868	***
f_{40}: The agent of p_2 is the patient of p_1	-0.61984	0.37		1.710374	101.606	***
f_{41}: The agents are the same entity	-1.50994	265.26	***	0.006720	0.100	
f_{42}: The patients are the same entity	-1.34141	94.45	***	0.233702	1.455	

Table 6: Features describing the sharing of participants ($-\Delta$ RD: drop in residual deviance; Sig.: Statistical significance, .: $p<0.1$; *: $p<0.05$; **: $p<0.01$; ***: $p<0.001$)

Feature id and description	Response variable					
	Subordinative combination			*p_2 subordinated to p_1*		
	Coefficient	$-\Delta$ RD	Sig.	Coefficient	$-\Delta$ RD	Sig.
Intercept	0.94877	–	–	0.002226	–	–
p_1 is a gerund	0.36027			-1.702426		
p_1 is an infinitive	0.11551	51.514	***	-1.187537	514.90	***
p_1 is a participle	-0.53580			-0.979405		
p_2 is a gerund	0.26939			1.835103		
p_2 is an infinitive	0.11392	24.017	***	1.014216	530.34	***
p_2 is a participle	-0.45433			1.154144		

Table 7: Features for the Morphological Model: verb form of p_1 and verb form of p_2. Each value is assigned a coefficient, but the drop in residual deviance is computed at the feature level. ($-\Delta$ RD: drop in residual deviance; Sig.: Statistical significance, .: $p<0.1$; *: $p<0.05$; **: $p<0.01$; ***: $p<0.001$)

We compare our Semantic/Discourse model to two other models. The first one, *Majority Baseline*, assigns every pair to the most frequent class. For the first task (subordination vs. coordination), this is subordination (75% of instances); for the second, this is subordination of p_1 under p_2 (52% of instances).

Our second point of comparison is the *Morphological Model*. This model is based on just two features, namely the morphological forms of the two verbs. These features allow the model to solve the second task in cases when subordinated predicate has a non-finite form. However, from our point of view, this model is not fit for our purposes since it uses information which from a generation perspective is not yet available at the point in time when syntactic decisions have to be made.

Table 7 lists these features in a similar manner to the semantic and discourse features used in Section 3. Both features are modelled as factors with four levels each (the three listed ones plus the base level of finite verb).[2]

The results of applying these models to our OntoNotes test set are shown in Table 8. For the first task, the accuracy of the Majority Baseline classifier corresponds to the proportion of the majority classes in the dataset (0.75). The Morphological Model follows the Baseline in assigning all cases to the subordination case and thus achieves the same overall accuracy. On the second task, it improves substantially over the baseline (accuracy 0.606) due to correct predictions in cases where subordinated clauses have non-finite predicates. At the same time, when both predicates have finite form (which is the majority of our data) the classifier cannot make any informed decision. However, although its intercept feature is very close to zero, it still has a little bias towards one of the classes, which is mirrored in the accuracy of prediction on different subsets of the data (0.921 vs. 0.316).

Our Semantics/Discourse Model is able to improve over the two other models for the subordination

[2]Consequently, there are three coefficients but just one drop in residual deviance resulting from the addition of the feature.

Model	Subordination vs. coordination			Direction of subordination		
	Overall	Subord.	Coord.	Overall	p_2 subord. to p_1	p_1 subord. to p_2
Majority Baseline	0.752	1.000	0.000	0.520	0.000	1.000
Morphological Model	0.752	1.000	0.000	0.606	0.921	0.316
Semantics/Discourse Model	0.779	0.946	0.368	0.576	0.668	0.420

Table 8: Prediction accuracy for the two tasks (Task 1: subordination vs. coordination; Task 2: direction of subordination) in terms of overall accuracy and class-specific accuracy.

vs. coordination task by learning how to recognize at least some cases of coordination. Concerning the direction of subordination, it improves over the baseline (0.576). While it does not achieve the overall accuracy of the Morphological Model, it is more balanced over the two classes. Also, recall that the good performance of the Morphological Model is due to its use of verb form information which is arguably unavailable at the decision time.

5 Related Work

The choice between subordination and coordination is related to work on various aspects of discourse and beyond in computational linguistics.

Rhetorical Relations. The closest area to our work consists of investigations of discourse relations in the context of Rhetorical Structure Theory (Mann and Thompson, 1988). Most studies in this area are primarily concerned with appropriate choice and positioning of the discourse cue, barely considering the differences between syntactic status of clauses to be combined. However, (Taboada, 2006) shows that some rhetorical relations are often expressed without any discourse cue, and such parameters of sentence structure as the order of phrases and their syntactic mode of combination become significant for the expression of rhetoric relation. There are several studies that consider syntactic means of expression of particular rhetorical relations. In particular, Grote et al. (1997) describe how syntactic structure and ordering of clauses correspond to the pragmatic subtypes of the *Concession* relation. Pitler et al. (2009) show that pairs of words taken from sentences linked by discourse relations, as well as Levin classes of verbs of the sentences and sentiment polarity information is useful for the prediction of implicit relations. The same authors also look into various entity-based features and show that again lexical information about mentioned entities correlates with the choice of discourse relation. In contrast, we focus on the correlation between the syntactic structure and the properties of events directly, since both types of clause combination may be used to encode the same rhetoric relation. We think that while the influence of pragmatic factors investigated by Grote et al. (1997) may be significant, we chose to explore other types of features in this study.

Lexical Models of Coherence Another direction of research of coherence relations within discourse is represented by Barzilay and Lapata (2008). They show that coherent discourse is characterized by chains of mentions of same entities. Hearst (1997) show that event chains that are formed only by the mentions of the same lexical item mirror the global structure of texts and can be used for discourse segmentation. The "shared participant" features that we use are similar to the approach of these studies. However, our work shows that coordination and subordination form distinct patterns of entity mentions which can be used to predict local text structure.

Generation and Summarization. We believe that our results may be useful to the natural language generation and summarization communities. In generation, many systems assume overgenerate-and-rank approach to sentence planning (for example, see Stent et al. (2004)). The description of features given in our work may help to create better ranking systems or even direct the generation of complex and compound sentences, in the spirit of Stent and Molina (2009). In summarization, Barzilay and McKeown (2005) present a sentence fusion technique for multidocument summarization which needs to restructure sentences to improve text coherence. Restructuring is currently done without regard to the underlying discourse structure. We believe that the features that we have identified can introduce a bias towards more appropriate structures during sentence fusion.

6 Conclusions

In this paper, we have reported on an examination of various semantic and discourse structure-based factors and their effect on the choice of clause combination (subordination vs. coordination) and the direction of relation within subordination pairs. On a dataset of clause pairs extracted from the OntoNotes corpus, our analysis led to the following results:

- The salience of events and their participants is connected with the syntactic position of corresponding clauses in the tree. However, in order to occupy the dominating position in the syntactic structure, the event only has to be more prominent than another event with which it forms a pair. It does not need to be the key, mainline event of the story.
- The presence of adjuncts of different types has an effect on the clause combination preferences. Locative adjuncts are different from other types of adjuncts and clauses in that they seem to support coordination more than subordination. On the other hand, the presence of causal adjuncts increases the likelihood of subordination constructions.
- Participant sharing between different argument positions of predicate is one of the decisive factors in the prediction of clause combination type. Coordination constructions are more likely to share one participant between same semantic roles of the predicates, whereas the in case of subordination participants are shared between patient and agent positions.

In sum, we find that the choice between subordination and coordination is not determined by "global" discourse factors alone, but also by the lexical and structural properties of the participating predicates and their immediate context. Moreover, the two prediction tasks involve different, often complimentary features. We interpret this as evidence for a richer, more interactive account of clause structuring in discourse context than previous work has suggested.

References

Baayen, H. (2011). *Analyzing Linguistic Data.* Cambridge University Press.

Barzilay, R. and M. Lapata (2008). Modeling Local Coherence: An Entity-Based Approach. *Computational Linguistics 34*(1), 1–34.

Barzilay, R. and K. McKeown (2005). Sentence fusion for multidocument news summarization. *Computational Linguistics 31*(3), 297–328.

BBN Technologies (2004-2007). *Co-reference guidelines for English OntoNotes.* BBN Technologies.

Bresnan, J., A. Cueni, T. Nikitina, and H. Baayen (2007). Predicting the dative alternation. In G. Bouma, I. Kraemer, and J. Zwarts (Eds.), *Cognitive Foundations of Interpretation*, pp. 69–94. Royal Netherlands Academy of Science.

Chiarcos, C. (2011). Evaluating salience metrics for the context-adequate realization of discourse referents. In *Proceedings of the 13th European Workshop on Natural Language Generation*, Nancy, France, pp. 32–43.

Culicover, P. W. and R. Jackendoff (1997). Semantic subordination despite syntactic coordination. *Linguistic Inquiry 28*(2), 195–217.

Goldsmith, J. (1985). A principled exception to the coordinate structure constraint. In *Proceedings of the 21st Regional Meeting of the Chicago Linguistic Society*. Chicago: Chicago Linguistic Society.

Grote, B., N. Lenke, and M. Stede (1997). Ma(r)king concessions in English and German. *Discourse Processes 24*, 87–117.

Haspelmath, M. (Ed.) (2004). *Coordinating constructions*. Amsterdam: Benjamins.

Hayes, B. and C. Wilson (2008). A maximum entropy model of phonotactics and phonotactic learning. *Linguistic Inquiry 39*, 379–440.

Hearst, M. A. (1997). Texttiling: segmenting text into multi-paragraph subtopic passages. *Computational Linguistics 23*(1), 33–64.

Mann, W. C. and S. A. Thompson (1988). Rhetorical structure theory: Toward a functional theory of text organization. *Text 8*(3), 243–281.

Marcus, M., B. Santorini, and M. A. Marcinkiewicz (1993). Building a Large Annotated Corpus of English: The Penn Treebank. *Computational Linguistics 19*(2), 313–330.

Matthiessen, C. and S. A. Thompson (1988). The structure of discourse and 'subordination'. In J. Haiman and S. A. Thompson (Eds.), *Clause combining in grammar and discourse*. Amsterdam: Benjamins.

Mitkov, R. (1998). Robust pronoun resolution with limited knowledge. In *Proceedings of ACL/COLING*, Montreal, Canada, pp. 869–875.

Palmer, M., D. Gildea, and P. Kingsbury (2005). The proposition bank: An annotated corpus of semantic roles. *Computational Linguistics 31*(2), 71–106.

Pitler, E., A. Louis, and A. Nenkova (2009). Automatic sense prediction for implicit discourse relations in text. In *ACL/AFNLP*, pp. 683–691.

Pradhan, S., E. H. Hovy, M. Marcus, M. Palmer, L. Ramshaw, and R. Weischedel (2007). OntoNotes: A Unified Relational Semantic Representation. In *Proceedings of the First IEEE International Conference on Semantic Computing*, pp. 517–526.

Ross, J. (1967). *Constraints on variables in syntax*. Ph. D. thesis, MIT.

Stent, A. and M. Molina (2009). Evaluating automatic extraction of rules for sentence plan construction. In *Proceedings of the SIGDIAL 2009 Conference*, London, UK, pp. 290–297.

Stent, A., R. Prasad, and M. Walker (2004). Trainable sentence planning for complex information presentation in spoken dialog systems. In *In Proc. of the Annual Meeting of the Association for Computational Linguistics*, pp. 79–86.

Taboada, M. T. (2006). Discourse markers as signals (or not) of rhetorical relations. *Journal of Pragmatics. 38*(4), 567–592.

Learning Corpus Patterns Using Finite State Automata

Octavian Popescu
FBK-irst, Trento, Italy
popescu@fbk.eu

1 Introduction

Words get their meaning in context and Harris's Distributional Hypothesis has been used in computational linguistics in order to identify the relationship between co-occurring words and their senses. In general, the local context contains the necessary information for word sense disambiguation (Stevenson&Wilks 2001). However, the exact extent of the local context varies significantly. To cope with this problem, previous research has shown that the regularity of word usage in natural language can be exploited (Pustejovsky&Hanks 2001). Many times, words are used in phrases with a patternable structure. On the basis of corpus evidence (Popescu&Magnini 2007), or on the basis of the lexicographer's intuition on the normal usage (Hanks 2005) a set of patterns can be built which makes the link between context and word senses.

In this paper [1] we focus on patterns centered on verbs. We show that their structure is learnable and by employing a learning algorithm we are able to build a recognizer able to match such patterns against previously unseen text. The CPA resource (Hanks & Pustejovsky 2005, Pustejovsky & Jezek 2008) contains a set of patterns for a part of the English verbs and is built through a systematic analysis of the patterns of meaning and use for each verb. Meaning is associated with prototypical sentences which are extracted from the BNC. The slots of the patterns are specified with semantic types. For example, the sentences:

(ACP) ... least that intense moment before the body abandons itself to passion.
(CCN) They danced wildly down the street, abandoning themselves to the night and the moon.

are instances of the pattern:

HUMAN abandon SELF {to ACTIVITY | to ATTITUDE}

HUMAN, SELF etc. are semantic types. The use of {} signals an optional slot of the pattern and | signals a choice. A semantic type characterizes a whole class of nouns, and as such, the semantic types are organized in a shallow ontology. The structure of these patterns is regular and we show that we can use the Angluin Algorithm to build a finite state automaton (FSA) which can recognize the patterns.

Going from the set of sentences associated to each pattern to the FSA recognizer is not trivial. The CPA does not contain information regarding the syntax of the patterns, or the senses of the words inside a pattern and it does not provide a resource which assigns a list of possible semantic types to the nouns of the English language. In order to obtain this information, we must rely on parsing and on other two resources, WordNet(Miller) and SUMO(Niles&Pease 2001). WordNet is a sense repository and SUMO is an ontology aligned to WordNet senses. We use SUMO to associate semantic types to the nouns. In the training phase, which results in the construction of the FSA recognizer, the system learns how to identify a certain pattern in a text where the words are replaced with SUMO semantic types. By matching a pattern, we obtain the syntactic structure of the context and the senses of the words in the context due to the SUMO alignment to WordNet. In the experiments we ran, we tested both the accuracy in finding the

[1] This research is supported by the BCROCE project. The author also thanks Nam Khanh Tran for helping implementing the Angluin Algorithm

correct syntactic structure and the accuracy in predicting the correct sense of the words of the matched context.

We introduce the task of pattern matching. Given an arbitrary sentence for which we know there is a unique pattern that matches it, the task consists in finding the appropriate pattern which matches the right words in the sentence. We analyzed the performances obtained by a baseline against a SVM approach and against the FSA recognizer. The results show that both the SVM and the FSA recognizer are over the baseline by several tens of percentages. The FSA recognizer reaches a significantly better accuracy than the SVM approach. We test the approaches both by a cross validation technique and by analyzing individually the performances on a list of verbs.

This paper is organized as follow: in the next Section we review the relevant literature on the interaction between meaning, syntax, ontology and patterns. In Section 3 we describe the form of corpus patterns and the CPA resource. in Section 4 we present the way in which the Angluin Algorithm for learning regular grammars from examples can be modified to learn to recognize the corpus patterns. In Section 5 the results of the experiments we carried out are presented and discussed. In the last section we present the conclusion and further research.

2 Related Work

Based on Harris Distributional Hypothesis, many approaches to WSD have focused on the contexts formed by the words surrounding the target word. With respect to verb behaviour, selectional restrictions have been used in WSD (see among others Resnik 1997, McCarthy, Caroll, Preis 2001, Briscoe et al. 2006). Also, (Hindle 1990) has tried to classify English nouns in similarity classes by using a mutual information measure with respect to the subject and object roles. Such information is very useful only in certain cases and, as such, it is difficult to use it directly in doing WSD.

Lin and Pantel (Lin, Pantel 2001) transpose the HDH from words to dependency trees. However, their measure of similarity is based on a frequency measure. They maintain that a (slotX, he) is less indicative than a (slotX, sheriff). While this might be true in some cases, the measure of similarity is given by the behaviour of the other components of the contexts: both he and $sheriff$ act either exactly the same with respect to certain verb meanings, or totally differently with respect to others. However, their method cannot be extended to take into account such differences. A classification of these cases is instrumental for WSD. Equally important is overcoming the limitation of considering only the subject and object. It has been shown that closed class categories, especially prepositions and particles, play an important role in disambiguation and wrong predictions are made if they are not taken into account (see, among others, Collins and Brooks 1995, Stetina&Nagao 1997). Our approach addresses both these issues.

Zhao, Meyers and Grishman (Zhao, Meyers and Grishman 2004) proposed a SVM application to slot detection, which combines two different kernels, one of them being defined on dependency trees. Their method tries to identify the possible fillers for an event, but it does not attempt to treat ambiguous cases; also, the matching score algorithm makes no distinction between the importance of the words, considering equal matching score for any word within two levels of the dependency tree.

(Pederson et al. 1997-2005) have clustered together the examples that represent similar contexts for WSD. However, given that they adopt mainly the methodology of ordered pairs of bigrams of substantive words, their technique works only at the word level, which may lead to a data sparseness problem. Ignoring syntactic clues may increase the level of noise, as there is no control over the relevance of a bigram. Many of the purely syntactic methods have considered the properties of the subcategorization frame of verbs. Verbs have been partitioned in semantic classes mainly on the basis of Levins classes of alternation. (Dorr&Jones 1996, Dang et al. 1998, Collins 1989, McCarthy 2001, Korhonen 2002, Lapata Brew 2004). These semantic classes can be used in WSD via a process of alignment with hierarchies of concepts as defined in sense repository resources (Shin&Mihalcea 2005). However the problem of the consistency of alignment is still an open issue and further research must be pursued before applying these methods to WSD.

The relationship between events and dependency parsing is analyzed in (McClosky et al. 2011). They extract events at the sentence granularity. However, the fact that the senses of the words are related in describing an event is not discussed. A semi-supervised technique for the discovery of semantic pattern is presented in (Sun&Grishman 2011). Their paper takes into account only the ACE named entities - PERSON, GPE, LOCATION etc. While the authors tried to catch meaning relations between their patterns, there is no clear meaning associated with each pattern. In fact, many times different senses are found in identically syntactic contexts. To capture the differences, the semantic types must be taken into account as well. The semantic binary relations discoverable in text are the focus of the paper (Chan&Roth 2011). They individuate syntactico-semantic structures which could be encoded as patterns but they do not discuss the complexity of learning them. The paper does not discuss possible extensions of the presented method to patterns matching a whole sentence.

3 Corpus Pattern Analysis

In CPA a pattern is understood as a corpus-derived predicate-argument structure with specification of the expected semantic type and subcategorization properties for the arguments (HanksPustejovski 2005). A pattern may not include, and usually it does not, all the phrases presented into the subcategorization frame. A pattern corresponds to a subgraph of the dependency graph of a set of sentences. In Table 1, in the first column, we present three patterns of the verb abandon, and in the second column we show prototypical examples.

Patterns	*Protypical examples*
HUMAN | INSTITUTION	he abandoned plans of working
abandon	are incapacitated or have abandoned their practices
ACTIVITY | PLAN	We should not abandon the search
HUMAN | INSTITUTION	he had abandoned immediate hopes
abandon	abandoned their principles
ATTITUDE	he had abandoned his commitment to persuasion
HUMAN | GROUP	citizens of Phocaea abandoned their town
abandon	The lands that they abandoned
LOCATION	before abandoning the site

Table 1: Patterns and Prototypical Examples

A semantic type outside a pattern is not functional. A word may be characterized by many semantic types, but only one of them is actuated in a pattern. The lexicologists task in CPA is to find the appropriate level of generalization of the semantic types on the basis of which senses are distinguished. The words collocating on the same syntactic position are grouped together according to their influence on the verb. Different patterns are often meaning contrastive. However, this is not always the case. Consider, for example, the three sentences below:

ex1 I drove him to the house.
ex2 I drove him to his father.
ex3 I drove him to despair.

which have the following corresponding patterns:

ex1pattern HUMAN drive_3 HUMAN to BUILDING
ex2pattern HUMAN drive_3 HUMAN to HUMAN
ex3pattern HUMAN drive_5 HUMAN to PSYCHOLOGICAL_STATE

Figure 1: Distribution of number of patterns

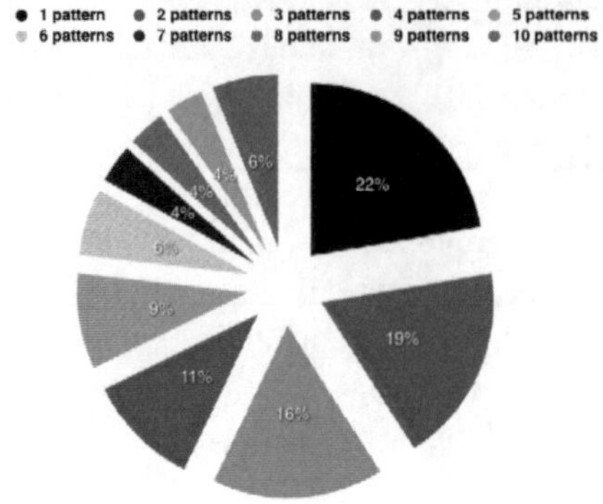

The patterns ex1pattern and ex2pattern, as opposed to ex3pattern, are not meaning contrastive. It would be hard to imagine that the same semantic type could cover both *house* and *father*. Rather, these remain separate patterns. However, the intuition is that in ex1 and in ex2, *house* and *father* are both understood as PLACE. The CPA treats such cases as "exploitation of the norm" (Hanks 2008). The CPA provides a different set of sentence contexts from BNC for exploitation cases. The CPA resource is freely available from http://deb.fi.muni.cz/pdev/. Table 2 summarizes the figures related to the actual coverage of the corpus. The number of patterns varies from 1 to 56.

Characteristics	*Dimension*
Number of Verbs	721
Number of Patterns	2745
Number of files with Examples	5447

Table 2: CPA corpus in Figures

Figure 1 shows the distributions of the number of patterns in CPA. There are roughly a couple of semantic types currently used in CPA. Two of them, namely "Human" and "Institution" are significantly more frequent than others; they are used 1,849 and 365 times, respectively. The CPA also provides the likelihood of a pattern in BNC. The distribution of the patterns in corpus is not uniform, the mode being that a dominant pattern is likely to have a few times more occurrences than the next most frequent pattern.

We computed how many times the dominant pattern for a verb has more than 40%, 60% or 80% of occurrences, by also considering the total number of patterns for the respective verbs grouped in intervals: verbs which have between 3 and 5 patterns, verbs which have between 5 and 20 patterns, verbs having between 20 and 40 patterns, and verbs having between 40 and 60 patterns. For example, 65.25% of the verbs with patterns between 5 and 20 have a dominant pattern that occurs more than 40% in the corpus, but only 23.72% of the verbs with the same number of patterns have a dominant pattern that occurs more than 60% of the time in the corpus. See Table 3.

coverage/patterns	*2-5*	*6-20*	*21-40*
40%	94.35%	65.25%	25%
60%	60.45%	23.72%	12.5%
80%	27.1%	14.23%	0%

Table 3: Dominant Pattern Frequency in Corpus

The SUMO ontology is aligned to the senses present in Wordnet1.6. In Table 4 we list the SUMO attributes for the direct object position for the examples listed in Table 2.

Considering all SUMO attributes of a word is likely to lead to confusion, for example in Table 4 the "NormativeAttribute" belongs both to practice and principle, which are the direct objects in different pat-

direct object	*SUMO attributes*
plan	Plan, Abstract, icon
practice	normativeAttribute, EducationalProcess
search	Pursuing, Investigating, ContentDevelopment
hope	EmotionalState, Reasoning
principle	NormativeAttribute, Proposition
commitment	TraitAttribute, Declaring
town	City, Geopolitical
land	LandArea, Geopolitical, Nation
site	LandArea, Located

Table 4: Patterns and Prototypical Examples

terns. However, the sense determination relationship characterizing the CPA patterns (explained below) , allows only a certain combination of senses, to which only certain SUMO attributes correspond, because SUMO is aligned to the sense repository. The pattern learning and recognizing algorithm must be able to retain for a word only the SUMO features which are instantiated in a particular corpus sentence. The algorithm presented in the next section learns the patterns, as well as which SUMO attributes are legible in a CPA pattern for each word.

Before concluding this section we discuss a relationship between the components of the corpus patterns which will be proven to be important for the construction of more accurate FSA. The relationships between the semantic types and the senses of the verbs are such that only certain combinations are valid. We are interested in corpus patterns for which a determination relationship holds: given either the sense of the verb or the semantic types of one of the components then all the other can be inferred. For example knowing that the direct object has the semantic type LAND then the verb *abandon* must have the sense 3. The disambiguation of the senses of the words matched by a pattern follow a chain like relationship - it is enough to disambiguate one component, and all the words get disambiguated. We call this relationship Chain Clarifying Relationship (CCR) (Popescu,Magnini 2007, Popescu 2012). CCR is instrumental in constructing accurate FSAs. By considering the difference between two CCRs we do not need to match the whole pattern, but to identify only the distinctive semantic types in the CCRs. In Section Experiments we analyze the influence of this relationship on the overall accuracy of the recognizer.

4 Angluin Algorithm

The Angluin's algorithm (AA) is proved to be able to learn the minimal regular grammar that produces or rejects a set of examples provided as input. In general, the problem of learning a regular grammar only from positive examples is an NP-hard problem. Angluin's algorithm is guided in learning by an oracle, which can answer yes/no questions or give a counter example, and it runs in linear time by considering the length of the input examples.

The AA exploits the fact that a language is regular if and only if it is prefix closed, which means that a language is regular if and only if there is a finite number of equivalence classes of the strings, prefixes, which affect the acceptability of the bigger strings that they initiate in the same way. As it learns new examples, the AA builds a table of observation of all possible prefixes and suffixes. When the acceptance of each of the strings formed by joining prefixes with suffixes is known, the table is considered closed. If a closed table also obeys the prefix closeness condition, then it is also considered consistent. The entries in a closed and consistent table describe a Finite State Automaton (FSA), which correctly accepts or rejects the examples given. However, there is more that one possible regular language that describes a set of finite examples. Therefore, when the table is closed and consistent the algorithm asks for a counter

Figure 2: System Flow

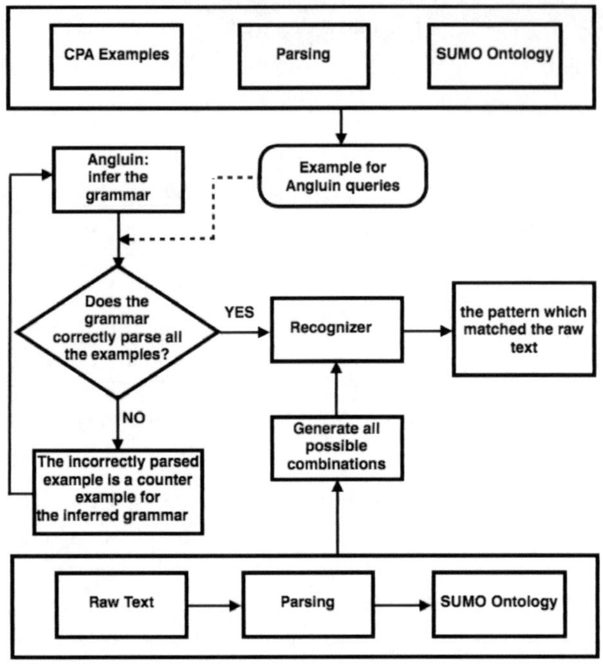

example - which is a string that is accepted or rejected by the language to be learned, and is rejected or accepted, respectively, by the language described in the actual table. If such a counter example is given, the operation of closing the table is carried out again; otherwise, the algorithm stops and the desired FSA is the one described in the table. (Angluin 1987).

The oracles questions about the acceptance of a new string formed by prefixing and suffixing parts of the previously seen strings are called the membership queries. The oracles questions regarding the equivalence between the FSA found by consistently closing the table and the FSA parsing the real grammar are called equivalence queries. A counter example to the equivalence query shows that the actual FSA is too general and new states must be found.

The AA receives as input all the strings created by considering all the SUMO attributes for the words in training and learns the correct prefixes and suffixes for the patterns. The membership queries are carried out in order to determine what SUMO attributes form valid strings in which slot. The equivalent queries are carried out to determine that no relevant SUMO attribute is left unanalyzed. If a word has many SUMO features, it generates more symbols: *practice*, for example, generates *EDUCATIONAL_PROCESS*, and *NORMATIVE_ATTRIBUTE*. The same string may be generated by two sentences with different patterns, for example *abandon practice* and *abandon principle*, which generates *HUMAN abandon NORMATIVE_ATTRIBUTE* (see Table 1 and Table 4). This is incorrect, because if the FSA accepts *HUMAN abandon NORMATIVE_ATTRIBUTE* then the FSA is unable to assign a unique pattern to the text. Such strings are considered counter examples for the AA algorithm and the system learns that they are not part of the language to be learned. Consequently, the respective SUMO feature for that particular slot will not be considered by the final FSA. Whether a SUMO attribute is considered or not depends entirely on the structure of the patterns for that verb. The flow is plotted in Figure 2.

The grammars we are interested in are finite. The role of the oracle can be skipped in this case. In an input file we provide the set of strings with the specification of their acceptances. The AA reads the examples from the input file and builds the table. The answer to both membership queries and equivalence queries is carried out automatically by assuming that if a string is not in the input file, then it is not accepted, and by assuming that if there are strings in the input file which are not generated by the

Figure 3: the FSA recognizer for a subset of examples for *move*

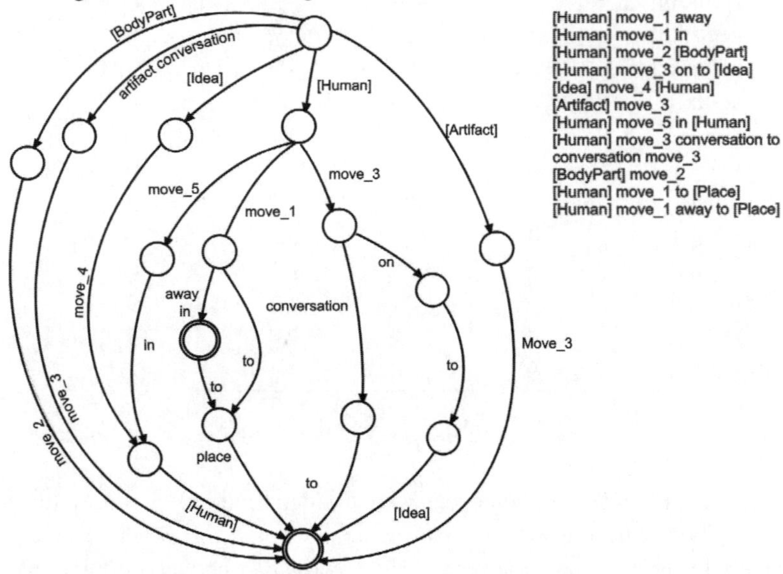

current FSA, then any of them can serve as a counter-example and the search for a new FSA resumes.

The input to the AA algorithm is a set of examples of patterns and the output is a FSA able to recognize only the strings that corresponds to the contexts which are matched by only one pattern. In Figure 3 we present the FSA generated by a subset of examples for *move*.

5 Experiments

We ran several experiments in order to evaluate the performances of pattern recognition via regular grammars. We started by running a 4 fold cross validation experiment. Because we wanted to analyze the results in more detail, we look for a set of verbs having a representative number of patterns and of examples for the whole set of verbs and we analyzed specifically the accuracy of various methods individually. The recognizing process using FSA can be made in two scenarios: using a parser or not. The second scenario, no parsing for the input text, is challenging, because the recognizer acts as syntactico-semantic parser which outputs a dependency path corresponding to the context matched and it also outputs the senses of the words . While the accuracy of pattern recognition is lower in this case, the results are promising.

The SUMO features are obtained for the noun phrases heads via a public available API (Pianta et al. 2002). At the test phase all the possible SUMO combinations inside the syntactic slots of a pattern are given to FSA. If the FSA is unable to find a derivation, or if it finds more than one, it means that we are unable to match a single pattern against the given sentence and these cases are considered errors.

The results for the 4 fold cross validation experiment are presented in Table 8. Both the SVM and the FSA reaches a good accuracy. However, the results may be biased by the existence of verbs having just one pattern or of verbs having a dominant pattern. In such cases, which represents more or less a quart of the total number, there is no ambiguity so we can hardly talk about a recognition process. For a clearer understanding of the behavior of the systems we chose a set of 12 verbs having a number of patterns between 3 and 9, half of them having exactly 5 patterns (see Table 5). The maximal and the minimal frequencies of a pattern are listed in the third and forth column, respectively.

We are interested in the maximal and minimal frequencies of the pattern, because, usually, there is little training available for those patterns with low frequency. The risk of not recognizing the minimal frequency is high. The approach presented here depends to a little extent on the dimension of the training corpus and to a large extent on its quality. That is why we wanted to analyze the performances for

verb	*pattern*	*max Freq*	*min Freq*	*# train 10%*
abandon	8	48%	1%	41
accompany	5	31%	1%	23
acknowledge	5	54%	1%	56
acquire	5	51%	2%	46
arrive	5	69%	1%	41
execute	5	36%	8%	60
fence	3	64%	2%	5
furnish	4	31%	14%	21
launch	6	60%	3%	41
maintain	5	67%	2%	9
saddle	4	71%	2%	9
yield	9	24%	4%	55

Table 5: Test Verbs

different types of patterns. The available sentences were divided randomly into training and test sets. We considered approximately two training sets containing approximately 10% and 30% of all the available sentences, respectively. With a training ratio of 10%, 8 verbs had between 40 and 50 sentences. Two verbs, *accompany* and *furnish*, have around 20 examples each, and two other verbs have only 5 and, respectively, 9 examples each (see column 5 Table 6). The 30% training sets had three times more examples. The very first run we tried was to use all SUMO features, which led to the acceptance of all the possible combinations. The result was very low; in more than 90 percent of the cases when the recognition set was not empty, it contained more than a pattern. This experiment showed the necessity of observing the CCR condition for the CPA patterns. If the CCR condition is observed, then not all the SUMO attribute combinations are accepted. All the following experiments are conducted by observing the CCR condition (see section 4). Using a 10% ratio for training was enough to obtain a very good precision, on average between 80% and 90%. However, *fence* expectedly performed poorer than the rest, with a precision of 45%, as it contained only 5 training examples. Considering the precision for two other verbs with a relatively low number of training examples, namely *accompany* and *furnish*, we can see that 20 examples seem to be enough for a precision around 96% (Table 7).

The low figure for recall has three main different causes: (1) the errors along the pipe generated at parsing time and at dependency extraction (2) the lack of SUMO features for pronouns and proper names and (3) the rigid condition of recognizing all the elements of a pattern, as requested by the FSA.

verb	*BasicFSA 10% train RECALL*	*ExtendedFSA 10% train RECALL*
abandon	.26	.36
accompany	.22	.49
acknowledge	.10	.12
acquire	.25	.48
arrive	.25	.37
execute	.10	.22
fence	.23	.23
furnish	.10	.32
launch	.2	.45
maintain	.1	.36
saddle	.22	.34
yield	.14	.4

Table 6: Recall for BasicFSA vs. ExtendedFSA with 10%

The first two causes are not directly linked to the methodology described here. These causes could be addressed in an independent manner. However, the third cause is directly linked to the way the

FSA works and we wanted to focus on it. When the string corresponding to a test sentence is not complete, the FSA rejects it. As many of the patterns may differ due to the direct object or due to the prepositional complement, it suffices to correctly recognize that part of the string in order to correctly categorize the test sentence as belonging to one group or another. These subparts of the patterns can be automatically generated by comparing the patterns against each other. We can include them in the training set as well. In a second experiment we provided to the AA the automatically generated subparts of the patterns. We refer to the new automaton as extended FSA in order to distinguish it from the initial FSA trained on complete patterns, which we called BasicFSA. The recall increased significantly by using the extendedFSA. For certain verbs the recall was doubled or nearly doubled. In Table 6 the results obtained are listed. We also ran the Extended FSA with a 30% training corpus. The results are listed in Table 7.

Basic+10%				Extended+30%		
verb	*precision*	*recall*	*F1*	*precision*	*recall*	*F1*
abandon	.95	.26	.41	.97	.6	.74
accompany	.96	.22	.35	.87	.71	.78
acknowledge	.88	.10	.18	.9	.25	.39
acquire	.98	.25	.39	.97	.6	.74
arrive	.60	.25	.35	1	.41	.58
execute	.78	.10	.15	.85	.46	.59
fence	.45	.23	.30	.57	.36	.44
furnish	1	.1	.16	.84	.42	.56
launch	.99	.20	.33	.95	.79	.87
maintain	.93	.10	.17	.9	.48	.63
saddle	1	.22	.36	1	.36	.68
yield	.96	.14	.24	.96	.51	.62

Table 7: BasicFSA + 10% vs. ExtendedFSA + 30% training set

Considering a training corpus which represents 30% of the total number of corpus sentences does not mean that the training was three times more informative than a 10% training corpus. This happens because it is not unusual for otherwise different sentences to have the same word on the same spot in the argument structure. If two such sentences were in the training set, there was nothing new to learn. It seemed that the precision is not affected by the dimension of the training set. We noticed that even the low frequency patterns were correctly identified. However, the increase in recall is significant. Both the increasing of the training set and the improvement brought by the ExtendedFSA are equally contributors to this.

A baseline of the most frequent pattern scores low. The precision never exceeds 40% and the recall is 18.65%. It is most likely that these low figures are due to the fact that the CPA corpus is not a random part of BNC; on a totally random corpus, the baseline is expected to perform better. A SVM approach which considers the right and the left context relatively to the target verb (Giuliano et all. 2009) did not

	method	*F1*
[cross validation]	BasicFSA	53.61
	ExtendedFSA	71.93
	SVM	68.58
	MostFrequent	48.12

	method	*F1*
[12 verbs]	BasicFSA+10%	26.58
	BasicFSA+30%	37.45
	ExtendedFSA+10%	45.08
	ExtendedFSA+30%	60.52
	SVM+30%	55.71
	MostFrequent	21.85

Table 8: Cross Validation and 12 Verb F1 results

perform better either. It reached an average precision of 65%, and a recall a little lower than 48%. The SVM approach works best with contexts that are bigger than the sentence, which were not available in this experiment. However the SVM figures reported above refer only to verb sense and not to pattern recognition. In Table 8 the F1 formula averaged for all verbs is presented for the 4-fold cross validation and for the set of the chosen 12 verbs respectively. A last experiment we conducted was to see how much the learned FSA matches against the raw text. The test sentences werent parsed anymore but all the nouns were considered together with their SUMO features and were sent into input to the FSA. For the 12 chosen verbs we obtained the results reported in Table 9. Using the FSA recognizer in this way means to have a deep semantic parser which provides in the same time the syntax, the dependency relationships, the senses of the words and ontological links. These are not separate operations carried in cascade, but the results of "understanding" a verbal phrase according to the grammar associated with the respective verb. The experiments on raw text show that it is possible to develop a technique which does not necessarily make use of a parser. However, the interaction between two CCRs which are recognized in the same sentence must be first resolved in order to adopt such technique.

verb	*subject F1*	*object F1*	*verb*	*subject F1*	*object F1*
abandon	.55	.59	fence	.22	.31
accompany	.42	.34	furnish	.44	.59
acknowledge	.39	.22	launch	.58	.48
acquire	.51	.58	maintain	.39	.37
arrive	.6	.54	saddle	.34	.41
execute	.46	.61	yield	.52	.49

Table 9: Applying FSA to raw text

6 Conclusion and Further Research

The CPA is a resource that creates links between word senses and word usage. A mutual sense dependency relationship acts between the slots of a pattern. We presented a methodology for pattern learning and recognition using finite state automata. A FSA is built for each verb by using dependency chains with SUMO attribute features. In the process of learning only the relevant SUMO features are retained. The results suggest that the methodology is stable and works properly when the slots of the patterns are filled. The method is very precise for frequent senses as well as for less frequent senses. However, in order to improve the coverage, a module which handles the pronouns and proper names should be implemented. This represents the next goal for us.

The experiments we carried out suggest that the quantity of data required for training is small. We start experimenting with a training set which is built iteratively by letting the algorithm decide what is the next training example expected to help in learning the patterns. In the same vein as the original Angluins Algorithm, the learning of patterns can be carried completely automatically. The states of the obtained FSAs, although nameless, may correspond to a set of semantic types.

An important direction of work is to improve the technique of using the FSA with raw text, and shortcut the role of the parser in the architecture pipe. Our initial experiments suggest that this could be done by bootstrapping. The results obtained so far are very good and they compare positively with the ones obtained by the state of the art approaches.

7 References

D. Angluin.1987. Learning regular sets from queries and counterexamples. Inf. Comp., 75(2):87106

Briscoe, E., J. Carroll and R. Watson. 2006 The Second Release of the RASP System. In Proceedings of the COLING/ACL 2006

S. Chan, D. Roth. 2011 Exploiting Syntactico-Semantic Structures for Relation Extraction. In Proceedings of ACL 2011, Portland

M. Collins, J. Brooks. 1995. Prepositional phrase attachment through a backed-off model. In Proceedings of the Third Workshop on Very Large Corpora, pages 27–38, Cambridge.

M. Collins. 1999. Head-Driven Statistical Models for Natural Language Parsing. Ph.D. thesis, University of Pennsylvania.

B. Dorr, D. Jones. 1999. Acquisition of Semantic Lexicons in Breadth and Depth of Semantic Lexicons. Edited by Evelyne Viegas. Kluwer Press.

C. Fillmore, C. Baker, S. Hiroaki. 2002. Seeing Arguments through Transparent Structures. Proceedings of the Third International Conference on Language Resources and Evaluation (LREC). Las Palmas. 787-91

T. Dang, K. Kipper, K. Palmer, J. Rosenzweig. 1998. Investigating regular sense extensions based on intersective Levin classes. Coling-ACL98 , Montreal CA, August 11-17

C. Giuliano, A. Gliozzo and C. Strapparava .2009. Kernel Methods for Minimally SupervisedWSD. Computational Linguistics, 35:4

P. Hanks, Pustejovsky 2005. A Pattern Dictionary for Natural Language Processing, Revue Francaise de Language Appliquee, 10:2

P. Hanks.2005.Immediate Context Analysis: distinguishing meaning by studying usage. Words in Context A tribute to John Sinclair on his Retirement.

P. Hanks.2009. The Linguistics Double Helix:Norm and Exploitations. Slavonic Natural Language Processing, Brno, Masaryk University, 63-80

D. Hindle,1990. Noun classification from predicate argument structures. Proceedings of the Annual Meeting of the Association for Computational Linguistics, pp 268–275.

D. Klein C. Manning. 2003. Accurate Unlexicalized Parsing. ACL 423-430

A. Korhonen. 2002. Subcategorization Acquisition. PhD thesis published as Techical Report UCAM-CL-TR-530. Computer Laboratory

M. Lapata, C. Brew. 2004. Verb Class Disambiguation Using Informative Priors. Computational Linguistics 30:1, 45-73.

C. Leacock, G. Towell, and E Voorhes. 1993. Towards Building Contextual Representations of Word Senses Using Statistical Models. In Proceedings, SIGLEX workshop: Acquisition of Lexical Knowledge from Text, ACL.

M. Marneffe, B. McCartney, C. Manning. 2006. Generating Typed Dependency from Phrase Structure Parses. LREC 2006.

Y. Lee, H. Ng. 2002. An empirical evaluation of knowledge sources and learning algorithms for word sense disambiguation. Proceedings of EMNLP02, pap 4148, Philadelphia, PA, USA.

D. Li, N. Abe. 1998. Word Clustering and Disambiguation Based on Co-occurrence Data. COLING-ACL : 749-755.

D. Lin, P. Pantel. 2001. Discovery of Inference Rules for Question Answering. Natural Language Engineering 7(4): 343-360.

D. McCarthy, J. Carroll, and J. Preiss. 2001 Disambiguating noun and verb senses using automatically acquired selectional preferences. Proceedings of the SENSEVAL-2 Workshop at ACL/EACL'01, Toulouse, France.

D. McClosky, M. Surdeanu, C. Manning 2011, Event Extractions as Dependency Parsing Exploiting Syntactico-Semantic Structures for Relation Extraction. In Proceedings of ACL 2011, Portland I. Niles, A. Pease. 2001. Towards a Standard Upper Ontology. FOIS 2001

E. Pianta, L. Bentivogli, C. Girardi.2002. MultiWordnet: developing an aligned multilingual database Global WordNet, 146-154

T. Pederson. 1998. Learning Probabilistic Models of Word Sense Disambiguation .Southern Methodist University (PhD Dissertation)

T. Pederson. 2005. SenseClusters: Unsupervised Clustering and Labeling of Similar Contexts. Proceedings of the Demonstration and Interactive Poster Session of the 43rd Annual Meeting of the Association for Computational Linguistics.

A. Ratnaparkhi. 1997. A Linear Observed Time Statistical Parser Based on Maximum Entropy Models.Proceedings of the Second Conference on Empirical Methods in Natural Language Processing.

O.Popescu, B. Magnini. Sense Discriminative Patterns for Word Sense Disambiguation. SCAR workshop, NODALIDA 2007

O. Popescu 2012. Building a Resource of Patterns Using Semantic Types. Proceedings of LREC, Istanbul

A. Sun, R. Grishman 2011 Semi-supervised Semantic Pattern Discovery with Guidance from Unsupervised pattern Clusters, Exploiting Syntactico-Semantic Structures for Relation Extraction. In Proceedings of ACL 2011, Portland

The Impact of Selectional Preference Agreement on Semantic Relational Similarity

Bryan Rink Sanda Harabagiu
University of Texas at Dalals
{bryan,sanda}@hlt.utdallas.edu

Abstract

Relational similarity is essential to analogical reasoning. Automatically determining the degree to which a pair of words belongs to a semantic relation (relational similarity) is greatly improved by considering the selectional preferences of the relation. To determine selectional preferences, we induced semantic classes through a Latent Dirichlet Allocation (LDA) method that operates on dependency parse contexts of single words. When assigning relational similarities to pairs of words, if the agreement of selectional preferences is considered alone, a correlation of 0.334 is obtained against the manual ranking outperforming the previously best reported score of 0.229.

1 Introduction

In natural language, words participate often in a variety of semantic relations. Both linguists and psychology researchers have been interested in categorizing semantic relations and to understand their usage in language and cognition. One particular interesting usage of semantic relations is provided by analogical reasoning. As reported by Gentner (1983) and Holyoak and Thagard (1996), whenever a new situation arises, humans tend to search for an analogous situation from their past experience. Analogical reasoning relies on relational similarity, as reported by Turney (2006) and Turney (2008). In analogical reasoning, the degree of relational similarity is an estimation of the likelihood of applicability of the knowledge transfer (from past to present). Thus, as postulated in the recent SemEval 2012 Task 2 (Jurgens et al., 2012), the automatic analysis of relational similarity may have practical benefits of indicating the appropriateness of an analogy.

Relational similarity, as reported in Turney (2006), is one of the forms of similarity, the other one being provided by attributional similarity. Relational similarity evaluates the correspondence between relations (Medin et al., 1990), while attributional similarity evaluates the correspondence between attributes. As stated by Turney: "*When two words have a high degree of attributional similarity, we call them* synonyms. *When two word* pairs *have a high degree of relational similarity, we say they are* analogous."

We claim that there is a special property that arguments of relations need to share. The arguments of relations are words which are predications of binary facts, properties, actions, etc. As such, we are aware from the work of Resnik (1996) that words which appear as arguments of a predicate define the selectional preferences of the predicate. Moreover, Pantel et al. (2007) have extended the notion of predicate selectional preferences to "relational selectional preferences" of binary relations. For a binary relation $r(x, y)$, the semantic classes $C(x)$ which can be instantiated for the argument x as well as $C(y)$, the semantic classes which can be instantiated for the argument y constitute the relational selectional preferences of the binary relation. Thus we believe and show in this paper that semantic relations have selectional preferences and that word pairs x:y are more similar to a relation when those words are more admissible under the relational selectional preferences.

Consider the semantic relation REFERENCE-*Expression*, with prototypical word pairs *smile*:*friendliness*, *lamentation*:*grief*, and *hug*:*affection*. In these pairs, the first word can be seen as a physical expression of the emotional state represented by the second word. Word pairs which are prototypical of the relation

Category	Example word pairs	Relations
CLASS-INCLUSION	flower:tulip, weapon:knife, clothing:shirt, queen:Elizabeth	5
PART-WHOLE	car:engine, fleet:ship, mile:yard, kickoff:football	10
SIMILAR	car:auto, stream:river, eating:gluttony, colt:horse	8
CONTRAST	alive:dead, old:young, east:west, happy:morbid	8
ATTRIBUTE	beggar:poor, malleable:molded, soldier:fight, exercise:vigorous	8
NON-ATTRIBUTE	sound:inaudible, exemplary:criticized, war:tranquility, dull:cunning	8
CASE RELATIONS	tailor:suit, farmer:tractor, teach:student, king:crown	8
CAUSE-PURPOSE	joke:laughter, fatigue:sleep, gasoline:car, assassin:death	8
SPACE-TIME	bookshelf:books, coast:ocean, infancy:cradle, rivet:girder	9
REFERENCE	smile:friendliness, person:portrait, recipe:cake, astronomy:stars	6

Table 1: The ten categories of semantic relations. Each word pair has been taken from a different subcategory of each major category.

should be assigned a high degree of membership for the REFERENCE-*Expression* relation, while word pairs such as *discourse:relationship* and *anger:slap* should not, either because the word pair expresses a different relation, or because the pair is in the wrong order (slap is an expression of anger, not the other way around). Table 1 shows the ten top-level categories of relations we consider, which is further divided into 79 relations covering multiple parts of speech (adjective, noun, adverb, and verb).

We show that a model which independently considers the semantic classes of each word in a word pair is effective at assigning degrees of membership (relational similarity). For instance, knowing that the relation REFERENCE-*Expression* selects for emotional states in the first argument (e.g., *grief*, *friendliness*, *affection*) and expressions of emotion in the second argument (e.g., *smile*, *hug*, *lamentation*) helps in determining word pair candidates which don't adhere to those classes. Clearly word pairs whose arguments do not fit these preferences should be given a lower degree of relatedness to the relation. We describe a method for inducing semantic classes for use as selectional preferences and a method for determining the distributions over argument classes for a relation. While selectional preferences are not the only phenomena responsible for assigning degrees of membership for word pairs to semantic relations, we choose to model it alone in this paper to examine its importance. We show that modeling selectional preference alone produces results which are better than the previously reported results for measuring relational similarity.

The rest of this paper is structured as follows: Section 2 gives some perspective on previous work, Section 3 describes how we used an LDA model to induce semantic classes. Section 4 describes the dataset we use for measuring relational similarity. Section 5 describes how the induced semantic classes are used to model the selectional preferences of semantic relations. Section 5 describes how we determine the extent to which a word pair matches a relation's selectional preferences. Section 6 gives our experimental setup and the results of our evaluation. Section 7 analyzes the types of semantic classes that were automatically induced and Section 8 concludes the paper.

2 Previous work

Prior work on relational similarity (Jurgens et al., 2012; Rink and Harabagiu, 2012; Turney, 2005, 2006) has understandably focused the actual relation between a pair of words under consideration. These approaches have all considered how the two words co-occur in a large corpus and what contexts can be found near the words when they co-occur. Contextual information is useful for determining the relationship between two words. Therefore we believe the selectional preference agreement method can complement these approaches. The best-performing relational similarity approach at the SemEval 2012 Task 2 utilized a graphical model to determine patterns likely to be found between the two words of a word pair within a large corpus (Rink and Harabagiu, 2012). Word pairs were then ranked by their likelihood of occurring with those patterns. Constraints on the arguments were not directly addressed. One of the limitations of the approach is that word pairs which never occurred near each other in the corpus could not be ranked, which occurred regularly for some relations. The approach we present does not have this sparsity issue because we treat the relation arguments independently.

The literature on selectional preferences has focused largely on well-known relations such as syntactic relations (Mechura, 2008; Resnik, 1996; Ó Séaghdha, 2010), considering typical subjects and direct objects of verbs, or typical nouns modified by specific adjectives. These approaches usually focus on semantic classes of nouns at the exclusion of other parts of speech. One recent example relevant to our work is a set of LDA-inspired models proposed by Ó Séaghdha (2010). His models directly induce semantic classes for each predicate (verb or adjective). One consequence of such approaches is that the semantic classes differ based on the type of relationship being modeled: verb-object, noun-noun, or adjective-noun. The set of classes derived for nouns which are objects of verbs will be different than the classes derived for nouns which are modified by adjectives for instance. In our approach we induce semantic classes independently of the relations whose selectional preferences we are modeling. We take this approach because our relational data consists only of word pairs with no context. Further, some of the word pairs may never occur in the same sentence even in a large corpus (e.g., *signature:acknowledgment*) yet we can still check the admissibility of the words as arguments to the desired relation (e.g, X represents Y).

An extension to Latent Dirichlet Allocation model has been used before by Ritter and Etzioni (2010) to model semantic relations and their selectional preferences. There are two distinct reasons their approach is not well-suited to the relational similarity task. First, they were additionally inducing the set of relations present in their data, while in the relational similarity task we aim to determine membership to an existing set of relations. The second difference in their approach is the large size of their dataset. While we were able to train our models using on average around 40 word pairs per relation, their data contained all tuples matching a relation over a large corpus.

There has been much previous research effort on inducing semantic classes as well. Most approaches use some form of context around words to induce the classes. Older approaches simply used a bag of words context (Roark and Charniak, 1998), but this leads to induced classes containing more paradigmatically similar words rather than syntagmatically similar words (Widdows and Dorow, 2002). More recent approaches have utilized a subset of semantically-rich syntactic relations such as verb-object, noun modifier, coordination, and preposition (Baroni and Lenci, 2010; Widdows and Dorow, 2002). Lin and Pantel (2001) induce semantic classes using dependency parse contexts. Their approach is based on a vector space rather than the probabilistic setting of an LDA. Rahman and Ng (2010) use a factor graph with various semantic, morphological, and grammatical features to induce a set of semantic classes with the goal of performing better named entity recognition. Pantel (2003) uses short contextual patterns to inform a clustering approach to category induction.

3 Inducing semantic word classes

We consider a *semantic class* to be a set of words which share a semantic property. For example, the semantic property "male" forms a semantic class which includes the words "man, bull, boy, boyfriend, groom". Under this definition, words can belong to many semantic classes. For example "man" could belong to semantic classes for "man", "adult", and "human". We adopt the "distributional hypothesis" that the meaning of words can be inferred from their context. We follow existing approaches which use syntactic dependency context (Lin and Pantel, 2001) for inducing semantic classes. n The basis of our model for selectional preference agreement uses a set of semantic word classes induced using a Latent Dirichlet Allocation model (Blei et al., 2003). The data for this model is structured differently than a standard LDA, so that rather than inducing topic distributions for documents, we induce semantic class distributions for words. We begin with a large corpus of documents and dependency parses (De Marneffe and Manning, 2008) for all the documents. Every time a word occurs in the corpus we collect all of the dependency edges which include the word. We then concatenate the label on the dependency edge and the other word to form what we call a *dependency context*. For instance, the syntactic dependency *sadness* $\xleftarrow{dobj}$ *expressed* would generate one dependency context for *sadness*: "←*dobj expressed*" and one dependency context for *expressed*: "→*dobj sadness*". Figure 1 shows the most frequent dependency contexts for the word *sadness*.

We train our LDA model by forming a pseudo-document for each unique word in the corpus consisting of all of the dependency contexts for that word, with repetitions. Figure 1 shows a small part of the pseudo-document formed for the word *sadness*. After forming such pseudo-documents, the LDA can be trained in the usual way to infer the parameters of the model.

More formally, the generative story for this LDA can be written as:

1. For each semantic class k, draw a distribution over dependency contexts $\phi_k \sim Dirichlet(\beta)$
2. For each unique word in the corpus w, draw a distribution over semantic classes $\theta_w \sim Dirichlet(\alpha)$
3. For each dependency context k of word w in the corpus, draw a semantic class $z_{w,k} \sim Multinomial(\theta_w)$
4. Draw a dependency context $d_{w,k} \sim Multinomial(z_{w,k})$

The LDA model trained on the pseudo-documents formed from dependency contexts will form two clusterings, a clustering of dependency contexts and a clustering of words. We argue that the clustering of words represent semantic classes. We evaluate this claim in Section 7. As an example of dependency context clustering, a *person* semantic class could be induced which would often be assigned to dependency contexts such as "←nsubj said", "→amod young", "→amod famous", or "→amod teenage".

The trained LDA model also assigns each pseudo-document a distribution over semantic classes (θ_w). Because the pseudo-documents correspond to unique words from the corpus, we can assess the affinity of each word to each semantic class and, in turn, compare two words to each other. For example, the most frequent dependency contexts for *sadness* include ←DOBJ *expressed*, →AMOD *great*, and →AMOD *deep*. Some other words sharing these contexts include *hope*, *sorrow*, *regret*, and *satisfaction*. We would therefore expect them to be clustered together by the LDA model. This allows us to compare two words based on the similarity of their semantic class distributions (θ_w).

Freq.	Context
1485	→det the
1233	←dobj expressed
978	→amod great
857	→det a
757	→punct "
601	→amod deep
532	→poss his
388	←prep_of sense
386	←prep_with is
342	→amod profound
318	←conj_and shock
300	←dobj express
297	←nsubj is
279	→poss their
259	→det the
248	←dobj feel
212	←dobj expressing
193	←dobj felt
189	←prep_with tinged
184	→conj_and anger
184	←conj_and anger
180	→det The
176	→det some
170	←nsubj 's
163	←prep_of lot

Figure 1: A compact representation of the pseudo-document associated with the word *sadness*. The most frequent contexts are shown.

4 SemEval-2012 Relational Similarity Task

The dataset we use for evaluating the degrees of relational similarity was developed as part of SemEval 2012 Task 2 - Measuring Degrees of Relational Similarity (Jurgens et al., 2012). In the task, organizers focused on 79 categories of relations taken from Bejar et al. (1991), which can be partitioned into the ten broader categories listed in Table 1. The task of obtaining word pairs that match closely with each type of relation was crowd-sourced to Amazon Mechanical Turk in two phases. In the first phase, participants were shown a description of the relation along with several prototypical word pairs. Then, they were asked to provide additional word pairs belonging to the same relation. The second phase focused on determining the similarity of each word pair to the relation. Participants were shown a description of the relation, several prototypical word pairs, and a set of four word pairs collected in Phase 1. They were then asked to choose both the word pair among those four which best represented the relation, and the word pair which least represented the relation. Each word pair appeared in multiple

	Semantic class distribution									
Word	44	17	13	47	24	32	36	41	3	45
sadness	.71	.07	.04	.04	.02	0	0	0	0	0
happiness	.73	.02	.01	0	0	0	0	0	0	0
sorrow	.75	.02	.01	.06	0	0	0	0	0	0
terror	.06	0	0	.26	0	0	0	0	0	.47
amusement	.19	0	0	0	0	.54	0	0	0	0
agreement	.01	.08	0	0	0	0	.03	0	.82	0
smile	.04	.40	.09	0	.33	0	0	0	0	0
nod	0	.42	.03	0	.02	0	.11	0	0	0
laugh	.01	.23	.31	0	.15	0	0	0	0	0
kiss	.04	.22	.19	0	.09	0	.03	.12	0	0
intoxicate	0	0	.2	0	0	0	0	.55	0	0

Table 2: A portion of the semantic class distribution vectors for several words participating in word pairs belonging to the REFERENCE:*Expression* relation.

Phase 2 questions, sometimes being chosen as the most representative, and other times being chosen as the least representative. This setup is known as a MaxDiff (Louviere and Woodworth, 1991) problem and is effective at deciding an absolute ranking among items without requiring participants to order all items.

Using the data collected from Amazon Mechanical Turk, the organizers were able to create a ranked list of word pairs for each relation in the following manner. Each word pair was assigned a score equal to the percentage of times it was chosen as the most representative minus the percentage of times it was chosen as the least representative. The word pairs were then ranked based on this score. An example ranking is shown in Figure 2. The goal of the SemEval task was to most accurately reproduce this ranking using automatic methods.

Word Pair	Similarity
laugh:happiness	50
nod:agreement	46
laugh:amusement	44
tears:sadness	44
crying:sadness	40
tears:sorrow	36
laughter:amusement	34
scream:terror	26
lie:dishonesty	16
laugh:hilarity	14
yawn:boredom	8
frown:discontent	6
frown:sadness	-2
sigh:exhaustion	-8
frown:anger	-28
wink:friendliness	-48
exhaustion:sigh	-50
anger:slap	-56
hilarity:laugh	-58
discourse:relationship	-60
friendliness:wink	-68

Figure 2: Ranking of a subset of the word pairs for the relation REFERENCE:*Expression* chosen by participants

5 Measuring selectional preference agreement

In order to measure how well a word pair matches the selectional preferences of a relation we must first model the selectional preferences for each argument of each relation. This is done using the induced semantic word classes described earlier.

We model the selectional preferences for an argument position of a relation using a distribution over semantic classes. These distributions are determined by first gathering all of the word pairs belonging to a relation (as collected in Phase 1). For each word pair $w1{:}w2$, we retrieve the semantic class distribution associated with each word (θ_{w1} and θ_{w2}). The distributions for all of the words appearing as a first argument are then averaged to obtain a class distribution for the first argument, which we call σ_1. This is repeated to obtain a distribution for the second argument as well to obtain σ_2. We then repeat this procedure for all relations to obtain selectional preferences for them. The assumption we make about our dataset is that the average word pair which needs to be ranked is representative of the arguments for that relation, or at least, that the contributions of non-representative word pairs will not overwhelm the contributions of those which are representative.

Measuring the agreement of a single word to the selectional preferences of a relation is then done by comparing the semantic class distribution associated with the word (θ_w) to the average distribution computed for that argument position (σ_1 or σ_2) of the relation. We consider several possible vector similarity metrics such as cosine similarity. Table 2 shows the most significant elements of the semantic class distributions (θ_w) for several words participating in the REFERENCE:*Expression* relation. The top half of Table 2 shows distributions for words participating in the second argument of a word pair, and the bottom half shows words participating in the first argument of a word pair (except *intoxicate*). Table 2 illustrates that similar words have similar vectors in the induced semantic class space. The words *sadness*, *happiness*, and *sorrow* are semantically similar. We have also included an outlier word *intoxicate* to show that the words in the bottom of the figure were not similar simply because they were all verbs. The distribution for *intoxicate* is zero for many of the classes that are significant for the other words confirming that we are capturing semantics beyond just part of speech.

We model relational similarity (how closely a word pair belongs to a relation) using only the selectional preferences of the relation. For a word pair w_1:w_2 we measure its relational similarity to relation r as:

$$sim(r, w_1 : w_2) = \frac{s(\theta_{w_1}, \sigma_{r,1}) + s(\theta_{w_2}, \sigma_{r,2})}{2} \quad (1)$$

where θ_w is the LDA-induced semantic class distribution for word w, $\sigma_{r,n}$ is the selectional preference distribution for the nth argument of relation r, and s is a similarity measure between vectors.

The measure in (1) compares each word pair's semantic class distributions against the average for all word pairs assigned to a relation. The similarities for all word pairs belonging to a relation are computed and the pairs are then ranked. Next, this ranking is compared against the ranking produced by annotators such as the ranking in Figure 2. Note that only the order in the ranking is considered, the particular similarity values are not. We chose to average over all class distributions for an argument position to capture a soft membership of each class to the selectional preferences. We evaluate several vector similarity measures in the next section.

6 Evaluation of the relational similarity method

For training our LDA model we used a corpus consisting of the 8 million documents from English Gigaword (LDC2009T13) (Parker and Consortium, 2009) and the 4 million documents from the 2011-12-01 dump of Wikipedia[1]. The dependency parses were obtained by using the Stanford dependency parser[2] (De Marneffe and Manning, 2008). The textual content from the Wikipedia XML files was extracted using WP2TXT (http://wp2txt.rubyforge.org/). Due to the large size of this corpus we used a parallel implementation of LDA known as PLDA (Liu et al., 2011) across eight quad-core machines. The parameters for the LDA were the suggested defaults of $\alpha = 0.1$ and $\beta = 0.01$. We arbitrarily chose 50 topics, but this is clearly a parameter that requires further investigation. Additionally, our input to the LDA only consisted of 3,357 pseudo-documents, corresponding to all of the unique words in all of the word pairs that we were interested in ranking. While this contains many commonly used words in English, many other words are not covered and the data would have to be expanded for use in other tasks.

We used the official testing set from the SemEval 2012 Task 2 (Jurgens et al., 2012), which consisted of 69 relations (another ten were released for training but we do not make use of them). The relations had an average of 40 word pairs, ranging from 25 to 45. We evaluate the performance of the relational similarity model using a Spearman correlation score between the model's word pair ranking and the ranking produced by the annotation effort. This is the same evaluation metric used during the official SemEval 2012 Task 2 (Jurgens et al., 2012). Table 3 shows the results of our approach under several common similarity measures. We expected the measures designed for probability distributions (Jensen Shannon/Hellinger) to perform best, however our evaluation showed that vector space metrics (cosine/Tanimoto) performed slightly better. During the official evaluation, the best performing system achieved a correlation of 0.229. The model presented in this paper achieved a significantly higher correlation of 0.334 using the Tanimoto

[1]http://dumps.wikimedia.org/

[2]http://nlp.stanford.edu/software/lex-parser.shtml

Model	Correlation
Best SemEval 2012 system	0.229
Jensen Shannon divergence	0.324
Hellinger distance	0.326
Cosine similarity	0.332
Tanimoto coefficient	0.334
Generalized Dice coefficient	0.307

Table 3: Spearman's correlation scores between rankings produced by our approach over different similarity metrics and the gold rankings made available for SemEval 2012 Task 2

metric, which is similar to cosine similarity defined as:

$$Tanimoto(a, b) = \frac{a \cdot b}{||a||^2 + ||b||^2 - a \cdot b} \quad (2)$$

The effectiveness of the simple model presented in this paper shows two things: (1) an LDA model can be used effectively to induce semantic classes from English text using dependency parse contexts, and (2) that those semantic classes can be used to model selectional preferences in semantic relations. These results also show the high importance of selectional preference agreement when measuring the degree to which a pair of words belongs to a semantic relation. This model outperforms reported results, without taking into consideration the actual relation between the two arguments of a word pair. Future work will involve combining the selectional preferences approach with a approach that also models the dependence between the two arguments.

7 Analysis of the induced semantic classes

We first present a manual inspection of the semantic class space that was induced by the LDA, followed by a more analytical evaluation. Table 4 illustrates the top dependency contexts associated with four semantic classes that were prominent for relation REFERENCE:*Expression* in Table 2. Table 5 shows the top words associated with the same four semantic classes. All of the top 16 words for class 44 are categorized as abstract entities in WordNet. Many of them can be further categorized as states (*independence, love, freedom, confidence, security*). We can see from the top dependency contexts of class 44 listed in Table 4 the types of contexts which indicate a state: ←prep_of lack, ←prep_of level, ←prep_of sense. From Table 2 we can see that class 44 is the predominant class for several emotional states participating in the first argument of a REFERENCE:*Expression* relation, so it is reassuring to see that this class consists of states.

Class 44	Class 17	Class 13	Class 24
access	day	take	white
progress	time	come	red
confidence	man	mean	black
independence	game	done	light
ability	victory	look	blue
freedom	question	understand	green
relationship	number	love	hair
responsibility	deal	call	suit
experience	member	give	rain
growth	team	ask	color
future	case	live	yellow
strength	state	agree	breeze
authority	sign	concerned	dress
love	person	remember	flag
security	record	read	shirt
life	attack	hear	smoke

Table 5: The top words (descending) occurring with with semantic classes 44, 17, 13, and 24.

The words in class 17 seem less related, but have some broad similarities. For instance, they appear to be countable nouns expressed in the singular form. When we examine the dependency contexts for class 17 we can understand why this is. The contexts include →det another, →amod first, →det every, →amod only, etc. These determiners and adjectives cannot modify mass nouns and the set of top words for the class do appear to fall in the category of countable nouns.

Class 44	Class 17	Class 13	Class 24
←prep_of lack	→det another	→nsubj I	→amod white
←nn process	→amod first	←ccomp said	→dobj wearing
→amod economic	→amod big	→neg n't	→amod black
←nn talks	←prep_of kind	→punct "	←prep_of pair
→amod political	←prep_of part	→neg not	→amod red
←prep_of kind	←dobj made	→nsubj they	→conj_and white
←prep_of level	→det every	→nsubj we	→amod green
→amod national	→amod only	→nsubj you	→amod blue
→amod great	→det any	→nsubj We	←conj_and red
←dobj expressed	→amod single	→aux do	→amod calm
←prep_of sense	→amod second	→nsubj he	←amod light
→amod public	→amod major	→aux to	←dobj wear
←dobj claimed	→det each	→complm that	←conj_and black
←nn plan	←nsubj came	→aux did	→amod dark
←nn agreement	→amod biggest	→aux does	→amod heavy
←dobj made	→amod great	→aux would	←dobj wore
←prep_of loss	→predet such	→nsubj They	←appos C.
→amod social	←dobj make	→nsubj who	←amod chips
←dobj give	←nsubj 's	→nsubj people	←prep_in dressed
→amod full	→advmod just	→nsubj You	→punct
←prep_of moment	←dobj has	→dobj it	←amod card

Table 4: The top dependency contexts for semantic classes 44, 17, 13, and 24. Some contexts which are common across many semantic classes were omitted.

Semantic class 13 consists largely of actions taken by humans. The dependency contexts reveal how this cluster came about: →nsubj I, →neg n't, →nsubj they, →aux would, etc. These dependencies apply to verbs, and many of them specifically contain pronouns (you, I) reserved primarily for humans. From Table 2 class 13 was largest for the "expression" words *smile*, *nod*, *laugh*, *kiss* which obviously are actions usually preformed by humans.

Semantic class 24 appears to contain words which are often described using colors or shades (e.g., dark, light). Examples for colors would include white flag, white suit, black smoke, while examples for shades would include dark hair and dark shirt, but also colors themselves as in dark green and light blue.

Overall, it appears that using the LDA model on dependency contexts performed well at clustering words into semantic classes, picking up on common-place but subtle linguistic phenomena such as countable nouns, and whether a verb tends to have a person as a subject.

We now present a more quantitative assessment of the induced semantic class space. We follow the evaluation proposed by Widdows and Dorow (2002). They selected the ten categories of objects shown in the first column of Table 6, along with a prototypical member word for each category. Using the prototype word as a seed, its twenty nearest neighbors are determined. The most appropriate distance metric for our approach is to use the Tanimoto coefficient between the semantic classes distributions of two words. The lists of nearest neighbors produced using our induced class distributions are illustrated in Table 6. Neighbors which are not subsumed by the WordNet synset represented in the first column have been italicized. Our method achieves a precision of only 59.4% on this evaluation. The results are considerably below previous approaches which have achieved 82% (Widdows and Dorow, 2002) and 90.5% (Davidov and Rappoport, 2006), however our method has several disadvantages in this comparison. Firstly, we have only generated semantic class vectors for the 3,357 words which occurred in the word pairs in the relation dataset which limits our recall. This particularly affects the retrieval of "easy" but rare neighbors of a word such as *fortepiano* from the seed *piano*. This also caused us to choose different seed words for the categories crimes, body parts, and academic subjects because the seeds used in prior literature did not

Class	Seed Word	Neighbors
crimes	theft	*abuse destruction* rape infringement *crimes violence* crime *explosion famine eruption scandal discrimination accident* assault *crash damage punishment controversy snowstorms slavery*
places	park	mall zoo hall marina stadium castle mill airport aquarium cafeteria hotel factory warehouse gym firehouse restroom shrine house casino garage
tools	screwdriver	knife trowel *mattress* spatula broom *stool* scalpel *flashlight stethoscope pillow microphone leash pouch beaker lid faucet pane fingertip glove scepter*
vehicle conveyance	train	ship *link* craft bus truck boat van airplane *route highway* wagon *mountain* vessel vehicle car *engine* kayak sedan rocket
musical instruments	piano	violin clarinet cello guitar flute *rock* bass *fairy jazz blues television art computer music* keyboard *dance soap opera cinema* Throughout
clothes	shirt	hat sweater frock blouse *earring* wig yarmulke *tiara* coat scarf *necklace bracelet* skirt *breeze eyeshadow* burka pants sandal ballpoint
body parts	neck	wrist ear finger nose waist mouth spine toe *glove coffin* foot eye *couch* hands fingers *door* During penis legs *lawn*
academic subjects	philosophy	geography logic chemistry religion composition psychology anatomy algebra architecture *voice vision* geometry genealogy *image* discourse art *memory signature* history *conception*
foodstuffs	cake	egg salad apple *cane* pie soup *blender* carrot *leaf* omelette *cigarette* pizza *pot polymer* dish beer *oven glass* dessert

Table 6: The nearest neighbors for nine seed words. Italics mark words which do not match the class of the seed word.

appear in the word pair corpus. Secondly, the previous approaches utilizing this evaluation metric have limited their class induction space to only nouns. Therefore, the candidate neighbors under the previous approaches are restricted to nouns, whereas our approach conflated words with the same surface form, but different parts of speech. The effects of this are quite clear for the tools category. Certain tool words which are also used as verbs are absent from our top neighbors such as rake, plow, and shovel, however they are top neighbors of each other. Both of these limitations can be alleviated, but are not addressed in this paper. We believe the results from Table 6 show that our semantic space based on an LDA model and Tanimoto coefficient do correspond to a semantic class space. While alternative semantic class induction techniques may improve our relational similarity results, this approach does show the merit in modeling the relational selectional preferences by semantic class membership of the relation arguments.

8 Conclusion

We showed that a simple model based on LDA using dependency parse contexts can be used effectively to model selectional preferences of semantic relations. Further, we can achieve state of the art results for measuring relational similarity by using only the agreement between a word pair and the expected semantic classes for the relation's arguments. While there remains more work to be done towards incorporating additional types of information beyond just argument semantic classes, our current results are promising. Future improvements to the method would include the use of word senses (or simply part of speech) information to form more semantically coherent classes, and incorporating information about relations into the semantic class induction process.

References

Baroni, M. and Lenci, A. (2010). Distributional memory: A general framework for corpus-based semantics. *Comput. Linguist.*, 36(4):673–721.

Bejar, I. I., Chaffin, R., and Embretson, S. E. (1991). *Cognitive and psychometric analysis of analogical problem solving. Recent research in psychology.* Springer-Verlag Publishing.

Blei, D. M., Ng, A. Y., and Jordan, M. I. (2003). Latent dirichlet allocation. *The Journal of Machine Learning Research*, 3:993–1022.

Davidov, D. and Rappoport, A. (2006). Efficient unsupervised discovery of word categories using symmetric patterns and high frequency words. In *Proceedings of the 21st International Conference on Computational Linguistics and the 44th annual meeting of the Association for Computational Linguistics*, pages 297–304. Association for Computational Linguistics.

De Marneffe, M. C. and Manning, C. D. (2008). The Stanford typed dependencies representation. In *Coling 2008: Proceedings of the workshop on Cross-Framework and Cross-Domain Parser Evaluation*, pages 1–8. Association for Computational Linguistics.

Gentner, D. (1983). Structure-mapping: A theoretical framework for analogy. *Cognitive Science*, 7(2):155 – 170.

Holyoak, K. and Thagard, P. (1996). *Mental leaps: Analogy in creative thought.* MIT press.

Jurgens, D. A., Mohammad, S. M., Turney, P. D., Holyoak, and J., K. (2012). SemEval-2012 Task 2: Measuring Degrees of Relational Similarity. In *Proceedings of the 6th International Workshop on Semantic Evaluation (SemEval 2012).*

Lin, D. and Pantel, P. (2001). Induction of semantic classes from natural language text. In *Proceedings of the seventh ACM SIGKDD international conference on Knowledge discovery and data mining*, KDD '01, pages 317–322, New York, NY, USA. ACM.

Liu, Z., Zhang, Y., Chang, E. Y., and Sun, M. (2011). PLDA+: Parallel Latent Dirichlet Allocation with Data Placement and Pipeline Processing. *ACM Transactions on Intelligent Systems and Technology, special issue on Large Scale Machine Learning*.

Louviere, J. J. and Woodworth, G. G. (1991). Best-worst scaling: A model for the largest difference judgments. Technical report, Working paper. University of Alberta.

Mechura, M. (2008). *Selectional Preferences, Corpora and Ontologies*. PhD thesis, University of Dublin.

Medin, D., Goldstone, R., and Gentner, D. (1990). Similarity involving attributes and relations: Judgments of similarity and difference are not inverses. *Psychological Science*, 1(1):64–69.

Ó Séaghdha, D. (2010). Latent variable models of selectional preference. In *Proceedings of the 48th Annual Meeting of the Association for Computational Linguistics (ACL-10)*, Uppsala, Sweden.

Pantel, P. (2003). *Clustering by committee*. PhD thesis, Citeseer.

Pantel, P., Bhagat, R., Coppola, B., Chklovski, T., and Hovy, E. H. (2007). ISP: Learning Inferential Selectional Preferences. In *North American Chapter of the Association for Computational Linguistics*, pages 564–571.

Parker, R. and Consortium, L. D. (2009). *English gigaword fourth edition*. Linguistic Data Consortium.

Rahman, A. and Ng, V. (2010). Inducing fine-grained semantic classes via hierarchical and collective classification. In *Proceedings of the 23rd International Conference on Computational Linguistics*, COLING '10, pages 931–939, Stroudsburg, PA, USA. Association for Computational Linguistics.

Resnik, P. (1996). Selectional constraints: an information-theoretic model and its computational realization. *Cognition*, 61(1-2):127 – 159. ¡ce:title¿Compositional Language Acquisition¡/ce:title¿.

Rink, B. and Harabagiu, S. (2012). UTD: Determining Relational Similarity Using Lexical Patterns. In *Proceedings of the 6th International Workshop on Semantic Evaluation (SemEval 2012), in conjunction with the First Joint Conference on Lexical and Computational Semantics (* SEM 2012)*.

Ritter, A. and Etzioni, O. (2010). A latent dirichlet allocation method for selectional preferences. In *In Proceedings of the Association for Computational Linguistics ACL2010*.

Roark, B. and Charniak, E. (1998). Noun-phrase co-occurrence statistics for semiautomatic semantic lexicon construction. In *Proceedings of the 17th international conference on Computational linguistics - Volume 2*, COLING '98, pages 1110–1116, Stroudsburg, PA, USA. Association for Computational Linguistics.

Turney, P. D. (2005). Measuring Semantic Similarity by Latent Relational Analysis. In *Proceedings of the 19th international joint conference on Artificial intelligence*, pages 1136–1141.

Turney, P. D. (2006). Similarity of semantic relations. *Comput. Linguist.*, 32(3):379–416.

Turney, P. D. (2008). A uniform approach to analogies, synonyms, antonyms, and associations. In *Proceedings of the 22nd International Conference on Computational Linguistics - Volume 1*, COLING '08, pages 905–912, Stroudsburg, PA, USA. Association for Computational Linguistics.

Widdows, D. and Dorow, B. (2002). A graph model for unsupervised lexical acquisition. In *Proceedings of the 19th international conference on Computational linguistics-Volume 1*, pages 1–7. Association for Computational Linguistics.

Recognizing Spatial Containment Relations between Event Mentions

Kirk Roberts
Human Language Technology Research Institute
University of Texas at Dallas
kirk@hlt.utdallas.edu

Michael A. Skinner
University of Texas Southwestern Medical Center
Children's Medical Center
michael.skinner@childrens.com

Sanda M. Harabagiu
Human Language Technology Research Institute
University of Texas at Dallas
sanda@hlt.utdallas.edu

Abstract

In this paper, we present an approach for recognizing spatial containment relations that hold between event mentions. Event mentions refer to real-world events that have spatio-temporal properties. While the temporal aspect of event relations has been well-studied, the spatial aspect has received relatively little attention. The difficulty in this task is the highly implicit nature of event locations in discourse. We present a supervised method that is designed to capture both explicit and implicit spatial relation information. Our approach outperforms the only known previous method by a 14 point increase in F_1-measure.

1 Introduction

Understanding the interaction of events expressed in natural language requires the ability to recognize spatio-temporal relations between event mentions. While the automatic recognition of temporal relations has received significant attention in the literature (Pustejovsky et al. 2003, Verhagen et al. 2009, UzZaman et al. 2012), the automatic recognition of spatial relations has received comparatively little attention. We believe this is partly due to the difficulty of the task as compared to temporal event relations. The difficulty stems from the fact that (i) spatial relations are multi-dimensional and therefore have a more complex representation, (ii) narrative structure is largely chronological in nature, and the events are often presented by their relative temporal order instead of their relative spatial arrangement, and (iii) by extension, spatial event relations are typically implicit in nature, relying on an intuitive understanding of the semantic properties of events.

Spatial relations between events that are explicitly expressed are typically indicated through syntactic relationships, such as "*The [presentation] at the [conference] was excellent*". Here, the preposition *at* indicates the *presentation* event is spatially contained within the *conference* event.

Far more common, however, are implicitly expressed spatial event relations. For example, in the sentence "*The [bombing] victim [died] immediately*", it is clear that the *died* event is spatially related to the *bombing* event. Specifically, we would say that the *bombing* event spatially contains the *died* event since the assumed bounds of the *bombing* is larger.

An automatic method for recognizing spatial relations between events would be useful for many extraction and reasoning tasks. For instance, mapping the location of entities mentioned in discourse has generally been accomplished through semantic role labeling, which links a predicate with its local semantic arguments. However, locations are relatively rare in discourse as compared to verbal and nominal predicates. Usually the location of an entity is not directly stated in the entity's local argument structure. Instead, this information is *implicit* as the relevant information is located outside a limited syntactic/semantic scope. Tying an entity to a location mentioned elsewhere in the discourse requires either co-reference (either entity or event co-reference), or an understanding of the spatial interactions present within the discourse structure so that relevant spatial inferences may be made.

The goal of this paper is to enable this type of spatial reasoning by connecting events through spatial containment relations.

These spatial relations allow for complex reasoning beyond simply placing an entity on a map. Consider the following sentence taken from a surgeon's operative note:

> A longitudinal [incision] through the umbilicus was [carried] down through to the fascia.

Here the nominalized *incision* event is spatially tied to the *carried* event. Understanding the spatial relation between these events allows us to recognize that a three-dimensional path exists from the point of the *incision* down to the *fascia*, a layer of tissue between the skin and muscles. This deep spatial understanding of text motivates new forms of information extraction, machine reading, and question answering.

In this paper, we present a mostly supervised approach to the detection of spatial event relations. Due to the presense of both explicitly and implicitly expressed relations, we rely on two different classes of features. The first class, which targets explicitly expressed relations, utilizes typical information extraction features, such as lexical and syntactic context. The second class, which targets implicitly expressed relations, focuses on identifying semantically related events that are more likely to be spatially related (such as *presentation* and *conference*, or *bombing* and *die*). This allows us to leverage unlabeled data to derive semantic similarity measures.

The remainder of this paper is organized as follows. Section 2 outlines related work in generalized event relations, generalized spatial relations, as well as current work in spatial event relations. Section 3 describes the data we use to train and evaluate our models. Section 4 details our supervised method, including our classifier, features, and feature selection technique. Section 5 contains the results of our experiments. Section 6 discusses the limitations of our approach and proposes future work. Finally, Section 7 concludes by summarizing our work.

2 Related Work

Event relations in general have received significant attention in the literature, but largely in the form of temporal event relations. The TimeML annotation standard (Pustejovsky et al., 2003) for temporal relations as well as the TimeBank corpus (Pustejovsky et al., 2003) have inspired a significant number of automatic systems for this task (Verhagen et al. 2009, Verhagen et al. 2010, UzZaman et al. 2012, Sun et al. 2013). Beyond temporal relations, work in other types of event relations has received less attention. Prominent among the other event relation types is causation (Bethard and Martin 2008, Beamer and Girju 2009, Rink et al. 2010, Do et al. 2011) and co-reference (Chen et al. 2009, Bejan and Harabagiu 2010). Beyond event relations, Chambers and Jurafsky (2008, 2009) and Bejan (2008) both create narrative schemas based on commonly co-occurring event structures, which is a useful tool for determining a prior likelihood of two or more events being related.

Spatial relations between non-events has likewise received much attention. Several such works are spatial annotation schemas. SpatialML (Mani et al., 2008) focuses on recognizing geographic regions and expressions. For example, the following text:

> a town some 50 miles south of Salzburg in the central Austrian Alps

SpatialML would recognize *town*, *Salzburg*, *Austrian*, and *Alps* as geographic locations, normalize *Salzburg* and *Austrian* to their respective geo-political entities, recognize the direction and distance relation between *town* and *Salzburg*, and the containment relations between *Salzburg* and *Austrian* and *Alps* and *Austrian*. SpatialML has no handling, however, for spatial event relations. Likewise, SpRL (Kordjamshidi et al., 2010) represents spatial relations beyond geographic relations, but would have difficulty representing event relations because SpRL requires an indicator (trigger, e.g., *in*, *on*, *at*, *to the left of*) that is rarely present in spatial event mentions. SpRL does, however, have an annotated corpus (Kordjamshidi et al., 2012) and several automatic approaches have been proposed (Kordjamshidi et al. 2011, Roberts and Harabagiu 2012). STML (Pustejovsky and Moszkowicz, 2008) focuses on the annotation of spatial relations for events, specifically motion events. But their scheme connects a motion event with its motion-specific arguments, and does not include event-event spatial relations.

Despite significant work in both event relations and spatial relations, work specific to spatial relations between events has been quite sparse. ISO-Space (Pustejovsky et al. 2011a, Pustejovsky et al. 2011b, Lee et al. 2011) is an on-going effort to develop a detailed annotation system for spatial information (beyond just spatial language). However, no publicly available corpus is known to exist.[1] Prior to this work, we have developed a corpus (Roberts et al., 2012) of spatial event relations, which is discussed in detail in the next section. While its spatial representation is not as rich as ISO-Space, it contains similar relation types and is designed to represent the highly implicit nature of spatial event relations.

3 Data

In order to conceptualize spatial relations between event mentions, the event itself must be spatially conceptualized. In Roberts et al. (2012), we suggest this can be done by approximating the spatial bounds of an event. For instance, an *election* event might assume the spatial bounds of the geo-political entity conducting the election; a sporting event may be bounded by the field or stadium in which it is played; and a *battle* event may be bounded by the immediate vicinity of the various battle participants. A spatial relation between events, then, can be determined by comparing the spatial bounds of two events, such as whether they are equal, overlap, or one event subsumes the other.

This corpus consists of 162 newswire documents, a subset of the SpatialML corpus (Mani et al., 2008). The corpus contains 5,029 events and 1,695 spatial relations. Annotators marked each event as "spatial" or not based on whether they had intuitive spatial bounds (e.g., "*the gas [attack]*" would be spatial while "*the stock price [increase]*" would not be spatial as it is not clear what the spatial bounds of *increase* might be). In order for a spatial relation to hold between two events, both events must be marked as spatial. For the purposes of this paper, we only evaluate on event pairs in which both events are manually marked as spatial. The data contains six different spatial relation types:

1. SAME: Two events E1 and E2 have indistinguishable spatial bounds.
2. CONTAINS: E1's spatial bounds contain E2's spatial bounds.
3. R_CONTAINS: E2's spatial bounds contain E1's spatial bounds.
4. OVERLAPS: E1 and E2 share partial spatial bounds but neither is a sub-set of the other.
5. NEAR: E1 and E2 do not share spatial bounds but they are within close proximity of each other.
6. DIFFERENT: E1 and E2 have distinguishably different spatial bounds.

These relation types are based on RCC-8 (Randell et al., 1992). Four of the part-of relations are collapsed into CONTAINS and R_CONTAINS. Also, NEAR and DIFFERENT replace the disconnected and externally connected relations, a design decision similar to SpatialML. An example sentence from this corpus exemplifies the CONTAINS relation:

> In October of 1985, four hijackers under his command [took] over the Italian cruise ship Achille Lauro and [killed] a wheelchair-bound American tourist, Leo Klinghoffer.

Here, the *took* event is determined to exhibit a CONTAINS relation with the *killed* event, as *took*'s spatial bounds are determined to be the entire cruise ship, while the spatial bounds of *killed* are the immediate vicinity of the victim.

In addition to annotating spatial events and spatial relations between events, the corpus contains annotated participants and locations of the events. In this way we can graphically represent the spatial relationships between various entities in the text, such as in Figure 1. This graph allows us to make the inference that *Leo Klinghoffer* was located on the *Achille Lauro* when he was killed. Without such a relation, we would have to make the (un-principled) assumption that the closest location (in this case a vehicle) is the location of the *killed* event.

4 Method

We utilize a mostly supervised, two-stage machine learning approach for detecting spatial event relations. A binary support vector machine (SVM) classifier is used for recognizing spatial relations and a multi-class SVM is used for determining the relation type. Previous SVM-based approaches to relation extraction have utilized advanced kernels (e.g., Nguyen et al. (2009)). In this work, however,

[1]Gaizauskas et al. (2012) have annotated a small corpus of facility design reports with a version of ISO-Space, but it is neither publicly available nor large enough to utilize as training data in a machine learning approach. Furthermore, the majority of its spatial relations (perhaps all) are not between events.

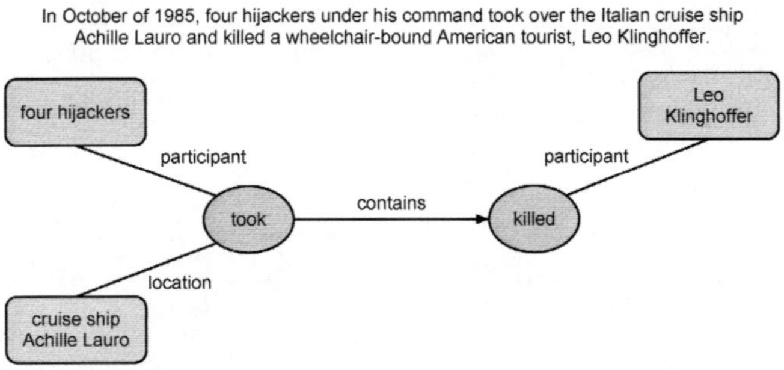

Figure 1: Example spatial event relation from our corpus.

we focus on the utility of different feature types and perform our experiments with a linear kernel using LibLinear (Fan et al., 2008). We evaluate on 3-sentence and 1-sentence windows for potentially related events (annotators were limited to relations in a 3-sentence window). Since the vast majority of event mentions are not spatially related, we adjust the negative weight to 0.05 (leaving the positive weight at 1.0). For the multi-class relation type classifier, SAME and CONTAINS make up the vast majority of relations and therefore get a weight of 0.1. These weights were tuned using a different cross-validation split than that used on our experiments below. Below we detail the features used by the two classifiers. For both classifiers, a large number of partially overlapping features were developed, most of which are described below. We utilize a greedy forward/backward technique known as floating forward feature selection (Pudil et al., 1994) to optimize the best sub-set of features.

4.1 Explicit Relation Features

These features are designed to recognize explicit statements of spatial relatedness based on the context of the relation. Sometimes explicit relations are expressed with spatial prepositions such as *in*, *on*, or *at*. In general, however, we consider explicit relations to be those in which the local context indicates a spatial relation is highly likely. For instance:

> After today's air [strikes], 13 Iraqi soldiers [abandoned] their posts and [surrendered] to Kurdish fighters.

Here, *abandoned* and *surrendered* share the same subject and are syntactically connected through the conjunction *and*. When an actor performs two actions at connected or overlapping time intervals, the actions are necessarily spatially related. While an *and* dependency doesn't necessarily guarantee temporal connectivity, it is highly suggestive and therefore acts as a good indicator.

We utilize the following classes of features:

- Words between arguments, which includes features that are ignored entirely when the arguments are separated by a certain number of tokens or sentences. These bag-of-word features provide useful lexical context that is not always available from a dependency parse (such as modifiers).
- Token-level and sentence-level distance. Event mentions that are lexically closer are more likely to be spatially related, and mentions in different sentences are much less likely to be spatially related.
- Dependency paths. We use the Stanford Dependency Parser (de Marneffe et al., 2006) with the collapsed representation so that preposition nodes (*prep*) become edges (e.g., *prep_at*). This also results in more semantic conjunction edges (*conj_and* instead of simply *conj*).
- TimeML relations from TARSQI (Verhagen et al., 2005), including TLinks, SLinks, and ALinks. TLinks are typical temporal links, such as one event occurring before or after another event. SLinks are a subordinate links, such as in "*John [promised] to [buy] wine for Mary*". ALinks are aspectual links, such as "*John [stopped] [talking]*".
- Event participants/locations from the manually annotated data. If necessary these could be automatically annotated by a semantic role labeler.

Top 5 Events via TLink PMI

bomb	PMI	**pass**	PMI	**drive**	PMI
strafe	0.298	touchdown	0.288	intoxicate	0.276
nuke	0.281	defense	0.277	floorboarding	0.271
landmark	0.273	exam	0.268	park	0.239
shell	0.242	interception	0.249	impair	0.231
machine-gun	0.242	amendment	0.233	bike	0.208

Top 5 Events via Gigaword Sentence PMI

bomb	PMI	**pass**	PMI	**drive**	PMI
strafe	0.295	touchdown	0.354	homer	0.289
plot	0.292	veto	0.237	intoxicate	0.260
nuke	0.291	vote	0.230	floorboarding	0.257
landmark	0.255	squash	0.212	reformat	0.256
scan	0.249	test	0.209	touchdown	0.234

Table 1: Highly associated events for *bomb*, *pass*, and *drive*, as acquired from unlabeled data.

4.2 Implicit Relation Features

These features are designed to recognize spatial relatedness between events based entirely on their semantic properties (i.e., without regard to context). Many times our intuitive understanding of event structures enables the omission of linguistic context clues of spatial relations. For instance:

> During a live broadcast, Geraldo [drew] a map in the sand [showing] the location of the unit in relation to Baghdad.

Here, we understand the purpose of *drew* is manifested in *showing*, and further that in such a relationship the two events are connected by a common object (in general a drawing, but specifically a *map* in this example) that forms an integral part of their spatial bounds. This kind of information requires a source of external knowledge, potentially from (i) a manually constructed knowledge base, (ii) knowledge built from training data, or (iii) knowledge built from unlabeled data. While manual knowledge sources such as ConceptNet (Liu and Singh, 2004) or FreeBase (Bollacker et al., 2008) could be utilized, they are quite sparse on event information (rather focusing on entity information). Instead, we focus on learning which individual events are likely to participate in a spatial relation (using the training data), which pairs of events are likely to participate in a spatial relation (also from the training data), and which pairs of events are likely to be related (from unlabeled data).

We utilize the following classes of features:

- Individual arguments (separate features for first and second arguments). Includes features based on event mention's surface form, caseless form, lemmatized form, part-of-speech from the Stanford Parser (Klein and Manning, 2003), General Inquirer categories (Stone et al., 1966), TimeML event classes from TARSQI (Verhagen et al., 2005), WordNet (Fellbaum, 1998) synsets and hypernyms, and VerbNet (Kipper et al., 1998) classes.
- Concatenation of the above individual argument features for both arguments (e.g., "*draw::show*" for lemmatized form, "*25.2::29.5-2*" for VerbNet classes).
- Intersection of feature values for individual argument features.
- Statistical association of events based on various resources:
  - Gigaword (Parker et al., 2009) sentence co-occurrence
  - TimeML relations on Gigaword
  - Wikipedia co-occurrence

The statistical association features discussed above are designed to elicit spatial information from data without spatial labels. To accomplish this, we start by extending the chronological narrative assumption to space. That is, the narrative not only expresses a directional path through time, but a path through space as well. Thus, events that are closer to each other in the narrative are more likely to be spatially related. The resources mentioned above are thus drawn from different representations of potential narratives. First, sentence co-occurrence in Gigaword is a means of discretizing the narrative into small, tightly related sets of events. Second, TimeML relations are designed to extract the narrative in a temporal structure. These relations have the advantage of including related cross-sentence events while excluding un-related within-sentence events. While this is more principled, TimeML is a difficult task, and any automatic technique would contain both noise and bias. Third, Wikipedia's article structure is more inclined to articles whose events take place in a single location. Thus, we can relax our local constraint to allow for document-wide context. This not only reduces sparsity, but is more likely to capture transitive spatial relations.

While all of these resources should be capable of providing related events, we require a method to increase the likelihood of the event associations being spatial. For this purpose, we use the statistical association metric known as pointwise mutual information (PMI):

$$PMI(x, y) = log\frac{p(x|y)}{p(y)}$$

Where co-occurrences with less than 10 instances are discarded. PMI is a simple technique that has been shown to be effective at natural language tasks, most appropriately narrative chain construction (Chambers and Jurafsky, 2008). Due to the large amount of data, we require a highly efficient technique, such as PMI, that only requires a limited view of the data.[2]

The result of these PMI calculations for three events (*bomb*, *pass*, and *drive*) are shown in Table 1. As can be seen, PMI across this data is able to capture spatially related events: *bomb* is spatially related to sub-types of bombing events such *nuke* and *shell* and other war activities such as *strafe* and *machine-gun*. PMI captures spatially related events for multiple senses of *pass* and *drive*. For instance, *touchdown*, *defense*, and *interception* are spatially related events to the sporting sense of *pass*, while *vote*, *veto* and *amendment* are spatially related events to the political sense of *pass* (as in, "*pass a bill into law*"). Further, as can be seen in Table 1, while the different data sources assign different weights, there is some degree of overlap between them.

Given the different data sources, and the myriad of potential features that could be written to represent this data (in addition to all the other feature types), we utilize the automated feature selection technique discussed above. This enables us to optimize how we present these partially overlapping features to the classifier, ultimately resulting in increased performance. We next discuss the actual features chosen by this technique.

4.3 Selected Features

The features chosen by the feature selector for relation detection are shown in Table 2. The feature selector chose four explicit relation features and eight implicit relation features. The chosen implicit relation features include the first feature chosen and five of the first six features. The features chosen by the feature selector for relation type classification are shown in Table 3. Here, the feature selector chose only two features, both of which are implicit features, suggesting the context is of little significance for determining specifically how two event mentions may be related. The next section evaluates these two classifiers on held-out data.

5 Experiments

We experiment under two different settings: (1) intra-sentence relations only, and (2) intra-sentence relations up to a 3-sentence window, the maximum relation length for the data. We evaluate both relation recognition (whether two event mentions have a spatial relation between them) and relation type classification (given a related pair of mentions, which is the proper relation type). These are both evaluated on the data described in Section 3. In Roberts et al. (2012), we present a baseline method for both spatial relation recognition and spatial relation type classification based on the event mention words, the words between the mentions, and the mention hypernyms. We consider this our baseline for the task. The results for spatial relation recognition are shown in Table 4, and the results for spatial relation classification are shown in Table 5.

Our method easily outperforms the baseline for spatial relation recognition with a 30% increase in F_1-measure. The overall score is still quite low, however, owing to the difficulty of the task. This is discussed more in the next section. Spatial relation type classification outperforms the baseline,

[2]For instance, our same sentence data has 837 million event pairs (14 million unique), while our TLink data has 360 million event pairs (12 million unique).

#	Type	Feature Description
1[a]	I	Concatenated event mention lemmas. Argument order is ignored by representing lemmas in orthographic order. E.g., *kill::take*
2	E	Dependency path between the event mentions. E.g., $\downarrow$*conj_and*
3	I	TLink co-occurrence from Gigaword, adjusted by point-wise mutual information (PMI). Specifically, we use a symmetric PMI so the feature is mention-order independent. This is done by taking the minimum of PMI(E1, E2) and PMI(E2, E1). (real-valued)
4	I	Concatenated event mentions in their caseless form. Argument order is preserved. E.g., *took::killed*
5	I	Co-occurrence from Wikipedia, adjusted using PMI. (real-valued)
6	I	Concatenated event mention lemmas. Argument order is preserved unlike Feature 1. E.g., *take::kill*
7	E	Whether the two event mentions have the same location. This feature uses the Stanford co-reference resolution system (Raghunathan et al., 2010) to expand locations so that two events have the same location if their respective locations belong to the same co-reference chain. (boolean-valued)
8	E	Whether the two event mentions have the same participant. (boolean-valued)
9	E	Token distance between the event mentions. Reduced to scalar between 0 and 1 by computing $1 - (\lvert t_1 - t_2 \rvert + 1)^{-1}$. (real-valued)
10	I	Intersection of event mention categories from the General Inquirer. E.g., *kill*'s categories are: ACTIVE, DAV, H4LVD, HOSTILE, NEGATIV, NGTV, NOUN, PFREQ, SOCREL, STRONG, SUPV, and TRNLOSS. *take*'s categories are: ACTIVE, AFFIL, BEGIN, DAV, FETCH, H4, HANDELS, IAV, MODIF, NEED, POWER, SOCREL, STRONG, SUPV, TRY, VARY, and VIRTUE. The intersection is thus ACTIVE (i.e., active orientation), DAV (descriptive action verb), SOCREL (socially defined inter-personal process), STRONG (strength), and SUPV (support verb).
11	I	Intersection of event mention VerbNet classes. E.g., $\emptyset$
12	I	Concatenated event mention surface form. Argument order is ignored. E.g., *killed::took*

Table 2: Spatial event relation recognition features, shown in the order chosen by the feature selector. Type 'E' refers to the explicit features (Section 4.1), Type 'I' refers to the implicit features (Section 4.2). Feature values taken from example in Figure 1.

#	Type	Feature Description
1	I	Whether the ALink co-occurrence PMI (from Gigaword) is greater than 0 (i.e., is the aspectual link positively correlated?). This does not use a symmetric PMI because the relation type order matters. (boolean-valued)
2	I	Co-occurrence from Gigaword sentences, adjusted using PMI. (real-valued)

Table 3: Spatial event relation type features.

[a]This was not technically the first feature chosen. Instead, the length of the dependency path was the first feature, but this was pruned after Feature 8 was added to the feature set.

Method	1-sentence P	R	F_1	3-sentence P	R	F_1
Baseline	35.1	41.3	37.9	29.1	35.5	32.0
Our Method	44.7	69.2	54.3	37.2	60.4	46.0

Table 4: Spatial event relation recognition experiments on our corpus.

Method	1-sentence %	3-sentence %
Baseline	59.3	58.3
Our Method	60.1	59.3

Table 5: Spatial event relation type classification experiments on our corpus.

but only slightly. Here, the issue is largely a matter of data imbalance: the SAME relation is favored by the classifier in almost all cases.

Reducing the context to a single-sentence window improves the relation recognition score by a further 8.3 points. While this would limit the reasoning power of any downstream system, it is useful to know that performance gains are possible by focusing on an easier sub-set of the data. This improvement in relation recognition does not apply to relation type classification, however. In the next section we place our results in greater context and analyze some typical errors.

6 Discussion

The performance gains seen in the previous section are encouraging: they validate our assumption that spatial information can be obtained from large amounts of unlabeled data in an efficient manner. The overall F_1-measure, though, still seems quite low compared to other natural language tasks such as named entity recognition (NER) and semantic role labeling (SRL). However, those tasks are limited to explicit context, such as contiguous tokens for NER and parse nodes within the syntactic scope for SRL. These tasks also utilize more predictable features, such as surface-level casing features for NER and predictable argument structures for SRL (e.g., the syntactic subject for an active verb is usually the ARG0). Proper comparison requires evaluating our results alongside other implicit tasks. One such work involves implicit SRL. Gerber and Chai (2010) perform nominal SRL and achieve an overall F_1 measure of 42.3. While the tasks are not directly comparable in terms of difficulty, this does suggest that implicit tasks require far more advanced methods to achieve superior performance and that downstream systems will likely need to be highly tolerant to noise. To address this, we discuss future work below, analyzing the types of errors that our system makes to give context to these ideas.

As might be guessed, rare event mentions with long dependency paths are highly likely to result in false negatives, such as the relation between *elected* and *disillusionment* here:

> Tehran had been governed by reformists since 1989, but a conservative city council was [elected] in the February 28 municipal polls in a result attributed to a meager turnout amid growing public [disillusionment] with electoral politics.

Here the *elected* and *disillusionment* events are judged to cover all of Tehran. The dependency path for this relation has five edges, including the rare dependency relation *prep_amid*. Further, the *disillusionment* event is fairly rare. Such long dependency relations with rare arguments is unlikely to be recognized by a simple machine learning classifier. Instead, this suggests an approach where either intermediate events are able to transitively suggest spatial relations, or the dependency parse is relaxed in certain cases to allow for longer-range relations.

As is common in semantic tasks, word sense presents an issue, resulting in a false negative:

> It was believed Naotia was a [practicing] sorcerer and through his black magic he had [cast] evil spells on villagers, prompting a group within the village to eliminate them.

Since our corpus-based method uses a lemmatized form only, when related but rare senses are used, such as the witchcraft sense of *cast*, PMI is unable to attribute the proper association between the two events.

In terms of false positives, our implicit features can result in errors when very similar events are clearly different based on their context:

> The British leader [travelled] to the United States before also [visiting] Japan, South Korea, China on a whistle-stop tour.

Here, the spatial bounds of *travelled* is interpreted as being the United States and the flight from Britain, while the *visiting* event is interpreted as being several Asian countries. While one might argue these two trips are spatially related since one is a continuation of the other, the annotator in this case chose to use neither the NEAR or OVERLAPS relations. This highlights another issue with such implicit tasks: the annotations rely heavily on the annotator's intuition. Not unexpectedly, the corpus has fairly low inter-annotator agreement (Roberts et al., 2012).

One final error highlights the difference between events that are related by a narrative, and events that are spatially related:

> Police have [arrested] four people in connection with the [killings].

This false positive resulted from the high degree of association between *arrested* and *killings*, but arrests are rarely made at the scene of the crime. One potential solution to this is to automatically extract event narrative structures, then check the locations of the events on that structure for unexpected location changes. This would be quite challenging: automatic narrative structures proposed thus far are quite simplistic, and most events within a narrative structure will not have an explicit location, so a very robust model of structure would be required.

Finally, despite the accuracy score being higher than the F_1-measure for relation recognition, spatial relation type classification may be the more difficult task. Almost all errors were the result of misclassifying a relation as SAME due to the class imbalance. While the classifier weights may be tuned to improve F_1-measure for recognition, this rarely improves a multi-class task significantly. Our main direction for future work is to actually classify the *size* of events. For example, we would like to recognize that an *election* has larger bounds than a *protest*. This would allow our classifier to recognize when two events are very different in size, and if so which is larger. Ideally, by constricting the set of classes for a containment relation using the sizes of the arguments, this would allow other semantic features to contribute to relation type classification.

7 Conclusion

We have presented an approach for recognizing spatial containment relations between event mentions. Using a corpus of event mentions from newswire texts, we have developed a supervised classifiers for (1) recognizing the presense of a spatial relation between two event mentions, and (2) classifying spatially related event pairs into one of five spatial containment relations. Our method combines features that are designed to extract explicit information from the relation context, as well as implicit information about the likelihood of two events being spatially related. We have evaluated our method and shown substantial improvements over the pre-existing baseline, achieving an F_1 of 46.0 on relation recognition and an accuracy of 59.3% on relation type classification. These gains, though, are largely limited to the task of recognizing whether a spatial relation exists. Finally, we have performed an error analysis to determine paths of future work on this challenging task.

References

Beamer, B. and R. Girju (2009). Using a Bigram Event Model to Predict Causal Potential. In *Proceedings of Computational Linguistics and Intelligent Text Processing*, pp. 430–441.

Bejan, C. A. (2008). Unsupervised Discovery of Event Scenarios from Texts. In *Proceedings of the 21st Florida Artificial Intelligence Research Society International Conference (FLAIRS)*.

Bejan, C. A. and S. Harabagiu (2010). Unsupervised Event Coreference Resolution with Rich Linguistic Features. In *Proceedings of the Association for Computational Linguistics*.

Bethard, S. and J. H. Martin (2008). Learning Semantic Links from a Corpus of Parallel Temporal and Causal Relations. In *Proceedings of the 46th Annual Meeting of the Association for Computational Linguistics: Human Language Technologies*, pp. 177–180.

Bollacker, K., C. Evans, P. Paritosh, T. Sturge, and J. Taylor (2008). Freebase: A Collaboratively Created Graph Database for Structuring Human Knowledge. In *Proceedings of ACM SIGMOD International Conference on Management of Data*, pp. 1247–1250.

Chambers, N. and D. Jurafsky (2008). Unsupervised Learning of Narrative Schemas and their Participants. In *Proceedings of the 46th Annual Meeting of the Association for Computational Linguistics: Human Language Technologies*.

Chambers, N. and D. Jurafsky (2009). Unsupervised Learning of Narrative Schemas and their Participants. In *Proceedings of the Joint Conference of the 47th Annual Meeting of the ACL and the 4th International Joint Conference on Natural Language Processing of the AFNLP*.

Chen, Z., H. Ji, and R. Haralick (2009). A pairwise event coreference model, feature impact and evaluation for event coreference resolution. In *Proceedings of the RANLP Workshop on Events in Emerging Text Types*, pp. 17–22.

de Marneffe, M.-C., B. MacCartney, and C. Manning (2006). Generating Typed Dependency Parses from Phrase Structure Parses. In *Proceedings of the Fifth International Conference on Language Resources and Evaluation*.

Do, Q. X., Y. S. Chan, and D. Roth (2011). Minimally Supervised Event Causality Identification. In *Proceedings of the 2011 Conference on Empirical Methods in Natural Language Processing*, pp. 294–303.

Fan, R.-E., K.-W. Chang, C.-J. Hsieh, X.-R. Wang, and C.-J. Lin (2008). LIBLINEAR: A Library for Large Linear Classification. *Journal of Machine Learning Research 9*, 1871–1874.

Fellbaum, C. (Ed.) (1998). *WordNet: An Electronic Lexical Database*. MIT Press.

Gaizauskas, R., E. Barker, C.-L. Chang, L. Derczynski, M. Phiri, and C. Peng (2012). Applying ISO-Space to Healthcare Facility Design Evaluation Reports. In *Seventh Workshop on Interoperable Semantic Annotation (ISA), Eighth International Conference on Language Resources and Evaluation*, pp. 13–20.

Gerber, M. and J. Y. Chai (2010). Beyond NomBank: A Study of Implicit Arguments for Nominal Predicates. In *Proceedings of the Association for Computational Linguistics*, pp. 1583–1592.

Kipper, K., H. T. Dang, and M. Palmer (1998). Class-based construction of a verb lexicon. In *Proceedings of AAAI/IAAI*.

Klein, D. and C. D. Manning (2003). Accurate Unlexicalized Parsing. In *Proceedings of the 41st Annual Meeting of the Association for Computational Linguistics*, pp. 423–430.

Kordjamshidi, P., S. Bethard, and M.-F. Moens (2012). SemEval-2012 Task 3: Spatial Role Labeling. In *Proceedings of the 6th International Workshop on Semantic Evaluation (SemEval)*.

Kordjamshidi, P., M. V. Otterlo, and M.-F. Moens (2011). Spatial Role Labeling: Towards Extraction of Spatial Relations from Natural Language. *ACM Transactions on Speech and Language Processing 8*(3).

Kordjamshidi, P., M. van Otterlo, and M.-F. Moens (2010). Spatial role labeling: Task definition and annotation scheme. In *Proceedings of the Seventh International Conference on Language Resources and Evaluation*, pp. 413–420.

Lee, K., A. C. Fang, and J. Pustejovsky (2011). Multilingual Verification of the Annotation Scheme ISO-Space. In *International Conference on Semantic Computing (ICSC)*, pp. 449–458.

Liu, H. and P. Singh (2004). ConceptNet – a practical commonsense reasoning tool-kit. *BT Technology Journal 22*(4), 211–226.

Mani, I., J. Hitzeman, J. Richer, D. Harris, R. Quimby, and B. Wellner (2008). SpatialML: Annotation Scheme, Corpora, and Tools. In *Proceedings of the Sixth International Conference on Language Resources and Evaluation*.

Nguyen, T.-V. T., A. Moschitti, and G. Riccardi (2009). Convolution kernels on constituent, dependency and sequential structures for relation extraction. In *Proceedings of the 2009 Conference on Empirical Methods in Natural Language Processing*, pp. 1378–1387.

Parker, R., D. Graff, J. Kong, K. Chen, and K. Maeda (2009). English Gigaword Fourth Edition. *The LDC Corpus Catalog. LDC2009T13.*

Pudil, P., J. Novovičová, and J. Kittler (1994). Floating search methods in feature selection. *Pattern Recognition Letters 15*, 1119–1125.

Pustejovsky, J., J. Castano, R. Ingria, R. Saurí, R. Gaizauskas, A. Setzer, G. Katz, and D. Radev (2003). TimeML: Robust Specification of Event and Temporal Expressions in Text. In *IWCS-5 Fifth International Workshop on Computational Semantics.*

Pustejovsky, J., P. Hanks, R. Saurí, A. See, R. Gaizauskas, A. Setzer, D. Radev, B. Sundheim, D. Day, L. Ferro, and M. Lazo (2003). The TIMEBANK Corpus. In *Proceedings of Corpus Linguistics.*

Pustejovsky, J. and J. L. Moszkowicz (2008). Integrating Motion Predicate Classes with Spatial and Temporal Annotations. In *Proceedings of COLING 2008*, pp. 95–98.

Pustejovsky, J., J. L. Moszkowicz, and M. Verhagen (2011a). Iso-space: The annotation of spatial information in language. In *Proceedings of the Sixth Joint ISO-ACL SIGSEM Workshop on Interoperable Semantic Annotation*, pp. 1–9.

Pustejovsky, J., J. L. Moszkowicz, and M. Verhagen (2011b). Using ISO-Space for Annotating Spatial Information. In *Proceedings of the International Conference on Spatial Information Theory.*

Raghunathan, K., H. Lee, S. Rangarajan, N. Chambers, M. Surdeanu, D. Jurafsky, and C. Manning (2010). A Multi-Pass Sieve for Coreference Resolution. In *Proceedings of the 2010 Conference on Empirical Methods in Natural Language Processing.*

Randell, D. A., Z. Cui, and A. G. Cohn (1992). A Spatial Logic based on Regions and Connection. In *Proceedings of the 3rd International Conference on Knowledge Representation and Reasoning*, Volume 117.

Rink, B., C. A. Bejan, and S. Harabagiu (2010). Learning Textual Graph Patterns to Detect Causal Event Relations. In *Proceedings of the 23rd Florida Artificial Intelligence Research Society International Conference (FLAIRS'10), Applied Natural Language Processing Track*, pp. 265–270.

Roberts, K., T. Goodwin, and S. M. Harabagiu (2012). Annotating Spatial Containment Relations Between Events. In *Proceedings of the Eighth International Conference on Language Resources and Evaluation*, pp. 3052–3059.

Roberts, K. and S. M. Harabagiu (2012). UTD-SpRL: A Joint Approach to Spatial Role Labeling. In *Proceedings of the 6th International Workshop on Semantic Evaluation (SemEval).*

Stone, P. J., D. C. Dunphy, and M. S. Smith (1966). *The General Inquirer: A Computer Approach to Content Analysis.* MIT Press.

Sun, W., A. Rumshisky, and O. Uzuner (2013). Evaluating Temporal Relations in Clinical Text: 2012 i2b2 Challenge Overview. *Journal of the American Medical Informatics Association Submitted.*

UzZaman, N., H. Llorens, J. F. Allen, L. Derczynski, M. Verhagen, and J. Pustejovsky (2012). TempEval-3: Evaluating Events, Time Expressions, and Temporal Relations. *arXiv.1206.5333v1.*

Verhagen, M., R. Gaizauskas, F. Schilder, M. Hepple, J. Moszkowicz, and J. Pustejovsky (2009). The TempEval challenge: identifying temporal relations in text. *Language Resources and Evaluation 43*, 161–179.

Verhagen, M., I. Mani, R. Saurí, R. Knippen, J. Littman, and J. Pustejovsky (2005). Automating Temporal Annotation with TARSQI. In *Proceedings of the 43rd Annual Meeting of the Association for Computational Linguistics, Demo Session.*

Verhagen, M., R. Saurí, T. Caselli, and J. Pustejovsky (2010). SemEval-2010 Task 13: TempEval-2. In *Proceedings of the 5th International Workshop on Semantic Evaluation*, pp. 57–62.

Regular Meaning Shifts in German Particle Verbs: A Case Study

Sylvia Springorum, Jason Utt and Sabine Schulte im Walde
Institut für Maschinelle Sprachverarbeitung
Universität Stuttgart
{riestesa|uttjn|schulte}@ims.uni-stuttgart.de

Abstract

This paper provides a corpus-based study on German particle verbs. We hypothesize that there are regular mechanisms in meaning shifts of a base verb in combination with a particle that do not only apply to the individual verb, but across a semantically coherent set of verbs. For example, the syntactically similar base verbs *brummen* 'hum' and *donnern* 'rumble' both describe an irritating, displeasing loud sound. Combined with the particle *auf*, they result in near-synonyms roughly meaning 'forcefully assigning a task' (in one of their senses). Covering 6 base verb groups and 3 particles with 4 particle meanings, we demonstrate that corpus-based information on the verbs' subcategorization frames plus conceptual properties of the nominal complements is a sufficient basis for defining such meaning shifts. While the paper is considerably more extensive than earlier related work, we view it as a case study toward a more automatic approach to identify and formalize meaning shifts in German particle verbs.

1 Introduction

Our focus of interest is on German particle verbs. We hypothesize that there are regular mechanisms that trigger a meaning shift of a base verb (such as *brummen* 'hum') in combination with a particle (such as *auf*, in this case referring to a contact relation) that do not only apply to the individual verb, but across a semantically coherent set of verbs. For example, *donnern* 'rumble' agrees with *brummen* in properties at the syntax-semantic interface in that both verbs are intransitive, and both describe an irritating, displeasing loud sound that the typically non-agentive, non-living subject produces. In addition, the resulting particle verbs *aufbrummen* and *aufdonnern* are near-synonyms, roughly meaning 'forcefully assigning a task' (in one of their senses). Furthermore, they agree in properties at the syntax-semantic interface in that both verbs (again, in one of their senses) are ditransitive, with an agentive subject imposing something on another person.

The example demonstrates that a coherent set of base verbs in combination with a particle meaning[1] may result in a coherent set of particle verbs. Equation (1) illustrates this pattern: a base verb **BV** with properties pBV_i in combination with a particle with meaning **PM** results in a particle verb **PV** with properties pPV_j.

(1) $$\mathbf{BV}\ \{pBV_1,\ pBV_2,\ \ldots,\ pBV_n\}\ +\ \mathbf{PM} \rightarrow \mathbf{PV}\ \{pPV_1,\ pPV_2,\ \ldots,\ pPV_m\}$$

The goal of this paper is to demonstrate that we can find such regular meaning shifts across semantically coherent verb groups and across particle meanings by using a property selection process. Our work is corpus-based, i.e., we identify coherent verb groups and particle meanings on the basis of large-scale corpus data. The empirical data is used to describe the base verbs as well as the particle verbs with regard to common properties at the syntax-semantic interface. Covering 6 base verb groups with 3 particles and 4 particle meanings, we consider this paper as considerably more extensive than earlier related work, but at the same time we view it as a case study toward an even more extensive, and also more automatically driven identification of meaning shifts in particle verbs. We therefore combine the corpus-based analyses with advice on future elaborations, mainly with regard to applying approaches of regular polysemy.

[1] Note that particles in German particle verbs are in general highly ambiguous.

The paper is organized as follows. Section 2 presents related work. Section 3 represents the core of the paper: We describe our corpus-based acquisition method, the empirical behavior for each of our BV–PV groups, and regularities in the meaning shift. In Section 4, we generalize over the concrete patterns in meaning shift, discuss elaborations of the existing method, and hypothesize about a more automatic approach to identifying and formalizing meaning shifts in German particle verbs.

2 Related Work

Previous work on meaning shifts of semantically coherent groups of verbs has shown that there are regularities at the syntax-semantic interface with regard to the literal vs. transferred meanings of the verbs. For example, Morgan (1997) uses schematic diagrams to illustrate the meaning shifts of particle verb constructions with English *out*. She claims that the source domain in a shift is systematically determined by the base verb, and the particle meanings are instantiated by cognitive image schemas. Ibarretxe-Antuñano (1999) describes systematic non-prototypical meanings of perception verbs cross-linguistically for English, Spanish, and Basque. She investigates the meaning shifts on the basis of corpus examples and introspection.

Given that there is substantial theoretical evidence for regular patterns in verb meaning shifts, it is surprising that—to our knowledge—no empirical, corpus-based work so far has applied approaches of regular polysemy to a large, coherent group of verbs. On the one hand, there has been an impressive increase in empirical work on modeling meaning shifts in recent years (mostly with regard to metonymy and metaphor). For example, Stefanowitsch and Gries (2006) edited a volume on corpus-based approaches and Markert and Nissim (2007) provided a shared task for metonymy resolution at SemEval 2007. On the other hand, the research has, in general, been restricted to small groups of target items. For example, the shared task by Markert and Nissim (2007) comprised only locations and organizations; Lönneker-Rodman (2008) describes the working environment and result of developing the *Hamburg Metaphor Database*, comprising a respectable framework that, up to now, covers few targets and less than 2,000 annotated sentences. Work by Birke (2005) provided an extensive automatic detection of non-literal use of English verbs in context, but did not specifically look at regular shifts in meanings across multiple verbs.

3 Corpus-based Acquisition of Base and Particle Verb Groups with a Meaning Shift

Our strategy to identify meaning shifts in BV–PV transfer is as follows. We searched our corpus for examples of base verbs and particle verbs, concentrating on one specific particle at a time. As corpus data, we rely on the SDEWAC corpus (Faaß et al., 2010), a cleaned version of the German web corpus DEWAC created by the WACKY group (Baroni et al., 2009). The SDEWAC contains approximately 880 million tokens and has been parsed by Bohnet's MATE dependency parser (Bohnet, 2010). The information we used for our search was effectively verb subcategorization information that had been extracted and quantified automatically from the corpus parses. That is, for each verb (including BVs as well as PVs), we have quantitative information about how often the verb appeared with a specific subcategorization frame, and how often and which nominal complements appeared within the frames.

In a first step, we searched the subcategorization database for all occurrences of particle verbs with a specific particle (such as *auf*), the particle verbs' subcategorization frames, and the nominal fillers of the various verb complements in the frames. In parallel, we searched for the same information with regard to all base verbs that combine with that particle. We focused on the empirically strongest subcategorization frames, and on the most dominant nominal complements, where empirical strength was determined by *Local Mutual Information (LMI)*, cf. Evert (2005).

On the basis of the parallel data on subcategorization frames and nominal complements for base verbs and for particle verbs, we then manually identified semantically coherent groups of base verbs and the respective particle verbs which showed regularities with regard to a meaning shift. For each of the regular meaning shifts that we identified, the following subsections present the corpus data on the base verbs and the particle verbs, and a description of the meaning shift. The corpus data is provided in tables capturing the following information:

- the base/particle verbs in the respective verb group, identified via a particular particle meaning;
- the predominant subcategorization frame that is relevant for the meaning shift;
- one illustrative example complement per literal and shifted sense, within a relevant slot for the meaning shift;
- the strongest connotations, and
- the concepts that play a role in the meaning shift.

Concerning base verb and particle verb senses, note that many of the verbs are ambiguous. Our analyses focus on those senses that are relevant for the meaning shift, i.e., we only refer to the subcategorization and conceptual information with regard to (a) the base verb sense that undergoes the meaning shift, (b) the literal meaning of the particle verb in relation to the base verb, if there is any, and (c) the particle verb sense that represents the respective meaning shift. For example, we find (a) *Die Sonne strahlt* 'The sun is shining' as a base verb example, with (b) a literal particle verb extension *Die Sonne strahlt das Gebirge an* 'The sun shines on the mountains' and with (c) a meaning shift in *Die Frau strahlt den Mann an* 'The woman smiles at the man'.

3.1 *an*: Emotional Communication

The German verb particle *an* has one very prominent meaning (among others), where it ascribes a direction to the verb complement realized as its direct object. All PVs with this meaning of *an* are transitive, and combining this *an* with communication verbs such as *sprechen* 'talk' or *schreiben* 'write' is productive.

However, there are PVs such as *anstrahlen* in Example (3) that can also be characterized as directed communication verbs, but the BVs do not themselves carry a communication meaning, cf. Example (1). The sun (as well as other intransitive subjects of the base verb *strahlen* which occurred in the data) does not communicate through shining. So there must be an additional extended particle reading which includes communication semantics to get a shift from a literal PV meaning, as exemplified in Example (2), which describes a directed shining event of the uplighter toward the ceiling, to a metaphorical PV meaning with a directed communication action between two persons, cf. Example (3). In this example, the girl has an intention to smile in the direction of the grumpy person and therefore she must also expect him to be a potential experiencer. Compare *'He smiled at the chair', which is odd. While there are many other verbs that describe the manner in which an object may shine, it is necessary for the verb to allow for a directed communication reading: One could assume that verbs such as *glitzern* 'glitter' and *glänzen* 'gleam' which are similar to *funkeln* 'twinkle' also allow such a reading, however, these verbs denote the reflection of light instead of emission, i.e. the object itself is the light source. The verb *scheinen* 'shine' is a near-synonym of *strahlen* 'beam'/'shine', while the latter suggests directed communication, the former does not necessarily.

(1) *Die Sonne strahlt.* 'The sun is shining.'

(2) *Der Deckenfluter strahlt den Deckenbereich an.* 'The uplighter shines at the ceiling area.'

(3) *Das Mädchen strahlt den Obermuffel an.* ' The girl smiles at the grumpy person.'

There are four different categories of non-communication BVs with such a shift to communication PVs. They can be sub-divided into two groups, one with a positive connotation as in Tables 1 & 2, and one with a negative connotation as in Tables 3 & 4.

verbs	frames	complements	connotations	properties
strahlen 'beam' *funkeln* 'twinkle'	intrans intrans	*Sonne* 'sun' / *Auge* 'eye' *Sternlein* 'little star' / *Auge* 'eye'	bright, warm pleasing, valuable	light emission
lächeln 'smile' *grinsen* 'grin'	intrans intrans	*Mädchen* 'girl' *Freund* 'friend'	happy, friendly expression	positive emotion

Table 1: Base verbs that combine with *an* to mean *positive directed communication*.

It is striking that positively connoted BVs are all perceivable by vision, either because of the brightness ('beam', 'twinkle') or because of a facial expression ('smile', 'grin'), and lead to a positive communication reading in Table 2. The negatively connoted BVs are either sound-related or refer to animal sounds ('bark', 'growl') that are frightening or bear an acoustic intensity, cf. Table 3. In contrast, the PV *anzwitschern*, derived from the rather quiet and non-threatening BV *zwitschern* ('tweet') does not exist in this communication reading, because it is missing the negative connotation.[2] These observations are in line with Ibarretxe-Antuñano (1999), who claims that auditory as well as olfactory perception often comes with a negative connotation, since these senses can be overloaded. This is not the case for the visual sense, which can easily be regulated and effectively 'shut off'.

verbs	frames	complements	connotations	properties
anstrahlen 'beam at'	trans	*Deckenbereich* 'ceiling area'		
		Obermuffel 'grumpy person'	pleasing,	pos. directed communication
anfunkeln 'beam at'	trans	*Großmaul* 'loudmouth'	positive	
anlächeln 'smile at'	trans	*Mädchen* 'girl'	communication	
angrinsen 'grin at'	trans	*Mädchen* 'girl'		

Table 2: *Positive directed communication* particle verbs with *an*.

Furthermore, there are negative communication PVs which are not derived by sounds, but by vulgar expressions like 'shit' or 'piss', with an inherent negative polarity, cf. Table 3. Taking the non-vulgar synonym *pinkeln* 'tinkle' for *pissen* results in the odd PV *anpinkeln*, which cannot be readily interpreted except literal. So again, the missing negative connotation excludes the PV from the meaning shift. The BV subjects in the negative cases are mostly animals, whereas the subjects and also the objects in the corresponding PVs are persons (e.g., *Gegner* 'opponent', *Fan* 'fan') if the reading is metaphorical, cf. Table 4. In the literal meaning of, for example, *anbellen* 'bark at', the subject is a dog and we can find also inanimate objects such as *Mond* 'moon' as objects.

verbs	frames	complements	connotations	properties
bellen 'bark'	intrans	*Schäferhund* 'German shepherd'	loud sound,	uncivilized communication
kläffen 'yap'	intrans	*Köter* 'mutt'	displeasing	
pissen 'piss'	intrans	*Hund* 'dog'	feces, vulgar,	uncivilized excretion
scheißen 'shit'	intrans	*Taube* 'pigeon'	unpleasant	

Table 3: Base verbs that combine with *an* to mean *negative directed communication*.

verb	frame	complements	connotations	properties
anbellen 'bark at'	trans	*Mond* 'moon'	negative,	
		Gutachter 'surveyor'	intense,	neg. directed communication
ankläffen 'yap at'	trans	*Gegner* 'opponent'	aggressive,	
anpissen 'irritate'	trans	*Fan* 'fan'	vulgar	
anscheißen 'pester'	trans	*Bulle* 'cop'		

Table 4: *Negative directed communication* particle verbs with *an*.

3.2 *auf*: Social Pressure

We now investigate a meaning shift in PVs with the particle *auf* that have a social pressure reading. The BVs which belong to this group (cf. Table 5) are on the one hand force verbs which bring about a state that would not come about on its own, e.g., *zwängen* 'pressure/wedge' or *lasten* 'charge/weight'. On the other hand, there are the verbs *brummen* 'hum' and *donnern* 'rumble' which describe a heavy

[2] Nowadays, it can have a special communication reading because of the social web service Twitter.

and intense sound. Their complements are affected with a heavy sound in the literal meaning ('skull', 'cannon') and with heavy activity in a metaphorical meaning ('business'). The complements of *zwängen* all indicate a literal meaning (cf. Example 5), whereas *lasten* has direct objects that indicate a literal (*Gewicht* 'weight') and a less literal (*Verantwortung* 'responsibility') meaning.

verbs	**frames**	**complements**	**connotations**	**properties**
zwängen 'pressure/wedge'	trans (in-comp)	*Bus* 'bus'	pressure, negative	
bürden 'burden'	trans (auf-comp)	*Mitschuld* 'complicity'	assignment, strain	pressure, burden
lasten 'charge/weigh'	intrans (auf-comp)	*Gewicht* 'weight'		
		Verantwortung 'responsibility'	pressure, negative	
brummen 'hum'	intrans	*Schädel* 'skull'	loud, heavy activity	
		Geschäft 'business'		sound
donnern 'rumble'	intrans	*Kanone* 'cannon'	loud, menacing force	

Table 5: Base verbs that combine with *auf* to mean *transfer of negative social pressure.*

Combining these verbs with the social pressure triggered by *auf*, we only find abstract objects such as *Risiko* 'risk', *Strafe* 'penalty', etc. (cf. Table 6). Thus we have a meaning shift from an interpretation mostly ascribed to the physical domain to an interpretation within an abstract social domain.

The fact that the verbs **aufquetschen* and *aufschieben* do not have this reading shows that there must be another constraint. In comparison to the previous BVs, *quetschen* 'squeeze' suggests equally opposed forces and *schieben* 'push' one single moving force. The verbs *zwängen, bürden* and *lasten* all imply power inequality with some kind of resistance (e.g. non-compliance if it is a person or inertial/spatial opposition otherwise). In light of this, we can compare the social pressure meaning with the support meaning of *auf*. In both cases we have the concept that something is above something else. In Example (6), with its abstract social pressure reading, Maria bears a more powerful social position and thus is, metaphorically speaking, above her friends. Here, the equivalent of contact is expressed in her friends being the supporter because they have to carry the abstract pressure of the will of somebody else. However, the sound verbs are not restricted to the power inequality constraint; instead, only the semantics of something heavy being involved plays a role. The non-existence of *auf* together with *summen* 'sum', which sounds similar to *brummen* (but with higher sound frequencies and therefore not as heavy) is evidence for this assumption. Similarly, such loud sounds as those denoted by *krachen* ('crash') and *knallen* ('bang') lack a clear presence of a long, low-frequency sound. By contrast, while not present in the standard German dictionary Duden[3], the heavy sound of *dröhnen* ('drone'), gives rise to *aufdröhnen*, which is attested on the web:

(4) *Gehen wir einmal davon aus, Ihnen wird kein Fahrtenbuch aufgedröhnt, um den privaten Nutzungsanteil nachzuweisen.* 'Let's assume you are not forced to keep a driver's logbook in order to account for private use.'

The social pressure meaning as in Example (7) can only come from *auf*. The shift occurs here from being a sound verb to a verb describing somebody exerting negative social force upon somebody else.

(5) *Der Fahrer zwängt den Bus in eine kleine Parklücke.* 'The driver wedges the bus in a small parking space.'

(6) *Maria zwängt ihren Freunden ihren Willen auf.* 'Maria imposes her will on her friends.'

(7) *Der Richter hat dem Einbrecher eine gerechte Strafe aufgebrummt.* 'The judge inflicted a justified punishment on the burglar.'

3.3 *auf*: Initialization/Intensification of Visual Perceivables

The second reading of PVs with *auf* we take into account describes a transient change in which something suddenly appears and usually shortly after disappears. In Example (8), it is Micha's cry which abruptly appears and shortly afterwards becomes silent.

[3] `http://www.duden.de`

verbs	frames	complements	connotations	properties
aufzwängen 'impose on'	ditrans	*Wille* 'will'	negative	
aufbürden 'impose on'	ditrans	*Schuld* 'blame/debt'	pressure,	negative
auflasten 'impose on'	ditrans	*Verantwortung* 'responsibility'	burden,	social
aufbrummen 'force s.o. to do s.th.'	ditrans	*Strafe* 'penalty'	strenuous	pressure
aufdonnern 'force s.o. to do s.th.'	ditrans	—		

Table 6: *Transfer of negative social pressure* particle verbs with *auf.*

(8) *Als Micha das Buch auf den Fuß fiel, schrie er auf.* 'Micha let out a cry when the book fell on his foot.'

Table 7 groups BVs that are intransitive and visually perceivable.The subjects can thereby be seen as the source of the perceivable impulse, e.g. a lamp or a star. In some cases this visually perceivable source optionally produces heat like in Example (9). Other subjects we found in this context are blaze, spark, flame, light, etc. Such stimuli can grow in intensity very quickly. Therefore we can already find some non-literal usages in the BVs describing an intense emotion like hate, however only with *flammen* and *lodern* (the heat-related verbs).

verbs	frames	complements	connotations	properties
glimmen 'glimmer'	intrans	*Funke* 'spark'	bright, warm,	visual
glühen 'glow'	intrans	*Licht* 'light' / *Auge* 'eye'	pleasant	perception
lodern 'blaze'	intrans	*Flamme* 'flame' / *Hass* 'hate'	hot, (emotionally)	visual, thermal
flammen 'flame'	intrans	*Feuer* 'fire'	intense, bright	perception

Table 7: Base verbs that combine with *auf* to mean *initialization/intensification of visual perceivable.*

Combining these BVs with the particle *auf*, the metaphorical meaning turns out to be prominent. This is consistent with the characteristics of emotions which can appear and disappear very quickly. Comparing something like anger with a heat source is very common and captured in Lakoff et al.'s (2005) INTENSE EMOTIONS ARE HEAT conceptual metaphor. Therefore the parallel usage sharing one PV is not surprising. The only difference between the literal Example (10) and the non-literal Example (11) is that the perceived heat belongs to another domain. Other examples of emotion subjects are *Hoffnungsschimmer*, 'glimpse of hope', *Mitleid* 'pity' and *Debatte* 'debate', which is not an emotion, but in context of the *auf*-verb it refers to an intense discussion which involves emotions.

(9) *Das Feuer flammt.* 'The fire flames.'

(10) *Das Feuer flammt auf.* 'The fire flared up.'

(11) *Die Debatte flammt auf.* 'The debate flared up.'

In summary, we can say that both light and heat in these verbs seems to be central. While there is a wide class of BVs that allow for such a meaning shift (including most verbs applicable to light coming from a fire, e.g., *flackern* 'glint'), we find counterexamples where such an emotional metaphorical meaning is not present: *aufleuchten* 'light up', *aufblinken* 'flash', *auffunkeln* 'twinkle', *aufglitzern* '(suddenly) glitter'—all of which do not necessitate a notion of heat. It seems the 'light' property, as opposed to 'heat', is more involved in the perception and cognition domain (cf. the conceptual metaphors IDEAS ARE LIGHT SOURCES, UNDERSTANDING IS SEEING). The mental enlightenment is more a process than a sudden appearance which explains the incompatibility with this particle meaning.

3.4 *auf*: Intensification/Initialization of Emotion

A completely different class of base verbs leads to the same reading of a quick increase in intensity as the 'flare up' verbs. These are verbs which describe internally caused processes, such as *brausen*

verbs	frames	complements	connotations	properties
aufglimmen 'light up/flicker'	intrans	*Glimmlampe* 'glow lamp'	(more) visible	
		Hoffnungsschimmer 'glimmer of hope'	(and vanish),	initialization
aufglühen 'light up'	intrans	*Rücklichter* 'tail lights' / *Auge* 'eye'	quickly become	(intensification)
auflodern 'become intense'	intrans	*Feuer* 'fire' / *Wut* 'anger'	perceivable	
aufflammen 'flare up'	intrans	*Kampf* 'fight' / *Debate* 'debate'		

Table 8: *Initialization/intensification of perceivable* particle verbs with *auf*.

'roar', *kochen* 'boil' which denote a forceful movement, cf. Examples (12,13). The force involved can be physical (e.g., *schaukeln* 'swing') but can also be conceptualized as emotional, as in the metaphorical meaning in Example (14):

(12) *Der Sturm braust.* 'The storm is roaring.'

(13) *Der Sturm braust auf.* 'The storm is roaring up.'

(14) *Der Jubel braust auf.* 'The cheering is roaring up.'

All such 'forceful movement' BVs have an intransitive frame that has as subject in the literal sense (a) the entity being moved (e.g., *Schiff* 'ship'), or (b) a mass which is in motion (e.g., *Wasser* 'water'). The metaphorical reading can involve strong emotions (*Blut* 'blood'), intense activity (*Verkehr* 'traffic'), or both (*Gerüchteküche* 'rumor mill'); the activity in the latter is also showing up in the term for those involved in spreading rumors, namely 'busybodies'.

verbs	frames	complements	connotations	properties
schaukeln 'swing'	intrans	*Schiff* 'ship'	intense,	internally caused
brausen 'roar/crash'	intrans	*Sturm* 'storm' / *Verkehr* 'traffic'	sweeping motion,	motion
wallen 'undulate/surge'	intrans	*Nebel* 'fog' / *Blut* 'blood'	emotions	
brodeln 'seethe'	intrans	*Wasser* 'water'	heat,	internally caused
		Gerüchteküche 'rumor mill'	bubbling,	motion (with heat),
kochen 'boil'	intrans	*Wasser* 'water'	motion	emotion

Table 9: Base verbs that combine with *auf* to mean *initialization/intensification of emotions*.

verbs	frames	complements	connotations	properties
aufschaukeln 'build up'	intrans	*Papierboot* 'paper boat'	to and fro,	
		Konflikt 'conflict'	intense	
aufwallen 'surge up'	intrans	*Staub* 'dust' / *Zorn* 'fury'	motion,	intensification
aufbrausen 'flare up'	intrans	*Sturm* 'storm' / *Jubel* 'cheering'	strong	
aufbrodeln 'bubble up'	intrans	*Milch* 'milk' / *Hass* 'hate'	negative	
aufkochen '(bring to a) boil'	intrans	*Wasser* 'water' / Wut 'anger'	emotion	

Table 10: *Initialization/intensification of emotions* particle verbs with *auf*.

The shared property between the visual BV group and these motion verbs is that heat is understood to be conceptually linked to emotions (Lakoff and Johnson, 1980). The contribution of *auf* in this context is a notion of surging up, i.e., things are coming from below (hidden) to the surface (perceivable). These are terms that are commonly used to describe emotions, when they cannot be perceived (i.e., when they are not intense enough), they are 'hidden'. If they grow in intensity, they are said to 'surface' (*Gefühle aufwühlen* 'churn up feelings'). It is worth noting that *aufschaukeln* gives rise to a 'discussion' image, as it describes a constant to and fro between two opposing sides.

The compositional reading is dispreferred, since it is not typical to have both a back and forth and an upwards motion combined. As expected, base verbs that describe a subsiding of motion (e.g., *flachen* 'flatten', *ebben* 'ebb', *sinken* 'sink') combined with the particle expressing the opposite of this *auf* reading (i.e., *ab*), give exactly the opposite meaning, namely to lessen, abate, diminish; both in a physical as well as emotional sense.

Although it is not attested in the corpus, there exists the same metaphor in German and English *Das bringt mich zum Kochen* 'It makes my blood boil', of an intense emotion—in this case, fury—being conceptualized as something seething within the experiencer.

3.5 *ab*: Successive Tasks

One of the multiple meanings of the particle *ab* involves the concept of a sequence of similar actions leading to the completion of a complex task. Kliche (2011) terms this the 'mereological reduction' sense of *ab*. On the one hand, this meaning can come from verbs that generally entail some form of work (e.g., *arbeiten* 'work', *leisten* 'perform'). On the other hand, there are verbs that suggest the actual event structure of the chain of sub-tasks being completed.

verbs	frames	complements	connotations	properties
klappern 'clatter'	intrans	*Storch* 'stork'	sharp, short,	rapid succession
rattern 'clatter'	intrans	*Nähmaschine* 'sewing machine'	repetitive,	
stottern 'stutter'	intrans	*Motor* 'motor'	sound/action	

Table 11: Base verbs that combine with *ab* to mean *successive task completion.*

This can arise when (a) the actions are performed on an area that is successively covered along the event chain (e.g., *grasen* 'graze', *kämmen* 'comb', *suchen* 'search'); or (b) when the verb that is combined with *ab* suggests a mass that diminishes progressively due to the performed action until it is completely gone (e.g., *abbezahlen, abstottern* 'pay off'). The successive character of the mereological reduction sense is thus already inherently present in these verbs.

verbs	frames	complements	connotations	properties
abklappern 'check all'	trans	*Sehenswürdigkeit* 'tourist sight'	successive	successive reduction
abrattern 'pay off (a debt)'	trans	—	accomplishing,	
abstottern 'pay off (a debt)'	trans	*Schuldenberg* 'mountain of debt'	stepwise reduction	

Table 12: *Successive task completion* particle verbs with *ab*.

Interestingly enough, it is sufficient for the mereological reduction *ab* to be available that only the event structure itself to be conveyed, even without the concept of work being present in the base verb. In our everyday experience, the rapid succession of similar short events can give rise to a particular repetitive acoustic pattern, which is captured in the onomatopoetic verbs: *klappern/rattern* 'clatter' and *stottern* 'stutter'. These verbs combined with *ab* then give the expected reading, namely a chain of similar actions being performed. However, this does not work with semelfactive sound verbs like *klicken* 'klick' or *ticken*, even if they can provide a repetitive reading by multiplying the single verb events. The verbs in this class are iterative and cannot be interpreted as semelfactive.

It is clear that the acoustic signal lends itself to a mapping to the event structure, since both are organized linearly in time. This also explains the inaccessibility of the same meaning for a visual signal, since there is no straightforward mapping of the visual field to the time axis. The only counterexample of a visual mereological reduction verb that we are aware of is *absuchen* 'scan'; which suggests a linear process of visual perception; e.g., along a linear path through a room, or via the linear searching through a telescope or magnifying glass.

4 Discussion

The previous section provided an extensive analysis of 6 different cases of BV–PV meaning shifts, with regard to 3 different particles. We briefly summarize these meaning shifts, concentrating on the main conceptual properties only. The presentation is done according to the pattern in Equation (1) as introduced in Section 1.

(1) $\texttt{BV}\ \{pBV_1,\ pBV_2,\ \ldots,\ pBV_n\}\ \texttt{+ PM} \rightarrow \texttt{PV}\ \{pPV_1,\ pPV_2,\ \ldots,\ pPV_m\}$

Meaning shift classes:

1. ***an: "positive emotional communication"***
   BV {pleasing, emission} **+ PM** {dir+com} → **PV** {positive directed communication}
   with BVs *funkeln, grinsen, lächeln, strahlen*

2. ***an: "negative emotional communication"***
   BV {displeasing, uncivilized} **+ PM** {dir+com} → **PV** {negative directed communication}
   with BVs *bellen, kläffen, pissen, scheißen*

3. ***auf: "negative social pressure"***
   BV {loud/heavy pressure} **+ PM** {vert. contact} → **PV** {negative social pressure}
   with BVs *brummen, bürden, donnern, lasten, zwängen*

4. ***auf: "initialization of perceivables (vision & emotion)"***
   BV {bright, vision} **+ PM** {sudden, initial} → **PV** {initialization of visual perceivable}
   with BVs *flammen, glimmen, glühen, lodern*

5. ***auf: "intensification of perceivables (emotion)"***
   BV {int. caused motion} **+ PM** {sudden, initial} → **PV** {intensification of emotions}
   with BVs *brausen, brodeln, kochen, schaukeln, wallen*

6. ***ab: "successive task completion"***
   BV {repetitive, sound} **+ PM** {mereol. reduction} → **PV** {successive task completion}
   with BVs *klappern, rattern, stottern*

The analyses were performed across several semantically coherent groups of verbs. We demonstrated that corpus-based information on the verbs' subcategorization frames and nominal complements (combined with intuitions about generalizations of the noun complements) is a sufficient basis for defining BV–PV meaning shifts. We thus confirmed our initial hypothesis that there are regular mechanisms with regard to the syntax-semantic interface that trigger a meaning shift of a base verb in combination with a particle meaning and that do not only apply to the individual verb but across a semantically coherent set of verbs. The identified meaning shift classes are effectively larger than those presented in the tables in Section 3 because the classes are productive. Relying on the productivity, we could easily enlarge our meaning shift classes with new members (which will be discussed below).

We briefly summarize the main findings from our analyses, with regard to the BV, PV and particle properties: (i) There is a very strong agreement across verbs (both BVs and PVs) within a meaning shift class with regard to the subcategorization frame types. This is a very impressive indicator for semantically coherent groups, where we had expected more diversity. (ii) Even restricting the nominal complements to only the 10-20 most strongly *LMI*-based associated types is a sufficient basis for investigating the conceptual properties that determine the respective slot. (iii) To our knowledge, a new aspect to meaning shifts in (German) particle verbs has been discovered: We found that particles actually adopt meaning aspects from the base verbs they combine with. For example, the particle *an* in meaning shift classes 1 and 2 a priori refers to a *direction* meaning. However, it obviously incorporates meaning aspects from communication base verbs that it typically combines with (when no meaning shift is involved), such as *ansprechen* 'speak to' and *anreden* 'address someone'. As a result, the particle meaning within the particle verbs in classes 1 and 2 contributes meaning aspects of *direction* as well as *communication*. To go deeper into this issue, future work will investigate the diachronic development of particle roots with regard to the particle meanings.

Our strategy can easily be replicated for another BV–PV data set in German or other languages, given that parsed corpus data is available. In addition, there are easy extensions to the strategy that however make the identification and factors of meaning shifts more objective: (i) co-occurrence of the BVs and PVs with particular *adverbs* should be useful as indicators of meaning shifts, as they are expected to agree across the respective base and particle verbs but might be different between the literal and shifted meanings of the particle verbs. (ii) Similarly, we expect *2nd-order co-occurrence adjectives*, i.e., those adjectives that modify the nominal complements of the verbs (Schulte im Walde,

2010), to be useful indicators of the kinds of connotations we so far collected manually. For example, concerning meaning shift class 4 above, strong adjectival modifiers of both *Feuer* 'fire' and *Flamme* 'flame' are *ewig* 'eternal' *lodernd* 'blazing', and *offen* 'open', while strong adjectival modifiers of both *Konflikt* 'conflict' and *Diskussion* 'discussion' are *aktuell* 'current', *politisch* 'political', and *weit* 'wide'. (iii) Instead of subjective definitions of conceptual generalizations over nominal complements, one could apply *GermaNet* (Kunze, 2000), the German pendant to *WordNet* (Fellbaum, 1998). For example, both *Feuer* 'fire' and *Flamme* 'flame' are generalized to *Ereignis* 'event' by GermaNet on level 3 (starting from the top node level) and to *Phänomen* 'phenomenon' on level 4, while both *Konflikt* 'conflict' and *Diskussion* 'discussion' are generalized to *Kommunikation* 'communication' and *Gespräch* 'conversation' on levels 3 and 4, respectively. (iv) A simple way to enlarge meaning shift classes is by looking up synonyms of the base and/or particle verbs in dictionaries. For example, Bulitta and Bulitta (2003) defines *aufdrängen*, *aufnötigen*, and *aufoktroyieren* as near-synonyms to *aufzwängen*, so we could check whether these three particle verbs fall into meaning shift class 3.

A long-term goal of our work is to extend it toward a more automatically driven identification of meaning shifts in particle verbs. Three examples of approaches that are potentially useful to complement our corpus-based search are the following: Reisinger and Mooney (2010) presented a multi-prototype vector-space model that discriminates multiple senses of a word by clustering contexts, an idea adopted from Schütze (1998). We could reduce their "contexts" to the crucial information about the BV and PV properties we identified, i.e., subcategorization frame types and concept properties, possibly refined by further meaning aspects as suggested above. The framework would then allow us to determine the similarity between the "contexts" of base verbs and particle verbs, and thus to identify the semantically coherent groups of base verbs as well as literal meanings of particle verbs with regard to their base verbs. To do this we could use a clustering approach similar to Reisinger and Mooney (2010). Birke (2005) also relied on clustering to discover literal and non-literal uses of English verbs in context. However, while her approach required a manually labeled set, we could envision an automatic detection of literality as done by Turney et al. (2011). Boleda et al. (2012) presented an approach to regular polysemy where meta-alternations capture regularities in meaning shifts. In a first step, the meta-alternations are instantiated by monosemous words exhibiting the respective meaning shift. In a second step, the meta-alternations are used to predict a meaning shift for a new item. With regard to our research, a meta-alternation should capture the BV and PV properties of a certain meaning shift. As in Boleda et al. (2012), we would instantiate the meta-alternations through monosemous base and particle verbs. For a new BV–PV pair, we could then predict the (non-)existence of the meaning shift by comparing the pair's conceptual properties to the properties of the meta-alternation. Note that this approach requires prior knowledge about some seed BV–PV pairs and their meaning shifts.

Last but not least, a major challenge in the automation of our work is in distinguishing between BV and PV verb polysemy vs. meaning shift. That is, most computational approaches such as Reisinger and Mooney (2010) will provide us with knowledge about the various meanings of the base and/or particle verbs. However, we not only want to detect different senses (e.g., the particle verb *abnehmen* has several senses with overlapping subcategorization properties that all but one differ from the literal meaning), but in addition which of the senses is a meaning shift, and why. Our goals are more addressed by the Boleda et al. (2012) approach, which however requires manual work in the outset.

5 Acknowledgements

We are thankful for the very fruitful discussions with Antje Roßdeutscher and Alessandra Zarcone as well as for the helpful suggestions made by the reviewers. The work has been supported by the DFG, with the SFB 732 funding Jason Utt and Sylvia Springorum, and the DFG Heisenberg Fellowship SCHU-2580/1-1 funding Sabine Schulte im Walde.

References

Baroni, M., S. Bernardini, A. Ferraresi, and E. Zanchetta (2009). The WaCky Wide Web: A Collection of Very Large Linguistically Processed Web-Crawled Corpora. *Language Resources and Evaluation 43*(3), 209–226.

Birke, J. (2005). *A Clustering Approach for the Unsupervised Recognition of Nonliteral Language*. Ph. D. thesis, Simon Fraser University.

Bohnet, B. (2010). Top Accuracy and Fast Dependency Parsing is not a Contradiction. In *Proceedings of the 23rd International Conference on Computational Linguistics*, Beijing, China.

Boleda, G., S. Padó, and J. Utt (2012). Regular Polysemy: A Distributional Model. In **SEM: The First Joint Conference on Lexical and Computational Semantics*, Montréal, Canada, pp. 151–160.

Bulitta, E. and H. Bulitta (2003). *Wörterbuch der Synonyme und Antonyme* (2nd ed.). Information und Wissen. Frankfurt, Germany: Fischer Taschenbuch Verlag.

Evert, S. (2005). *The Statistics of Word Co-Occurrences: Word Pairs and Collocations*. Ph. D. thesis, Institut für Maschinelle Sprachverarbeitung, Universität Stuttgart.

Faaß G., U. Heid, and H. Schmid (2010). Design and Application of a Gold Standard for Morphological Analysis: SMOR in Validation. In *Proceedings of the 7th International Conference on Language Resources and Evaluation*, Valletta, Malta, pp. 803–810.

Fellbaum, C. (Ed.) (1998). *WordNet – An Electronic Lexical Database*. Language, Speech, and Communication. Cambridge, MA: MIT Press.

Ibarretxe-Antuñano, B. I. (1999). *Polysemy and Metaphor in Perception Verbs*. Ph. D. thesis, University of Edinburgh.

Kliche, F. (2011). Semantic Variants of German Particle Verbs with *ab*. *Leuvense Bijdragen* (97).

Kunze, C. (2000). Extension and Use of GermaNet, a Lexical-Semantic Database. In *Proceedings of the 2nd International Conference on Language Resources and Evaluation*, Athens, Greece, pp. 999–1002.

Lakoff, G., J. Espenson, and A. Schwartz (2005). Master Metaphor List. Technical Report.

Lakoff, G. and M. Johnson (1980). *Metaphors we live by*. University of Chicago Press.

Lönneker-Rodman, B. (2008). The Hamburg Metaphor Database Project: Issues in Resource Creation. *Language Resources and Evaluation 42*, 293–318.

Markert, K. and M. Nissim (2007). Data and Models for Metonymy Resolution. *Language Resources and Evaluation 43*(2), 123–138.

Morgan, P. S. (1997). Figuring out *figure out*: Metaphor and the Semantics of English Verb-Particle Constructions. *Cognitive Linguistics 8*(4), 327–357.

Reisinger, J. and R. J. Mooney (2010). Multi-Prototype Vector-Space Models of Word Meaning. In *Proceedings of the 11th Annual Conference of the NAACL*, pp. 109–117.

Schulte im Walde, S. (2010). Comparing Computational Approaches to Selectional Preferences: Second-Order Co-Occurrence vs. Latent Semantic Clusters. In *Proceedings of the 7th International Conference on Language Resources and Evaluation*, Valletta, Malta, pp. 1381–1388.

Schütze, H. (1998). Automatic Word Sense Discrimination. *Computational Linguistics 24*(1), 97–123. Special Issue on Word Sense Disambiguation.

Stefanowitsch, A. and S. T. Gries (Eds.) (2006). *Corpus-Based Approaches to Metaphor and Metonymy*. Berlin: de Gruyter.

Turney, P., Y. Neuman, D. Assaf, and Y. Cohen (2011). Literal and Metaphorical Sense Identification through Concrete and Abstract Context. In *Proceedings of the 2011 Conference on Empirical Methods in Natural Language Processing*, Edinburgh, Scotland, UK., pp. 680–690.

Semantic Annotation of Textual Entailment

Assaf Toledo
a.toledo@uu.nl

Stavroula Alexandropoulou
s.alexandropoulou@uu.nl

Sophia Katrenko
sophia@katrenko.com

Heidi Klockmann
h.e.Klockmann@uu.nl

Pepijn Kokke
pepijn.kokke@gmail.com

Yoad Winter
y.winter@uu.nl

Utrecht University

1 Abstract

We introduce a new formal semantic model for annotating textual entailments, that describes restrictive, intersective and appositive modification. The model contains a formally defined interpreted lexicon, which specifies the inventory of symbols and the supported semantic operators, and an informally defined annotation scheme that instructs annotators in which way to bind words and constructions from a given pair of premise and hypothesis to the interpreted lexicon. We explore the applicability of the proposed model to the Recognizing Textual Entailment (RTE) 1-4 corpora and describe a first-stage annotation scheme based on which manual annotation work was carried out. The constructions we annotated were found to occur in 80.65% of the entailments in RTE 1-4 and were annotated with cross-annotator agreement of 68% on average. The annotated RTE corpora are publicly available for the research community.

2 Introduction

The RTE challenges (Dagan et al., 2006) aim to automatically determine whether an entailment relation obtains between a naturally occurring **text** sentence (T) and a **hypothesis** sentence (H). The RTE corpus (Bar Haim et al., 2006; Giampiccolo et al., 2007, 2008; Bentivogli et al., 2009), which is currently the only available resource of textual entailments, marks entailment candidates as valid/invalid.[1]

Example 1

- T: The head of the Italian opposition, Romano Prodi, was the last president of the EC.
- H: Romano Prodi is a former president of the EC.[2]
- Entailment: Valid

This categorization contains no indication of the linguistic processes that underlie entailment. In the lack of a gold standard of inferential phenomena, entailment systems can be compared based on their performance, but their inferential processes are not directly accessible for analysis.

The goal of this work is to elucidate some central inferential processes underlying entailments in the RTE corpus. By doing that, we aim to advance the possibility of creating a benchmark for modeling entailment recognition. We presume that this goal is to be achieved incrementally by modeling increasingly complex semantic phenomena. To this end, we employ a standard model-theoretic approach to entailment in order to combine gold standard annotations with a computational framework. The model

[1] Pairs of sentences in RTE 1-3 are categorized in two classes: *yes-* or *no-entailment*; pairs in RTE 4-5 are categorized in three classes: *entailment*, *contradiction* and *unknown*. We label the judgments *yes-entailment* from RTE 1-3 and *entailment* from RTE 4-5 as *valid*, and the other judgments as *invalid*.

[2] Pair 410 from the test set of RTE 2. *EC* stands for European Commission

contains a formally defined interpreted lexicon, which specifies the inventory of symbols and semantic operators that are supported, and an informally defined annotation scheme that instructs annotators how to bind words and constructions from a given T-H pair to entries in the interpreted lexicon. Our choice to focus on the semantic phenomena of restrictive, intersective and appositive modification is driven by their predominance in the RTE datasets, the ability to annotate them with high consistency and the possibility to capture their various syntactic expressions by a limited set of concepts.

However, currently we are only at the first stages of implementing the theoretical semantic model using an annotation platform combined with a theorem prover. In the course of the development of this model we adopted a narrower annotation scheme by which modification phenomena were annotated in all valid entailment pairs from RTE 1-4 without accounting for the way in which the annotated phenomena contribute to the inference being made. This work allowed us to perform data analysis and to further learn about the phenomena of interest as part of the development of the semantic model.

The structure of this paper is as follows. Section 3 reviews some related methods used in Bos et al. (2004) and MacCartney and Manning (2007). In Section 4 we introduce the formal semantic model on which we rely and use it for analyzing some illustrative textual entailments. Section 5 points out a challenge in applying this model to parts of the RTE data and describes our first-stage annotation scheme. We elaborate on the methods employed in applying this scheme to the datasets of RTE 1-4, and present some quantitative data on the targeted phenomena and inter-annotator agreement. Section 6 concludes.

3 Related Work

Bos and Markert (2005) utilizes a CCG parser (Bos et al., 2004) to represent the text and hypothesis in discourse representation structures (DRSs, Kamp and Reyle 1993) that encapsulate information on argument structure, polarity, etc. The DRSs of the text and hypothesis are then translated into formulae in first order logic, and a theorem prover is used in order to search whether there is a logical proof from the text formula to the hypothesis formula. The system reached a relatively high precision score of 76% in recognizing the positive cases in RTE 2 but suffered from a very low recall of 5.8%.

MacCartney and Manning (2007)'s system recognizes monotonic relations (or lack thereof) between aligned lexical items in the text and hypothesis and employs a model of compositional semantics to calculate a sentence-level entailment prediction. The recognition of monotonic relations is done using an adapted version of Sanchez Valencia's Natural Logic (Valencia, 1991), the alignment between the text and hypothesis is based on a cost function that extends Levenshtein string-edit algorithm, and the entailment is classified by a decision tree classifier, trained on a small data set of 69 handmade problems. The system was tested on RTE 3 and achieved relatively high precision scores of 76.39% and 68.06% on the positive cases in the development and test sets respectively. This system also suffers from low recall scores of 26.70% and 31.71% respectively.

The model we propose in this work diverges from these systems in two respects: (a) its first goal is to develop gold standard semantic annotations based on a general formal semantic model; (b) it does not aim to represent phenomena that are not accounted for in this model. For example, consider the following inference, which is based on causal reasoning: *Khan sold nuclear plans* $\Rightarrow$ *Khan possessed nuclear plans*.[3] Causal reasoning and lexical relations are not part of the semantic phenomena addressed in this paper, and a pattern in the form of *X sold Y* $\Rightarrow$ *X possessed Y* should be defined ad-hoc by annotators to align the instances of the verbs *sell* and *possess*. This approach allows us to concentrate on the logical aspects of textual entailment, while phenomena involving lexical semantics and world knowledge are handled by a shallow analysis.[4]

[3]This example of causal reasoning is taken from MacCartney and Manning (2007).

[4]Another related work, which approaches inference in natural language as part of a semantic paradigm, is the FraCaS test suite (Cooper et al., 1996). This suit concerns examples that mainly rely on generalized quantification, argument monotonicity, plurality, anaphora resolution, ellipsis, etc. Entailments based on these phenomena are not very common in the RTE data that are analyzed here. Further research is needed in order to integrate data like those in FraCaS into a formal annotation scheme like the one suggested in this paper.

4 Theoretical background and RTE examples

To model entailment in natural language, we assume that entailment describes a *preorder* on natural language sentences. Thus, we assume that any sentence trivially entails itself (reflexivity); and given two entailments $T_1 \Rightarrow H_1$ and $T_2 \Rightarrow H_2$ where H_1 and T_2 are identical sentences, we assume $T_1 \Rightarrow H_2$ (transitivity). A computational theory of entailment should describe an approximation of this preorder on natural language sentences. We use a standard model-theoretical extensional semantics, based on the simple *partial order* on the domain of *truth-values*. Each model M assigns sentences a truth-value in the set $\{0, 1\}$. Such a Tarskian theory of entailment is considered adequate if the intuitive entailment preorder on sentences can be described as the pairs of sentences T and H whose truth-values $[\![T]\!]^M$ and $[\![H]\!]^M$ satisfy $[\![T]\!]^M \leq [\![H]\!]^M$ for all models M. In this section we give the essentials of this model-theoretic approach to entailment that are relevant to the annotated phenomena and illustrate it using a small interpreted lexicon, simplifying the analysis of some representative examples from the RTE.

4.1 An interpreted lexicon

The interpreted lexicon presented in Table 1 illustrates our treatment of major lexical categories over types e, t and their functional compounds. Our aim is to allow binding of words and expressions in entailment data to the lexicon. Each word is stated in its literal form, the type assigned to it, and its denotation in intended models. Denotations that are assumed to be arbitrary in intended models are given in boldface. For example, the intransitive use of the verb *sit* is assigned the type et and its denotation **sit** is an arbitrary function of this type. By contrast, other lexical items have their denotations restricted by the intended models. For example, the definite article *the* is assigned the type $(et)e$ and its denotation is fixed as the *iota* operator. The functions that we use for defining denotations are specified in Figure 1. Several items in the lexicon are assigned more than one type and/or more than one denotation due to ambiguity in natural language. The following list explains some of the main items in the lexicon:

- The coordinator *and*, when appearing as predicate conjunction, is analyzed as a function - AND, mapping any two et predicates A and B to a predicate that sends every entity e to the truth-value of the conjunction $A(x) \wedge B(x)$.
- The copular *is* and the article *a* in copular sentences (e.g. *Dan is a man / Dan is short*) are analyzed as identity functions IS and A of type $(et)(et)$ respectively. In copula sentences that express an equality relation (e.g. *Dan is Jan*), *is* is analyzed by the equality function IS_{eq} of type $e(et)$.
- The word *some* denotes the existential quantifier SOME, as it is used in intransitive sentences such as *some man sat* (transitive sentences like *Jan saw some man* are not treated here).
- The relative pronoun *who* allows noun modification either by a restrictive relative clause denoted by WHO_R or by an appositive clause denoted by WHO_A. WHO_R is expressed in sentences such as *the alien who is a nun sat*, in which the pronoun creates a complex predicate, *alien who is a nun*. WHO_A appears in sentences such as *the alien, who is a nun, sat* where the pronoun adds information on a given entity x. The resulting entity is x if A holds of x, and undefined otherwise.
- The adjectives *short* and *Dutch*, when appearing as modifiers, restrict the denotation of the noun they attach to: *a short/Dutch man* is *a man*. *Dutch* is furthermore *intersective*: *a Dutch man* is invariably *Dutch*. The predicate *Dutch* is defined as an arbitrary constant **dutch** of type et. The modifier is derived by a function I_m identical to AND. The restrictive modifier *short* is defined by the function R_m and a constant **short** of type $(et)(et)$. The predicative denotation of *short* is defined using the function P_r as the set of "short things" - by applying the constant to all entities.

See Pratt-Hartmann and Moss (2009) for a wider coverage of some of the same semantic ground that goes further in dealing with comparative constructions and transitive verbs.

4.2 Analyzing entailments using the interpreted lexicon

Some central logical semantic aspects of entailments from the RTE can be formally analyzed using the lexicon in Table 1. We analyze entailments by binding expressions in the RTE data to structurally equivalent expressions containing items in the interpreted lexicon. This analysis is three-fold:

Word	Type	Denotation	Remarks
Dan, Jan, Vim	e	$\mathbf{dan, jan, vim}$	proper name
man, nun, alien	et	$\mathbf{man, nun, alien}$	intrans. noun
sat	et	$\mathbf{sit}$	intrans. verb
saw	$e(et)$	$\mathbf{see}$	trans. verb
and	$(et)((et)(et))$	AND	pred. conj. (coordinator)
is	$(et)(et)$	IS	copula (modifier)
is	$e(et)$	IS_{eq}	copula (equality)
a	$(et)(et)$	A	indef. article (modifier)
the	$(et)e$	THE	def. article (iota)
some	$(et)((et)t)$	SOME	indef. determiner
who	$(et)((et)(et))$	WHO_R	res. rel. pronoun (coordinator)
who	$(et)(ee)$	WHO_A	app. rel. pronoun
Dutch, black	et	$\mathbf{dutch}_{et}$, $\mathbf{black}_{et}$	int. adjective (predicate)
Dutch, black	$(et)(et)$	$I_m(\mathbf{dutch}_{et})$, $I_m(\mathbf{black}_{et})$	int. adjective (modifier)
short	et	$P_r(\mathbf{short}_{(et)(et)})$	res. adjective (predicate)
short	$(et)(et)$	$R_m(\mathbf{short}_{(et)(et)})$	res. adjective (modifier)
slowly	$(et)(et)$	$R_m(\mathbf{slowly}_{(et)(et)})$	res. adverb (modifier)

Table 1: An Interpreted Lexicon

$$\text{AND} = \lambda A_{et}.\lambda B_{et}.\lambda x_e.B(x) \wedge A(x)$$
$$\text{IS} = \lambda A_{et}.A$$
$$\text{IS}_{eq} = \lambda x_e.\lambda y_e.x = y$$
$$\text{A} = \text{IS} = \lambda A_{et}.A$$
$$\text{THE} = \iota_{(et)e} = \lambda A_{et}.\begin{cases} a & \text{if } A = (\lambda x_e.x = a) \\ \text{undefined} & \text{otherwise} \end{cases} \quad \text{(iota operator)}$$
$$\text{SOME} = \lambda A_{et}.\lambda B_{et}.\exists x_e.A(x) \wedge B(x)$$
$$\text{WHO}_R = \text{AND} = \lambda A_{et}.\lambda B_{et}.\lambda x_e.B(x) \wedge A(x)$$
$$\text{WHO}_A = \lambda A_{et}.\lambda x_e.\iota(\lambda y.y = x \wedge A(x))$$
$$P_r = \lambda M_{(et)(et)}.\lambda x_e.M(\lambda y_e.1)(x) \quad \text{deriving a predicate from a general modifier}$$
$$I_m = \text{AND} = \lambda A_{et}.\lambda B_{et}.\lambda x_e.B(x) \wedge A(x) \quad \text{deriving an intersective modifier}$$
$$R_m = \lambda M_{(et)(et)}.\lambda A_{et}.\lambda x_e.M(A)(x) \wedge A(x) \quad \text{deriving a restrictive modifier}$$

Figure 1: Functions used in the interpreted lexicon

1. Phenomena Simplification: we simplify the text and hypothesis to exclude inferential phenomena that we do not handle in the scope of this work. For instance, in Example 2, the inference *Google operates on the web* ⇒ *Google is on the web* is based on lexical knowledge, which we do not address here, and therefore it is handled as part of the simplification step.
2. Binding to Lexicon: we bind the constructions in the data to parallel constructions in the interpreted lexicon that share the same structure and semantic properties. This step produces a text $\text{T}_{Lexicon}$ and a hypothesis $\text{H}_{Lexicon}$ as new structurally equivalent versions of the simplified text and hypothesis. The parse trees are assumed in a way that allows to apply the interpreted lexicon.
3. Proof of Entailment: using predicate calculus and lambda calculus reductions, we establish a logical proof between $\text{T}_{Lexicon}$ and $\text{H}_{Lexicon}$.[5]

Example 2

- Data:
  - T: The largest search engine on the web, Google receives over 200 million queries each day through its various services.

[5]The only higher-order constants in the above lexicon are the $(et)(et)$ constants attributed to non-intersective restrictive modifiers. Treating them in predicate calculus theorem provers may require some *ad hoc* assumptions.

- H: Google operates on the web.[6]

1. Phenomena Simplification:
   In the text: adding an overt appositive WH pronoun to match the interpreted lexicon:
   - $\mathrm{T}_{Original}$: The largest search engine on the web, Google receives...
   - T_{Simple}: The largest search engine on the web, which is Google, receives...

   In the hypothesis: reducing the meaning of 'X operates on Y' to 'X is on Y':
   - $\mathrm{H}_{Original}$: Google operates on the web
   - H_{Simple}: Google is on the web
2. Binding to Lexicon:
   Text[7,8]:
   - T_{Simple}: [The largest search engine on the web, which is Google,] receives...
   - $\mathrm{T}_{Lexicon}$: [The short Dutch man, who is Jan,] saw Dan

   Hypothesis:
   - H_{Simple}: Google [is [on the web]]
   - $\mathrm{H}_{Lexicon}$: Jan [is Dutch]
3. Proof of entailment $\mathrm{T}_{Lexicon} \Rightarrow \mathrm{H}_{Lexicon}$: Let M be an intended model,
   $[\![$ [[*The* [*short Dutch man*]], [*who* [*is Jan*]],] *saw Dan* $]\!]^M$

   $= (\mathbf{see}(\mathbf{dan}))((\textsc{who}_A(\textsc{is}_{eq}(\mathbf{jan})))(\iota((R_m(\mathbf{short}))((I_m(\mathbf{dutch}))(\mathbf{man})))))$ — analysis

   $= (\mathbf{see}(\mathbf{dan}))(\iota(\lambda y.y = (\iota((R_m(\mathbf{short}))((I_m(\mathbf{dutch}))(\mathbf{man})))) \wedge \mathbf{jan} = (\iota((R_m(\mathbf{short}))((I_m(\mathbf{dutch}))(\mathbf{man}))))))$ — def. of $\textsc{who}_A$ + $\textsc{is}_{eq}$, func application

   By definition of ι: $\mathbf{jan} = \iota((R_m(\mathbf{short}))((I_m(\mathbf{dutch}))(\mathbf{man})))$

   $\Rightarrow \mathbf{jan} = \iota(\lambda y_e.(\mathbf{short}(\lambda x_e.\mathbf{man}(x) \wedge \mathbf{dutch}(x)))(y) \wedge \mathbf{man}(y) \wedge \mathbf{dutch}(y))$ — def. of R_m, I_m, $\wedge$ + func. application

   By definition of ι: $(\mathbf{short}(\lambda x_e.\mathbf{man}(x) \wedge \mathbf{dutch}(x)))(\mathbf{jan}) \wedge \mathbf{man}(\mathbf{jan}) \wedge \mathbf{dutch}(\mathbf{jan})$

   $\leq \mathbf{dutch}(\mathbf{jan}) = (\textsc{is}(\mathbf{dutch}))(\mathbf{jan}) = [\![$*Jan [is Dutch]*$]\!]^M$ — def. of $\wedge$, $\textsc{is}$ + analysis

A crucial step in this analysis is our assumption that *on the web* is an intersective modifier of *search engine*. This allows the subsumption of *search engine on the web* by *on the web*. In the interpreted lexicon we describe this behavior using the intersective denotation of the modifier *Dutch*. Let us investigate further the implications of this annotation in the following hypothetical example.

Example 3

1. Pair 1: T_1: Jan is a short Dutch man $\not\Rightarrow$ H_1: Jan is a short man — no entailment
2. Pair 2: T_2: Jan is a black Dutch man $\Rightarrow$ H_2: Jan is a black man — entailment

From a purely textual/syntactic point of view, these two T-H pairs are indistinguishable. The lexical overlap between the text and hypothesis in both pairs is 100%. This does not allow entailment systems to rely on textual measurements to identify that the pairs need to be classified differently. Such a perfect score of overlap may lead to a false positive classification in Pair 1 or conversely, to a false negative in Pair 2. Also syntactically, both *short* and *black* serve as adjectives attached to a noun phrase - *Dutch man*. There is nothing in this syntactic configuration to suggest that omitting *Dutch* in Pair 1 might result in a different entailment classification than omitting it in Pair 2. However, from a semantic point of view, based on annotations of abstract relations between predicates and their modifiers, we can correctly analyze both the non-validity of the entailment in Pair 1 and the validity of the entailment in Pair 2.

- Analysis of Pair 1

  To validate that there is no entailment between a text and a hypothesis means to show that there is an intended model $M = \langle E, I \rangle$ in which there is no $\leq$ relation between their denotations.

[6] Pair 955 from the test set of RTE 4 (Giampiccolo et al., 2008).

[7] Note that the post-nominal intersective modifier *on the web* is bound to a pre-nominal modifier *Dutch*. This is done in order to match the vocabulary of the interpreted lexicon, in which the only intersective modifier is *Dutch*.

[8] In this example, T_{Simple} (consequently from $T_{Original}$) is structurally ambiguous between *The* [*largest* [*search engine on the web*]], *which is Google, receives...* and *The* [[*largest search engine*] *on the web*], *which is Google, receives....* We illustrate the former analysis here. The latter analysis can be handled in a similar vein.

Let M be an intended model that satisfies the following:

- $\mathbf{man}_{et}$ characterizes $\{\mathbf{dan}, \mathbf{jan}, \mathbf{vim}\}$
- $\mathbf{dutch}_{et}$ characterizes $\{\mathbf{jan}, \mathbf{vim}\}$
- $\mathbf{short}(\mathbf{man})_{et}$ characterizes $\{\mathbf{dan}\}$
- $\mathbf{short}(\lambda y_e.\mathbf{man}(y) \wedge \mathbf{dutch}(y))_{et}$ characterizes $\{\mathbf{jan}\}$

Let us assume parse trees as follows:

- Text: *Jan* [*is* [*a* [*short* [*Dutch man*]]]]
- Hypothesis: *Jan* [*is* [*a* [*short man*]]]

Consider the denotations of the text and hypothesis in the model M:

- Text:

$[\![$ *Jan* [*is* [*a* [*short* [*Dutch man*]]]] $]\!]^M$

$= (\textsc{is}(\textsc{a}((R_m(\mathbf{short}))((I_m(\mathbf{dutch}))(\mathbf{man})))))(\mathbf{jan})$	analysis
$= ((R_m(\mathbf{short}))((I_m(\mathbf{dutch}))(\mathbf{man})))(\mathbf{jan})$	def. of A, IS
$= (((\lambda M_{(et)(et)}.\lambda A_{et}.\lambda y_e.M(A)(y) \wedge A(y))(\mathbf{short}))$ $(((\lambda A_{et}.\lambda B_{et}.\lambda x_e.B(x) \wedge A(x))(\mathbf{dutch}))(\mathbf{man})))(\mathbf{jan})$	def. of I_m, R_m
$= 1 \wedge 1 \wedge 1 = 1$	func. application + denotations in M

- Hypothesis:

$[\![$ *Jan* [*is* [*a* [*short man*]]] $]\!]^M$

$= (\textsc{is}(\textsc{a}((R_m(\mathbf{short}))(\mathbf{man}))))(\mathbf{jan})$	analysis
$= ((R_m(\mathbf{short}))(\mathbf{man}))(\mathbf{jan})$	def. of A, IS
$= (((\lambda M_{(et)(et)}.\lambda A_{et}.\lambda y_e.M(A)(y) \wedge A(y))(\mathbf{short}))(\mathbf{man}))(\mathbf{jan})$	def. of R_m
$= 0 \wedge 1 = 0$	func. application + denotations in M

Intuitively, *Jan* can be a man who is considered to be short in the population of Dutch men, hence $(\mathbf{short}(\lambda x_e.\mathbf{man}(x) \wedge \mathbf{dutch}(x)))\ (\mathbf{jan}) = 1$, but not in the population of all men, hence $(\mathbf{short}(\mathbf{man}))(\mathbf{jan}) = 0$. This is a consequence of having *short* denoting a non-intersective modifier: the set denoted by $\mathbf{short}(\lambda x_e.\mathbf{man}(x) \wedge \mathbf{dutch}(x))$ is not necessarily a subset of $\mathbf{short}(\mathbf{man})$.

- Analysis of Pair 2

Let us assume parse trees as follows:

- Text: *Jan* [*is* [*a* [*black* [*Dutch man*]]]]
- Hypothesis: *Jan* [*is* [*a* [*black man*]]]

In analyzing this pair we can show a proof of entailment. Let M be an intended model,

$[\![$ *Jan* [*is* [*a* [*black* [*Dutch man*]]]] $]\!]^M$

$= (\textsc{is}(\textsc{a}((I_m(\mathbf{black}))((I_m(\mathbf{dutch}))(\mathbf{man})))))(\mathbf{jan})$	analysis
$= (((\lambda A_{et}.\lambda B_{et}.\lambda y_e.B(y) \wedge A(y))(\mathbf{black}))(((\lambda A_{et}.\lambda B_{et}.\lambda x_e.B(x) \wedge A(x))(\mathbf{dutch}))(\mathbf{man})))(\mathbf{jan})$	def. of A, IS, I_m
$= \mathbf{dutch}(\mathbf{jan}) \wedge (\mathbf{man}(\mathbf{jan}) \wedge \mathbf{black}(\mathbf{jan}))$	func. application
$\leq \mathbf{man}(\mathbf{jan}) \wedge \mathbf{black}(\mathbf{jan})$	def. of $\wedge$
$= (\textsc{is}(\textsc{a}((I_m(\mathbf{black}))(\mathbf{man}))))(\mathbf{jan}) = [\![$ *Jan* [*is* [*a* [*black man*]]] $]\!]^M$	beta reduction + def. of I_m, A, IS + analysis

In this case we rely on the intersectivity of *black*, which in conjunction with the intersectivity of *Dutch* licenses the inference that the set characterized by the *et* function $[\![$ *black* [*Dutch man*] $]\!]^M$ equals to the set characterized by $[\![$ *Dutch* [*black man*] $]\!]^M$, which is a subset of the set characterized by $[\![$ *black man* $]\!]^M$.

5 Current Annotation Scheme

In the first stages of our attempt to implement the theoretical model described above, we faced a practical problem concerning the binding of expressions in the RTE data to structurally equivalent expressions in the interpreted lexicon: we currently lack an annotation scheme and a user interface that allows annotators to consistently and effectively annotate RTE data. The root of this problem lies in the intricate ways in which the semantic phenomena that we are concerned with are combined with other phenomena or with each other. Simplifying RTE material to an extent that allows binding it to the lexicon as in the above example is often not straightforward. Consider the following example:

Example 4

- T: *Comdex – once among the world's largest trade shows, the launching pad for new computer and software products, and a Las Vegas fixture for 20 years - has been canceled for this year.*
- H: *Las Vegas hosted the Comdex trade show for 20 years.*[9]

Validating the entailment in this pair requires a lexical alignment between an expression in the text and the word *hosted* in the hypothesis. However, there is no expression in the text to establish this alignment. In the text, the noun *Comdex* is in an appositive relation with three conjoined propositions: (i) *once among the world's largest trade shows*; (ii) *the launching pad for new computer and software products*; and (iii) *a Las Vegas fixture for 20 years*. The third element contains a locative restrictive modification in which *Las Vegas* modifies *fixture*. The apposition licenses the inference that *Comdex* IS *a Las Vegas fixture* and serves as a prerequisite for the alignment: *Comdex is a Las Vegas fixture* $\Rightarrow$ *Las Vegas hosted Comdex* that simplifies the lexical inference. This alignment is also required for validating the modification by the temporal prepositional phrase *for 20 years* which in the text modifies a noun, *fixture*, and in the hypothesis modifies a verb, *host* - apparently two unrelated lexical items. This example illustrates the difficulty in separating lexical inferences from the semantic relations that underlie the constructions they appear in. In this sense, the manual annotation process that we exemplified in Section 4, in which the stage of *Phenomena Simplification* takes place before the semantic machinery applies, is challenging and requires further investigation with RTE data in order to see what part of the RTE can be annotated using this paradigm, and what elements are needed in order to extend its coverage.

Due to this challenge, and in order to enhance our understanding of the phenomena in the RTE corpora, we adopted a narrower annotation scheme that was carried out on RTE 1-4, named SemAnTE 1.0 - *Semantic Annotation of Textual Entailment*.[10] In this annotation work we focused on valid entailments involving restrictive, intersective and appositive modification that contribute to the recognition of the entailment.[11] In this approach, a construction is annotated if its semantics are required for validating the entailment, but no account is made of the compositional method in which the meaning of the full sentence is obtained. Annotations were marked in 80.65% of the entailments in the RTE 1-4 corpora and reached cross-annotator agreement of 68% on average in four consistency checks. The internal structure of the annotated XML files and a use-case of the annotations for evaluating an entailment component in the BIUTEE recognizer (Stern and Dagan, 2011) are presented in Toledo et al. (2012). See Garoufi (2007) for other relevant work on semantic analysis and annotation of textual entailment done on RTE 2.

5.1 Phenomena Annotated

Our annotations mark inferences by aligning strings in the text and the hypothesis. This is done by pairing each annotation in the text with a corresponding annotation in the hypothesis that marks the output of the inferential process of the phenomenon in question. In the rest of this section we illustrate the phenomena and underline the annotated part in the text with its correspondence in the hypothesis.

[9] Pair 214 from the development set of RTE 1.(Dagan et al., 2006)

[10] The annotated files of SemAnTE are publicly available for download at http://sophia.katrenko.com/CorpusDownload/

[11] Annotators were instructed to construct a full inferential process informally and then to recognize the contribution of the phenomena we aimed to annotate. This method could be applied efficiently only to valid entailments. Invalid entailments marked as *unknown* exhibit an unidentified relation between the text and hypothesis, and pairs marked as *contradictory* rarely center upon the phenomena in question.

5.2 Restrictive modification (RMOD)

- T: *A Cuban*$_{Modifier}$ *American*$_{Modifiee}$ *who is accused of espionage pleads innocent.*
- H: *American accused of espionage.*

In this case, *Cuban* modifies *American* and restricts the set of Americans to Cuban Americans. This instance of RMOD validates the inference from *Cuban American* to *American* which is required for establishing the entailment. The intersective nature of the process is not exploited in the actual inference, since the hypothesis does not report that the accused person is Cuban. Thus, only the restrictive property of the modifier *Cuban* is here relevant for the validity of the entailment. More syntactic configurations:

- A verb phrase restricted by a prepositional phrase:
  - T: *The watchdog International Atomic Energy Agency meets in Vienna*$_{Modifiee}$ *on September 19*$_{Modifier}$.
  - H: *The International Atomic Energy Agency holds a meeting in Vienna.*
- A noun phrase restricted by a prepositional phrase:
  - T: *U.S. officials have been warning for weeks of possible terror attacks*$_{Modifiee}$ *against U.S. interests*$_{Modifier}$.
  - H: *The United States has warned a number of times of possible terrorist attacks.*

5.3 Intersective Modification (CONJ)

- T: *Nixon was impeached and became the first president ever to resign on August 9th 1974.*
- H: *Nixon was the first president ever to resign.*

This conjunction intersects the two verb phrases *was impeached* and *became the first president ever to resign.* The entailment relies on a subsumption of the full construction to the second conjunct. In addition to canonical conjunctive constructions, CONJ appears also in Restrictive Relative Clauses whereby the relative clause is interpreted intersectively with the noun being modified:

- T: *Iran will soon release eight British servicemen detained along with three vessels.*
- H: *British servicemen detained.*

5.4 Appositive modification (APP)

- Appositive subsumption (left part):
  - T: *Mr. Conway, Iamgold's chief executive officer, said the vote would be close.*
  - H: *Mr. Conway said the vote would be close.*
- Identification of the two parts of the apposition as referring to one another:
  - T: *The incident in Mogadishu, the Somali capital, came as U.S. forces began the final phase of their promised March 31 pullout.*
  - H: *The capital of Somalia is Mogadishu.*

In addition to appositions, APP is annotated in several more syntactic constructions:

- Non-Restrictive Relative Clauses:
  - T: *A senior coalition official in Iraq said the body, which was found by U.S. military police west of Baghdad, appeared to have been thrown from a vehicle.*
  - H: *A body has been found by U. S. military police.*
- Title Constructions:
  - T: *Prime Minister Silvio Berlusconi was elected March 28 with a mandate to reform Italy's business regulations and pull the economy out of recession.*
  - H: *The Prime Minister is Silvio Berlusconi.*

5.5 Marking Annotations

Given a pair from the RTE in which the entailment relation obtains between the text and hypothesis, the task for the annotators is defined as follows:

Table 2: Counters of annotations in RTE 1-4 separated into development and test sets. $A_{\#}$ indicates the number of annotations, $P_{\#}$ indicates the number of entailment pairs containing an annotation and $P_{\%}$ indicates the portion of annotated pairs relative to the total amount of entailment pairs.

(a) RTE 1

	Dev set			Test set		
Ann.	$A_{\#}$	$P_{\#}$	$P_{\%}$	$A_{\#}$	$P_{\#}$	$P_{\%}$
APP	97	87	31	161	134	34
CONJ	90	79	28	126	112	28
RMOD	180	124	44	243	167	42
Any	367	210	74	530	297	74

(b) RTE 2

	Dev set			Test set		
Ann.	$A_{\#}$	$P_{\#}$	$P_{\%}$	$A_{\#}$	$P_{\#}$	$P_{\%}$
APP	179	149	37	155	135	34
CONJ	141	119	30	161	144	36
RMOD	314	205	51	394	236	59
Any	634	318	80	710	350	88

(c) RTE 3

	Dev set			Test set		
Ann.	$A_{\#}$	$P_{\#}$	$P_{\%}$	$A_{\#}$	$P_{\#}$	$P_{\%}$
APP	188	150	38	166	136	34
CONJ	176	138	35	162	134	34
RMOD	300	201	50	307	193	48
Any	664	329	82	635	328	82

(d) RTE 4

	Test set		
Ann.	$A_{\#}$	$P_{\#}$	$P_{\%}$
APP	259	200	40
CONJ	192	164	33
RMOD	429	271	54
Any	880	413	83

1. Read the data, verify the entailment and describe informally why the entailment holds.
2. Annotate all instances of RMOD, APP and CONJ that play a role in the inferential process.

5.6 Annotation Statistics and Consistency

The annotated corpus is based on the scheme described above, applied to the datasets of RTE 1-4 (Dagan et al., 2006; Bar Haim et al., 2006; Giampiccolo et al., 2007, 2008). We report annotation statistics in Table 2 and consistency measurements in Table 3. In each consistency check we picked 50-70 entailment pairs that both annotators worked on independently, and compared the phenomena that were annotated.

5.7 Annotation Platform

We used GATE Developer (Cunningham et al., 2011) to annotate the original RTE XML files. The work was performed in two steps using GATE annotation schemes that correspond to RMOD, APP and CONJ: (1) marking the relevant string in the text using one of GATE's schemes (e.g. a scheme of appositive modification), and (2) - marking a string in the hypothesis that corresponds to the output of the inferential process. The annotation in the hypothesis was done using a dedicated *reference_to* scheme.

5.8 Connection to the interpreted lexicon approach

Consider the following pair from RTE 2:
Example 5

- T: *The anti-terrorist court found two men guilty of murdering Shapour Bakhtiar and his secretary Sorush Katibeh, who were found with their throats cut in August 1991.*
- H: *Shapour Bakhtiar died in 1991.*

Several entailment patterns in this example can be explained by appealing to the semantics of APP, CONJ and RMOD, as follows:

- APP: The appositive modification in *Shapour Bakhtiar and his secretary Sorush Katibeh, who were found with their throats cut in August 1991* licenses the inference that *Shapour Bakhtiar and his secretary Sorush Katibeh were found with their throats cut in August 1991.*
- RMOD: The restrictive modification in *August 1991* licenses a subsumption to *1991.*

Table 3: Results of Four Consistency Checks. Each check examined 50-70 annotated pairs from RTE 1-4. In these four checks 66%, 74.11%, 66.67% and 64.66% of the annotations were identical, respectively. On average, 68.03% of the annotations we checked were identical. The rubric *Incorrect Ann.* presents cases of annotations done with an incorrect scheme or with an incorrect scope. *Ambig.-Struct.* are cases of structural or modifier-attachment ambiguity in the text that led to divergent annotations. *Ambig.-Infer.* are cases of divergent annotations stemming from several possible analyses of the inference. *Ambig.-Scheme* refers to instances of divergent annotations due to unclarity or limited specification in the annotation scheme. The last two measures are reported only for the second, third and forth checks.

Measure	RTE 1	RTE 1+2	RTE 3	RTE 4
Data Source(s)	Dev set	Test sets	Dev+Test sets	Test set
Entailment Pairs	50	70	70	70
Total Ann.	93	112	99	133
Identical Ann.	62	83	66	86
Missing Ann.	2	7	7	10
Incorrect Ann.	10	1	2	2
Ambig.-Struct.	9	16	20	15
Ambig.-Infer.	N/A	8	13	12
Ambig.-Scheme	N/A	0	9	7
Consistency (%)	66.67	74.11	66.67	64.66

- CONJ: The conjunction in *Shapour Bakhtiar and his secretary Sorush Katibeh* licenses a subsumption of this expression to *Shapour Bakhtiar*.

By combining these three patterns, we can infer that *Shapour Bakhtiar was found with his throat cut in 1991*. However, additional world knowledge is required to infer that *found with his throat cut* entails *died*. In our current annotation scheme this inference cannot be handled since lexical alignment of unmodeled phenomena is not supported . This motivates a more robust approach as proposed in Section 4.

6 Conclusions

The goal of this research is to establish a model-theoretic benchmark explaining entailment data. We have presented a model that utilizes standard semantic principles and illustrated the way it accounts for textual entailment from the RTE corpora. The model centers upon an interpreted lexicon that comprises words and operators. These elements are used to represent a fragment of English to which premises and hypotheses may be bound.

We focus on the annotation of semantic phenomena which are predominant in the RTE corpora and can be annotated with high consistency, but which may have several syntactic expressions and therefore allow us to generalize regarding abstract entailment patterns. Non-modeled phenomena that exist in the data are simplified in a preparatory step but cases in which such phenomena are deeply intertwined with the semantic phenomena that we model pose a challenge for the formalization of an annotation scheme.

At a first stage, we carried out a restricted annotation scheme by which instances of restrictive, intersective, and appositive modification are marked in entailment pairs with no account for the full inferential process between the premise and the hypothesis. These phenomena were found in 80.65% of the entailments in RTE 1-4 and were marked with cross-annotator agreement of 68% on average.

We are currently investigating different directions in the formulation of an extensive annotation scheme coincident with the model we described and are aiming to develop a corresponding annotation platform. This platform would allow annotators to bind constructions manifesting supported semantic phenomena to representations in the interpreted lexicon as well as to simplify lexical/syntactic phenomena of the kind illustrated in Examples 2 and 4 by textual alignment. In the next stages of this project, we plan to use an external theorem prover to automatically validate the entailment relation (or lack thereof).

References

Bar Haim, R., I. Dagan, B. Dolan, L. Ferro, D. Giampiccolo, B. Magnini, and I. Szpektor (2006). The second pascal recognising textual entailment challenge. In *In Proceedings of the Second PASCAL Challenges Workshop on Recognising Textual Entailment*.

Bentivogli, L., I. Dagan, H. T. Dang, D. Giampiccolo, and B. Magnini (2009). The fifth pascal recognizing textual entailment challenge. *Proceedings of TAC 9*, 14–24.

Bos, J., S. Clark, M. Steedman, J. R. Curran, and J. Hockenmaier (2004). Wide-coverage semantic representations from a CCG parser. In *Proceedings of the 20th international conference on Computational Linguistics*, pp. 12–40.

Bos, J. and K. Markert (2005). Recognising textual entailment with logical inference. In *Proceedings of the conference on Human Language Technology and Empirical Methods in Natural Language Processing*, pp. 628–635.

Cooper, R., D. Crouch, J. Van Eijck, C. Fox, J. Van Genabith, J. Jaspars, H. Kamp, D. Milward, M. Pinkal, M. Poesio, S. Pulman, T. Briscoe, H. Maier, and K. Konrad (1996). *Using the Framework*. The Fracas Consortium.

Cunningham, H., D. Maynard, K. Bontcheva, V. Tablan, N. Aswani, I. Roberts, G. Gorrell, A. Funk, A. Roberts, D. Damljanovic, T. Heitz, M. A. Greenwood, H. Saggion, J. Petrak, Y. Li, and W. Peters (2011). *Text Processing with GATE (Version 6).*

Dagan, I., O. Glickman, and B. Magnini (2006). The pascal recognising textual entailment challenge. *Machine Learning Challenges. Evaluating Predictive Uncertainty, Visual Object Classification, and Recognising Tectual Entailment*, 177–190.

Garoufi, K. (2007). Towards a better understanding of applied textual entailment: Annotation and evaluation of the rte-2 dataset. Master's thesis, Saarland University.

Giampiccolo, D., H. T. Dang, B. Magnini, I. Dagan, and E. Cabrio (2008). The fourth pascal recognising textual entailment challenge. In *In TAC 2008 Proceedings*.

Giampiccolo, D., B. Magnini, I. Dagan, and B. Dolan (2007). The third pascal recognizing textual entailment challenge. In *In Proceedings of the ACL-PASCAL Workshop on Textual Entailment and Paraphrasing*, RTE '07, Stroudsburg, PA, USA, pp. 1–9. Association for Computational Linguistics.

Kamp, H. and U. Reyle (1993). *From discourse to logic: Introduction to model-theoretic semantics of natural language, formal logic and discourse representation theory*, Volume 42. Kluwer Academic Dordrecht,, The Netherlands.

MacCartney, B. and C. D. Manning (2007). Natural logic for textual inference. In *Proceedings of the ACL-PASCAL Workshop on Textual Entailment and Paraphrasing*, pp. 193–200.

Pratt-Hartmann, I. and L. S. Moss (2009). Logics for the relational syllogistic. *Review of Symbolic Logic*, 647–683.

Stern, A. and I. Dagan (2011). A confidence model for syntactically-motivated entailment proofs. In *Proceedings of RANLP 2011*.

Toledo, A., S. Katrenko, S. Alexandropoulou, H. Klockmann, A. Stern, I. Dagan, and Y. Winter (2012). Semantic annotation for textual entailment recognition. In *Proceedings of the Eleventh Mexican International Conference on Artificial Intelligence (MICAI)*.

Valencia, V. S. (1991). *Studies on natural logic and categorial grammar*. Ph. D. thesis, University of Amsterdam.

Parsimonious Semantic Representations with Projection Pointers

Noortje J. Venhuizen
University of Groningen
n.j.venhuizen@rug.nl

Johan Bos
University of Groningen
johan.bos@rug.nl

Harm Brouwer
University of Groningen
harm.brouwer@rug.nl

Abstract

The influential idea by van der Sandt (1992) to treat presuppositions as anaphora in the framework of Discourse Representation Theory (DRT, Kamp and Reyle, 1993) has inspired a lot of debate as well as elaborations of his account. In this paper, we propose an extension of DRT, called Projective DRT, which adds pointers to all DRT referents and conditions, indicating their projection site. This means that projected content need not be moved from the context in which it is introduced, while it remains clearly discernible from asserted content. This approach inherits the attractive properties from van der Sandt's approach to presupposition, but precludes a two-step resolution algorithm by treating projection as variable binding, which increases compositionality and computational efficiency. The result is a flexible representational framework for a descriptive theory of projection phenomena.

1 Introduction

When it comes to presupposition projection, or more general 'projection phenomena', there seems to be some unpleasant friction between neat compositional approaches to discourse representation, and empirically driven theories. A case in point is Discourse Representation Theory (DRT), in which proper names are treated with a special procedure in order to account for their availability as antecedent for subsequent anaphora (Kamp and Reyle, 1993). This behaviour is due to the *projective* nature of proper names, that is, their existential indifference to logical operators such as negation and conditionals. In van der Sandt's (1992) empirically-driven theory of presupposition projection, formalized in the DRT framework, this discrepancy between compositionality and empirical soundness becomes very clear: presuppositions are only resolved in a second stage of processing by moving them from an embedded context to their context of interpretation. In purely compositional accounts of DRT, on the other hand, treatment of projection phenomena is usually simply left out (Muskens, 1996).

The goal of this paper is to investigate whether van der Sandt's idea to treat presuppositions in the same way as anaphora can be generalized to account for other projection phenomena, such as Potts's (2005) conventional implicatures, in a more compositional manner. To this purpose, we propose a representational extension of DRT, called Projective DRT (PDRT), that deals with presuppositions and other projection phenomena without moving semantic material within the representation. The approach is a simplification of Layered DRT, as proposed by Geurts and Maier (2003), since presuppositions and asserted content are treated on the same level. In PDRT, projection is represented by assigning variables ranging over DRSs, just as anaphora in dynamic frameworks are dealt with by assigning variables ranging over entities. This results in semantic representations that are close to the linguistic surface structure, while clearly distinguishing between asserted and projected content.

This paper is organized as follows. First, a theoretical background on projection phenomena in DRT is provided, focusing on van der Sandt's (1992) approach to presuppositions. In Section 3 we introduce Projective DRT, describing its preliminaries and how it deals with different types of (projective) content. The interpretation of PDRT is given via a translation to standard DRT, described in Section 4. Finally, Section 5 presents the conclusion and indicates directions for future work, describing an ongoing effort to implement PDRT into a large corpus of semantically annotated texts: the Groningen Meaning Bank (Basile et al., 2012).

2 Background

Presuppositions have a long history in the formal semantics and pragmatics literature (see, e.g., Beaver and Geurts, 2011, for an overview). In this paper, we focus on a specific representational theory of presuppositions based on Discourse Representation Theory (DRT; Kamp and Reyle, 1993).

2.1 Presuppositions as anaphora

In the theory of van der Sandt (1992), presupposition projection is treated on a par with anaphora resolution. This approach is motivated by the observation that presuppositions and anaphora display similar behaviour, since they both project their content from the scope of entailment-cancelling operators and show a preference for binding to an accessible antecedent. Unlike anaphora, however, presuppositions can occur felicitously in contexts where no suitable antecedent can be found. In these cases a new antecedent is created at an accessible discourse level, a process that has been called '*accommodation*'. The framework used by van der Sandt to implement his theory is DRT. In this account, each DRS is associated with a so-called A-structure, in which all presuppositions of that DRS are collected. In a second stage of processing, these presuppositions are resolved by either *binding* them to earlier introduced discourse referents or *accommodating* them at a suitable level of discourse. Presupposition resolution is secured by applying several constraints that determine relative preferences between alternative interpretations. These constraints include, for example, that binding is preferred over accommodation, and that global accommodation is preferred over local accommodation (see also Geurts, 1999).

An example of the working of van der Sandt's algorithm is shown in (1) (the A-structure introduced by the presuppositional content is indicated by a dashed box). In the unresolved representation in (1a) the presupposition triggered by the definite description "the cyclist" occurs in the A-structure at the introduction site. In the second stage of processing, this A-structure is resolved by accommodating the presupposition in the global DRS, resulting in the representation shown in (1b).

(1) Someone did not see the cyclist.

a. Unresolved DRS:

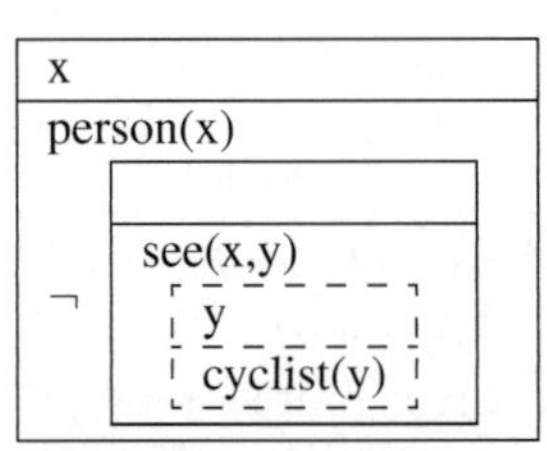

b. Resolved DRS:

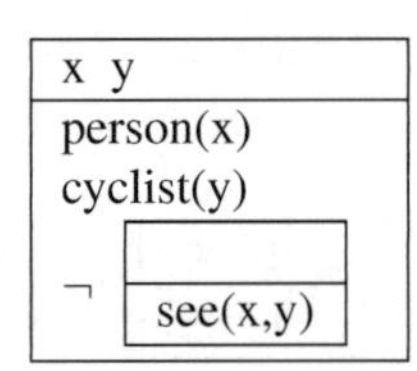

One of the main issues with van der Sandt's analysis of presuppositions in DRT is that, after presupposition projection, accommodated presuppositions and asserted content are indistinguishable. For example, in (1b) the accommodated presupposition "the cyclist" is added to the global context and therefore obtains the same status as the asserted content introduced by "someone". Krahmer (1998) argues, following Kracht (1994), that accommodated presuppositions should maintain their *presupposition-hood* because they are interpreted different from asserted content. For example, falsehood of a presupposition, also called *presupposition failure*, makes the sentence in which it occurs undefined (as in "The king of France is bald", where the existence of a king of France is presupposed), while in the case of falsely asserted content, the sentence is simply false (as in "France is a monarchy"). Moreover, given a compositional approach to semantics, we have to take into account that accommodated presuppositions may become bound later on, when more information of the surrounding context becomes available. This is not the case for asserted content, which implies that at each stage of processing these types of content should be distinguishable.

In order to resolve this issue, Krahmer (1998) introduces a marker for presuppositional content, such that presuppositions are accommodated at a higher discourse level *as presuppositions*, allowing for an interpretation distinct from asserted content. While this increases compositionality, the presupposition is still moved away from its introduction site in case of accommodation, which makes it difficult to retrieve the linguistic surface structure. This is problematic for applications such as surface realisation – text generation from semantic representations – and for the treatment of phenomena that depend on this surface structure, such as factive constructions and VP-ellipsis. Introducing yet another marker to identify the introduction site of a presupposition would clutter the representation and severely reduce readability and computational efficiency. Another issue with this approach is that recently the property of projection has been associated with a wider range of linguistic expressions outside of presuppositions (see Simons et al., 2010, for an overview). An important example are conventional implicatures (CIs), as described by Potts (2005). An example of a CI is shown in (2) (adapted from Potts, 2005).

(2) It is not true that Lance Armstrong, an Arkansan, won the 2002 Tour de France.

The conventional implicature triggered in the appositive (that Lance Armstrong is an Arkansan), is projected from out of the scope of the negation, just like the presupposition triggered by the proper name. However, CIs show a different projective behaviour than presuppositions, since they have a strong resistance against binding to an antecedent. This is explained by the observation that they intuitively convey 'new' information, like asserted content. This preference for accommodation contrasts with the theoretical assumptions of van der Sandt (1992) and Krahmer (1998), who implement accommodation as a repair strategy.

In sum, we need a single representational framework that allows for a separate treatment of asserted and projected content. An important step in this direction is Layered DRT (Geurts and Maier, 2003) where different types of information are treated on different layers. We will show that although this representation accounts for the differences between asserted, presupposed and conventionally implied content, it fails to capture their similarities and interactions.

2.2 Layered DRT

In Layered DRT (LDRT), the distinction between different types of information is implemented by introducing different layers (Geurts and Maier, 2003). Each discourse referent and condition is associated with a set of labels that indicate the layers on which the information is interpreted. These layers allow for a distinction between asserted and presupposed content, but also for a separate interpretation of implicated, indexical and formal content. An example is shown in (3), where the label p indicates presupposed content, the label a implicates asserted content and ci indicates a conventional implicature.

(3) Bill, a linguist, does not like Mary.

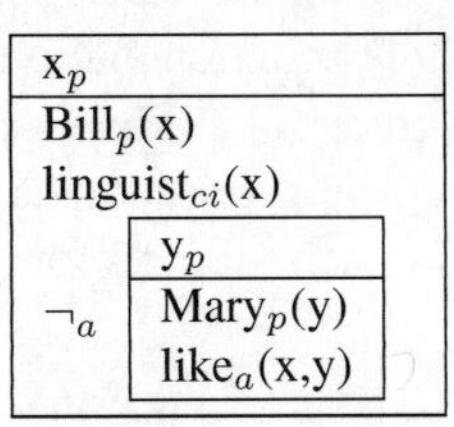

This example shows that the different types of content are represented within a single framework, while being clearly distinguishable through the labels. The different layers are connected by sharing discourse referents, indicating the interaction between different types of content. Since all conditions are indexed with a label, projected material can remain at its introduction site, because it is interpreted at a separate layer and therefore it is not targeted by logical operators. The interpretation of LDRT is defined on the basis of the truth-conditional content of sets of layers. For example, the presupposed meaning of (3) is true in the set of worlds in which the individuals called Bill and Mary exist. The asserted content can only be defined in combination with the presupposed content, representing the set of worlds in which Bill does not like Mary.

Although LDRT nicely captures the differences and dependencies between the various types of information, the separation into different layers comes at a cost. Firstly, it is unclear under which conditions a new layer is created. According to Geurts and Maier (2003, pp.15–16), all information that has a "special status" may be put on a separate layer. However, this may result in abundance of layers that all have their specific interpretation, which would fail to account for any similarities between phenomena interpreted on different layers. In particular, the similar felicity conditions for anaphora and presuppositions described by van der Sandt (1992) and the strong correspondence between asserted content and conventional implicatures (see, e.g., Amaral et al., 2007) cannot be captured in a multi-dimensional (multi-layered) framework.

Secondly, not all material seems to strictly belong to a specific layer. For example, Maier (2009) adapts Layered DRT to account for the special behaviour of proper names and indexicals, which are taken to constitute a special layer for 'reference-fixing' content (Maier calls this the *'kripke-kaplan'* or kk-layer, separating its content from the *'fregian'* fr-layer). However, some expressions, such as proper names and third person pronouns must be allowed to 'hop' between layers in order to account for their different usages (e.g., third person pronouns are regularly used in both deictic and anaphoric constructions). This solution is criticized by Hunter (2012), who argues that a relaxation of the separation between layers seems to defeat their purpose, since apparently they do not represent strictly distinct parts of meaning. Hunter provides an alternative analysis in which she shows that no extra layer is needed for indexical content; the behaviour of reference-fixing expressions can be accounted for by adding an extra-linguistic context level to standard DRT, the content of which is determined by the actual state of the world. This context allows indexicals to pick out a unique object in the actual world, without the need for a separate layer of meaning.

The goal of the current paper is to apply a similar kind of dimension reduction for projection phenomena, and to show that their behaviour can be accounted for within a unidimensional framework. To this purpose, we develop Projective DRT, which extends standard DRT with a set of pointers to indicate the accommodation site of linguistic material. The framework can be seen as a refinement of Layered DRT, which integrates a subset of its layers into one and thereby accounts for the distinction, as well as the similarities between the different phenomena.

3 Projective Discourse Representation Theory

Projective DRT (PDRT) is an extension of standard DRT in which each referent and condition is associated with a pointer to indicate projection behaviour. The basic idea of PDRT is that all projected content is represented locally, i.e., at the introduction site, and that projection is signalled by means of pointers that indicate where the content is to be interpreted. This means that projection is not realised by physically moving semantic material in the resolution stage, but by setting a variable equation on pointers and PDRS labels. This representation stays closer to the linguistic surface structure, and reduces computational complexity born out of a two-stage resolution mechanism. Moreover, presupposed and asserted (i.e. non-projected) content are clearly discernible in the representation at each step of composition, while remaining subject to the same interpretation mechanism.

3.1 Projection as variable binding

In PDRT, asserted and projected material is treated in the same way, by associating the content with a pointer to its context of interpretation. The differences between asserted and projected material arise from the different contexts they point to. Asserted material gets as pointer the label of the PDRS in which it is introduced, and is thus interpreted locally. In the case of projected material, the pointer may refer to the label of an accessible PDRS (in van der Sandt's terminology: a PDRS on the projection path), or it may be a free variable. As a result, projected content is interpreted in the appointed PDRS or in the global PDRS in case the pointer is a free variable. An example is shown in (4), where we use integers to denote labels and bound pointers, and f for free pointers.

(4) a. A man smiles. b. The man smiles. c. It is not the case that the man smiles.

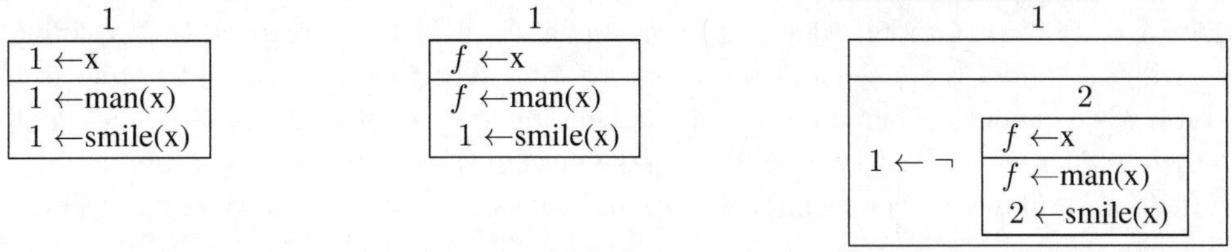

Each PDRS introduces a label, represented on top of the PDRS, and all referents and conditions associate with a label via a pointer, represented with an inverted arrow. If no material is projected, as in (4a), all material points to the PDRS in which it is introduced (the PDRS labeled '1'). In (4b) and (4c), on the other hand, the definite description 'the man' triggers a presupposition about the existence of its referent. In PDRT this is indicated by using a free variable as pointer for the presupposed material (here, 'f'). Free pointers are interpreted as pointing to the outermost PDRS (representing the discourse context), which both in (4b) and (4c) is the PDRS labeled '1'. As a result, the interpretations of (4a) and (4b) are equivalent, as desired, but on the representational level they are clearly distinguishable in order to account for their different compositional properties.

3.2 Preliminaries

The vocabulary of PDRT extends the standard DRT language with labels for DRSs and pointers for referents and conditions. A structure in PDRT (a PDRS) consists of a label ϕ, a set of projected referents D and a set of projected conditions C, resulting in a triple: $\langle \phi, D, C \rangle$. The projected referents and conditions are defined as follows:

Definition 1 (Projected referents).
If p is a pointer and d is a discourse referent, then $\langle p, d \rangle$ is a projected discourse referent.

Definition 2 (Projected conditions).

- If p is a pointer and P is an n-place predicate and $u_1, ..., u_n$ are discourse referents, then $\langle p, P(u_1, ..., u_n) \rangle$ is a projected condition.
- If p is a pointer and ϕ and ψ are PDRSs, then $\langle p, \neg\phi \rangle$, $\langle p, \phi \vee \psi \rangle$, $\langle p, \phi \rightarrow \psi \rangle$ are projected conditions.

Furthermore, accessibility between PDRSs and free variables are defined just as in standard DRT (Kamp and Reyle, 1993). Below, when possible, we will simply refer to the referents and conditions of PDRSs, instead of projected referents and projected conditions.

In the current implementation, the semantics of a PDRS is provided via a translation to standard DRT (see Section 4). This is computationally advantageous because of the model-theoretic properties of standard DRT, which are interpretable via first order logic (Muskens, 1996). This means that although in PDRT the movement of projected material is precluded at the representational level, in the interpretation it will be moved in order to obtain equivalence to DRT. This way, the theory inherits some attractive properties from the DRT account to presupposition, such as its inference mechanisms and predictions with respect to, for example, the proviso problem (cf. Geurts, 1999). However, the approach can easily be adapted to incorporate other interpretative models, for example a three-valued logic to account for presupposition failure in terms of undefinedness (see, e.g., Krahmer, 1998).

3.3 PDRS composition

Most presuppositional theories are lexically driven, i.e., based on the assumption that specific lexical items give rise to presuppositions (so-called 'presupposition triggers'). Therefore, projected material will be manifested in the lexical semantics of projection triggers. Various authors have proposed a compositional treatment of DRT using basic tools from Montague Grammar and lambda calculus (Muskens, 1996; Bos, 2003; de Groote, 2006). Compositionality in PDRT is realised by providing every lexical item with an (unresolved) semantics in the form of a typed lambda term. In order to combine these unresolved semantics, a merge operation can be applied that combines two PDRSs into one by means of *merge-reduction* (see, e.g., Bos, 2003). In the current framework, we use different types of merge for asserted, presupposed and conventionally implied material in order to account for their different compositional properties.

In PDRT, projected material is not interpreted on a different level than asserted material, it only contributes to the context in a different way. This is realised by implementing distinct types of merge for asserted and presupposed material: assertive merge ($+$) and projective merge ($*$). Assertive merge between two (unresolved) PDRSs can be defined in the usual way by the union of the referents and conditions. Additionally, however, the pointers that refer to the merged PDRSs (i.e., the bound pointers) must be unified with the label of the resulting PDRS, in order to secure that asserted material is interpreted locally. The definition of assertive merge operations is shown below. For the renaming of pointers we use the notation '$A[x/y]$', which is taken to represent the set resulting from replacing every instance of y in the set A by x.

Definition 3 (Assertive merge).
$$\begin{array}{c} i \\ \hline \multicolumn{1}{|c|}{D_i} \\ \hline \multicolumn{1}{|c|}{C_i} \\ \hline \end{array} \quad + \quad \begin{array}{c} j \\ \hline \multicolumn{1}{|c|}{D_j} \\ \hline \multicolumn{1}{|c|}{C_j} \\ \hline \end{array} \quad := \quad \begin{array}{c} j \\ \hline \multicolumn{1}{|c|}{D_i[j/i] \cup D_j} \\ \hline \multicolumn{1}{|c|}{C_i[j/i] \cup C_j} \\ \hline \end{array}$$

In words, the definition for assertive merge defines the merge of two asserted PDRSs as the union of the domains and conditions of the PDRSs, with the local pointers of the PDRS in the first argument of the merge (labeled i) replaced by the label of the second argument of the merge (labeled j).

Projected material, on the other hand, is not affected by the local context, but keeps its own pointer, which either refers to its accommodation site or is a free variable. Therefore, projective merge only involves adding the projected referents and conditions to the resulting DRS, without affecting their interpretation. This results in the following definition:

Definition 4 (Projective merge).
$$\begin{array}{c} i \\ \hline \multicolumn{1}{|c|}{D_i} \\ \hline \multicolumn{1}{|c|}{C_i} \\ \hline \end{array} \quad * \quad \begin{array}{c} j \\ \hline \multicolumn{1}{|c|}{D_j} \\ \hline \multicolumn{1}{|c|}{C_j} \\ \hline \end{array} \quad := \quad \begin{array}{c} j \\ \hline \multicolumn{1}{|c|}{D_i \cup D_j} \\ \hline \multicolumn{1}{|c|}{C_i \cup C_j} \\ \hline \end{array}$$

Conventional implicatures, in turn, exhibit yet a different type of compositional behaviour (Potts, 2005). Like presuppositions, CIs project out of their local context. Unlike presuppositions, however, they cannot bind to an antecedent, nor accommodate locally (i.e., non-globally). In PDRT, this is realised by always projecting conventionally implied content to the outermost context (the "global" PDRS). This way, conventional implicatures receive an interpretation that is in some way between that of presuppositions and assertions: CIs accommodate at the highest possible context, while assertions accommodate locally and presuppositions remain free to indicate binding possibilities. In the definition for implicative merge, this means that all (bound) pointers of the conventionally implied content are replaced by a constant, say '0', which always refers to the outermost discourse context. This results in the following definition:

Definition 5 (Implicative merge).
$$\begin{array}{c} i \\ \hline \multicolumn{1}{|c|}{D_i} \\ \hline \multicolumn{1}{|c|}{C_i} \\ \hline \end{array} \quad \bullet \quad \begin{array}{c} j \\ \hline \multicolumn{1}{|c|}{D_j} \\ \hline \multicolumn{1}{|c|}{C_j} \\ \hline \end{array} \quad := \quad \begin{array}{c} j \\ \hline \multicolumn{1}{|c|}{D_i[0/i] \cup D_j} \\ \hline \multicolumn{1}{|c|}{C_i[0/i] \cup C_j} \\ \hline \end{array}$$

3.4 Projection in PDRT

Next we will show how the different merge definitions are implemented in the lexical semantics of the linguistic material, resulting in a unified compositional framework for the representation of asserted content, presuppositions and conventional implicatures.

3.4.1 Asserted versus projected content

The distinction between asserted content and projected content is achieved by making use of different merge operations, reflecting the different ways in how the content is added to the discourse context. As an example, we look at the lexical semantics of definite descriptions and indefinites. In order to obtain the representations shown in (4), the indefinite should be added to the local context and the definite description should project using a free variable as pointer. This can be achieved by using different types of merge in the lexical semantics of "a" and "the". An indefinite description combines with the local context using an assertive merge, which means that the referent inherits the label from the merged PDRS and thus becomes asserted content. Definite descriptions, on the other hand, project out of their local context, which can be achieved using projective merge. The resulting lexical semantics for the determiners "a" and "the" are shown in (5).

(5) a. "a": $\lambda p.\lambda q.((\overset{i}{\begin{array}{|c|}\hline i \leftarrow x \\ \hline \\ \hline \end{array}} + p(x)) + q(x))$

b. "the": $\lambda p.\lambda q.((\overset{i}{\begin{array}{|c|}\hline i \leftarrow x \\ \hline \\ \hline \end{array}} + p(x)) * q(x))$

The lexical semantics of the indefinite article "a" introduces a discourse referent in a local PDRS. This PDRS is first combined with a predicate (e.g. a noun like "man") using assertive merge. The result of this merge operation is then combined with another predicate (e.g. a verb like "smiles"), again using *assertive* merge. This results in a representation where the indefinite description ("a man") is interpreted locally in the PDRS introduced by the rest of the context ("smiles"). For the definite article "the", on the other hand, the *projective* merge is used to combine the result of the first, assertive merge with the rest of the context. This means that the definite description keeps its own pointer, which will either be bound by an accessible PDRS, or become a free variable in the final representation, indicating accommodation.

Other presupposition triggers, such as pronouns and proper names, receive a lexical semantics similar to definite descriptions, using projective merge. In case a presupposition gets bound, the standard DRT analysis can be used, introducing an equality relation between the referent and the antecedent (Kamp and Reyle, 1993). Alternatively, we can unify the referent with the antecedent, as in van der Sandt (1992).

3.4.2 Conventional Implicatures

Potts (2005) defined the class of conventional implicatures on the basis of a set of specific criteria, including non- cancellability, not at-issueness, scopelessness and speaker orientation. He roughly categorizes CIs into two groups: supplemental expressions (including appositives, non-restrictive relative clauses – NRRCs– and parenthetical adverbs) and expressives (including expressive attributive adjectives, epithets and honorifics). Potts (2005) presents a multi-dimensional framework in order capture the distinction between CIs and asserted content. However, there is strong evidence against such a multi-dimensional approach, as Amaral et al. (2007) argue that there is a strong interaction between CIs and asserted content and Simons et al. (2010) unify presuppositions and CIs as projection phenomena. Therefore, in Projective DRT conventional implicatures are treated in the same way as presuppositions and asserted content, with the peculiarity that CIs always accommodate to the global discourse level. This is realised by projecting CIs using the implicative merge defined in Section 3.3.

Conventional implicatures are often triggered by constructions rather than lexical items, for example the subordinating constructions of appositives and NRRCs. In PDRT this is reflected by creating a special semantics for the subordinating comma, which projects its second argument. Because of the directionality of the merge operator, this means that the subordinating comma must reorder its arguments, such that the subordinated content is projected. The resulting semantics is shown in (6).

(6) subordinating comma ",": $\lambda p.\lambda q.(q \bullet p)$

An example of the PDRT representation of an appositive is shown in (7). Note that the pointer of the appositive is '0', which is a constant referring to the label of the current global context, here '1'. Thus, both the presupposition introduced by the proper name and the CI introduced by the appositive accommodate to the global discourse context. The difference is that the pointer of the presupposition (indicated with 'f') remains available for binding, while the pointer of the appositive will always refer to the most global context.

(7) It is not true that Lance Armstrong, a former cyclist, is a Tour-winner.

1	
	2
$1 \leftarrow \neg$	$f \leftarrow$x
	$f \leftarrow$Lance_Armstrong(x) 0 $\leftarrow$former_cyclist(x) 2 $\leftarrow$Tour-winner(x)

3.5 Comparison with related approaches

As described above, Layered DRT, as proposed in Geurts and Maier (2003), is a multi-dimensional framework that can account for different linguistic phenomena within a single representation. Projective DRT provides a unidimensional treatment for a subset of the phenomena covered in LDRT, including asserted content, presuppositions and conventional implicatures. The advantage of treating these different phenomena on a single 'layer' is that they are not treated as different kinds of meaning; they merely contribute their content to the context in a different way. A similar endeavour was taken by Hunter (2012), who argues for a unidimensional account of indexicals and asserted content. She proposes a DRT-style analysis in which an extra context is created for reference-fixing content, which is interpreted relative to the actual state of the world. This fits neatly within the idea of Projective DRT, where linguistic expressions are differentiated on the basis of the context the project ('point') to, and thus allows for a straightforward extension along these lines. We will leave an implementation of this and other extensions of PDRT for future work.

The account presented here is also related to the work of Schlenker (2011), who proposes a DRT account in the spirit of Heim (1983). In his representation, presupposed propositions are indexed with context variables that explicitly represent local contexts in the logical form. In this sense, his analysis is in line with approaches that use update semantics (e.g., Zeevat, 1992), because the context variable defines the context in which the presupposition is interpreted. The anaphoric aspect is therefore not in the presupposition itself, but in the context variables, which can anaphorically refer to accessible contexts. The consequence of this analysis is that accommodation does not imply adding the presuppositional content to a higher context, but rather interpreting it within this higher context. So, the interpretation of the presupposition itself, rather than that of the context in which it is accommodated is affected. In this respect Schlenker's approach crucially differs from Projective DRT, since in PDRT the traditional DRT strategy of adding presuppositions to their context of interpretation is applied. This allows for a straightforward analysis of cases of intermediate accommodation, which are difficult to capture in Schlenker's account. Moreover, PDRT allows for a more fine-grained analysis, since each referent and condition is associated with an interpretation site, while Schlenker only projects complete propositions.

4 Translation PDRT to DRT

The semantics of PDRSs can be described via a translation to standard DRT (Kamp and Reyle, 1993). As described above, PDRT is not strictly limited to this interpretation and may be extended to incorporate other interpretation models. We implemented PDRT as part of the wide-coverage semantic parser Boxer (Bos, 2008), including an automatic translation to standard DRT. Below we only provide a sketch of the algorithmic translation to DRT, as space limitations do not permit a description of the full translation.

4.1 Translation procedure

For the translation to DRT we make use of PDRT's separation of logical structure and linguistic content. Since each referent and condition is associated with a pointer to its accommodation site, it is possible to first separate this content from the embedded PDRS structure and accordingly project each condition to its appointed site. We assume that α-conversion is applied to the PDRS in order to make sure that all labels, pointers and referents use unique variables.

For convenience, we here describe the algorithm for translating PDRSs to DRSs in three steps. In the first step, all accommodation sites referents and conditions are gathered in separate sets. In the second step, the referents and conditions are added to their appointed accommodation site. In the third and final step, the PDRSs in the set of accommodation sites are combined to form a DRS.

Step 1. We start by creating three empty sets: one for accommodation sites (Π), one for discourse referents (Δ) and one for conditions (Γ). Starting from a PDRS $\Phi = \langle \varphi, D, C \rangle$, we define the pointer of Φ to be a constant: $p(\Phi) = g$, and we add this pointer, together with an empty PDRS with the label of Φ to Π: $\Pi \cup \langle p(\Phi), \langle \varphi, \{\}, \{\} \rangle \rangle$. All referents $d \in D$ are added to Δ. For the conditions $c \in C$, the base case is that c contains no embedded PDRSs, i.e., $c = \langle p, R(x_1, ..., x_n) \rangle$. In this case c is added to Γ. If c does contain an embedded PDRS, e.g., $c = \langle p, \neg \langle l, D_l, C_l \rangle \rangle$, then a fresh label is created, say l_0. This label is used as a sort of 'trace' to indicate where the embedded PDRS was introduced. We add $\langle l_0, \langle l, \{\}, \{\} \rangle \rangle$ to Π and $\langle p, \neg \langle l_0, \{\}, \{\} \rangle \rangle$ to Γ. This way, the context introduced by the embedded PDRS becomes available as an accommodation site, and the condition containing the embedded PDRS is added to the list of conditions. Accordingly, the referents (D_l) and conditions (C_l) of the embedded PDRS are recursively resolved in the same manner as described above, with respect to the current Δ, Γ and Π. This procedure can also be applied for other complex conditions, such as disjuctions, implications, modal expressions or propositional PDRSs (e.g., $c = \langle p, v : \langle l, D_l, C_l \rangle \rangle$).

Step 2. In this step, all referents in Δ and all conditions in Γ are projected to an appropriate PDRS in the list of accommodation sites, Π. For each referent $\langle l, u \rangle \in \Delta$, this means that if $\langle p, \langle l, D_l, C_l \rangle \rangle \in \Gamma$, then u is added to the domain: $D_l \cup u$ (so without the pointer). Otherwise, the label occurs free, so u is added to the domain of the outermost PDRS, which has g as pointer: $\langle g, \langle m, D_m \cup u, C_m \rangle \rangle$. The same strategy can be applied for conditions and the process continues until Δ and Γ are empty.

Step 3. The last step is to put the accommodation sites in Π (which now contain all the accommodated material) back together in order to form a translated DRS. We start with the DRS $\Phi = \langle D_1, C_1 \rangle$, such that: $\langle g, \langle l_1, D_1, C_1 \rangle \rangle \in \Pi$. This accommodation site is accordingly removed from Π. Then we check the conditions of Φ for embedded PDRSs. If such a complex condition is found, e.g. $c = \neg \langle l_c, D_c, C_c \rangle$, then the embedded PDRS is replaced by the DRS $\Psi = \langle D_m, C_m \rangle$, such that: $\langle l_c, \langle l_m, D_m, C_m \rangle \rangle \in \Pi$, which is accordingly removed from Π. Then, the set of conditions C_m of Ψ is again checked for embedded PDRSs. Once no embedded PDRSs remain, the remainder of the conditions of the dominating DRS (in this case, Φ) are checked. This recursive process goes on until Π is empty. At that point we will have a DRS with all the projected (and asserted) material at its accommodation site.

4.2 Example translation

We now provide an example of the translation procedure explained in the last subsection. The PDRS is shown in (8a), the desired DRS translation is shown in (8b) and its first-order logic equivalent in (8c).

(8) a.

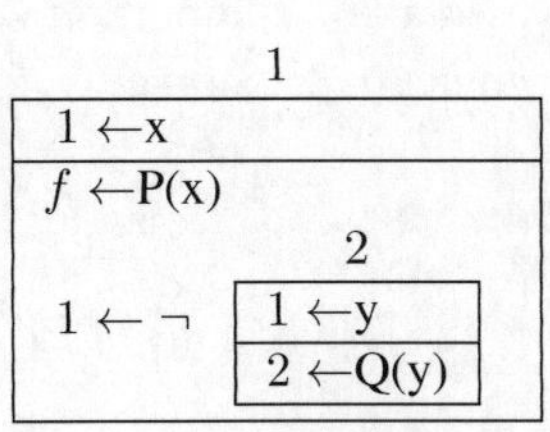

b.

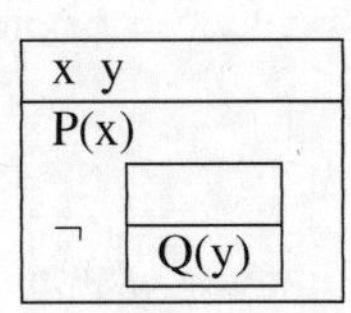

c. $\exists x \exists y (P(x) \wedge \neg Q(y))$

Step 1. We start with three empty sets: Δ, Γ and Π. First, we add an empty PDRS with the label of the outermost PDRS Φ and a fixed pointer, say 0, to the set of accommodation sites: $\Pi = \{\langle 0, \langle 1, \emptyset, \emptyset\rangle\rangle\}$. We add the referents and simple conditions of Φ to the correct sets: $\Delta = \{\langle 1,\mathrm{x}\rangle\}$; $\Gamma = \{\langle f,\mathrm{P(x)}\rangle\}$. Then, we create a fresh label, say 3, and add an empty PDRS with the label of the embedded PDRS and the fresh label as pointer to Π: $\Pi = \{\langle 0, \langle 1, \emptyset, \emptyset\rangle\rangle, \langle 3, \langle 2, \emptyset, \emptyset\rangle\rangle\}$. The condition with the operator and an empty PDRS with the fresh label is then added to Γ: $\Gamma = \{\langle f,\mathrm{P(x)}\rangle, \langle 1, \neg\langle 3, \emptyset, \emptyset\rangle\rangle\}$. Finally, we add the content of the embedded PDRS to the corresponding sets: $\Delta = \{\langle 1,\mathrm{x}\rangle, \langle 1,\mathrm{y}\rangle\}$; $\Gamma = \{\langle f,\mathrm{P(x)}\rangle, \langle 1, \neg\langle 3, \emptyset, \emptyset\rangle\rangle, \langle 2,\mathrm{Q(y)}\rangle\}$.

Step 2. Now, we simply project each of the elements of Δ and Γ to the correctly labeled PDRS in Π, i.e., to the PDRS that has the pointer of the referent/condition as label, or to the PDRS with the pointer 0 in case of a free variable: $\Pi = \{\langle 0, \langle 1, \{x, y\}, \{\mathrm{P(x)}, \neg\langle 3, \emptyset, \emptyset\rangle\}\rangle\rangle, \langle 3, \langle 2, \emptyset, \{\mathrm{Q(y)}\}\rangle\rangle\}$.

Step 3. Finally, we create a DRS Ψ from the accommodation site in Π that has 0 as pointer: $\Psi = \langle\{x, y\}, \{\mathrm{P(x)}, \neg\langle 3, \emptyset, \emptyset\rangle\}\rangle$. We check for embedded PDRSs in the conditions of Ψ and replace them with the DRS from the corresponding element in Π (matching the pointer to the label). The result is the following DRS: $\langle\{x, y\}, \{\mathrm{P(x)}, \neg\langle\emptyset, \{\mathrm{Q(y)}\}\rangle\}\rangle$, which is exactly the desired DRS shown in (8b).

5 Conclusions and future work

In this paper we presented Projective DRT, and extension of DRT in which all linguistic material is associated with a pointer to indicate its accommodation site. This way, semantic material does not need to be moved or copied at the representational level, as projection is secured by using free variables as pointers, or by binding the pointers of projected material to labels introduced by higher level PDRSs. This is in line with van der Sandt's (1992) idea to treat presuppositions as anaphora, since in DRT anaphora resolution is also based on variable binding. The theory results in a simple and parsimonious representation of different linguistic phenomena, with a unified treatment of asserted content, presuppositions and conventional implicatures. Moreover, it allows for compositional construction of discourse structures with projected content while precluding a two-step resolution algorithm. The resulting representation structures have a straightforward interpretation via translation to standard DRT.

Projective DRT can be extended to account for other phenomena, as well as other interpretation models. For example, we above mentioned a possible extension with a special context for indexical content, as described by Hunter (2012). Other directions for future work include the incorporation of phenomena such as factive constructions and VP-ellipsis with presupposed content in PDRT. A proper treatment of such phenomena may ask for an extension of the PDRT syntax (for example, allowing multiple pointers for one condition) or a more elaborate semantics that is not necessarily interpretable via a translation to standard DRT.

All in all, PDRT provides a transparent and flexible compositional framework for investigating projection phenomena. The robustness of the framework has already been put to test through an implementation into Bos's (2008) wide-coverage semantic parser: Boxer. Future work will aim at evaluating and refining the PDRSs produced by Boxer via an integration into the Groningen Meaning Bank, a large-scale corpus of semantically annotated texts (Basile et al., 2012). PDRT allows for a coherent and easy-to-read representation of projection phenomena, since all content appears locally and the representation is therefore closer to the linguistic surface structure. This is important for a proper evaluation of semantic representations, as well as for studying the behaviour of linguistic phenomena. Implementation of PDRT into a large resource of semantically annotated texts will make an important contribution to corpus-based investigations into the behaviour of projection phenomena in discourse.

Acknowledgements

We thank Emar Maier for an interesting discussion about one of the earlier versions of PDRT.

References

Amaral, P., C. Roberts, and E. Smith (2007). Review of "The Logic of Conventional Implicatures" by Chris Potts. *Linguistics and Philosophy 30*(6), 707–749.

Basile, V., J. Bos, K. Evang, and N. J. Venhuizen (2012). Developing a large semantically annotated corpus. In *Proceedings of the Eighth International Conference on Language Resources and Evaluation (LREC'12)*, Istanbul, Turkey, pp. 3196–3200. European Language Resources Association (ELRA).

Beaver, D. I. and B. Geurts (2011). Presupposition. In E. N. Zalta (Ed.), *The Stanford Encyclopedia of Philosophy* (Summer 2011 ed.). Metaphysics Research Lab, CSLI, Stanford University.

Bos, J. (2003). Implementing the binding and accommodation theory for anaphora resolution and presupposition projection. *Computational Linguistics 29*(2), 179–210.

Bos, J. (2008). Wide-coverage semantic analysis with boxer. In *Semantics in Text Processing. STEP 2008 Conference Proceedings*, Volume 1, pp. 277–286.

de Groote, P. (2006). Towards a montagovian account of dynamics. In *Proceedings of SALT*, Volume 16, pp. 1–16.

Geurts, B. (1999). *Presuppositions and pronouns*. Elsevier.

Geurts, B. and E. Maier (2003). Layered DRT. Ms. To appear as: Layered Discourse Representation Theory. In Alessandro Capone (Ed.), *Perspectives on pragmatics and philosophy*. Springer, Berlin.

Heim, I. (1983). On the projection problem for presuppositions. In *Proceedings of the West Coast Conference on Formal Linguistics*, Volume 2, pp. 144–226.

Hunter, J. (2012). Presuppositional indexicals. *Journal of Semantics 0*, 1–41.

Kamp, H. and U. Reyle (1993). *From discourse to logic: Introduction to modeltheoretic semantics of natural language, formal logic and Discourse Representation Theory*. Kluwer Academic Dordrecht, The Netherlands.

Kracht, M. (1994). Logic and control: How they determine the behaviour of presuppositions. In J. van Eijck and A. Visser (Eds.), *Logic and Information Flow*, pp. 89–111. Cambridge, MA: MIT press.

Krahmer, E. (1998). *Presupposition and anaphora*. CSLI Publications.

Maier, E. (2009). Proper names and indexicals trigger rigid presuppositions. *Journal of Semantics 26*(3), 253–315.

Muskens, R. (1996). Combining Montague Semantics and Discourse Representation. *Linguistics and Philosophy 19*(2), 143–186.

Potts, C. (2005). *The Logic of Conventional Implicatures*. Oxford University Press, USA.

Schlenker, P. (2011). DRT with local contexts. *Natural language semantics 19*(4), 373–392.

Simons, M., J. Tonhauser, D. Beaver, and C. Roberts (2010). What projects and why. In *Proceedings of SALT*, Volume 20, pp. 309–327.

van der Sandt, R. (1992). Presupposition projection as anaphora resolution. *Journal of Semantics 9*, 333–377.

Zeevat, H. (1992). Presupposition and accommodation in update semantics. *Journal of Semantics 9*(4), 379–412.

Subgraph-based Classification of Explicit and Implicit Discourse Relations

Yannick Versley
SFB 833
University of Tübingen
versley@sfs.uni-tuebingen.de

Abstract

Current approaches to recognizing discourse relations rely on a combination of shallow, surface-based features (e.g., bigrams, word pairs), and rather specialized hand-crafted features. As a way to avoid both the shallowness of word-based representations and the lack of coverage of specialized linguistic features, we use a graph-based representation of discourse segments, which allows for a more abstract (and hence generalizable) notion of syntactic (and partially of semantic) structure. Empirical evaluation on a hand-annotated corpus of German discourse relations shows that our graph-based approach not only provides a suitable representation for the linguistic factors that are needed in disambiguating discourse relations, but also improves results over a strong state-of-the-art baseline by more accurately identifying *Temporal*, *Comparison* and *Reporting* discourse relations.

1 Introduction

Discourse relations between textual spans capture essential structural and semantic/pragmatic aspects of text structure. Besides anaphora and referential structure, discourse relations are a key ingredient in understanding a text beyond single clauses or sentences. The automatic recognition of discourse relations is therefore an important task; approaches to the solution of this problem range from heuristic approaches that use reliable indicators (Marcu, 2000) to modern machine learning approaches such as Lin et al. (2009) that apply broad shallow features in cases without such indicators.

Especially on *implicit discourse relations*, where no discourse connective could provide a reliable indication, broad, shallow features such as bigrams or word pairs conceivably lack the precision that would be needed to improve disambiguation results beyond a certain level. Conversely, hand-crafted linguistic features allow one to encode certain relevant aspects, but they have often limited coverage. Encoding detailed linguistic information in a structured representation, as in the work presented here, allows us to bridge this divide and potentially find a golden middle between linguistic precision and broad applicability.

We propose a graph-based representation of discourse segments as a way to overcome both the shallowness of a word-based representation and the non-specificity or lack of coverage of specialized linguistic features. In the rest of the paper, section 2 discusses the current state of the art in discourse relation classification. Section 3 introduces feature graphs as a general representation and learning mechanism, and section 4 provides an overview of the used corpus, as well as feature-based and graph-based representations for discourse relations. Section 5 presents empirical evaluation results.

2 Classification of Discourse Relations

Most early work on recognizing discourse relations was tailored towards unambiguously marked, explicit discourse relations, such as those introduced by *because* (e.g. in "[*Peter despises Mary*] because [*she stole his yoghurt*]") since connectives unambiguously signal one particular relation.

In other cases, a connective can be ambiguous, as in the case of German '*nachdem*' (as/after/since). *Nachdem* can signal multiple types of discourse relations (e.g. purely temporal or temporal and causal), as in (1):[1]

(1) [$_{\text{arg1}}$ Nachdem sowohl das Verwaltungsgericht als auch das Oberverwaltungsgericht das Verbot bestätigt hatten,]
[$_{\text{arg2}}$ rief die NPD am Freitag nachmittag das Bundesverwaltungsgericht an].
[$_{\text{arg1}}$ *After both the Administrative Court and the Higher Administrative Court had confirmed the interdiction,*]
[$_{\text{arg2}}$ *the NPD appealed to the Federal Administrative Court.*] *(Temporal+cause)*

Another type of discourse relations are *implicit discourse relations*, which can occur between neighbouring spans of text without any discourse connective signaling them:[2]

(2) [$_{\text{arg1}}$ Mittlerweile ist das jedoch selbstverständlich]
[$_{\text{arg2}}$ Die gemeinsame Arbeit hilft, den anderen zu verstehen.]
[$_{\text{arg1}}$ *In the meantime, this has become a matter of course*] (implied:since) *(Explanation)*
[$_{\text{arg2}}$ *The common work helps to appreciate the other.*]

Researchers concerned with classifying the explicit discourse relations signalled by ambiguous discourse connectives, such as Miltsakaki et al. (2005) or Pitler and Nenkova (2009), claim that a small number of linguistic indicators (e.g., tense or syntactic context) can be used for successful disambiguation of discourse connectives, while Versley (2011) claims that additional semantic and structural information can help improving the classification accuracy in such cases.

In the case of implicit discourse relations, the absence of overt clues suggests that a combination of weak linguistic indicators and world knowledge is needed for successful disambiguation. Sporleder and Lascarides (2008) use positional and morphological features, as well as subsequences of words, lemmas or POS tags to disambiguate implicit relations in a reannotated subset of the RST discourse treebank (Carlson et al., 2003). Sporleder and Lascarides also show that (despite the corpus size of about 1000 examples) actual annotated relations are more useful than artificial examples derived from non-ambiguous explicit discourse relations.

Research using the implicit discourse relations annotated in the second release of the Penn Discourse Treebank (Prasad et al., 2008) shows a focus on shallow features: Pitler et al. (2009) find that the most important feature in their work on implicit discourse relations are word pairs. Lin et al. (2009) identify production rules from the constituent parse, as well as word pairs, to be the most important features in the system, with dependency triples not being useful as a features, and information from surrounding (gold-standard) discourse relations having only a minimal impact.

Most recent research, such as Feng and Hirst (2012), who classify a mixture of explicit and implicit discourse relations in the RST Discourse Treebank (Carlson et al., 2003), or Park and Cardie (2012), use these shallow features as their mainstay, adding surrounding relations and either semantic similarity (Feng and Hirst) or verb classes (Park and Cardie), leaving open the question how to incorporate more general linguistic information.

3 Feature-Node Graphs

Different information sources extract features that are relevant to subparts of an argument clause (e.g., information status and semantic class of a noun phrase), extracting features locally loses the information on each part. In contrast, we hope to maintain the information contained in these local features by representing them in *feature-node graphs*. This formalism also allows us to take into account more

[1]TüBa-D/Z corpus, sentence 7462
[2]TüBa-D/Z corpus, sentence 448

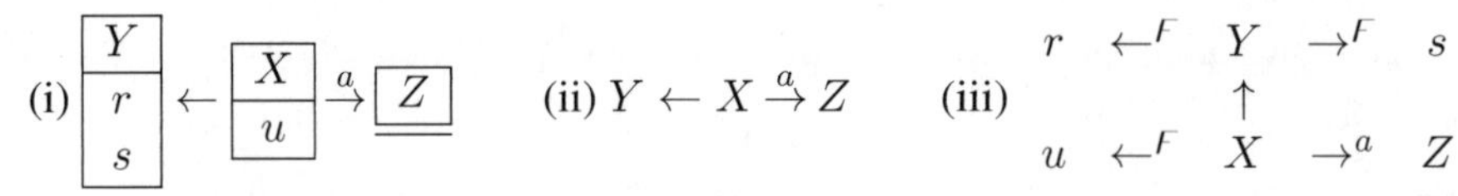

Figure 1: Example Feature-Node Graph (i), its backbone (ii), and its expansion (iii)

structure than n-grams (which are limited to relatively shallow information) or dependency triples (which would be too sparse in the case of typical discourse corpora). [3]

Formally, a feature-node graph consists of a set V of vertices with labels $L_V : V \to L$, a set of edges $E \subseteq V \times V$ with labels $L_E : E \to L$, with the addition of a set $F : V \to \mathcal{P}(L)$ that assigns to each vertex a set of *feature* labels.

The *backbone* of a feature-node graph is simply the labeled directed graph (V, L_V, E, L_E), without any features.

The *expansion* of a feature-node graph is the labeled directed graph (V', L'_V, E', L'_E) built by expanding the set of nodes to $V' = V \uplus \{(v, l) \in V \times L | l \in F(v)\}$ with labels $L'_V(v) = L_V(v)$ for all $v \in V$ and $L'_V((v, l)) = l$ for all $v \in V, l \in F(v)$ and correspondingly adding edges to get the complete set $E' = E \uplus \{(v, (v, l)) | l \in F(v)\}$, with a special symbol F for the labels of newly introduced edges, i.e. $L_E(v, (v, l)) = F$.

Figure 1 gives an example of a feature-node graph with the vertices X, Y and Z with $F(X) = \{u\}$, $F(Y) = \{r, s\}$, and $F(Z) = \emptyset$, edges $E = \{(X, Y), (X, Z)\}$ and edge labels $L_E((X, Y)) = \varepsilon$, $L_E((X, Z)) = a$.

Representing desired information as features (instead of, e.g., using words, or POS tags, as the node labels in a dependency graph) is advantageous because that two feature-node graphs of similar structures will have a common substructure as long as the backbone of that structure is identical. In the case of words as node labels, any non-identical word would prevent the detection of the common substructure.

Machine Learning on Feature-Node Graphs Using an attributed graph representation, we can apply general substructure mining and structured learning approaches to extract good candidates for informative substructures. In contrast to other fields where these approaches have been used (computational chemistry, computer vision), computational linguistics problems tend to have both larger data sets as well as larger structures. As a consequent, the naïve application of these structure mining algorithms would suffer from combinatorial explosion. In particular, a star-shaped graph (i.e., the typical case of a node with a large number of features) has exponentially many substructures, which would lead to both efficiency and performance problems, while an explicit distinction between features and backbone nodes can help by explicitly or implicitly limiting the number of features that a substructure can have in order to be considered.

In general, all approaches to learn from structure fall into one of three groups: *linearization* approaches, which decompose a structure into parts that can be presented to a linear classifier as a binary feature, *structure boosting* approaches, which determine the set of included substructures as an integral part of the learning task, and *kernel-based methods* which use dynamic programming for computing the dot product in an implied vector space of substructures. Kernel-based methods on trees have been used in the re-ranking of answers in a question answering system (Moschitti and Quarteroni, 2011), whereas Kudo et al. (2004) use boosting of graphs for a sentiment task (classifying reviews into positive/negative instances). Arora et al. (2010) use subgraph features in a linearization-based approach to sentiment classification.

For simplicity reasons, we use a linearization-based approach based on subgraph mining. Generating candidate subgraphs is done using a version of gSpan (Yan and Han, 2002) that we modified to distin-

[3]For reasons of efficiency as well as learnability, the structures we use to represent each discourse unit are simpler and more compact than the annotated corpus data from which they are derived.

Relation	# total	# implicit	% implicit	% relation
Contingency				
├Causal				
│ ├Result	133	88	66.2%	11.0%
│ └Explanation	122	81	66.4%	10.1%
├Conditional				
│ ├Consequence	26	5	19.2%	0.6%
│ ├Alternation	7	2	28.6%	0.2%
│ └Condition	13	—	0.0%	—
└Denial				
├ConcessionC	60	9	15.0%	1.1%
├Concession	34	5	14.7%	0.6%
└Anti-Explanation	3	3	100.0%	0.4%
Expansion				
├Elaboration				
│ ├Restatement	149	140	94.0%	17.4%
│ ├Instance	63	39	61.9%	4.9%
│ └Background	119	109	91.6%	13.6%
├Interpretation				
│ ├Summary	2	1	50.0%	0.1%
│ └Commentary	36	28	77.8%	3.5%
└Continuative				
├Continuation	89	71	79.8%	8.8%
└Conjunction	45	1	2.2%	0.1%
Temporal				
├Narration	127	70	55.1%	8.7%
└Precondition	34	23	67.6%	2.9%
Comparison				
├Parallel	55	23	41.8%	2.9%
└Contrast	66	26	39.4%	3.2%
Reporting				
├Attribution	67	67	100.0%	8.3%
└Source	65	65	100.0%	8.1%

%implicit: proportion of relation instances that are implicit, rather than explicit. *% rel*: percentage of given relation among all implicit. About 10% of the implicit instances have multiple labels (e.g. *Result+Narration*).

Table 1: Frequencies of discourse relations in the corpus of Gastel et al. (2011)

guish between 'backbone' nodes and features, and restrict the search space to subgraphs with at most three feature nodes by stopping the expansion of a subgraph pattern whenever it exceeds this limit.

4 Disambiguating Discourse Relations

In order to test our approach to discourse relation classification, we rely on two German data sets annotated with discourse relations: The first contains explicit discourse relations signalled by ambiguous temporal connectives (in particular *nachdem* – corresponding to English 'after/as/since' as the most ambiguous connective in that dataset), with an annotation scheme that has been described by Simon et al. (2011). The corpus contains 294 instances of *nachdem*, along with other, less ambiguous connectives. The second data set stems from a subcorpus that has received full annotation for all discourse relations, according to an annotation scheme described by Gastel et al. (2011). This corpus contains 803 implicit discourse relations that are not marked by a connective (using the criteria set forth by Pasch et al., 2003).

As can be seen from tables 1 and 2, the two annotation schemes include overlapping groups of relations (*Causal*, *Temporal* and *Comparison* relations), but the implicit relations cover a broader set of relations, whereas the temporal connectives are annotated with a finer granularity.

Relation	# total	% relation
Temporal	276	93.9%
Result		
├ situational		
│ ├ enable	94	31.6%
│ └ cause	65	21.7%
└ rhetorical		
├ evidence	12	4.1%
└ speech-act	6	2.4%
Comparison		
├ parallel	14	4.8%
└ contrast	16	5.8%

About 65% of *nachdem* instances have multiple labels.

Table 2: Frequencies of discourse relations in the *nachdem* data from Simon et al. (2011)

Among the most frequent unmarked relations are *Restatement* and *Background* from the Expansion/Elaboration group, which predominantly occur as implicit discourse relations, as well as *Result* and *Explanation*, which occur unmarked in about two thirds of the cases. In other cases, such as *Consequence*, *Concession* (is limited to cases of contraexpectation) and *ConcessionC* (which also includes more pragmatic concession relations), only a minority of relation instances is implicit whereas the majority is marked by an explicit connective.

Relations that are typically marked, such as *Contrast* – see example (3) – or *Concession/ConcessionC* – see example (4) – often contain weak indicators for the occurring discourse relation, such as the opposition *policemen-demonstrators* in the first case, or the negation of a reference to Arg1 ("*this wish will not be fullfilled soon*").

(3) [$_{\text{arg1}}$ 159 Polizisten wurden verletzt.]
[$_{\text{arg2}}$ Zahlen über verletzte DemonstrantInnen liegen nicht vor.] *(Contrast)*
[$_{\text{arg1}}$ *159 policemen were injured.*][arg2 *No data is available regarding injured demonstrators.*]

(4) [$_{\text{arg1}}$ "Nun will ich endlich in Frieden leben."]
[$_{\text{arg2}}$ Dieser Wunsch Ahmet Zeki Okcuoglus wird so bald nicht in Erfüllung gehen.]
[$_{\text{arg1}}$ *"Now I finally want to live in peace."*] (implied: However,)
[$_{\text{arg2}}$ *This wish of Ahmet Zeki Okcuoglu will not be fulfilled any time soon.*] *(ConcessionC)*

Improving the performance on explicit discourse relations beyond the easiest cases, especially in the case of the notoriously ambiguous temporal connectives, is only possible by exploiting weak indicators for a relation. Features exploiting these weak indicators are a key ingredient to successfully predicting both implicit discourse relations and the non-majority readings of explicit discourse relations with ambiguous temporal connectives.

4.1 Linguistic Features

We implemented a group of specialized linguistic features, which are inspired by those that were successfully used in related literature (Sporleder and Lascarides, 2008; Pitler et al., 2009; Versley, 2011).

As implicit discourse relations can occur intra- as well as intersententially, the **topological relation** between the arguments is classified by syntactic embedding (if one argument is in the pre- or post-field of the other), or as one preceding, succeeding or embedding the other.

Several features reproduce simple **morphosyntactic properties**: One feature signals the presence or of *negation* in either argument, either as a negating adverb (English *not*), determiners (*no*), or pronouns (*none*). A negated Arg1 would be tagged `1N+`, a non-negated one as `1N-`. *Tense and mood* of clauses in either argument are also incorporated as features (e.g. `1tense=t` for an Arg1 in pas(t) tense). The

head lemma(s) of each argument, which is normally the main verb, is also included as a feature (e.g. `1Lverletzen` for the Arg1 of example 3).

We also mark the **semantic type of adjuncts** present in either relation argument, with categories for temporal, causal, or concessive adverbials, conjunctive focus adverbs (*also*, *as well*), and commentary adverbs (*doubtlessly*, *actually*, *probably* ...). As an example, an Arg1 containing "*despite the cold*" would receive a feature `1adj_concessive`.

The detection of **cotaxonomic relations** between words in both arguments using the German wordnet GermaNet (Henrich and Hinrichs, 2010). Such pairs of contrasting lemmas, such as *hot-cold* or *policeman-demonstrator* commonly indicate a *parallel* or *contrast* relation. If two words share a common hyperonym (excluding the uppermost three levels of the noun hierarchy, which are not informative enough), feature values indicating the least-common-subsumer synset (such as *temperature adjective*) and up to two hyperonyms are added.

A **sentiment** feature uses the lists of emotional words and of 'shifting' words (which invert the emotional value of the phrase) by Klenner et al. (2009) as well as the most reliable emotional words from Remus et al. (2010). The combination of emotional words and shifting words into a feature is similar to Pitler et al. (2009): according to the presence of positive- or negative-emotion words, each relation argument is tagged as `POS`, `NEG` or `AMB`. When a negator or shifting expression is present, a "`-NEG`" is added to the tag, yielding, e.g. "`1pol NEG-NEG`" for an Arg1 phrase containing the words '*not bad*'.

4.2 Shallow Features

As mentioned in section 2, shallow lexical features empirically constitute a very important ingredient in the automatic classification of implicit (and ambiguous explicit) discourse relations, despite the fact that they lack most – semantic or structural – generalization capabilities. We implemented three groups of features that have been identified as important in the prior work of Sporleder and Lascarides (2008), Lin et al. (2009) and Pitler et al. (2009).

A first group of features captures (unigrams and) **bigrams** of words, lemmas, and part-of-speech tags. In this fashion, the bigram "*Zahlen über*" from Arg2 of (3) would be represented by word forms `2w_Zahlen_über`, lemmas `2l_Zahl_über` and POS tags `2p_NN_APPR`.[4]

Word pairs, i.e., pairs consisting of one word from each of the discourse relation arguments, have been identified as a very useful feature for the classification of implicit discourse relations in the Penn Discourse Treebank (Lin et al., 2009; Pitler et al., 2009), and, quite surprisingly, also for smaller datasets such as the discourse relations in the RST Discourse Treebank targeted by Feng and Hirst (2012) or the ambiguous connective dataset used by Versley (2011).[5] Because of the morphological richness of German, we use lemma pairs across sentences; for example (3), the lemma *Polizist* from Arg1 and the lemma *DemonstrantIn* from Arg1, among others, would be combined into a feature value `wp_Polizist_DemonstrantIn`.

Finally, **CFG productions** were used by Lin et al. (2009) to capture structural information, including parallelism. Context-free grammar expansions are extracted from the subtrees of the relation arguments and used as features by marking whether the corresponding rule type occurs only in one, or in both, arguments. In example (3), the CFG rule 'PX → APPR NX' for prepositional phrases occurs in both arguments, yielding a feature "`pr B PX=APPR-NX`", whereas the preterminal rule "APPR → über" only occurs in Arg2 (yielding "`pr 2 APPR=über`").

[4]Sporleder and Lascarides (2008) use a Boosting classifier (BoosTexter) that can extract and use arbitrary-length subsequences from its training data. As our dataset is small enough that we do not expect a significant contribution from longer sequences, we approximate the sequence boosting by extracting unigrams and bigrams. As with the other shallow features, unigrams and bigrams are subject to the same supervised feature selection that is also applied to subgraph features.

[5]For an illustration of the differences in size, consider that the Penn Discourse Treebank contains about 20 000 implicit discourse relations in 2159 articles, and the RST Discourse Treebank contains a lower number of 385 documents; Sporleder and Lascarides used a sample of 1 051 annotated implicit relations which were derived from the RST Discourse Treebank but manually relabeled according to an SDRT-like annotation scheme.

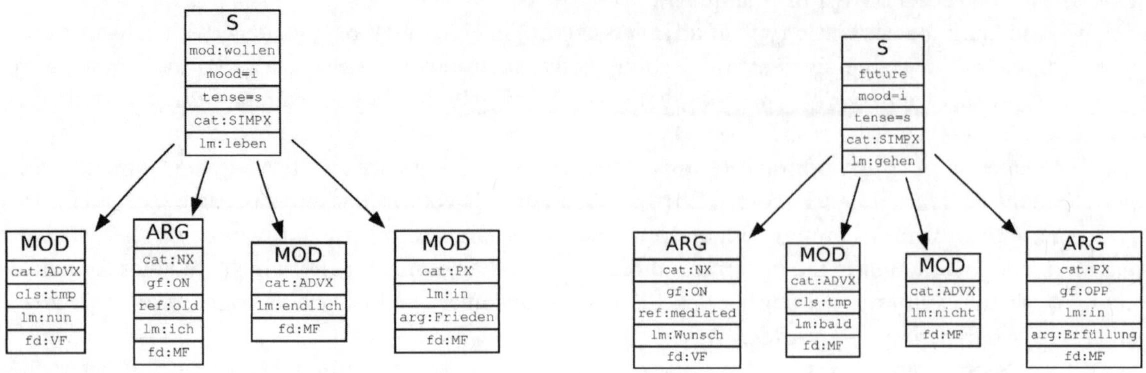

Figure 2: The complete graphs built from the implicit relation arguments "*Nun will ich endlich in Frieden leben.*" and "*Dieser Wunsch Ahmet Zeki Okcuoglus wird so bald nicht in Erfüllung gehen.*" – cf. ex. (4).

4.3 Graph construction

The **backbone** of the graph is built using nodes for a clause (`S`), and including children nodes for any clause adjuncts (`MOD`), verb arguments (`ARG`). In the case of relation arguments being in a (syntactic) matrix clause - subclause relationship (e.g. [$_{\text{arg1}}$ *Peter wears his blue pullover,*] [$_{\text{arg2}}$ *which he bought last year*]), the graph corresponding to the matrix clause receives a special node (`SUB-CL`, or `REL-CL` for relative clauses). This is universally the case for the explicit relations in the case of *nachdem*, but may also occur in the case of unmarked relations. For example, *Background* relations are frequently realized by relative clauses. Non-referring noun phrases (which are tagged as 'expletive' or 'inherent reflexive' in the referential layer of TüBa-D/Z), receive a node label `expletive` instead of `ARG`.

In each of the adjunct/argument nodes, we include **syntactic information** such as the category of the node (nominal/prepositional/adverbial phrase, e.g. `cat:NX` for a noun phrase), the topological field (cf. Höhle, 1986, e.g. `fd:MF` for a constituent occurring in the middle field) and, for clause arguments, the grammatical function (subject, accusative or dative object or predicative complement – e.g., `gf:OA` for the accusative object). Clauses nodes contain features for tense and mood based on the main and auxiliary/modal verb(s) of that clause (e.g., `mood=i`, `tense=s` for an indicative/past clause).

In the realm of **semantic information**, we use the heuristics of Versley (2011) to identify *semantic classes of adverbials*, in particular temporal, causal or concessive adverbials, conjunctive focus adverbs, and commentary adverbs. As the backbone of our graph structure abstracts from syntactic categories and only distinguishes adjuncts and arguments, it is possible to learn generalizations over different realizations of the same type of adjunct: for example, temporal adjuncts may be realized as a noun phrase (*next Monday*), a prepositional phrase (*in the last week*), an adverb (*later*), or a clause (*when Peter was ill*).

Noun phrase arguments are annotated with information pertaining to their **information status**, marking them either as *old* (if their referent has already been introduced), *mediated* (if a modifier – e.g. the genitive *John's* in *John's hat* – has been previously introduced), or *new* (if neither the phrase nor any of its modifiers has a previous mention). Additionally, we use a semantic categorization into persons (PER), organizations (ORG), locations (LOC), events (EVT) and other entities. In the case of named entities, this information is derived from the existing named entity annotation in the TüBa-D/Z treebank (by simply mapping the GPE label to LOC); for phrases with a nominal head, this information is derived using the heuristics of Versley (2006), which use information from GermaNet, semantic lexicons, and heuristics based on surface morphology. Clauses as well as arguments and adjuncts are annotated with their **semantic head**; prepositional phrases are, in addition, annotated with the semantic head of the preposition's argument (*in the next year*).

From the graph representations of relation arguments that are created in this step, frequent subgraphs are extracted. The subgraphs must occur at least five times in either the Arg1 or Arg2 graph, have at most seven nodes, of which at least two must be backbone nodes, and at most three can be feature nodes.

For the learning task, features are created by concatenating an identifier for the subgraph (e.g. `graph1234`) with a suffix specifying whether it occurs only in the main clause (_1), only in the subclause (_2), or in both clauses (_12). Detecting subgraphs that occur in both clauses allows the system to take into account parallelism in terms of syntactic and/or semantic properties of parts of each clause.

Both the shallow features and the subgraph features are subject to **supervised feature selection**: In each fold of the 10-fold crossvalidation, the training portion is used to score each feature and only include the most informatives one in each fold. For this, an association measure between the examples from that training portion and, for each relation label, the examples in the training portion that the label occurs in, is determined. The best score over all the labels is kept, and is used to filter out features that score less than the top-N features of that group. Supervised feature selection has been used by Lin et al. (2009), using pointwise mutual information (PMI) on candidate productions and word pairs, and in the work of Arora et al. (2010) using Pearson's χ^2 statistic on candidate subgraphs. We tried PMI, χ^2 and the Dice coefficient $\frac{2|A \cap B|}{|A||B|}$ as association measures, and empirically found that the Dice coefficient worked best in the case of implicit discourse relations.

5 Evaluation Results

For both the 294 explicit *nachdem* relations and the 803 implicit discourse relations, we use a 10-fold cross-validation scheme where, successively, one tenth of the data is automatically labeled by a model from the remaining nine tenth of the data. Multiple relation labels are predicted by using binary classifiers (one-vs-all reduction) and using confidence values to choose one or several labels among those that have the most confident positive classification. In the case of multiple positive classifications (e.g., if *Reporting*, *Temporal* and *Expansion* all receive a positive classification), relations are only considered for the 'second' label if the most-confident label and the potential second label have been seen together in the training data (e.g. *Contingency* and *Temporal* can occur together, but *Reporting* will not be extended by a second relation labels). In a second step, the coarse grained relation label (or labels) is extended up to the finest taxonomy level (e.g., an initial coarse-grained *Contingency* label is extended to *Contingency.Causal.Explanation*). In our experiments, we use SVMperf, an SVM implementation that is able to train classifiers optimized for performance on positive instances (Joachims, 2005).

Tables 3 and 4 provide evaluation figures for different subsets of the presented features, using aggregate measures over relations both at the coarsest level (for implicit discourse relations, the five categories *Contingency, Expansion, Temporal, Comparison, Reporting*), and the finest level (which contains twenty-one relations in the case of implicit relations).

For each level of granularity, we can measure the quality of the classifier's predictions in terms of an average over relation tokens, giving partial credit for partially matching labelings (e.g., a system prediction of *Narration* or *Narration+Comparison*, instead of gold-standard *Narration+Result*). This measure, the **dice score**, assigns partial credit for a relation token when system and/or gold standard contain multiple labels and both label sets overlap, calculated as $\frac{2|G \cap S|}{|G|+|S|}$ – an exact match would be scored as 1.0, whereas guessing a sub- or superset (e.g. only *Result* instead of *Result+Narration*) would give a contribution of 0.66 for that example, and overlapping predictions (*Result+Comparison* instead of *Result+Narration*) would get a partial credit of 0.5. As an average over relation types, we can also calculate an average of the F-score over all relations, yielding the **macro-averaged F-score** (MAFS).

Because the label distribution is heavily skewed – some relations, such as *Restatement*, are relatively frequent with 140 occurrences, while, e.g., *Contrast* with 26 occurrences, is much less frequent – a classification that is biased towards the more frequent relations will receive higher token-weighted (dice) scores and lower type-weighted (MAFS) scores, whereas an unbiased system would receive lower dice and higher macro-averaged F scores.

	3 relations Dice	3 relations MAFS	7 relations Dice	7 relations MAFS	Temp F_1	Result F_1	Comp F_1	contr F_1	cause F_1	evid F_1
Temp+enable	0.829	0.573	0.680	0.208	0.97	0.75	0.00	0.00	0.00	0.00
random	0.751	0.562	0.626	0.211	0.94	0.62	0.13	0.06	0.23	0.00
ling	0.830	0.666	0.698	0.358	0.97	0.75	0.28	0.00	0.35	0.37
Ver11	0.846	0.751	0.717	0.361	0.97	0.76	0.52	0.40	**0.38**	0.26
gr(2000,χ^2)	0.839	0.727	0.688	0.381	0.97	0.77	0.45	0.31	0.13	0.23
Ver11+gr(5k,χ^2)	**0.859**	**0.774**	**0.734**	**0.472**	0.97	**0.78**	**0.57**	**0.51**	0.36	**0.47**

Table 3: Results for disambiguation of *nachdem*. Rows include the specialized linguistic features of Versley (2011), as *ling*, a system additionally using word pairs and CFG (with unsupervised feature selection), as *Ver11*, and finally versions including the graph representation (*gr* and *Ver11+gr*). Shaded rows indicate variants using the graph representation.

Disambiguating *nachdem* For the disambiguation of the ambiguous temporal connective *nachdem*, we use a set of linguistic and shallow features to reproduce the results of Versley (2011), similar to that described in section 3, but with very few exceptions.[6] Looking at the aggregate measures, we see that the graph-based features in isolation already perform quite well, surpassing a version with linguistic features, but no word pairs or CFG productions. Adding subgraph features with appropriate feature selection to the complete system (including linguistic and shallow features) yields a further improvement over a relatively strong baseline.

Implicit relations Table 4 presents both aggregate measures (Dice, macro-averaged F-measure) as well as scores for the most important coarse-grained relations. We provide results for the full graph (*grA*), a version with all features except information status (*grB*), and finally a minimal version that excludes all semantic features and lemmas (*grC*).

In general, both the linguistic features and the graph features perform much better than the shallow features (with the best single source of information being the complete graph), and also that a combination of linguistic and all shallow features (*all–gr*) suffers from

In the second section of the table, the influence of different information sources is detailed. We see that, despite the skewed distribution of relations, all information sources outperform the most-frequent-sense baseline by themselves. By providing a higher precision on *Expansion* relations, and generally better performance on *Reporting* relations, the graph-based representation performs better than any of the other information sources, and is the only information source to provide enough information for the identification of *Comparison* relations. The third group of rows, showing combinations of the linguistic features with the shallow information sources and with the graph representation, shows that, while the addition of specialized features to the shallow ones yields a general improvement, the graph-based representation still works best; for *Temporal* relations, we see that the noise brought in by the shallow features hinders their identification more than in the case of the graph-based representation.

The last part of table 4 provides evaluation results for a system using the complete set of information sources (*all*), for systems leaving out one of the shallow information sources (*all–bi*, *all–wp*, *all–pr*), and a system using only linguistic and shallow features but no graph information (*all–gr*). We see that, in general, the identification of rare relations such as *Temporal*, *Comparison*, and *Reporting* is helped by the graph representation (the full system obtains the best MAFS scores of 0.438 and 0.208, for coarse- and fine-grained relations, respectively, against 0.388 and 0.145 for the system without graph information). System variants with graph information also obtain higher coarse-grained dice scores (0.564–0.571) than the version without graph information (0.551 for *all–gr*). In the same vein, we see that the parsimonious *grC* graph gives the best combination result (*allC–pr*, including linguistic, word pair, unigram/bigram, and graph features) despite the more informative *grA* giving the best results in isolation.

[6]The *nachdem* relations are predicted without *sentiment* feature, but with the earlier system's punctuation and compatible pronouns features. The shallow features of Versley (2011) include word pairs and context-free rules, with unsupervised feature selection.

	5 relations Dice	5 relations MAFS	21 relations Dice	21 relations MAFS	Cont F_1	Expn F_1	Temp F_1	Comp F_1	Rept F_1
Restatement	0.474	0.129	0.161	0.014	0.00	0.00	0.65	0.00	0.00
random	0.338	0.233	0.096	0.056	0.06	0.27	0.50	0.21	0.14
ling only	0.540	**0.396**	**0.274**	0.127	0.40	0.68	0.32	0.00	0.58
bi(5k)	0.516	0.301	0.260	0.098	0.40	0.65	0.00	0.00	0.45
wp(2k)	0.494	0.307	0.198	0.084	0.42	0.65	0.02	0.05	0.40
pr(5k)	0.478	0.154	0.192	0.034	0.12	0.65	0.00	0.00	0.00
grA(20k)	**0.559**	0.381	0.269	0.163	0.39	0.69	0.24	0.00	0.59
grB(20k)	0.549	0.387	**0.274**	**0.187**	0.36	0.69	0.22	0.09	0.57
grC(20k)	0.544	0.382	0.268	0.164	0.36	0.68	0.23	0.09	0.55
ling+bi(5k)	0.545	0.399	0.300	0.141	0.39	0.69	0.33	0.00	0.59
ling+wp(2k)	0.552	0.408	0.277	0.144	0.42	0.68	0.33	0.00	0.61
ling+pr(5k)	0.546	0.399	0.297	0.142	0.40	0.68	0.33	0.00	0.58
ling+grA(20k)	0.574	0.389	0.285	0.161	0.37	0.70	0.28	0.00	0.59
ling+grB(20k)	0.579	0.394	0.294	0.173	0.36	0.71	0.30	0.00	0.60
ling+grC(20k)	**0.580**	**0.411**	**0.307**	**0.179**	0.37	0.70	0.35	0.03	0.60
all-gr	0.538	0.343	0.273	0.116	0.42	0.68	0.10	0.00	0.52
allA	0.572	0.408	0.306	0.178	0.43	0.70	0.29	0.00	0.62
allB	0.573	0.411	0.301	0.171	0.40	0.70	0.32	0.00	0.63
allC	0.579	0.422	0.309	0.177	0.38	0.70	0.35	0.04	0.65
allA-pr	0.576	0.407	0.300	0.174	0.41	0.70	0.32	0.00	0.61
allB-pr	**0.581**	0.410	0.298	0.171	0.40	0.70	0.32	0.00	0.62
allC-pr	**0.581**	**0.425**	**0.310**	**0.185**	0.36	0.70	0.36	0.07	0.64

Table 4: Implicit discourse relations: specialized linguistic features (*ling*), word/lemma/pos bigrams (*bi*), word pairs (*wp*), CFG productions (*pr*), and different methods for constructing graphs (*grA*, *grB* and *grC*). Shaded rows indicate variants using the graph representation.

6 Conclusion

In this article, we presented a novel way to identify discourse relations using feature-node graphs to represent rich linguistic information. We evaluated our approach on two datasets: one dataset containing implicit discourse relations and one containing explicit discourse relations with the ambiguous temporal connective *nachdem*. We showed in both cases that using the graph-based representation, with appropriate heuristics for supervised feature selection, yields an improvement even over a strong state-of-the-art system using linguistic and shallow features.

Besides applying the techniques on other corpora, issues for future work would include the use of unlabeled data to improve the generalization capability of the classifier, or the use of reranking techniques to combine local decisions into a global labeling.

Acknowledgements The author is grateful to the Deutsche Forschungsgemeinschaft (DFG) for funding as part of SFB 833, and to Corina Dima, Erhard Hinrichs, Emily Jamison and Verena Henrich, as well as the three anonymous reviewers, for suggestions and constructive comments on earlier versions of this paper.

References

Arora, S., E. Mayfield, C. Penstein-Rosé, and E. Nyberg (2010). Sentiment classification using automatically extracted subgraph features. In *NAACL 2010*.

Carlson, L., D. Marcu, and M. E. Okurowski (2003). Building a discourse-tagged corpus in the framework of rhetorical structure theory. In *Current Directions in Discourse and Dialogue*. Kluwer.

Feng, V. W. and G. Hirst (2012). Text-level discourse parsing with rich linguistic features. In *ACL 2012*.

Gastel, A., S. Schulze, Y. Versley, and E. Hinrichs (2011). Annotation of implicit discourse relations in the TüBa-D/Z treebank. In *GSCL 2011*.

Henrich, V. and E. Hinrichs (2010). GernEdiT - the GermaNet editing tool. In *Proceedings of the Seventh Conference on International Language Resources and Evaluation (LREC 2010)*, pp. 2228–2235.

Höhle, T. (1986). Der Begriff "Mittelfeld", Anmerkungen über die Theorie der topologischen Felder. In *Akten des Siebten Internationalen Germanistenkongresses 1985*, pp. 329–340.

Joachims, T. (2005). A support vector method for multivariate performance measures. In *Proceedings of the International Conference on Machine Learning (ICML)*.

Klenner, M., S. Petrakis, and A. Fahrni (2009). Robust compositional polarity classification. In *Recent Advances in Natural Language Processing (RANLP 2009)*.

Kudo, T., E. Maeda, and Y. Matsumoto (2004). An application of boosting to graph classification. In *NIPS 2004*.

Lin, Z., M.-Y. Kan, and H. T. Ng (2009). Recognizing implicit discourse relations in the Penn Discourse Treebank. In *EMNLP 2009*.

Marcu, D. (2000). The rhetorical parsing of unrestricted texts: A surface-based approach. *Computational Linguistics 26*, 3.

Miltsakaki, E., N. Dinesh, R. Prasad, A. Joshi, and B. Webber (2005). Experiments on sense annotations and sense disambiguation of discourse connectives. In *TLT 2005*.

Moschitti, A. and S. Quarteroni (2011). Linguistic kernels for answer re-ranking in question answering systems. *Information Processing and Management 47*, 825–842.

Park, J. and C. Cardie (2012). Improving implicit discourse relation recognition through feature set optimization. In *SIGDIAL 2012*, pp. 108–112.

Pasch, R., U. Brauße, E. Breindl, and U. H. Waßner (2003). *Handbuch der deutschen Konnektoren*. Berlin / New York: Walter de Gruyter.

Pitler, E., A. Louis, and A. Nenkova (2009). Automatic sense prediction for implicit discourse relations in text. In *ACL-IJCNLP 2009*.

Pitler, E. and A. Nenkova (2009). Using syntax to disambiguate explicit discourse connectives in text. In *ACL 2009 short papers*.

Prasad, R., N. Dinesh, A. Lee, E. Miltsakaki, L. Robaldo, A. Joshi, and B. Webber (2008). The Penn Discourse Treebank 2.0. In *Proceedings of LREC 2008*.

Remus, R., U. Quasthoff, and G. Heyer (2010). SentiWS — a publicly available German-language resource for sentiment analysis. In *Proceedings of LREC 2010*.

Simon, S., E. Hinrichs, S. Schulze, and Y. Versley (2011). Handbuch zur Annotation expliziter und impliziter Diskursrelationen im Korpus der Tübinger Baumbank des Deutschen (TüBa-D/Z) Teil I: Diskurskonnektoren. Technical report, Seminar für Sprachwissenschaft, Universität Tübingen.

Sporleder, C. and A. Lascarides (2008). Using automatically labelled examples to classify rhetorical relations: An assessment. *Natural Language Engineering 14*(3), 369–416.

Versley, Y. (2006). A constraint-based approach to noun phrase coreference resolution in German newspaper text. In *Konferenz zur Verarbeitung Natürlicher Sprache (KONVENS 2006)*.

Versley, Y. (2011). Multilabel tagging of discourse relations in ambiguous temporal connectives. In *Proceedings of Recent Advances in Natural Language Processing (RANLP 2011)*.

Yan, X. and J. Han (2002). gSpan: Graph-based substructure pattern mining. In *Proceedings fo the Second IEEE Conference on Data Mining (ICDM 2002)*.

What excludes an Alternative in Coherence Relations?

Bonnie Webber
School of Informatics
University of Edinburgh
bonnie.webber@ed.ac.uk

Abstract

This paper identifies features that occur frequently in coherence relations labelled CHOSEN ALTERNATIVE. This achieves two goals: (1) to identify evidence for an argument being considered an alternative excluded from further consideration, and (2) to contribute to the automatic identification of coherence relations and their arguments. It is shown that the simplest of these features occur significantly more often in implicit CHOSEN ALTERNATIVE relations than in explicit CHOSEN ALTERNATIVE relations, where a connective helps signal this sense.

1 Introduction

There have been two main approaches to identifying what coherence relations can hold between the segments in a discourse. Knott (1996) calls one *theoretical*, grounded in a philosophical view of language, and the other *empirical*, grounded in the discourse connectives that can be taken as explicit expressions of coherence relations. Knott's own approach starts with the first, characterizing patterns of meaning-preserving *substitutability* between connectives — whether two connectives are freely substitutable wherever they occur as connectives (hence *synonyms*), contingently substitutable (one a *hyponym* of the other), or non-substitutable (hence *exclusive*). He then explains these patterns in terms of connectives being more or less specific with respect to one or more theoretically-motivated features and their (exclusive) values. In later work, Knott and Sanders (1998) show how the approach works for subsets of connectives in both English and Dutch. It does not, however, explain how the same coherence relations may be seen to hold when connectives are absent.

Automated approaches to recognizing coherence relations do not assume that their sense arises solely from connectives. Rather, these approaches take as evidence, lexical and syntactic features of the arguments of the coherence relation, nearby coherence relations, high-level text structure, etc. (Feng and Hirst, 2012; Ghosh et al., 2011; Hernault et al., 2010; Lin et al., 2010; Lin, 2012; Marcu, 2000; Marcu and Echihabi, 2002; Sagae, 2009; Sporleder and Lascarides, 2008; Subba et al., 2006). As one might expect, automated approaches use simple features that can be computed reliably. However, performance in recognizing coherence relations in the absense of connectives is still low, and significant improvement is unlikely to come from simply trying new Machine Learning methods over the same set of simple features. A bigger pay-off might come from identifying more predictive features. That is the goal of the current work.

The particular coherence relation of interest here is one that holds when the discourse connective *instead* is present, but can also hold when it isn't. In the Penn Discourse TreeBank 2.0 (Prasad et al., 2008), the sense is called CHOSEN ALTERNATIVE. It is defined as holding when "two alternatives are evoked in the discourse but only one is taken" — meaning still being considered while the other isn't (The PDTB Research Group, 2008).

Such a definition leads to two questions: What, if any, features suggest that the two arguments of a coherence relation denote *alternatives*, and what, if any, features indicate that one of them has been *excluded* from further consideration? As Sporleder and Lascarides (2008) argue, one should not assume *a priori* that the same features will be at work when a connective is present and when it isn't. However, one satisfying outcome of the current effort is that when the most common features are present, an explicit connective is often absent. When the evidence is more subtle, explicit connectives are more often present.

The PDTB 2.0 provides a good basis for starting to address these questions because it contains over 40K manual annotations of coherence relations that are either signalled by explicit discourse connectives or that hold between adjacent sentences that lack such an explicit signal (Prasad et al., 2008). Additional evidence is taken from a corpus of >300 singly-annotated tokens of the discourse connective *instead* and its arguments gathered over several years (the *Instead Corpus*).

The paper is structured as follows: Section 2 presents the connective *instead* and its place in earlier approaches to coherence relations. It then presents the annotation of coherence relations in the PDTB 2.0. Within this framework, *instead* is taken to be an unambiguous signal of the coherence relation CHOSEN ALTERNATIVE, one of three types of ALTERNATIVE relations annotated in the PDTB 2.0. The section concludes by laying out the scope of the current study with respect to CHOSEN ALTERNATIVE, which is to argue for what characterizes the argument that serves as its *excluded alternative*. Section 3 describes several constructions that commonly appear there in explicit CHOSEN ALTERNATIVE. Section 4 then shows that three of them (negation markers, *downward-entailing* constructions, and event *modals*) are even more frequent in the even larger percentage of implicit CHOSEN ALTERNATIVE. Finally, Section 5 lays out some open issues and some thoughts on further work that should be done.

2 *Instead* and CHOSEN ALTERNATIVE

2.1 Background

As noted in the Introduction, approaches to coherence relations differ in whether they start from an abstract theory of what relations can hold between units of text, or from empirical data on the discourse connectives that serve as explicit ways of expressing those relations.

Rhetorical Structure Theory (Mann and Thompson, 1988) belongs to the first sort. In the first large corpus annotated in the framework of RST — the *RST Corpus* (Carlson et al., 2003) — coherence relations are annotated on the basis of definitions that do not link them with any particular discourse connectives (Carlson and Marcu, 2001). Still, examining the corpus for those elementary discourse units (EDUs) that begin *"Instead, ...* ", one finds eleven such EDUs: three in CONTRAST relations, four in PREFERENCE and two in ANTITHESIS relations (both being types of COMPARISON relations), one in a REASON relation and one in an ELABORATION relation. Given this, one can not associate the connective *instead* with any particular coherence relation (or relations, if it is ambiguous) because there is no record for why any of these relations has been taken to hold between EDUs other than their definitions.

Instead is one of the discourse connectives that Knott (1996) has analysed. He places it at a very high level of his substitutability structure, taking it to be specified only for the feature *polarity* with value *negative*. *Polarity* is defined in terms of a defeasible rule $P \rightarrow Q$. Given two segments A and C connected by a connective whose polarity is *positive*, A=P, C=Q and the defeasible rule is specified to succeed. If the polarity of the connective is *negative*, A=P, C is inconsistent with Q, and the rule is specified to fail. If a connective is unspecified for *polarity*, then neither case holds. But *instead* having negative polarity does not provide any information about its arguments beyond the fact that the speaker must believe in the existence of such a rule and that it fails for the given arguments.

While Martin (1992) also approaches coherence relations from theory (here, systemic-functional grammar (Halliday and Hasan, 1976)), he illustrates each relation with one or more English connectives. One can see from this that he takes *instead* to convey the COMPARATIVE relation he calls REPLACEMENT. In later work on families of coherence relations and connectives in English and German, Stede (2012) similarly mentions both English *instead* and German *anstatt*, as both expressing the SUBSTITUTION relation, a sub-type of CONTRASTIVE RELATION. Both REPLACEMENT and SUBSTITUTION seem intuitively to represent the same notion as CHOSEN ALTERNATIVE in the Penn Discourse TreeBank.

2.2 The Penn Discourse TreeBank 2.0

As noted in the Introduction, the Penn Discourse TreeBank 2.0 (or PDTB 2.0) contains over 40K manual annotations of coherence relations over the *Penn Wall Street Journal Corpus*, over 18K signalled by explicit discourse connectives and over 16K holding between adjacent sentences that lack this explicit signal (Prasad et al., 2008). In the latter case, readers are taken to infer an *implicit* discourse connective relating the adjacent units, and their annotation includes an indication of the connective that best conveys the inferred relation. The remaining annotation includes around 5K tokens of *entity relations*, where the second sentence only serves to provide some further description of an entity in the first, akin to *entity-based coherence* (Knott et al., 2001), plus another 624 tokens in which the coherence relation is signalled by some alternative lexicalization (such as "that means") other than a conjunction or discourse adverbial and another 254 in which no relation is inferred as holding between the adjacent sentences.

Annotated for each coherence relation are its arguments, the one or more sense relations taken to hold between them, and any attribution relations taken to hold over either the relation as a whole or either of its arguments.

All coherence relations have two and only two arguments. When a relation is realised with an explicit connective or alternative lexicalization (ALTLEX), one of those arguments derives from the clause that is syntactically bound to the connective. In the PDTB 2.0, this is called **Arg2**. The other argument, called *Arg1*, may be linked syntactically to **Arg2** if the connective is a subordinating conjunction or coordinating conjunction (Ex. 1). Or it may be elsewhere in the sentence or previous discourse, if the connective is a discourse adverbial (Ex. 2). If the coherence relation is realized through sentence adjacency and an *implicit connective*, the second sentence is taken to provide **Arg2** and the first sentence, *Arg1*.

(1) Several years ago he gave up *trying to persuade Miami to improve its city-owned Orange Bowl*, **and** instead **built his own $100 million coliseum with private funds**. [wsj_0126]

(2) The tension was evident on Wednesday evening during Mr. Nixon's final banquet toast, normally an opportunity *for reciting platitudes about eternal friendship*. Instead, **Mr. Nixon reminded his host, ..., that Americans haven't forgiven China's leaders for the military assault of June 3-4 that killed hundreds, and perhaps thousands, of demonstrators**. [wsj_0093]

The senses used in annotation are drawn from a hierarchy of semantic classes whose top level consists of four abstract classes: TEMPORAL, CONTINGENCY, COMPARISON and EXPANSION. Each of these is further divided into several types, which may themselves be further divided into sub-types (The PDTB Research Group, 2008). Annotators could associate one or more senses with each explicit or implicit connective or ALTLEX, with each sense at the level of sub-type or type, if the annotator couldn't decide among its sub-types.

In the PDTB 2.0, 108 of the 112 tokens of *instead* are annotated EXPANSION.ALTERNATIVE.CHOSEN ALTERNATIVE (here, simply CHOSEN ALTERNATIVE). Its higher sense type ALTERNATIVE is taken to hold "when the two arguments denote alternative situations" (The PDTB Research Group, 2008) and its sister sub-types are CONJUNCTIVE (taken to hold when both alternatives are possible) and DISJUNCTIVE (taken to hold when only one alternative needs to be possible). CHOSEN ALTERNATIVE itself is taken to hold when "two alternatives are evoked in the discourse but only one is taken".

Of the four tokens not annotated as CHOSEN ALTERNATIVE, Ex. 3 is annotated ALTERNATIVE rather than the more specific ALTERNATIVE.CHOSEN ALTERNATIVE, though it is hard to imagine the annotators being uncertain about which sub-type holds, Examples 4–5 have been annotated COMPARISON.CONTRAST and Ex. 6, COMPARISON.CONTRAST.JUXTAPOSITION. The latter is defined in terms of a comparison between a shared property having values taken to be *alternatives*. While there will be more to say about CONTRAST versus CHOSEN ALTERNATIVE in Section 5, there is no reason not to consider all four as instances of CHOSEN ALTERNATIVE, if only for considering the set of features its first argument dispays, which are no different than other instances of *instead*.

(3) *The group didn't make a formal offer*, **but** instead [EXPANSION.ALTERNATIVE] **told UAL's advisers before the most-recent board meeting that it was working on a bid valued at between $225 and $240 a share**. [wsj_1010]

(4) *At the 50%-leveraged Zenith Income Fund, portfolio manager John Bianchi recently dumped Mesa Petroleum, Wickes and Horsehead Industries, among others, ...* **Because of the recent junk-market turmoil, the fund is considering investing in other issues** instead [COMPARISON.CONTRAST], **including mortgage-backed bonds**. [wsj_0983]

(5) This ministry has done nothing *to correct the misunderstandings and misperceptions that are at the root of Japan's deteriorating image*. Instead, **it seems to be using foreign pressure and even the trade conflict to expand its sphere of influence vis a vis other ministries.**

(6) *It presents no great issue of legal principle, no overriding question of family law or the law of contempt.* Instead [COMPARISON.CONTRAST.JUXTAPOSITION], **it turns on the disputed and elusive facts of "who did what to whom"**. [wsj_0946]

2.3 The Scope of the Current Study

The current study addresses the second question raised in Section 1: What, if any, features indicate that one of the *alternatives* of a CHOSEN ALTERNATIVE relation has been *excluded* from further consideration? This is of practical, as well as of theoretical interest because in English, the *excluded alternative* derives from *Arg1* of the relation.[1] Because this argument is not syntactically linked to the connective, its location and identity is more difficult for automated methods to determine (Webber et al., 2012). Also, for implicit coherence relations, the same features that can be used to identify *Arg1* of an explicit CHOSEN ALTERNATIVE may also be used to suggest that CHOSEN ALTERNATIVE holds in the absense of an explicit connective.

3 Features manifest in CHOSEN ALTERNATIVE

For brevity, instances of CHOSEN ALTERNATIVE that have an explicit connective will simply be called explicit CHOSEN ALTERNATIVE, while those that lack an explicit connective associated with this sense will be called implicit CHOSEN ALTERNATIVE.

This analysis of features characteristic of the arguments of explicit and implicit CHOSEN ALTERNATIVE is based on 289 multiply-annotated tokens in the PDTB 2.0 (118 explicit and 171 implicit), and seven multiply-annotated tokens in the BioDRB corpus (Prasad et al., 2011). The *Instead Corpus* mentioned in Section 1 is used as a source of shorter, simpler examples.

Approximately 70% of the cases of explicit CHOSEN ALTERNATIVE in the PDTB and BioDRB manifest features discussed in Sections 3.1–3.3 below. And ~87% of the even larger number of implicit CHOSEN ALTERNATIVE do the same (Section 4).

3.1 Negation markers

Of the 118 tokens of explicit CHOSEN ALTERNATIVE, the largest subset have an explicit *negation* marker associated with *Arg1*. Such a marker is sufficient to allow the sense that *Arg1* is an alternative that is no longer in consideration. Negation markers here include *not* (Ex. 8), *no* (Ex. 9), *never* (Ex. 10), and *no one*.

(8) If the flex is worn, *do not use insulating tape to repair it*. Instead, **you should replace it ...**.

[1] Paola Merlo has suggested [personal communication] that this doesn't hold in all languages. She identifies the connective *invece* as expressing CHOSEN ALTERNATIVE in Italian and the closest in meaning to English *instead*. While *Invece* allows either alternative in *Arg1* (Ex. 7), cases like (7b) do not occur in English.

(7) a. John non ha mangiato gli spinaci. Invece Maria si'.
(John didn't eat spinach. Instead Mary did.)

b. John ha mangiato gli spinaci. Invece Maria no.
(John ate spinach. *Instead Mary didn't.)

(9) *There are no separate rafters in a flat roof*; instead, **the ceiling joists of the top story support the roofing**.

(10) *Sue Grafton has never bowed to fad or fashion.* Instead, **she's kept her whip-smart private investigator, Kinsey Millhone, focused on modestly scaled domestic crimes ....**

That the negation marker is critical to interpreting *Arg1* as excluded from consideration, can be seen by the infelicity of similar examples without the negation marker.

(11) If the flex is worn, *use insulating tape to repair it.* *Instead, **you should replace it ....**

(12) *There are separate rafters in a flat roof*; *instead, **the ceiling joists of the top story support the roofing**.

(13) *Sue Grafton has bowed to fad or fashion.* *Instead, **she's kept her whip-smart private investigator, Kinsey Millhone, ...**

3.2 Downward Entailment

Since negation markers are *downward entailing* (DE), one might check whether all DE constructions can exclude *Arg1* of explicit CHOSEN ALTERNATIVE from consideration, or if not all, whether a larger set of DE constructions than just negation markers can do so.

Constructions that are *downward entailing* (⇓) support valid reasoning from a set to a member. Ones that are *upward entailing* (⇑) support valid reasoning in the opposite direction, from a member to a set. Upward entailment means that one can reason from *John owns a beagle* to *John owns a dog*. Negation markers, being downward entailing, support valid reasoning from *John doesn't own a dog* to *John doesn't own a beagle*.

In the corpora analyzed in this study, the second largest set of explicit CHOSEN ALTERNATIVE relations have a DE predicate associated with *Arg1* that is other than a negation marker. Examples 14–15 below show two of them: *reject* (from *John* ***rejected*** *dogs*, conclude *John* ***rejected*** *beagles*) and *too* *<modifier>* (from *John was* ***too ill*** *to own a dog*, conclude *John was* ***too ill*** *to own a beagle*).

(14) *In India, he* ***rejects*** *the identification of Indianness with Hinduism, ...* Instead **he champions Mr Tagore's view ....** [The Economist, 18 June 2005]

(15) *The current system is too bureaucratic ....* Instead, **research councils should "pay the full costs of the projects they fund ...".** [Research Fortnight, 28 April 2004]

Other DE predicates that appear in *Arg1* of explicit CHOSEN ALTERNATIVE in the PDTB or BioDRB are shown in Figure 1: This list, although long, is only a subset of DE constructions. What about other ones? Since neither dictionaries nor other lexical resources record direction of entailing as a property, Danescu-Niculescu-Mizil et al. (2009) attempted to extract DE constructions from the large BLLIP corpus (LDC catalogue LDC2000T43), using cooccurence with *Negative Polarity Items* (NPI) like "any" as a cue.

Figure 2 shows the 55 most frequent DE lemmas that Danescu-Niculescu-Mizil et al. (2009) extracted from the corpus: Four are *negation markers* or contain them (cannot, never, nobody, nothing), twelve have attested occurences in *Arg1* of *instead* in the PDTB or BioDRB (as indicated in Figure 1), and all but two of the others (*compensate for* and *essential for*) can be found on the web in similar *Arg1* position as the attested forms. Why does neither *compensate for* nor *essential for* seem to license an alternative being excluded from consideration, as in

(16) Olivia compensates for eating by exercising. *Instead she ???

(17) Talent is essential for singing. *Instead ???

First, observe that all the DE constructions in Figure 1 and all the lemmas in Figure 2 except for *compensate for* and *essential for* are negative assertions: e.g., *bar*, *block*, *prevent*, and *prohibit* assert that something does **not** occur. In contrast, what is negative in *compensate for* and *essential for* is what they presuppose: *Compensate for* presupposes that one has done something that one should **not** have; *essential for* presupposes that something **cannot** occur without it. While a negative presupposition is sufficient to allow cooccurence with NPIs, as in

abandon	deny	leave	renounce
absence	disagree	less	resist
avoid	discourage from	little	scoff at
banish	dispense with	lose	shy away
be/remain disdainful	dismiss	miss the chance	stop
be futile	do away	miss the opportunity	suspend
be/remain oblivious	drop plans	omit	swear off
be/remain unconvinced	eliminate	pass up	tone down
call off	eschew	prevent X from	vault over
cease	fail	put off	veto
cut X off	give up	rebuff	waste
dare not	hurt	refuse	withdraw
decline	ignore		

Figure 1: DE constructions found in *Arg1* of explicit CHOSEN ALTERNATIVE

absense of **	defer	hardly	premature to	rule out	veto **
absent from	deny **	lack	prevent	skeptical	wary of
anxious about	deter	innocent of	prohibit	suspend **	warn about
avoid **	discourage **	minimize	rarely	thwart	whenever
bar	dismiss **	never *	refrain from	unable to	withstand
barely	doubt	nobody *	refuse **	unaware of	
block	eliminate **	nothing *	regardless	unclear on	
cannot *	essential for	oppose	reject	unlike	
compensate for	exclude	postpone	reluctant to	unlikely	
decline **	fail **	preclude	resist **	unwilling to	

Figure 2: The 55 most common downward entailing lemmas that Danescu-Niculescu-Mizil et al. (2009) found in the BLLIP corpus. * marks *negative* constructions (Section 3.1), and ** marks lemmas also identified as DE constructions in *Arg1* of *instead* in Figure 1.

(18) An online presence is essential for any business today. [www.alpha360.net/online-presence-essential-business-today]

(19) The car's on-board diagnostic systems compensate for any of these blends to keep it running according to manufacturer's specifications. [http://auto.howstuffworks.com]

it is insufficient to license the exclusion of an alternative from further consideration: That requires a negative assertion. Of course, *compensate for* and *essential for* are not alone in this: The same holds for *repent, atone, repair, make amends for*, etc. All have negative presuppositions and so can cooccur with NPIs, but do not make a negative assertion, so do not license an excluded alternative.

While I will continue to refer to DE predicates as evidence for alternatives being excluded from consideration, I only mean those DE predicates that make a negative assertion and not those that only have a negative presupposition.

3.3 Modals

The third largest set of explicit CHOSEN ALTERNATIVE have a *modal* associated with *Arg1*. However, because there are so many different modals, it makes sense to examine whether all of them license the *excluded alternative* of this relation, and for those which do, it makes sense to examine why they can do so.

Palmer (2001) divides modality into two types:

- *propositional modality*, involving the speaker's attitude towards the factual status of a proposition, as in Ex. 20;
- *event modality*, involving events that are not actualized, but are merely potential, as in Ex. 21.

(20) Kate **must** be eating dinner at home tonight. (Otherwise, you would see her at that table.)

(21) Kate **must** eat dinner at home tonight. (She hasn't spent any time with her children yet this week.)

Palmer further divides *event modality* into:

- *deontic modality*, involving obligation or permission, and conditional factors "that are *external* to the individual"
- *dynamic modality*, involving factors "internal to the individual" (including purpose, wishes, effort, fears, etc.)

Both types of event modality are found associated with *Arg1* of CHOSEN ALTERNATIVE relations. Ex. 22–23 illustrate *deontic modals* (obligation and permission), while Ex. 24–25 illustrate *dynamic modals* (want/wish/desire/hope and effort).

(22) *Charles Kennedy's advisors should have told him the truth.* Instead, **they covered up for him to an unacceptable extent and for far too long**. [The Economist, 14 January 2006]

(23) *Lynn Sherr could have availed herself of one of the 10.4m private pools in the United States.* Instead, **she became determined to swim the Hellespont in western Turkey**. [The Economist, 2 June 2012]

(24) *Anne Compoccia wanted to be a nun.* Instead, **she found herself in prison for embezzling city funds**. [http://www.nytimes.com/2002/12/22/nyregion/22DECA.html?todaysheadlines]

(25) *Lyndon B Johnson was trying to have the parallel presidency that Dick Cheney secured for himself under a compliant George Bush.* Instead, **he was consigned to an office in the Executive Office Building**. [NYRB, 2012]

On the other hand, while Palmer (2001) further divides *propositional modality* into:

- *epistemic modality*, involving the speaker's *judgment* about the factual status of a proposition;
- *evidential modality*, involving the speaker's *evidence* for the factual status of a proposition.

neither seems appropriate in the argument conveying the alternative that is excluded from consideration, and there are no such tokens in the PDTB 2.0, the BioDRB, or the *Instead Corpus*. The examples in (26) illustrate the inappropriateness of *instead* with *epistemic modals*, while those in (27) show the same is true of *evidential modals* (where *they* in Example 27b should be taken as generic, for this to be evidential).

(26) a. John always arrives promptly, so he **must/may** have been delayed. *Instead, he decided not to come.

b. John has a senior pass, so he **must/may** be over 60. *Instead, he's not.

(27) a. John seems to have left the house. *Instead, he has locked himself in the lavatory.

b. They say John drinks. *Instead, he smokes weed.

This pattern suggests that modals associated with the *excluded alternative* of a CHOSEN ALTERNATIVE relation are ones that mark their associated state-of-affairs as not holding. In her study of alternatives in disjunction, Mauri (2008) uses the term *irrealis* to describe an alternative that doesn't hold. If we follow Mauri, then we can say that *Event modals* mark their associated SoA as *irrealis* because neither factors external to the individual (obligations, permissions, etc.) nor factors internal to the individual (purposes, wishes, effort, fear, etc.) can guarantee that the SoA will come to pass.

3.4 Other features

In addition to these three constructions that appear frequently with excluded alternatives are some other sets that can be characterized by lexico-syntactic features. One is a set of predicates that specify an actual state-of-affairs (SoA) that lead one to *expect* some particular next SoA. While expected, this next SoA does not hold, and so is *irrealis*. Thus, while not modals, these predicates can be associated with alternatives that are excluded from consideration for the same reason as modals can. Among such predicates are *expect* (Ex. 28), *encourage* (Ex. 29), and *prepare to* (Ex. 30).

(28) *They expected a new barrage of demands that Japan do something quickly to reduce its trade surplus with the U.S.* Instead, **they got a discussion of the need for the U.S. and Japan to work together ....**[wsj_2321]

(29) *Their broker encouraged them to take a month in Europe*; instead **they moved to South Carolina, where they began building a dream house on the beach**. [NYTimes, 14 July 2002]

(30) A gynecologist is slain at home by his wife, *who was preparing to serve him coq au vin that evening*. Instead, **she thrusts a kitchen knife through his heart**. [NYTBR, 4 May 2003]

Other state-expecting predicates found in *Arg1* of explicit CHOSEN ALTERNATIVE include: *anticipate*, *be about to*, *plan*, *promise*, *propose*, *raise expectations*, *suggest* and *wait for*. As with downward entailing, state-expecting is not a feature marked in dictionaries, and one may simply have to search for examples in a large corpus based on what it cooccurs with.

A second set comprises **Arg2** of non-factual *if* clauses and constructions indicating hypotheticals such as sentence-initial *Had*. Although downward entailing, they seem sufficiently different from the DE predicates to warrant separate mention. The three examples of this in the PDTB 2.0 include:

(31) *If government or private watchdogs insist, however, on introducing greater friction between the markets (...)*, the end loser will be the markets themselves. Instead, **we ought to be inviting more liquidity with cheaper ways to trade and transfer capital among all participants**. [wsj_0118]

Feature	Implicit tokens	Explicit tokens
Negation marker	**116 (67.8%)**	47 (39.8%)
Downward-entailment	24 (14.0%)	18 (15.3%)
Event Modal	9 (5.3%)	13 (11.0%)
Other	22 (12.9%)	**40 (33.9%)**
Total	171	118

Table 1: Absolute and relative frequency of features found in the excluded alternative of CHOSEN ALTERNATIVE relations in the PDTB 2.0. Other includes state-expecting predicates and if clauses. Bold indicates the largest differences.

4 Implicit Chosen Alternatives

Having described features commonly found on *Arg1* of explicit CHOSEN ALTERNATIVE that are usually, but not always, signalled by *instead*, I now turn to the even larger number of implicit CHOSEN ALTERNATIVE relations in the PDTB 2.0 and BioDRB. Here, the three features that are most common with explicit CHOSEN ALTERNATIVE are even more common with implicit CHOSEN ALTERNATIVE — negation markers (Ex 32), DE predicates (Ex 33), and event modals (Ex 34):

(32) *It isn't just exercise gear that isn't getting a good workout.* **The fitness craze itself has gone soft**, the survey found. [wsj_0409]

(33) *Copper futures prices failed to extend Friday's rally.* **Declines came because of concern that demand for copper may slow down**. [wsj_0437]

(34) ...Ortega indicated *that renewed U.S. military aid to the Contras could thwart the balloting*. He said **U.S. assistance should be used to demobilize the rebels**. [wsj_0174]

Table 1 shows just how much more common they are, both with respect to absolute and relative frequency. In fact, with an implicit CHOSEN ALTERNATIVE, either a negation marker, DE predicate or event modal is present ∼87% of the time.

5 Conclusion

I have left three questions unresolved:

1. What is behind the view that *instead* is evidence for a type of COMPARISON relation (Martin, 1992) or a type of CONTRASTIVE relation (Stede, 2012) and behind the decision of PDTB 2.0 annotators to label three of the 112 tokens of *instead* as conveying a COMPARISON.CONTRAST relation?

2. Are the features that allow *Arg1* to be interpreted as an excluded alternative, sufficient to label an implicit discourse relation as having the sense CHOSEN ALTERNATIVE, or do negation markers, DE constructions, event modals and other less frequent licensers of excluded alternatives occur in *Arg1* of other constructions?

3. What features suggest that the two arguments of a coherence relations denote *alternatives*?

With respect to the first question, researchers since Mann and Thompson (1988) have drawn a distinction between SEMANTIC and PRAGMATIC relations, which Moore and Pollack (1992) call INFORMATIONAL and INTENTIONAL, respectively. Moore and Pollack (1992) make a convincing arguement that relations of both types can hold simultaneously. With respect to *instead,* I think it can be argued that it conveys a purely informational relation. That is, *instead* (when it is not in construction with *of,* followed by the alternative being excluded) is *anaphoric*: Its excluded alternative must be derived from the (previous) discourse context. The most common thing that a speaker does with this excluded alternative may be to compare or contrast it with the alternative still in consideration, so that COMPARISON or CONTRAST become the most common intentional relation to hold when *instead* is used. But other intentional relations are possible, as evidenced by the many instances of explicit *and instead*, *because instead*, and *so instead*, etc. (again, not in construction with *of*). This will be discussed in a companion paper.

As for the second question, negation markers, DE constructions, event modals and state-expecting predicates are indeed found in the first (and second) arguments of relations other than CHOSEN ALTERNATIVE, including purely temporal relations (Example 35) and causal relations (Example 36):

(35) *they may not buy new episodes*, when [TEMPORAL.SYNCHRONY] **their current contracts expire** [wsj_0060]

(36) *The president could probably not avoid this restriction by choosing people willing to serve without pay* because [CONTINGENCY.CAUSE.REASON] **the Anti-Deficiency Act prohibits voluntary service to the government** [wsj_0112]

So a procedure for recognizing *Arg1* of a CHOSEN ALTERNATIVE relation would use the absense of all these features as evidence against a possible candidate.

As for the third question – deciding whether two arguments can and should be interpreted as alternatives – it may be that this does not have to be addressed independently, but rather falls out as a consequence of strong lexico-syntactic cues. This too will be discussed in a companion paper.

Acknowledgements

I would like to thank my three anonymous reviewers for their very valuable comments on the submitted version of this paper. In addition, earlier versions of this material were presented as invited talks at ACL ExProm Workshop in Jeju, South Korea (July 2012) and later at the TAG+11 Conference in Paris (September 2012). Members of the audience at both meetings were a source of additional valuable comments, some of which are addressed here and others of which I hope to address in the companion paper.

References

Carlson, L. and D. Marcu (2001). Discourse tagging reference manual. Technical Report ISI-TR-545, Information Sciences Institute.

Carlson, L., D. Marcu, and M. E. Okurowski (2003). Building a discourse-tagged corpus in the framework of rhetorical structure theory. In J. van Kuppevelt & R. Smith (Ed.), *Current Directions in Discourse and Dialogue*. New York: Kluwer.

Danescu-Niculescu-Mizil, C., L. Lee, and R. Ducott (2009). Without a 'doubt'? unsupervised discovery of downward-entailing operators. In *Proceedings of Human Language Technologies: The 2009 Annual Conference of the North American Chapter of the Association for Computational Linguistics*, Boulder, Colorado, pp. 137–145. Association for Computational Linguistics.

Feng, V. W. and G. Hirst (2012). Text-level discourse parsing with rich linguistic features. In *Proc. 50th Annual Meeting of the Association for Computational Linguistics*, Jeju Island, Korea, pp. 60–68.

Ghosh, S., R. Johansson, G. Riccardi, and S. Tonelli (2011). Shallow discourse parsing with conditional random fields. In *Proceedings, International Joint Conference on Natural Language Processing*.

Halliday, M. and R. Hasan (1976). *Cohesion in English*. Longman.

Hernault, H., H. Prendinger, D. A. duVerle, and M. Ishizuka (2010). Hilda: A discourse parser using support vector machine classication. *Dialogue and Discourse 1*(3), 1–33.

Knott, A. (1996). *A Data-driven Methodology for Motivating a Set of Coherence Relations*. Ph. D. thesis, Department of Artificial Intelligence, University of Edinburgh.

Knott, A., J. Oberlander, M. O'Donnell, and C. Mellish (2001). Beyond elaboration: The interaction of relations and focus in coherent text. In T. Sanders, J. Schilperoord, and W. Spooren (Eds.), *Text Representation:Linguistic and psycholinguistic aspects*, pp. 181–196. John Benjamins Publishing.

Knott, A. and T. Sanders (1998). The classification of coherence relations and their linguistic markers. *Journal of Pragmatics 30*, 135–175.

Lin, Z. (2012). *Discourse Parsing: Inferring Discourse Structure, Modelling Coherence, and its Applications*. Ph. D. thesis, National University of Singapore.

Lin, Z., H. T. Ng, and M.-Y. Kan (2010, November). A PDTB-styled end-to-end discourse parser. Technical report, Department of Computing, National University of Singapore. http://arxiv.org/abs/1011.0835.

Mann, W. and S. Thompson (1988). Rhetorical Structure Theory: Toward a functional theory of text organization. *Text 8(3)*, 243–281.

Marcu, D. (2000). *The theory and practice of discourse parsing and summarization*. MIT Press.

Marcu, D. and A. Echihabi (2002). An unsupervised approach to recognizing discourse relations. In *Proceedings of ACL'02*.

Martin, J. (1992). *English Text: System and Structure*. Philadelphia: John Benjamins.

Mauri, C. (2008). Towards a typology of disjunction. *Studies in Language 32*, 22–55.

Moore, J. and M. Pollack (1992). A problem for RST: The need for multi-level discouse analysis. *Computational Linguistics 18(4)*, 537–544.

Palmer, F. (2001). *Mood and Modality* (2 ed.). Cambridge: Cambridge University Press.

Prasad, R., N. Dinesh, A. Lee, E. Miltsakaki, L. Robaldo, A. Joshi, and B. Webber (2008). The Penn Discourse TreeBank 2.0. In *Proceedings, 6th International Conference on Language Resources and Evaluation*, Marrakech, Morocco, pp. 2961–2968.

Prasad, R., S. McRoy, N. Frid, A. Joshi, and H. Yu (2011). The Biomedical Discourse Relation Bank. *BMC Bioinformatics 12*(188), 18 pages. http://www.biomedcentral.com/1471-2015/12/188.

Sagae, K. (2009). Analysis of discourse structure with syntactic dependencies and data-driven shift-reduce parsing. In *In Proceedings of IWPT 2009*.

Sporleder, C. and A. Lascarides (2008). Using automatically labelled examples to classify rhetorical relations: an assessment. *Natural Language Engineering 14(3)*, 369–416.

Stede, M. (2012). *Discourse Processing*. Morgan & Claypool Publishers.

Subba, R., B. D. Eugenio, and S. N. Kim (2006). Discourse parsing: Learning fol rules based on rich verb semantic representations to automatically label rhetorical relations. In *Proc. EACL Workshop on Learning Structured Information in Natural Language Applications*.

The PDTB Research Group (2008). The Penn Discourse TreeBank 2.0 Annotation Manual. Available at http://www.seas.upenn.edu/~pdtb/, or as part of the download of LDC2008T05.

Webber, B., M. Egg, and V. Kordoni (2012). Discourse structure and language technology. *Natural Language Engineering 18*(4), 437–490.

A Search Task Dataset for German Textual Entailment

Britta D. Zeller and Sebastian Padó
Department of Computational Linguistics, Heidelberg University, Germany
{zeller,pado}@cl.uni-heidelberg.de

Abstract

We present the first freely available large German dataset for Textual Entailment (TE). Our dataset builds on posts from German online forums concerned with computer problems and models the task of identifying relevant posts for user queries (i.e., descriptions of their computer problems) through TE. We use a sequence of crowdsourcing tasks to create realistic problem descriptions through summarisation and paraphrasing of forum posts. The dataset is represented in RTE-5 Search task style and consists of 172 positive and over 2800 negative pairs. We analyse the properties of the created dataset and evaluate its difficulty by applying two TE algorithms and comparing the results with results on the English RTE-5 Search task. The results show that our dataset is roughly comparable to the RTE-5 data in terms of both difficulty and balancing of positive and negative entailment pairs. Our approach to create task-specific TE datasets can be transferred to other domains and languages.

1 Introduction

Textual Entailment (TE) is a binary relation between two utterances, a *Text T* and a *Hypothesis H*, which holds if "a human reading T would infer that H is most likely true" (Dagan et al., 2005). Example 1 shows a positive entailment (T entails H_1) and a negative entailment (T does not entail H_2).

(1) **T:** Yoko Ono unveiled a bronze statue of her late husband, John Lennon, to complete the official renaming of England's Liverpool Airport as Liverpool John Lennon Airport.

H_1: Yoko Ono is John Lennon's widow.

H_2: John Lennon renamed Liverpool Airport.

The appeal of Textual Entailment is that it can arguably meet a substantial part of the semantic processing requirements of a range of language processing tasks such as Question Answering (Harabagiu and Hickl, 2006), Information Extraction (Romano et al., 2006), or Summarisation (Harabagiu et al., 2007). Consequently, there is now a research community that works on and improves Textual Entailment technology. In this spirit, the main TE forum, the yearly Recognising Textual Entailment (RTE) Challenge, has created a number of datasets that incorporate the properties of particular tasks, such as Semantic Search in RTE-5 (Bentivogli et al., 2009) or Novelty Detection in RTE-7 (Bentivogli et al., 2011).

At the same time, work on RTE on has focused almost exclusively on English. There is at most a handful of studies on Textual Entailment in other languages, notably German and Italian (Wang and Neumann, 2008; Negri et al., 2009; Bos et al., 2009) as well as a study on cross-lingual entailment (Mehdad et al., 2010).[1] Consequently, virtually no TE technology is available for non-English languages. What is more, it is not clear how well existing algorithms for English RTE carry over to other languages, which might show very different types of surface variation from English. The same limitation exists in terms of genre/register. Virtually all existing datasets have been created from "clean" corpora – that is, properly tokenised, grammatical text, notably Wikipedia. Again, the question arises how well TE

[1]There is also a translation of the RTE-3 dataset into German, but it is so far unpublished, although available from http://www.dfki.de/~neumann/resources.html

algorithms would do on noisier genres like transcribed speech or user-generated content. Arguably, it would benefit the community to have a larger variety of datasets at hand for such investigations.

This paper reports our creation and analysis of a German dataset for TE that is derived from social media data, as is produced every day on a large scale by of non-professional web users. This type of data respects linguistic norms such as spelling and grammar less than traditional textual entailment datasets (Agichtein et al., 2008), which present challenges to semantic processing.

We concentrate on a search task on a computer user forum that deals with computer problems: given a problem statement formulated by a user, identify all relevant forum threads that describe this problem. We created queries for a sample of forum threads by crowdsourcing. We asked annotators to summarise the threads and to paraphrase the summaries to achieve high syntactic and lexical variability. The resulting summaries can be understood as queries (problem statements) corresponding to the original posts. The search for relevant posts given a query can be phrased as a TE problem as follows: queries are hypotheses that are entailed by forum posts (texts) T iff the forum post is relevant for the query (Peñas et al., 2008).

Plan of the paper. Section 2 defines the task in more detail and describes the rationale behind our definition of the crowdsourcing tasks. Section 3 provides a detailed analysis of the queries that were produced by crowdsourcing. Section 4 assesses the difficulty of the dataset by modelling it with the RTE system EDITS (Kouylekov and Negri, 2010). Finally we relate our study to prior work and sum up.

2 Creating a German Social Media TE Dataset with Crowdsourcing

2.1 Rationale

As mentioned above, the promise of TE lies in its ability to model NLP tasks. One of the best-established of these tasks is search, which has been a part of the RTE challenges since RTE-5 (Bentivogli et al., 2009). In this setup, given a query statement and a set of documents, a document is relevant if it entails the query. That is, the documents serve as candidate texts T for a hypothesis H given by the query. We apply this setup to social media texts that discuss computer problems. Our use case is that a user has a particular problem with their machine and wants to retrieve the set of relevant documents from computer problem forums. In terms of the entailment-based search task, the Ts are given by a corpus of German computer forum threads. More specifically, we use the first post of each thread, since an analysis showed that the first post usually contains the problem description. What is missing, however, are plausible queries (i.e., Hs). We create these queries by asking laypersons to summarise posts through Amazon Mechanical Turk (AMT) (Snow et al., 2008). This involves three steps:

Summarisation. Given the first post of a forum thread (T), summarise the content in one sentence (H*).

Paraphrasing. Paraphrase H* into another sentence (H) by changing both syntax and lexical choice.

Validation. Given original post (T) and paraphrased summary (H), assess if H correctly summarises T.

Step 1 maps documents onto potential queries; these queries might however be still very close to the original verbalisation in the document. On the semantic level, we assume that summarisation can lose information, but not create new information; thus, summaries should be entailed by the original texts (Harabagiu et al., 2007). Step 2 allows that there is an amount of syntactic and lexical variance between T and H that is realistic for a search task. On the semantic level, we assume that paraphrasing preserves information; that is, input and output of this step should generally exhibit a high degree of semantic equivalence. Finally, Step 3 allows us to detect and remove bad queries produced by unmotivated or sloppy turkers. Thus, queries validated by Step 3 will be entailed by the original documents.

2.2 Crowdsourcing Details

We sampled 25 first posts of threads from a corpus of German computer self-help forums as Ts, each for which we generate several Hs. The posts were selected so that their length matches the distribution over lengths for all first posts in the corpus. All 25 posts have a length between 50 and 120 words.

	ps	is	ns
ps	168	211	47
is	0	132	87
ns	0	0	36

Table 1: Confusion matrix for pairs of AMT validation annotations

Task 1: Summarisation. In the first step, we asked AMT workers to write a concise summary of a forum post, summarising the central points of the original text in a declarative sentence. We also provide an example text with summary. Turkers could mark a text as unsummarisable, but had to indicate a reason.

The task was conducted by five turkers for each forum post, leading to $25 * 5 = 125$ potential summaries. Two posts were discarded as unsummarisable since they referred heavily to another forum post, which left us with 115 summaries. We paid 0.20 USD for each summary. (Total: 23 USD)

Task 2: Paraphrasing. In this task, workers had to reformulate the summaries produced in the first task. They were asked to replace words by appropriate synonyms and to change the sentence structure, while still maintain the meaning of the original sentence. The workers of Task 2 were not shown the original forum posts, only the summaries. Again, there was the possibility to leave the text unparaphrased, indicating a reason. Each sentence was paraphrased by two turkers, resulting in $115 * 2 = 230$ paraphrases.

We decided to discard four of the 230 paraphrases, including their two input sentences (summaries from Task 1). We found that these input sentences provide overly generic summaries of their posts to be usable. For example, a post which dealt with various strategies to solve pop-up problems in Firefox was summarised as "Mein Rechner öffnet selbstständig Webseiten [...]." (*"My computer opens web pages on its own [...]."*). We paid 0.10 USD for each of the 230 paraphrases. (Total: 23 USD)

Task 3: Validation. This task asked workers to judge whether the paraphrased summaries resulting from Task 3 are correct summaries of the problem described in T.[2] Possible answers were (a) perfect summary ("ps"); (b) incomplete summary that is missing central concept ("is"); (c) no ("ns"). We also asked turkers to verify that the paraphrased summaries were complete, grammatical, declarative sentences. Each T/H pair was assessed by 3 turkers who were paid 0.05 USD for each assessment. (Total: 35 USD)

Surprisingly, the most frequently chosen category was not "is" (41% of all assessments), but "ps" (43%). About 16% of the paraphrases summaries are judged as "ns". To assess reliability, we computed a confusion matrix. In our three-annotation AMT setup where annotators are not necessarily constant across sentences, we decided to count the three pairwise annotations (*a1-a2, a2-a3, a1-a3*) for each sentence. Since the order of the annotators is random, we normalised to the order "ps" < "is" < "ns". Table 1 shows the results. Satisfactorily, the diagonal, corresponding to matching judgements, shows the highest numbers. In total, 49% of the judgement pairs agree. The largest group of disagreements is "ps"/"is"; the number of "is"/"ns" cases is lower by a factor of two, and the number of "ns"/"ps" cases smaller by another factor of 2. We interpret these number as indication that the annotation task is fairly difficult, but that there is in particular a large number of clear correct cases. We build on this observation below.

2.3 Compilation of the Dataset

For each T/H pair, Task 3 provides us with three judgements on an ordinal scale with three categories: perfect summary ("ps"), incomplete summary ("is"), no summary ("ns"). The next question is how to select cases of true entailment and true non-entailment from this dataset.

Positive entailment pairs. As for entailment, we start by discarding all pairs that were tagged as "ns" by at least one rater. The situation is less clear for "is" cases: on one hand, hypotheses can drop information

[2]We used the term "summary" to describe the concept to our lay taggers which are unfamiliar with the term "entailment".

Assessments	ps-ps-ps	ps-ps-is	ps-is-is	is-is-is	ns-ns-ns	ns-ns-is	ns-is-is
Entailment	Y	Y	Y	Y	N	N	N
Occurrence	38	45	50	20	7	11	21
Selected as (Non-)Entailment	37	41	42	7	7	2	1

Table 2: Association between AMT assessments and final entailment relations

present in the text while preserving entailment; on the other hand, the absence of important information in the summary can indicate difficulties with the original text or the summary. Thus, to keep precision high, we decided to manually check all "is"/"ps" T/H pairs. The left-hand part of Table 2 shows that in fact, the ratio of proper entailments trails off from almost 100% for "ps-ps-ps" to about one third for "is-is-is". In total, we obtained 127 positive entailment pairs in this manner.

During the extraction, we noted that one of the 23 forum posts did not yield reliable assessments for any of its generated hypotheses and discarded it.

Negative entailment pairs. Negative entailment pairs come from two sources. First, "ns" T/H pairs are cases where turkers missed the semantic core of the original text. These cases might be particularly informative non-entailment pairs because they are near the decision boundary. For example, one author asks whether a virus can settle down on the motherboard. The corresponding generated hypothesis turned the question into a fact, stating that "My BIOS has been infected by a virus.". Again, we checked all pairs with at least one "ns" judgement by hand. As the right-hand side of Table 2 shows, we find the same pattern as for positive pairs: perfect non-entailment for instances with perfect agreement on "ns", and lower non-entailment ratio for increasing "is" ratio. Rejected pairs are e.g. very generic and fuzzy summaries or refer only to a minor aspect of the problem described in the forum. Unfortunately, this strategy only results in 10 negative entailment T/H pairs. The second source of negative pairs are combinations of verified Hs with "other" Ts, that is, Ts from which they were not created. In fact, we can pair each of the 137 validated distinct Hs with all other Ts, resulting in $21 * 137 = 2877$ additional non-entailment T/H pairs.

However, since the domain of computer problems is relatively narrow, a few post topics are so close to each other that generated hypotheses are entailed by multiple texts. While this effect is usually ignored in machine learning (Bergsma et al., 2008), our goal is a clean dataset. Therefore, we manually checked all cross-pairs with similar topics (e.g. virus attacks) for positive entailment relations. Indeed, we found hypotheses which were general enough to match other texts. We removed 45 such pairs from the negative entailment pairs and added them to the set of positive pairs.

In total, we obtained 172 positive and 2842 negative entailment T/H pairs for 22 Ts and 137 distinct Hs. At a cost of 82 USD, this corresponds to an average of 50 cents for each explicitly generated positive pair, but just 3 cents for each T/H pair in the complete dataset. From the 226 AMT-generated pairs, we use 56% as positive pairs and 4% as negative pairs. We discard the remaining, inconsistently judged, 40%.

2.4 Discussion

The three tasks vary in their nature and difficulty. As mentioned above, we paid more for Task 1 than for Task 2, since it involved authoring a text. The amount of time needed for the tasks confirms this assumption: Task 1 took about 80 seconds per annotation, Task 2 only about 60 seconds. In terms of difficulty, Task 1 seems to be the easier one, though: We removed only a small number of post summaries from Task 1, but had to disregard a number of paraphrases from Task 2 (cf. Section 2.3). We believe that two factors contribute to this observation: (a), it is easier to summarise a complete text than to paraphrase a sentence out of context; (b), we deliberately asked workers in Task 2 to introduce as much variance as possible, which can lead to somewhat unnatural statements. Finally, the assessment Task 3 is the fastest one, requiring only about 30 seconds per annotation.

Post/Summary ID	Example (German/English)	Phenomenon
1/1	Rechner mit Virus infiziert. – *Computer infected with virus.*	Incomplete sentence
1/2	Mein Rechner ist von einem Virus befallen. – *My computer is infected by a virus.*	Personal point of view, short summary
1/3	Der Virtumonde-Virus lässt sich nicht entfernen. – *The Virtumonde virus cannot be removed.*	Pseudo-passive
25/1	Ich möchte, dass mein Board dauerhaft auf GB LAN schalten. – *I want that my board permanently to switch to GB LAN.*	Ungrammatical sentence
25/3	Wie lässt sich bei einer GB-Netzwerkkarte ein Fallback auf 100mbit verhindern? – *How can a fallback to 100mbit in a GB network adapter be prevented?*	Question
20/2	Heute ist schon 4 mal beim aufrufen des p5q deluxe-sammelthreads mein trendmicro virenscanner angeschlagen er meldet den Virus: TSPY_ONLINEG.FXG was kann ich dagegen machen? – *Today while calling the p5q deluxe collective threads my trendmicro virus scanner has given mouth already 4 times it reports the virus: TSPY_ONLINEG.FXG what can i do against this?*	Long summary, writing errors

Table 3: Linguistic phenomena in summarisation task

Our results show that both with regard to positive and negative entailment, three consistent judgements are sufficient for an almost perfect guarantee of the respective relation (cf. Table 2), but only a comparatively small sample of our data fall into these categories (around 15% for positive and 3% for negative entailment, respectively). Creators of a dataset therefore have the option of either making up for this loss by starting with more initial data, which leads to a higher overall cost, or to perform a subsequent expert-driven manual pass over the inconsistent candidates, as we did.

3 Analysis of Created Data

This Section illustrates the properties and problems of each step.

3.1 Task 1: Summarisation

Linguistic properties. Table 3 illustrates some of the phenomena appearing in the summarisation task, which seem to be largely specific to the particular genre (web forum texts) that we consider, while appearing less frequent in standard trainig data like newswire. Example 1/1 shows a typical "telegram style" summary which omits determiners and copula; Example 25/1 shows that not all summaries are even grammatical (underlined word). A comparison of examples 1/2 and 1/3 shows that the summaries either retain the personal point of view typically used by the original posts (using first-personal personal or possessive pronouns) or employ generic, impersonal formulations such as (pseudo-)passives. In one example, the AMT worker even cited the author of the original post using the introduction "Micha fragt, ob [...]" (*"Micha asks whether [...]"*). Similarly, 12 summaries use interrogative form (Example 25/3) like the original posts even though we explicitly asked the turkers to generate declarative sentences. Finally, example 20/2 illustrates typical writing errors, including the omission of punctuation and the defiance of German capitalisation rules. It is notable that turkers used this style, which is typically used for writing forum posts, even in the rather more formal AMT task environment. It occurs more frequently for original posts with the same style. Arguably, the turkers perceived this as the "correct" manner to summarise such posts, as our guidelines did not address this question.

Post/Summary/ Paraphrase ID	Example (German/English)	Phenomenon
2/1/1, 2/1/2	PC ⇒ Computer/Rechner *(computer)*	Abbreviation, loanword
10/2/1	CPU ⇒ Prozessor *(processor)*	Abbreviation
3/3/1	AntiVir *(specific anti-virus program)* ⇒ Anti-Viren-Programm – *anti-virus program*	Hypernym
9/5/2	starten – *to start* ⇒ booten – *to boot*	Synonym
5/4/2	wird Hilfe benötigt – *help is needed* ⇒ bedarf es Unterstützung – *support is required*	Support verb construction changes
8/3/2	Ich habe XP neu installiert – *I reinstalled XP* ⇒ Neuinstallation von XP – *Reinstallation of XP*	Nominalisation
13/5/2	starten – *to start* ⇒ gestartet werden – *to be started*	Active/passive switch
4/4/2	ich möchte [...] löschen – *I want to delete [...]* ⇒ [...] lässt sich nicht entfernen – *[...] cannot be removed* (literally: *does not let itself be removed*)	Change of perspective (pseudo-passive)
17/3/2	User frägt ob eine Schadsoftware sich auch in der Hardware einnisten kann. – *User asks if malware can also infect hardware.* ⇒ Kann die Hardware ebenfalls von Maleware befallen sein? – *Can hardware be affected by malware, too?*	Declarative/interrogative switch

Table 4: Linguistic phenomena in paraphrasing task

Content properties. Most summaries reproduced the original content correctly. The turkers apparently concentrated more on the content, i.e. writing a good summary, than formal task details, resulting, e.g. in interrogative formulations. This is not untypical for crowdsourcing tasks (Chen and Dolan, 2010).

Nonetheless, reproducing the context correctly was not trivial: some forum posts are rambling or vague and difficult to summarise. Summaries of such posts often either (a) do not cover the whole content or (b) are incorrect. Cases (a) lead to assessments of medium reliability in Task 3 ("H is an incomplete, but valid summary of T"). Cases (b) lead to negative entailment cases.

As intended, the results of Task 1 are significantly shorter than the original texts, with an average length of 11 words (min 3, max 39 words). Often, they use more general wording, e.g. "Der Prozessor läuft schnell heiß." (*"The processor runs hot quickly"*) for a description containing a concrete temperature.

3.2 Task 2: Paraphrasing

Linguistic properties. In the paraphrasing task, workers were asked to change both syntax and word choice whenever possible. Although texts can contain many content words that are hard to paraphrase (e.g. basic level terms such as *table*), the problem is alleviated in the software domain where abbreviations and English loanwords that can be substituted easily are frequent (examples 2/1/1, 2/1/2, 10/2/1 in Table 4). The most frequent change was the replacement of verbs by synonyms and nouns by synonyms or hypernyms, as in examples 3/3/1 and 9/5/2. Some turkers modified both syntax and lexemes to vary support verb constructions (5/4/2).

While these phenomena are all "generic" paraphrasing devices that have been observed in previous studies on English and newswire text (Lin and Pantel, 2002; Bannard and Callison-Burch, 2005), we find two more classes of paraphrasing patterns that are specific to German and the social media domain, respectively. Prominent among German-specific changes are the large number of nominalisations (8/3/2) as well as active/passive switches (13/5/2). Next to the regular passive construction with the auxiliary *werden*, we often see "pseudo-passives" which use *lassen* combined with the reflexivised verb (4/4/2).

As for domain-specific patterns, we frequently observe the alternation of interrogative and declarative sentences (17/3/2) noted before which is caused by the tendency of the original posts to formulate problems as questions. Again, personalised and generic expressions alternate (4/4/2), which typically involves rephrasing first-person statements as third-person or impersonal ones – often though (pseudo-)passives.

The quality is generally higher in Task 2 than it is in Task 1. Although we asked the turkers to generate paraphrases by changing both syntax and lexis, they frequently modified just the syntax. However, this is not critical, since the summaries already exhibit varied word choice, so that there is enough variance between T and the corresponding true entailment Hs to avoid oversimplifying the TE task.

Content properties. Recall that no context was given in the paraphrasing task to avoid influencing the turkers with regard to vocabulary and syntax. In most cases, context was also not necessary. However, this also meant that some semantic errors occurred as a result of ambiguous formulations in summaries that were propagated into the paraphrase. For example, the author of one forum post explains that a BIOS update has failed and that he is afraid of restarting the computer. The corresponding summary "Fehlermeldung nach Bios-Update, Rechner trotzdem neustarten?" (*"Error message after Bios update, restart computer anyway?"*) is paraphrased with "Ich erhalte nach dem Update meines BIOS eine Fehlermeldung, soll ich den PC neu starten?" (*"I get an error message after the BIOS update, should I restart the PC?"*), which has rather the meaning of restarting the PC *in order to* overcome the problem. Consequently, the assessment in Task 3 was controversial (ps-is-ns, see Section 2.3) and lead to a rejection of the T/H pair. In the best case, such errors can also lead to clear rejections (ns-ns-ns).

A specific problem that we observed was the lack of domain knowledge by turkers. For example, the summary "Anschluss von einem zusätzlichem SATA-Gerät . . . " (*"Connection of an additional SATA device . . . "*) becomes "ich möchte Hardware von SATA . . . anschließen" (*"I want to connect hardware (made) by SATA . . . "*). This is an incorrect paraphrase: SATA is not a hardware manufacturer, but a type of interface. This problem extended to Task 3, where assessments were controversial (ps-is-ns).

Finally, some turkers, contrary to instructions, produced summaries of the summaries. These texts became very short and were often marked as "is" (valid but incomplete) in Task 3. We observed that it was mostly turkers who already participated in Task 1 who acted in this manner. We feel that there is a tension regarding re-employing workers who participated in previous tasks: quality may profit from their previous training, but suffer from their bias to approach the second task with the same mindset as the first one.

3.3 Task 3: Validation

The output of the validation task allows us to correlate the quality ratings of T/H pairs to their linguistic properties. We observe a broad overlap between assessments of the type "is" and hypotheses which are very short or whose content is very general, e.g. due to the usage of hypernyms. Accordingly, T/H pairs which are marked consistently as "ps" concern either hypotheses which are relatively comprehensive, or texts which describe rather simple situations. At the opposite end of the scale, T/H pairs with three "ns" assessments arise from to propagated errors. T/H pairs marked with all three categories, ps-is-ns, make up only about 3%. These cases frequently refer to posts with complex queries such as users describing a sequence of problems. Such posts are hard to summarise and to evaluate, but are also unlikely search queries. The average length of the Hs selected through Task 3 is 11.4 words (min 5, max 22).

In sum, we interpret the three-stage crowdsourcing task as a success: The first two tasks generate a broad variation of potentially true T/H pairs, while the third task enables a filtering of dubious pairs. Although the linguistic quality of the obtained hypotheses shows clear imperfections, the quality of the original texts is equally low: the resulting T/H pairs reflect particularities of the social media domain. Example 2 shows (part of) a T/H pair; note the ungrammaticality in both T and H.

(2) **T:** [...] Ich habe heute alles zusammengebaut, aber aheb folgende probleme... 1.Der PC brauch ca 5-10min zum booten. 2.Nach dem Starten hängt der pc sich ständig auf. [...] 4.beim booten wird "Pri Master Hard Disk : S.M.A.R.T. Status BAD, Backup and Replace Press F1 to Resume." wenn ich denn F1 drücke fährt der pc weiter hoch. MFG

	Accuracy	P	R	F_1
		for positive entailment		
Word overlap	.93	.38	.38	.38
EDITS (edit distance)	.95	.63	.34	.44

Table 5: Test set results on social media dataset for two simple Textual Entailment algorithms

[...] I have assembled everything today, but haev the following problems: 1.The PC take ca 5-10min to boot. 2.After starting the pc locks up constantly. [...] 4. while booting is "Pri Master Hard Disk : S.M.A.R.T. Status BAD, Backup and Replace Press F1 to Resume." than when I press F1 the pc continues booting. RSVP

H: Meinen Computer benötig für das Hochfahren sehr lange und zeigt mir dann eine Meldung für einen Fehler an.
Mine computer need a long time for booting and then shows me a message for an error.

4 Modelling the Dataset with Textual Entailment Systems

In order to evaluate the difficulty of the dataset that we have created, we performed experiments with two different TE engines. We split our dataset into a development and a test set. Both sets are identical in terms of size (1507 T/H pairs) and amount of positive and negative pairs (86 and 1421 pairs, respectively).

The first system is EDITS (Negri et al., 2009), version 3.0.[3] EDITS uses string edit distance as a proxy of semantic similarity between T and H and classifies pairs as entailing if their normalised edit distance is below a threshold θ which can be optimised on a development set. While additional entailment knowledge can be included, no such knowledge is currently available for German and we use the default weights. The second system is a simple word overlap strategy which approximates semantic similarity through the fraction of H words that also occur in T (Monz and de Rijke, 2001). Again, pairs are classified as entailing if this fraction is larger than a threshold θ.

We preprocessed the data by lemmatising it with TreeTagger (Schmid, 1994) and removing stop words, employing a German stop word list which includes keywords from the social media domain.[4] The thresholds θ for both systems were set by optimising the F_1 score for positive entailment on the train set.

Table 5 shows the results for the word overlap model and EDITS. The very high accuracy values merely reflect the predominance of the negative entailment class; we therefore concentrate on the F-score statistics for positive entailment. We find that edit distance outperforms word overlap with F_1 scores of .44 and .38, respectively. Since the main difference between the two approaches is that edit distance is sensitive to word order, order information appears to be indeed informative: reordering between T and H do not incur costs in the word overlap model, but they do in the edit distance model. Example 3 shows a T/H pair with high word overlap, but negative entailment. It is correctly classified by EDITS, but misclassified by the word overlap model.

(3) **T:** Hallo PC-Freunde, ich habe letzte Woche XP neu installiert. Heute ist mir aufgefallen das die CPU-Auslastung immer zwischen 60% und 80% liegt obwohl im Taskmanager der Lerlaufprozess mit 90-99% angezeigt wird. Kann es vieleicht sein das im Taskmanager nicht alle Programme erfasst werden(währe mir neu) oder könnte vieleicht ein Virus, Trojaner sein der diese ununterbrochen hohe Auslastung bewirkt? Vobei mein Antivirusprogramm (Awast) keinen Virus oder ähnliches erkennt. [...]
[...] Today I realised that the CPU load is always between 60% and 80% although the idle task is always displayed with 90-99% in the task manager. Is it mabe possible thet not all

[3]Downloadable from `http://sourceforge.net/projects/edits/files/`
[4]`http://solariz.de/649/deutsche-stopwords.htm`

programs are captured in the task manager(whould be new to me) or could mabe be a virus, trojan horse which causes this steadily high load? Hovever my anti virus program (Awast) does not recognise a virus or the like. [. . .]

H: Die Prozessorauslastung ist bei 100% und Antivirenprogramme funktionieren nicht.
The processor load is at 100% and anti virus programs do not work.

Example 4 shows the opposite case, namely a positive T/H entailment pair that hardly shares any vocabulary since many T details are omitted in H. Both systems are unable to correctly label this instance.

(4) **T:** Es gibt bei m ir zwei Probleme bei der Ausführung des Tools unter Vista. 1) Vista blockiert die Ausführung mit dem Kommentar " ...Sie verfügen eventuell nicht über ausreichende Berechtigungen... " und 2) F-Secure gibt eine Malware-Warnung aus " W32/ Suspicious_U.gen " Virus. Ist die Viruswarnung nur ein Fehlalarm?
I h ave two problems with the execution of the tool under Vista. 1) Vista blocks the execution with the comment " ...You might not have sufficient authorisation... " and 2) F-Secure gives a malware warning " W32/ Suspicious_U.gen " Virus. Is the virus warning just a false alarm?

H: Wegen fehlenden Systemrechten des Anwenders in Windows kann die Datei nicht gestartet werden. – *The file cannot be started due to missing system rights by the user in Windows.*

The most direct point of comparison for our dataset is the RTE-5 search pilot (Bentivogli et al., 2009). The two main differences are language (English vs. German) and genre (newswire vs. social media). We found our dataset to be slightly easier to model. Part of the reason is the somewhat more balanced positive/negative distribution in our dataset: a random baseline achieves an F-Score of 8.4% on RTE-5 and 10.4% on our data. However, the improvement of informed models is also somewhat higher: EDITS without additional knowledge resources achieves 32.6% F-Score on RTE-5 (+24% over the baseline) (Bentivogli et al., 2009) and 44% F-Score on our dataset (+34% over the baseline). We believe that this is due to the greater coherence of our dataset: it deals with just one topic, while the RTE-5 dataset covers ten topics. We also observe that the Hs in RTE-5 are shorter than ours (avg. length 8.75 words vs. 11.4) which presumably leads to worse sparsity problems. Nevertheless, the results on the two datasets for baselines and simple methods are still remarkably similar.

5 Related work

In the Textual Entailment community, particularly in the studies who create datasets and resources, there is a strong focus on the English language (Androutsopoulos and Malakasiotis, 2010). All RTE datasets, the most widely used experimental materials, are in English. A few datasets have been created for other languages. To our knowledge, only an Italian one (Bos et al., 2009) and a Spanish one are freely available (Peñas et al., 2006). Datasets for other languages have been created in the context of the CLEF QA Answer Validation and Machine Reading tasks, but do not appear to be available to the general community.

We have employed crowdsourcing, a technique whose practice has expanded greatly over the last years (Snow et al., 2008). It has rarely been used for Textual Entailment, though, since high-quality crowdsourcing relies on the ability to formulate the task in layman's terms, which is challenging for entailment. We avoided this problem by asking turkers to provide summaries and paraphrases in two separate steps. Wang and Callison-Burch (2010) also use crowdsourcing to collect hypotheses for TE. In contrast to us, they do not ask turkers for full summaries and paraphrases, but have them extract facts from texts and create counter-facts from facts by inserting negations, using antonyms, or changing adverbs.

Finally, Bernhard and Gurevych (2008) present a study on data that is similar to ours. Their goal is the automatic collection of paraphrases for English questions on social Q&A sites. Employing similar methods to us (e.g., word overlap and edit distance), they achieve very good results. Their task is simpler in that in concentrates on paraphrase relations among statements rather than summarisation relations between texts and statements.

6 Conclusions

This paper makes two contributions. The first one is a freely available dataset[5] for Textual Entailment tasks which covers (a) a new language, namely German; and (b), a new genre, namely web forum text. The dataset models a search task on web forums, with short queries as hypotheses and forum posts as text candidates. Being constructed from real social media data, our data is more noisy than existing RTE datasets and shows novels linguistic paraphrasing phenomena such as switches between interrogative and declarative sentences. We consider our dataset to be a test bed for TE algorithms that have to deal with spontaneous and sloppy language, e.g. for other social media areas or on transcribed spoken language.

Our second contribution is a crowdsourcing-based procedure to create the dataset which can be applied to other languages and data sources in order to create comparable datasets quickly and at modest expense. The three-step setup that we introduce consists of a summarisation step, a paraphrasing step, and a validation step. This setup guarantees syntactic and lexical variation and makes it possible to detect and remove the sizable portion of the data that consists of queries that are either invalid or hard to judge. The number of summaries and paraphrases can be chosen according to the requirements of the dataset; as for validation, we found that three judgments were sufficient for a final categorisation. An alternative to our rather artificial way to collect data is presented in (Baldwin et al., 2010), employing web forum structure.

We have presented an experiment with two basic TE algorithms which establishes that the difficulty of the dataset is roughly comparable with the RTE-5 Search task testset. However, both algorithms were essentially knowledge-free, and we will conduct experiments with more informed algorithms. We expect the inclusion of lexical entailment knowledge (such as hyponymy relations) to provide a clear benefit. However, the top systems on the RTE-5 Search-Task, where the best result was 46% F-Score (+13% F-Score over edit distance) crucially employed lexico-syntactic paraphrase knowledge à la DIRT (Lin and Pantel, 2002). It remains to be seen how such syntax-based TE algorithms do on our dataset, where we expect parsing results to be substantially more noisy than for traditional RTE datasets.

Acknowledgments. This work was supported by the EC project EXCITEMENT (FP7 ICT-287923).

References

Agichtein, E., C. Castillo, D. Donato, A. Gionis, and G. Mishne (2008). Finding high-quality content in social media. In *Proceedings of WSDM*, Stanford, CA, pp. 183–194.

Androutsopoulos, I. and P. Malakasiotis (2010). A Survey of Paraphrasing and Textual Entailment Methods. *Journal of Artificial Intelligence Research 38*, 135–187.

Baldwin, T., D. Martinez, R. B. Penman, S. N. Kim, M. Lui, L. Wang, and A. MacKinlay (2010). Intelligent linux information access by data mining: the ILIAD project. In *Proceedings of the NAACL Workshop on Computational Linguistics in a World of Social Media*, Los Angeles, CA, pp. 15–16.

Bannard, C. and C. Callison-Burch (2005). Paraphrasing with bilingual parallel corpora. In *Proceedings of ACL*, Ann Arbor, MI, pp. 597–604.

Bentivogli, L., P. Clark, I. Dagan, H. Trang Dang, and D. Giampiccolo (2011). The seventh PASCAL recognising textual entailment challenge. In *Proceedings of TAC*, Gaithersburg, MD.

Bentivogli, L., I. Dagan, H. T. Dang, D. Giampiccolo, M. L. Leggio, and B. Magnini (2009). Considering discourse references in textual entailment annotation. In *Proceedings of the 5th International Conference on Generative Approaches to the Lexicon*, Pisa, Italy.

Bentivogli, L., B. Magnini, I. Dagan, H. Trang Dang, and D. Giampiccolo (2009). The fifth PASCAL recognising textual entailment challenge. In *Proceedings of TAC*, Gaithersburg, MD.

[5]Can be downloaded from `http://www.excitement-project.eu/`.

Bergsma, S., D. Lin, and R. Goebel (2008). Discriminative Learning of Selectional Preference from Unlabeled Text. In *Proceedings of EMNLP*, Honolulu, Hawaii, pp. 59–68.

Bernhard, D. and I. Gurevych (2008). Answering learners' questions by retrieving question paraphrases from social Q&A sites. In *Proceedings of the ACL Workshop on Innovative Use of NLP for Building Educational Applications*, Columbus, Ohio, pp. 44–52.

Bos, J., M. Pennacchiotti, and F. M. Zanzotto (2009). Textual entailment at EVALITA 2009. In *Proceedings of the 11th Conference of the Italian Association for Artificial Intelligence*, Reggio Emilia.

Chen, D. L. and W. B. Dolan (2010). Building a persistent workforce on Mechanical Turk for multilingual data collection. In *Proceedings of the AAAI Human Computation Workshop*, San Francisco, CA.

Dagan, I., O. Glickman, and B. Magnini (2005). The PASCAL Recognising Textual Entailment Challenge. In *Proceedings of the First PASCAL Challenges Workshop on Recognising Textual Entailment*, Southampton, UK.

Harabagiu, S. and A. Hickl (2006). Methods for using textual entailment in open-domain question answering. In *Proceedings of COLING/ACL*, Sydney, Australia, pp. 905–912.

Harabagiu, S., A. Hickl, and F. Lacatusu (2007). Satisfying information needs with multi-document summaries. *Information Processing and Management 43*(6), 1619–1642.

Kouylekov, M. and M. Negri (2010). An open-source package for recognizing textual entailment. In *Proceedings of the ACL 2010 System Demonstrations*, Uppsala, Sweden, pp. 42–47.

Lin, D. and P. Pantel (2002). Discovery of inference rules for question answering. *Journal of Natural Language Engineering 7*(4), 343–360.

Mehdad, Y., M. Negri, and M. Federico (2010). Towards cross-lingual textual entailment. In *Proceedings of HLT/NAACL*, Los Angeles, CA, pp. 321–324.

Monz, C. and M. de Rijke (2001). Light-weight entailment checking for computational semantics. In *Proceedings of ICoS*, Siena, Italy, pp. 59–72.

Negri, M., M. Kouylekov, B. Magnini, Y. Mehdad, and E. Cabrio (2009). Towards Extensible Textual Entailment Engines: the EDITS Package. In *Proceeding of IAAI*, Reggio Emilia, Italy.

Peñas, A., Á. Rodrigo, V. Sama, and F. Verdejo (2008). Testing the reasoning for question answering validation. *Journal of Logic and Computation 18*, 459–474.

Peñas, A., Á. Rodrigo, and F. Verdejo (2006). SPARTE: a test suite for recognising textual entailment in spanish. In A. Gelbukh (Ed.), *Proceedings of CICLing*, Lecture Notes in Computer Science.

Romano, L., M. Kouylekov, I. Szpektor, I. Dagan, and A. Lavelli (2006). Investigating a generic paraphrase-based approach for relation extraction. In *Proceedings of EACL*, Trento, Italy, pp. 401–408.

Schmid, H. (1994). Probabilistic part-of-speech tagging using decision trees. In *Proceedings of ICNLP*, Manchester, UK.

Snow, R., B. O'Connor, D. Jurafsky, and A. Ng (2008). Cheap and fast—but is it good?: evaluating non-expert annotations for natural language tasks. In *Proceedings of EMNLP*, Honolulu, HI, pp. 254–263.

Wang, R. and C. Callison-Burch (2010). Cheap facts and counter-facts. In *Proceedings of the NAACL HLT 2010 Workshop on Creating Speech and Language Data with Amazons Mechanical Turk*, pp. 163–167.

Wang, R. and G. Neumann (2008). Information synthesis for answer validation. In *Proceedings of CLEF 2008*, Aarhus, Denmark.

Pre-Processing MRSes

Tore Bruland
Norwegian University of Science and Technology
Department of Computer and Information Science
torebrul@idi.ntnu.no

Abstract

We are in the process of creating a pipeline for our HPSG grammar for Norwegian (NorSource). NorSource uses the meaning representation Minimal Recursion Semantics (MRS). We present a step for validating an MRS and a step for pre-processing an MRS. The pre-processing step connects our MRS elements to a domain ontology and it can create additional states and roles. The pipeline can be reused by other grammars from the Delph-In network.

1 Introduction

NorSource[1] (Beermann and Hellan, 2004; Hellan and Beermann, 2005), a grammar for Norwegian, is a Head-Driven Phrase Structure Grammar (HPSG) (Sag et al., 2003), developed and maintained with the Linguistic Knowledge Builder (LKB) tool (Copestake, 2002), and originally based on the HPSG Grammar Matrix, which is a starter kit for developing HPSG grammars (Bender et al., 2002). An HPSG grammar can use Minimal Recursion Semantics (MRS) as meaning representation (Copestake et al., 2005). In order to speed up the parsing process (the unification algorithm), a HPSG grammar can be compiled and run (parsing) with the PET[2] tool (Callmeier, 2001). The Flop program in PET compiles the LKB grammar and the Cheap program runs it. An alternative to the PET system is the Answer Constraint Engine (ACE)[3] created by Woodley Packard. ACE can parse and generate using the compiled grammar.

Our goal is to create a pipeline for the NorSource grammar and use it to create small question-answer systems or dialogue systems. The first step in the pipeline is the parsing process with ACE. The next step is to select the most suitable MRS. We use Velldal's ranking model (Velldal, 2008). The model is based on relevant sentences from our system, treebanked with [tsdb++] (Oepen et al., 2002; Oepen and Flickinger, 1998). The selected MRS is checked with the Swiss Army Knife of Underspesification (Utool) (Koller and Thater, 2006b) and our own validating procedure. Only well-formed MRSes are used in our pipeline. We also use Utool to solve the MRS and to eliminate any logically equivalent readings. The next step is to pre-process the MRS (calculate event structure and generate roles), and the last step in our pipeline creates a First-Order Logic formula from the MRS (only the easy cases).

Our contribution is the validating step and the pre-processing step.

In the next section, we give a brief introduction to MRS. Then we present details from our validating procedure. Next, we solve an MRS and eliminate logically equivalent readings with Utool. We pre-process the selected MRS in section 6. At last, we look at a way to create a First-Order Logic formula from a solved MRS and we present a few challenges from our research.

[1] http://typecraft.org/tc2wiki/Norwegian_HPSG_grammar_NorSource
[2] http://pet.opendfki.de/
[3] http://moin.delph-in.net/AceTop

2 Minimal Recursion Semantics

The elements of an MRS can be defined by the structure mrs(T, I, R, C), where *T* is the top handle, *I* is the index, *R* is a bag of elementary predictions (EP), and *C* is a bag of constraints.

Every dog chases some white cat (1)

(1) can have the following MRS (created for demonstration purposes):

T h_0,

I e_1,

R { h_1:every(x_1,h_3,h_8), h_3:dog(x_1), h_7:white(x_2), h_7:cat(x_2), h_5:some(x_2,h_{10},h_9), h_4:chase(e_1,x_1,x_2) }

C $h_{10} =_q h_7$

An MRS can be in two states: unsolved or solved. An algorithm (LKB and Utool) brings an MRS from the unsolved state into one or more solved states. An unsolved MRS has holes that are not in the set of labels, and a solved MRS has holes that are from the set of labels. The set of labels in our example: $\{h_1$, h_3, h_4, h_5 and $h_7\}$. The set of holes: $\{h_3$, h_8, h_9 and $h_{10}\}$. A hole can be either open or closed. A hole is open when it isn't in the set of labels, and a hole is closed when the hole is in the set of labels. Hole h_3 is closed in our example.

3 Validate MRSes From NorSource

We want to search our MRSes for properties that can lead to problems. The Utool solvable function checks if an unsolved MRS can be transformed into one or more solved MRSes without violating the MRS definitions.[4] Our validating procedure contains a set of functions. We create variables or list of variables for each function that is positive. The functions are: *empty index*, *empty feature*, *empty reference*, *key conjunction*, and *argument EP conjunction*. An *empty index* exist when the index value refers to a variable that is not an EP's arg_0. An *empty feature* exist when a feature value refers to a variable that is not found in the EP's arguments. An *empty reference* exist when an argument refers to a variable that is not an EP's arg_0 and the variable is not in the set of feature values. A *key conjunction* exist when more than one EP in an MRS have the same arg_0 and they are not quantifiers. An *argument EP conjunction* exists when an argument contains a label that is an EP conjunction. In Table 1, the variable

EP	Feature
h_3:pred$_1$(arg_0(e_1),arg_1(h_9))	e_1,feature$_1$,value$_1$
h_9:pred$_2$(arg_0(u_1),arg_1(x_1),arg_2(u_{10}))	u_{12},feature$_2$,value$_2$
h_9:pred$_3$(arg_0(u_1),arg_1(x_1),arg_2(x_2),arg_3(u_{15}))	u_{15},feature$_3$,value$_3$
h_2:pred$_4$(arg_0(x_1))	u_{16},feature$_4$,value$_4$
h_4:pred$_5$(arg_0(x_2))	

Table 1: Eps and Features

u_{12} is an empty feature. The variable u_{10} is a empty reference. The arg_0 of pred_2 and pred_3 form a key conjunction. The argument h_9 in arg_1 of pred_1 is an argument EP conjunction.

[4]Utool is stricter than the LKB software, see Fuchss et al. (2006).

4 Selecting An MRS

Before we create a ranking model, we analyze and compare the MRSes from our domain.[5] We use the variable-free solution Oepen and Lønning introduced (Oepen and Lønning, 2006). We compare parts from the syntax tree, the EPs, the features, and if the MRS is solvable or not. We also present results from our validation procedure. If we parse (2) with NorSource, it yields 9 MRSes. Parts of the EP information is presented in Table 2.

	1	2	3	4	5	6	7	8	9
legge_v ARG1 addressee-rel	x	x	x	x	x	x	x	x	x
legge_v ARG2 bok_n	x	x	x	x	x	x	x	x	x
legge_v ARGX på_p		x	x						
på_p ARG1 bok_n	x	x	x			x	x	x	x
på_p ARG1 legge_v				x	x				
på_p ARG2 bord-1_n	x	x	x	x	x	x	x	x	x

Table 2: Compare MRSes

Legg boken på bordet
Put the book on the table (2)

We use the LOGON software to treebank ([tsdb++]) and to create our ranking model (we have copied adjusted the scripts in folder lingo/redwoods). We parse with the ranking model and we select the first MRS.

5 Solving The MRS

Utool solves an MRS using a dominance graph and a chart (Niehren and Thater, 2003). The redundancy elimination algorithm (Koller and Thater, 2006a) takes a chart and a redundancy elimination file as input and returning the chart without the redundancy. We have created a redundancy elimination file according to (Koller and Thater, 2006b) for our quantifiers.

6 Pre-Processing The Selected MRS

In the pre-processing step we focus on the event structure and roles. By event structure we mean: sub events, aspectual and causal notions. Vendler grouped verbs into classes based on their temporal properties (Vendler, 1967). The verbs are classified according to duration and presence of a terminal point. A verb with a terminal point is called telic (the verb culminates). Vendler's classes are also known by other terms such as: eventualities, situations, lexical aspect or Aktionsart. The classes are: state, point, process, achievement, and accomplishment. The verb's connection to a class is not static, because a verb argument can move an event from one class into another. This phenomenon is called aspectual composition or coercion (Moens and Steedman, 1988).

A predicate string in an EP can contain the prefix "_", the suffix "_rel", a name, a part-of-speech type and a sense number. The name, the part-of-speech type and the sense number can be connected to a domain ontology definition. If we don't have the sense number, we can have a list of domain ontology definition candidates. A predicate string can also be a unique name like in "first_position_prominent".

Our goal with the pre-processing is:

- to connect the names in the predicate strings to a domain ontology
- to check if the predicate and the predicate arguments are valid according to the domain

[5] A demo for NorSource: `http://regdili.idi.ntnu.no:8080/comparemrs/compare`

- to create a common structure for a set of verbs
- implement an algorithm for roles and states

The main elements of our solution are a predicate tree, an algorithm, a domain ontology, and a set of object-oriented classes. The predicate tree is created from the predicates and their arguments.

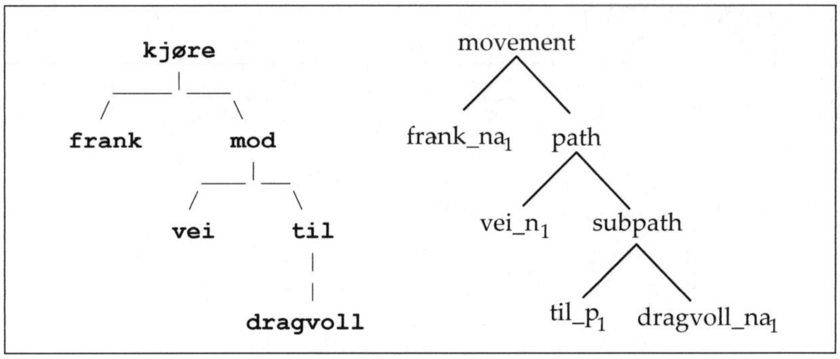

Figure 1: The Predicate Tree and the Movement Class

Frank kjører veien til Dragvoll
Frank drives the road to Dragvoll (3)

The predicate tree on the left in Figure 1 is created from (3). The algorithm searches the predicate tree and for each node in the tree it finds templates from the domain ontology. A template contains checks against the domain ontology, a return function and a return class. One of the templates used in our example is shown in Table 3. The variable X is replaced by vei_n$_1$ in our example. The final class for

key	nodes	check list	return	class
mod$_5$	node(n,X) node(subpath,til_p$_1$)	isa(X,path_n$_1$)	new	path

Table 3: Template Example

(3) is shown on the right in Figure 1. We have defined three return functions: "new", "call" and "fork". "New" creates the return class from its arguments. "Call" is used when one node consumes another. For example in "VP PP", the PP can be consumed by the VP. "Fork" is used when different classes are connected. For example in "My uncle goes to town" we have a Family class and a Movement class that are connected through the variable for the uncle. The Movement class for (3) contains the following information:

movement
  event(e_1:kjøre_v$_1$)
  subject(x_2:frank_na$_1$)
  path
    object(x_9:vei_n$_1$)
    end-point(x_1:dragvoll_na$_1$,t_2)

checks
  has(dragvoll_na$_1$,location)
  isa(vei_n$_1$,path_n$_1$)
templates
  [tv$_2$, pp$_2$, mod$_5$]

The Movement class is a result from analyzing a number of different sentences about objects changing location. The Movement class is a process and it can contain a path, a departure, an arrival, a road (named path), a vehicle etc. A number of these objects are connected. For example the beginning of the process and the beginning of the path. The beginning of the path and the departure. We have implemented an algorithm for detecting the roles *work* and *cargo*. *Work* indicates an object that is using energy. *Cargo* indicates an object that is being transported.

The classes can be used as they are in a further reasoning process, or they can generate EPs and features that are inserted into the MRS. For example, the state *at_location*(x_4,x_1) can be inserted in an EP conjunction.

7 Logic Form

The solved MRSes are not yet formulas in First-Order Logic. We have to convert arguments that are in a Higher-Order Logic, insert the *not* operator, and use the quantifiers from First-Order Logic. An argument that has an Ep conjunction or has a handle needs to be rewritten. An argument with a handle is replaced with the arg_0 from the EP of the handle. We can give a reference and a predicate to the conjunction or we can find a candidate in the conjunction. We use the latter method. The predicate *_neg_adv_rel* is converted to the operator *not*. We have connected some of the NorSource quantifiers to the First-Order Logic quantifiers *exist* and *all*. Quantifiers like *some*, *few*, etc can be assigned to a group / type of their own. We place an operator between the arguments "RSTR" and "BODY" in our quantifiers:

$$\exists(y)[pred_1(y)\ \mathbf{operator}_1\ \forall(x)[pred_2(x)\ \mathbf{operator}_2\ pred_3(x,y)]]$$

We have defined **operator**$_1$ as $\wedge$ and **operator**$_2$ as $\rightarrow$. The formula from (3) is:

$$\exists(x_1)[na(x_1, dragvoll) \wedge \exists(x_2)[na(x_2, frank) \wedge \exists(x_9)[vei\_n(x_9) \wedge kjøre\_v(e_1, x_2, x_9) \wedge til\_p(u_1, x_9, x_1)]]]$$

The meaning of the MRS quantifiers are preserved with the extra predicates: q_meaning(u100,x_1,def), q_meaning(u101,x_2,def) and q_meaning(u102,x_9,def). These predicates need to be inserted into the logic formula.

8 Challenges

The first challenge is to find a representative selection of sentences from the domain. The sentences are treebanked and used in our ranking model, and their selected MRSes are also used for creating domain ontology definitions. We use a virtual profile where we can add new annotated profiles.

We need to find a way to process our quantifiers that are not in First-Order Logic. At this early stage we can use off-the-shelf theorem provers and model finders as described in Blackburn's and Bos' reasoning framework for First-Order logic (Blackburn and Bos, 2005). We must classify different kinds of questions and commands, and we need to describe how to process them.

So far, we have connected types for each Ep together, but sometimes a more detailed structure is required in order to express meaning. A part of one structure can connect to a part of another. In the examples: "the cat sits in the car", "the cat sits on the car", and "the cat sits under the car", there are three different locations related to the car. We have a container in the car, an area on top of the car, and a space under the car. This extra information needs to be used together with the MRS. Sometimes more ambiguities are introduced and we need a ranking. For example in "Fred poured coffee on the thermos", the most probable is when the coffee ends up inside the thermos and the less probable version where the coffee is poured on the outside of the thermos. We also want to use previous situations and the discourse so far in our pre-processing step.

References

Beermann, D. and L. Hellan (2004). A treatment of directionals in two implemented hpsg grammars. In S. Müller (Ed.), *Proceedings of the HPSG04 Conference*. CSLI Publications.

Bender, E. M., D. Flickinger, and S. Oepen (2002). The grammar matrix: An open-source starter-kit for the rapid development of cross-linguistically consistent broad-coverage precision grammars. In

J. Carroll, N. Oostdijk, and R. Sutcliffe (Eds.), *Proceedings of the Workshop on Grammar Engineering and Evaluation at the 19th International Conference on Computational Linguistics*, Taipei, Taiwan, pp. 8–14.

Blackburn, P. and J. Bos (2005). *Representation and Inference for Natural Language*. CSLI Publications.

Callmeier, U. (2001). *Efficient Parsing with Large-Scale Unification Grammars*. Master thesis, Universit¨at des Saarlandes.

Copestake, A. (2002). *Implementing Typed Feature Structure Grammars*. CSLI.

Copestake, A., D. Flickinger, C. Pollard, and I. A. Sag (2005). Minimal Recursion Semantics. An introduction. *Journal of Research on Language and Computation 3*(4), 281 – 332.

Fuchss, R., A. Koller, J. Niehren, and S. Thater (2006). Minimal recursion semantics as dominance contraints: Translation, evaluation and analysis. In *Proceedings of the 42nd ACL*. Association for Computational Linguistics.

Hellan, L. and D. Beermann (2005). Classification of prepositional senses for deep grammar applications. In V. Kordoni and A. Villavicencio (Eds.), *Proceedings of the 2nd ACL-Sigsem Workshop on The Linguistic Dimensions of Prepositions and their Use in Computational Linguistics Formalisms and Applications*, Colchester, United Kingdom.

Koller, A. and S. Thater (2006a). An improved redundancy elimination algorithm for underspecified representations. In *Proceedings of the 21st International Conference on Computational Linguistics and the 44th annual meeting of the Association for Computational Linguistics*, pp. 409–416. Association for Computational Linguistics.

Koller, A. and S. Thater (2006b). *Utool: The Swiss Army Knife of Underspesification*. Saarland University, Saarbrücken.

Moens, M. and M. Steedman (1988). Temporal ontology and temporal reference. *Computational Linguistics 14*(2).

Niehren, J. and S. Thater (2003). Bridging the gap between underspesification formalisms: Minimal recursion semantics as dominance constraints. In *41st Meeting of the Association of Computational Lingustics*, pp. 367–374.

Oepen, S. and D. Flickinger (1998). Towards systematic grammar profiling. test suite technology ten years after. *Journal of Computer Speech and Language 12*(4), 411–436.

Oepen, S. and J. Lønning (2006). Discriminant-based mrs banking. In *Proceedings of the 5th International Conference on Language Resources and Evaluation (LREC 2006)*.

Oepen, S., K. Toutanova, S. Shieber, C. Manning, D. Flickinger, and T. Brants (2002). The lingo redwoods treebank: Motivation and preliminary applications. In *Proceedings of the 19th international conference on Computational linguistics-Volume 2*, pp. 1–5. Association for Computational Linguistics.

Sag, I. A., T. Wasow, and E. M. Bender (2003). *Syntactic Theory: a formal introduction* (2. ed.). CSLI Publications.

Velldal, E. (2008). *Empirical realization ranking*. Ph. D. thesis, The University of Oslo.

Vendler, Z. (1967). *Linguistics in Philosophy*. Cornell Univerity Press.

The semantic annotation of quantification

Harry Bunt
TiCC, Tilburg Center for Cognition and Communication
Tilburg University, The Netherlands
harry.bunt@uvt.nl

Abstract

This paper presents an approach to the annotation of quantification, developed in the context of an ISO project aiming to define standards for semantic annotation. The approach is illustrated for a range of quantification phenomena, including cumulative, collective, and group quantification.

1 Introduction

In 2012, two ISO standards for semantic annotation were established, one for time and events (ISO 24617-1), and one for dialogue acts (ISO 24617-2); others are under development for semantic roles, spatial information, and discourse relations. Quantification turns up as a problem in nearly all of these efforts. ISO 24617-1 has some provisions for dealing with quantification (see Pustejovsky et al., 2010), but these are too limited and do not always give correct results (Bunt and Pustejovsky, 2010).

The annotation of quantification faces three main issues:

1. Which set of semantic features, expressed most likely as XML attributes and values, adequately characterize a wide range of forms of quantification;
2. Is it possible to define a formal semantics of these expressions;
3. How can the relevant features (attributes and values) be defined as components of the semantic annotations in a way that respects compositional semantics?

Bunt (2005) proposed a way to representing quantifications in terms of feature structures, however, in this proposal the properties of a quantification are all expressed as properties of an event, which is inconvenient for annotators and is hard to combine with a compositional NP semantics. This paper presents an approach where quantification features are distributed over annotation structure components in a way that corresponds to their linguistic expression in syntactic structures, and shows the semantic adequacy of the proposal by a compositional translation into discourse representation structures.

2 Aspects of quantification

Quantification occurs when a predicate is applied to sets of arguments. Questions then arise concerning the precise way that the predicate is applied to members of these sets. As an example, consider the sentence (1a); some of the questions that may be asked (and answered) are (1b) - (1f):

(1) a. *Although a threat had been made before, three men rather unexpectedly moved both pianos.*
   b. How many men were involved? (Answer: *Three.*)
   c. How many pianos were involved? (Answer: *Two.*)
   d. Did the same men move both pianos? (Answer: *Yes.*)
   e. Did the men act collectively or individually? (Answer: *Collectively, probably.*)
   f. Were the pianos acted upon collectively or individually? (Answer: *Individually, probably.*)

Given the *restriction* part of a quantification, that specifies a domain from which elements can be taken that participate in certain events individually, in groups, or collectively, the *distribution* is a function that computes the set of those entities that participate in the events as agents, as themes, as instruments, etc. We call such a set of participants a *predication domain*, and the domain, defined by the restriction, the *reference domain*. In the case of individual distribution, the two are the same.

A common function of proportional quantifier words like *all, some,* and *most*, and of absolute quantifiers like *three, more than five, 2 litres of* is to specify the fraction of the reference domain that is involved in the events under consideration. Numerical and amount quantifiers may also be used to indicate the size of a reference domain, like *twelve* in *The twelve students in this room all speak two languages.*

Proportional and absolute quantifiers can also be used to indicate the number/amount of a predication domain per element of another predication domain, like *five* in *Each of the dogs ate five sausages.*

Some of the most important aspects of quantification, distinguished in (Bunt, 1985) are:

(2)
1. the quantifier's restriction, describing the reference domain of the quantification;
2. the distribution, defining the predication domain;
3. size of the reference domain;
4. involvement of the reference domain (in absolute or relative terms);
5. relative scoping of the quantifications associated with argument NPs;
6. scoping of NP-quantifications relative to quantified events;
7. size of groups of elements from a reference domain;
8. number of elements of a reference domain involved per element of a predication domain.

3 Events, participants, and quantification annotation

In a davidsonian approach to meaning, we may view the combination of a verb with its arguments as introducing a set of events ('eventualities', more generally) of the type indicated by the verb, and with a number of properties concerning the way in which the participants of these events are involved. Applying this view to sentence (1a), we obtain a descriptions in terms of a set of move-events, a set of men, participating in these events as agents, and a set of pianos that participate as themes. This is exactly what is expressed in an annotation of semantic roles according to the ISO standard 24617-4 under development (see Bunt & Palmer, 2013):

(3)
```
[v1:] <event xml:id="e1" target="#m2" eventType="move"/>
[p1:] <participant xml:id="x1" target="#m1" entityType="man"/>
[p2:] <participant xml:id="x2" target="#m3" entityType="piano"/>
[L1:] <srLink event="#e1" participant="#x1" semRole="agent"/>
[L2:] <srLink event="#e1" participant="#x2" semRole="theme"/>
```

Since quantification occurs when two or more sets of arguments are related by a predicate, we can view the quantifications in (1a) as due to the Agent and Theme predicate relating sets of events and participants. This information can thus be represented as properties of the semantic role links (<srLink>), adding features to these links as follows, where the feature @signature="set" expresses that the sentence is about sets of events and participants :

(4)
```
[v1:] <event xml:id="e1" target="#m2" eventType="move" signature="set"/>
[p1:] <participant xml:id="x1" target="#m1" entityType="man”
       signature ="set" involvement="3"/>
[p2:] <participant xml:id="x2" target="#m3" entityType="piano"
       signature ="set" definiteness="def" involvement="2"/>
[L1:] <srLink event="#e1" participant="#x1" semRole="agent"/>
       distribution="collective"/>
[L2:] <srLink event="#e1" participant="#x2" semRole="theme"
       distribution="individual"/>
```

The correctness and usefulness of annotating quantification this way depends on how well it deals with the three issues mentioned in Section 1: expressive adequacy of attributes and values; their semantic adequacy; and compatibility with compositional phrase semantics. These issues are addressed next.

4 Representational and semantic adequacy

Of the information types listed in (2), those numbered 1, 2, 4, and 8 can be represented by the attributes and values shown in (4). For types 3, 5, 6 and 7, the attribute `@cardinality` is defined for `<event>` (for *"say twice"* etc.) and `<participant>` elements; the attribute `@outScoping` allows the expression of relative scope restrictions; and the values of the `@groupCard` attribute can be used to indicate group sizes in group quantifications. This provides the expressive power to represent a wide range of quantification phenomena.

The issue of compatibility with compositional NP semantics arises because we propose to represent some of the properties of a quantification as parts of semantic role links, where traditionally the semantic representation of quantification is considered to be part of NP semantics. This is in particular the case with distribution, as in (4). Having `@distribution` as an attribute of `<participant>` elements would run into problems for a sentence such as *The men had a beer before they moved the piano*, where the subject NP should be interpreted individually for the drinking, but collectively for the lifting.

The semantic adequacy of the proposed annotation format can be shown by defining a systematic translation of annotations into DRSs, following Bunt (2011; 2013). XML elements describing sets of events or participants, like those in (4), are translated to a DRS which introduces a higher-order (i.e. set-valued) discourse marker,[1] and conditions translating the other features. DRSs interpreting linking elements introduce discourse markers for the linked sets of elements, and conditions that further characterize the link, e.g.:

[v1:] $\rightsquigarrow \langle\{E_1\},\{\langle\langle\{e\},\{e \in E_1\}\rangle \Rightarrow \langle\{\},\{move(e)\}\rangle\rangle\}\rangle$, or in box form: 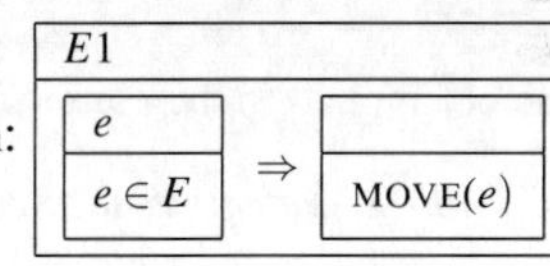

[p1]: $\rightsquigarrow$ 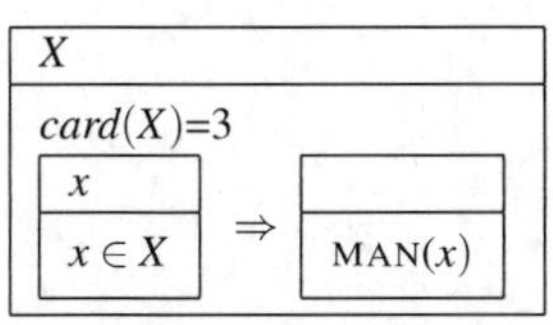

[L1:] $\rightsquigarrow$ 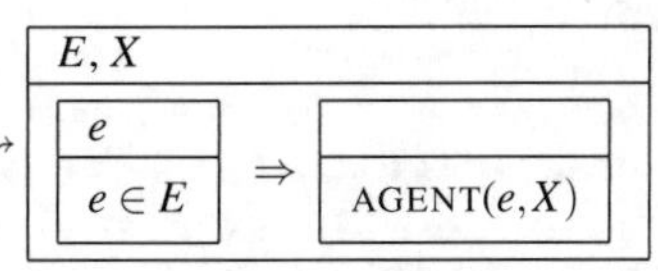

The merge of these DRSs plus those translating [p2] and [L2] yields the satisfactory result:[2]

$[p1 \cup L1] \cup [p2 \cup L2] \cup v1 =$ 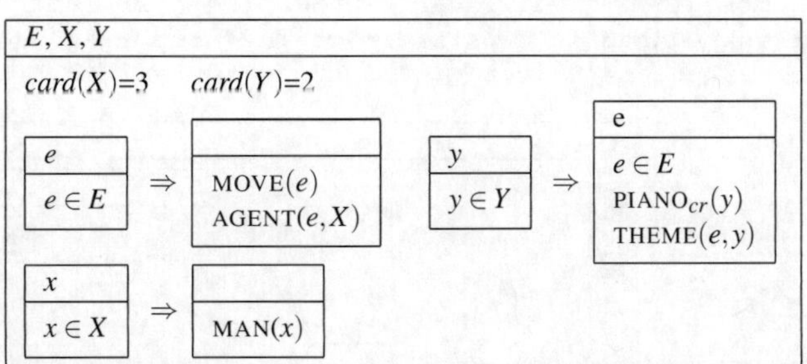

Note that in this example both NPs outscope the verb; their relative scoping is irrelevant since the group of three men acted collectively, as a single entity. While verbs very often have narrow scope relative to argument NPs, this is not always the case, as (5) illustrates. Using the attributes and values introduced so far, the wide-scope interpretation of *"die"* is easily annotated:[3]

(5) a. *Everybody will die.*
b. Annotation for wide-scope 'die':

[1]The presentation is simplified here; see Bunt (2013) for the use of pairs $\langle m,x\rangle$ of markables and discourse markers, where the markables make sure that only the intended marker variables are unified upon DRS-merging.

[2]The subscript 'cr' (for 'contextually relevant') indicates the interpretation of the definiteness of the NP *both pianos*.

[3]We assume here an approach to semantic roles which allows an event to have more than one theme, such as the LIRICS annotation scheme (Petukhova & Bunt, 2007).

```
[v1:] <event xml:id="e1" target="#m1" eventType="die" signature="set"
      cardinality="1"/>
[p1:] <participant xml:id="x1" target="#m2" entityType="person"
      signature="set" involvement="all"/>
[L1:] <srLink event="#e1" participant="x1" semRole="theme"
      outScoping="#e1 #x1"/>
```

c. Semantics:

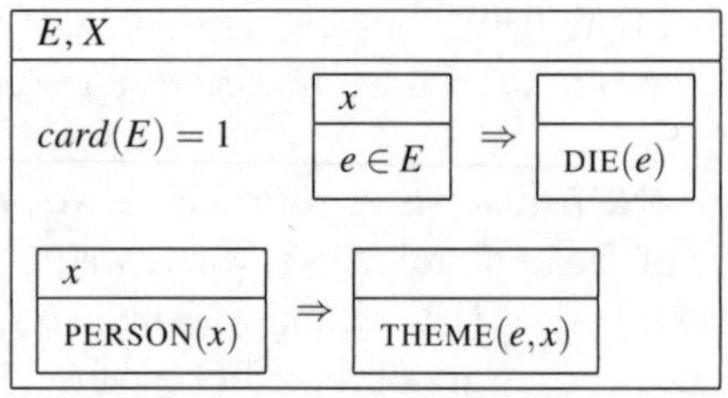

Cases of quantified NPs with unequal scope are readily annotated in the format outlined here, but in order to support these annotations by a well-defined semantics a new kind of merge operation on DRSs is neede, the *scoped merge*, which is defined as follows:

(6)

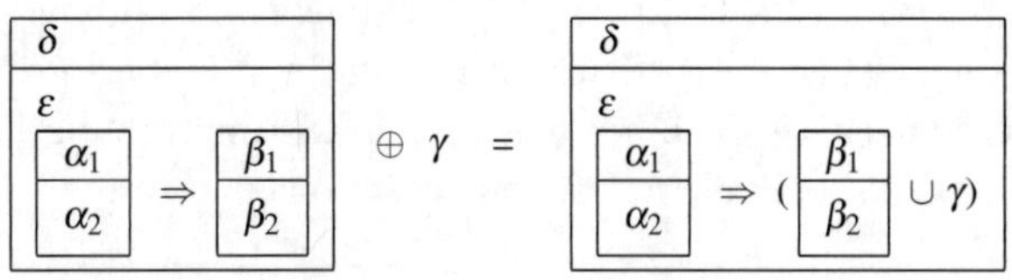

For instance, applied to the classical scoping example (7a), we obtain the semantics (7c) of the annotation (7b):

(7) a. *All the students read two papers*

b. Annotation for wide-scope *two papers*:

```
[v1:] <event xml:id="e1" target="#m1" eventType="read" signature="set"/>
[p1:] <participant xml:id="x1" target="#m2" entityType="student"
      definiteness="def" signature ="set" involvement="all"/>
[p2:] <participant xml:id="x2" target="#m3" entityType="paper"
      signature ="set" cardinality="2" involvement="all"/>
[L1:] <srLink event="#e1" participant="x1" semRole="agent"
      distribution="individual" outScoping="#x1 #e1"/>
[L2:] <srLink event="#e1" participant="x2" semRole="theme"
      distribution="individual" outScoping="#x2 #x1"/>
```

c. Semantics:

$[p2 \cup L2] \oplus [p1 \cup L1 \cup v1] =$

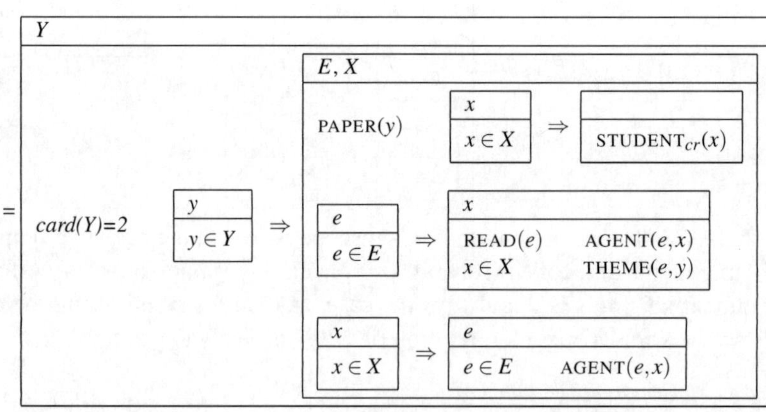

Besides scoped quantifications, also unscoped, partially scoped, and equally scoped quantifications have to be considered. Partially and unscoped scoped cases, where there is no or incomplete information about relative scoping, are easily annotated by not specifying values for `@outScoping` attributes, and interpreted with underspecified DRSs (see Reyle 1993; 1994). Equally scoped quantifications, as occurring in *cumulative quantification* (Scha, 1981) and in group quantification (Bunt, 1985), can be annotated using the attribute `@eqScope`, as shown in (8) and (9). The semantics is obtained simply by using the ordinary rather than the scoped merge of the sub-DRSs.

(8) a. *Three breweries supplied fifteen inns.*

b. Annotation of cumulative reading (*In total 3 breweries supplied in total 15 inns*):

```
[v1:] <event xml:id="e1" target="#m2" eventType="supply" signature="set"/>
[p1:] <participant xml:id="x1" target="#m1" entityType="brewery"
      signature ="set" involvement="3"/>
[p2:] <participant xml:id="x2" target="#m3" entityType="inn"
      signature ="set" involvement="15"/>
[L1:] <srLink event="#e1" participant="#x1" semRole="agent"
      distribution="individual" eqScope="#x1 #x2"/>
[L2:] <srLink event="#e1" participant="x2" semRole="theme"
      distribution="individual" eqScope="#x2 #x1"/>
```

c. Semantics:

$(p1 \cup L1) \cup (p2 \cup L2) \cup v1 =$

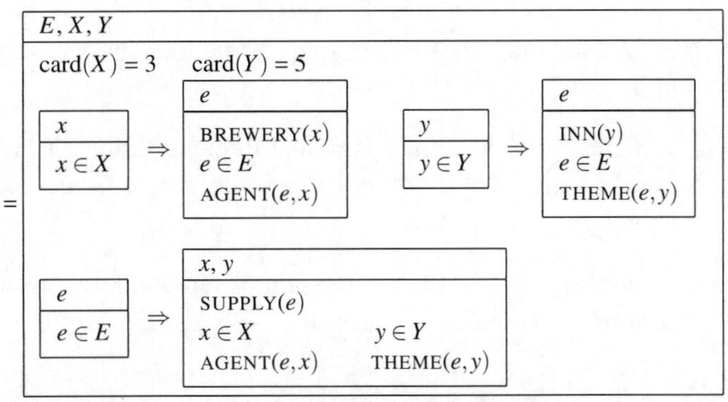

Group quantification, as in *Three boys played soccer against five girls* on the reading where teams of 3 boys played against teams of 5 girls, can be annotated by using, besides the `@eqScope` attribute, the `@groupCard` attribute. The semantics is obtained by interpreting the participant annotations as DRSs introducing discourse markers for sets of sets of 3 boys and 5 girls.

(9)

```
[e1:] <event xml:id="e1" target="#m2" eventType="play" signature="set"/>
[p1:] <participant xml:id="x1" target="#m1" entityType="boy"
      signature ="set" groupCard="3"/>
[p2:] <participant xml:id="x2" target="#m3" entityType="girl"
      signature ="set" distribution="group" groupCard="5"/>
[L1:] <srLink event="#e1" participant="x1" semRole="agent"
      distribution="group" eqScope="#x1 #x2"/>
[L2:] <srLink event="#e1" participant="x2" semRole="co-agent"
      distribution="group" eqScope="#x2 #x1"/>
```

5 Concluding Remarks

We have described the essentials of a way of annotating quantification phenomena where the features that characterize different forms of quantification and their properties are distributed over components of annotation structures in a way that corresponds to their linguistic expression (e.g., involvement and cardinality are features of `<participant>` components, corresponding to their expression in NPs).

Taking a davidsonian approach, we have introduced attributes and values for events, event participants, and the semantic roles of participants in events. However, the view of quantification which underlies this is more general; when predicate and argument structures are used, rather than events with participants and semantic roles, that is easily accommodated, by introducing `<predicate>`. `<argument>`, and `<argLink>` elements, and e.g. attaching distribution and scoping features to the letter, as in:

(10)
```
<argLink pred="#P1" arg="#x1" argNum="arg1" distr="collective"/>
```

Quantification over events, time and place can be annotated in a similar way. As suggested by Lee & Bunt (2012), Temporal quantification can be annotated by adding features to the `<event>` and `<timex3>` elements defined in ISO 24617-2 and to the `<tLink>` that represents the semantic relation between a set of events and a set of temporal entities (as in *Most of the professors teach every Monday*.

Clearly, something similar can be done for the annotation of quantifications over events and space, as occurring in *Policemen can be found at every streetcorner*, adding the same features to the elements defined in the ISO-Space language under development (see Pustejovsky et al., 2012).

References

Bunt, H. (1985). *Mass Terms and Model-Theoretic Semantics.* Cambridge University Press.

Bunt, H. (2005). Quantification and Modification Represented as Feature Structures. In *Proceedings 6th International Workshop on Computational Semantics (IWCS-6)*, Tilburg, Netherlands, pp. 54–65.

Bunt, H. (2011). Abstract syntax and semantics in semantic annotation, applied to time and events. In E. Lee and A. Yoon (Eds.), *Recent Trends in Language and Knowledge Processing*. Seoul: Hankukmunhwasa.

Bunt, H. (2013). A Methodology for Designing Semantic Annotations. *Language Resources and Evaluation (forthc.).*

Bunt, H. and M. Palmer (2013). Conceptual and Representational Choices in Defining an ISO Standard for Semantic Role Annotation. In *Proceedings of the Ninth Joint ACL-ISO Workshop on Interoperable Semantic Annotation ISA-9*, Potsdam.

Bunt, H. and J. Pustejovsky (2010). Annotation of temporal and event quantification. In *Proceedings of the Fifth Joint ACL-ISO Workshop on Interoperable Semantic Annotation ISA-5*, Hong Kong, pp. 15–22.

ISO24617-1:2012 (2012). *Language Resource Management - Semantic Annotation Framework, Part 1: Time and Events (SemAF/Time).* ISO Standard 24617-1, March 2012, Geneva. March 2012.

ISO24617-2:2012 (2012). *Language Resource Management - Semantic Annotation Framework, Part 2: Dialogue Acts (SemAF/Dialogue acts).* ISO Standard 24617-2, September 2012, ISO, Geneva.

Lee, K. and H. Bunt (2012). Counting time and events. In *Proceedings of the Eighth Joint ACL-ISO Workshop on Interoperable Semantic Annotation ISA-8*, Pisa, pp. 34–41.

Petukhova, V. and H. Bunt (2008, May). LIRICS Semantic Role Annotation: Design and Evaluation of a Set of Data Categories. In *Proceedings of the Sixth International Conference on Language Resources and Evaluation (LREC 2008)*, Genova, Italy.

Pustejovsky, J., K. Lee, H. Bunt, and L. Romary (2010). ISO-TimeML: An International Standard for Semantic Annotation. In *Proceedings of the Sevenfth International Conference on Language Resources and Evaluation (LREC 2010), Malta*, Paris, pp. 394–397. ELDA.

Pustejovsky, J., J. Moszkowics, and M. Verhagen (2012). The Current Status of ISO-Space. In *Proceedings of Joint ISA-7, SRSL-3 and I@MRT Workshop at LREC 2012), Istanbul*, Paris. ELDA.

Reyle, U. (1993). Dealing with Ambiguity by Underspecification. *Journal of Semantics 10(2)*, 123–179.

Reyle, U. (1994). Monotonic Disambiguation and Plural Pronoun Resolution. In H. Kamp (Ed.), *Ellipsis, Tense, and Questions. Esprit project 6852 DYANA-2, Deliverable R2.2.B.* Stuttgart: IMS.

Scha, R. (1981). Distributive, Collective and Cumulative Quantification. In J. Groenendijk and M. Stokhof (Eds.), *Formal Methods in the Study of Language*. Amsterdam: Mathematical Center.

Scope Disambiguation as a Tagging Task

Kilian Evang
CLCG, Rijksuniversiteit Groningen
k.evang@rug.nl

Johan Bos
CLCG, Rijksuniversiteit Groningen
johan.bos@rug.nl

Abstract

In this paper we present a pragmatic account of scope alternation involving universal quantifiers in a lexicalist framework based on CCG and DRT. This account can derive the desired reading for 96% of all cases of scope interaction involving universal quantification mediated by prepositions in a real corpus. We show how this account allows for recasting scope resolution as a simple token classification task, providing a simpler handle for statistical approaches to scope resolution than previous accounts.

1 Introduction

The correct handling of scope-bearing operators such as quantifiers, negation and intensional verbs is crucial for constructing logical form from text that capture the intended meaning. A lot of work has been done to describe the scope alternation behavior especially of quantifiers and to construct underspecified meaning representations from which all (theoretically) possible readings of a sentence containing them can be enumerated (Reyle, 1993; Bos, 1996; Copestake et al., 2005; Egg et al., 2001). The problem of finding the preferred reading in each concrete case has also been addressed, using machine learning (Higgins and Sadock, 2003; Andrew and MacCartney, 2004; Srinivasan and Yates, 2009; Manshadi and Allen, 2011).

Despite these efforts, existing wide-coverage semantic parsers do not typically resolve scope. Either the semantic representations they output are shallow and do not use logical quantifiers, which is sufficient for many applications but not for model-theoretic reasoning. Or they leave the output underspecified or always deterministically pick the same scoping behavior for a given quantifier.

How to make a semantic parser aware of scope alternation? We argue that an additional layer of tags is a good way. A semantic parser can use these tags to guide its decisions—just like it might use a layer of word sense tags and a layer of named-entity tags, and just like a syntactic parser uses part-of-speech tags. Scope tags can guide the construction of logical forms from the start and thereby avoid the additional computational and representational complexity of underspecified representations. At the same time, this approach avoids the need to change the syntactic parsing model.

In this paper we show how we applied this technique to the semantic parsing system of Curran et al. (2007). It consists of C&C, a statistical syntactic parser whose output includes predicate-argument structures, and Boxer, a semantic construction component which builds interpretable semantic representations. The resulting enhanced system is being used in constructing the Groningen Meaning Bank (GMB), a large corpus of English text annotated with logical form (Basile et al., 2012).

2 Formal Background

Boxer's lexical-semantic framework (Bos, 2009) uses the output of the C&C parser, which consists of derivations in Combinatory Categorial Grammar (CCG; Steedman, 2001). In these derivations, words and smaller constituents combine into larger constituents using combinatory rules such as forward application, which combines a *functor* category $X/Y : f$ with an *argument* category $Y : a$ to yield a new constituent with category $X : f@a$ (1-place function f applied to a). Left of the colon are syntactic

$$\lambda p.(\begin{array}{|c|}\hline x \\ \hline \text{member}(x) \\ \hline \end{array} ; (p@x)) \qquad \lambda p.\begin{array}{|c|}\hline \\ \hline \begin{array}{|c|}\hline x \\ \hline \text{member}(x) \\ \hline \end{array} \Rightarrow (p@x) \\ \hline \end{array}$$

Figure 1: Generalized quantifiers denoted by the NPs *a member* and *every member*

$$\lambda io.\lambda do.\lambda su.\lambda mp.(su@\lambda x.(io@\lambda y.(do@\lambda z.(\begin{array}{|c|}\hline e \\ \hline \text{give}(e) \\ \text{Agent}(e,x) \\ \text{Recipient}(e,y) \\ \text{Theme}(e,z) \\ \hline \end{array} ; (mp@e)))))$$

Figure 2: Semantics of the verb *give*, ignoring tense. The core consists of a DRS introducing an event discourse referent e and relating it to the arguments using thematic role relations. The modifier semantics is applied to e, the result is combined with the core DRS using merge reduction (;). The rest is largely for dealing with NP arguments.

categories that determine the ways in which constituents are allowed to combine, right of it are semantic categories that specify the semantics of a constituent based on the semantics of the constituents that combined to form it. There are a number of combinatory rules besides forward application, and each specifies syntax and semantics in a similar way. Boxer's most important task is thus to assign a semantics to each word; given the derivation, the semantics of each phrase then follows deterministically.

The semantics of all functor categories, such as verbs and prepositions, must be prepared to combine with their arguments and therefore must be functions. They are specified using the notation of the lambda calculus. For example, the semantics of a ditransitive verb has the form $\lambda io.\lambda do.\lambda su.\mathbf{sent}$ where *io*, *do*, *su* are variables standing for the semantics of the indirect object, the direct object and the subject respectively, reflecting the order in which the verb arguments combine syntactically, and $\mathbf{sent}$ is the semantics of the resulting sentence, specified in terms of the verb meaning and *io*, *do*, *su*.

Boxer uses a neo-Davidsonian event semantics, expressing verb meanings using event individuals that permit an unlimited number of verb modifiers. This motivated a decision to represent sentence meanings themselves as functions—from event properties to sentence meanings—to allow modifiers to combine with them. $\mathbf{sent}$ above is therefore always of the form $\lambda mp.\mathbf{drs}$ where *mp* is a variable standing for an event property and $\mathbf{drs}$ is an expression that evaluates to a proper truth-theoretic meaning representation in the form of a discourse representation structure (DRS; Kamp and Reyle, 1993).

All noun phrases are analyzed as generalized quantifiers, i.e. functions from individual properties to DRSs. Figure 1 shows the semantics of *a member* and *every member* as examples. Verb semantics take the status of NPs as generalized quantifiers into account by using *predicate abstraction*: they apply an NP semantics to a property that expresses the core verb meaning, modifier meanings, and meanings of any previously absorbed arguments. For example, for a ditransitive verb, the $\mathbf{drs}$ part above has the form $(su@\lambda x.(do@\lambda y.(io@\lambda z.\mathbf{drs}')))$. Figure 2 shows a full semantics of the verb *give*.

3 Scope-mediating Categories

3.1 Verbs

It is easy to see from Figure 2 that in our lexical-semantic framework, it is the semantics of a verb that determines the relative scope of its arguments. For example, with the given lexical entry, the sentence *A lecturer gave every student a book* receives an interpretation with a unique lecturer, but if we swap the substrings $su@\lambda x$ and $io@\lambda y$, every student got a book from a potentially distinct lecturer. We thus account for scope ambiguity by giving verbs different interpretations, as in the proposal of Hendriks (1993). Boxer can generate an appropriate lexical entry for any scope order given a tag on the verb encoding the scope order of arguments—e.g., for a three-place verb, one of 312, 321, 132, 123, 231, 213.

Table 1: Eight types of scope interaction involving universal quantifiers, mediated by a preposition. Columns indicate what the preposition attaches to (verb or noun phrase), which of its arguments contains the universal quantifier (object or the phrase it attaches to), and whether the universal quantifier has wide or narrow scope. All examples are from the Groningen Meaning Bank (GMB); numbers in brackets are GMB document identifiers.

	att	∀ in	∀ scope	example	count
(a)	NP	obj	wide	Finally the gorgeous jewel of the order, gleaming upon *the breast* **of** *every member*, suggested "your Badgesty," which was adopted, and the order became popularly known as the Kings of Catarrh. [72/0696]	115
(b)	NP	att	wide	*All such attacks* **by** *drone aircraft* are believed to be carried out by U.S. forces. [76/0357]	32
(c)	VP	obj	wide	Jobs *grew* **in** *every sector except manufacturing*, with much of the growth due to hurricane clean-up efforts in Florida. [97/0059]	57
(d)	VP	att	wide	NATO says militants surrounded the outpost, *firing from all directions* **with** *rocket-propelled grenades, small arms and mortars*. [92/0311]	25
(e)	NP	obj	narrow	He is the former director of national intelligence, *the head* **of** *all U.S. intelligence agencies*. [59/0286]	44
(f)	NP	att	narrow	The official Xinhua news agency says *all 28 workers* **in** *a mine in northwestern Shaanxi province* died when an underground cable caught fire on Saturday night. [40/0608]	16
(g)	VP	obj	narrow	Responsibility for Africa is *currently fractured* **under** *all three*. [90/0450]	11
(h)	VP	att	narrow	Opening batsman Jamie How *led all scorers* **with** *88 runs* as New Zealand reached 203-4 in 42.1 overs. [13/0199]	17
(i)	NP	obj	neutral	He said methods such as abortion do not fight poverty or help a country's development but actually constitute "*the destruction* **of** *the poorest of all human beings*." [13/0428]	1
(j)	NP	att	neutral	It tacitly encouraged Iraq's minority Sunni Muslims to vote, saying *all segments* **of** *the Iraqi people* must go to the polls. [52/0038]	83
(k)	VP	obj	neutral	The preferred stock, which would have a dividend rate of $ 1.76 a year, would *be convertible into Heritage common* **at** *a rate of four common shares for each preferred*. [38/0686]	3
(l)	VP	att	neutral	The program airs in 40 countries worldwide, and *every Idolwinner records* **through** *Sony BMG*. [75/0494]	52

3.2 Prepositions

Scope interactions involving universal quantifiers and mediated by prepositions can roughly be classified along three binary distinctions: whether the preposition attaches to a verb or a noun, whether it is the object of the preposition or the phrase it attaches to that contains the universal quantifier, and whether the universal quantifier takes wide scope over the other argument of the preposition. Table 1 has an example for each situation.

Whether the universal quantifier must take wide scope depends on the desired interpretation. It should take wide scope if the non-universal argument introduces an entity that is non-specific, i.e. whose extension depends on the instantiation of the universally quantified-over variable. In this case, the universal argument should take wide scope. This is the case in (a–d). On the other hand, if the non-universal argument introduces an existentially quantified-over variable that is necessarily the same for all instantiations of the universally quantified-over variable, the non-universal argument must take wide scope. This is the case in (e–h). There are also cases were neither of the two criteria applies, e.g. because the non-universal argument is a definite that should be interpreted at a global level. Examples are shown

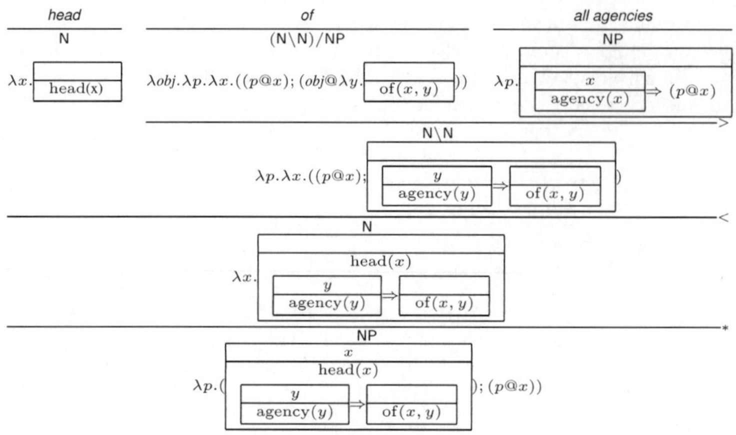

Figure 3: NP derivation with narrow-scope modifier

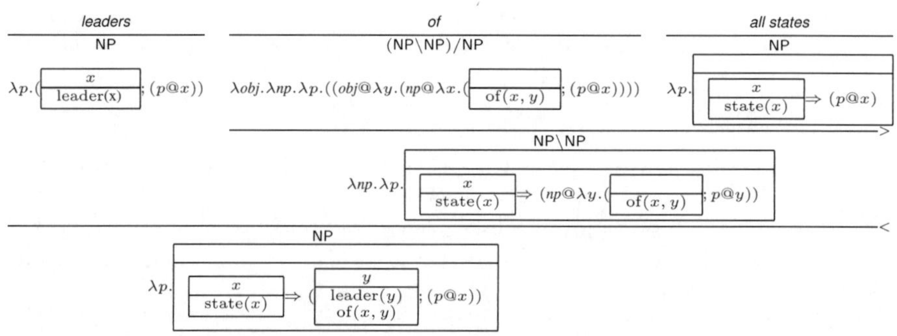

Figure 4: NP derivation with wide-scope modifier

in (i–l). Finally, in rare cases, both of the aforementioned criteria may apply simultaneously. The only example we found of this in the corpus is given in (1) below, where the modifier *in all major cities and towns* should be outscoped by *an Islamic alliance*, but outscope *members*. In such cases, our scheme is too coarse-grained to derive the desired semantics.

(1) *Members of an Islamic alliance and other parties took to the streets Saturday* **in** *all major cities and towns*, where speakers denounced General Musharraf for breaking his promise. [50/0210]

Scope alternation in these configurations can be effected using just two scope tags on prepositions, indicating modifier wide scope (inv as in a,c,f,h) vs. modified constituent wide scope (noninv as in b,d,e,g). For cases like (i–l), one tag can be used as the default.

In the case of verb phrase modifiers, preposition semantics effecting the desired scope behavior are straightforward to implement (Figure 5). For noun phrase modifiers, things are trickier. Firstly, narrow-scope modifiers need to apply to individual properties whereas wide-scope modifiers need to apply to generalized quantifiers. The easiest way to ensure this is to give the preposition the syntactic type $((N\backslash N)/NP)$ in the former case and $((NP\backslash NP)/NP)$ in the latter before parsing. Thus, in this case, the syntactic structure is affected. Both categories are well supported in the standard model of the C&C parser trained on CCGbank (Hockenmaier and Steedman, 2007), and although the assignment of lexical categories is integrated with parsing, the parser can be forced using tricks to pick a particular category. Example derivations for both cases are shown in Figures 3 and 4.

The second issue with noun phrase modifiers is more severe: specific modifiers of universally quantified noun phrases as in (f) cannot be accounted for in a similar way without heavily modifying the lexical-semantic framework because universally quantified noun phrases keep only their nuclear scope open for modification, not their restrictor. We will return to this limitation in the discussion.

$$\lambda obj.\lambda vp.\lambda subj.\lambda mp.((vp@subj)@\lambda e.(obj@\lambda y.(\boxed{\begin{array}{c} \\ \hline \text{with(e, y)} \end{array}}\,;(mp@e))))$$

$$\lambda obj.\lambda vp.\lambda subj.\lambda mp.(obj@\lambda y.((vp@subj)@\lambda e.(\boxed{\begin{array}{c} \\ \hline \text{with(e, y)} \end{array}}\,;(mp@e))))$$

Figure 5: Two possible semantics of a preposition attaching to a VP. Syntactically, it combines first with its object, then with the VP, then the resulting extended VP combines with the subject, hence $\lambda obj.\lambda vp.\lambda subj....$ Semantically, in the first entry, *vp* is first applied to *subj*, yielding a sentence meaning, which is then modified by applying it to an event property ($\lambda e....$). In the second entry, application to the preposition object to the corresponding property is moved out of the scope of all of this to give it scope over the verb and its arguments. In both cases, the additional λmp ensures that a proper sentence meaning results, allowing for additional modifiers.

4 Annotation and Results

For studying quantifier scope interactions in the wild, we use the Groningen Meaning Bank (GMB), a freely available annotated English corpus of currently a little over 1 million tokens in 7,600 documents, made up mainly of political news, country descriptions, fables and legal text. Since a pilot study showed that clear deviations from the default scope order of verbal arguments (subject > objects in surface order) is very rare (only 12 of 206 cases), we decided to focus on scope interactions mediated by prepositions.

Using the syntactic annotation of the GMB we extracted all prepositions where either the object or the modified constituent contains one of the universally-quantifying determiners *every*, *each* and *all*. We discarded prepositions serving as discourse connectives as in ***With** all ballots cast, people are awaiting the results* because they relate propositions to each other rather than individuals with which we are concerned. We also discarded prepositions that are part of fixed expressions such as ***in** all*, ***at** all*, as well as the *of* in NPs such as *all **of** the leaders*, which we assume to mean the same as *all leaders*. Finally, we cast aside the prepositions *including*, *excluding* and *except* as deserving special treatment not within the scope of this work. This left us with 456 instances which were manually annotated by one annotator for scope behavior. The counts are shown in the last column of Table 1.

In cases of doubt, we generally preferred annotations resulting in the logically weaker reading. For example, in (2), we could either assume a separate termination event for each banking license or a single termination event for them all, and we preferred the former by giving the universal quantifier wide scope.

(2) the International Banking Repeal Act of 2002 resulted in *the termination* **of** *all offshore banking licenses* [03/0688]

5 Discussion

Our approach deals with scope alternation at the level of functor semantics, thus is syntactically constrained. There are some scope orderings, such as interleaved verb arguments and modifiers, that it cannot derive. Also, specific indefinites pose problems in cases such as (f), and will probably show need for special treatment even more clearly once we broaden our attention to their interactions with intensional verbs and negation, see e.g. Geurts (2010). A more powerful account of indefinites is proposed within CCG in Steedman (2012). However, it remains to be seen whether it can be implemented efficiently within a wide-coverage parser, see Kartsaklis (2010). Another phenomenon we haven't dealt with yet is scope interaction between universals and negation.

Nevertheless, our approach is empirically successful at accounting for 96% of all cases in some of the most common syntactic configurations giving rise to scope ambiguities involving universal quantifiers, namely modification of NPs and VPs by preposition phrases. It is also a straightforward extension to an existing semantic parsing system given an annotation of the input text with a layer of scope tags. In future work, we plan to provide this layer automatically by adapting techniques for the statistical resolution of scope, such as that of Manshadi and Allen (2011).

References

Andrew, G. and B. MacCartney (2004). Statistical resolution of scope ambiguity in natural language. Unpublished manuscript.

Basile, V., J. Bos, K. Evang, and N. Venhuizen (2012). Developing a large semantically annotated corpus. In *Proceedings of the Eighth International Conference on Language Resources and Evaluation (LREC-2012)*, Istanbul, Turkey, pp. 3196–3200.

Bos, J. (1996). Predicate Logic Unplugged. In P. Dekker and M. Stokhof (Eds.), *Proceedings of the Tenth Amsterdam Colloquium*, ILLC/Dept. of Philosophy, University of Amsterdam, pp. 133–143.

Bos, J. (2009). Towards a large-scale formal semantic lexicon for text processing. In C. Chiarcos, R. Eckart de Castilho, and M. Stede (Eds.), *Proceedings of the Biennal GSCL Conference 2009*, pp. 3–14. Gunter Narr Verlag.

Copestake, A., D. Flickinger, I. Sag, and C. Pollard (2005). Minimal recursion semantics: An introduction. *Journal of Research on Language and Computation 3*(2–3), 281–332.

Curran, J., S. Clark, and J. Bos (2007). Linguistically Motivated Large-Scale NLP with C&C and Boxer. In *Proceedings of the 45th Annual Meeting of the Association for Computational Linguistics Companion Volume Proceedings of the Demo and Poster Sessions*, Prague, Czech Republic, pp. 33–36.

Egg, M., A. Koller, and J. Niehren (2001). The constraint language for lambda structures. *Logic, Language and Information 10*, 457–485.

Geurts, B. (2010). Specific indefinites, presuppositions, and scope. In R. Buerle, U. Reyle, and T. E. Zimmermann (Eds.), *Presuppositions and discourse*, pp. 125–158. Emerald Group.

Hendriks, H. (1993). *Studied Flexibility: Categories and Types in Syntax and Semantics.* Ph. D. thesis, University of Amsterdam.

Higgins, D. and J. Sadock (2003). A machine learning approach to modeling scope preferences. *Computational Linguistics 29*(1), 73–96.

Hockenmaier, J. and M. Steedman (2007). Ccgbank: a corpus of ccg derivations and dependency structures extracted from the penn treebank. *Computational Linguistics 33*(3), 355–396.

Kamp, H. and U. Reyle (1993). *From Discourse to Logic; An Introduction to Modeltheoretic Semantics of Natural Language, Formal Logic and DRT.* Dordrecht: Kluwer.

Kartsaklis, D. (2010). Wide-coverage CCG parsing with quantifier scope. Master's thesis, University of Edinburgh.

Manshadi, M. and J. Allen (2011). Unrestricted quantifier scope disambiguation. In *Proceedings of TextGraphs-6: Graph-based Methods for Natural Language Processing*, Portland, Oregon, pp. 51–59. Association for Computational Linguistics.

Reyle, U. (1993). Dealing with ambiguities by underspecification: Construction, representation and deduction. *Journal of Semantics 10*, 123–179.

Srinivasan, P. and A. Yates (2009). Quantifier scope disambiguation using extracted pragmatic knowledge: Preliminary results. In *Proceedings of the 2009 Conference on Empirical Methods in Natural Language Processing: Volume 3-Volume 3*, pp. 1465–1474. Association for Computational Linguistics.

Steedman, M. (2001). *The Syntactic Process.* The MIT Press.

Steedman, M. (2012). *Taking Scope.* The MIT Press.

What is in a text, what isn't, and what this has to do with lexical semantics

Aurelie Herbelot
Universität Potsdam
aurelie.herbelot@cantab.net

Abstract

This paper queries which aspects of lexical semantics can reasonably be expected to be modelled by corpus-based theories such as distributional semantics or techniques such as ontology extraction. We argue that a full lexical semantics theory must take into account the *extensional* potential of words. We investigate to which extent corpora provide the necessary data to model this information and suggest that it may be partly learnable from text-based distributions, partly inferred from annotated data, using the insight that a concept's features are extensionally interdependent.

1 Introduction

Much work in computational linguistics relies on the use of corpora as evidential data, both for investigating language and for 'learning' about the world. Indeed, it is possible to inspect a great variety of phenomena, and get access to a lot of world knowledge, simply by having a large amount of text available. The purpose of this paper is to both acknowledge corpora as an invaluable data source for computational linguistics and point at their shortcomings. In particular, we want to argue that an appropriate representation of lexical meaning requires information beyond what is provided by written text and that this can be problematic for lexical models which rely entirely on corpora. Specifically, we wish to highlight how corpora fail to supply the information necessary to represent the *extension* of a term. In a nutshell, our argument is that the aspect of meaning represented by model theory is, in the best case, hard to extract and in the worst case not available at all when looking at corpus data. Building on this first discussion, we show that a concept's features are *extensionally* interdependent and, using this insight, propose that the part of model theory dealing with set relations (how much of set X is included in set Y?) may be learnt by exploiting a mixture of annotated (non-textual) data and standard distributional semantics. We present preliminary experiments investigating this hypothesis.

2 Text and extension

1. My cat – a mammal – likes sitting on the sofa.
2. There are more than two trees in this forest.
3. Cats have two eyes.

Sentences like 1–3 are not often found in corpora, or any kind of speech, for that matter. This is fortunate from the point of view of communication. In all three examples, the Gricean maxim of quantity is violated: 1 repeats information which is already implicitely given by the encyclopedic definition of the lexical item *cat*, while the other two express something obvious to anyone who has been in contact with forests/cats in their life (or indeed, who has read the encyclopedic definitions of *forest*/*cat*).

From the point of view of standard computational linguistics, this state of affairs is however undesirable. We will consider here two major approaches to extracting 'conceptual' knowledge from text:

distributional semantics and ontology extraction. Distributional semantics accounts for the lexical meaning of words by modelling, via appropriate weighting, their co-occurrence with other words (or any larger lexical context). The representation of a target word is thus a vector in a space where each dimension corresponds to a possible context. (Curran, 2003 and Turney and Pantel, 2010 are good overviews of this line of work). Ontology extraction, on the other hand, retrieves facts from text by searching for specific patterns: for instance, it is possible to find out that 'cat' is a hyponym of 'feline' by examining lexical patterns of the type 'X such as Y' (Hearst, 1992).

It should be clear that neither method can extract information which is simply absent from text. 3, for instance, may never occur in a corpus. This issue has been noted before, in particular in the psycholinguistics literature (Devereux et al., 2009; Andrews et al., 2009). To compensate, the use of manually obtained 'feature norms' is often advocated to complete corpus-based representations of concepts (e.g. a human might associate *bear* with the sensory-motor norms *claw, big, brown*, etc). But missing features are not the only issue. Let us return to 1. If we mentioned the word *mammal* everytime we speak of a cat, distributional semantics systems would be able to appropriately reflect the hyponymic relation between the two concepts – which in turn translates into an inclusion relation in model theory. But precisely because of the strong association between them, we (as good Griceans) are careful to leave the mammal out of the cat. Consequently, it is usual for a distribution to assign fairly low weights to features which we would argue are essential to the lexical representation of a word (see Geffet and Dagan, 2005 or Baroni et al., 2012 for attempts to capture the inclusion relation despite the flaws in the data).

Pattern-based methods obviously fare better when attempting to extract standard lexical relations. They do not, however, provide a true *extensional* analysis of the information they retrieve. For instance, from the snippet *four-legged animals such as cats and dogs*, we should not conclude that the set of dogs is included in the set of four-legged animals – a fair amount of dogs only have three legs. Our point is that relations obtained from corpora (or by coding feature norms) are essentially intensional: they do not model the part of semantics dealing with set relations and thus do not reflect our *expectations* with regard to a particular concept (i.e. how *likely* is it that a given bear is big, brown, etc?) We argue that such expectations are part of lexical semantics, as they mediate our use of words.[1] For instance, we strongly expect a dog to have four legs, but are not overly surprised when seeing a three-legged dog (the set of dogs is mostly, but not entirely, included in the set of four-legged things) and so would still call it a dog. Conversely, a forest with one tree is not intuitively a forest (the sets of trees making up each instance in the set of forests *all* have a 'large' cardinality).

In what follows we investigate how such set relations can be inferred from prior knowledge: we recall that features (whether of the distributional type or the sensory-motor type) are dependent on each other and that this dependency can be exploited to learn human-like expectations with regard to extension.

3 The extensional dependency hypothesis

Let us assume a particular kind of conceptual representation which consists of a vector of weighted features, as in distributional semantics, but where the weights are the *expected probabilities* of an instance of the concept to be associated with a particular distributional feature in the real world. So for instance, the feature *mammal* has a weight of 1 for the concept *cat* because all cats are mammals. In the same concept, *black* has perhaps a weight of 0.1 (assuming that one cat in ten is black). We call such representations **extensional distributions**, because each probability reflects some expectation about the inclusion relation between two sets.

Let us further assume a distributional space with n dimensions and let us refer to the extensional distribution of A as A$^\circ$. We hypothesise that the value of A$^\circ$ along a dimension d_k is dependent on the value of A$^\circ$ along all other dimensions $d_{1...n}$ in that space. Intuitively, this means that the probability that a cat (habitually) eats is dependent on the probability of that cat to (habitually) sleep, run, communicate, to be made of stone or to write books. In other words, the extensional distribution of a typical cat x

[1]Of course, expectations reflect certain common beliefs and no extensionally true facts about the world. But those beliefs can be modelled using the set-theory machinery, i.e. they can be regarded as a possible world.

reflects its status as a living (non-human) being, which in turn implies a high probability of cat ° along the dimension *eat*. We call this the **extensional dependency hypothesis** (see Devereux et al., 2009 for related comments on this effect).

Such dependencies mean that learning the probabilities of certain features in relation to instances of a given target word can be greatly facilitated by learning another, information-rich feature. For instance, knowing that a is a bird allows us to infer many properties about a, e.g. that it lays eggs if it is female, that it probably flies, or that it perhaps builds nests.

In the absence of any supervision, it is hard to find out which features are most inference-producing. However, we can adopt a different strategy to learn inference rules. Let us assume that there *is* a correspondence between distributional data and the real world for at least some features. For example, we might find that as long as the predicate *be_v+fish_n* has been seen next to *pike* – be it only once –, we can infer that all pikes are fish. It is a property of the feature that if it applies to one individual of a kind, it will apply to all of them (contrast this with, e.g. *black_a*). If we can be reasonably certain that, given enough data, *be_v+fish_n* will be seen next to *pike*, we have a way to learn a real world probability from corpus data which we are confident in and which may be used for producing inferences. The rest of this paper investigates this hypothesis.

4 Experiments

4.1 A distributional system

Talking of '(expected) probabilities in the real world' has consequences in terms of choosing a particular notion of context for building our corpus-based distributions. Consider a system where context is defined by a word window around the target. *mouse* may be one of the terms sometimes appearing in the context of *cat*, but having a feature *mouse* does not tell us anything about how mice and cats are related in the real world (do mice eat cats? are made of cats? sell cats?) and so, the 'association' *mouse-cat* cannot be assigned a probability. In contrast, if we choose as context semantic dependencies of the type *_+eat+mouse* or *_+be+kept+as+pet*, where _ indicate the position of the target word, there is a clear interpretation of the context as being related to the target in the real world (what is the probability of a cat to eat mice? to be kept as a pet?) Consequently, we build a distributional system using dependency relations. Our data is the Wikiwoods corpus (Flickinger et al., 2010), a Wikipedia snapshot parsed with the English Resource Grammar (ERG), which we convert into a Dependency Minimal Recursion Semantics (DMRS, Copestake, 2009) format for our experiments. We only consider a number of dependency structures as context for a target word: adjectives, adverbs, prepositions and verbs, with their direct arguments, possessive constructs and coordination. The weight of a target word along a particular dimension of the semantic space is given by the normalised PMI measure proposed by Bouma (2007).

To speed up processing, we only retain dimensions which do occur with the lexical items in our experimental set (see 4.3 for a description). This results in our semantic space having 15799 dimensions.

4.2 The learning system

We design a system based on bootstrapping, which learns extensional distributions. The idea is to learn from our corpus the features which we are most confident in and use those to further the learning process.

Let us assume we wish to learn real-world probabilities for some features $F_1...F_n$, as applied to instances of various target words $w_k...w_m$ (F_1 might be *lay_v+egg_n* while w_k might be *aardvark*). Let us also assume that we have some annotated data which provides us with 'rough' probabilities for a number of feature-instance pairs. For convenience of annotation – and because we do not expect humans to have an accurate probabilistic model of the world –, we express those probabilities using the natural language quantifiers *no, few, some, most, all* (see Herbelot and Copestake, 2011 for related work on resolving underspecified quantification). So we might already know that *most* swallows migrate.

The first iteration of our bootstrapping process runs over each feature F in $\{F_1...F_n\}$. A machine learning algorithm is fed the corpus-based distributions of the training instances (let us call them

$w_1...w_j$), together with the probabilities $p_m(F|w_1...j)$ from the annotated data. A classifier is learnt for F and its precision estimated by performing leave-one-out cross-validation on the training data. The classifier with the best precision, say $C(F_i)$ is recorded, together with its decisions, $p(F_i|w_1...j)$. The feature F_i is considered 'learnt'.

From the second iterations on, the following process takes place. For each feature F which has not yet been learnt, the machine learning algorithm is fed the corpus-based distributions of $w_1...w_j$, together with the values of the learnt features $p(F_{learnt}|w_1...j)$ and the manually annotated probabilities $p_m(F|w_1...j)$. As before, a classifier is learnt and its precision calculated by performing leave-one-out cross-validation on the training data and the classifier with the best precision, as well as its decisions on the training data, are recorded for use in the next iteration.

When classifying new, unseen instances, the classifiers are applied to the data in the order they were learnt during the training process. As an example, let us assume that we have learnt the probabilities of the features *be_v+fish_n* and *aquatic_a* for the animals *aardvark, cod* and *dolphin.* Let us also assume that *be_v+fish_n* was learnt first (it was classified with higher precision than *aquatic_a* in the first iteration of the algorithm). Let us further suppose that in the second iteration, the initial classifier for *aquatic_a* was modified to take into account the learnt feature *be_v+fish_n* (i.e. the precision of the classifier was increased by using the new information). Presented with a new classification problem, say *salmon,* the system would first try to find out the probability *p(be_v+fish_n|salmon)* and then use that figure to estimate *p(aquatic_a|salmon).*

4.3 The dataset

We attempt to learn the quantification of a number of animal-feature pairs. The animals and features used in our experiment are chosen as follows.

The animals are picked by selecting the entries in the Wikipedia 'List of animals'[2] which have an occurrence count over 2000 in our corpus. This results in a set of 72 animals.

The features are chosen manually amongst the 50 most highly weighted vector components of ten different animal distributions. The animals considered are selected semi-randomly: we make sure that the most common types are included (mammals, fish, insects, birds, invertebrates). Features which satisfy the following conditions are included in the experiment: a) the feature must be applicable to the animal at the 'individual' level, i.e. it cannot be a temporary state of the animal, or apply to the species collectively (*black_a* is appropriate while *wounded_a* or *endangered_a* are not) b) the feature must be semantically 'complete', i.e. make sense when applied to the animal in isolation (*be_v+mammal_n* is appropriate while *behaviour_n+of_p* is not).

The feature selection exercise results in 54 vector components being selected.

Given our 72 animals and 54 features, we ask a human annotator to mark each animal-feature pair with a 'probability', expressed as a quantifier. Possible values are *no, few, some, most, all.* The guidelines for the annotation task can be seen at `http://www.cl.cam.ac.uk/~ah433/material/iwcs13-annot.pdf`.

5 Results

The following is based on an implementation of our system using Weka's[3] C4.5 (also referred to as J48) classifier (Quinlan, 1993). The C4.5 classifier produces a decision tree which can be inspected and is therefore particularly appropriate to 'check' learnt rules against human intuition. We perform leave-one-out validation on the first 10 animals in our dataset (for instance, we predict the values of our 54 features for *ant* using a training set consisting of all other animals). For each animal, the system therefore runs 1485 iterations of the classifier.

[2] `http://en.wikipedia.org/wiki/List_of_animals#Animals_.28by_common_name.29`

[3] `http://http://www.cs.waikato.ac.nz/~ml/weka/`

5.1 Finding relationships between corpora and the real world

In order to investigate whether real-world probabilities can be derived from corpus data, we first run a baseline system which classifies animal-feature pairs into our five quantifier classes, *no, few, some, most, all*, using only the corpus-based distributions of the animals in our training set.

The overall precision of the baseline system over our 540 predicted values is 0.51. As hypothesised, some features are learnt with high precision using word distributions only: *be_v+bird_n* is one such example, classifying all but one instances correctly (its estimated performance on the training data, as per cross-validation, is 0.95). Others, such as *carnivorous_a* consistently receive an incorrect classification (precision of 0 on the test data and 0.24 on the training data).

5.2 Learning inferences

We now turn to the question of learning rules which reflect real-world relationships. Because of space constraints, we are unable to reproduce actual output from the system, but examples can be seen at `http://www.cl.cam.ac.uk/~ah433/material/iwcs13-examples.pdf`. As illustration, we consider here the classifiers produced for the feature *aquatic_a*.

The baseline classifier (the one learnt from distributional data only) does use distributional features that are associated with water (*mediterranean_a, in_p()+water_n*), but overall, the decision tree is rather far from the way we might expect a human to attribute the feature *aquatic_a* to an animal species, and mostly includes seemingly irrelevant features such as *variant_of* or again *fascinating*.

The final classifier produced by our learning system, in contrast, involves the learnt probability for the feature *terrestrial_a*. It captures the facts that a) non-terrestrial species are aquatic and b) terrestrial species which live near water can also be said to be aquatic (cf. otters or beavers).

Other examples of real world dependencies learnt in the iterative process include *lay_v+egg_n* and *woolly_a* being dependent on *be_v+mammal_n*, *have_v+hair_n* depending on *woolly_a* and *be_v+insect_n*, or again *walk_v* depending on *be_v+mammal_n* and *fly_v*.

5.3 Overall performance

The overall precision of the iterative system is 0.48, which makes it lag behind the baseline by 3%. The result is disappointing but can be explained when inspecting the output. The strength of the system in catching meaningful dependencies between features, which we illustrated in the previous section, is also what makes it lose accuracy on our small dataset. Indeed, the dependencies integrated in the final classifiers assume that the learnt features were correctly predicted for the animal under consideration. This is unfortunately not the case, and errors accumulate during bootstrapping. For instance, when running on the test instance *ape*, the system classifies the features *woolly_a* and *lay_v+egg_n* by relying on the prediction for *be_v+mammal_n*. The precision of the system on that feature, however, is only 0.5. In order to truly evaluate the performance of the system, we suggest experimenting with a larger dataset.

6 Conclusion

This paper argued that there is a part of lexical semantics which is not dealt with by modelling techniques relying entirely on corpora. Indeed, standard speech tends to omit information which is true from an extensional point of view but irrelevant for successful communication. In order to retrieve the extensional potential of lexical terms, we proposed a separate, distribution-like representation which provides the *expected* real-world probabilities of instance-feature pairs and which we refer to as extensional distribution. We argued that a) for *some* features, there is a correspondence between corpus data and real world which can be learnt b) probabilities in the extensional distribution are dependent on each other and it is possible to infer unknown values from already learnt ones (including those learnt from corpus data).

Acknowledgement

The author is in receipt of a postdoctoral fellowship from the Alexander von Humboldt foundation.

References

Andrews, M., G. Vigliocco, and D. Vinson (2009). Integrating experiential and distributional data to learn semantic representations. *Psychological Review 116*(3), 463.

Baroni, M., R. Bernardi, N.-Q. Do, and C.-c. Shan (2012). Entailment above the word level in distributional semantics. In *Proceedings of the 15th Conference of the European Chapter of the Association for Computational Linguistics (EACL12).*

Bouma, G. (2007). Normalized (Pointwise) Mutual Information in Collocation Extraction. *Proceedings of GSCL*, 31–40.

Copestake, A. (2009). Slacker semantics : why superficiality , dependency and avoidance of commitment can be the right way to go. In *Proceedings of the 12th Conference of the European Chapter of the Association for Computational Linguistics (EACL09)*, Athens, Greece, pp. 1–9.

Curran, J. (2003). *From Distributional to Semantic Similarity*. Ph. D. thesis.

Devereux, B., N. Pilkington, T. Poibeau, and A. Korhonen (2009). Towards unrestricted, large-scale acquisition of feature-based conceptual representations from corpus data. *Research on Language and Computation 7*, 137.

Flickinger, D., S. Oepen, and G. Ytrestol (2010). Wikiwoods: Syntacto-semantic annotation for english wikipedia. In *Proceedings of the Seventh International Conference on Language Resources and Evaluation (LREC10).*

Geffet, M. and I. Dagan (2005). The distributional inclusion hypothesises and lexical entailment. In *Proceedings Of the 43rd Annual Meeting of the Association for Computational Linguistics*, pp. 107–114.

Hearst, M. (1992). Automatic acquisition of hyponyms from large text corpora. Volume 14th International Conference on Computational Linguistics (COLING 92), pp. 539.

Herbelot, A. and A. Copestake (2011). Formalising and specifying underquantification. In *Proceedings of the Ninth International Conference on Computational Semantics*, IWCS '11, Oxford, United Kingdom, pp. 165–174.

Quinlan, J. R. (1993). *Programs for Machine Learning*. Morgan Kaufman.

Turney, P. D. and P. Pantel (2010). From frequency to meaning: Vector space models of semantics. *Journal of Artificial Intelligence Research 37*, 141–188.

Semantic Similarity Computation for Abstract and Concrete Nouns Using Network-based Distributional Semantic Models

Elias Iosif*, Alexandros Potamianos*, Maria Giannoudaki*, Kalliopi Zervanou†
* Dept. of Electronics & Computer Engineering, Technical University of Crete, Greece
{iosife,potam,maria}@telecom.tuc.gr
†Centre for Language Studies, Radboud University Nijmegen, The Netherlands
k.zervanou@let.ru.nl

Abstract

Motivated by cognitive lexical models, network-based distributional semantic models (DSMs) were proposed in [Iosif and Potamianos (2013)] and were shown to achieve state-of-the-art performance on semantic similarity tasks. Based on evidence for cognitive organization of concepts based on degree of concreteness, we investigate the performance and organization of network DSMs for abstract vs. concrete nouns. Results show a "concreteness effect" for semantic similarity estimation. Network DSMs that implement the maximum sense similarity assumption perform best for concrete nouns, while attributional network DSMs perform best for abstract nouns. The performance of metrics is evaluated against human similarity ratings on an English and a Greek corpus.

1 Introduction

Semantic similarity is the building block for numerous applications of natural language processing (NLP), such as grammar induction [Meng and Siu (2002)] and affective text categorization [Malandrakis et al. (2011)]. Distributional semantic models (DSMs) [Baroni and Lenci (2010)] are based on the distributional hypothesis of meaning [Harris (1954)] assuming that semantic similarity between words is a function of the overlap of their linguistic contexts. DSMs are typically constructed from co-occurrence statistics of word tuples that are extracted from a text corpus or from data harvested from the web. A wide range of contextual features are also used by DSM exploiting lexical, syntactic, semantic, and pragmatic information. DSMs have been successfully applied to the problem of semantic similarity computation. Recently [Iosif and Potamianos (2013)] proposed *network-based DSMs* motivated by the organization of words, attributes and concepts in human cognition. The proposed semantic networks can operate under either the *attributional similarity* or the *maximum sense similarity* assumptions of lexical semantics. According to attributional similarity [Turney (2006)], semantic similarity between words is based on the commonality of their sense attributes. Following the maximum sense similarity hypothesis, the semantic similarity of two words can be estimated as the similarity of their two closest senses [Resnik (1995)]. Network-based DSMs have been shown to achieve state-of-the-art performance for semantic similarity tasks.

Typically, the *degree of semantic concreteness* of a word is not taken into account in distributional models. However, evidence from neuro- and psycho-linguistics demonstrates significant differences in the cognitive organization of abstract and concrete nouns. For example, Kiehl et al. (1999) and Noppeney and Price (2004) show that concrete concepts are processed more efficiently than abstract ones (aka "the concreteness effect"), i.e., participants in lexical decision tasks recall concrete stimuli faster than abstract. According to dual code theory [Paivio (1971)], the stored semantic information for concrete concepts is both verbal and visual, while for abstract concepts stored information is only verbal. Neuropsychological studies show that people with acquired dyslexia (deep dyslexia) face problems in reading abstract nouns aloud [Coltheart (2000)], *verifying that concrete and abstract concepts are stored in different regions of the human brain anatomy* [Kiehl et al. (1999)]. The reversal concreteness effect is also reported for people with semantic dementia with a striking impairment in semantic memory [Papagno et al. (2009)].

Motivated by this evidence, we study the semantic network organization and performance of DSMs for estimating the semantic similarity of abstract vs. concrete nouns. Specifically, we investigate the validity of the maximum sense and attributional similarity assumptions in network-based DSMs for abstract and concrete nouns (for both English and Greek).

2 Related Work

Semantic similarity metrics can be divided into two broad categories: (i) metrics that rely on knowledge resources, and (ii) corpus-based metrics. A representative example of the first category are metrics that exploit the WordNet ontology [Miller (1990)]. Corpus-based metrics are formalized as DSM [Baroni and Lenci (2010)] and are based on the distributional hypothesis of meaning [Harris (1954)]. DSM can be categorized into unstructured (unsupervised) that employ a bag-of-words model [Agirre et al. (2009)] and structured that rely on syntactic relationships between words [Pado and Lapata (2007)]. Recently, motivated by the graph theory, several aspects of the human languages have been modeled using network-based methods. In [Mihalcea and Radev (2011)], an overview of network-based approaches is presented for a number of NLP problems. Different types of language units can be regarded as vertices of such networks, spanning from single words to sentences. Typically, network edges represent the relations of such units capturing phenomena such as co-occurrence, syntactic dependencies, and lexical similarity. An example of a large co-occurrence network is presented in [Widdows and Dorow (2002)] for the automatic creation of semantic classes. In [Iosif and Potamianos (2013)], a new paradigm for implementing DSMs is proposed: a two tier system in which corpus statistics are parsimoniously encoded in a network, while the task of similarity computation is shifted (from corpus-based techniques) to operations over network neighborhoods.

3 Corpus-Based Baseline Similarity Metrics

Co-occurrence-based: The underlying assumption of co-occurrence-based metrics is that the co-existence of words in a specified contextual environment indicates semantic relatedness. In this work, we employ a widely-used co-occurrence-based metric, namely, Dice coefficient [Iosif and Potamianos (2010)]. The Dice coefficient between words w_i and w_j is defined as follows: $D(w_i, w_j) = \frac{2f(w_i,w_j)}{f(w_i)+f(w_j)}$, where $f(.)$ denotes the frequency of word occurrence/co-occurrence. Here, the word co-occurrence is considered at the sentential level, while D can be also defined with respect to broader contextual environments, e.g., at the paragraph level [Véronis (2004)].
Context-based: The fundamental assumption behind context-based metrics is that *similarity of context implies similarity of meaning* [Harris (1954)]. A contextual window of size $2H + 1$ words is centered on the word of interest w_i and lexical features are extracted. For every instance of w_i in the corpus the H words left and right of w_i formulate a feature vector v_i. For a given value of H the context-based semantic similarity between two words, w_i and w_j, is computed as the cosine of their feature vectors: $Q^H(w_i, w_j) = \frac{v_i \cdot v_j}{||v_i||\,||v_j||}$. The elements of feature vectors can be weighted according various schemes [Iosif and Potamianos (2010)], while, here we use a binary scheme.

4 Network-based Distributional Semantic Models

Here, we summarize the main ideas of network-based DSMs as proposed in [Iosif and Potamianos (2013)]. The network is defined as an undirected (under a symmetric similarity metric) graph $F = (V, E)$ whose the set of vertices V are all words in our lexicon L, and the set of edges E contains the links between the vertices. The links (edges) between words in the network are determined and weighted according to the pairwise semantic similarity of the vertices. The network is a parsimonious representation of corpus statistics as they pertain to the estimation of semantic similarities between word-pairs in the lexicon. In addition, the network can be used to *discover relations that are not directly observable in the data*; such relations emerge via the systematic covariation of similarity metrics. For each word (reference word) that is included in the lexicon, $w_i \in L$, we consider a sub-graph of F, $F_i = (N_i, E_i)$, where the set of vertices N_i includes in total n members of L, which are linked with w_i via edges E_i. The F_i sub-graph is referred to as the semantic neighborhood of w_i. The members of N_i (neighbors of w_i) are selected according to a semantic similarity metric (co-occurrence-based D or context-based Q^H defined in Section 3) with respect to w_i, i.e., the n most similar words to w_i are selected. Next, we present two semantic similarity metrics that utilize the notion of semantic neighborhood [Iosif and Potamianos (2013)].

4.1 Maximum Similarity of Neighborhoods

This metric is based on the hypothesis that the similarity of two words, w_i and w_j, can be estimated by *the maximum similarity of their respective sets of neighbors*, defined as follows:

$$M_n(w_i, w_j) = \max\{\alpha_{ij}, \alpha_{ji}\}, \quad \text{where } \alpha_{ij} = \max_{x \in N_j} S(w_i, x), \;\; \alpha_{ji} = \max_{y \in N_i} S(w_j, y). \tag{1}$$

α_{ij} (or α_{ji}) denotes the maximum similarity between w_i (or w_j) and the neighbors of w_j (or w_i) that is computed according to a similarity metric S: in this work either D or Q^H. N_i and N_j are the set of neighbors for w_i and w_j, respectively. The definition of M_n is motivated by the maximum sense similarity assumption. Here the underlying assumption is that the most salient information in the neighbors of a word are semantic features denoting senses of this word.

4.2 Attributional Neighborhood Similarity

The similarity between w_i and w_j is defined as follows:

$$R_n(w_i, w_j) = \max\{\beta_{ij}, \beta_{ji}\}, \quad \text{where } \beta_{ij} = \rho(C_i^{N_i}, C_j^{N_i}), \;\; \beta_{ji} = \rho(C_i^{N_j}, C_j^{N_j}) \tag{2}$$

$$\text{where } C_i^{N_i} = (S(w_i, x_1), S(w_i, x_2), \ldots, S(w_i, x_n)), \quad \text{and } N_i = \{x_1, x_2, \ldots, x_n\}.$$

Note that $C_j^{N_i}$, $C_i^{N_j}$, and $C_j^{N_j}$ are defined similarly as $C_i^{N_i}$. The ρ function stands for the Pearson's correlation coefficient, N_i is the set of neighbors of word w_i, and S is a similarity metric (D or Q^H). Here, we aim to exploit the entire semantic neighborhoods for the computation of semantic similarity, as opposed to M_n where a single neighbor is utilized. The motivation behind this metric is attributional similarity, i.e., we assume that semantic neighborhoods encode attributes (or features) of a word. Neighborhood correlation similarity in essence compares the distribution of semantic similarities of the two words on their semantic neighborhoods. The ρ function incorporates the covariation of the similarities of w_i and w_j with respect to the members of their semantic neighborhoods.

5 Experimental Procedure

Lexica and corpora creation: For English we used a lexicon consisting of $8,752$ English nouns taken from the SemCor3[1] corpus. In addition, this lexicon was translated into Greek using Google Translate[2], while it was further augmented resulting into a set of $9,324$ entries. For each noun an individual query was formulated and the $1,000$ top ranked results (document snippets) were retrieved using the Yahoo! search engine[3]. A corpus was created for each language by aggregating the snippets for all nouns of the lexicon.
Network creation: For each language the semantic neighborhoods of lexicon noun pairs were computed following the procedure described in Section 4 using either co-occurrence D or context-based $Q^{H=1}$ metrics [4].
Network-based similarity computation: For each language, the semantic similarity between noun pairs was computed applying either the max-sense M_n or the attributional R_n network-based metric. The underlying semantic similarity metric (the S metric in (1) and (2)) can be either D or Q^H. Given that for both neighborhood creation and network-based semantic similarity estimation we have the option of D or Q^H, a total of four combinations emerge for this two-phase process: (i) D/D, i.e., use co-occurence metric D for both neighborhood selection and network-based similarity estimation, (ii) D/Q^H, (iii) Q^H/D, and (iv) Q^H/Q^H.

6 Evaluation Datasets

The performance of network-based similarity metrics was evaluated for the task of semantic similarity between nouns. The Pearson's correlation coefficient was used as evaluation metric to compare estimated similarities against the ground truth (human ratings). The following datasets were used:
English (WS353): Subset of WS353 dataset [Finkelstein et al. (2002)] consisting of 272 noun pairs (that are also included in the SemCor3 corpus).
Greek (GIP): In total, 82 native speakers of modern Greek were asked to score the similarity of the noun pairs in a range from 0 (dissimilar) to 4 (similar). The resulting dataset consists of 99 nouns pairs (a subset of pairs translated from WS353) and is freely available [5].
Abstract vs. Concrete: From each of the above datasets two subsets of pairs were selected, where both nouns in the pair are either abstract or concrete, i.e., pairs consisting of one abstract and one concrete nouns were ruled out. More specifically, 74 abstract and 74 concrete noun pairs were selected from WS353, for a total of 148 pairs. Regarding GIP, 18 abstract and 18 concrete noun pairs were selected, for a total of 36 pairs.

---

[1] http://www.cse.unt.edu/~rada/downloads.html
[2] http://translate.google.com/
[3] http://www.yahoo.com//
[4] We have also experimented with other values of context window H not reported here for the sake of space. However, the highest performance was achieved for $H = 1$.
[5] http://www.telecom.tuc.gr/~iosife/downloads.html

7 Results

The performance of the two proposed network-based metrics, M_n and R_n, for neighborhood size of 100, is presented in Table 1 with respect to the English (WS353) and Greek (GIP) datasets. Baseline performance (i.e., no use of the network) is also shown for co-occurrence-based metric D and context-based metric Q^H. For the max-sense

Language: dataset	Number of pairs	Baseline D	Baseline Q^H	Network metric	Neighbor selection / Similarity computation D/D	D/Q^H	Q^H/D	Q^H/Q^H
English: WS353	272	0.22	0.30	$M_{n=100}$	**0.64**	**0.64**	0.47	0.46
				$R_{n=100}$	0.50	0.14	**0.56**	**0.57**
Greek: GIP	99	0.25	0.13	$M_{n=100}$	**0.51**	**0.51**	0.04	0.04
				$R_{n=100}$	-0.11	0.03	**0.66**	0.11

Table 1: Pearson correlation with human ratings for neighborhood-based metrics for English and Greek datasets. Four combinations of the co-occurrence-based metric D and the context-based metric Q^H were used for the definition of semantic neighborhoods and the computation of similarity scores. Baseline performance is also shown.

similarity $M_{n=100}$ metric, the use of the co-occurrence metric D for neighbor selection yields the best correlation performance for both languages. For the attributional similarity $R_{n=100}$ metric, best performance is achieved when using the context-based metric D for the selection of neighbors in the network. As explained in [Iosif and Potamianos (2013)], the neighborhoods selected by the D metrics tend to include words that denote word senses (yielding best results for similarity), while neighborhoods computed using the Q^H metric are semantically broader including word attributes (yielding best results for attributional similarity). The network-based DSM results are also significantly higher compared to the baseline for both languages. The best results achieved by D/Q^H for the $M_{n=100}$, and Q^H/D for the $R_{n=100}$ are consistent with the results reported in [Iosif and Potamianos (2013)] for English. The best performing metric for English is $M_{n=100}$ (max-sense) while for Greek $R_{n=100}$ (attributional). Overall, utilizing network neighborhoods for estimating semantic similarity can achieve good performance[6], and the type of metric (feature) used to select the neighborhood is a key performance factor.

Next, we investigate the performance of the network metrics with respect to the neighborhood size n for the abstract and concrete noun pairs included in English and Greek datasets. The performance of the max-sense M_n (D/Q^H) metric is shown in Fig. 1(a),(c) for the (subsets of) WS353 and GIP, respectively. The performance over the whole (abstract and concrete) dataset is shown with a solid line. Similarly the results for the attributional R_n (Q^H/D) metric are shown in Fig. 1(b),(d). The main conclusions for these experiments (for both languages) are: 1) The correlation performance for concrete noun pairs is higher than for abstract noun pairs. 2) For concrete nouns the max-sense M_n metric achieves best performance, while for abstract nouns the attributional R_n metric is the top performer. 3) For the R_n network metric, very good performance is achieved for abstract noun pairs for a small neighborhood size n (around 10), while for concrete nouns larger neighborhoods are needed (up to 40 and 30 neighbors, for English and Greek, respectively).

Neighbor selection metric	Number of reference nouns	Type of reference nouns	Type of neighbors (abstract/concrete) English (WS353) abstract	English (WS353) concrete	Greek (GIP) abstract	Greek (GIP) concrete
D	15	abstract	**76%**	24%	**82%**	18%
D	15	concrete	36%	**64%**	23%	**77%**
Q^H	15	abstract	**82%**	18%	**91%**	9%
Q^H	15	concrete	31%	**69%**	31%	**69%**

Table 2: Distribution of abstract vs. concrete nouns in (abstract/concrete noun) neighbourhoods.

In order to further investigate the network organization for abstract vs. concrete nouns, we manually inspected the top twenty neighbors of 30 randomly selected nouns (15 abstract and 15 concrete) and classified each neighbor as either abstract or concrete. The distributions of abstract/concrete neighbors are shown in Table 2 as a function of neighbor selection metric (D vs. Q^H) and reference noun category. It is clear, that the neighborhoods of abstract nouns contain mostly abstract concepts, especially for the Q^H neighbor selection metric (similarly the neighborhoods of concrete nouns contain mainly concrete concepts). The neighbors of concrete nouns mainly belong to the same semantic class (e.g., "vehicle", "bus" for "car") often corresponding to relevant senses. The

[6]The best correlation score for the WS353 dataset does not exceed the top performance (0.68) of unsupervised DSMs [Agirre et al. (2006)]. However, we have found that the proposed network metrics obtain state-of-the-art results for other standard datasets, e.g., 0.87 for [Rubenstein and Goodenough (1965)] and 0.91 for [Miller and Charles (1998)].

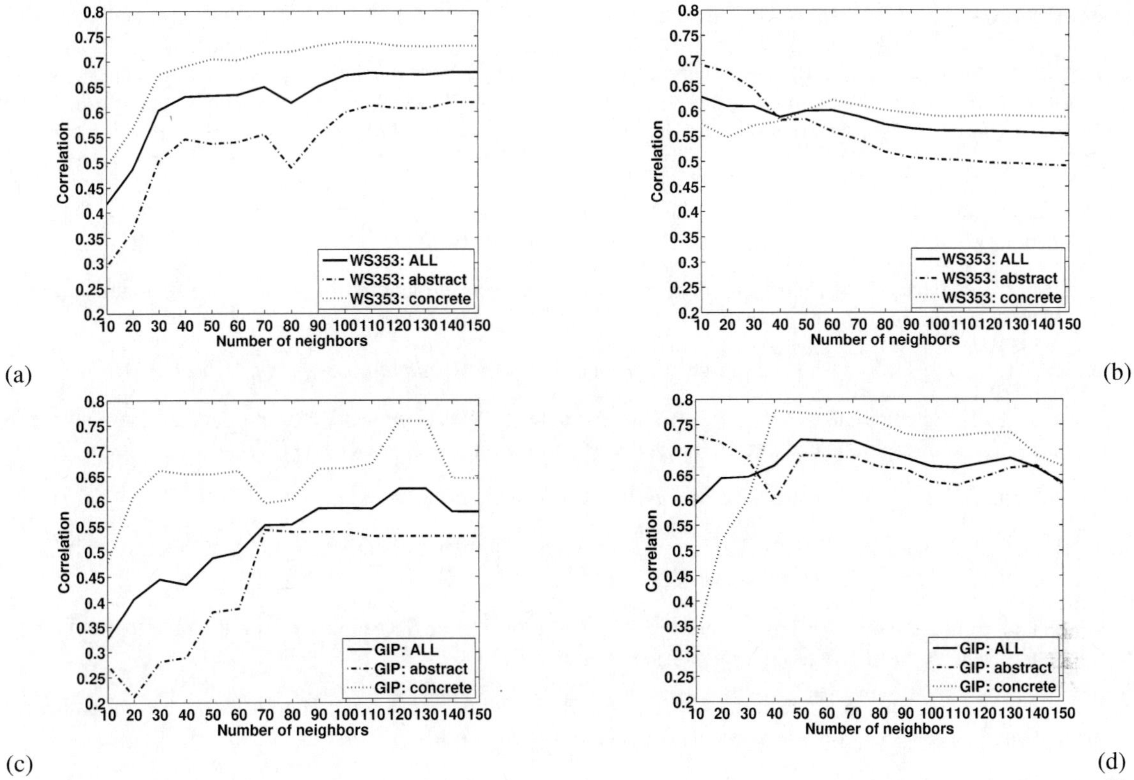

Figure 1: Correlation as a function of number of neighbors for network-based metrics. Max-sense M_n (D/Q^H) for datasets: (a) English and (c) Greek. Attributional R_n (Q^H/D) for datasets: (b) English and (d) Greek.

neighbors of the abstract nouns have an attributive function, reflecting relative attributes and/or aspects of the referent nouns (e.g., "religion", "justice" for "morality").

8 Discussion

We investigated the performance of network-based DSMs for semantic similarity estimation for abstract and concrete noun pairs of English and Greek. We observed a "concreteness effect", i.e., performance for concrete nouns was better than for abstract noun pairs. The assumption of maximum sense similarity as encoded by the M_n metric consistently yielded higher performance for the case of concrete nouns, while the semantic *similarity of abstract nouns was better estimated via the attributional similarity assumption* as implemented by the R_n metric. The results are consistent with the initial hypothesis that differences in cognitive organization may warrant different network organization in DSMs. In addition, abstract concepts were best modeled using an attributional network DSM with small semantic neighborhoods. This is a first step towards the better understanding of the network organization of DSMs for different categories of concepts. In terms of computation algorithms of semantic similarity, it might prove advantageous to define a metric that combines the maximum sense and attributional assumptions based on the semantic concreteness of the words under investigation. Further research on more data and languages is needed to verify the universality of the findings.

9 Acknowledgements

Elias Iosif, Alexandros Potamianos, and Maria Giannoudaki were partially funded by the PortDial project ("Language Resources for Portable Multilingual Spoken Dialogue Systems") supported by the EU Seventh Framework Programme (FP7), grant number 296170.

References

Agirre, E., E. Alfonseca, K. Hall, J. Kravalova, M. Pasca, and A. Soroa (2009). A study on similarity and relatedness using distributional and wordnet-based approaches. In *Proc. of the Annual Conference of the North American Chapter of the Association for Computational Linguistics: Human Language Technologies*, pp. 19–27.

Agirre, E., D. Martínez, O. L. de Lacalle, and A. Soroa (2006). Two graph-based algorithms for state-of-the-art WSD. In *Proc. of Conference on Empirical Methods in Natural Language Processing*, pp. 585–593.

Baroni, M. and A. Lenci (2010). Distributional memory: A general framework for corpus-based semantics. *Computational Linguistics 36*(4), 673–721.

Coltheart, M. (2000). Deep dyslexia and right-hemisphere reading. *Brain and Language 71*, 299–309.

Finkelstein, L., E. Gabrilovich, Y. Matias, E. Rivlin, Z. Solan, G. Wolfman, and E. Ruppin (2002). Placing search in context: The concept revisited. *ACM Transactions on Information Systems 20*(1), 116–131.

Harris, Z. (1954). Distributional structure. *Word 10*(23), 146–162.

Iosif, E. and A. Potamianos (2010). Unsupervised semantic similarity computation between terms using web documents. *IEEE Transactions on Knowledge and Data Engineering 22*(11), 1637–1647.

Iosif, E. and A. Potamianos (2013). Similarity Computation Using Semantic Networks Created From Web-Harvested Data. *Natural Language Engineering (submitted)*.

Kiehl, K. A., P. F. Liddle, A. M. Smith, A. Mendrek, B. B. Forster, and R. D. Hare (1999). Neural pathways involved in the processing of concrete and abstract nouns. *Human Brain Mapping 7*, 225–233.

Malandrakis, N., A. Potamianos, E. Iosif, and S. Narayanan (2011). Kernel models for affective lexicon creation. In *Proc. Interspeech*, pp. 2977–2980.

Meng, H. and K.-C. Siu (2002). Semi-automatic acquisition of semantic structures for understanding domain-specific natural language queries. *IEEE Transactions on Knowledge and Data Engineering 14*(1), 172–181.

Mihalcea, R. and D. Radev (2011). *Graph-Based Natural Language Processing and Information Retrieval*. Cambridge University Press.

Miller, G. (1990). Wordnet: An on-line lexical database. *International Journal of Lexicography 3*(4), 235–312.

Miller, G. and W. Charles (1998). Contextual correlates of semantic similarity. *Language and Cognitive Processes 6*(1), 1–28.

Noppeney, U. and C. J. Price (2004). Retrieval of abstract semantics. *NeuroImage 22*, 164–170.

Pado, S. and M. Lapata (2007). Dependency-based construction of semantic space models. *Computational Linguistics 33*(2), 161–199.

Paivio, A. (1971). *Imagery and Verbal Processes*. New York, Holt, Rinehart and Winston.

Papagno, C., R. Capasso, and G. Miceli (2009). Reversed concreteness effect for nouns in a subject with semantic dementia. *Neuropsychologia 47*(4), 1138–1148.

Resnik, P. (1995). Using information content to evaluate semantic similarity in a taxanomy. In *Proc. of International Joint Conference for Artificial Intelligence*, pp. 448–453.

Rubenstein, H. and J. B. Goodenough (1965). Contextual correlates of synonymy. *Communications of the ACM 8*(10), 627–633.

Turney, P. (2006). Similarity of semantic relations. *Computational Linguistics 32*(3), 379–416.

Véronis, J. (2004). Hyperlex: Lexical cartography for information retrieval. *Computer Speech and Language 18*(3), 223–252.

Widdows, D. and B. Dorow (2002). A graph model for unsupervised lexical acquisition. In *Proc. of the 19th International Conference on Computational Linguistics*, pp. 1093–1099.

Finite State Temporality and Context-Free Languages

Derek Kelleher
Trinity College Dublin
kellehdt@tcd.ie

Carl Vogel
Trinity College Dublin
vogel@tcd.ie

Abstract

In the finite-state temporality approach, events in natural language semantics have been characterized in regular languages, with strings representing sequences of temporal observations. We extend this approach to natural language constructions which are not regular. Context-free constructions are detailed and discussed. Superposition, the key operator in the finite-state temporality approach is investigated for context-free languages. The set of context-free languages is found to not be closed under superposition. However, as with intersection, the superposition of a context-free language and a regular language results in a context-free language. Previous work on subsumption and entailment is inapplicable to context-free languages, due to the undecidability of the subset relation for context-free languages.

1 Introduction

In recent years, events have been encoded as strings of a regular language, where a symbol in the language represents a set of predicate logic formulae that hold at a particular temporal instant, and the order of the symbols is associated with temporal order. Temporal granularity is revealed by the "superposition" of languages, essentially forming a more specific representation by collecting together formulae that hold at the same time. The representation is supplemented by notions of subsumption and entailment, allowing comparisons of information content, logical soundness, and completeness.

However, some natural language constructions concerning events are difficult to represent in this regular framework. These constructions suggest a relationship between the frequency of events, similar to the dependency of symbol frequencies on other symbol frequencies found in many context-free languages ($L = a^n b^n$). Together with their increase in complexity over regular langauges, this makes context-free languages a natural area of interest in this field.

As an example, take the expression "A as often as B", where A and B can be thought of as events. This construction implies a frequency relationship between the occurrence of two events, where A occurs at least as many times as B, possibly more. These events do not have to occur in an ordered sequence, where a sequence of As are followed by a sequence of Bs, As and Bs can occur in any order as long as the overall frequncy relationship is maintained. To be accurate, we must also allow for "instants" of time that separate any occurrence of the events we are interested in. Representing event A as the symbol a, event B as the symbol b, and an instant of time in which events may be occurring, but which are not relevant to our analysis by $\Box$, we get strings of the form $a\Box^*b$, $a\Box^*b\Box^*b\Box^*a$, $b\Box^*b\Box^*a\Box^*a\Box^*a$ etc. These strings form a context-free language.

Moens and Steedman (1988) highlight the complicated nature of the phrase "when". They suggest that "When A, B" implies not a strictly temporal relationship, but a causal one, making it a prime candidate for representation by a context-free language. Note that "When I swear, I put money into the swear jar" implies that if I swear twice, I put money into the jar twice, but not necessarily in a particular temporal order. I may swear twice during the day, and have to wait until I get home to put money in the jar.

More formal (and seemingly less natural) constructions such as "an equal number of times as", while rare, do have a place in more formal literature such as legal documents. This particular construction appears in locations as varied as "The Federal Code of the United States of America" and the bye-laws of the town of New Canaan,CT: "he shall choose alternates in rotation so that the alternates chosen by the Chairman shall be seated as nearly an equal number of times as is possible".[1]

Our analysis is restriced to the case of there being a frequency relationship between two types of events. It should be noted that the addition of a third event would lead to strings characterised by languages that are not context-free, similar to the difference between $a^n b^n$ and $a^n b^n c^n$. While these constructions tend to seem less natural ("I cried as often as I laughed, and I laughed as often as I sang"), they cannot be discounted.

The above linguistic data, while by no means exhaustive, provides a steady base from which to explore context-free languages in a finite-state temporality framework. The ubiquity of the phrases "when" or "whenever" highlights the need for this extension, while their causal nature, as opposed to temporal nature, suggests further ontological applications.

2 Background

Envisaging events as a sequence of "snapshots", Fernando (2004) has encoded event-types as regular languages, made up of symbols representing sets of "fluents"(Φ), similar to those found in McCarthy and Hayes (1969). As well as representing event types, a regular language can represent sequences of temporal observations. The diagram below represents these two concepts:

$$L = \boxed{\sim swim(john, x)}\ \boxed{swim(john, x)}^{+}\ \boxed{swim(john, m)}$$

$$L' = \qquad \boxed{mile(m)}^{*}$$

The "superposition" of two langauges is the componentwise union of their strings:

$$L\&L' = \bigcup_{k \geq 1} \{(\alpha_1 \cup \alpha'_1) \ldots (\alpha_k \cup \alpha'_k) \mid \alpha_1 \ldots \alpha_k \in L \text{ and } \alpha'_1 \ldots \alpha'_k \in L'\}$$

Intuitively, snapshots taken at the same temporal instant are merged, forming a larger picture of the world at that time:

$$\boxed{\sim swim(john, x) mile(m)}\boxed{swim(john, x) mile(m)}^{+}\boxed{swim(john, m) mile(m)}$$

The set of regular languages is closed under superposition ensuring that the superposition operation does not take us to a higher level of complexity(Fernando (2003)). Superposition allows us to define a reflexive, transitive relation (a pre-order) associated with the concept of subsumption. To preserve reflexivity subsumption $\trianglerighteq$ is defined by:

$$L \trianglerighteq L' \quad \text{iff} \quad L \subseteq L'$$

Subsuption can be thought of as relating to "information content". A language that subsumes another is more specific than that language. It contains all the information of the other language, and more.

3 Superposition and Context-Free Languages

Superposition, as the central operation in the finite-state temporality framework, must be re-examined in light of our inclusion of context-free languages. The key question is whether the result of superposing a context-free language with either a regular language or another context-free language, is itself regular, context-free, or otherwise.

[1] http://ecode360.com/9045062 - accessed on 30/11/12.

Proposition 1 *The set of context-free languages is not closed under superposition.*

Proof(by counter-example): Let the set $\{\phi\}$ be represented by the symbol $\boxed{\phi}$, and the set $\{\psi\}$ be represented by the symbol $\boxed{\psi}$. The language $L_1 = \boxed{\phi}^n \boxed{\psi}^n$ is context-free, as is the language $L_2 = \boxed{\phi}^m \boxed{\psi}^{2m}$. L_1 is given by the grammar:

$S \rightarrow \boxed{\phi} S \boxed{\psi}$
$S \rightarrow e$

and L_2 by the grammar:

$S \rightarrow \boxed{\phi} S \boxed{\psi}\boxed{\psi}$
$S \rightarrow e$

The superposition of these two languages will contain strings consisting of three possible symbols: $\{\phi\} \cup \{\phi\} = \{\phi\}$ represented as $\boxed{\phi}$, $\{\phi\} \cup \{\psi\} = \{\phi, \psi\}$ represented as $\boxed{\phi\psi}$, and $\{\psi\} \cup \{\psi\} = \{\psi\}$ represented as $\boxed{\psi}$.

Strings in the language L_1 have length 2n, and strings in the language L_2 have length 3m. Strings can only be superposed if they have equal length, therefore only strings of length 6r from both languages can be superposed, resulting in strings of the same length. Strings in L_1 will consist of 3r $\boxed{\phi}$s followed by 3r $\boxed{\psi}$s, and strings in L_2 will consist of 2r $\boxed{\phi}$s followed by 4r $\boxed{\psi}$s. The superposition of these two strings will consist of 2r $\boxed{\phi}$s superposed with $\boxed{\phi}$s, r $\boxed{\phi}$s superposed with $\boxed{\psi}$s, and 3r $\boxed{\psi}$s superposed with $\boxed{\psi}$s, resulting in strings of the form $\boxed{\phi}^{2r} \boxed{\phi\psi}^{r} \boxed{\psi}^{3r}$. Introducing a homomorphism from $\boxed{\phi}$ to 'a', from $\boxed{\phi\psi}$ to 'b', and from $\boxed{\psi}$ to 'c', we have an equivalent language $a^{2r}b^{r}c^{3r}$.

If this language were context-free, given that it is infinte, there would be some constant K such that any string longer than K would be representable as a string uvxyz such that v and y are not empty and are pumpable. If we choose the string $a^{2K}b^{K}c^{3K}$ as a string longer than K, we should be able to factorize it in this manner. If we chose v to have both as and bs or both bs and cs, then upon pumping it, we would have bs before as or cs before bs, which would result in a string not in our language. The same considerations apply to choosing y. Therefore v and y must each contain only as, or only bs, or only cs. Pumping v and y would therefore increase the number of one or two of the symbols but not all three, thereby losing the frequency relationship between the three symbols. The language cannot be context-free.□

Proposition 2 *The superposition of a context-free language with a regular language is context-free.*

Proof: Given L_1, a context-free language, and L_2, a regular language, let $P = \langle Q_P, \Sigma, \Gamma, \Delta_P, q_{P0}, F_P \rangle$ be a pushdown-automaton accepting L_1 and $A = \langle Q_A, \Sigma, \delta_A, q_{A0}, F_A \rangle$ be a finite-state-automoton accepting L_2. Δ_P is the set of transitions of the form $(q_i, a, A) \rightarrow (q_j, \gamma)$ interpreted as: when in state q_i, with input symbol a, and symbol A at the top of the stack, go to state q_j and replace A by the string γ, and δ_A is the set of transitions of the form $(q_i, a) \rightarrow (q_j)$ interpreted as: when in state q_i with input symbol a, go to state q_j. We form a pushdown automaton $R = \langle Q_P \times Q_A, \Sigma, \Gamma, \Delta_{P\times A}, (q_{P0}, q_{A0}), F_P \times F_A \rangle$, with transitions $\Delta_{P\times A}$ constructed as follows:

1. If Δ_P contains a rule of the form $(q_0, e, e) \rightarrow (q_1, S)$, then $\Delta_{P\times A}$ contains a rule of the form $((q_0, q_0), e, e) \rightarrow ((q_1, q_0), S)$.

2. If Δ_P contains a rule of the form $(q_1, e, A) \rightarrow (q_1, \gamma)$, then $\Delta_{P\times A}$ contains rules of the form $((q_1, q_x), e, A) \rightarrow ((q_1, q_x), \gamma)$ for every $q_x \in Q_A$.

3. If Δ_P contains a rule of the form $(q_1, a, a) \rightarrow (q_1, e)$, then $\Delta_{P\times A}$ contains rules of the form $((q_1, q_x), a \cup b, a) \rightarrow ((q_1, q_y), e)$ if and only if there is a transition $(q_x, b) \rightarrow (q_y)$ in δ_A.

The new transitions are akin to running the PDA and FSA in tandem, where a state (q_x, q_y), while strictly a state of R, can be thought to represent the simultaneous states of P and A. A rule of type 1 and rules of type 2 perform the same stack operations as the PDA they were derived from. Therefore, R can produce on its stack the same set of strings that P produces on its stack. No input symbol is being read while these stack operations are performed, therefore R should remain in state (q_x, q_y). Rules of type 3 ensure that if R is in a state (q_1, q_y) with an input symbol $a \cup b$, and encounters the terminal symbol a on its stack, along with there being a transition in A from q_y to q_z on input b, then R will transition to state (q_1, q_z), and delete a from its stack. These are exactly the states that P and A would seperately be in upon reading input a and b respectively. Thus, if P reads a string $a_1 \ldots a_n$ and is in a final state with an empty stack (i.e. P accepts this string), and A reads a string $b_1 \ldots b_n$ and is in a final state (i.e. A accepts this string), then R will be in a final state upon reading the superposition of these two strings. If P accepts a language L_1 and A accepts a language L_2, then R will accept $L = L_1 \& L_2$.$\Box$

If we superpose the context-free language that represents "I laughed as often as I cried" with the regular langauge that represents "an hour" to get a language representing "In an hour, I cried as often as I laughed", this language, as the superposition of a context-free langauge and a regular language, will be context-free.

4 Final Remarks

Further work will involve investigating how the concepts of subsumption and entailment can be related to context-free languages. In this framework, entailment is defined in terms of subsumption, which is defined in terms of the subset relation (Fernando and Nairn (2005)). However, according to Hopcroft et al. (1979), the problem of whether a context-free language is a subset of another context-free language is undecidable. If the subset relation cannot be calculated for context-free languages, subsumption and entailment relations break down.

One possible avenue of exploration is the making of regular approximations of context-free languages (Mohri et al. (2001)). This would preserve the subsumption and entailment relations, but at a possible cost to accurately representing the context-free construction, possibly losing the exact relationship between the frequencey of two symbols.

References

Fernando, T. (2003). Finite-state descriptions for temporal semantics. In *Proceedings of the Fifth International Workshop on Computational Semantics (IWCS-5)*.

Fernando, T. (2004). A finite-state approach to events in natural language semantics. *Journal of Logic and Computation 14*(1), 79–92.

Fernando, T. and R. Nairn (2005). Entailments in finite-state temporality. In *Proc. 6th International Workshop on Computational Semantics*, pp. 128–138.

Hopcroft, J., R. Motwani, and J. Ullman (1979). *Introduction to automata theory, languages, and computation*, Volume 2. Addison-wesley Reading, MA.

McCarthy, J. and P. Hayes (1969). Some philosophical problems from the standpoint of artificial intelligence. In M. Meltzer and D. Michie (Eds.), *Machine Intelligence 4*. Edinburgh University Press.

Moens, M. and M. Steedman (1988). Temporal ontology and temporal reference. *Computational Linguistics 14*(2), 15–28.

Mohri, M., M. Nederhof, et al. (2001). Regular approximation of context-free grammars through transformation. *Robustness in language and speech technology 17*, 153–163.

Logic Programs vs. First-Order Formulas in Textual Inference

Yuliya Lierler
University of Nebraska at Omaha
ylierler@unomaha.edu

Vladimir Lifschitz
University of Texas at Austin
vl@cs.utexas.edu

Abstract

In the problem of recognizing textual entailment, the goal is to decide, given a text and a hypothesis expressed in a natural language, whether a human reasoner would call the hypothesis a consequence of the text. One approach to this problem is to use a first-order reasoning tool to check whether the hypothesis can be derived from the text conjoined with relevant background knowledge, after expressing all of them by first-order formulas. Another possibility is to express the hypothesis, the text, and the background knowledge in a logic programming language, and use a logic programming system. We discuss the relation of these methods to each other and to the class of effectively propositional reasoning problems. This leads us to general conclusions regarding the relationship between classical logic and answer set programming as knowledge representation formalisms.

1 Introduction

In the problem of recognizing textual entailment, the goal is to decide, given a text T and a hypothesis H expressed in a natural language, whether a human reasoner would call H a consequence of T. The following example is No. 115 in the collection of problems proposed as the Second PASCAL Recognizing Textual Entailment Challenge Bar-Haim et al. (2006):

> T: The World Bank has also been criticized for its role in financing projects that have been detrimental to human rights and the natural environment.
>
> H: The World Bank is criticized for its activities.
>
> *Expected answer*: Yes.

Recognizing textual entailment is a special case of a more general and practically important problem, textual query answering.

To recognize the fact that H is "entailed" by T, we often need to use some background commonsense knowledge. For instance, in the example above it is essential that financing is an activity.

The approach to recognizing textual entailment employed in Bos and Markert (2005) and implemented in the system Nutcracker[1] can be summarized as follows:

(i) T and H are represented first by discourse representation structures Kamp and Reyle (1993) and then by first order formulas,

(ii) potentially relevant background knowledge is identified and expressed by a first-order formula *BK*,

(iii) an automated reasoning system is used to check whether the implication

$$T \wedge BK \rightarrow H \tag{1}$$

is logically valid.

[1] http://www.cogsci.ed.ac.uk/~jbos/RTE/.

Related work is described in Akhmatova (2005); Fowler et al. (2005).

The approach to the problem proposed in Baral et al. (2005); Tari and Baral (2005); Nouioua and Nicolas (2006) is similar, except that it relies on logic programs as the representation language instead of first-order formulas, and on logic programming systems as computational tools instead of first-order reasoners. The following example comes from the introduction to Baral et al. (2005):

> T: In Paris, on March 15th, John packed his laptop in the carry-on luggage and took a plane to Baghdad.
>
> H: His laptop was in Baghdad on March 16th.
>
> *Expected answer*: Yes.

Here again some background commonsense knowledge is needed to recognize that *yes* is the correct answer: a trip from Paris to Baghdad by air does not normally take more than a day; a person and his carry-on luggage are normally in the same city. Baral *et al.* represent the text T by a set of rules,[2] along with background knowledge *BK*; H is represented by a ground atom. Then an answer set solver and a constraint logic programming system are used to establish the fact that H is entailed by logic program $T \cup BK$.

Each of the two knowledge representation languages—first-order formulas and logic programs—has its own advantages. A first-order formula may have a complex, nested form; this is essential because discourse representation structures are often deeply nested. On the other hand, the semantics of logic programs is nonmonotonic; this is crucial when background commonsense knowledge is expressed by defaults (note the word "normally" in the examples above).

In this paper we argue, however, that these two versions of the logic approach to textual entailment have more in common than meets the eye. A large part of the work done by Bos and Markert can be understood in terms of the logic programming methodology advocated by Baral *et al.* Many textual entailment problems used to test the Nutcracker system can be solved by the answer set solver DLV[3] instead of the first-order theorem prover VAMPIRE[4] and the model builder PARADOX[5] that were actually employed in Nutcracker experiments.

The first-order reasoning problems that can be naturally expressed by logic programs have a distinctive syntactic feature: they belong to the "effectively propositional," or "near-propositional" formulas Schulz (2002). The relationship between effectively propositional reasoning (EPR) and answer set programming (ASP) Lifschitz (1999); Marek and Truszczyński (1999); Niemelä (1999) is one of the topics discussed in this paper. This will bring us, at the end of the paper, to some general conclusions regarding the relationship between classical logic and answer set programming as knowledge representation formalisms.

2 Representing EPR Formulas by Logic Programs

We consider here first-order formulas that may contain equality and object constants, but not function constants of arity > 0. An *EPR formula* is the universal closure of a quantifier-free formula in conjunctive normal form. We will show how to turn any EPR formula F into a logic program $\pi(F)$ such that $\pi(F)$ has a stable model iff F is satisfiable.

In the definition of π we assume that every clause in F is written as an implication with a conjunction of atoms (possibly empty) in the antecedent, and a disjunction of atoms (possibly empty) in the consequent:

$$A_1 \wedge \cdots \wedge A_m \to A_{m+1} \vee \cdots \vee A_n. \tag{2}$$

[2] This is done manually; automating the translation is mentioned in the paper as future work.

[3] `http://www.dbai.tuwien.ac.at/proj/dlv/`.

[4] `http://en.wikipedia.org/wiki/Vampire_theorem_prover`.

[5] `http://www.math.chalmers.se/~koen/paradox/`.

Besides the predicate constants occurring in F, the program $\pi(F)$ will contain two new predicate constants: the unary constant u (for "universe") and the binary constant eq (for "equals"). For any atomic formula A, by A^{eq} we denote $eq(t_1, t_2)$ if A is an equality $t_1 = t_2$, and A otherwise.

Program $\pi(F)$ consists of

(i) the facts $u(c)$ for all object constants c occurring in F;

(ii) the rules

$$\begin{array}{l} eq(X, X) \leftarrow u(X) \\ eq(Y, X) \leftarrow eq(X, Y) \\ eq(X, Z) \leftarrow eq(X, Y), eq(Y, Z); \end{array}$$

(iii) the rules

$$p(Y_1, \ldots, Y_k) \leftarrow p(X_1, \ldots, X_k), eq(X_1, Y_1), \ldots, eq(X_k, Y_k)$$

for all predicate constants p occurring in F;

(iv) the disjunctive rules

$$A^{eq}_{m+1}; \ldots; A^{eq}_n \leftarrow A^{eq}_1, \ldots, A^{eq}_m, u(X_1), \ldots, u(X_k)$$

corresponding to the conjunctive terms (2) of F, where $X_1, \ldots, X_k$ are the variables that occur in the consequent $A_{m+1} \vee \cdots \vee A_n$ of (2) but do not occur in its antecedent $A_1 \wedge \cdots \wedge A_m$.

If, for instance, F is

$$\forall X(p(a) \wedge p(b) \wedge \neg p(c) \wedge (p(X) \to X = a)) \tag{3}$$

then $\pi(F)$ consists of the rules

$$\begin{array}{l} u(a) \leftarrow \quad u(b) \leftarrow \quad u(c) \leftarrow \\ eq(X, X) \leftarrow u(X) \\ eq(Y, X) \leftarrow eq(X, Y) \\ eq(X, Z) \leftarrow eq(X, Y), eq(Y, Z) \\ p(Y) \leftarrow p(X), eq(X, Y) \\ p(a) \\ p(b) \\ \leftarrow p(c) \\ eq(X, a) \leftarrow p(X). \end{array} \tag{4}$$

As usual in answer set programming, by a model (stable model) Gelfond and Lifschitz (1988, 1991) of $\pi(F)$ we understand a model (stable model) of the corresponding ground program. It is clear that $\pi(F)$ is a (possibly disjunctive) program without negation. Its stable models are simply minimal models. Each rule of $\pi(F)$ is safe—every variable occurring in its head occurs also in its body. The stable models of this program can be generated by the answer set solver DLV.

Theorem *For any EPR formula F, the following conditions are equivalent:*

(i) F is satisfiable,

(ii) $\pi(F)$ has a model,

(iii) $\pi(F)$ has a stable model.

If F does not contain equality then this assertion remains valid if all rules containing eq are dropped from $\pi(F)$.

For instance, formula (3) is satisfiable; accordingly, program (4) has a stable model:

$$\{u(a),\ u(b),\ u(c),\ p(a),\ p(b),\ eq(a,a),\ eq(b,b),\ eq(c,c),\ eq(a,b),\ eq(b,a)\}.$$

Proof We begin by proving the second claim, that is, assume that F does not contain equality and that the rules containing *eq* are dropped from the program $\pi(F)$. *From (i) to (ii).* F is the universal closure of a quantifier-free formula, and it is satisfiable. Consequently F has an Herbrand model. By adding to this model the atoms $u(c)$ for all object constants c we get a model of $\pi(F)$. *From (ii) to (iii).* The result of grounding $\pi(F)$ is a finite program without negation; since it has a model, it has a minimal model. *From (iii) to (i).* By removing the atoms $u(c)$ from a model of $\pi(F)$ we get an Herbrand model of F. Consider now the general case, when F may contain equality. Let F^* be the formula obtained from F by

- replacing each equality $t_1 = t_2$ with $eq^*(t_1, t_2)$, where eq^* is a new binary predicate constant;
- conjoining the result with the universal closures of the formulas

$$eq^*(X,X),$$
$$eq^*(X,Y) \rightarrow eq^*(Y,X),$$
$$eq^*(X,Y) \wedge eq^*(Y,Z) \rightarrow eq^*(X,Z)$$

  and

$$p(X_1,\ldots,X_k) \wedge eq^*(X_1,Y_1) \wedge \cdots \wedge eq^*(X_k,Y_k) \rightarrow p(Y_1,\ldots,Y_k)$$

  for all predicate constants p occurring in F;
- converting the result to prenex form.

It is clear that F^* is an EPR formula that does not contain equality, and that it is satisfiable iff F is satisfiable. The rules of $\pi(F^*)$ that do not contain *eq* can be obtained from the rules of $\pi(F)$ by replacing each occurrence of *eq* with eq^*. Consequently $\pi(F^*)$ has a model (stable model) iff $\pi(F)$ has a model (stable model). It remains to apply the part of the theorem proved above to F^*.

This proof shows that, in the case when F does not contain equality, the models of $\pi(F)$ are essentially identical to the Herbrand models of F.

From the theorem we see that testing an EPR formula for satisfiability can be accomplished using an answer set solver. In the next section we investigate the applicability of this idea to the problem of recognizing textual entailment.

3 EPR Formulas in Experiments with Textual Entailment

Recall that Bos and Markert [2005] recognize textual entailment by determining whether implication (1) is logically valid.[6] In many cases, the negation

$$T \wedge BK \wedge \neg H \qquad (5)$$

of formula (1) can be converted to a prenex form with all existential quantifiers in front of the universal quantifiers ("$\exists\forall$-prenex form"). Then the sentence F, obtained from this prenex form by Skolemization and then converting the quantifier-free part to conjunctive normal form, is an EPR formula. It is clear that (1) is logically valid iff F is unsatisfiable.

The possibility of converting (5) to $\exists\forall$-prenex form is essential because it guarantees that no function constants of arity > 0 are introduced in the process of Skolemization. It is clear that conjunction (5) can be written in $\exists\forall$-prenex form if every conjunctive term can be written in this form.

[6]Like other existing systems for recognizing textual entailment, Nutcracker is not completely reliable. Generally, formulas H and T only approximate the meanings of RTE sentence pairs. For instance, Nutcracker currently ignores the semantics of plurals, tense, and aspect. Also, formula *BK* may not adequately represent all relevant background knowledge.

How restrictive is this requirement? The website shown in Footnote 1 gives the first-order formulas corresponding to 799 textual entailment problems from the second PASCAL collection that were produced by Nutcracker. In 711 cases (89%), both T and $\neg H$ can be converted to $\exists\forall$-prenex form. The conjunctive terms of *BK* come from two sources: most are automatically extracted from WordNet, the others are hand-coded. All conjunctive terms of the first kind are universal sentences, so that each of them is $\exists\forall$-prenex. Among the hand-coded parts of *BK* that Bos and Markert chose to include we found several exceptions, but they are never essential: dropping the "difficult" hand-coded part of *BK* from any of the 711 implications (1) that we have studied never makes a logically valid formula invalid.

The model builder PARADOX terminates, in principle, on any EPR formula; it generates a model if the formula is satisfiable, and reports that it is unsatisfiable otherwise. For this reason, in each of the 711 cases (with the inessential "difficult" terms dropped) Bos and Markert would be able to test the formula for satisfiability by running PARADOX alone, without invoking also the theorem prover VAMPIRE.

In these 711 cases we could also test the logical validity of (1) by running the answer set solver DLV, as described in the previous section. Interestingly, the runtime of DLV was smaller than the runtime of the model builder PARADOX in most cases, even though DLV did some redundant work: whenever the program $\pi(F)$ has a model, it computed one of its *minimal* models.[7] We should add that all these runtimes are pretty small, usually less than a second.

The main computational difference between model builders, such as PARADOX, and answer set solvers, such as DLV, is that model builders typically start by looking for a finite model with a small universe (say, a singleton); if there is no such model then search is extended to larger universes. If the input is an EPR formula containing N object constants, then answer set solvers ground the given program with the universe of size N, which means essentially that they only look for a model of cardinality N. Good answer set solvers, such as DLV, perform grounding "intelligently" and sometimes introduce auxiliary predicates that make the size of the grounded program smaller.

It is interesting also that among the 711 EPR formulas from Nutcracker experiments that we have investigated, 514 are Horn—all their conjunctive terms (2) are definite ($n = m+1$) or negative ($n = m$). If F is a Horn EPR formula then the program $\pi(F)$ is nondisjunctive; since there is no negation in this program, it can have at most one stable model. Note that deciding whether a ground nondisjunctive program without negation has a model can be done in linear time.

4 Conclusion

The properties of the translation π established in this paper suggest that EPR reasoning can be described as the common part of classical first-order logic and logic programming under the stable model semantics: (Figure 1). In terms of expressiveness, the availability of formulas more complex than EPR is

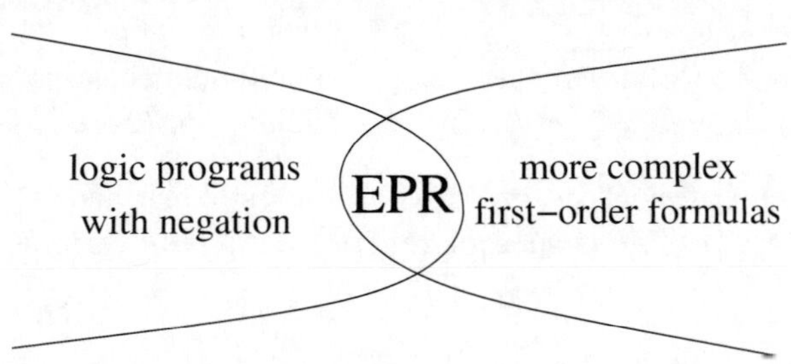

Figure 1: Logic programs vs. first-order formulas: a comparison

a strong side of classical logic; the availability of negation as failure is a strong side of declarative logic programming. Representations used in the existing work on the analysis of textual inference in terms of classical logic belong mostly to the common part of the two areas.

[7]System DLV has the option `-OM-` that disables testing for minimality, but in our experiments it did not have a noticeable effect on runtimes.

References

Akhmatova, E. (2005). Textual entailment resolution via atomic propositions. In *Proceedings of the PASCAL Challenges Workshop on Recognising Textual Entailment.*

Bar-Haim, R., I. Dagan, B. Dolan, L. Ferro, D. Giampiccolo, B. Magnini, and I. Szpektor (2006). The Second PASCAL Recognising Textual Entailment Challenge. In *Proceedings of the Second PASCAL Challenges Workshop on Recognising Textual Entailment.*

Baral, C., G. Gelfond, M. Gelfond, and R. Scherl (2005). Textual inference by combining multiple logic programming paradigms. In *AAAI Workshop on Inference for Textual Question Answering.*

Bos, J. and K. Markert (2005). Recognising textual entailment with logical inference. In *Proceeding of the Conference on Empirical Methods in Natural Language Processing (EMNLP)*, pp. 628–635.

Fowler, A., B. Hauser, D. Hodges, I. Niles, A. Novischi, and J. Stephan (2005). Applying COGEX to recognize textual entailment. In *Proceedings of the PASCAL Challenges Workshop on Recognising Textual Entailment.*

Gelfond, M. and V. Lifschitz (1988). The stable model semantics for logic programming. In R. Kowalski and K. Bowen (Eds.), *Proceedings of International Logic Programming Conference and Symposium*, pp. 1070–1080. MIT Press.

Gelfond, M. and V. Lifschitz (1991). Classical negation in logic programs and disjunctive databases. *New Generation Computing 9*, 365–385.

Kamp, H. and U. Reyle (1993). *From discourse to logic*, Volume 1,2. Kluwer.

Lifschitz, V. (1999). Action languages, answer sets and planning. In *The Logic Programming Paradigm: a 25-Year Perspective*, pp. 357–373. Springer Verlag.

Marek, V. and M. Truszczyński (1999). Stable models and an alternative logic programming paradigm. In *The Logic Programming Paradigm: a 25-Year Perspective*, pp. 375–398. Springer Verlag.

Niemelä, I. (1999). Logic programs with stable model semantics as a constraint programming paradigm. *Annals of Mathematics and Artificial Intelligence 25*, 241–273.

Nouioua, F. and P. Nicolas (2006). Using answer set programming in an inference-based approach to natural language semantics. In *Proceedings of the Fifth Workshop on Inference in Computational Semantics (ICoS).*

Schulz, S. (2002). A comparison of different techniques for grounding near-propositional CNF formulae. In *Proceedings of the 15th International FLAIRS Conference*, pp. 72–76.

Tari, L. and C. Baral (2005). Using AnsProlog with Link Grammar and WordNet for QA with deep reasoning. In *AAAI Workshop on Inference for Textual Question Answering.*

Using Network Approaches to Enhance the Analysis of Cross-Linguistic Polysemies

Johann-Mattis List
Philipps-University Marburg
mattis.list@uni-marburg.de

Anselm Terhalle
Heinrich Heine University Düsseldorf
terhalle@phil.hhu.de

Matthias Urban
Philipps-University Marburg
matthias.urban@uni-marburg.de

Abstract

Since long it has been noted that cross-linguistically recurring polysemies can serve as an indicator of conceptual relations, and quite a few approaches to model and analyze such data have been proposed in the recent past. Although – given the nature of the data – it seems natural to model and analyze it with the help of network techniques, there are only a few approaches which make explicit use of them. In this paper, we show how the strict application of weighted network models helps to get more out of cross-linguistic polysemies than would be possible using approaches that are only based on item-to-item comparison. For our study we use a large dataset consisting of 1252 semantic items translated into 195 different languages covering 44 different language families. By analyzing the community structure of the network reconstructed from the data, we find that a majority of the concepts (68%) can be separated into 104 large communities consisting of five and more nodes. These large communities almost exclusively constitute meaningful groupings of concepts into conceptual fields. They provide a valid starting point for deeper analyses of various topics in historical semantics, such as cognate detection, etymological analysis, and semantic reconstruction.

1 Introduction

What do "milk" and "udders" have to do with each other? Conceptually, they are closely related, since the former is the product and the content of the latter. Linguistically, they may even look the same, being referred to by identical word forms in many different languages, such as, e.g., by [nax] in Judeo-Tat (an Indo-European language), by [ukun] in Oroqen (an Altaic language), or by [mis] in Miao (a Hmong-Mien language, all data taken from Key and Comrie 2007). Historically, the conceptual relation between "milk" and "udders" may show up in the form of semantic shifts where a word which was formerly used to express one of the concepts in a given language is henceforth used to express the other one. Thus, in Standard Chinese, the word [niou^{35}nai^{214}] "milk" is a compound of [niou^{35}] "cow" and [nai^{214}] "milk" which originally meant "udder" (as well as "breast").[1]

The situation in which a set of conceptually related meanings is expressed by the same form in a given language is known as *polysemy*. In this paper, we show how an analysis of a weighted network reconstructed from a large database of cross-linguistic polysemies can help to shed light on common conceptual associations in the world's languages. We find that the reconstructed network has a strong *community structure*: it can be easily separated into communities, i.e. groups of nodes that share more connections with each other than with nodes outside the group. We detected 104 large communities consisting of five and more nodes. These communities cover 879 out of 1286 concepts (68%) and almost exclusively constitute meaningful groupings of concepts into conceptual fields, thus providing a valid starting point for further analyses in historical linguistics.

[1]Superscript numbers indicate tones.

2 Polysemy and Conceptual Relations in Synchrony and Diachrony

The term *polysemy* was first used by Bréal (1897, 154), who explicitly introduced the notion as a direct consequence of semantic change. Indeed, recent approaches to semantic change (e.g. Traugott and Dasher 2002) emphasize that the development of an initially secondary polysemous reading is the first stage of a complete semantic change to take place. Given that for semantic change a certain 'association [...] between the old meaning and the new [...] might be regarded as a necessary condition' (Ullmann, 1972, 211), the same kind of "association" can also be assumed to hold for polysemy. There are recent approaches in historical semantics that explicitly start from polysemous lexical items to extract information about what kinds of concepts are associated and what kinds of semantic change seem to be plausible (Croft et al., 2009). This procedure has the great advantage of providing 'an important antidote to the unbridled imagination in postulating etymologies' (Evans and Wilkins, 2000, 550), where intuitive assessments regarding plausibility as far as semantics is concerned are still frequent. Our approach operates in a similar vein.

3 Modeling Cross-Linguistic Polysemies as Weighted Networks

The idea to model polysemies as networks itself is not new. It was already underlying Haspelmath's (2003) *semantic map* approach which is used as a heuristic tool to analyze grammatical categories in linguistic typology. François (2008) applied this approach to the lexical domain, followed by further work by Croft et al. (2009), Perrin (2010), Cysouw (2010a, 2010b), and Steiner et al. (2011), who also introduced a simplified procedure to retrieve putative polysemies from semantically aligned word lists. What is new in our approach, however, is the strict modeling of cross-linguistic polysemies as *weighted* networks that shall be briefly introduced in the following.

3.1 Reconstruction

Networks (or graphs) constitute a system representation tool which is used by many different disciplines (Newman, 2004). We make use of a weighted network model to display and analyze conceptual relations reconstructed on the basis of cross-linguistic polysemies. Our network has the following structure:

> Let C be a set of n concepts $c_1, \ldots, c_n$ whose linguistic representation we want to analyze on the basis of a set L of m different languages belonging to $o \leq m$ language families. Our network is an undirected weighted graph $G = (V, E, f)$, with $V = C$ and $E \subseteq \{e_{ij} := \{c_i, c_j\} \mid c_i, c_j \in C \text{ and } i \neq j\}$. f is a mapping from E into $\mathbb{N}$ with $f(e_{ij}) \leq o$ being the number of language families which use one word for both c_i and c_j, and $f(E) = \{f(e_{ij}) \mid e_{ij} \in E\}$.[2]

In less formal terms, we reconstruct a weighted network by representing all concepts in a given multilingual word list as nodes (vertices), and draw edges between all nodes that show up as polysemies in the data. The edge weights reflect the number of language families in which these polysemies are attested.

3.2 Analysis

Statistical accounts on cross-linguistic polysemies retrieved from semantically aligned word lists make it possible to define the similarity between concepts on an item-to-item basis. Here, problems may arise from the fact that our approach cannot make an a priori distinction between polysemy and semantic vagueness on the one hand (Geeraerts, 1993), and polysemy and homophony on the other (compare François' 2008 notion of *colexification*). While, as Haspelmath (2003, 231) and François (2008, 169f) argue, the distinction between (true) polysemy and semantic vagueness does not matter from a cross-linguistic perspective (and we will make no attempt to distinguish the two), the failure to single out homophones can lead to wrong assessments regarding concept relations. In German, Dutch, and Yiddish, for example, the stems expressing the concepts "arm" and "poor" are identical in form. If one naively counted the number

[2] Many thanks to Daniel Schulzek for helpful comments on the maths.

of languages where the concepts are expressed by the same word, the link would appear to find much more support in the languages of the world than that between "udder" and "chest", which is only reflected in two languages in our data, namely in Aymara and Sirionó (see Supplemental Material), although in this latter case, the connection between the two concepts seems much more meaningful than in the former one.

A first way to solve this problem is to count occurrences of links between concepts not on the basis of languages but of language families, thus avoiding that they result from genetic inheritance. This would resolve the problem in favor of "udder" and "chest", since the link between "arm" and "poor" only occurs in the closely related Germanic languages, whereas Aymara and Sirionó belong to different language families. The problem can further be addressed by setting up a threshold of occurrences and to ignore links that exhibit less occurrences. Such an analysis is illustrated in Figure 1, where, starting from a given concept network, the threshold is successively increased and more and more edges are successively removed. While such an analysis surely yields the most reliable links, it has the drawback of ignoring many links that might reflect true – although less frequently attested – conceptual relations.

In order to solve the problem of separating the wheat from the chaff without losing too much wheat, the network perspective as opposed to the item-to-item perspective can be of great help. For the kind of networks we are dealing with in this study, an analysis of *community structure* seems to be specifically useful. Community structure refers to the property of many networks that do not consist of random collections of nodes with random connections between them but of 'distinct "communities" – groups of vertices within which the connections are dense but between which they are sparser' (Newman, 2004, 4). It is straightforward to assume that a network reflecting relations between concepts should exhibit some kind of community structure, given that it is often assumed that concepts can be grouped into specific conceptual fields. Analyzing the community structure of cross-linguistic polysemy networks should therefore give us some interesting insights into general concept relations.

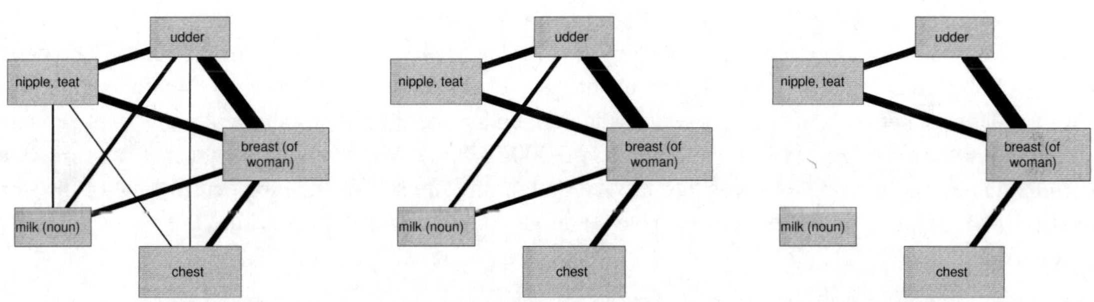

(a) no cutoff (b) cutoff < 5 (c) cutoff < 10

Figure 1: Setting up a Threshold of Occurrences.

4 Application

4.1 Data

Our analysis is based on a large multilingual word list consisting of 1252 glosses ("concepts") translated into 195 different languages, covering 44 different language families (see Supplemental Material). The data was taken from three different sources, namely the Intercontinental Dictionary Series (IDS, Key and Comrie 2007, 133 languages), the World Loanword Database (WOLD, Haspelmath and Tadmor 2009, 30 languages), and a multilingual dictionary provided by the Logos Group (Logos, Logos Group 2008, 32 languages). The data from each of these sources was automatically cleaned and normalized with help of Python scripts. While the original sources of IDS and WOLD have a total of 1310 glosses, we selected only those glosses which were at least reflected in 100 languages. The structure of the input data is illustrated in Figure 2, with two instances of polysemies in Russian and German marked in bold font.

Key	Concept	Russian	German	...
1.1	world	mir, svet	Welt	...
1.21	earth, land	zemlja	**Erde**, Land	...
1.212	ground, soil	počva	**Erde**, Boden	...
1.420	tree	**derevo**	Baum	...
1.430	wood	**derevo**	Wald	...
...	...	...	...	...

Figure 2: Structure of the Data

(a) Complete Network (b) Community Structure

Figure 3: Comparing the Network and its Community Structure.

4.2 Analysis

We created a weighted network from the data, using the number of language families in which a particular polysemy was reflected as edge weights. We further analyzed the community structure of the data with help of a weighted version (Newman, 2004) of the Girvan-Newman algorithm for community detection (Girvan and Newman, 2002).[3] This algorithm successively removes the edges with the highest *betweenness* from a given network. Edge betweenness is defined as 'the number of shortest paths between pairs of vertices that run along it' (Girvan and Newman, 2002, 7822). We followed Newman (2004) in using *modularity*, i.e. the 'fraction of edges that fall within communities minus the expected value of the same quantity if edges are assigned at random' (Newman, 2004, 6), as a criterion to find the best split for the analysis.

4.3 Results

In Figure 3 the original network (a) and the network's community structure (b) are contrasted. The original network consists of one very large connected component of 1141 nodes and only a spurious number of unconnected nodes. The analysis of the network with help of the Girvan-Newman algorithm yielded a total of 337 communities of which 104 are rather large, consisting of 5 and more nodes, and covering a majority of the concepts (879 out of 1289, 68%). Most of these large communities constitute meaningful groupings of concepts into conceptual fields. Community 5, for example, groups concepts that deal with the cover of bodies ("feather", "hair", "bark", etc.). Community 28 deals with learning ("study", "count", "try, attempt", etc.). And community 70 contains concepts related to transport vehicles ("canoe", "boat", and "carriage, wagon, cart", etc., see Supplemental Material).

Apart from the general question of which items are grouped together in one community, it is also interesting to investigate the internal structure of the communities more closely. Community 3, for example, consists of 18 items which all center around the concepts "tree" and "wood" (see the network representation using force-directed layout in Figure 4). Cross-linguistically, the conflation of "tree" and

[3]We are well aware of the fact that there are many other, supposedly better, algorithms for community detection. However, given that this is a pilot study, we decided to take a rather simple algorithm whose basic ideas are nicely described and easy to understand, thus limiting our presuppositions about conceptual structures to a minimum.

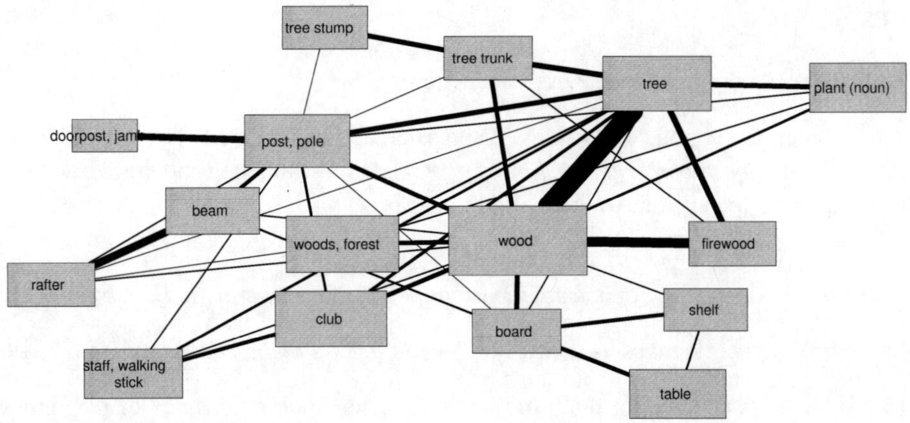

Figure 4: Force-Directed Representation of Cluster 3.

"wood" into one lexical form occurs very frequently, and it has been identified previously by several scholars (Hjelmslev, 1963; Witkowski et al., 1981). Our data is congruent with the traditional literature in this respect. However, in our network, these central concepts are connected with a substantial number of contiguously related ones. Thus, "wood" has something to do with "clubs", "staffs", "walking sticks", and the like, in that these all are artifacts "made from wood", and "trees" (and "wood") have also a contiguous relation with "forests" in so far as forests are, simply spoken, "agglomerations of trees". Unlike the well-documented association between "wood" and "tree", to our knowledge most of these further semantic connections have not yet been documented explicitly from a cross-linguistic point of view. Hence, as even this single example shows, our analysis contributes to enhancing our knowledge regarding cross-linguistically common conceptual associations. From the perspective of historical semantics, as Witkowski et al. (1981) argue, polysemies between "tree" and "wood" can be interpreted in diachronic terms, with terms for "wood" frequently giving rise to terms for "tree". But there is a diachronic correlate also for other concepts in this cluster. For example, the Proto-Indo-European root **dóru-* has a direct descendant in Russian *dérevo* "tree, wood". In other languages, however, reflexes are used to denote all kinds of weapons that were originally made from wood, such as Avestan *dāuru* "club" (but also "tree trunk"), or Modern Greek δόρυ "spear", which regularly meant "wood, tree" (but also "beam, pole") in Old Greek (Nussbaum 1968, 147, footnote).

5 Conclusion

Polysemies offer powerful evidence to study conceptual relations and semantic change. In this paper, we tried to show how the analysis of such data can be enhanced with the help of weighted network approaches. By applying them to a large dataset, we illustrated the potential of cross-linguistic polysemy data for semantic analyses. The analysis of the community structure of our network not only reproduces findings from the literature, but also reveals additional cross-linguistic regularities in the conceptual structures underlying semantic change.

Supplemental Material

The supplemental material accompanying this study contains the word lists of all 195 languages, upon which the reconstruction of the weighted network was based, and all essential results in form of text files, including the network, a detailed list and description of all inferred communities, and additional statistics regarding the languages.

References

Bréal, M. (1897). *Essai de sémantique*. Paris: Hachette.

Croft, W., C. Beckner, L. Sutton, T. Wilkins, J.and Bhattacharya, and D. Hruschka (2009). *Quantifying semantic shift for reconstructing language families*. Talk, held at the 83rd Annual Meeting of the Linguistic Society of America. PDF: `http://www.unm.edu/~wcroft/Papers/Polysemy-LSA-HO.pdf`.

Cysouw, M. (2010a). Drawing networks from recurrent polysemies. *Linguistic Discovery 8*(1), 281–285.

Cysouw, M. (2010b). Semantic maps as metrics on meaning. *Linguistic Discovery 8*(1), 70–95.

Evans, N. and D. Wilkins (2000). In the mind's ear: The semantic extensions of perception verbs in Australian languages. *Language 76*(3), 546–592.

François, A. (2008). Semantic maps and the typology of colexification: intertwining polysemous networks across languages. In M. Vanhove (Ed.), *From polysemy to semantic change*, pp. 163–215. Amsterdam: Benjamins.

Geeraerts, D. (1993). Vagueness's puzzles, polysemy's vagaries. *Cognitive Linguistics 4*(3), 223–272.

Girvan, M. and M. E. Newman (2002). Community structure in social and biological networks. *Proceedings of the National Academy of Sciences of the United States of America 99*(12), 7821–7826.

Haspelmath, M. (2003). The geometry of grammatical meaning: semantic maps and cross-linguistic comparison. In M. Tomasello (Ed.), *The new psychology of language*, pp. 211–242. Mahwah, NJ: Lawrence Erlbaum.

Haspelmath, M. and U. Tadmor (2009). *World Loanword Database*. Munich: Max Planck Digital Library.

Hjelmslev, L. (1963). *Prolegomena to a theory of language*. Madison: University of Wisconsin Press.

Key, M. R. and B. Comrie (2007). *IDS – The Intercontinental Dictionary Series*. URL: `http://lingweb.eva.mpg.de/ids/`.

Logos Group (2008). *Logos Dictionary*. URL: `http://www.logosdictionary.org/index.php`.

Newman, M. E. J. (2004). Analysis of weighted networks. *Physical Review E 70*(5), 056131.

Nussbaum, A. J. (1968). *Head and horn in Indo-European. The words for "horn," "head," and "hornet"*. Berlin and New York: de Gruyter.

Perrin, L.-M. (2010). Polysemous qualities and universal networks, invariance and diversity. *Linguistic Discovery 8*(1), 259–280.

Steiner, L., P. F. Stadler, and M. Cysouw (2011). A pipeline for computational historical linguistics. *Language Dynamics and Change 1*(1), 89–127.

Traugott, E. C. and R. B. Dasher (2002). *Regularity in semantic change*. Cambridge: Cambridge University Press.

Ullmann, S. (1972). *Semantics*. Blackwell.

Witkowski, S. R., C. H. Brown, and P. K. Chase (1981). Where do tree terms come from? *Man 16*(1), 1–14.

A corpus-based taxonomy of question responses

Paweł Łupkowski*
Institute of Psychology
Adam Mickiewicz University, Poznan
Pawel.Lupkowski@amu.edu.pl

Jonathan Ginzburg
UFR Études anglophones
Université Paris-Diderot (Paris 7)
yonatan.ginzburg@univ-paris-diderot.fr

Abstract

In this paper we consider the issue of answering a query with a query. Although these are common, with the exception of Clarification Requests, they have not been studied empirically. After briefly reviewing different theoretical approaches on this subject, we present a corpus study of query responses in the British National Corpus and develop a taxonomy for query responses. We sketch a formal analysis of the response categories in the framework of KoS.

1 Introduction

Responding to a query with a query is a common occurrence, representing on a rough estimate more than 20% of all responses to queries found in the British National Corpus.[1] Research on dialogue has long recognized the existence of such responses. However, with the exception of one of its subclasses—albeit a highly substantial one—the class of query responses has not been characterized empirically in previous work. The class that has been studied in some detail are Clarification Requests (CRs) (Rodriguez and Schlangen, 2004; Rieser and Moore, 2005). However, CRs can be triggered by any utterance, interrogative or otherwise. Researchers on the semantics and pragmatics of questions (see e.g. Carlson, 1983; Wiśniewski, 2003) have been aware for many years of the existence of one class of query responses—responses that express questions dependent on the question they respond to, as in (1a,b). This lead Carlson to propose (1c) as a sufficient condition for a query response, which can be formalized using (1d), assuming notions of resolvedness and aboutness (for which see e.g. Ginzburg and Sag, 2000).

(1) a. **A:** Who murdered Smith? **B:** Who was in town?

b. **A:** Who is going to win the race? **B:** Who is going to participate?

c. Who killed Smith depends on who was in town at the time.

d. q_2 can be used to respond to q_1 if q_1 $\mathsf{depends\ on}$ q_2.

e. q_1 $\mathsf{depends\ on}$ q_2 iff any proposition p such that p $\mathsf{Resolves}$ q_2, also satisfies p entails r such that r is About q_1.

Larsson (2002) and Asher and Lascarides (2003) argue that the proper characterization of question responses is pragmatically based. Asher and Lascarides (2003) propose to characterize non-CR query responses by means of the rhetorical relation *question elaboration* (Q-Elab) with stress on the plan-oriented relation between the initial question and the question expressed by the response. Q-Elab might be informally summarized as follows:

(2) If Q-Elab(α, β) holds between an utterance α uttered by A, where g is a goal associated by convention with utterances of the type α, and the question β uttered by B, then any answer to β must elaborate a plan to achieve g.

*The author was supported by the Iuventus Plus grant (IP2011-031-771).

[1] In the spoken part of the BNC, using SCoRE (Purver, 2001), we found 11312 ?/? cross-turn sequences, whereas 41041 ?/. cross-turn sequences, so the ?/? pairs constitute 21.6%. (For the SCoRE syntax see `http://www.dcs.qmul.ac.uk/imc/ds/score/help.html`.)

Table 1: Tags used to annotate question—question-response sample

Tag	Question-response category
CR	clarification requests
DP	dependent questions
FORM	questions considering the way of answering $q1$
MOTIV	questions about the underlying motivations behind asking $q1$
NO ANSW	questions aimed at avoiding answering $q1$
QA	questions providing an answer to $q1$
IGNORE	questions ignoring $q1$
IND	questions with a presupposed answer

The relation of Q-Elab, motivated by interaction in cooperative settings, is vulnerable to examples such as those in (3). (3a) has one understanding that might be characterized using dependence (*What I like depends on what* YOU *like*), but can also be used simply as a coherent retort. (3b) could possibly be used in political debate without it necessarily involving an attempt to discover an answer to the first question asked.

(3) a. **A:** What do you like? **B:** What do you like?

b. **A:** What is Sarkozy going to do about it? **B:** What is Papandreou?

In order to better understand the nature of question responses, we ran a corpus study on the British National Corpus (BNC). The results we obtained show that, apart from CRs, dependent questions are indeed by far the largest class of question responses. However, they reveal also the existence of a number of response categories, characterizable neither as dependent questions nor as plan supporting responses. They include (a) a class akin to what Conversation Analysts refer to as *counters* (Schegloff, 2007)—responses that attempt to foist on the conversation a distinct issue from the current discourse topic and (b) responses that ignore the current topic but address the situation it concerns.

Attaining completeness in characterizing the response space of a query is of fundamental importance for dialogue management and the design of user interfaces. Beyond that general goal, a better understanding of e.g. *counters* and *situation–relevant responses*, which we believe are rare in task–oriented dialogue, is important for adversarial interaction (courtroom, interrogation, argumentation, certain games). Characterizing their coherence is challenging for all approaches that ground dialogue on cooperativity principles (e.g. Asher and Lascarides, 2003; Roberts, 2011).

The rest of the paper is structured as follows: in section 2 we present the taxonomy underlying our corpus study; section 3 describes the results; in section 4 we sketch a formal analysis of one of the response categories in the framework of KoS (Ginzburg and Fernández, 2010). We conclude with a summary and future work.

2 A corpus-based taxonomy of answering by means of questions

The study sample The taxonomy of query responses was designed after an analysis of 1051 examples of query-query response pairs obtained from the BNC. The sample was obtained from blocks D, F, G, H, J, K of the BNC (so it covers a wide range of dialogue domains, like interviews, radio and TV broadcasts, tutorials, meetings, training sessions or medical consultations). Initially, examples were obtained with the search engine SCoRE (Purver, 2001) (the search string was `?$ | ?$`). Subsequently, cross talk and tag questions were eliminated manually. The sample was classified and annotated by the first author with tags presented in Table 1 (we discuss the reliability of this annotation in section 3).

In what follows we describe and exemplify each class of the resulting taxonomy. To make the description clear we will use $q1$ for the initial question posed and $q2$ for a question given as a response to $q1$. The taxonomy was built with attention paid to the function of $q2$ in the dialogue.

Clarification requests (CR) Clarification requests are all question-responses that concern the content or form of $q1$ that was not completely understood. This class contains intended content queries (4a), repetition requests (4b) and relevance clarifications (4c).

(4) a. **A:** What's Hamlet about? **B:** Hamlet? [KPW, 945–946][2]

b. **A:** Why are you in? **B:** What? **A:** Why are you in? [KPT, 469–471]

c. **A:** Is he knocked out? **B:** What do you mean? [KDN, 3170–3171]

In this paper we will not consider this class in detail, mainly because of existing, detailed work on this subject such as (Purver, 2006).

Dependent questions (`DP`) By a *dependent question* we understand $q2$ where a dependency statement as in (1c) could be assumed to be true. The following examples illustrate this:

(5) a. **A:** Do you want me to <*pause*> push it round? **B:** Is it really disturbing you? [FM1, 679–680]
(cf. *Whether I want you to push it depends on whether it really disturbs you*

b. **A:** Any other questions? **B:** Are you accepting questions on the statement of faith at this point? [F85, 70–71]
(cf. *Whether more questions exist depends on whether you are accepting questions on the statement of faith at this point.*)

'How should I answer this?' questions (`FORM`) This class consists of question-responses addressing the issue of the *way* the answer to $q1$ should be given. It is the case where the *form* of answer to $q1$ depends on the answer given to $q2$. This relation between $q1$ and $q2$ might be noticed in following examples. Consider (6a). The way B answers A's question in this case will be dictated by A's answer to $q2$—whether or not, A wants to know details point by point.

(6) a. **A:** Okay then, Hannah, what, what happened in your group?
B: Right, do you want me to go through every point? [K75, 220–221]

b. **A:** Where's that one then?
B: Erm, you know Albert Square? [KBC, 506–507]

Requests for underlying motivation (`MOTIV`) In the case of *requests for underlying motivation* $q2$ addresses the issue of motivation behind asking $q1$. What is important here is that the fact of answering $q1$ depends on the answer to $q2$ (i.e. providing proper reasons for asking $q1$). In this aspect this class differs form the previous ones, where we may assume that an agent wishes to provide answer to $q1$. Most of question responses of this kind are of the form "Why?" (32 out of 41 gathered examples, cf. (7a)), but also other formulations were observed (8 out of 41, cf. (7b)). Most direct questions of this kind are: *What's it got to do with you?*; *what's it to you?*; *Is that any of your business?*; *what's that gotta do with anything?*.

(7) a. **A:** What's the matter? **B:** Why? [HDM, 470–471]

b. **A:** Out, how much money have you got in the building society? **B:** What's it got to do with you? [KBM, 2086–2087]

I don't want to answer your question (`NO ANSW`) The role of query responses of this class is to give a clear signal that an agent does not want to provide an answer to $q1$. Instead of answering $q1$ the agent provides $q2$ and attempts to 'turn the table' on the original querier.

(8) a. **A:** Yeah what was your answer? **B:** What was yours? [KP3, 636–637]

b. **A:** Why is it recording me? **B:** Well why not? [KSS, 43–44]

[2]This notation indicates the BNC file (KPW) together with the sentence numbers (945–946).

Table 2: Frequency of question—question-response categories. The parenthesized percentage is the category's percentage of the sample that *excludes* CRs.

Category	Frequency	% of the Total
CR	832	79.16
DP	108	10.28 (49)
MOTIV	41	3.90 (18)
NO ANSW	26	2.47 (12)
FORM	16	1.52 (7)
QA	13	1.24 (6)
IND	9	0.85 (4)
IGNORE	6	0.57 (3)
Total	**1051** (219)	100

Indirect answers/responses (IND/QA) This class consists of query responses, which provide (indirectly) an answer to $q1$. Interestingly, answering $q2$ is not necessary in this case. Consider (9a). B by asking the question *Do you know how old this sweater is?* clearly suggests that the answer to A's question is negative. Moreover, B does not expect to obtain an answer to his/her question. This might also be observed in (9b) ('of course I am Gemini').

(9) a. **A:** Is that an early Christmas present, that sweater? **B:** Do you know how old this sweater is? [HM4, 7–8]

b. **A:** Are you Gemini? **B:** Well if I'm two days away from your, what do you think? [KPA, 3603–3604]

Another means of providing indirect answers can be observed in the corpus data. It is the case that by asking $q2$ an agent already presupposes the answer to $q1$. If we take a look on (10) we note that positive answer to $q1$ is presupposed in B's question (I will help you).

(10) **A:** Will you help with the *<pause>* the paint tonight? **B:** What can I do? [KE4, 3263–3264]

I ignore your question (IGNORE) The last observed class is somewhat harder to grasp. This is the case where $q2$ is related to the situation, but ignores $q1$. This is evident in (11). A and B are playing *Monopoly*. A asks a question, which is ignored by B. It is not that B does not want to answer A's question and that's why he/she asks $q2$. Rather, B ignores $q1$ and asks a question related to the situation (in this case the board game).

(11) **A:** I've got Mayfair *<pause>* Piccadilly, Fleet Street and Regent Street, but I never got a set did I?
B: Mum, how much, how much do you want for Fleet Street? [KCH, 1503–1504]

3 Results and annotation reliability

The results of the performed classification are presented in Table 2. Putting aside CRs, the majoritarian class is indeed DP. What is striking is the relatively large frequency of adversarial responses (the classes MOTIV, NO ANSW, IGNORE). FORM, as we discuss below, is the sole class whose coherence clearly requires reasoning about the querier's intentions. It is relatively infrequent.

In order to check the reliability of the classification process, the decision tree was tested by three other annotators. Annotators obtained the sample of 90 (randomly chosen) question-question pairs[3] and decision tree. The instruction was to annotate question-reply to the first question in each example. Some of the examples were enriched with additional context (after q2). Two annotators reported that the annotation task would be easier if the context would be present for all examples.

The reliability of the annotation was evaluated using κ (Carletta, 1996). The agreement on the coding of the control sample by four annotators was moderate (Fleiss $\kappa = 0.44$, $SE = 0.0206$, $95\%CI =$

[3]The distribution of the classes was in line with the distribution observed by the primary annotator: CR: 39 examples; DP: 18 examples; MOTIV: 10 examples; NO ANSW: 10 examples; FORM: 4 examples; QA: 4 examples; IGNORE: 3 examples; OTHER: 2 examples.

0.3963 to 0.4770)[4]. One of the control sample annotators is an experienced linguist with extensive past work with dialogue transcripts. In this case agreement on the coding was strong (71% agreement with Cohen's $\kappa = 0.62$, $SE = 0.0637$, $95\% CI = 0.4902$ to 0.7398). Two other control sample annotators are logicians, but with little experience in corpus annotation. For them agreement on the coding was somewhat lower, i.e. moderate (66% agreement with Cohen's $\kappa = 0.56$, $SE = 0.0649$, $95\% CI = 0.4266$ to 0.6810; and 54% agreement with Cohen's $\kappa = 0.42$, $SE = 0.0674$, $95\% CI = 0.2829$ to 0.5472). The most unproblematic cases were `CR`, `MOTIV` and `IGNORE` (the largest groups of examples with at least 3 annotators' agreement). Also `DP`, `NO ANSW` and `QA` had high agreement between annotators. The main problem was with `FORM`. We assume that this is caused by the unclarity in the question introducing this class in the decision tree ('The way the answer to $q1$ will be given depends on the answer to $q2$', while for DP it was 'Is it the case that the answer to $q1$ depends on the answer to $q2$?'). Feedback from two of three control sample annotators reported this as a confusing case. There were two cases in the control sample on which annotators completely disagreed. These were the following:

(12) a. **A:** You know the one you just took out? **B:** You want it back? [F77, 86–87]

b. **A:** You want a drink dear? **B:** Have your sweets for what? [KD1, 5132–5133]

4 Modeling Query Response Categories in KoS

In this section we show how to explicate the coherence relation that underlies the `DP` query responses within the framework of KoS. It is worth mentioning that this framework allows to model also the other query responses types described in this article, as we will show in an extended version of this paper. KoS is a framework for dialogue whose logical underpinning is Type Theory with Records (TTR) (Cooper, 2005) and which underlies dialogue systems such as GoDiS and CLARIE (Larsson, 2002; Purver, 2006). On the approach developed in KoS, there is actually no single context—instead of a single context, analysis is formulated at a level of information states, one per conversational participant. The type of such information states is given in (13a). We leave the structure of the private part unanalyzed here, as with one exception all our characterizations do not make reference to this; for one approach to $private$, see e.g. (Larsson, 2002). The dialogue gameboard represents information that arises from publicized interactions. Its structure is given in (13b)—the *spkr,addr* fields allow one to track turn ownership, *Facts* represents conversationally shared assumptions, *Pending* and *Moves* represent respectively moves that are in the process of/have been grounded, *QUD* tracks the questions currently under discussion:

(13) a. TotalInformationState (TIS) $=_{def}$

$$\begin{bmatrix} \text{dialoguegameboard : DGB} \\ \text{private : Private} \end{bmatrix}$$

b. DGBType $=_{def}$

$$\begin{bmatrix} \text{spkr: Ind} \\ \text{addr: Ind} \\ \text{utt-time : Time} \\ \text{c-utt : addressing(spkr,addr,utt-time)} \\ \text{Facts : Set(Proposition)} \\ \text{Pending : list(locutionary Proposition)} \\ \text{Moves : list(locutionary Proposition)} \\ \text{QUD : poset(Question)} \end{bmatrix}$$

The basic units of change are mappings between dialogue gameboards that specify how one gameboard configuration can be modified into another on the basis of dialogue moves. We call a mapping between DGB types a *conversational rule*. The types specifying its domain and its range we dub, respectively, the *preconditions* and the *effects*, both of which are supertypes of DGBType.

We start by characterizing the moves that typically involve accepting $q1$ into the DGB. The potential for `DP` responses is explicated on the basis of the two conversational rules in (14a,b): (14a) says that given a question q and ASK(A,B,q) being the LatestMove, one can update QUD with q as QUD–maximal.

[4]All the data established with `http://www.stattools.net`. Access 25.11.2012.

QSPEC is what characterizes the contextual background of reactive queries and assertions. (14b) says that if q is QUD–maximal, then subsequent to this either conversational participant may make a move constrained to be q–specific (14c):

(14) a. Ask QUD–incrementation

$$\begin{bmatrix} \text{pre :} & \begin{bmatrix} \text{q : Question} \\ \text{LatestMove = Ask(spkr,addr,q): IllocProp} \end{bmatrix} \\ \text{effects :} & \begin{bmatrix} \text{qud} = \langle \text{q,pre.qud} \rangle \text{: poset(Question)} \end{bmatrix} \end{bmatrix}$$

b. QSPEC

$$\begin{bmatrix} \text{pre :} \begin{bmatrix} \text{qud} = \langle \text{q, Q} \rangle \text{: poset(Question)} \end{bmatrix} \\ \text{effects : TurnUnderspec} \wedge_{merge} \\ \begin{bmatrix} \text{r : AbSemObj} \\ \text{R: IllocRel} \\ \text{LatestMove = R(spkr,addr,r) : IllocProp} \\ \text{c1 : Qspecific(r,q)} \end{bmatrix} \end{bmatrix}$$

c. q-specific utterance: an utterance whose content is either a proposition p About q or a question q_1 on which q Depends

5 Summary and Future Work

The paper provides the first empirically-based study of query responses to queries. The most interesting finding here is the existence of a number of classes of adversarial responses, that involve the rejection/ignoring of the original query. Indeed, in such cases the original query is rarely responded to in subsequent interaction.

We conducted our study in the BNC since it is a general corpus with a variety of domains and genres. It is of course important to extend this study to more detailed consideration of specific genres and domains. A significant challenge for future work is automatic classification of query responses into a taxonomy like the one provided here. We intend to address this in future work.

References

Asher, N. and A. Lascarides (2003). *Logics of Conversation.* Cambridge: Cambridge University Press.

Carletta, J. (1996). Assessing agreement on classification tasks: The kappa statistic. *Computational Linguistics 22*(2), 249–254.

Carlson, L. (1983). *Dialogue Games.* Synthese Language Library. Dordrecht: D. Reidel.

Cooper, R. (2005). Austinian truth in Martin-Löf type theory. *Research on Language and Computation 3*(4), 333–362.

Ginzburg, J. and R. Fernández (2010). Computational models of dialogue. In A. Clark, C. Fox, and S. Lappin (Eds.), *Handbook of Computational Linguistics and Natural Language*, Oxford. Blackwell.

Ginzburg, J. and I. A. Sag (2000). *Interrogative Investigations: the form, meaning and use of English Interrogatives.* Number 123 in CSLI Lecture Notes. Stanford: California: CSLI Publications.

Larsson, S. (2002). *Issue based Dialogue Management.* Ph. D. thesis, Gothenburg University.

Purver, M. (2001, October). SCoRE: A tool for searching the BNC. Technical Report TR-01-07, Department of Computer Science, King's College London.

Purver, M. (2006). Clarie: Handling clarification requests in a dialogue system. *Research on Language & Computation 4*(2), 259–288.

Rieser, V. and J. Moore (2005). Implications for generating clarification requests in task-oriented dialogues. In *Proceedings of the 43rd Meeting of the Association for Computational Linguistics*, Michigan.

Roberts, C. (2011). Information structure: Afterword. *Semantics and Pragmatics*.

Rodriguez, K. and D. Schlangen (2004). Form, intonation and function of clarification requests in german task-oriented spoken dialogues. In J. Ginzburg and E. Vallduvi (Eds.), *Proceedings of Catalog'04, The 8th Workshop on the Semantics and Pragmatics of Dialogue*, Universitat Pompeu Fabra, Barcelona.

Schegloff, E. (2007). *Sequence Organization in Interaction*. Cambridge: Cambridge University Press.

Wiśniewski, A. (2003). Erotetic search scenarios. *Synthese 134*, 389–427.

Learning Semantic Representations in a Bigram Language Model

Jeff Mitchell
mitchelljeff@hotmail.com

Abstract

This paper investigates the extraction of semantic representations from bigrams. The major obstacle to this objective is that while these word to word dependencies do contain a semantic component, other factors, e.g. syntax, play a much stronger role. An effective solution will therefore require some means of isolating semantic structure from the remainder. Here, the possibility of modelling semantic dependencies within the bigram in terms of the similarity of the two words is explored. A model based on this assumption of semantic coherence is contrasted and combined with a relaxed model lacking this assumption. The induced representations are evaluated in terms of the correlation of predicted similarities to a dataset of noun-verb similarity ratings gathered in an online experiment. The results show that the coherence assumption can be used to induce semantic representations, and that the combined model, which breaks the dependencies down into a semantic and a non-semantic component, achieves the best performance.

1 Introduction

Distributional semantics derives semantic representations from the way that words are distributed across contexts. The assumption behind this approach is that words that occur in similar contexts will tend to have similar meanings. Firth (1957) expressed this in a well known slogan - *you shall know a word by the company it keeps*. In application, these representations have proven successful in automatic thesaurus generation (Grefenstette, 1994), enhancing language models (Coccaro and Jurafsky, 1998) and modelling of reading times (Pynte et al., 2008) and the effects of priming (Landauer and Dumais, 1997).

However, the high level identification of meaning with distributional properties leaves the question of exactly which distributional properties are relevant to semantics a little vague. In practice, researchers evaluate various approaches and select those that produce the best performance. Moreover, other linguistic characteristics, such as syntax, are also analysed in terms of distributional properties. Bigram distributions, for example, are commonly used to induce POS classes (e.g Brown et al., 1992; Clark, 2003), but they have also been investigated as a basis for semantic representations (Bullinaria and Levy, 2007).

Here we examine the question of what statistical properties can be used to distinguish semantic factors from other dependencies in the distribution of words across bigram contexts. We carry this out in terms of class based bigram language models, and explore the possibility that semantic dependencies can be characterised in terms of coherence or similarity across the bigram. We then evaluate the induced representations in terms of their ability to predict human similarity ratings for noun-verb pairs. By evaluating the similarity predictions of our models across POS classes in this way, we assess the ability of the model to focus purely on the semantic content while ignoring other information, such as syntax.

2 Models

The intention is to induce semantic representations within a bigram model based on the assumption that semantic content is coherent across the bigram. Assume that semantic information can be captured in terms of a set, S, of semantic topics, with each word, w, having some independent probability of being used in a topic, $p(w|s)$. Then, if the probabilities of the topics are given by $p(s)$ and each bigram, w_1w_2, belongs to a single topic, then the joint probability, $p(w_1w_2)$, is given by:

$$p(w_1 w_2) = \sum_{s \in S} p(s) p(w_2|s) p(w_1|s) \tag{1}$$

Rewriting this in conditional form, with $p(s|w_1) = \frac{p(s)p(w_1|s)}{p(w_1)}$, gives:

$$p(w_2|w_1) = \sum_{s \in S} p(w_2|s) p(s|w_1) \tag{2}$$

This can also be expressed in a form that explicitly connects to the idea of a probability based on semantic similarity.

$$p(w_2|w_1) = p(w_2) \sum_{s \in S} \frac{p(s|w_2)}{p(s)} p(s) \frac{p(s|w_1)}{p(s)} \tag{3}$$

Equation 3 can be thought of as the unigram probability of w_2 modulated by its similarity to w_1, measured in terms of a weighted dot product between vectors representing the two words. In this case, the vector components are a ratio of probabilities measure, $\frac{p(s|w)}{p(s)}$, which has been widely used in distributional semantics (e.g. Bullinaria and Levy, 2007).

The key feature of this model is that the word probabilities in Equation 1 are independent of position in the bigram. It is this assumption that serves to ensure that the induced topics identify a characterisitic that is stable across the bigram, which, it is hoped, will relate to semantic content.

Relaxing this assumption produces a more general class based model, specifically the aggregate markov model of Saul and Pereira (1997). Using superscripts to indicate the position a word occurs in within the bigram, we write this model as:

$$p(w_2^r|w_1^l) = \sum_{z \in Z} p(w_2^r|z) p(z|w_1^l) \tag{4}$$

In contrast to Equation 1, this model makes no assumption of stability of content across the bigram, and instead allows the word distributions, $p(w|z)$ to be very different in the left and right positions. Thus, this model ought to more suited to handling the word order effects that the similarity based model cannot.

To construct a combined model, the bigram probabilities are expressed in terms of a sum over both S and Z.

$$p(w_2^r|w_1^l) = \sum_{s \in S, z \in Z} p(w_2^r|s, z) p(s, z|w_1^l) \tag{5}$$

These terms can be broken down further based on conditional independence of s and z. The rightmost probability, $p(s, z|w_1^l)$ separates straightforwardly.

$$p(s, z|w_1^l) = p(s|w_1) p(z|w_1^l) \tag{6}$$

On the other hand, s and z cannot in general also be conditionally independent given w_2. However, we can use this as an approximation and then normalise the final probabilities.

$$\hat{p}(w_2^r|s, z) = \frac{p(w_2^r) p(s|w_2) p(z|w_2^r)}{p(s, z)} \tag{7}$$

The final model then combines these components and divides through by a normalising constant $N(w_1)$.

$$p(w_2^r|w_1^l) = \sum_{s \in S, z \in Z} \frac{\hat{p}(w_2^r|s, z) p(s, z|w_1^l)}{N(w_1)} \tag{8}$$

$$N(w_1) = \sum_{w_2} \sum_{s \in S, z \in Z} \hat{p}(w_2^r|s, z) p(s, z|w_1^l) \tag{9}$$

	High	Medium	Low
Group 1	*anticipation - predict* *withdrawal - retire*	*analysis - derive* *invasion - merge*	*opinion - vanish* *disappearance - believe*
Group 2	*disappearance - vanish* *invasion - occupy*	*anticipation - believe* *opinion - predict*	*withdrawal - derive* *implication - retire*
Group 3	*opinion - believe* *implication - derive*	*disappearance - retire* *withdrawal - vanish*	*anticipation - succeed* *invasion - predict*

Table 1: Example items from the noun-verb similarity rating experiment.

2.1 Construction

Models were constructed based on three approaches: similarity based models, as defined by Equation 2, aggregate models, defined by Equation 4, and combined models, defined by Equation 8. The parameters of these bigram models were optimised over a set of sentences extracted from the BNC (BNC Consortium, 2001). 80,775,061 words from the written component of this corpus were used as a training set, with 9,759,769 words forming a development set and the final 9,777,665 words held back as a test set. Preprocessing included conversion to lowercase, addition of $\langle start \rangle$ and $\langle stop \rangle$ at the beginning and ends of sentences, and replacement of words that occurred fewer than 100 times in the training set with an $\langle unk \rangle$ token.

Optimisation of the parameters was based on the EM algorithm (Dempster et al., 1977), with training stopped when the log-likelihood over the development set began to increase. For the pure similarity and aggregate approaches, models were trained with numbers of induced classes ranging from 10 to 2,000. The numbers of classes, $|S|$ and $|Z|$, for the two components of the combined models, each ranged from 10 to 100. The ratio of probabilities measure from Equation 3 was used to construct the components of vectors which then formed the word representations, and similarity of these vectors was measured in terms of the cosine measure.

For comparison, a bigram language model with back-off and Kneser-Ney smoothing (Kneser and Ney, 1995) was also constructed using the SRILM toolkit (Stolcke, 2002).

3 Evaluation

The induced representations were evaluated in terms of their ability to predict semantic similarity ratings for a set of word pairs. We measured the cosine similarity of our word representations and correlated that with the human ratings to produce a measure of agreement. Because the strongest dependencies within the bigrams are likely to be syntactic effects based on the POS classes of the two words, measuring semantic similarity across POS classes is particularly relevant. That is, the semantic representations should contain as much information about the meaning of the words as possible, while containing as little part-of-speech information as possible, which should instead be shifted into the other part of the model. Predicting the similarity between nouns and verbs should therefore be an effective evaluation, as these two word classes contain the core of a sentence's semantic content while having substantially divergent distributional properties in regards of syntax. In this way, we can test whether the POS differences are genuinely being ignored to allow just the semantic similarity to be focussed on.

Thus, an experiment was run to collect similarity ratings for noun-verb pairs. Each participant rated one of three groups of 36 noun-verb pairs, giving a total of 108 items. Each group consisted of 12 high similarity pairs, 12 medium similarity pairs and 12 low similarity pairs.

Table 1 contains a small sample of these items, with rows corresponding to the three experimental groups of participants and columns corresponding to the high, medium and low similarity sets of items seen by each group. The items in the high similarity set (e.g. *anticipation-predict*) are related, via an intermediary word, by a combination of morphology (e.g. *anticipation-anticipate*) and synonymy (e.g. *anticipate-predict*), drawing on Catvar (Habash and Dorr, 2003) and WordNet (Miller, 1995) to identify these relationships. The medium and low sets are then recombinations of nouns and verbs from the high set, with the medium items being the most similar such pairings, as rated by WordNetSimilarity (Pedersen et al., 2004), and low being the least similar.

60 participants were paid $2 each to rate all 36 items from a single group, with equal numbers

seeing each group. The experiments were conducted online, with participants instructed to rate the similarity in meaning of each pair of words on a scale of 1 to 5. They were initially presented with five practice items before the experimental materials were presented with randomisation of both within and between item orders.

Individual Spearman correlations were calculated for each participant's ratings against the predicted similarities, and the average of these values was used as the evaluation measure for the semantic representations induced by a model. A t-test on the z-transformed participant correlations was used to assess the significance of differences between these averages.

The performance of these models simply as language models was also evaluated, in terms of their perplexity over the test set, T, calculated in terms of the probability assigned to the test set, $p(T)$, and the number of words it contains, $|T|$.

$$perplexity = p(T)^{-\frac{1}{|T|}} \tag{10}$$

4 Results

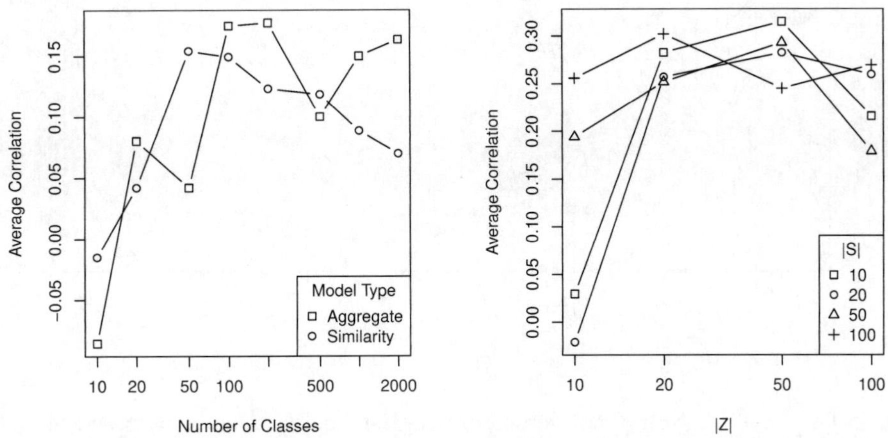

(a) Average correlations by model size for the Similarity and Aggregate models.

(b) Average correlations by model size for the Combined models.

Figure 1: Correlations of model similarities with human ratings.

Figure 1(a) plots the average correlation between the model similarities and the human ratings for the similarity and aggregate representations. Both models show similar strengths of correlation and a similar pattern in relation to the size of the model, with a peak around the 50 - 200 range. The highest correlation is 0.18, achieved by the aggregate model with 200 classes, while the similarity model achieves a peak of 0.15 at $|S| = 50$. These values are not significantly different, $t(59) = 0.71$, $p = 0.24$. The equivalence in performance of the aggregate and similarity models is not entirely surprising, as both models, despite their differing forms, are directed at the problem of predicting the same bigram dependencies. It may therefore be expected that the weaker semantic factors play only a minor role within the representations generated.

In contrast, the combined models, which allow a separation of the dependencies into distinct components, are able to achieve higher correlations, as plotted in Figure 1(b). Among these models, the highest correlation of 0.31, which is significantly greater than the best aggregate model, $t(59) = 9.35$, $p < 0.001$, is achieved by a model having $|Z| = 50$ and $|S| = 10$. In fact, all the correlations over 0.2 in Figure 1(b) are significantly greater at the $p < 0.001$ level, except $|Z| = 100$, $|S| = 10$ and $|Z| = 20$, $|S| = 20$, which are only significant at the $p < 0.05$ and $p < 0.01$ levels respectively. This leaves only the four lowest performing combined models as not significantly outperforming the best aggregate model. Nonetheless, these values are substantially lower than the inter-subject correlations ($mean = 0.74$, $min = 0.64$), suggesting that the model could be improved further. In particular, extending the span of the model to longer ngrams ought to allow the induction of stronger and more detailed semantic representations. The fact that the best performing model only contains 10 semantic classes underscores the limitations of extracting such representations from bigrams.

In addition to the ability of these models to induce semantic representations, their performance simply as language models was also evaluated. Figure 2 plots perplexity on the test set against number of parameters per word ($|S| + 2|Z|$) for the aggregate and combined models. In general lower perplexities are achieved by larger models for both approaches, as is to be expected. Within this trend, the combined model tends to have a lower perplexity than the aggregate model by about 5%. The single case in which the combined model is above the trend line of the aggregate model occurs for a model with in which a very small aggregate component, $|Z| = 10$, is dominated by a large similarity component, $|S| = 100$.

The performance of these models does not, however, rival that of a standard bigram model with back-off and Kneser and Ney (1995) smoothing, which achieves a perplexity of 185. On the other hand, neither the aggregate nor combined models are explicitly designed to address the issue of small or zero counts.

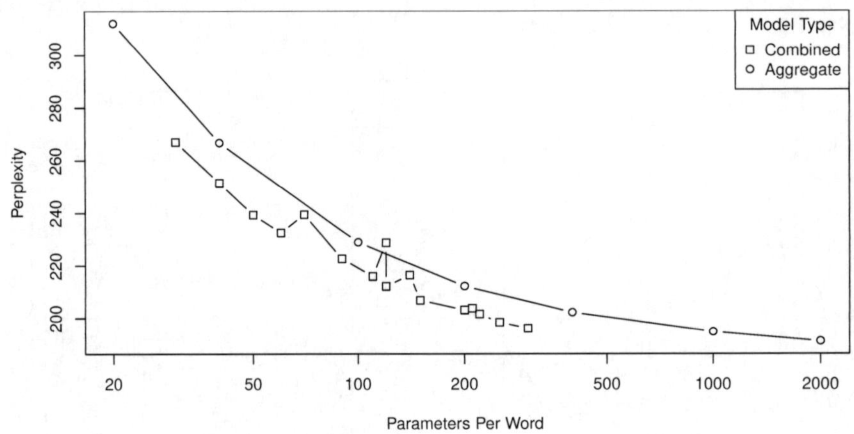

Figure 2: Perplexity by Number of Parameters for the Aggregate and Combined Models

5 Conclusions

Our experiments produced two novel results.

Firstly, we have shown that semantic representations can be induced from the dependencies within bigram word sequences, using an approach that derives word probabilities from similarity. This is similar in form to prior models (e.g Coccaro and Jurafsky, 1998; Bellegarda, 1997), but whereas they imported distributional representations from outside the model to enhance their performance, we use this model form to induce semantic representations within the model.

Secondly, we have shown that this approach is most effective when the model breaks these dependencies down into both a semantic and a non-semantic component. Typically, semantic classes have been induced in isolation (Landauer and Dumais, 1997; Bullinaria and Levy, 2007) or applied to long-range structure while short-range structure is handled by a separate component (Boyd-Graber and Blei, 2008; Griffiths et al., 2004; Wallach, 2006). Here, we have shown that even simple bigram dependencies can be conceived as breaking down into semantic and non-semantic components, as opposed to using those components to model two different types of dependency.

We also introduced a novel evaluation dataset for semantic representations, containing noun-verb similarity ratings. Correlation of these human ratings with the model similarities allows a quantification of the extent to which a model ignores POS information to focus on semantic content.

In future work, we hope to extend the span of our model and to characterise syntax, semantics and their interaction in a more sophisticated manner. Particularly interesting is the question of the extent to which the form of our model is specific to languages, such as English, in which syntax is identified with word order and how this might be adapted to free word order languages.

References

Bellegarda, J. R. (1997). A latent semantic analysis framework for large-span language modeling. In G. Kokkinakis, N. Fakotakis, and E. Dermatas (Eds.), *EUROSPEECH*. ISCA.

BNC Consortium (2001). The British National Corpus, Version 2. Distributed by Oxford University Computing Services on behalf of the BNC Consortium.

Boyd-Graber, J. L. and D. M. Blei (2008). Syntactic topic models. In D. Koller, D. Schuurmans, Y. Bengio, and L. Bottou (Eds.), *NIPS*, pp. 185–192. Curran Associates, Inc.

Brown, P. F., V. J. D. Pietra, P. V. de Souza, J. C. Lai, and R. L. Mercer (1992). Class-based n-gram models of natural language. *Computational Linguistics 18*(4), 467–479.

Bullinaria, J. and J. Levy (2007). Extracting semantic representations from word co-occurrence statistics: A computational study. *Behavior Research Methods 39*(3), 510–526.

Clark, A. (2003). Combining distributional and morphological information for part of speech induction. In *EACL*, pp. 59–66. The Association for Computer Linguistics.

Coccaro, N. and D. Jurafsky (1998). Towards better integration of semantic predictors in statistical language modeling. In *ICSLP*. ISCA.

Dempster, A. P., N. M. Laird, and D. B. Rubin (1977). Maximum Likelihood from Incomplete Data via the EM Algorithm. *Journal of the Royal Statistical Society. Series B (Methodological) 39*(1), 1–38.

Firth, J. R. (1957). A synopsis of linguistic theory 1930-1955. In *Studies in Linguistic Analysis*, pp. 1–32. Oxford: Philological Society.

Grefenstette, G. (1994). *Explorations in Automatic Thesaurus Discovery*. Norwell, MA, USA: Kluwer Academic Publishers.

Griffiths, T. L., M. Steyvers, D. M. Blei, and J. B. Tenenbaum (2004). Integrating topics and syntax. In *NIPS*.

Habash, N. and B. J. Dorr (2003). A categorial variation database for english. In *HLT-NAACL*.

Kneser, R. and H. Ney (1995). Improved backing-off for M gram language modeling. In *International Conference on Acoustics, Speech, and Signal Processing, 1995.*, Volume 1, pp. 181–184 vol.1.

Landauer, T. and S. Dumais (1997). A solution to plato's problem: The latent semantic analysis theory of acquisition, induction, and representation of knowledge. *Psychological Review; Psychological Review 104*(2), 211.

Miller, G. A. (1995). Wordnet: A lexical database for english. *Commun. ACM 38*(11), 39–41.

Pedersen, T., S. Patwardhan, and J. Michelizzi (2004). Wordnet: : Similarity - measuring the relatedness of concepts. In D. L. McGuinness and G. Ferguson (Eds.), *AAAI*, pp. 1024–1025. AAAI Press / The MIT Press.

Pynte, J., B. New, and A. Kennedy (2008). On-line contextual influences during reading normal text: A multiple-regression analysis. *Vision Research 48*, 2172–2183.

Saul, L. K. and F. Pereira (1997). Aggregate and mixed-order markov models for statistical language processing. In *Proceedings of the Second Conference on Empirical Methods in Natural Language Processing*, New York, NY, pp. 81–89. ACM Press.

Stolcke, A. (2002). SRILM - an extensible language modeling toolkit. In J. H. L. Hansen and B. L. Pellom (Eds.), *INTERSPEECH*. ISCA.

Wallach, H. M. (2006). Topic modeling: beyond bag-of-words. In W. W. Cohen and A. Moore (Eds.), *ICML*, Volume 148 of *ACM International Conference Proceeding Series*, pp. 977–984. ACM.

Predicate-specific Annotations for Implicit Role Binding: Corpus Annotation, Data Analysis and Evaluation Experiments

Tatjana Moor Michael Roth Anette Frank
Department of Computational Linguistics, Heidelberg University
{moor,mroth,frank}@cl.uni-heidelberg.de

Abstract

Current research on linking implicit roles in discourse is severely hampered by the lack of sufficient training resources, especially in the verbal domain: learning algorithms require higher-volume annotations for specific predicates in order to derive valid generalizations, and a larger volume of annotations is crucial for insightful evaluation and comparison of alternative models for role linking.

We present a corpus of predicate-specific annotations for verbs in the FrameNet paradigm that are aligned with PropBank and VerbNet. A qualitative data analysis leads to observations regarding implicit role realization that can guide further annotation efforts. Experiments using role linking annotations for five predicates demonstrate high performance for these target predicates. Using our additional data in the SemEval task, we obtain overall performance gains of 2-4 points F_1-score.

1 Introduction

Automatic annotation of semantic predicate-argument structure (PAS) is an important subtask to be solved for high-quality information access and natural language understanding. Semantic role labeling (SRL) has made tremendous progress in addressing this task, using supervised and recently also semi- and unsupervised methods (Palmer et al., 2010).

Traditional SRL is restricted to the local syntactic domain. In discourse interpretation, however, we typically find locally unrealized argument roles that are contextually bound to antecedents beyond their local structure. Thus, by using strictly local methods, we are far from capturing the full potential offered by semantic argument structure (Fillmore and Baker, 2001; Burchardt et al., 2005).

The task of resolving the reference of implicit arguments has been addressed in previous work: Gerber and Chai (2012) address the task in the nominal domain by learning a model from manually annotated data following the NomBank paradigm (Meyers et al., 2004). In contrast, Ruppenhofer et al. (2010) follow the FrameNet paradigm, which is not restricted to nominal predicates. However, their data set suffers from considerable sparsity with respect to annotation instances per predicate (cf. Section 2).

Our contribution addresses the problem of sparse training resources for implicit role binding by providing a higher volume of predicate-specific annotations for non-local role binding, using OntoNotes (Weischedel et al., 2011) as underlying corpus. A qualitative analysis of the produced annotations leads to a number of hypotheses on implicit role realization. Using the extended set of annotations, we perform experiments to measure their impact, using a state-of-the-art system for implicit role binding.

2 Motivation and Related Work

The main motivation for this work relates to the SemEval 2010 Task 10 on implicit role linking[1] and the problem of data sparsity that became evident by the poor performance of the participating systems, at 1% F_1-score (Tonelli and Delmonte, 2010; Chen et al., 2010).[2] Later systems could only marginally improve

[1] http://www.coli.uni-saarland.de/projects/semeval2010_FG

[2] The data set provides 245/259 instances of resolvable implicit roles for training/testing. All cases of implicit roles (580/710) are distributed over 317/452 frame types and a small overall number of frame instances (1,370/1,703 training/testing).

on these results, with performance up to 19% F_1-score due to improved recognition of resolvable implicit roles, heuristic data acquisition, and variations in model properties.[3] Gerber and Chai (2010, 2012), working on a related task following the NomBank/PropBank paradigm, achieved higher performance of 50% F_1-score, using as training data a substantial amount of annotations for 10 noun predicates.

3 Corpus and Annotation

3.1 Corpus

While there is a rich source of annotated sentences in the FrameNet paradigm, contextualized FrameNet annotations are restricted in coverage. As we target high-frequency annotations for specific verbs, and in order to make annotations available for a corpus that is widely used, we chose OntoNotes (V.4.0) (Weischedel et al., 2011) as underlying corpus. OntoNotes contains semantic role annotations following the PropBank annotation style (Palmer et al., 2005). We map these annotations to FrameNet using the mapping specified in the SemEval 2010 Task 10 data, which is based on SemLink (Loper et al., 2007).

3.2 Selection of Annotation Targets

Our goal was to produce a high volume of annotations for specific verb predicates, ideally reaching a margin of 100-200 instances involving locally unfilled argument roles (cf. Gerber and Chai (2010)). In order to make the task feasible for the annotators, we selected predicates and frame readings that are relatively easy to discriminate, so that the annotators can concentrate on the role linking task.

We applied a number of further selection criteria to make the resulting annotations as useful as possible: (i) We excluded light verbs, as they are not well covered in FrameNet, and typically involve difficult sense distinctions. (ii) We only chose predicates (and senses) that are covered in VerbNet, PropBank and FrameNet, according to the Unified Verb Index.[4] This ensures that the corpus can also be used for experimentation using the VerbNet or PropBank paradigm. Finally, (iii) for the selected candidate predicates and readings, we investigated the FrameNet annotation data base to determine whether the annotated frames involve a critical number of non-instantiated roles that can be resolved from discourse context.[5] In case we found little or no such cases for the candidate reading, the predicate was not chosen.

The list of predicates that resulted from this selection process is given in Table 1. They exhibit varying numbers of core roles (2-7), frame ambiguity (1-7), and different syntactic properties.

3.3 Annotation Process and Categories

Data preparation. We extracted annotation instances for the selected target predicates from the OntoNotes corpus. The resulting corpus consists of overall 1.992 instances. Each annotation instance was embedded within its full document context. The average document length is 612 words.

Annotation Categories. Our annotation maily follows the SemEval task guidelines for role linking (Ruppenhofer et al., 2010, 2012), with the exception that we differentiate between non-instantiated (NI) roles that are *resolvable* vs. *non-resolvable* within discourse instead of classifying them as 'definite (DNI)' vs. 'indefinite (INI)'. This distinction makes the task of linking NIs much clearer, as definite null-instantiations may or may not be resolvable within the discourse context.[6]

Two examples of NI occurrences are given below: (1) illustrates a (resolvable) DNI: the implicit role's referent is anaphorically bound within the prior discourse. In (2) the non-instantiated role can only be interpreted existentially within the given discourse (non-resolvable, INI).

[3] See Tonelli and Delmonte (2011); Ruppenhofer et al. (2011); Silberer and Frank (2012); Laparra and Rigau (2012).

[4] `http://verbs.colorado.edu/verb-index`

[5] Even though FrameNet annotations are out of context, non-realized core roles are marked for definite vs. indefinite interpretation.

[6] In fact, only 80.9%/74.2% of all DNIs in the SemEval training/test corpus are linked within discourse.

(1) (s3) Nearly 200 American agents went to [Yemen]$_{Source}$ right after the attack on the "Cole".
(s9) They$_{Theme}$ are *leaving* frustrated. (*Source*: resolvable, DNI)

(2) I$_{Donor}$ tried to *give* as good as I got. (*Recepient*, non-resolvable, INI; *Theme*, non-resolvable, INI)

The annotation consists of three sub-tasks that are applied to null-instantiated core roles (NIs) only: (a) classifying each NI as a *resolvable or non-resolvable null instantiation*; (b) distinguishing between *Lexical* and *Constructional Licensing* of each NI;[7] and (c) *linking resolvable DNIs* to the closest antecedent mention within the preceding context.[8]

Before proceeding to these decisions, the annotator determines whether the mapped frame corresponds to the actual predicate meaning in the given context. If not, it is marked as 'NgFNS' (no genuine FN sense). We also flag roles whose filler does not correspond to the role definition given in FrameNet (e.g., roles categorized as 'Physical object' that are filled by an abstract concept). For each predicate, we record the chosen frame as well as the mapping to the corresponding readings in PropBank and VerbNet.

Calibration of Annotation Quality. The annotation was performed by two annotators, both students of Computational Linguistics. Both of them studied the SemEval guidelines and used the first 50 sentences of the SemEval corpus as a trial corpus, in order to validate their understanding of the guidelines.

We performed two calibration experiments, in which we measured Kappa (Cohen, 1960) for the assignment of role interpretation type (resolvable vs. non-resolvable role), and percentage of agreement on the chosen antecedent for resolvable roles.

(I) **Agreement with SemEval:** After initial training, we measured IAA between our main annotator and the SemEval gold annotations for sentences 51-100 of the SemEval data set. For *interpretation type* (resolvable/non-resolvable classification) we achieved a Kappa of 0.77. For NI-linking, we measured 71.43% agreement (15 out of 21 resolvable roles were correctly linked).

(II) **Agreement between Annotators:** We determined agreement between both annotators on all annotation instances pertaining to the predicate *give*. For *interpretation type*, the annotators achieved a Kappa value of 0.94. For *linking*, the annotators agreed on the marked antecedent in 85.7% of all cases (48 out of 56 cases).

After this calibration phase, the annotation was done independently by the two annotators.

4 Data Analysis

Table 1 gives an overview of the annotations we obtained. Overall we annotated 630 NI occurrences for genuine frame meanings, distributed over 438 verb occurrences (i.e., 1.44 NIs/verb).[9] We observe great variation in the number of NI occurrences for the different predicates (e.g., *leave* vs. *pay*). We find a predominance of non-resolvable over resolvable role classifications (61.6% vs. 38.4%). 78% of the resolvable NIs are realized within a window of 3 sentences,[10] as opposed to 69.6% in the SemEval and 90% in Gerber&Chai's data. This can be explained by variation in text genre and target categories.

Considering the distribution of NI-realizations and the properties of the corresponding predicates, we note some tendencies that seem worth investigating on a larger scale, as potential factors determining null instantiation of roles. Predicates with low frame ambiguity rate (*pay, bring, give*) tend to have a higher NI-realization rate than frames with a higher ambiguity rate (*leave, put*). A higher number of core roles of the target frame tends to go along with a higher NI-realization potential (*bring, pay*).

[7] As the SemEval guidelines for lexical and constructional licensing are not very explicit, and given these annotations are not required for evaluating system annotations, we do not report details about this part of the annotation.

[8] If the antecedent is not found in the preceding context, we also inspect the following discourse.

[9] 204 out of all 834 NIs (24.5%) do not pertain to genuine frame readings. These were held out from further data statistics.

[10] 9.9% of the fillers were found in the following discourse.

verb	frame	verb occ.	core roles	frame ambig.	NI occurrences all	other reading	frame reading	frame occ.	NIs per frame	resolvable abs.	resolvable %	non-resolv. abs.	non-resolv. %
give	GIVING	524	3	1	218	63	155	144	1.08	62	40.0	93	60.0
put	PLACING	427	4	3	39	17	22	22	1.00	10	45.5	12	54.5
leave	DEPARTING	354	2	7	70	30	40	39	1.03	25	62.5	15	37.5
bring	BRINGING	351	7	2	103	38	65	45	1.44	28	43.1	37	56.9
pay	COMMERCE_PAY	336	5	1	404	56	348	188	1.85	117	33.6	231	66.4
all		1992	–	–	834	204	630	438	–	242	–	388	–

Table 1: Annotated predicates and data analysis: Implicit role interpretation and linking.

give: GIVING		all	**Donor**	**Recepient**	**Theme**		
Interpretation	resolvable	40.0	**25.2**	13.5	1.3		
	non-resolvable	60.0	19.4	**37.4**	3.2		
put: PLACING		all	**Agent**	**Cause**	**Theme**	**Goal**	
Interpretation	resolvable	45.5	**40.9**	4.6	0.0	0.0	
	non-resolvable	54.4	**45.5**	9.1	0.0	0.0	
leave: DEPARTING		all	**Theme**	**Source**			
Interpretation	resolvable	62.5	0.0	**62.5**			
	non-resolvable	37.5	7.5	30.0			
bring: BRINGING		all	**Agent**	**Goal**	**Source**	**Carrier**	
Interpretation	resolvable	43.1	9.3	16.9	16.9	0.0	
	non-resolvable	56.9	21.5	1.5	**23.1**	10.8	
pay: COMMERCE_PAY		all	**Buyer**	**Seller**	**Goods**	**Money**	**Rate**
Interpretation	resolvable	33.6	6.6	**14.6**	9.2	2.9	0.3
	non-resolvable	66.4	2.5	**25.3**	17.2	10.9	10.3

Table 2: Distribution of resolvable vs. non-resolvable NI roles over predicate roles (in percent).

Further data statistics for particular predicates and which roles they omit under the different NI-interpretations are given in Table 2. Typically, we find NI-realization concentrated on one or two roles for a given predicate. Yet, these are observations on a small number of predicates that need substantiation by further data annotation, with systematic exploration of other determining properties, such as role meaning or perspectivation (*pay/sell*; *leave/arrive*) and the influence of constructional licensing.

5 Evaluation Experiments

We evaluate the impact of predicate-specific annotations for classification using two scenarios: (**CV**) we examine the linking performance of models trained and tested on the same predicate by adopting the 10-fold Cross-Validation scenario used by Gerber and Chai (2012) (G&C).[11] (**SemEval**) Secondly, we examine the direct effect of using our annotations as additional training data for linking NIs in the SemEval 2010 task on implicit role binding. We use the state-of-the-art system and best performing feature set described in Silberer and Frank (2012) (S&F) to make direct comparisons to previous results.

CV. As positive training and test samples for this scenario, we use all annotated (and resolvable) NIs and randomly split them into 10 folds. Negative training samples (i.e., incorrect NI fillers) are automat-

[11] Note that this is not a direct comparison as both the annotation paradigm and the data sets are different.

	Cross-Validation				SemEval 2010 test set				
verb	precision	recall	F_1	**training data**	FS	NgFNS	precision	recall	F_1
give	48.8	33.3	39.6	**S&F'12**					
put	33.3	20.0	25.0	no additional data	+	n.a.	25.6	25.1	25.3
leave	48.3	**56.0**	**51.9**	+ best heuristic data	+	n.a.	30.8	25.1	27.7
bring	**72.7**	27.6	40.0	**this paper**					
pay	35.4	20.0	25.6	+ our annotations	–	–	21.7	21.2	21.5
—	—	—	—	+ our annotations	+	–	33.3	22.0	26.5
average	47.7	31.4	36.4	+ our annotations	+	+	**34.3**	**26.3**	**29.8**

Table 3: Results for both evaluations (all figures are percentages). FS indicates whether feature selection was applied. NgFNS indicates the use of frame annotations that do not match the contextual meaning.

ically added by extracting constituents that overtly fill a role according to the semantic annotations in the OntoNotes gold standard. We only consider phrases of type NPB, S, VP, SBAR and SG within the current and the two preceding sentences as potential fillers.[12]

SemEval. This setting is identical with the linking evaluation in S&F. Like them, we (optionally) apply an additional step of feature selection (±FS) on the SemEval training data to select a feature subset that generalizes best across data sets, i.e., the fully annotated novel from the shared task and our predicate-specific annotations based on OntoNotes. We further compare models trained w/ and w/o non-genuine frame annotations (±NgFNS). As in the CV setting, we assume that all resolvable NIs are known and only the correct fillers are unknown. Thus, our results are not comparable to those of participants of the *full* SemEval task, who solved two further sub-tasks. Instead we compare to the NI linking results in S&F, with models trained on the SemEval data and using additional heuristically labelled data.

Table 3 summarizes our results for both settings. They are not strictly comparable due to varying properties, i.a., the number of available annotations. The **CV** results show that few annotations can be sufficient to achieve a high linking precision and f-score (up to 72.7 P, 51.9 F_1). However, this is highly dependent on the target predicate (cf. *bring* vs. *pay*). Overall, the results exhibit a similar variance and lie within the same range as those reported by G&C. Even though the numbers are not directly comparable, they generally indicate a similar difficulty of linking implicit arguments across lexical predicate types.

In the **SemEval** setting, we obtain improved precision and recall over S&F's results (± additional heuristic data, cf. Silberer&Frank, 2012)) when linking NIs using our additional training data and feature selection. Using our full additional data set (+NgFNS) we obtain higher performance compared to S&F's best setting with heuristically labelled data, yielding highest scores of 34.3% precision and 26.3% recall. The resulting F_1-score of 29.76% lies 2.1 points above the best model of S&F, whose full system also achieved state-of-the-art performance on the *full* SemEval task.

6 Conclusions

We presented an annotation effort for implicit role linking targeting five verb predicates. The FrameNet annotations are mapped to PropBank and VerbNet and will be available for the community. Annotations follow the SemEval guidelines and were quality-controlled. We annotated 630 NI realizations for the intended predicate senses. Our experiments show that even a moderate amount of annotations per predicate yield substantial performance gains of 2.1-4.5 points F_1-score. Our data set complements the SemEval corpus in terms of text genre and Gerber&Chai's data set in terms of category and explicit annotation for interpretation type. Due to higher-volume predicate-specific annotations, it enables more insightful evaluation and comparison between different models, including comparison across frameworks. In future work, we plan to extend the annotation to further predicates using, i.a., active learning techniques.

[12]This corresponds to the *SentWin* setting in Silberer and Frank (2012) and is motivated by the fact that most NI fillers both in the SemEval training data and in our annotations are located within a span of the current and two preceding sentences.

References

Burchardt, A., A. Frank, and M. Pinkal (2005). Building Text Meaning Representations from Contextually Related Frames – A Case Study. In *Proceedings of the 6th International Workshop on Computational Semantics*, IWCS-6, Tilburg, The Netherlands, pp. 66–77.

Chen, D., N. Schneider, D. Das, and N. A. Smith (2010, July). SEMAFOR: Frame Argument Resolution with Log-Linear Models. In *Proceedings of the 5th International Workshop on Semantic Evaluation*, Uppsala, Sweden, pp. 264–267.

Cohen, J. (1960). A coefficient of agreement for nominal scales. *Educational and Psychological Measurement 20*(1), 37–46.

Fillmore, C. J. and C. F. Baker (2001, June). Frame Semantics for Text Understanding. In *Proceedings of the NAACL 2001 Workshop on WordNet and Other Lexical Resources*, Pittsburgh.

Gerber, M. and J. Chai (2010). Beyond NomBank: A Study of Implicit Arguments for Nominal Predicates. In *Proceedings of the 48th Annual Meeting of the Association for Computational Linguistics*, Uppsala, Sweden, pp. 1583–1592.

Gerber, M. and J. Y. Chai (2012). Semantic role labeling of implicit arguments for nominal predicates. *Computational Linguistics 38*(4), 755–798.

Laparra, E. and G. Rigau (2012). Exploiting Explicit Annotations and Semantic Types for Implicit Argument Resolution. In *6th IEEE International Conference on Semantic Computing (ICSC'12)*, Palermo, Italy.

Loper, E., S. Yi, and M. Palmer (2007). Combining Lexical Resources: Mapping between PropBank and VerbNet. In *Proceedings of the 7th International Workshop on Computational Semantics*, Tilburg, the Netherlands.

Meyers, A., R. Reeves, C. Macleod, R. Szekely, V. Zielinska, B. Young, and R. Grishman (2004). Annotating Noun Argument Structure for NomBank. In *Proceedings of the 4th International Conference on Language Resources and Evaluation*, LREC-2004, Lisbon, Portugal, pp. 803–806.

Palmer, M., D. Gildea, and P. Kingsbury (2005). The Proposition Bank: An Annotated Corpus of Semantic Roles. *Computational Linguistics 31*(1), 71–106.

Palmer, M., D. Gildea, and N. Xue (2010). *Semantic Role Labeling*. Synthesis Lectures on Human Language Technologies. Morgan & Claypool Publishers.

Ruppenhofer, J., P. Gorinski, and C. Sporleder (2011). In Search of Missing Arguments: A Linguistic Approach. In *Proceedings of RANLP*, Hissar, Bulgaria, pp. 331–338.

Ruppenhofer, J., R. Lee-Goldman, C. Sporleder, and R. Morante (2012). Beyond sentence-level semantic role labeling: linking argument structures in discourse. *Language Resources and Evaluation*. DOI: 10.1007/s10579-012-9201-4.

Ruppenhofer, J., C. Sporleder, R. Morante, C. Baker, and M. Palmer (2010). SemEval-2010 Task 10: Linking Events and Their Participants in Discourse. In *Proceedings of the 5th International Workshop on Semantic Evaluations*, Uppsala, Sweden, pp. 45–50.

Silberer, C. and A. Frank (2012). Casting Implicit Role Linking as an Anaphora Resolution Task. In **SEM 2012: The First Joint Conference on Lexical and Computational Semantics*, Montréal, Canada, pp. 1–10.

Tonelli, S. and R. Delmonte (2010). VENSES++. Adapting a Deep Semantic Processing System to the Identification of Null Instantiations. In *Proceedings of the 5th International Workshop on Semantic Evaluations*, Uppsala, Sweden, pp. 296–299.

Tonelli, S. and R. Delmonte (2011). Desperately Seeking Implicit Arguments in Text. In *Proceedings of the ACL 2011 Workshop on Relational Models of Semantics*, Portland, pp. 54–62.

Weischedel, R., E. Hovy, M. Palmer, M. Marcus, R. Blevin, S. Pradhan, L. Ramshaw, and N. Xue (2011). OntoNotes: A Large Training Corpus for Enhanced Processing. In J. Olive, C. Christianson, and J. McCary (Eds.), *Handbook of Natural Language Processing and Machine Translation*. Springer.

A Pilot Experiment in Knowledge Authoring as Dialogue*

Artemis Parvizi† Caroline Jay‡ Christopher Mellish† Jeff Z. Pan† Yuan Ren†
Robert Stevens‡ Kees van Deemter†

Abstract

This project aims to build an ontology authoring interface in which the user is engaged in a dialogue with the system in controlled natural language. To investigate what such a dialogue might be like, a layered annotation scheme is being developed for interactions between ontology authors and the Protégé ontology authoring environment. A pilot experiment has been conducted with ontology authors, which reveals the complexity of mapping between user-interface actions and acts that appear in natural language dialogues; it also suggests the addition of some unanticipated types of dialogue acts and points the way to some possible enhancements of the authoring interface.

1 Introduction

Ontology authoring – the process of creating and modifying an ontology in order to capture the knowledge about a domain – is hard. Studies such as (Rector et al., 2004) and (Dzbor et al., 2006), for example, have shown that ontology authors frequently misunderstand axioms in the ontology. These studies also suggest that current ontology authoring tools fail to support some of the actions that authors would like to perform, and that users would like to be warned against potential mis-uses of axioms and unforeseen consequences of those axioms.

This paper reports on work in progress, in which we study the interaction of human users with an ontology authoring interface, with the ultimate aim of developing a tool that will permit a much richer knowledge authoring experience, thereby addressing the above-mentioned problems associated with existing knowledge authoring. We envisage developing a plugin to the knowledge authoring interface Protégé[1] that will allow authors to interact with the ontology via a controlled natural language (CNL) dialogue that offers users some of the freedom of natural language without causing insurmountable natural language understanding problems to the system. Specifically, we report on a pilot experiment in which we observed human editors who were invited to use Protégé while talking to an experimenter, and on a layered annotation scheme that we are developing for annotating the resulting interactions. Once a stable annotation scheme has been reached, we shall use the scheme to obtain annotations involving a larger number of users and a larger number of knowledge authoring tasks, the results of which will inform the design of the new knowledge authoring interface. In this paper, we focus on the following questions:

- If knowledge authoring is viewed as a dialogue, what would be the main moves that one would expect to see in these dialogues?
- How are these dialogue moves grounded in lower-level actions like "Finding subsumers for a given concept", or "Looking at a concept"?
- How does the annotation of a knowledge authoring dialogue compare to the annotation of real spoken dialogue?

*This work was supported by EPSRC grants EP/J014354/1 and EP/J014176/1.
†University of Aberdeen, UK
‡University of Manchester, UK
[1] http://protege.stanford.edu

Ontology authoring aided by CNL has been addressed from various points. ACE (Fuchs et al., 1999) and PENG (Schwitter, 2002) allow users to express specifications that can be translated into an unambiguous logical language, understandable to machines. CLCE (Sowa, 2004) resembles ACE but, being closer to English, its output is more readable. SWAT (Power, 2009) uses natural language generation to enable users to produce description logic statements. Similar to CLCE, (Bernardi et al., 2012)'s work is another example of a novel controlled language capable of assisting ontology authoring.

Whereas this previous work has addressed the problem of producing isolated utterances relevant to knowledge authoring using CNL, this project attempts to further develop knowledge authoring by adopting new interactive methods inspired by human dialogue. For example, we hypothesise that by allowing an author to pose *what-if* questions prior to authoring an axiom in an ontology, the authoring process will run in a more informed manner. The following dialogue is an example of the type of communication that this project is attempting to make possible during knowledge authoring:

U1 I want a Moral Right to be able to have a date.
S1 Moral Rights currently have no date property.
U2 What if I import timeframe.owl?
S2 That is consistent. There is now a date property.
U3 What if a Moral Right must have exactly one date?
S3 That implies that Attribution Rights and Integrity Rights must have exactly one date.

2 A new dialogue annotation scheme for Knowledge Authoring

We decided to use a layered model of human-computer interaction to analyse the interactions between knowledge editors and Protégé. This general idea has a long pedigree. Moran (1981) proposed a command language grammar, Foley et al. (1982) suggested a 4-layer design model, Buxton (1983) expanded Foley et al.'s model into a 5-layer design model, and Nielsen (1986) presented a virtual communication protocol. Generally, the aim is to have a better understanding of various aspects of human machine interaction, recognising that a high-level action may be "implemented" in various ways. In this section, we sketch our intial three-level scheme for analysing the interaction between users and Protégé, which was then modified in light of our experiment.

KLM level. The lowest level of analysis is akin to the Keystroke Level Model (KLM) (Card et al., 1986). This level records the physical interactions of the user with the system. KLM level includes acts such as clicks, mouse hovers, and eye movements.

Authoring level. At a higher level of analysis, we wanted to record what it is that users attempt to do and the high-level actions that they perform to accommodate these goals. Some existing analyses (Goncalves et al., 2011; Abgaz et al., 2012) have attempted to understand and categorise changes to the knowledge base during its development. The intention of the present work is not only to categorise such change, but also to understand users' thinking and, ultimately, to work towards a greater knowledge authoring functionality. We decided to group authoring-level acts into general acts and interface acts. *General acts* are grouped into (1) various types of observations (for example, looking whether a class of a given name exists in the ontology; looking to see what instances of a class exist), (2) addition, updating, and deletion of axioms, (3) noticing and resolving inconsistencies. *Interface acts* include (1) common interface features such as undoing or redoing a previous action, and (2) seeking explanations of inconsistencies.

Dialogue level. Annotation at this level involves a creative step where actions are analysed *as if* they were instances of acts in a natural language dialogue. These dialogue acts will provide basis for the design of an interface for knowledge authoring that is similar to natural dialogue. Annotation of dialogue acts is standard in the analysis of Natural Language dialogues (Bunt, 1994; Ginzburg, 1994), but this is not yet used in ontology authoring. Figures 1 and 2 show our initial intuition of dialogue acts, which are categorised into user and system's dialogue acts.

- *Informative Questions* The aim of this type of question is to acquire some information, for example, "Where does class X appear in the classification hierarchy?". The system is intended to search

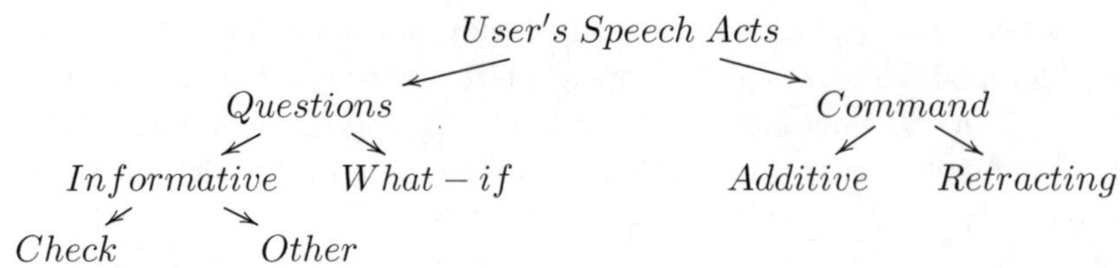

Figure 1: User's Dialogue Acts

through the inferred hierarchy for a response.

- *What-if Questions* Based on the current context, this type of question informs the user about a possible future state of the system. The system needs to perform an action and report its consequences. However, the decision to apply the change is made by the user later.
- *Check Questions* Similar in nature to informative questions, check questions provide answers to user's inquiries, but where the user has a strong expectation about the answer.
- *Additive Command* Informing the system of a certain statement that has to be added or made true in the ontology. The consistency of the ontology needs to be checked and reported to the user. The decision how and when to address the inconsistency has to be made by the user later.
- *Retracting Command* In certain circumstances when the ontology has become inconsistent, the user can either ask an informative question, or a check question and based on the answer decide to retract a change; or, the user can simply retract one or more of the uttered statements.

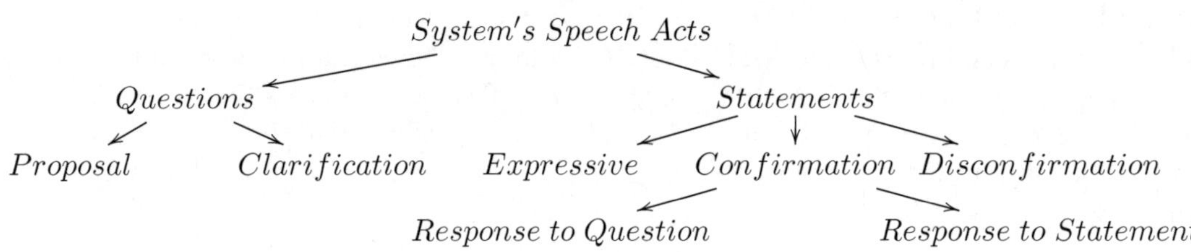

Figure 2: System's Dialogue Acts

- *Expressive Statements* A response to an information seeking or a *what-if* question. Based on the type of question to be addressed, the system may or may not be involved in an authoring process.
- *Confirmation Statements in Response to Questions* Informing the user that an authoring act had the desired effect.
- *Disconfirmation Statements in Response to Question* Informing the user of the consequences to an authoring act, which may not be desired.
- *Confirmation Statements in Response to Statements* Confirmation of a successful authoring act.
- *Proposal Questions* A suggestion by the system to undertake an action.
- *Clarification Questions* A question posed to the user to clarify a command.

3 A Pilot Experiment

The 5 participants in the pilot study were computer scientists who were experienced users of OWL and Protégé. They were asked to set up the Protégé interface as they normally operated it. They were asked to explore the People and Pet ontology acquired from the Tones repository [2], and manipulate it as they saw fit. They were asked to follow the *think aloud* protocol, and describe their moves. In addition, their interactions and eye movements were video-recorded. Where the experimenters were unclear about a description of what was happening, they asked the subject for clarification. Occasionally, when the

[2]http://owl.cs.manchester.ac.uk/repository/

subject felt unsure how to proceed, the experimenter suggested an action (for example, Why don't you look at the axioms now appearing in red?")

Table 1: A pilot experiment and various levels of annotation

	Speech/Action	Authoring level	Dialogue Level
7:35	"he's a car driver"	Adopt goal 1: (Mick is a car driver)	Expression of intention
⋮	⋮	⋮	⋮
8:57	"make the ... thing that he's driving ..."	Adopt goal 2: (Q123 is a car)	Expression of intention
9:01	"I will just remove whatever was there and ..."	Adopt goal 3: (Q123 is only a car)	Expression of intention
9:03	"oh I know!"	Abandon goal 3	Retraction of intention
9:03	clicks 'Types+' in 'Description Q123'	Add axiom: (Q123 is a car)	Additive command
9:04	"add car as well"		
9:04	types 'car' in 'Q123' dialogue		
9:05	"and see whether it's invalid"	Check: (Mick is a car driver)	Check Question
9:08	runs reasoner		
9:08	"if it is really the same thing then it should be disjoint"	Notice: (vehicle type not disjoint)	–
		Note goal: (vehicle types disjoint)	Expression of desire
9:11	"mm-hm"	Confirm check	Confirmation statement
9:16	clicks 'Mick' in 'individuals' window	Goal achieved: (Mick is a car driver)	Retraction of intention

Knowledge authoring sessions were annotated with reference to the scheme outlined above but, crucially, annotators wrote annotations in a free style: the interface did not limit them to a fixed set of labels implied by our initial annotation scheme. A small annotated segment of one session is presented in Table 1. In the speech/action column, speech refers to the user's comments and is displayed within quotations, and actions refers to the physical interactions between the user and the Protégé interface.

Our initial intuitions about dialogue acts were shown to be far from perfect. Perhaps unsurprisingly, it became clear that the mapping between KLM, Protégé and dialogue levels can be very complex. An annotation in one layer can correspond to more than one in another layer. For example, a subject may observe the definition or the location in the hierarchy of a concept for various *conceptual reasons*, for instance to check consistency (a *Check Question* in our scheme) or to prepare for adding a new concept (an *Additive Command*). Difficulties of a similar kind are well known from the annotation of natural language dialogue, for instance whether a given spoken utterance (for example, "You are 29 years old") has declarative or interrogative meaning (Beun, 1989). It also became clear that a separate category is required where a command is both Additive and Retracting at the same time, such as a *Modifying Command*. Furthermore, as displayed in Table 1 at 9:08, an action at one layer may not correspond to an action in another layer at all. Most interestingly, we discovered that knowledge authoring is full of what we call *Hidden Acts*, which do not correspond with actual Protégé actions, but which turn out to play an important role in the interaction, as evidenced by subjects' spoken utterances. These include, most prominently, various types of goal handling, such as the adoption, revision, satisfaction, and abandonment of goals. At the dialogue level, these correspond to the expression of desires (when a goal is set aside for later) and intentions (when a goal is starting to be pursued).

How does our annotation scheme compare to schemes for the analysis of natural language dialogue, such as the ISO-standard of (Bunt et al., 2010)? Similarities with our own scheme are easy to find: the distinction between information seeking and informative providing is an obvious example. Important differences exist as well. The ISO standard has been developed for annotating a wide class of dialogues. Our own scheme targets a specific kind of "asymmetric" dialogue, between a person and a machine. Goals can only be expressed by the person; *what-if* questions can only be posed by the person (the system responds, for example, with an *Expressive Statement*). Furthermore, the person cannot, at present, make

Expressive Statements (given that the addition of an axiom has been modelled as a *Command*). *Proposals* (as opposed to *Commands*) are only open to the system. Perhaps the most interesting differences between the two schemes relate to the expression of goals, which appears to be absent from the ISO standard. A few other natural-language related annotation schemes (e.g, (Leech and Weisser, 2003)) do allow the expression of "desires", though the distinction between desires and intentions – reminiscent of Bratman-style "Beliefs, Desires and Intentions" (Bratman, 1999) – is not made.

4 Where do we go from here?

Our annotation scheme has been updated to reflect the observations reported in the previous section, adding categories like *Expression of Intention* and *Expression of Desire*. Having offered tentative answers to the three questions mentioned at the end of the introduction to this paper, how do we plan to proceed?

First, we aim to further improve our understanding of knowledge authoring. Our experiment has given us some relevant insights, as incorporated in our modified annotation scheme, but the validity of these insights has yet to be proven. To do this we shall write an explicit annotation manual, and ask annotators to use these in a full-scale experiment. As before, the study proper will have as participants ontologists working on an ontology they either own or collaborate on in authoring and will not necessarily be computer scientists. Thus the study proper will observe participants in their everyday work, rather than a task that was merely an artefact of the study. In such a setting, there is the potential for a *think aloud* protocol to distort 'normal working practices', which was not an issue in the pilot study. After the experiment they will be asked to clarify their actions (retrospective think-aloud), and to elaborate on what they were trying to do (Olmsted-Hawala et al., 2010). Next, we shall ask annotators to use the annotation manual (and an annotation tool based on the categories defined in the manual) to annotate a number of episodes from the full-scale experiment. Inter-annotator agreement will then be measured using standard methods (for example, the κ test), which should tell us whether our annotation scheme, and the annotations that are based on it, are clear. Where necessary the scheme will be adapted in light of the experiment and the editors' clarifications.

As explained in the Introduction, we aim to exploit our improved understanding of knowledge authoring by designing an improved knowledge authoring interface. This will be a difficult step, which will start with an in-depth study of the outcomes of the full-scale experiment, trying to understand what ontology authors were attempting to do, and how their actions may be better supported by an improved knowledge authoring interface. It is too early to say with certainty what these improvements will be but, in light of our pilot studies, it seems plausible that the new interface will allow ontology authors to manipulate goals at different levels ("I'd like this concept to be subsumed by concept X", "I'd like this concept to have an infinite extension", "This goal has now been fulfilled and can therefore be deleted"), ask competency questions (such as questions that knowledge authors are often asked to write down before starting the authoring process proper) and ask *what-if* questions that allow users to explore the consequences of potential actions without as yet committing to them. Ultimately, we envisage implementing the new dialogue moves as a plug-in to Protégé-style knowledge authoring software.

References

Abgaz, Y., M. Javed, and C. Pahl (2012). Analyzing impacts of change operations in evolving ontologies. In *ISWC Workshops: Joint Workshop on Knowledge Evolution and Ontology Dynamics*.

Bernardi, R., D. Calvanese, and C. Thorne (2012). Designing efficient controlled languages for ontologies. In *Computating Meaning* (Vol 4 ed.). Springer.

Beun, R. (1989). *The recognition of declarative questions in information dialogues*. Ph. D. thesis, University of Tilburg.

Bratman, M. (1999). *Intention, plans, and practical reason*. Cambridge University Press.

Bunt, H. (1994). Context and dialogue control. *Think Quarterly 3*(1), 19–31.

Bunt, H., J. Alexandersson, J. Carletta, J.-W. Choe, A. C. Fang, K. Hasida, K. Lee, V. Petukhova, A. Popescu-Belis, L. Romary, C. Soria, and D. Traum (2010). Towards an iso standard for dialogue act annotation. In *Proceedings of the 7th International Conference on Language Resources and Evaluation*, Valletta, Malta. European Language Resources Association.

Buxton, W. (1983). Lexical and pragmatic considerations of input structures. *Computer Graphics 17*(1), 31–37.

Card, S., T. Moran, and A. Newell (1986). *The psychology of human-computer interaction*. L. Erlbaum Associates Inc.

Dzbor, M., E. Motta, J. M. Gomez, C. Buil, K. Dellschaft, O. Görlitz, and H. Lewen (2006). D4.1.1 analysis of user needs, behaviours & requirements wrt user interfaces for ontology engineering. Technical report, NeOn Project.

Foley, J. and A. Van Dam (1982). *Fundamentals of interactive computer graphics*, Volume 1. Addison Wesley Longman Publishing Co.

Fuchs, N., U. Schwertel, and R. Schwitter (1999). Attempto controlled english not just another logic specification language. In *Logic-Based Program Synthesis and Transformation*, Volume 1559, pp. 1–20. Springer.

Ginzburg, J. (1994). An update semantics for dialogue. In *Proceedings of the 1st International Workshop on Computational Semantics*.

Goncalves, R. S., B. Parsia, and U. Sattler (2011). Categorising logical differences between owl ontologies. In *Proceedings of the 20th ACM international conference on Information and knowledge management*, pp. 1541–1546. ACM.

Leech, G. and M. Weisser (2003). *Generic speech act annotation for task-oriented dialogues*, pp. 441–446. Centre for Computer Corpus Research on Language Technical Papers, Lancaster University.

Moran, T. (1981). The command language grammar: A representation for the user interface of interactive computer systems. *International Journal of Man-Machine Studies 15*(1), 3–50.

Nielsen, J. (1986). A virtual protocol model for computer-human interaction. *International Journal of Man-Machine Studies 24*(3), 301–312.

Olmsted-Hawala, E., E. Murphy, S. Hawala, and K. Ashenfelter (2010). Think-aloud protocols: a comparison of three think-aloud protocols for use in testing data-dissemination web sites for usability. In *the 28th international conference on Human factors in computing systems*, pp. 2381–2390.

Power, R. (2009). Towards a generation-based semantic web authoring tool. In *Proceedings of the 12th European Workshop on Natural Language Generation*, Stroudsburg, PA, USA, pp. 9–15. Association for Computational Linguistics.

Rector, A., N. Drummond, M. Horridge, J. Rogers, H. Knublauch, R. Stevens, H. Wang, and C. Wroe (2004). Owl pizzas: Practical experience of teaching owl-dl: Common errors & common patterns. In *Engineering Knowledge in the Age of the Semantic Web*, Volume 3257, pp. 63–81. Springer.

Schwitter, R. (2002). English as a formal specification language. In *Database and Expert Systems Applications, 2002. Proceedings. 13th International Workshop on*, pp. 228 – 232.

Sowa, J. (2004). Common logic controlled english. `http://www.jfsowa.com/clce/specs.htm`. Accessed: 27/11/2012.

Towards a Tight Integration of Syntactic Parsing with Semantic Disambiguation by means of Declarative Programming*

Yuliya Lierler
University of Nebraska at Omaha
ylierler@unomaha.edu

Peter Schüller
Sabancı University
peterschueller@sabanciuniv.edu

Abstract

We propose and advocate the use of an advanced declarative programming paradigm – answer set programming – as a uniform platform for integrated approach towards syntax-semantic processing in natural language. We illustrate that (a) the parsing technology based on answer set programming implementation reaches performance sufficient for being a useful NLP tool, and (b) the proposed method for incorporating semantic information from FRAMENET into syntactic parsing may prove to be useful in allowing semantic-based disambiguation of syntactic structures.

1 Introduction

Typical natural language processing (NLP) system consists of at least several components including syntactic and semantic analyzers. A common assumption in the design of an NLP system is that these components are separate and independent. On one hand, this allows researchers an abstraction necessary to promote substantial steps forward in each task, plus such a separation permits for more convenient, modular software development. On the other hand, constraints from "higher level" processes are frequently needed to disambiguate "lower level" processes. For example, consider the syntactically ambiguous sentence

I eat spaghetti with chopsticks. (1)

Its verb phrase allows for two syntactic structures:

$$\dfrac{\dfrac{\dfrac{eat}{(VP/PP)/NP} \quad \dfrac{spaghetti}{NP}}{VP/PP} \quad \dfrac{with\ chopsticks}{PP}}{VP} \qquad\qquad \dfrac{\dfrac{eat}{VP/NP} \quad \dfrac{\dfrac{spaghetti}{NP} \quad \dfrac{with\ chopsticks}{NP\backslash NP}}{NP}}{VP} \tag{2}$$

In the former, the prepositional phrase "*with chopsticks*" modifies the verbal phrase "*eat spaghetti*", and in the latter, it modifies the noun phrase "*spaghetti*". The sentence

I eat spaghetti with meatballs (3)

is syntactically ambiguous in a similar manner. In order to assign the proper syntactic structure to each of these sentences one has to take into account *selectional restrictions*, i.e., the semantic restrictions that a word imposes on the environment in which it occurs. For instance, in (1) the fact that a chopstick is an instrument suggests that "*with chopsticks*" modifies "*eat spaghetti*" as a tool for eating. Thus, an approach that integrates syntactic and semantic processing is essential for proper analysis of such sentences. Modern statistical methods, dominant in the field of syntactic analysis, take into account

*We would like to thank Vladimir Lifschitz and Ray Mooney for useful discussions and comments related to the topic of this work. Peter Schüller was supported by a TUBITAK scholarship.

selectional restrictions *implicitly* by assigning most probable syntactic structure based on observed co-occurrences of words and structures in corpora. Yet, this is often not sufficient. Sentences (1) and (3) illustrate this point, as the advanced parsers, including Stanford and Berkeley systems, do not produce proper syntactic representations for these sentences: instead they favor the same structure for both of them.[1] Similarly, semantic role labelers (joint syntactic-semantic parsers) such as SEMAFOR (Das et al., 2010) and LTH (Johansson and Nugues, 2007) display the same issue. The FRAMENET project (Baker et al., 1998) provides information that can disambiguate sentences (1) and (3). For instance, the frame *food* corresponds to the word "*spaghetti*". This frame contains information that *food* only takes other *food* as constituents. Thus modifying "*spaghetti*" with "*chopsticks*" in a parse tree for (1) yields a forbidden situation.

In this paper we present preliminary work on a system for natural language parsing that targets a tight integration of syntax and semantics. We illustrate its ability to take into account both quantitative and qualitative data available for processing natural language, where the former stems from statistical information available for natural language and the latter stems from lexical and commonsense knowledge available in lexical datasets such as FRAMENET.

Lierler and Schüller (2012) developed a Combinatory Categorial Grammar (CCG) parser ASPCCGTK[2]. A distinguishing feature of ASPCCGTK is that its design allows for synergy of both quantitative and qualitative information. First, it relies on the C&C part-of-speech *supertagger* (Clark and Curran, 2007) – built using latest statistical and machine learning advances in NLP. Second, its implementation is based on a prominent knowledge representation and reasoning formalism — answer set programming (ASP), see Brewka et al. (2011). ASP constitutes a convenient framework for representing constraints posed by selectional restrictions *explicitly*; thus we can augment implicit information available from statistical part-of-speech tagging with qualitative reasoning. We believe that the ASPCCGTK parser is a strong ground for designing a systematic, elaboration tolerant, knowledge intensive approach towards an integrated syntax-semantics analysis tool. Performance results on ASPCCGTK reported in (Lierler and Schüller, 2012) suggest that the "planning" approach adopted for parsing in the system scales to sentences of length up to 15 words. It may be sufficient for a number of applications: for example, 6.87 is the average number of words in sentences in the GEOQUERY corpus (Zelle and Mooney, 1996). But, in order for ASPCCGTK to become a viable NLP technology it is important to address the issue of its scalability.

The two contributions of this paper are as follows. First we demonstrate how use of the Cocke-Younger-Kasami (CYK) algorithm (Kasami, 1965) enhances the performance of ASPCCGTK. We evaluate the new approach implemented in ASPCCGTK on the CCGbank corpus (Hockenmaier and Steedman, 2007) and report the results. Second we propose and illustrate the method on how (a) FRAMENET can be used for properly disambiguating sentences (1) and (3), and (b) how this information is incorporated into the ASPCCGTK system. As a result we are able to use the ASPCCGTK parser to generate only the expected syntactic structures for the sentences in question.

In the future, we will automate a process of extracting selection restriction constraints from the data available in FRAMENET, by building an interface between ASPCCGTK and FRAMENET. CCGbank will provide us with extensive real world data for evaluating our approach. Once successful, we will look into expanding the approach to the use of other semantic annotations datasets for lexical items such as VERBNET, PROPBANK, NOMBANK and others for more complete sets of lexical constraints.

2 Extending ASPCCGTK for parsing CCG with CYK in ASP

Combinatory Categorial Grammar (Steedman, 2000) is a formalism that uses a small set of combinatory rules and a rich set of categories. Categories are either atomic such as NP, or complex such as $S\backslash NP$, which is a category for English intransitive verbs. The category $S\backslash NP$ states that an NP to the left of the

[1] Thanks to Nathan Schulte for carrying out the research supporting this claim by investigating the behavior of nine state-of-the-art parsers listed at `http://nlp.stanford.edu/software/stanford-dependencies.shtml`.

[2] `http://www.kr.tuwien.ac.at/staff/former_staff/ps/aspccgtk`

word will result in a sentence S. Given a sentence and a lexicon containing a set of word-category pairs, we replace words by appropriate categories and then apply combinators. For example, in the former derivation in (2), "*eat*" has category $(VP/PP)/NP$ and "*spaghetti*" has category NP. The combinator used in this derivation is *forward application* (*fa*)

$$\frac{A/B \quad B}{A}\, fa \tag{4}$$

where A and B are variables that can be substituted for CCG categories. Applying forward application to "*eat*" and "*spaghetti*" substitutes A with VP/PP and B with NP and yields VP/PP. An input sentence is part of a grammar if some sequence of applying combinators results in the category S at the root of the parse tree.

The implementation of ASPCCGTK is based on answer set programming – a declarative logic programming paradigm. ASP roots in answer set semantics of logic programs (Gelfond and Lifschitz, 1988). The idea of ASP is to represent a problem by a program whose answer sets correspond to solutions. For example, for parsing we encode the grammar and the input sentence in a way that each answer set corresponds to a valid parse tree of the input. Unlike in an imperative style of programming, in declarative programming we describe a specification of the problem, which expresses what the program should accomplish rather than prescribing how to do it. Answer set solvers use this specification to efficiently navigate through a search space and find solutions to the problem. For a more detailed and yet brief introduction of CCG and ASP we refer the reader to (Lierler and Schüller, 2012).

The CYK (Cocke, Younger, and Kasami) algorithm for context-free-grammars was initially published by Kasami (1965). It can be extended to CCG using ideas from Lange and Leiß (2009). Given an input of n words, CYK operates on an $n \times n$ triangular chart. Words in the input are associated with categories in the diagonal of the chart. Combinatory rules combine categories from two chart cells into a single category in another "corresponding" cell. We illustrate these intuitions using a 3×3 chart:

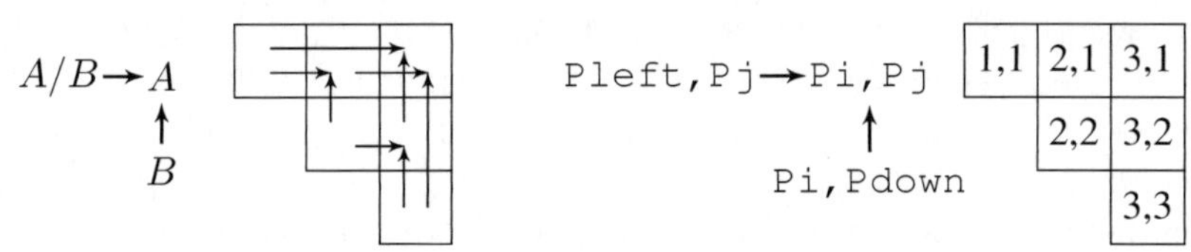

(5)

An input is recognized as part of the grammar if the top right chart cell contains the category `S` after successive application of combinators to the chart. A realization of CYK for recognition of context-free grammars in ASP was described by Drescher and Walsh (2011). First, we adapt their approach to CCG. Second, we extend it to the task of generating parse trees as we are not only interested in recognizing grammatical inputs but also in producing appropriate parses.

We now show parts of our realization of CYK in the ASP formalism. We represent a chart using a predicate `grid(Pi,Pj,Cat)` and initialize the diagonal using the rule

```
grid(P,P,C) :- category_at(C,P).
```

where the `category_at` predicate is obtained from tagging the input with the C&C supertagger.

Forward application is realized as follows (grid variables are shown in (5), X and Y are variables that stand for CCG categories):

```
applicable(fa,Pj,Pi,Pleft,Pdown,X,rfunc(X,Y),Y) :-
  grid(Pleft,Pi,rfunc(X,Y)), grid(Pj,Pdown,Y).
grid(Pj,Pi,X) :- applicable(_,Pj,Pi,_,_,X,_,_).
```

where `rfunc(X,Y)` encodes complex category of the form X/Y. The first rule defines where the *fa* combinator can be applied to within the chart. The second rule defines which categories this application creates. For obtaining parse trees, we "guess" for each instance of `applicable` if that combinator is actually applied (`SrcLeft`, `SrcDown`, and `Result` stand for CCG categories in the CYK grid):

```
{ applied(Comb,Pj,Pi,Pleft,Pdown,Result,SrcLeft,SrcDown) } :-
  applicable(Comb,Pj,Pi,Pleft,Pdown,Result,SrcLeft,SrcDown).
```

The curly bracket construct in the head of this rule is what expresses the guess as we can intuitively read this rule as follows: an expression in the head *may* hold in case if the body of the rule holds.

To obtain only valid parse trees, we furthermore (i) add rules that constraint the selection of multiple `applied` combinators in one cell, (ii) define reachability of diagonal chart cells from the S category in the top right cell, and (iii) add rules that require all diagonal cells to be reachable.

We believe that the possibility of explicitly representing alternatives and then restricting them by expressing appropriate conditions using declarative means makes ASP a powerful tool for working with ambiguities in the field of NLP.

We conducted empirical experiments to compare the performance of the original ASPCCGTK and the ASPCCGTK enhanced with CYK as described here. We report average times and number of timeouts when parsing all sentences of Section 00 of the CCGbank corpus (Hockenmaier and Steedman, 2007) using a timeout of 1200 seconds. The sentences were chunked and tagged by the C&C supertagger. The benchmark results show that the CYK approach has a significant performance advantage over the old approach. Columns show average time in seconds for groups of sentences of a certain length. Number in parenthesis represents the number of timeouts.

Number of Words	1-10	11-15	16-20	21-25	26-30	31-35	36-40	41+
Number of Sentences	195	285	345	330	287	224	118	129
ASPCCGTK (CYK)	0.04	0.18	0.49	1.04	2.11	3.21	6.66	27.01(3)
ASPCCGTK (original)	0.13	1.07	4.90	20.93	68.21(1)	194.59(2)	342.88(24)	497.93(75)

3 Semantic Disambiguation using FRAMENET

FRAMENET is a dataset of semantic relations based on Frame Semantics (Fillmore and Baker, 2001). Lexical items *evoke* certain *frames* that contain *frame elements*; for example, "*eat*" evokes an *ingestion* frame and everything that is of *semantic type* **food** evokes a *food* frame. Sample information available in the *ingestion* and *food* frames follow:

Frame	*Frame Element*	*Semantic Type*
ingestion	INGESTOR	**sentient**
	INGESTIBLE	**ingestible**
	INSTRUMENT	**tool**
	MANNER	**manner**

Frame	*Frame Element*	*Semantic Type*
food	CONSTITUENT	**food_constituent**

Each frame element is a slot that *may* be filled only by elements of the correct semantic type. Types are organized in a taxonomy. For instance, the following part of the taxonomy is relevant to this presentation:

tool is_a **instrument** **food** is_a **ingestible** **food** is_a **food_constituent**.

We propose a concept of a "semantically coherent" parse tree. Information from FRAMENET allows us to disambiguate semantically coherent and incoherent trees. We now make these ideas precise. Each node in a tree is annotated with a *tag* – either a distinguished tag $\perp$ or a pair $T||F$ where both T and F are sets consisting of semantic types. Each leaf of a tree is assigned a tag $T||F$ in accordance with FRAMENET information for a corresponding word. The set T contains the semantic types associated with the leaf-word. For instance, for word "*spaghetti*", this set T_{sp} is {**food**, **food_constituent**, **ingestible**}. The set F contains the semantic types associated with the frame elements of a frame evoked by a leaf-word. For instance, for word "*eat*" that evokes the *ingestion* frame, this set F_{eat} is

{**sentient**, **ingestible**, **tool**, **manner**}.

To define a tag for a non-leaf node of a tree we introduce the following terminology. Any non-leaf node in a CCG parse tree is a parent of two children: a *functor* and an *argument*. Depending on semantic information assigned to nodes, they act as functors or arguments. For a non-leaf node p, we define a tag $T_p||F_p$ as follows

$$T_p||F_p = \begin{cases} \perp & \text{if a tag of either } f \text{ or } a \text{ is } \perp \\ \perp & \text{if } F_f \cap T_a = \emptyset \\ T_f||(F_f \setminus \{s\}) & \text{if there is a semantic type } s \in F_f \cap T_a \end{cases}$$

where f and a stand for a functor and an argument children of p, respectively. Pairs $F_f||T_f$ and $F_a||T_a$ correspond to tags of these children. We say that a parse tree is *semantically coherent* if there is no node in the tree annotated by the $\perp$ tag.

Recall the syntactic structures (2) corresponding to the verb phrase of sentence (1). The annotated counterpart of the former structure follows[3]:

$$\cfrac{\cfrac{\cfrac{eat}{(VP/PP)/NP : \emptyset||F_{eat}} \quad \cfrac{spaghetti}{NP : T_{sp}||\{\textbf{food\_constituent}\}}}{VP/PP : \emptyset||\{\textbf{sentient}, \textbf{tool}, \textbf{manner}\}} \quad \cfrac{with\ chopsticks}{PP : \{\textbf{tool}, \textbf{instrument}\}||\emptyset}}{VP : \emptyset||\{\textbf{sentient}, \textbf{manner}\}}$$

This subtree is semantically coherent. On the other hand, part of the later structure in (2) constitutes semantically incoherent subtree:

$$\cfrac{\cfrac{spaghetti}{NP : T_{sp}||\{\textbf{food\_constituent}\}} \quad \cfrac{with\ chopsticks}{NP\backslash NP : \{\textbf{tool}, \textbf{instrument}\}||\emptyset}}{NP : \perp}$$

To implement described process within ASPCCGTK approach, we first manually specify a dictionary that contains FRAMENET information sufficient for annotating leaf nodes stemming from the words in an input sentence. We then use logic rules to (a) define annotations for non-leaf nodes of parse trees and (b) restrict the produced parse trees only to these that are semantically coherent. On the sentences (1) and (3), the ASPCCGTK parser implementing this approach is capable to enumerate only and all semantically coherent parses that correspond to syntactic structures expected for the sentences.

4 Conclusions and Future Work

In this work we propose and advocate the use of advanced declarative programming paradigm – answer set programming – as a uniform platform for integrated approach towards syntax-semantic processing in NLP. We illustrate that the CCG parser ASPCCGTK based on an ASP implementation reaches performance sufficient for being a useful NLP technology by taking advantage of the data structures of the CYK algorithm. Even though ASP has a high worst-case complexity, a related declarative paradigm with the same worst-case complexity was shown to be effective for solving NLP problems: the usage of Integer Linear Programming in (Roth and Yih, 2007). We also propose a method for disambiguating syntactic parse trees using the semantic information stemming from the FRAMENET dataset and implement it within the ASPCCGTK parser. This implementation results in the first step towards a synergistic approach in syntax-semantic processing by means of technology such as ASP. There is an open question on how to automatically fetch relevant information from FRAMENET in order to make the proposed implementation widely usable. This is the subject of ongoing and future work. One reasonable direction to explore is assess the usability of FRAMENET-based semantic role labeling systems for our purposes, in particular, LTH and SEMAFOR. The CCGbank will serve us as a test bed for evaluating the effectively of proposed method and directing this research. The source code of the reported implementation is available online at the ASPCCGTK website under version 0.3.

[3]The definition of semantically coherent trees presented here is a simplified version of a more complex construct, which takes into account functors that carry no semantic type information by themselves (for example, a functor corresponding to a word "*with*") but rather inherit this information from its argument.

References

Baker, C. F., C. J. Fillmore, and J. B. Lowe (1998). The Berkeley FrameNet Project. In *Proceedings of the 36th Annual Meeting of the Association for Computational Linguistics and 17th International Conference on Computational Linguistics*, San Mateo, CA, pp. 86–90.

Brewka, G., I. Niemelä, and M. Truszczyński (2011). Answer set programming at a glance. *Communications of the ACM 54(12)*, 92–103.

Clark, S. and J. R. Curran (2007). Wide-coverage efficient statistical parsing with CCG and log-linear models. *Computational Linguistics 33*(4), 493–552.

Das, D., N. Schneider, D. Chen, and N. A. Smith (2010). Probabilistic frame-semantic parsing. In *Human Language Technologies: The 2010 Annual Conference of the North American Chapter of the Association for Computational Linguistics*, HLT '10, Stroudsburg, PA, USA, pp. 948–956. Association for Computational Linguistics.

Drescher, C. and T. Walsh (2011). Modelling grammar constraints with answer set programming. In *International Conference on Logic Programming*, Volume 11, pp. 28–39.

Fillmore, C. J. and C. F. Baker (2001). Frame semantics for text understanding. In *WordNet and Other Lexical Resources, NAACL Workshop*.

Gelfond, M. and V. Lifschitz (1988). The stable model semantics for logic programming. In R. Kowalski and K. Bowen (Eds.), *Proceedings of International Logic Programming Conference and Symposium (ICLP'88)*, pp. 1070–1080. MIT Press.

Hockenmaier, J. and M. Steedman (2007). CCGbank: A corpus of CCG derivations and dependency structures extracted from the Penn Treebank. *Computational Linguististics 33*(3), 355–396.

Johansson, R. and P. Nugues (2007). Lth: semantic structure extraction using nonprojective dependency trees. In *Proceedings of the 4th International Workshop on Semantic Evaluations*, SemEval '07, Stroudsburg, PA, USA, pp. 227–230. Association for Computational Linguistics.

Kasami, T. (1965). An efficient recognition and syntax analysis algorithm for context-free languages. Technical Report AFCRL-65-758, Air Force Cambridge Research Laboratory, Bedford, Massachusetts.

Lange, M. and H. Leiß (2009). To CNF or not to CNF? An efficient yet presentable version of the CYK algorithm. In *Informatica Didactica 8*. Universität Potsdam.

Lierler, Y. and P. Schüller (2012). Parsing combinatory categorial grammar via planning in answer set programming. In *Correct Reasoning*, Volume 7265 of *Lecture Notes in Computer Science*, pp. 436–453. Springer.

Roth, D. and W. Yih (2007). Global inference for entity and relation identification via a linear programming formulation. In L. Getoor and B. Taskar (Eds.), *Introduction to Statistical Relational Learning*. MIT Press.

Steedman, M. (2000). *The syntactic process*. London: MIT Press.

Zelle, J. M. and R. J. Mooney (1996). Learning to parse database queries using inductive logic programming. In *Proceedings of the Thirteenth National Conference on Artificial Intelligence (AAAI-96)*, Portland, OR, USA, pp. 1050–1055.

Situated Utterances and Discourse Relations

Matthew Stone[†§], Una Stojnic[‡§] and Ernest Lepore[‡§*]
[†]Computer Science, [‡]Philosophy, [§]Cognitive Science
Rutgers University
matthew.stone@rutgers.edu, ustojnic@eden.rutgers.edu, lepore@ruccs.rutgers.edu

Abstract

Utterances in situated activity are about the world. Theories and systems normally capture this by assuming references must be resolved to real-world entities in utterance understanding. We describe a number of puzzles and problems for this approach, and propose an alternative semantic representation using discourse relations that link utterances to the nonlinguistic context to capture the context-dependent interpretation of situated utterances. Our approach promises better empirical coverage and more straightforward system building. Substantiating these advantages is work in progress.

1 Introduction

People exhibit sophisticated strategies for using language to coordinate their ongoing practical activities (Clark and Krych, 2004). Applications such as human–robot interaction must also also support these strategies (Kruijff et al., 2012). A key question is how to track speakers' reference to the environment. Julia Child's (1), from the "omelette" episode of *The French Chef*, illustrates the issues:

(1) There's your omelette, forming itself in the bottom of the pan.

The accompanying video is a close-up of a stovetop from above, with the omelette Child is cooking front and center. To understand what Child is doing, we need to track the obvious connection between her utterance and *that omelette* in *that pan*.

In this paper, we explore a novel and surprising proposal about how do this: *discourse relations*. Discourse relations are kinds of speech acts, which can connect an utterance to ongoing conversation, establish the coherence of what is said, and allow inference to implicatures and other aspects of the speaker's mental state (Asher and Lascarides, 2003, 2013). Child's (1) we suggest, gets its coherence, in part, as a *report of what's visible in that situation*. Child's reference to the omelette and the pan is a consequence of this interpretation, and so need not and should not be separately represented.

Prior work focuses on symbols that refer directly to the world and placeholders that abstract reference; see Section 2. We introduce our alternative and contrast it with these approaches in Section 3. On the theoretical side, we argue in Section 4, our approach captures meaning more precisely and provides a better account of what's needed to understand and disambiguate situated utterances. On the practical side, we argue in Section 5, our approach provides a more tractable interface between linguistic processing, situated perception, and deliberation.

2 Background

Our work arises out of an interest in combining grounded representations of meaning with coherence approaches to discourse. To appreciate the issues, consider a classic case (Bolt, 1980). A user utters (2), while pointing first at an object in the environment and then at the place it should go.

(2) Put that there.

*This paper is based on work supported by NSF IIS-1017811. We acknowledge the helpful anonymous reviews.

Kaplan (1989) urges us to treat demonstratives in cases such as (2) as *directly referential*. In using them, the speaker gives information about *those very things*. Computationally, this means that the objects of demonstrations should be represented using symbols that are locked onto their referents system-wide. In multimodal interfaces, like Bolt's (1980), the targets are graphical objects and other locations on a computer display, for which appropriate internal representations are readily available. For robotics, the natural strategy is to represent referents using perceptually-grounded symbols anchored in the real world, as do Yu and Ballard (2004) for example.

Speakers *use* many utterances referentially, even if the utterances don't have referential semantics (Kripke, 1977). Systems need to recognize and represent the speaker's referential communicative intentions in those cases too (Allen and Perrault, 1980). Bolt's system, for example, responded to definite descriptions, as in (3), the same way as it did to demonstratives: it moved *those things*.

(3) Put the cruise ship north of the Dominican Republic.

When it's problematic to use grounded symbols, we can use *discourse referents* alongside them. Formally, a discourse referent is just a free variable, but it can be associated with *anchoring constraints* that describe how it is supposed to be linked up with the world (Zeevat, 1999). In practice, anchoring involves representing interpretation in two separate tiers (Luperfoy, 1992). Meaning is represented via variables, the world is represented via suitably grounded symbols, and an evolving assignment of values to variables embodies the system's understanding of the real-world reference of expressions in discourse.

Reconciling grounded reference and discourse anaphora is the job of discourse semantics. We can see this in the planning dialogue of (4), for example.

(4) a. A: Let's put the cruise ship south of Florida.
b. B: That won't fit there.

We need to represent A's utterance as a proposal—a specific kind of problem-solving move that advocates a particular course of action and commits the speaker to following through on it if others concur. The move focuses attention on the entities involved in carrying it out: here, the ship, Florida and the region to its south. Meanwhile, B's response in (4b) is a rejection—a move that offers a negative assessment of the current proposal and commits the speaker against adopting it. Note that B's references with *that* and *there* succeed even if B produces the utterance without any accompanying gesture or demonstration, because the referent has been activated by an earlier mention in a related utterance (Gundel et al., 1993).

The simplest approach to discourse organization is to represent the state of the discourse with an information state (Poesio and Traum, 1997) and associate each move with an appropriate update. For example, we can model utterances such as (2) and (3) as making moves that contribute step-by-step to broader problem-solving activity; see Lochbaum (1998) or Blaylock (2005). Normally, the information state specifies once and for all how each thread of ongoing activity places relevant real-world entities at the center of attention (Grosz and Sidner, 1986; Poesio and Traum, 1997).

We advocate a different approach, based on *discourse coherence* (Kehler, 2002; Asher and Lascarides, 2003). The idea is that discourse is fundamentally composed of *relational* contributions, which establish connections that link each utterance by inference to segments of the preceding conversation. The interpretation of an utterance therefore implicitly refers to the interpretation of some prior discourse and comments on it. On coherence approaches, how an utterance *attaches* to the discourse determines what entities are prominent in interpreting it (Hobbs, 1979). Coherence theory does *not* naturally characterize discourse in terms of state-by-state updates to an overarching model of information and attention. Kehler and colleagues' (5) illustrates what's at stake (Kehler et al., 2008).

(5) Phil tickled Stanley, and Liz poked him.

When we understand the second clause of (5) as a description of a parallel to the first, we prefer to resolve *him* to Stanley. When we understand it to describe its results, we prefer to resolve *him* to Phil. For coherence theory, the two interpretations of the second clause *relate* it to the first, and the relation is what suggests prominent resolutions for its references. The relation in turn structures the discourse into higher level units that shape possibilities for attaching subsequent utterances.

3 Our Proposal

Coherence theories start from the observation that understanding utterances involves recognizing the implicit relationships that connect ideas together. The same is true, we argue, for utterances like (1). Child is not just giving the next step in making an omelette, or giving her audience new information about the principles of cooking. She's describing what's happening on the screen, in terms she expects her audience to confirm for themselves by examining what they see. An interpreter who doesn't recognize this about (1) has failed to understand it.

To sketch the key formal ingredients of our account, we use a simple dynamic semantics (Muskens, 1996) and an expressive ontology of situations and eventualities (Hobbs, 1985; Kratzer, 2002). Dynamic semantics represents meanings as sequences of updates $[\mathbf{v}|\varphi]$ that introduce discourse referents $\mathbf{v}$ and characterize them with conditions φ. We add an update $\langle \pi x c\rangle$ introducing a discourse referent x perceptually grounded in c, and an update $\langle \sigma x s\rangle$ introducing x as the central entity in grounded situation s (provided s does uniquely distinguish one). Where necessary, ∂K marks update K as presupposed.

Situations are parts of the world, capturing particular states of particular objects, perhaps as located in particular spatial regions and changing over particular temporal intervals. Propositions are true in situations; this is important for perceptual, causal and default reasoning. Eventualities, including Davidsonian events, turn out to be situations that exemplify propositions in characteristic ways. We capture discourse coherence by specifying relations among situations; these can be discourse referents for situations introduced by utterances or grounded references to parts of the speech situation.[1]

We capture the interpretation of (2) by specifying the dynamics of discourse referents and their grounded interpretations as in (6), using c_1 for *that* and c_2 for *there*.

(6) $\langle \pi x c_1\rangle; \langle \pi y c_2\rangle; [e|command(e), put(e,x,y)]$

Things get more interesting when we factor in coherence. We formalize (1) as in (7).

(7) $[e|Summary(s_0,e)]; \partial[o,p|omelette(o), pan(p)]; [|forming\text{-}self\text{-}in(e,o,p)]$

The discourse relation $Summary(s_0,e)$ captures the interpretive connection between the utterance describing e and what's happening simultaneously on the screen in situation s_0. Like all coherence relations, *Summary* reflects semantic and pragmatic constraints. Semantically, e must be part of s_0. Following Kratzer (2002), this entails that the information describing e is true in s_0. Pragmatically, $Summary(s_0,e)$ holds only if the information describing e provides a good answer about "what's happening" in s_0. A summary appeals to broad, basic categories to provide essential information. We have in mind something like the "vital nuggets of information" needed to answer definition questions (Voorhees, 2003).

For "That's an omelette" we offer (8), which defines the central entity in situation s_0 as an omelette:

(8) $[e|Summary(s_0,e)]; \langle \sigma o s_0\rangle; [|omelette(e,o)]$

The update $\langle \sigma o s_0\rangle$ formalizes how the *discourse relation* makes entities prominent for reference, as we observed in (5). Such updates can capture the interpretation of demonstratives when there's no explicit pointing or demonstration in the utterance.

Not all situated utterances offer a *Summary* of an unfolding situation. For example, utterances can offer *Assessments* that invite the audience not to define what's happening but to appraise it. Take "Yummy!" In commenting on the food this way, the speaker expects the audience to join in her appreciation. A formal characterization of *Assessment* would appeal to the semantics of predicates of personal taste and the distinctive pragmatic functions of such judgments, perhaps following Crespo and Fernández (2011). And speakers can also link up questions and instructions to ongoing activity by suitable relations.

Summary and *Assessment* could also be used to formalize the interpretation of successive utterances by relating two described situations. In fact, utterances can relate both to ongoing activity and to previous

[1]Thus we use situations to capture discourse meaning, *not* to formalize events of speech or the common ground as in Poesio and Traum (1997). An alternative approach would follow Zeevat (1999) and Asher and Lascarides (2003) and use labels for DRSs to capture perceptual and discourse content in discourse relations.

discourse. For example, consider (9) and (10), taken from Vi Hart's origami proof of the Pythagorean theorem—a visual narrative much like Child's where utterances describe ongoing events on the screen.[2]

(9) We're just taking advantage of the symmetries of the square for the next step.

(10) This is where you're choosing how long and pointy or short and fat the right triangle is.

Hart uses (9) while folding a square into eight identical segments to explain how to do the folds. Hart uses (10) as she describes the next step of folding, to highlight its result for the proof. Thus, these utterances are linked to the accompanying activity but do not just report what's going on; and they're linked to the ongoing discourse as well. In fact, coherence theory already allows that utterances can bear multiple connections to prior discourse (Asher and Lascarides, 2003). The closest parallel may be that of multimodal communication, where Lascarides and Stone (2009) argue that utterances bear discourse relations both to prior utterances and to simultaneous gesture.

4 Empirical Adequacy

Combining grounded representations with discourse relations, specifically as in (8), makes it possible to give a better characterization of the logical form of demonstrative utterances in otherwise problematic cases. In particular, it captures how speakers and interpreters can rely on the world to disambiguate what they say and to understand one another.

Here's a telling case. It's the beginning of spring, 2012, and Jupiter and Venus are shining brightly very close together—just a few degrees apart—in the evening sky. The speaker has deployed a telescope facing a window over the western sky. When a visitor arrives, the speaker adjusts the telescope, then says, without any further demonstration, either (11) or (12).

(11) That's Jupiter. You can even see four moons.

(12) That's Venus. You can see the crescent.

We (and our informants) find these utterances unproblematic. But the coherence theory is required to get their interpretations right. These are comments on what's visible through the telescope. You can't see four of Jupiter's moons or the crescent of Venus with the naked eye and the speaker isn't suggesting otherwise. Moreover, the coherence relation is what's making it possible for the speaker to refer to Jupiter or Venus as *that*. To comment on the view through the telescope is to evoke whatever entity is centrally imaged in the telescope as a prominent candidate for reference. And nothing else will do. Given the astronomical conjunction, the speaker couldn't distinguish Jupiter from Venus by pointing, nor could the visitor judge which body the telescope was pointed at by the direction of the tube. Letting s_1 name the view through the telescope, we can formalize the key bits of interpretation:

(13) $[e|Summary(s_1,e)];\langle \sigma x s_1\rangle;[|jupiter(e,x)]$

(14) $[e|Summary(s_1,e)];\langle \sigma x s_1\rangle;[|venus(e,x)]$

The representations get the meaning right. More importantly, they explain how the visitor can recover the logical form and understand the speaker's point by recognizing the relationship that makes the speaker's utterance coherent, even though the visitor can't identify which specific body the speaker is referring to until the visitor looks through the telescope for herself. By contrast, if all you had was representations like (6), grounded representations of deixis that made reference explicit, you'd incorrectly predict that there's an ambiguity to resolve in (11) and (12) even *after* you understand them as comments about the view through the scope. You'd have two grounded symbols for bright objects in the western sky, and you'd have to *pick* one as the referent of the speaker's demonstration—or ask for clarification. We take this as strong evidence against the idea that speakers and hearers must coordinate directly on demonstrative referents, a common view in both formal and computational semantics (Neale, 2004; Stone, 2004).

[2] `http://www.youtube.com/watch?v=z61L83w131E`

5 Cognitive Architecture

Systems with grounded language interpretation have to integrate language and perception. Real robotic understanding systems use a complicated inference process to resolve reference in situated utterances, in order to figure out what thing in the world is a reference of a demonstration, for example (Kruijff et al., 2012). It's not just a matter of selecting the right referent from a set of salient candidates based on linguistic constraints. Like people, robots have cameras with limited fields of view that must be pointed at what they see. So when you do a demonstration for a robot, it has to track the pointing movement to find the possible targets, much as a person would. There is substantial problem solving involved.

The same is true of many other grounded inference tasks involving domain reasoning. We may need the results to calculate the implications of what we hear, or even to select the most likely interpretation. But it's normally prohibitive to try to interleave that problem solving with fine-grained disambiguation, because it requires systems to solve these hard reasoning problems not just for the intended interpretation but for any candidate interpretation it considers.

Representing context dependence via coherence provides an attractive framework to divide interpretation into stages and minimize the problem solving that's necessary to compute logical form. Take (11) and its representation in (13). Here is a formalism that captures the meaning of the utterance while spelling out the further work that will be required to resolve reference. According to (13), when you look through the telescope, you'll find out what the referent of *that* is. Recognizing the logical form of the utterance this way should suffice for understanding. We expect that the discourse relation could be resolved based on shallow constraints on what information counts as a summary. And the system only needs to be tracking the ongoing activity enough to link utterances to relevant situations. It can ground its provisional understanding in perception and action as needed separately.

6 Conclusion and Future Work

We have considered grounded interpretations in coherent discourse, and argued that referential interpretations in cases like (1), (2) and (11) are understood and derived relationally. This requires representations of interpretation that explicitly link discourse entities with grounded symbols and track the heterogeneous prominence that these entities get in virtue of the diverse relationships that utterances can bear to ongoing activity. In brief: we relate our talk to the world around us through suitable discourse relations.

Our approach commits us to representing utterances with specific kinds of interpretive connections to the world. Our characterization of these connections is obviously provisional, and corpus and modeling work is necessary to flesh out the parameters of the approach. We have also suggested that these representations will be useful in designing systems that communicate about the environment where they can perceive and act. Experiments with prototypes are clearly necessary to substantiate this claim.

References

Allen, J. F. and C. R. Perrault (1980). Analyzing intention in utterances. *AIJ 15*(3), 143–178.

Asher, N. and A. Lascarides (2003). *Logics of Conversation.* Cambridge: Cambridge University Press.

Asher, N. and A. Lascarides (2013). Strategic conversation. *Semantics and Pragmatics.*

Blaylock, N. J. (2005). *Towards Tractable Agent-Based Dialogue.* Ph.D. dissertation, Rochester.

Bolt, R. (1980). Put-that-there: Voice and gesture at the graphics interface. *Computer Graphics 14*(3), 262–270.

Clark, H. H. and M. A. Krych (2004). Speaking while monitoring addressees for understanding. *Journal of Memory and Language 50*, 62–81.

Crespo, I. and R. Fernández (2011). Expressing taste in dialogue. In *SEMDIAL 2011: Proceedings of the 15th Workshop on the Seantics and Pragmatics of Dialogue*, pp. 84–93.

Grosz, B. J. and C. L. Sidner (1986). Attention, intentions, and the structure of discourse. *Computational Linguistics 12*(3), 175–204.

Gundel, J. K., N. Hedberg, and R. Zacharski (1993). Cognitive status and the form of referring expressions in discourse. *Language 69*(2), 274–307.

Hobbs, J. R. (1979). Coherence and coreference. *Cognitive Science 3*(1), 67–90.

Hobbs, J. R. (1985). Ontological promiscuity. In *Proceedings of ACL*, pp. 61–69.

Kaplan, D. (1989). Demonstratives. In J. Almog, J. Perry, and H. Wettstein (Eds.), *Themes from Kaplan*, pp. 481–563. Oxford: Oxford University Press.

Kehler, A. (2002). *Coherence, Reference and the Theory of Grammar*. Stanford: CSLI.

Kehler, A., L. Kertz, H. Rohde, and J. L. Elman (2008). Coherence and coreference revisited. *Journal of Semantics 25*(1), 1–44.

Kratzer, A. (2002). Facts: Particulars or information units? *Linguistics & Philosophy 25*(5–6), 655–670.

Kripke, S. (1977). Speaker's reference and semantic reference. In P. A. French, T. Uehling, Jr., and H. K. Wettstein (Eds.), *Midwest Studies in Philosophy, Volume II*, pp. 255–276. Minneapolis: University of Minnesota Press.

Kruijff, G.-J., M. Janicek, and H. Zender (2012). Situated communication for joint activity in human-robot teams. *IEEE Intelligent Systems 27*(2), 27–35.

Lascarides, A. and M. Stone (2009). Discourse coherence and gesture interpretation. *Gesture 9*(2), 147–180.

Lochbaum, K. E. (1998). A collaborative planning model of intentional structure. *Computational Linguistics 24*(4), 525–572.

Luperfoy, S. (1992). The representation of multimodal user interface dialogues using discourse pegs. In *Proceedings of ACL*, pp. 22–31.

Muskens, R. (1996). Combining Montague semantics and discourse representation. *Linguistics & Philosophy 19*(2), 143–186.

Neale, S. (2004). This, that, and the other. In A. Bezuidenhout and M. Reimer (Eds.), *Descriptions and Beyond*, pp. 68–181. Oxford: Oxford University Press.

Poesio, M. and D. R. Traum (1997). Conversational actions and discourse situations. *Computational Intelligence 13*(3), 309–347.

Stone, M. (2004). Intention, interpretation and the computational structure of language. *Cognitive Science 28*(5), 781–809.

Voorhees, E. M. (2003). Evaluating answers to definition questions. In *Companion Volume of the Proceedings of HLT-NAACL – Short Papers*, pp. 109–111.

Yu, C. and D. H. Ballard (2004). On the integration of grounding language and learning objects. In *Proceedings of the Nineteenth National Conference on Artificial Intelligence (AAAI)*, pp. 488–494.

Zeevat, H. (1999). Demonstratives in discourse. *Journal of Semantics 16*(4), 279–313.

Gamification for Word Sense Labeling

Noortje J. Venhuizen
University of Groningen
n.j.venhuizen@rug.nl

Valerio Basile
University of Groningen
v.basile@rug.nl

Kilian Evang
University of Groningen
k.evang@rug.nl

Johan Bos
University of Groningen
johan.bos@rug.nl

Abstract

Obtaining gold standard data for word sense disambiguation is important but costly. We show how it can be done using a "Game with a Purpose" (GWAP) called *Wordrobe*. This game consists of a large set of multiple-choice questions on word senses generated from the Groningen Meaning Bank. The players need to answer these questions, scoring points depending on the agreement with fellow players. The working assumption is that the right sense for a word can be determined by the answers given by the players. To evaluate our method, we gold-standard tagged a portion of the data that was also used in the GWAP. A comparison yielded promising results, ranging from a precision of 0.88 and recall of 0.83 for relative majority agreement, to a precision of 0.98 and recall of 0.35 for questions that were answered unanimously.

1 Introduction

One of the core aspects of semantic annotation is determining the correct sense of each content word from a set of possible senses. In NLP-related research, many models for disambiguating word senses have been proposed. Such models have been evaluated through various public evaluation campaigns, most notably SenseEval (now called SemEval), an international word sense disambiguation competition held already six times since its start in 1998 (Kilgarriff and Rosenzweig, 2000).

All disambiguation models rely on gold standard data from human annotators, but this data is time-consuming and expensive to obtain. In the context of constructing the Groningen Meaning Bank (GMB, Basile et al., 2012), a large semantically annotated corpus, we address this problem by making use of crowdsourcing. The idea of crowdsourcing is that some tasks that are difficult to solve for computers but easy for humans may be outsourced to a number of people across the globe. One of the prime crowdsourcing platforms is Amazon's Mechanical Turk, where workers get paid small amounts to complete small tasks. Mechanical Turk has already been successfully applied for the purpose of word sense disambiguation and clustering (see, e.g., Akkaya et al., 2010; Rumshisky et al., 2012). Another crowdsourcing technique, "Game with a Purpose" (GWAP), rewards contributors with entertainment rather than money. GWAPs challenge players to score high on specifically designed tasks, thereby contributing their knowledge. GWAPs were successfully pioneered in NLP by initiatives such as 'Phrase Detectives' for anaphora resolution (Chamberlain et al., 2008) and 'JeuxDeMots' for term relations (Artignan et al., 2009). We have developed an online GWAP platform for semantic annotation, called Wordrobe. In this paper we present the design and the first results of using Wordrobe for the task of word sense disambiguation.

2 Method

Wordrobe[1] is a collection of games with a purpose, each targeting a specific level of linguistic annotation. Current games include part-of-speech tagging, named entity tagging, co-reference resolution and

[1] http://www.wordrobe.org/

word sense disambiguation. The game used for word sense disambiguation is called *Senses*. Below we describe the design of Wordrobe and the data used for *Senses*.

2.1 Design of Wordrobe

Wordrobe is designed to be used by non-experts, who can use their intuitions about language to annotate linguistic phenomena, without being discouraged by technical linguistic terminology. Therefore, the games include as little instructions as possible. All games share the same structure: a multiple-choice question with a small piece of text (generally one or two sentences) in which one or more words are highlighted, depending on the type of game. For each question, players can select an answer or use the skip-button to go to the next question.

In order to encourage players to answer a lot of questions and to give good answers, they are rewarded in two ways: they can collect *drawers* and *points*. A drawer is simply a unit of a few questions – the more difficult the game, the fewer questions are in one drawer. By completing many drawers, players unlock achievements that decorate their profile page. While drawers are used to stimulate answering many questions, points are used to motivate players to play with attention. The points are calculated on the basis of two factors: the *agreement* with other players who answered the same question and the *bet* that the player put at stake. Players can place a bet reflecting the certainty about their answer. The bet is always between 10% and 100% of the points that a question is worth. The default choice is a bet of 10% and once a player adjusts the bet, this new value is remembered as the new preset value for the next question. Higher bets will result in higher gains when the answer is correct, and lower points when the answer is wrong. Since Wordrobe is designed to create gold standard annotations, the correct choice is not defined (this is exactly what we want to obtain!). Therefore, the points are calculated on the basis of the answers given by other players, as in Phrase Detectives (Chamberlain et al., 2008). The idea is that the majority rules, meaning that the choice that gets selected most by human players is probably the correct one. So, the more players agree with each other, the more points they gain. As a consequence, the score of a player is continually updated – even when the player is not playing – in order to take into account the answers provided by other players answering the same questions.

2.2 Generation of questions for the Senses game

All Wordrobe games consist of automatically generated multiple-choice questions. In the case of *Senses*, the word sense labeling game, each question consists of one or two sentences extracted from the Groningen Meaning Bank with one highlighted word for which the correct word sense in the given context must be determined. Currently, the game only focuses on nouns and verbs, but it can be easily extended to include, e.g., adjectives and adverbs. The choices for the questions are automatically generated from the word senses in WordNet (Fellbaum, 1998).

Of all the occurrences (tokens) of nouns and verbs in the GMB, 92.3% occurs in WordNet. This results in a total of 452,576 candidate questions for the *Senses* game. For the first version of Wordrobe, we selected a subset of the tokens that have at most five different senses in WordNet, such that the number of choices for each question is restricted. Figure 1 shows a screenshot of a question of *Senses*.

3 Results

The number of automatically generated questions for the first version of *Senses* was 3,121. After the first few weeks of Wordrobe going live, we had received 5,478 answers. Roughly half (1,673) of the questions received at least one answer, with an average of three answers per question. In order to test the validity of the method of using a GWAP to obtain reliable word sense annotations, we selected a subset of the questions with a reasonable response rate and created a gold standard annotation.

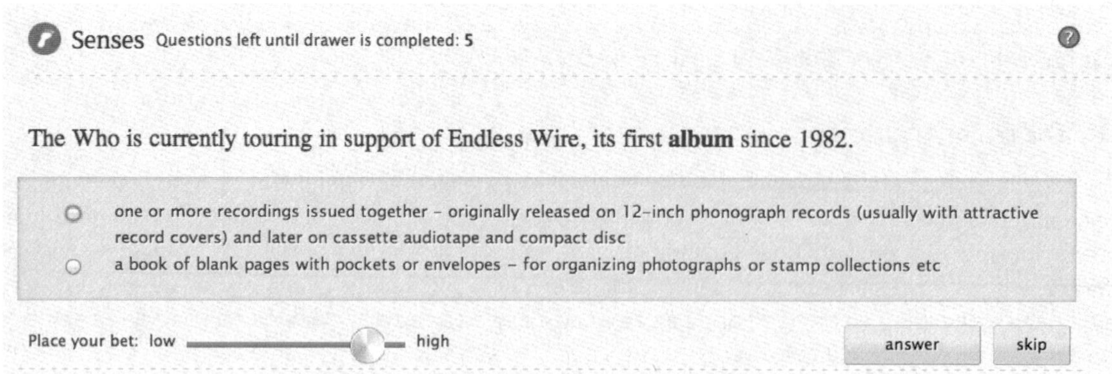

Figure 1: Screenshot from Wordrobe game *Senses*.

3.1 Gold standard annotation

We created a gold standard annotation for a test set of 115 questions with exactly six answers each, which was used to evaluate the answers given by the players of Wordrobe. Four trained human annotators individually selected the correct sense for each of the target words in the test set. Fleiss's kappa was calculated to evaluate inter-annotator agreement, resulting in $\kappa = 0.79$, which is generally taken to reflect substantial agreement. Unanimity was obtained for 64% of the questions and 86% of the questions had an absolute majority vote. In a second step of evaluation, the non-unanimous answers were discussed between the annotators in order to obtain 100% agreement on all questions, the result of which was used as the gold standard annotation.

3.2 Agreement measures

Given a question and a set of player answers, we need a procedure to decide whether to accept a particular choice into our annotated corpus. One important factor is agreement: if a great majority of players agrees on the same choice, this choice is probably the correct one. Smaller majorities of players are more likely to be wrong. Another important factor is the number of answers: the more players have answered a question, the more we can presumably rely on the majority's judgement. In this work, we focus on the first factor (agreement) because the average answer rate per question is quite low throughout our data set. We tested a couple of simple agreement measures that determine whether a choice is counted as a winning answer. We measure recall and precision for each measure with respect to the gold standard.

The simplest measure accepts every choice that has a relative majority. It always accepts some choice, unless the two choices with the most answers are tied. A stricter measure ("absolute majority") accepts only the choices that were chosen by at least a certain fraction of players who answered the question, with some threshold $t \geq 0.5$. We used the values 0.5, 0.7 and 1.0 as threshold, the latter only accepting choices unanimously picked by players.

The measures described above simply choose the majority answer relative to some threshold, but fail to take into account the total number of players that answered the question and the number of possible choices for a question. These factors will become more important when we evaluate questions with a higher number of answers. We need a measure that determines whether the majority answer is chosen significantly more often than the other answers. This means that the answers should be significantly skewed towards one answer. In order to test such an effect, we can use Pearson's chi-square test, which determines the goodness-of-fit of a given distribution relative to a uniform distribution. If we take the distribution of answers over the set of possible choices, we can say that only those questions for which this distribution significantly differs from a uniform distribution ($p < 0.05$) are considered to provide an acceptable answer. Because the number of answers per question in our test set is relatively small, a significant result means that there is one choice towards which the answers accumulate. Determining which choice this is can accordingly be done using the relative-majority measure described above.

3.3 Evaluation

We evaluate the annotations obtained from Wordrobe by comparing the data of the test set (115 questions) to the gold standard. We used each of the agreement measures described above to select the answers with a high enough majority, and calculated precision (the number of correct answers with respect to the total number of selected answers), recall (the number of correct answers with respect to the total number of questions), and the corresponding F-score. The results are shown in Table 1.

Table 1: Precision and recall based on different agreement measures

Strategy	Precision	Recall	F-score
Relative majority	0.880	**0.834**	**0.857**
Absolute majority ($t = 0.5$)	0.882	0.782	0.829
Absolute majority ($t = 0.7$)	0.945	0.608	0.740
Unanimity ($t = 1$)	**0.975**	0.347	0.512
Chi-square test ($p < 0.05$)	0.923	0.521	0.666

As expected, the highest recall is obtained using the relative majority measure since this measure is the least conservative in accepting a majority choice. As the threshold for accepting a choice is set higher, recall drops and precision rises, up to a very high precision for the unanimity measure, but with a significant loss in recall. The measure based on Pearson's chi-square test is similar in being conservative; having only six answers per question in the test set, only the questions that are very skewed towards one choice give a significant result of the chi-square test.

As described above, each answer is associated with a bet between 10% and 100% of the points available for a question, which players can adjust based on how certain they are about their answer. The distribution of bets over all answers shows two significant peaks for these extremes: in 66% of the cases the maximum bet was chosen, and the default minimum bet was chosen in 12% of the cases. The main motivation for inserting the betting function was to be able to identify questions that were more difficult for players by looking for low bets. We tested the correlation between the average bet per question and the relative size of the majority (indicating agreement between players) over all questions using Pearson's product-moment correlation and found a small but significant positive effect ($r = 0.150$, $p < 0.01$). We expect that this effect will increase if more data is available.

In order to test whether questions with high average bets were easier, we repeated the evaluation, including only questions with a high average bet: $\bar{b} \geq 80\%$ (see Table 2). Recall is reduced strongly, as one would expect, but we do observe an increase in precision for all measures except unanimity. This higher precision suggests that indeed the results of the questions for which players on average place a high bet are more similar to the gold standard. However, we will need more data to confirm this point.

Table 2: Precision and recall based on different agreement measures for questions with $\bar{b} \geq 80\%$

Strategy	Precision	Recall	F-score
Relative majority	0.917	**0.478**	**0.629**
Absolute majority ($t = 0.5$)	0.930	0.461	0.616
Absolute majority ($t = 0.7$)	0.956	0.383	0.547
Unanimity ($t = 1$)	**0.961**	0.217	0.355
Chi-square test ($p < 0.05$)	0.950	0.330	0.355

4 Discussion

The goal of Wordrobe is to obtain annotations from non-expert annotators that are qualitatively close to gold standard annotations created by experts. This requires automatic techniques for filtering out low-quality answers. We evaluated the results obtained using some simple selection techniques with respect to a gold standard created by experts. We found that even with very conservative settings, optimizing for precision, we could still get a reasonably high recall (0.347). The highest precision, obtained using this most conservative measure (unanimity), was 0.975. In fact, a closer look at the data showed that there was exactly one question on which the choice unanimously picked by players differed from the gold standard annotation. This question is shown in (1).

(1) Although the last Russian **troops** left in 1994, the status of the Russian minority (some 30% of the population) remains of concern to Moscow.

   a. soldiers collectively (synonyms: military personnel, soldiery)
   b. a group of soldiers
   c. a cavalry unit corresponding to an infantry company
   d. a unit of Girl or Boy Scouts (synonyms: troop, scout troop, scout group)
   e. an orderly crowd (synonyms: troop, flock)

While according to the gold standard annotation the correct answer was (1b), the six players who answered this question in the game unanimously chose (1a) as the correct answer. This example illustrates the difficulty of the task at hand very well; one could argue for the correctness of both of the possible answers. In this case, the average bet posed by the players (83%) is not helpful either in determining the difficulty of the question. This example suggests that using a more fine-grained gold standard annotation, with a ranking rather than selection of possible answers, may result in higher quality results.

Overall, the measures for calculating agreement show high numbers for precision, which were improved even more by only taking into account the questions that received a high average bet. The main drawback for this evaluation procedure is the restricted average number of answers per question. Although the recall for the unanimity measure remains at an acceptable level for the test set, this number is likely to decrease severely for questions with a higher number of answers. On the other hand, the measure based on the chi-square test is expected to become more reliable in the case of a larger dataset. In general, the evaluation measures discussed in section 3 are very basic and not robust against small datasets or unreliable annotators. With the recent uprise of crowdsourcing platforms such as Amazon's Mechanical Turk, there has been a revived interest in the task of obtaining reliable annotations from non-expert annotators. Various methods have been proposed to model annotated data such that it can be used as a gold standard (see, e.g., Carpenter, 2008; Snow et al., 2008; Beigman Klebanov and Beigman, 2009; Raykar et al., 2010). The goal of this paper was to provide a general idea of the quality of the data that can be obtained using games with a purpose. However, creation of a proper gold standard will require the collection of more data, and the use of more advanced techniques to obtain reliable annotations. As a first step towards this goal, we will make the data used in this paper available online,[2] such that interested readers can perform their own evaluation methods on this data.

5 Conclusions and future work

In this paper we described and evaluated the first results about the use of a 'Game with a Purpose' for annotating word senses. Although the amount of data obtained for each question is still relatively small (the largest amount of answers given to a reasonably sized amount of questions was 6), the results on precision and recall compared to the gold standard annotation are promising. We proposed several measures for determining the winning answer of a question, and compared them with respect to the precision and recall results. In this paper we focused on obtaining high precision scores, because the goal of the project is to obtain gold standard annotations which can be used to improve the Groningen Meaning Bank (Basile et al., 2012). Future work will focus on obtaining larger amounts of data and evaluating the annotations as part of an integration into the GMB. Moreover, this method for obtaining annotations will be applied and evaluated with respect to other linguistic phenomena, such as named entity tagging, noun-noun compound interpretation, and co-reference resolution.

[2]http://gmb.let.rug.nl/

Acknowledgements

We'd like to thank Bob Carpenter for comments and discussion of the Wordrobe data, and the pointers he provided to related work. Obviously we also thank all Wordrobe players (962 so far) that generated so many answers (41,541 so far) in such a short time.

References

Akkaya, C., A. Conrad, J. Wiebe, and R. Mihalcea (2010). Amazon mechanical turk for subjectivity word sense disambiguation. In *Proceedings of the NAACL HLT 2010 Workshop on Creating Speech and Language Data with Amazon's Mechanical Turk*, pp. 195–203. Association for Computational Linguistics.

Artignan, G., M. Hascoët, and M. Lafourcade (2009). Multiscale visual analysis of lexical networks. In *13th International Conference on Information Visualisation*, Barcelona, Spain, pp. 685–690.

Basile, V., J. Bos, K. Evang, and N. J. Venhuizen (2012). Developing a large semantically annotated corpus. In N. Calzolari, K. Choukri, T. Declerck, M. U. Doğan, B. Maegaard, J. Mariani, J. Odijk, and S. Piperidis (Eds.), *Proceedings of the Eighth International Conference on Language Resources and Evaluation (LREC'12)*, Istanbul, Turkey. European Language Resources Association (ELRA).

Beigman Klebanov, B. and E. Beigman (2009). From annotator agreement to noise models. *Computational Linguistics 35*(4), 495–503.

Carpenter, B. (2008). Multilevel bayesian models of categorical data annotation. Tech. report, Alias-i.

Chamberlain, J., M. Poesio, and U. Kruschwitz (2008). Addressing the Resource Bottleneck to Create Large-Scale Annotated Texts. In J. Bos and R. Delmonte (Eds.), *Semantics in Text Processing. STEP 2008 Conference Proceedings*, Volume 1 of *Research in Computational Semantics*, pp. 375–380. College Publications.

Fellbaum, C. (Ed.) (1998). *WordNet. An Electronic Lexical Database*. The MIT Press.

Kilgarriff, A. and J. Rosenzweig (2000). Framework and results for English SENSEVAL. *Computers and the Humanities 34*(1), 15–48.

Raykar, V., S. Yu, L. Zhao, G. Valadez, C. Florin, L. Bogoni, and L. Moy (2010). Learning from crowds. *The Journal of Machine Learning Research 11*, 1297–1322.

Rumshisky, A., N. Botchan, S. Kushkuley, and J. Pustejovsky (2012). Word sense inventories by non-experts. In N. Calzolari, K. Choukri, T. Declerck, M. U. Doğan, B. Maegaard, J. Mariani, J. Odijk, and S. Piperidis (Eds.), *Proceedings of the Eighth International Conference on Language Resources and Evaluation (LREC'12)*, Istanbul, Turkey. European Language Resources Association (ELRA).

Snow, R., B. O'Connor, D. Jurafsky, and A. Ng (2008). Cheap and fast—but is it good?: evaluating non-expert annotations for natural language tasks. In *Proceedings of the Conference on Empirical Methods in Natural Language Processing*, pp. 254–263. Association for Computational Linguistics.

Fitting, Not Clashing!
A Distributional Semantic Model of Logical Metonymy

Alessandra Zarcone[1], Alessandro Lenci[2], Sebastian Padó[3], Jason Utt[1]
[1]Universität Stuttgart, [2]Universität Heidelberg, [3]Università di Pisa
[1]zarconaa,uttjn@ims.uni-stuttgart.de,
[2]alessandro.lenci@ling.unipi.it, [3]pado@cl.uni-heidelberg.de

Abstract

Logical metonymy interpretation (e.g. *begin the book* → *writing*) has received wide attention in linguistics. Experimental results have shown higher processing costs for metonymic conditions compared with non-metonymic ones (*read the book*). According to a widely held interpretation, it is the type clash between the event-selecting verb and the entity-denoting object (*begin the book*) that triggers coercion mechanisms and leads to additional processing effort. We propose an alternative explanation and argue that the extra processing effort is an effect of thematic fit. This is a more economical hypothesis that does not need to postulate a separate type clash mechanism: entity-denoting objects simply have a low fit as objects of event-selecting verbs. We test linguistic datasets from psycholinguistic experiments and find that a structured distributional model of thematic fit, which does not encode any explicit argument type information, is able to replicate all significant experimental findings. This result provides evidence for a graded account of coercion phenomena in which thematic fit accounts for both the trigger of the coercion and the retrieval of the covert event.

1 Introduction

Type clash in logical metonymy. Logical metonymy, also known as enriched composition (e.g. *The writer began the novel*), is generally explained in terms of a type clash between an event-selecting metonymic verb (*begin*) and an entity-denoting object (*novel*), triggering the recovery of a covert event (*writing*). Extensive psycholinguistic work (McElree, Traxler, Pickering, Seely, and Jackendoff (2001) and Traxler, Pickering, and McElree (2002), among others) has demonstrated extra processing costs for metonymic constructions. For example, Traxler et al. (2002) combine metonymic and non-metonymic verbs with entity-denoting and event-denoting nouns (*The boy [started/saw]$_V$ [the puzzle/fight]$_{NP}$*) and report significantly higher processing costs for the coercion combination (metonymic verb combined with entity-denoting object, e.g. *The boy started the puzzle*).

Building on this and similar experiments, Frisson and McElree (2008) ascribe the extra processing cost to "the deployment of operations to construct a semantic representation" of the event (*writing the novel*) that is supposed to be triggered by the type clash. However, this explanation remains problematic. Notably, metonymic interpretations are also possible for event-denoting objects given suitable contexts (e.g. *John is a wrestling fan, he really enjoyed the fight last night* → *watching the fight*).

Thematic fit in logical metonymy. Another pervasive aspect of language processing is thematic fit in the shape of selectional preferences, that is, expectations of predicative lemmas about plausible fillers for their argument slots (e.g., the fact that *eat* requires a *[+edible]* object or that *crook* is a more fitting object for *arrest* than *cop*). While early formalizations of selectional preferences aimed at modeling a binary distinction between "sensical" and "nonsensical" predicate-argument combinations, later work such as Wilks (1975) adopted a graded notion of selectional preference. In psycholinguistics, thematic fit has emerged as a pivotal concept to explain effects on expectations about upcoming input in language comprehension (McRae, Spivey-Knowlton, and Tanenhaus 1998; Ferretti, McRae, and Hatherell 2001; Matsuki, Chow, Hare, Elman, Scheepers, and McRae 2011).

Concerning logical metonymy, there is considerable behavioral as well as modeling evidence that thematic fit plays an important role in metonymy *interpretation*, that is, the retrieval of covert events for metonymical constructions. Behavioral studies (Zarcone and Padó 2011; Zarcone, Padó, and Lenci 2012) as well as computational models (Lapata and Lascarides 2003; Zarcone, Utt, and Padó 2012) found that the retrieved event will be the event most compatible with our knowledge about typical events and their participants (as captured, e.g. by generalized event knowledge, (McRae and Matsuki 2009)), that is the interpretation with the highest thematic fit with the context. This is in contrast to traditional accounts of logical metonymy (Pustejovsky 1995) which ascribe covert event retrieval to complex lexical entries associating entities with events corresponding to their typical function or creation mode (qualia: *book* $\rightarrow$ *read / write*). The advantage of thematic fit-based accounts is that they can account for the influence of context on interpretation. For example, given *baker* and *child* as subjects of *finish the icing*, *baker* will cue *spread* as a covert event, while *child* will cue *eat*, even though it is possible that bakers eat icing or that children spread it.

Thematic fit as a trigger of logical metonymy. In this paper, we propose that thematic fit can explain not only the interpretation phase of metonymy (that is implicit event recovery), but also to the *triggering phase*. We claim that thematic fit can provide a convincing explanation for the triggering of the coercion operation: metonymic verbs prefer event-denoting objects, and sentences that have traditionally been analysed involving a coercion operation have a low thematic fit between the verb and the object. This account preserves the observation that metonymic verbs disprefer entity-denoting objects, but can explain it purely in terms of standard graded accounts of selectional preferences[1]. A thematic-fit based account of logical metonymy would bring a clear advantage of theoretical economy: it accounts for two phenomena (triggering and interpretation) with a single mechanism, that is, generalized event knowledge (quantified in terms of thematic fit). Furthermore, generalized event knowledge / thematic fit operate in any type of predicate-argument composition (McRae and Matsuki 2009). Thus, an explanation in terms of thematic fit would bring metonymy closer to "normal" online language comprehension process.

We test this hypothesis by modeling three datasets from well-known experimental studies on metonymy. We compute thematic fit predictions of all items relying solely on distributional information, without any information about predicate semantic types, and compare differences in thematic fit across conditions with corresponding differences in processing cost from the experiments. As we show below, our distributional model of thematic fit predicts all significant effects that have been found in the experiments previous experiments and that were interpreted as type-clash effects.

2 Experimental Setup

2.1 A Distributional Model of Thematic Fit

Distributional semantic models (Turney and Pantel 2010) build on the Distributional Hypothesis (Harris 1954; Miller and Charles 1991) which states that the meaning of a word can be modelled by observing the contexts in which it is used. Current distributional models are typically built by collecting contexts of word occurrences in large corpora, where "context" can be defined in many possible ways. Pairwise word similarity is then computed by comparing the similarity between the vectors which record the word co-occurrences in the data. Distributional models have been successful in modelling a range of cognitive tasks, including lexical development (Li, Farkas, and MacWhinney 2004), category-related deficits (Vigliocco, Vinson, Lewis, and Garrett 2004), and thematic fit (Erk, Padó, and Padó 2010).

Distributional Memory (DM, Baroni and Lenci (2010)) is a general framework for building distributional semantic models from syntactically analysed corpora. It constructs a three-dimensional tensor of

[1]Similarly, thematic-fit based accounts of selectional preferences encompass binary distinctions (e.g., *eat* requires a *[+edible]* object), while still including more fine-grained differences (e.g., *crook* is a more fitting object for *arrest* than *cop*).

weighted word-relation-word tuples each tuple is mapped onto a score by a function $\sigma\colon \langle w_1\ r\ w_2\rangle \rightarrow \mathbb{N}$, where w_2 is a target word, r as a relation and w_1 an argument or adjuct of the target word. For example, ⟨*marine subj shoot*⟩ has a higher weight than ⟨*teacher subj shoot*⟩. The set of relations can be defined in different ways, which gives rise to different flavors of DM. We use TypeDM, which uses generic syntactic relations as well as lexicalized relations (see Baroni and Lenci (2010) for details).

For our experiments, we project the DM tensor onto a $W_1 \times RW_2$ matrix, and we represent each target word W_1 in terms of a vector with dimensions corresponding to pairs of context words and their relations ($R \times W_2$). On this matrix, we compute a verb's expectations for its most typical object with a method similar to Erk et al. (2010) and Lenci (2011): For each verb v, we determine the 20 highest-scoring nouns in object relation and compute the centroid $c_o(v)$ of their context vectors. The thematic fit of a new noun n for v's object position is then defined as the cosine of the angle between n's own context vector and $c_o(v)$. Since all the vectors' components are positive, the thematic fit values range between 0 and 1.

2.2 Datasets

As stated above, we model three datasets from psycholinguistic experiments. The datasets fall into two categories: sentence triplets, and sentence quadruplets. Please refer to the corresponding psycholinguistic studies (McElree et al. 2001; Traxler et al. 2002) for further details about how the datasets were built.

Sentence Triplets The two datasets in this group consist of sentence triplets: one sentence with a metonymic verb ("type-shift" in the original papers), paired with two non-metonymic sentences, where one condition shows high thematic fit and one low thematic fit ("preferred" and "non-preferred" in the original papers). An example is *the writer [finished / wrote / read]*$_V$ *the novel.*

McElree dataset. This dataset is composed of 31 triplets of sentences from the self-paced reading experiment in McElree et al. (2001), for a total of 93 sentences. We excluded two triplets from the original dataset for problems of coverage, as they included low-frequency words.

Traxler dataset 1. This dataset is composed of 35 triplets of sentences from the eye-tracking experiment (experiment 1) in Traxler et al. (2002), for a total of 105 sentences. We excluded one triplet from the original dataset for problems of coverage, as it included low-frequency words.

The finding for these materials was a main effect of verb type on reading times (McElree et al. 2001) and eye tracking times (Traxler et al. 2002). Pairwise comparisons in both studies yielded (a) higher processing costs for the metonymic condition and (b) no significant differences between the high- and low-typicality condition.

Sentence Quadruplets The dataset in this group consists of sentence quadruplets which cross two factors: (i) metonymic verb vs. non-metonymic verb and (ii) event-denoting object vs. entity-denoting object. As an example, consider *The boy [started / saw]*$_V$ *[the fight / puzzle]*$_{NP}$.

Traxler dataset 2. This dataset is composed of 32 sentence quadruplets from experiments 2 (eye-tracking) and 3 (self-paced reading) in Traxler et al. (2002), for a total of 120 sentences. We exclude one triplet from the original dataset for problems of coverage.

The findings for this dataset were a main effect of object type on eye tracking times (experiment 2) and on reading times (and experiment 3), and a significant verb$*$object interaction, with higher processing costs for the metonymic condition (metonymic verb combined with entity-denoting object).

2.3 Evaluation Method

For each test sentence, we compute the verb-object thematic fit in DM. We assume that processing load increases with lower thematic fit and that processing cost (reading time and eye tracking time) corresponds to 1 − thematic fit. We manipulate thematic fit in DM as a dependent variable, and we employ linear

		high-typicality	low-typicality	metonymic
triplets from McElree et al. (2001)	reading times at the obj. + 1 position	360	361	385
	1 − thematic fit	0.484	0.571	0.763
triplets from Traxler et al. (2002)	eye tracking (total time)	397	405	444
	1 − thematic fit	0.482	0.576	0.744

Table 1: Comparing behavioral data from McElree et al. (2001) and Traxler et al. (2002) and thematic fit data from the computational model

regression analyses to test for main effects of factors (object type, verb type) on the dependent variable, as well as Wilcoxon rank sum task to test the significance of pairwise differences between conditions in terms of thematic fit. We then verify if the same main effects and significant pairwise differences were yielded by the psycholinguistic models and by the computational model.

3 Results

Sentence Triplets On the McElree dataset, the model mirrors all effects reported by the experimental studies, namely by yielding a main effect of the object type ($F = 20.247, p < 0.001$), and significant differences between the metonymic condition and both high-typicality ($W = 877, p < 0.001$) and low-typicality ($W = 740, p < 0.001$) conditions, but no significant difference between the high- and low-typicality conditions ($W = 595, p > 0.5$).

The model also mirrors the experimental effects found for the Traxler dataset 1. It yields a main effect of the object type ($F = 18.084, p < 0.001$), and significant differences between the metonymic condition and both high-typicality ($W = 1050, p < 0.001$) and low-typicality ($W = 889, p < 0.01$) conditions, but only a marginal difference between the high- and low-typicality conditions ($W = 780.5, p = 0.5$).

Sentence Quadruplets On the Traxler dataset 2, the model mirrors the main effect of the object type ($F = 8.0039, p < 0.01$) and the verb$*$object type interaction ($F = 8.3455, p < 0.01$) reported both by the self-paced reading and by the eye tracking studies. This result is visualized in Figure 1, which shows the close correspondence between experimental results from self-paced reading and modeling results.

The model also yields the same pair-wise differences reported by the eye-tracking study: within the sentences with entity-denoting objects, metonymic verbs yield lower thematic fit compared to non-metonymic sentences ($W = 300, p < 0.05$). Within the sentences with metonymic verbs, entity-denoting objects also yield lower thematic fit compared to entity-denoting objects ($W = 208, p < 0.01$).

4 Discussion and Conclusions

The distributional models successfully replicate the pattern of results of the psycholinguistic experiments. For the triplet dataset, the model yields a main effect of verb type, and produces the lowest thematic fit for the metonymic condition (corresponding to the longest reading times and eye fixations in the experiments); also, the significant differences detected by the model are the same as those in the experimental studies: high-typicality vs. metonymic and low-typicality vs. metonymic. Interestingly enough, while the computational model does not reveal a significant difference between what we called high- and low-typicality conditions (preferred and non-preferred conditions according to the paper's terminology), the psycholinguistic experiments were not able to show one either, suggesting that in the experimental materials that were employed, the preferred and non-preferred conditions do not differ significantly with regard to typicality.

For the quadruplet dataset, the model yields a main effect of object type and a significant verb$*$object interaction, producing the lowest thematic fit for metonymic verbs combined with entity-denoting objects.

		metonymic verb		non-metonymic verb	
		EN obj.	EV obj.	EN obj.	EV obj.
quadruplets from Traxler et al. (2002)	self-paced reading times at obj. + 1	512	427	467	455
	1 − thematic fit	0.230	0.336	0.283	0.287

Table 2: Comparing behavioral data (self-paced reading) from Traxler et al. (2002) and thematic fit data from the computational model. Eye-tracking data mirror the findings of the self-paced reading study.

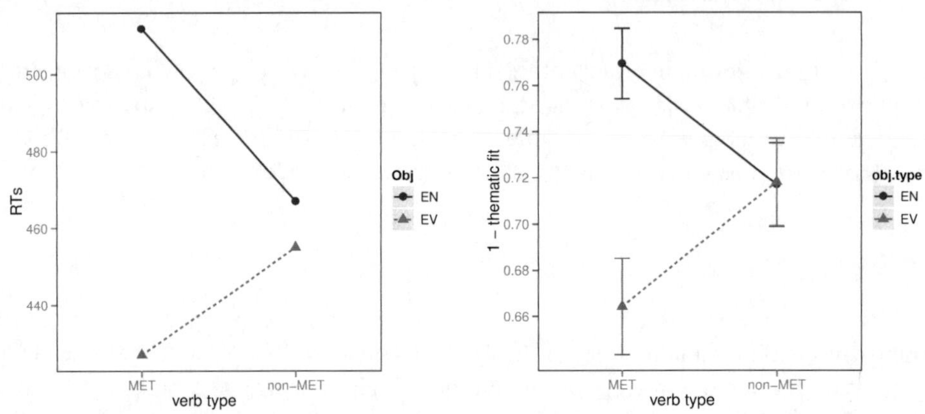

Figure 1: Comparing reading times in Traxler et al. (2002) (left, experiment 3) and results from thematic fit from our model (right).

The significant differences detected by the model were the same as those in the experimental studies: for the entity-denoting objects, metonymic verbs yielded lower thematic fit than non-metonymic verbs, whereas this difference was not significant for event-denoting objects; for the metonymic verbs, entity-denoting objects yielded lower thematic fit than event-denoting objects, whereas this difference was not significant for non-metonymic verbs.

The model's success in replicating the results from the psycholinguistic experiments shows that distributional similarity-based estimates of thematic fit are sufficient to account for the behavioral correlates of logical metonymy processing (such as longer reading and eye-tracking times) found so far in cognitive experiments. More precisely, the model, which did not encode any explicit type information, was able to replicate all significant experimental findings which were formulated based on type distinctions. This result supports the following general claims that we are currently testing on further experiments: i.) the two phenomena of triggering and interpretation in logical metonymy can be explained with a single mechanism relying on general event knowledge activation and integration; ii.) metonymy is actually much more closer to "normal" online predicate-argument composition processes, both being based on thematic fit computation. The structured distributional model of the latter proves to be an interesting tool to critically reanalyze psycholinguistic datasets, by (a) highlighting possible implicit lexical-semantic biases which may influence the results and (b) providing alternative explanations for them.

Acknowledgements The research for this paper was funded by the German Research Foundation (Deutsche Forschungsgemeinschaft) as part of the SFB 732 "Incremental specification in context" / project D6 "Lexical-semantic factors in event interpretation" at the University of Stuttgart.

References

Baroni, M. and A. Lenci (2010). Distributional memory: A general framework for corpus-based semantics. *Computational Linguistics 36*(4), 1–49.

Erk, K., S. Padó, and U. Padó (2010). A flexible, corpus-driven model of regular and inverse selectional preferences. *Computational Linguistics 36*(4), 723–763.

Ferretti, T. R., K. McRae, and A. Hatherell (2001). Integrating verbs, situation schemas and thematic role concept. *Journal of Memory and Language 44*, 516–547.

Frisson, S. and B. McElree (2008). Complement coercion is not modulated by competition: Evidence from eye movements. *Journal of Exp. Psychology: Learning, Memory, and Cognition 34*(1), 1.

Harris, Z. S. (1954). Distributional structure. *Word 10*(23), 146–162.

Lapata, M. and A. Lascarides (2003). A probabilistic account of logical metonymy. *Computational Linguistics 29*(2), 263–317.

Lenci, A. (2011). Composing and updating verb argument expectations: A distributional semantic model. In *Proceedings of CMCL*, Portland, Oregon, pp. 58–66.

Li, P., I. Farkas, and B. MacWhinney (2004). Early lexical development in a self-organizing neural network. *Neural Networks 17*, 1345–1362.

Matsuki, K., T. Chow, M. Hare, J. L. Elman, C. Scheepers, and K. McRae (2011). Event-based plausibility immediately influences on-line language comprehension. *Journal of Exp. Psychology: Language, Memory, and Cognition 37*(4), 913–934.

McElree, B., M. Traxler, M. Pickering, R. Seely, and R. Jackendoff (2001). Reading time evidence for enriched composition. *Cognition 78*(1), B17–B25.

McRae, K. and K. Matsuki (2009). People use their knowledge of common events to understand language, and do so as quickly as possible. *Language and Linguistics Compass 3/6*, 1417–1429.

McRae, K., M. Spivey-Knowlton, and M. Tanenhaus (1998). Modeling the influence of thematic fit (and other constraints) in on-line sentence comprehension. *Journal of Memory and Language 38*(3), 283–312.

Miller, G. A. and W. G. Charles (1991). Contextual correlates of semantic similarity. *Language and Cognitive Processes 6*(1), 1–28.

Pustejovsky, J. (1995). *The Generative Lexicon*. MIT Press.

Traxler, M. J., M. J. Pickering, and B. McElree (2002). Coercion in sentence processing: evidence from eye-movements and self-paced reading. *Journal of Memory and Language 47*, 530–547.

Turney, P. D. and P. Pantel (2010). From frequency to meaning: Vector space models of semantics. *Journal of Artificial Intelligence Research 37*, 141–188.

Vigliocco, G., D. P. Vinson, W. Lewis, and M. F. Garrett (2004). Representing the meanings of object and action words: The featural and unitary semantic space hypothesis. *Cognitive Psychology 48*(4), 422–488.

Wilks, Y. (1975). A preferential, pattern-seeking, semantics for natural language inference. *Artificial Intelligence 6*(1), 53–74.

Zarcone, A. and S. Padó (2011). Generalized event knowledge in logical metonymy resolution. In *Proceedings of CogSci*, Austin, TX, pp. 944–949.

Zarcone, A., S. Padó, and A. Lenci (2012). Inferring covert events in logical metonymies: a probe recognition experiment. In *Proceedings of CogSci*, Austin, TX.

Zarcone, A., J. Utt, and S. Padó (2012). Modeling covert event retrieval in logical metonymy: Probabilistic and distributional accounts. In *Proceedings of CMCL*, Montreal, Canada.

AUTHOR INDEX

Association for Computational Linguistics
209 N. Eighth Street
Stroudsburg, Pennsylvania 18360

CURRAN ASSOCIATES INC
proceedings.com